CLASSIC TEXTS SERIES

ELEMENTARY ALGEBRA FOR SCHOOLS

CLASSIC TEXTS SERIES

ELEMENTARY ALGEBRA FOR SCHOOLS

HS HALL & SR KNIGHT

arihant
SUCCESS AND NOTHING LESS

ARIHANT PRAKASHAN (Series), MEERUT

Administrative & Production Offices

Regd. Office

'Ramchhaya' 4577/15, Agarwal Road, Darya Ganj, New Delhi -110002
Tele: 011- 47630600, 43518550

Head Office

Kalindi, TP Nagar, Meerut (UP) - 250002
Tel: 0121-7156203, 7156204

Sales & Support Offices

Agra, Ahmedabad, Bengaluru, Bareilly, Chennai, Delhi, Guwahati, Hyderabad, Jaipur, Jhansi, Kolkata, Lucknow, Nagpur & Pune.

PRICE ₹350.00

PO No. : TXT-59-T069968-3-26

Published by Arihant Publications (India) Ltd.

For further information about the books published by Arihant, log on to www.arihantbooks.com or e-mail at info@arihantbooks.com

Follow us on

PREFACE

The last edition of Hall and Knight's *Elementary Algebra* published in Dr Knight's lifetime was the sixth, issued in 1890. Since his death in 1894 many alterations and additions have been made, as occasion required. These, for which I am solely responsible, may be summarized as follows:

Extract from the Preface to the Seventh Edition (Jan. 1897):

"The distinctive features are :

"(1) The definitions of *dimension, degree, homogeneous expression* are transferred from Art. 10' to Art. 24.

"(2) Greater prominence has been given to the *fundamental Laws of Algebra* (see Arts. 22, 29-32. 46-48). With this object, parts of the chapters on Multiplication and Division have been re-written.

"(3) A short section on the use of *Detached Coefficients* has been given on page 39.

"(4) A fuller treatment of the *Remainder Theorem* and its applications will be found on pages 261, 262.

"(5) Five new sets of *Miscellaneous Examples* have been added at convenient intervals beginning with one on page 34, which replaces Examples IV, c."

Extract from the Preface to the New Edition (Oct. 1907):

"The leading features are:

"(1) A full treatment of Graphs occupying more than 50 pages.

"(2) A new set of Easy Examples on Substitution in Chapter I.

"(3) The greater part of Chapter VIII, on Simple Equations, has been re-written so as to bring the use of the fundamental axioms into greater prominence, and to urge the importance of verifying solutions.

"(4) Chapter IX, on Symbolical Expression, has been enlarged. In particular, the section on Formulae has been illustrated by a new set of Examples.

"(5) A section on Square Root by inspection has been inserted in Chapter XVI.

"(6) In Chapter XVII, on Factors, a section on factorization of trinomials, by completing the square, has been introduced. Also a large number of *easy* miscellaneous examples take the place of the Exercise XVII, 1, of earlier editions.

"(7) Considerable additions to the chapters on Quadratic Equations. In particular, a set of examples involving applications to Geometry will be found at the end of Chapter XXVII.

"(8) The chapter on Logarithms has been re-written so as to introduce and explain the use of Four-Figure Tables. The Tables of Logarithms and Antilogarithms have been taken, with slight modifications, from those published by the Board of Education, South Kensington.

"(9) An easy first course has been mapped out enabling teachers to postpone, if they wish, the harder cases of 'Long' Multiplication and Division, and the rules dependent on these processes."

1 am thus responsible for more than 100 pages of new matter. In particular, pages 407-453 are my sole work, being taken verbatim from my little book, *A Short Introduction to Graphical Algebra,* which was first published in 1902.

H. S. HALL

SUGGESTIONS FOR A FIRST COURSE

In the first thirty chapters an asterisk has been placed before all articles and examples which may conveniently be omitted in a first course. Notes are occasionally given suggesting the most suitable place for a section which may have to be postponed.

For those who wish to defer to a later stage all the rules dependent on "Long" Multiplication and Division, so as to reach Quadratic Equations earlier, the following detailed course is recommended.

CHAP. 1. Arts. 1-11, 13-15. [Omit Art.-12, Examples I.C.]

CHAPS. II-V. Arts. 16-40. [Omit all the rest of Chap. V, except Art. 44.]

CHAP. VI. Arts. 46-50. [Omit Arts. 51-55.]

CHAPS. VII-XIII. Arts. 56-107. In connection with Chap. XIII

Arts. 417-424 on Elementary Graphs may be read.

CHAPS. XIV, XV. Arts. 108-113. [Omit Arts. 114, 115.]

CHAP. XVI. Arts. 116-118 A. [Omit Arts. 119-124.]

CHAP. XVII. Arts. 125-136. [Omit Arts. 136A-137.]

CHAP. XVIII. Arts. 138, 139. [Omit Arts. 140—148.]

CHAP. XIX. [Omit Arts. 152, 153.]

CHAP. XX. [Omit Arts. 159-163.]

CHAP. XXI. [Omit Arts. 171, 172.]

CHAP. XXII. Arts. 173-179. [Omit Arts. 180-185.]

[CHAPS. XXIII, XXIV may be taken later.]

CHAP. XXV. Quadratic Equations. In connection with this chapter

Arts. 425-428, 437-440 may be read.

From this point the omitted sections must be taken at the discretion of the Teacher.

CONTENTS

PART ONE
ELEMENTARY ALGEBRA

1
DEFINITIONS. SUBSTITUTIONS

1. ALGEBRA treats of quantities as in Arithmetic, but with greater generality; for while the quantities used in arithmetical processes are denoted by *figures* which have one single definite value, algebraical quantities are denoted by *symbols* which may have any value we choose to assign to them.

The symbols employed are letters, usually those of our own alphabet; and, though there is no restriction as to the numerical values a symbol may represent, it is understood that in the same piece of work it keeps the same value throughout. Thus, when we say "let $a = 1$", we do not mean that a must have the value 1 always, but only in the particular example we are considering. Moreover, we may operate with symbols without assigning to them any particular numerical value at all; indeed it is with such operations that Algebra is chiefly concerned.

We begin with the definitions of Algebra, premising that the symbols $+, -, \times, \div, =$, will have the same meanings as in Arithmetic. Also, for the present it will be assumed that all the algebraical symbols employed denote integral numbers.

2. An algebraical expression is a collection of symbols; it may consist of one or more terms, which are separated from each other by the signs + and –. Thus $7a + 5b - 3c - x + 2y$ is an expression consisting of five terms.

NOTE. When no sign precedes a term the sign + is understood.

3. Expressions are either simple or compound. A *simple expression* consists of *one* term, as $5a$. A *compound expression* consists of *two or more* terms. Compound expressions may be further distinguished. Thus an expression of *two* terms, as $3a - 2b$, is called a binomial expression; one of *three* terms, as $2a - 3b + c$, a trinomial; one of *more than three* terms a multinomial. Simple expressions are also spoken of as monomials.

4. When two or more quantities are multiplied together the result is called the product. One important difference between the notation of Arithmetic and Algebra should be here remarked. In Arithmetic the product of 2 and 3 is written 2×3, whereas in Algebra the product of a and b may be written in any of the forms $a \times b$, $a.b$, or ab. The form ab is the most usual. Thus, if $a = 2, b = 3$, the product $ab = a \times b = 2 \times 3 = 6$; but in Arithmetic 23 means "twenty-three", or $2 \times 10 + 3$.

5. Each of the quantities multiplied together to form a product is called a factor of the product. Thus, 5, a, b, are the factors of the product $5ab$.

6. When one of the factors of an expression is a numerical quantity, it is called the coefficient of the remaining factors. Thus, in the expression $5ab$, 5 is the coefficient. But the word coefficient is also used in a wider sense, and it is sometimes convenient to consider any factor, or factors, of a product as the coefficient of the remaining factors. Thus, in the product $6abc$, $6a$ may be appropriately called the coefficient of bc. A coefficient which is not merely numerical is sometimes called a literal coefficient.

NOTE. When the coefficient is unity it is usually omitted. Thus we do not write $1a$, but simply a.

7. If a quantity be multiplied by itself any number of times, the product is called a power of that quantity, and is expressed by writing the number of factors to the right of the quantity and above it. Thus $a \times a$ is called the *second power of a*, and is written a^2;

$a \times a \times a$ .... *third power* of a .... a^3;

and so on.

The number which expresses the power of any quantity is called its index or exponent. Thus 2, 5, 7 are respectively the indices of a^2, a^5, a^7.

NOTE. a^2 is usually read "a squared"; a^3 is read "a cubed"; a^4 is read "a to the fourth"; and so on.

When the index is unity it is omitted. Thus we do not write a^1, but simply a. Thus $a, 1a, a^1, 1a^1$ all have the same meaning.

8. The beginner must be careful to distinguish between *coefficient* and *index*.

Example 1. What is the difference in meaning between $3a$ and a^3?

By $3a$ we mean the product of the quantities 3 and a.

By a^3 we mean the third power of a; that is, the product of the quantities a, a, a.

Thus, if $a = 4$,

$$3a = 3 \times a = 3 \times 4 = 12;$$

$$a^3 = a \times a \times a = 4 \times 4 \times 4 = 64.$$

Example 2. If $b = 5$, distinguish between $4b^2$ and $2b^4$.

Here, $4b^2 = 4 \times b \times b = 4 \times 5 \times 5 = 100$;

whereas $2b^4 = 2 \times b \times b \times b \times b = 2 \times 5 \times 5 \times 5 \times 5 = 1250$.

Example 3. If $a = 4$, $x = 1$, find the value of $5x^a$.

Here, $5x^a = 5 \times x \times x \times x \times x = 5 \times 1 \times 1 \times 1 \times 1 = 5$.

NOTE. The beginner should observe that every power of 1 is 1.

9. In arithmetical multiplication the order in which the factors of a product are written is immaterial. For instance 3×4 means 4 sets of 3 units, and 4×3 means 3 sets of 4 units; in each case we have 12 units in all. Thus, $3 \times 4 = 4 \times 3$.

In a similar way, $3 \times 4 \times 5 = 4 \times 3 \times 5 = 4 \times 5 \times 3$;

and it is easy to see that the same principle holds for the product of any number of arithmetical quantities.

In like manner in Algebra ab and ba each denote the product of the two quantities represented by the letters a and b, and have therefore the same value. Again, the expressions $abc, acb, bac, bca, cab, cba$ have the same value, each denoting the product of the three quantities a, b, c. It is immaterial in what order the factors of a product are written; it is usual, however, to arrange them in alphabetical order.

Fractional coefficients which are greater than unity are usually kept in the form of improper fractions.

Example. If $a = 6$, $x = 7$, $z = 5$, find the value of $\frac{13}{10}axz$.

Here, $\frac{13}{10}axz = \frac{13}{10} \times 6 \times 7 \times 5 = 273$.

EXAMPLES I-a

If $a = 7, b = 2, c = 1, x = 5, y = 3$, find the value of

1. $14x$. **2.** x^3. **3.** $3ax$. **4.** a^3.

5. $5by$. **6.** b^5. **7.** $3b^2$. **8.** $2xa$.

9. $6c^4$. **10.** $4y^3$. **11.** $7c^3$. **12.** $9b^4$.

13. $8bcy$. **14.** $7y^3$. **15.** $8x^2$.

If $a = 8, b = 5, c = 4, x = 1, y = 3$, find the value of

16. $9xy$. **17.** $8b^3$. **18.** $3x^5$. **19.** x^8.

20. $7y^4$. **21.** c^x. **22.** b^y. **23.** y^a.

24. x^b. **25.** y^b. **26.** a^y. **27.** b^x.

28. a^c. **29.** c^y. **30.** $6bxy$.

If $a = 5, b = 1, c = 6, x = 4$, find the value of

31. $\frac{3}{8}x^3$. **32.** $\frac{1}{10}ax$. **33.** 3^x. **34.** 2^c.

35. 8^b. **36.** 7^x. **37.** $\frac{7}{15}acx$. **38.** $\frac{1}{8}bcx$.

39. $\frac{2}{9}c^3$. **40.** $\frac{x^5}{64}$.

10. When several different quantities are multiplied together a notation similar to that of Art. 7 is adopted. Thus, *aabbbbcddd* is written $a^2b^4cd^3$. And conversely $7a^3cd^2$ has the same meaning as $7 \times a \times a \times a \times c \times d \times d$.

Example 1. If $x = 5, y = 3$, find the value of $4x^2y^3$.

$$4x^2y^3 = 4 \times 5^2 \times 3^3 = 4 \times 25 \times 27 = 2700.$$

Example 2. If $a = 4, b = 9, x = 6$, find the value of $\frac{8bx^2}{27a^3}$.

$$\frac{8bx^2}{27a^3} = \frac{8 \times 9 \times 6^2}{27 \times 4^3} = \frac{8 \times 9 \times 36}{27 \times 64} = \frac{3}{2} = 1\frac{1}{2}.$$

11. If one factor of a product is equal to 0, the whole product must be equal to 0, *whatever values the other factors may have.* A factor 0 is usually called a zero factor.

For instance, if $x = 0$, then ab^3xy^2 contains a zero factor. Therefore $ab^3xy^2 = 0$, when $x = 0$ whatever be the values of a, b, y.

Again, if $c = 0$, then $c^3 = 0$; therefore $ab^2c^3 = 0$, whatever values a and b may have.

NOTE. Every power of 0 is 0.

EXAMPLES I-b

If $a = 7, b = 2, c = 0, x = 5, y = 3$, find the value of

1. $4ax^2$. **2.** a^3b. **3.** $8b^2y$. **4.** $3xy^2$.

5. $\frac{3}{4}b^2x$. **6.** $\frac{5}{6}b^3y^2$. **7.** $\frac{2}{5}xy^4$. **8.** a^3c.

9. a^2cy. **10.** $8x^3y$. **11.** $\frac{7}{20}ab^3x$. **12.** $\frac{1}{9}x^2y^4$.

If $a = 2, b = 3, c = 1, p = 0, q = 4, r = 6$, find the value of

13. $\frac{3a^2r}{8b}$. **14.** $\frac{8ab^2}{9q^2}$. **15.** $\frac{6a^3c}{b^2}$. **16.** $\frac{4cr^2}{9a^3}$.

17. $3a^2b^2$. **18.** $\frac{5}{6}ba$. **19.** $\frac{8b^q}{9a^r}$. **20.** $5a^bc^r$.

21. $\frac{2a^2p}{7r}$. **22.** 3^a2^b. **23.** 2^ra^5. **24.** a^bb^q.

25. $\frac{5a^rb^a}{64r^a}$. **26.** $\frac{27a^q}{32}$. **27.** $\frac{64}{q^r}$. **28.** $\frac{b^r}{r^b}$.

[*The articles and examples marked with an asterisk may be postponed and taken in connection with* Chap. XVI.]

***12. DEFINITION.** The square root of any proposed expression is that quantity whose square, or second power, is equal to the given expression. Thus the square root of 81 is 9, because $9^2 = 81$.

The square root of a is denoted by $\sqrt[2]{a}$, or more simply $\sqrt{a}$.

Similarly the cube, fourth, fifth, etc., root of any expression is that quantity whose third, fourth, fifth, etc., power is equal to the given expression.

The roots are denoted by the symbols $\sqrt[3]{\ }$, $\sqrt[4]{\ }$, $\sqrt[5]{\ }$, etc.

Examples. $\sqrt[3]{27} = 3$; because $3^3 = 27$. $\sqrt[5]{32} = 2$; because $2^5 = 32$.

The symbol $\sqrt{\ }$ is sometimes called the radical sign.

Example 1. Find the value of $5\sqrt{(6a^3b^4c)}$, when $a = 3, b = 1, c = 8$.

$$5\sqrt{(6a^3b^4c)} = 5 \times \sqrt{(6 \times 3^3 \times 1^4 \times 8)} = 5 \times \sqrt{(6 \times 27 \times 8)}$$
$$= 5 \times \sqrt{1296} = 5 \times 36 = 180.$$

Example 2. Find the value of $\sqrt[3]{\left(\frac{ab^4}{8x^3}\right)}$, when $a = 9, b = 3, x = 5$.

$$\sqrt[3]{\left(\frac{ab^4}{8x^3}\right)} = \sqrt[3]{\left(\frac{9 \times 3^4}{8 \times 5^3}\right)} = \sqrt[3]{\left(\frac{9 \times 81}{8 \times 125}\right)} = \sqrt[3]{\left(\frac{9 \times 9 \times 9}{1000}\right)} = \frac{9}{10}.$$

*EXAMPLES I-c

If $a = 8, c = 0, k = 9, x = 4, y = 1$, find the value of

1. $\sqrt{(2a)}$. **2.** $\sqrt{(kx)}$.

3. $\sqrt{(2ax)}$. **4.** $\sqrt{(2ak^2)}$.

5. $\sqrt[3]{3k}$. **6.** $\sqrt[3]{(ax^3)}$.

7. $\sqrt[3]{(8x^3y^3)}$. **8.** $\sqrt[3]{(cy^5)}$.

9. $2x\sqrt{(2ay)}$. **10.** $5y\sqrt{(4kx)}$.

11. $3c\sqrt{(kx)}$.

12. $2xy\sqrt{(4y^5)}$.

13. $\sqrt{\left(\frac{8x^3}{ak}\right)}$.

14. $\sqrt{\left(\frac{25a}{2k}\right)}$.

15. $\sqrt{\left(\frac{16x}{49y^3}\right)}$.

16. $\sqrt{\left(\frac{ca^2}{16k}\right)}$.

17. $\sqrt[3]{\left(\frac{3a}{k^2}\right)}$.

18. $\sqrt[3]{\left(\frac{ax^3}{27y^3}\right)}$.

19. $\sqrt[3]{\left(\frac{ca}{3k}\right)}$.

20. $\sqrt[3]{\left(\frac{a^2k^2}{3x^3}\right)}$.

21. $\sqrt{\left(\frac{kax^2}{18y^3}\right)}$.

13. In the case of expressions which contain more than one term, each term can be dealt with singly by the rules already given, and by combining the terms the numerical value of the whole expression is obtained. When brackets ( ) are used, they will have the same meaning as in Arithmetic, indicating that the terms enclosed within them are to be considered as one quantity.

Example 1. When $c = 5$, find the value of $c^4 - 4c + 2c^3 - 3c^2$.

Here $c^4 = 5^4 = 5 \times 5 \times 5 \times 5 = 625$; $4c = 4 \times 5 = 20$;

$2c^3 = 2 \times 5^3 = 2 \times 5 \times 5 \times 5 = 250$;

$3c^2 = 3 \times 5^2 = 3 \times 5 \times 5 = 75$.

Hence the value of the expression

$$= 625 - 20 + 250 - 75 = 780.$$

Example 2. If $a = 7, b = 3, c = 2$, find the value of $a(b + c)^2 - c(a - b)^3$.

The expression $= 7(3 + 2)^2 - 2(7 - 3)^3 = 7 \cdot 5^2 - 2 \cdot 4^3$

$$= 175 - 128 = 47.$$

Example 3. When $a = 5, b = 3, c = 1$, find the value of

$$a^2 \cdot \frac{a-b}{b+2c} - b^2 \cdot \frac{a-c}{(a+c)^2}.$$

The expression $= 5^2 \times \frac{5-3}{3+(2\times 1)} - 3^2 \times \frac{5-1}{(5+1)^2}$

$$= 25 \times \frac{2}{5} - 9 \times \frac{4}{36} = 10 - 1 = 9.$$

14. By Art. 11 any term which contains a *zero factor* is itself zero, and may be called a *zero term.*

Example 1. If $a = 2, b = 0, x = 5, y = 3$, find the value of

$$5a^3 - ab^2 + 2x^2y + 3bxy.$$

$$\text{The expression} = (5 \times 2^3) - 0 + (2 \times 5^2 \times 3) + 0$$
$$= 40 + 150 = 190.$$

NOTE. The two zero terms do not affect the result.

Example 2. Find the value of $\frac{3}{5}x^2 - a^2y + 7abx - \frac{5}{2}y^3$,

when $a = 5, b = 0, x = 7, y = 1$.

$$\frac{3}{5}x^2 - a^2y + 7abx - \frac{5}{2}y^3 = \frac{3}{5}\cdot 7^2 - 5^2\cdot 1 + 0 - \frac{5}{2}\cdot 1^3$$
$$= 29\frac{2}{5} - 25 - 2\frac{1}{2} = 1\frac{9}{10}.$$

Example 3. Find the values of the expression $x^2 - 10x + 21$ when x has the values 0, 2, 3, 7, 8.

Here the following arrangement will be found convenient.

x	0	2	3	7	8
x^2	0	4	9	49	64
$10x$	0	20	30	70	80
$x^3 - 10x + 21$	21	5	0	0	5

Thus the required values are 21, 5, 0, 0, and 5.

15. In working examples the student should pay attention to the following hints.

1. Too much importance cannot be attached to neatness of style and arrangement. The beginner should remember that neatness is in itself conducive to accuracy.
2. The sign = should never be used except to connect quantities which are equal. Beginners should be particularly careful not to employ the sign of equality in any vague and inexact sense.
3. Unless the expressions are very short the signs of equality in the steps of the work should be placed one under the other.
4. It should be clearly brought out how each step follows from the one before it: for this purpose it will sometimes be advisable to add short verbal explanations; the importance of this will be seen later.

EXAMPLES I-d

If $a=2, b=3, c=1, d=0$, find the numerical value of

1. $6a+5b-8c+9d$.

2. $3a-4b+6c+5d$.

3. $5a+3c-2b+6d$.

4. $ab+bc+ca-da$.

5. $6ab-3cd+2da-5cb+2db$.

6. $abc+bcd+cda+dab$.

7. $3abc-2bcd+2cda-4dab$.

8. $2bc+3cd-4da+5ab$.

9. $3bcd+5cda-7dab+abc$.

10. $a^2+b^2+c^2+d^2$.

11. $2a^2+3b^3-4c^4$.

12. $a^4+b^4-c^4$.

If $a=1, b=2, c=3, d=0$, find the numerical value of

13. $a^3+b^3+c^3+d^3$.

14. $\frac{1}{2}bc^3-a^3-b^3-\frac{3}{4}ab^3c$.

15. $3abc-b^2c-6a^3$.

16. $2a^2+2b^2+2c^2+2d^2-2bc-2cd-2da-2ab$.

17. $c^3+\frac{4}{5}ad^4-3a^3+b^2d$.

18. $a^2+2b^2+2c^2+d^2+2ab+2bc+\frac{2}{7}cd$.

19. $2c^2+2a^2+2b^2-4cb+6abcd$.

20. $13a^2+\frac{11}{9}c^4+20ab-16ac-16bc$.

21. $6ab-\frac{4}{3}ac^2-2a+\frac{1}{8}b^4-3d+\frac{4}{9}c^3$.

22. $a^2-c^2+b^2-d^2+2ab-2cd$.

23. $2ab-\frac{3}{4}b^3+3ac-2c-d+\frac{4}{15}ad$.

24. $125b^4c-9d^5+3abc^2d$.

If $a=2, b=1, c=3, x=4, y=6, z=0$, find the value of

25. $c^2(y-x)-b^2(c-a)$.

26. $(2a-c)(x+2y-z)$.

27. $\frac{2}{3}(c^2-z^2)+\frac{3}{5}(y^2-x^2)$.

28. $\frac{4}{9}(cy-2c^2)+\frac{3}{7}(xy-bc)$.

29. $\frac{a^2}{b^2}+\frac{b^2}{a^2}-\frac{2y}{x^2}$.

30. $\frac{a^2}{b^2}\cdot c^2+\frac{a^2}{b^2}+c^2$.

31. $\frac{(a+y)^2}{(x-z)^3}-\frac{6(c^2-a)}{7(a^2+x)}$.

32. $\frac{a^2-b^2}{a^2b^2}-\frac{(a+b+z)^2}{(b+c-z)^2}$.

33. $\frac{(a+b)^2}{(y-c)^2}-\frac{a(y-z)}{c(x+z)}$.

34. $\frac{(a+b+c)^2}{c(y-z)}-\frac{4(c-a)^3}{3(a+y)}$.

EXAMPLES I-e

1. When x has the values, 0, 3, 6, 8, 10 find the values of $x^2 - 9x + 20$.
2. Find the values of $3 + 2x + \frac{x^4}{4}$ when x has the values 0, 1, 2, 3, 4.
3. Shew that $y^2 - 15y + 56$ is 0 if $y = 7$, and also if $y = 8$. What is its value when $y = 10$?
4. Find the values of the expression $\frac{x^3}{100} + \frac{x^2}{10} + 2x$ when x has the values 2, 6, 8, 10.
5. Shew by substituting 10 for a and 3 for b that the two expressions $4(a-b) + 3(a+b), 5(a+b) + 2(a-3b)$ are equal.
   Test the equality also when $a = 6, b = 0$.
6. Shew that $x^3 - 6x^2 + 11x - 6$ is 0 for each of the values $x = 1, 2, 3$. What is its value when $x = 10$?
7. Shew that the expression $x^3 - 13x^2 + 44x$ is equal to 32 when $x = 1, 4$, or 8.
8. Shew that $x^3 + 10x$ is equal to $7x^2$ for each of the values $x = 0, 2, 5$. Which of the expressions is the greater, and by how much, when $x = 6$?
9. By substituting 3 for x and 2 for y shew that the expressions $6x^3 + 7x^2y - y^3$ and $(2x + y)(3x - y)(x + y)$ are equal.
10. Find the value of $4x^2 + 4x - 3$ when $x = 2$, and when $x = \frac{1}{2}$.
11. When $x = 5$, shew that $4x^2 + 4x - 3$ is equal to $9(x + 8)$.
12. Shew that $6x^3 - 11x^2 + 3x$ is equal to 0 when $x = \frac{1}{3}$, and when $x = \frac{3}{2}$.
    Find its value in the form of a decimal when $x = \frac{1}{10}$.

Examples for Revision (Oral)

1. What do you understand by 63 and by 6.3?
2. What is meant by $45xy$ and $4.5xy$? If $x = 4$, $y = 5$, give the arithmetical value of each.
3. Which is the greater 245 or $2 \cdot 4 \cdot 5$, and by how much?
4. Give the product of t and u in three ways.
5. If 5 boys have p marbles each, express algebraically how many they have in all. If $p = 25$ what is the number?

6. If x cakes are to be shared equally among 6 boy's, express algebraically how many each will have. If $x = 42$ what is the number?
7. If 54 books are divided equally among c boys, express each boy's share algebraically. What is the arithmetical value if $c = 6$?
8. What is the difference between "twice 3" and "3 squared"?
9. Give the expression for "thrice d", also that for the "cube of d". Give the arithmetical values if $d = 2$.
10. Distinguish between "four times x " and "x to the fourth". Give the respective values when $x = 3$.
11. The quantity c is to be multiplied by the quantity x. How is this expressed? Give the product if $c = 7$ and $x = 3$.
12. If x factors, each equal to c, are to be multiplied together, express this algebraically. What is the value if $x = 3$ and the factor $c = 7$?
13. The quantities a, b, c are to be added together. Express this algebraically. What is the answer if $a = 5, b = 7, c = 11$?
14. The quantity r is to be taken from the quantity s. Give the algebraical expression that denotes this. What is the answer if $r = 27$ and $s = 41$?
15. A boy starts playing with x marbles and wins y. Express the number then he has. If $x = 25$ and $y = 9$, what number has he?
16. The same boy plays with his increased number and loses z. Express the number then he has. If $z = 17$, how many has he left?
17. A shepherd takes f sheep to market and sells g of them. How many has he left? What is the remainder if $f = 64$ and $g = 48$?
18. Another shepherd takes k sheep to market and returns with l of them. How many has he sold? If $k = 75$, and $l = 32$. what is the number he has sold?
19. Give the sum and product of the three quantities a, b, c; and if $a = 5$, $b = 7, c = 6$, give the arithmetical value of each.
20. If I walk y km per hour for y hours, what is the algebraical expression for the length of my walk? If $y = 4$, what is the answer?

2

NEGATIVE QUANTITIES ADDITION OF LIKE TERMS

16. In the preceding examples the sum of the terms to be subtracted has never been greater than the sum of the terms to be added; that is to say, every operation has been capable of being worked by Arithmetic. But in an example that reduces to a result such as 4−9 the subtraction cannot be arithmetically performed, yet as an algebraical result such an expression can be explained; and, moreover, a subtractive term may stand alone and its meaning be quite plain.

17. Algebraical quantities which are preceded by the sign + are said to be positive; those to which the sign — is prefixed are said to be negative. When no sign is prefixed the + sign is to be understood. These signs are frequently used to denote a *quality* possessed by the quantities to which they are attached, as explained in the following illustrations:

(i) Suppose a trader gains Rs 100 and then losses Rs 70, the result of his trading is a *gain* of Rs 30, that is + Rs 100 – Rs 70 = + Rs 30; and the + Rs 30 denotes that he is Rs 30 better off than when he began.

But if he had first gained Rs 70 and then lost Rs 70, the loss would exactly balance the gain, that is + Rs 70 – Rs 70 = Rs 0. Thus, he would be in the same position as when he began.

If, however, he had first gained Rs 70 and then lost Rs 100, the result of his trading would be a *loss* of Rs 30, that is + Rs 70 — Rs 100 = — Rs 30, and the — Rs 30 denotes that he is Rs 30 worse off than when he began, or that he now has a *debt* of Rs 30.

Thus, we see that the – Rs 30 denotes a quantity *equal in magnitude, but opposite in character* to the + Rs 30.

(ii) Again, suppose a man to row 60 meters up a stream, and then to drift down with the current for 40 meters, his position relative to the starting point would be + 60 meters – 40 meters = + 20 meters the + 20 meters denoting the distance he was *up* stream from his starting point.

If he had rowed 40 meters up stream and then drifted down 60 meters, his position relative to the starting point would be + 40 meters – 60 meters = – 20 meters, the – 20 metres denoting the distance he was *down* stream from his starting point.

Thus, we see that – 20 metres denotes a distance *equal in magnitude, but opposite in direction to* that denoted, by + 20 metres.

(iii) On a Centigrade thermometer +15°C means 15° *above* the freezing point and – 15°C denotes 15° *below* freezing point.

From the above examples it will be understood that +5, for example, will denote a quantity *greater* than 0 by 5 units, whereas – 5 will denote a quantity that is *less* than 0 by 5 units, the two quantities being of the same *absolute value* but *of opposite character.*

EXAMPLES II-a

1. A trader gains Rs 20, loses Rs 42, and then gains Rs 10. Express algebraically the result of his three transactions.
2. Two cricket counties play 16 matches; one wins 10 and loses 6, and the other wins 7 and loses 9. Express the two results, allowing a gain of one point for a win and a loss of one point for a defeat.
3. In the night a Centigrade thermometer falls to –8°, and in the day-time it rises to 12°. How many degrees are there between the readings?
4. A Centigrade thermometer rises to 9° in the day-time and falls 15° during the night; what is the night reading?
5. A snail climbs 6 dm vertically upwards from a given point on a wall, slips down 15 dm, and then climbs 6 dm upwards again. Express algebraically his final position from his starting point.
6. Two men each fire 20 shots at a mark and agree to register 4 points for every hit and to deduct 3 points for every miss. One hits the mark 12 times, the other 8 times. Express algebraically their separate scores.
7. Each of three football teams plays 20 matches during the season. The *A* team wins 9 and loses 5, the *B* team wins 6 and loses 8, and the *C* team wins 9 and loses 9, the other games being drawn. If one point be allowed for a win, and one point deducted for a loss, place the three teams in order of merit and give the expressions that denote the results of the season's play.

Addition of Like Terms

18. DEFINITION. When terms do not differ, or when they differ only in their numerical coefficients, they are called like, otherwise they are called unlike. Thus $3a, 7a; 5a^2b, 2a^2b, 3a^3b^2, -4a^3b^2$ are pairs of like terms, and $4a, 3b; 7a^2, 9a^2b$ are pairs of unlike terms.

The rules for adding like terms are:

Rule 1. *The sum of a number of like terms is a like term.*

Rule II. *If all the terms are positive, add the coefficients.*

Example. Find the value of $8a + 5a$.

Here, we have to increase 8 things by 5 like things, and the aggregate is 13 of such things;

for instance, $8 \text{ kg} + 5\text{kg} = 13 \text{ kg}.$

Hence also, $8a + 5a = 13a.$

Similarly, $8a + 5a + a + 2a + 6a = 22a.$

Rule III. *If all the terms are negative, add the coefficients numerically and prefix the minus sign to the sum.*

Example. To find the sum of $-3x, -5x, -7x, -x$

Here we have to express, as one subtractive quantity, the *sum*, or total, of four subtractive quantities of like character. To subtract in succession 3, 5, 7, 1 like things would have the same effect as to take away $3 + 5 + 7 + 1$, or 16, such things in one operation. Thus, the sum of $-3x, -5x, -7x, -x$ is $-16x$.

Rule IV. *If the terms are not all of the same sign, add together separately the coefficients of all the positive terms and the coefficients of all the negative terms; the difference of these two results, preceded by the sign of the greater, will give the coefficient of the sum required.*

Example 1. Find the sum of $17x$ and $-8x$.

A gain of 17 followed by a loss of 8 would give as a result a gain of 9, for the difference of 17 and 8 is 9, and the gain, or positive term, is the greater.

Thus the sum of $17x$ and $-8x = 9x$.

Example 2. The sum of $-17x$ and $8x = -9x$.

Example 3. Find the sum of $8a, -9a, -a, 3a, 4a, -11a, a$.

The sum of the coefficients of the positive terms is 16.

The sum of the coefficients of the negative terms is 21.

The difference of these is 5, and the sign of the greater is negative: hence the required sum is $-5a$.

When a number of quantities are connected together by the signs + and −, the value of the result is the same in whatever order the terms are taken. For example, in a series of combined losses and gains, the result is the same in whatever order the gains and losses are taken. We may, therefore, add or subtract the terms in the most convenient order, which is usually that stated in Rule IV above. This process is called collecting terms.

19. When quantities are connected by the signs + and −, the resulting expression is called their algebraical sum.

Thus $11a - 27a + 13a = -3a$ states that the algebraical sum of $11a, -27a, 13a$ is equal to $-3a$.

NOTE. The sum of two quantities numerically equal but with opposite signs is zero. Thus, the sum of $5a$ and $-5a$ and $-5a$ is 0.

EXAMPLES II-b

Find the sum of

1. $5a, 7a, 11a, a, 23a.$
2. $4x, x, 3x, 7x, 9x.$
3. $7b, 10b, 11b, 9b, 2b.$
4. $6c, 8c, 2c, 15c, 19c, 100c, c.$
5. $-3x, -5x, -11x, -7x.$
6. $-5b, -6b, -11b, -18b.$
7. $-3y, -7y, -y, -2y, -4y.$
8. $-c, -2c, -50c, -13c.$
9. $-11b, -5b, -3b, -b.$
10. $5x, -x, -3x, 2x,, -x.$
11. $26y, -11y, -15y, y, -3y, 2y.$
12. $5f, -9f, -3f, 21f, -30f.$
13. $2s, -3s, s, -s, -5s, 5s.$
14. $7y, -11y, 16y, -3y, -2y.$
15. $5x, -7x, -2x, 7x, 2x, -5x.$
16. $7ab, -3ab, -5ab, 2ab, ab.$

Find the value of

17. $-9x^2 + 11x^2 + 3x^2 - 4x^2.$
18. $3a^2x - 18a^2x + a^2x.$
19. $3a^3 - 7a^3 - 8a^3 + 2a^3 - 11a^3.$
20. $4x^3 - 5x^3 - 8x^3 - 7x^3.$
21. $4a^2b^2 - a^2b^2 - 7a^2b^2 + 5a^2b^2 - a^2b^2.$
22. $-9x^4 - 4x^4 - 12x^4 + 13x^4 - 7x^4.$
23. $7abcd - 11abcd - 41abcd + 2abcd.$
24. $\frac{1}{2}x - \frac{1}{3}x + x + \frac{2}{3}x.$
25. $\frac{3}{2}a + \frac{3}{5}a - \frac{1}{2}a.$
26. $-5b + \frac{1}{4}b - \frac{3}{2}b + 2b - \frac{1}{2}b + \frac{7}{4}b.$
27. $-\frac{5}{3}x^2 - 2x^2 - \frac{2}{3}x^2 + x^2 + \frac{1}{2}x^2 + \frac{11}{6}x^2.$
28. $-ab - \frac{1}{2}ab - \frac{1}{3}ab - \frac{1}{4}ab - \frac{1}{6}ab + ab + \frac{5}{12}ab.$
29. $\frac{2}{3}x - \frac{3}{4}x + \frac{5}{6}x - 2x + \frac{11}{6}x - \frac{1}{8}x + x.$
30. $-\frac{5}{3}x^2 - \frac{3}{4}x^2 - \frac{4}{3}x^2 - \frac{1}{4}x^2 - x^2.$

3

SIMPLE BRACKETS ADDITION

20. WHEN a number of arithmetical quantities are connected together by the signs + and –, the value of the result is the same in whatever order the terms are taken. This also holds in the case of algebraical quantities.

Thus $a-b+c$ is equivalent to $a+c-b$, for in the first of the two expressions b is taken from a, and c, added to the result; in the second c is added to a. and b taken from the result. Similar reasoning applies to all algebraical expressions. Hence we may write the terms of an expression in any order we please.

Thus it appears that the expression $a-b$ may be written in the equivalent form $-b+a$.

To illustrate this we may suppose, as in Art. 17, that a represents a gain of a pounds, and $-b$ a loss of b pounds: It is clearly immaterial whether the gain precedes the loss or the loss precedes the gain.

21. Brackets () are used to indicate that the terms enclosed within them are to be considered as one quantity. The full use of brackets will be considered in Chap. VII; here we shall deal only with the simpler cases.

$8+(13+5)$ means that 13 and 5 are to be added and their sum added to 8. It is clear that 13 and 5 may be added separately or together without altering the result.

Thus $\quad 8+(13+5)=8+13+5=26.$

Similarly $a+(b+c)$ means that the sum of b and c is to be added to a.

Thus $\quad a+(b+c)=a+b+c,$

$8+(13-5)$ means that to 8 we are to add the excess of 13 over 3; now if we add 13 to 8 we have added 5 too much, and must therefore take 5 from the result.

Thus $\quad 8+(13-5)=8+13-5=16.$

Similarly $a+(b-c)$ means that to a we are to add b, diminished by c.

Thus $\quad a+(b-c)=a+b-c \qquad \ldots(1).$

In like manner, $a+b-c+(d-e-f)=a+b-c+d-e-f \qquad \ldots(2).$

Conversely, $a+b-c+d-e-f=a+b-c+(d-e-f) \qquad \ldots(3).$

Again, $a-b+c=a+c-b$, = the sum of a and $c-b$, [Art. 20]

= the sum of a and $-b+c$. [Art. 20]

therefore $a-b+c=a+(-b+c) \qquad \ldots(4).$

By considering the results (1), (2), (3), (4) we are led to the following rule:

Rule. *When an expression within brackets is preceded by the sign +, the brackets can be removed without making any change in the expression.*

Conversely: *Any part of an expression may be enclosed within brackets and the sign + prefixed, the sign of every term within the brackets remaining unaltered.*

Thus the expression $a - b + c - d + e$ may be written in any of the following ways,

$$a + (-b + c - d + e),\ a - b + (c - d + e),\ a - b + c + (-d + e).$$

22. The expression $a - (b + c)$ means that from a we are to take the sum of b and c. The result will be the same whether b and c are subtracted separately or in one sum. Thus

$$a - (b + c) = a - b - c.$$

Again, $a - (b - c)$ means that from a we are to subtract the excess of b over c. If from a we take b we get $a - b$; but by so doing we shall have taken away c too much, and must therefore add c to $a - b$. Thus

$$a - (b - c) = a - b + c.$$

In like manner,

$$a - b - (c - d - e) = a - b - c + d + e.$$

Accordingly the following rule may be enunciated.

Rule. *When an expression within brackets is preceded by the sign –, the brackets may be removed if the sign of every term within the brackets be changed.*

Conversely: *Any part of an expression may be enclosed within brackets and the sign – prefixed, provided the sign of every term within the brackets be changed.*

Thus the expression $a - b + c + d - e$ may be written in any of the following ways,

$$a - (+b - c - d + e),\ a - b - (-c - d + e),\ a - b + c - (-d + e).$$

We have now established the following results:

I. *Additions and subtractions may be made in any order.*

Thus $a + b - c + d - e - f = a - c + b + d - f - e$

$$= a - c - f + d + b - e$$

This is known as the Commutative Law for Addition and Subtraction.

II. *The terms of an expression may be grouped in any manner.*

Thus $a + b - c + d - e - f = (a + b) - c + (d - e) - f$

$$= a + (b - c) + (d - e) - f = a + b - (c - d) - (e + f).$$

This is known as the Associative Law for Addition and Subtraction.

Addition of Unlike Terms

23. When two or more *like* terms are to be added together we have seen that they may be collected and the result expressed as a *single* like term. If however, the terms are *unlike* they cannot be collected; thus in finding the sum of two unlike quantities a and b, all that can be done is to connect them by the sign of addition and leave the result in the form $a + b$.

Also by the rules for removing brackets, $a + (-b) = a - b$; that is, the algebraic sum of a and $-b$ is written in the form $a - b$.

It will be observed that in Algebra the word *sum* is used in a wider sense than in Arithmetic. Thus, in the language of Arithmetic, $a - b$ signifies that b is to be subtracted from a, and bears that meaning only; but in Algebra it is also taken to mean the sum of the two quantities a and $-b$ without any regard to the relative magnitudes of a and b.

Example 1. Find the sum of $3a - 5b + 2c$; $2a + 3b - d$; $-4a + 2b$.

$$\begin{aligned}\text{The sum} &= (3a - 5b + 2c) + (2a + 3b - d) + (-4a + 2b)\\ &= 3a - 5b + 2c + 2a + 3b - d - 4a + 2b\\ &= 3a + 2a - 4a - 5b + 3b + 2b + 2c - d\\ &= a + 2c - d,\end{aligned}$$

by collecting like terms. The addition is, however, more conveniently effected by the following rule:

Rule. *Arrange the expressions in lines so that the like terms may be in the same vertical columns: then add each column, beginning with that on the left.*

$$\begin{array}{rrrr} 3a & -5b & +2c & \\ 2a & +3b & & -d \\ -4a & +2b & & \\ \hline a & & +2c & -d \end{array}$$

The algebraical sum of the terms in the first column is a, that of the terms in the second column is zero. The single terms in the third and fourth columns are brought down without change.

Example 2. Add together $-5ab + 6bc - 7ac$; $8ab + 3ac - 2ad$; $-2ab + 4ac + 5ad$; $bc - 3ab + 4ad$.

$$\begin{array}{rrrr} -5ab & +6bc & -7ac & \\ 8ab & & +3ac & -2ad \\ -2ab & & +4ac & +5ad \\ -3ab & +bc & & +4ad \\ \hline -2ab & +7bc & & +7ad \end{array}$$

Here we first rearrange the expressions so that like terms are in the same vertical columns, and then add up each column separately.

EXAMPLES III - a

Find the sum of

1. $a+2b-3c; -3a+b+2c; 2a-3b+c.$
2. $3a+2b-c; -a+3b+2c; 2a-b+3c.$
3. $-3x+2y+z;\ x-3y+2z;\ 2x+y-3z.$
4. $-x+2y+3z; 3x-y+2z; 2x+3y-z.$
5. $4a+3b+5c; -2a+3b-8c;\ a-b+c.$
6. $-15a-19b-18c; 14a+15b+8c; a+5b+9c.$
7. $25a-15b+c;\ 13a-10b+4c;\ a+20b-c.$
8. $-16a-10b+5c;\ 10a+5b+c;\ 6a+5b-c.$
9. $5ax-7by+cz;\ ax+2by-cz;\ -3ax+2by+3cz.$
10. $20p+q-r;\ p-20q+r;\ p+q-20r.$

Add together the following expressions.

11. $-5ab+6bc+4ac; 8ab-4bc+3ca; -2ab-2bc+4ca.$
12. $15ab-27bc-6ca;\ 14ab-18bc+10ca;\ 45bc-3ac-49ab.$
13. $5ab+bc-3ca; ab-bc+ca; -ab+2ca+bc.$
14. $pq+qr-rp;\ -pq+qr+rp;\ pq-qr+rp.$
15. $x+y+z; 2x+3y-2z; 3x-4y+z.$
16. $2a-3b+c;\ 15a-21b-8c; 24b+7c+3a.$
17. $4xy-9yz+2zx; -25xy+24yz-zx; 23xy-15yz+zx.$
18. $17ab-13bc+8ca; -5ab+9bc-7ca; -7bc-ca+2ab.$
19. $47x-63y+z; -25x+15y-3z; -22x+15z+48y.$
20. $-17b-2c+23a; -9a+15b+7c; -13a+3b-4c.$

Dimension and Degree

Ascending and Descending Powers

24. Each of the letters composing a term is called a dimension of the term, and the number of letters involved is called the degree of the term. Thus the product abc is said to be *of three dimensions*, or *of the third degree*; and ax^4 is said to be *of five dimensions*, or *of the fifth degree*.

A numerical coefficient is not counted. Thus $8a^2b^5$ and a^2b^5 are each of *seven* dimensions.

The degree of an expression is the degree of the term of highest dimensions contained in it; Thus a^4-8a^3+3a-5 is *an expression of the fourth degree*, and $a^2x-7b^2x^3$ is *an expression of the fifth degree*. But it is sometimes useful to speak of the dimensions of an expression with regard to some one of the letters it involves. For instance the expression ax^3-bx^2+cx-d is said to be of *three dimensions in x*.

A compound expression is said to be homogeneous when all its terms are of the same dimensions. Thus $8a^6 - a^4b^2 + 9ab^5$ is a *homogeneous expression of six dimensions.*

25. Different powers of the same letter are unlike terms; thus the result of adding together $2x^3$ and $3x^2$ cannot be expressed by a single term, but must be left in the form $2x^3 + 3x^2$.

Similarly the algebraical sum of $5a^2b^2$, $-3ab^3$, and $-b^4$ is $5a^2b^2 - 3ab^3 - b^4$. This expression is in its simplest form and cannot be abridged.

In adding together several algebraical expressions containing terms with different powers of the same letter, it will be found convenient to arrange all expressions in *descending* or *ascending* powers of that letter. This will be made clear by the following examples.

Example 1. Add together $3x^3 + 7 + 6x - 5x^2; 2x^2 - 8 - 9x;$ $4x - 2x^3 + 3x^2; 3x^3 - 9x - x^2; x - x^2 + 4.$

$$\begin{array}{rrrr} 3x^3 & -5x^2 & +6x & +7 \\ & 2x^2 & -9x & -8 \\ -2x^3 & +3x^2 & +4x & \\ 3x^3 & -x^2 & -9x & \\ -x^3 & -x^2 & +x & +4 \\ \hline 3x^3 & -2x^2 & -7x & +3 \end{array}$$

In writing down the first expression we put in the first term the highest power of x, in the second term the next highest power, and so on till the last term, in which x does not appear. The other expressions are arranged in the same way, so that in each column we have *like powers of the same letter.*

Example 2. Add together $3ab^2 - 2b^3 + a^3$; $5a^2b - ab^2 - 3a^3$; $8a^3 + 5b^3$; $9a^2b - 2a^3 + ab^2$.

$$\begin{array}{rrrr} -2b^3 & +3ab^2 & & +a^3 \\ & -ab^2 & +5a^2b & -3a^3 \\ 5b^3 & & & +8a^3 \\ & ab^2 & +9a^2b & -2a^3 \\ \hline 3b^3 & +3ab^2 & +14a^2b & +4a^3 \end{array}$$

Here each expression contains powers of two letters, and is arranged according to *descending* powers of b, and *ascending* powers of a.

EXAMPLES III- b

Find the sum of

1. $2ab + 3ca + 6abc; -5ab + 2bc - 5abc; 3ab - 2bc - 3ca.$
2. $2x^2 - 2xy + 3y^2; 4y^2 + 5xy - 2x^2; x^2 - 2xy - 6y^2.$
3. $3a^2 - 7ab - 4b^2; -6a^2 + 9ab - 3b^2; 4a^2 + ab + 5b^2.$

4. $x^2 + xy - y^2; - z^2 + yz + y^2; - x^2 + xz + z^2.$

5. $-x^2 - 3xy + 3y^2; 3x^2 + 4xy - 5y^2; x^2 + xy + y^2.$

6. $x^3 - x^2 + x - 1; 2x^2 - 2x + 2; - 3x^3 + 5x + 1;$

7. $2x^3 - x^2 - x; 4x^3 + 8x^2 + 7x; - 6x^3 - 6x^2 + x.$

8. $9x^2 - 7x + 5; -14x^2 + 15x - 6; 20x^2 - 40x - 17.$

9. $10x^3 + 5x + 8; 3x^3 - 4x^2 - 6; 2x^3 - 2x - 3.$

10. $a^3 - ab + bc; ab + b^3 - ca - bc + c^3.$

11. $5a^3 - 3c^3 + d^3;\ b^3 - 2a^3 - 3d^3; 4c^3 - 2a^3 - 3d^3.$

Find the sum of

12. $6x^3 - 2x + 1; 2x^3 + x + 6; x^2 - 7x^3 + 2x - 4.$

13. $a^3 - a^2 + 3a; 3a^3 + 4a^2 + 8a; 5a^3 - 6a^2 - 11a.$

14. $x^2 + y^2 - 2xy; 2z^3 - 3y^2 - 4yz; 2x^2 - 2z^2 - 3xz.$

15. $x^3 - 2y^3 + x; y^3 - 2x^3 + y; x^2 + 2y^2 - x + y^3.$

16. $x^3 + 3x^2y + 3xy^2; -3x^2y - 6xy^2 - x^3; 3x^2y + 4xy^2.$

17. $a^3 + 5ab^2 + b^3; b^3 - 10ab^2 - a^3; 5ab^2 - 2b^3 + 2a^2b.$

18. $x^5 - 4x^4y - 5x^3y^3; 3x^4y + 2x^3y^3 - 6xy^4; 3x^3y^3 + 6xy^4 - y^5.$

19. $a^2 - 4a^2b + 6abc; a^2b - 10abc + c^3; b^3 + 3a^2b + abc.$

20. $x^3 - 4x^2y + 6xy^2; 2x^2y - 3xy^2 + 2y^3; y^3 + 3x^2y + 4xy^2.$

Add together the following expressions:

21. $\frac{1}{2}a - \frac{1}{3}b; - a + \frac{2}{3}b; \frac{3}{4}a - b.$ **22.** $-\frac{1}{3}a - \frac{1}{4}b; -\frac{2}{3}a + \frac{3}{4}b; - 2a - b.$

23. $-2a + \frac{5}{2}c; -\frac{1}{3}a - 2b; \frac{8}{3}b - 3c.$ **24.** $-\frac{13}{8}a - \frac{11}{4}c;\ 2a - 3b; \frac{11}{5}b - c.$

25. $\frac{2}{3}x^2 + \frac{1}{3}xy - \frac{1}{4}y^2; - x^2 - \frac{2}{3}xy + 2y^2; \frac{2}{3}x^2 - xy - \frac{5}{4}y^2.$

26. $3a^2 - \frac{2}{5}ab - \frac{1}{2}b^2; -\frac{3}{2}a^2 + 2ab - \frac{2}{3}b^2; -\frac{2}{3}a^2 - ab + b^2.$

27. $\frac{5}{8}x^2 - \frac{1}{3}xy + \frac{3}{10}y^2; -\frac{3}{4}x^2 + \frac{14}{15}xy - y^2; \frac{1}{2}x^2 - xy + \frac{1}{5}y^3.$

28. $-\frac{3}{4}x^3 + 5ax^2 - \frac{5}{8}a^2x; x^3 - \frac{37}{8}ax^2 + \frac{1}{2}a^2x; -\frac{1}{2}x^3 + \frac{3}{4}a^2x.$

29. $\frac{3}{8}x^2 - \frac{5}{3}xy - 7y^2; \frac{2}{3}xy + \frac{18}{5}y^2; -\frac{5}{8}x^2 + 4y^2.$

30. $\frac{1}{2}a^3 - 2a^2b - \frac{3}{2}b^3; \frac{3}{2}a^2b - \frac{3}{4}ab^2 + 2b^3; -\frac{3}{2}a^3 + ab^2 + \frac{1}{2}b^3.$

4

SUBTRACTION

26. THE simplest cases of Subtraction have already come under the head of addition of *like* terms, of which some are negative, [Art. 18.]

Thus $5a - 3a = 2a,$

$3a - 7a = -4a,$

$-3a - 6a = -9a,$

Also, by the rule for removing brackets [Art. 22],

$$3a - (-8a) = 3a + 8a = 11a,$$

and $$-3a - (-8a) = -3a + 8a = 5a.$$

Subtraction of Unlike Terms

27. The method is shown in the following example.

Example. Subtract $3a - 2b - c$ from $4a - 3b + 5c$.

The difference

$$= 4a - 3b + 5c - (3a - 2b - c)$$
$$= 4a - 3b + 5c - 3a + 2b + c$$
$$= 4a - 3a - 3b + 2b + 5c + c$$
$$= a - b + 6c.$$

The expression to be subtracted is first enclosed in brackets with a minus sign prefixed, then on removal of the brackets the like terms are combined by the rules already explained in Art. 18.

It is, however, more convenient to arrange the work as follows, the signs of all the terms in the lower line being changed.

$$\begin{array}{r} 4a - 3b + 5c \\ -3a + 2b + c \\ \hline a - b + 6c \end{array}$$

by *addition* ,

The like terms are written in the same vertical. column, and each column is treated separately.

Rule. *Change the sign of every term in the expression to be subtracted, and add to the other expression.*

Note. It is not necessary that in the expression to be subtracted the signs should be *actually* changed; the operation of changing signs ought to be performed mentally.

Example 1. From $5x^2 + xy$

take $2x^2 + 8xy - 7y^2$.

$$
\begin{array}{l}
5x^2 + xy \\
\underline{2x^2 + 8xy - 7y^2} \\
3x^2 - 7xy + 7y^2
\end{array}
$$

In the first-column we combine mentally $5x^2$ and $-2x^2$, the algebraic sum of which is $3x^2$. In the last column the sign of the term $-7y^2$ has to be changed before it is put down in the result.

Example 2. Subtract $3x^2 - 2x$ from $1 - x^3$.

Terms containing different powers of the same letter being *unlike* must stand in different columns.

$$
\begin{array}{l}
-x^3 + 1 \\
\underline{3x^2 - 2x} \\
-x^3 - 3x^2 + 2x + 1
\end{array}
$$

In the first and last columns, as there is nothing to be subtracted, the terms are put down without change of sign. In the second and third columns each sign has to be changed.

The re-arrangement of terms in the first line is not *necessary*, but it is convenient, because it gives the result of subtraction in descending powers of x.

EXAMPLES IV-a

Subtract

1. $4a - 3b + c$ from $2a - 3b - c$.
2. $a - 3b + 5c$ from $4a - 8b + c$.
3. $2x - 8y + z$ from $15x + 10y - 18z$.
4. $15a - 27b + 8c$ from $10a + 3b + 4c$.
5. $-10x - 14y + 15z$ from $x - y - z$.
6. $-11ab + 6cd$ from $-10bc + ab - 4cd$.
7. $4a - 3b + 15c$ from $25a - 16b - 18c$.
8. $-16x - 18y - 15z$ from $-5x + 8y + 7z$.
9. $ab + cd - ac - bd$ from $ab + cd + ac + bd$.
10. $-ab + cd - ac + bd$ from $ab - cd + ac - bd$.

From

11. $3ab + 5cd - 4ac - 6bd$ take $3ab + 6cd - 3ac - 5bd$.

12. $yz - zx + xy$ take $- xy + yz - zx$.

13. $- 2x^3 - x^2 - 3x + 2$ take $x^3 - x + 1$.

14. $- 8x^2y + 15xy^2 + 10xyz$ take $4x^2y - 6xy^2 - 5xyz$.

15. $\frac{1}{2}a - b + \frac{1}{2}a$ take $\frac{1}{3}a + \frac{1}{2}b - \frac{1}{2}c$.

16. $\frac{3}{4}x + y - z$ take $\frac{1}{2}x - \frac{1}{2}y - \frac{1}{3}z$.

17. $- a - 3b$ take $\frac{3}{2}a + \frac{1}{3}b - \frac{1}{2}c$.

18. $\frac{1}{2}x - \frac{3}{7}y + \frac{1}{10}z$ take $-\frac{1}{2}x + \frac{4}{7}y - \frac{1}{10}z$.

19. $-\frac{2}{3}x - \frac{3}{5}y - 5z$ take $\frac{2}{3}x - \frac{3}{5}y - \frac{11}{3}z$.

20. $-\frac{1}{2}x + \frac{2}{3}y - \frac{1}{6}z$ take $\frac{1}{3}x - \frac{3}{2}y - \frac{1}{6}z$.

EXAMPLES IV-b

From

1. $3xy - 5yz + 8zx$ take $- 4xy + 2yz - 10zx$.

2. $- 8x^2y^2 + 15x^3y + 13xy^3$ take $4x^2y^2 + 7x^3y - 8xy^3$.

3. $- 8 + 6ab + a^2b^2$ take $4 - 3ab - 5a^2b^2$.

4. $a^2bc + b^2ca + c^2ab$ take $3a^2bc - 5b^2ca - 4c^2ab$.

5. $- 7a^2b + 8ab^2 + cd$ take $5a^2b - 7ab^2 + 6cd$.

6. $- 8x^2y + 5xy^2 - x^2y^2$ take $8x^2y - 5xy^2 + x^2y^2$.

7. $10a^2b^2 + 15ab^2 + 8a^2b$ take $- 10a^2b^2 + 15ab^2 - 8a^2b$.

8. $4x^2 - 3x + 2$ take $-5x^2 + 6x - 7$.

9. $x^3 + 11x^2 + 4$ take $8x^2 - 5x - 3$.

10. $- 8a^2x^2 + 5x^2 + 15$ take $9a^2x^2 - 8x^2 - 5$.

Subtract

11. $x^3 - x^2 + x + 1$ from $x^3 + x^2 - x + 1$.

12. $3xy^2 - 3x^2y + x^3 - y^3$ from $x^3 + 3x^2y + 3xy^2 + y^3$.

13. $b^3 + c^3 - 2abc$ from $a^3 + b^3 - 3abc$.

14. $7xy^2 - y^3 - 3x^2y + 5x^3$ from $8x^3 + 7x^2y - 3xy^2 - y^3$.

15. $x^4 + 5 + x - 3x^3$ from $5x^4 - 8x^3 - 2x^2 + 7$.

16. $a^3 + b^3 + c^3 - 3abc$ from $7abc - 3a^3 + 5b^3 - c^3$.

17. $1 - x + x^5 - x^4 - x^3$ from $x^4 - 1 + x - x^2$.

18. $7a^4 - 8a^2 + 3a^5 + a$ from $a^2 - 5a^3 - 7 + 7a^5$.

19. $10a^2b + 8ab^2 - 8a^3b^3 - b^4$ from $5a^2b - 6ab^2 - 7a^3b^3$.

20. $a^3 - b^3 + 8ab^2 - 7a^2b$ from $-8ab^2 + 15a^2b + b^3$.

From

21. $\frac{1}{2}x^2 - \frac{1}{3}xy - \frac{3}{2}y^2$ take $-\frac{3}{2}x^2 + xy - y^2$.

22. $\frac{2}{3}a^2 - \frac{5}{2}a - 1$ take $-\frac{2}{3}a^2 + a - \frac{1}{2}$.

23. $\frac{1}{3}x^2 - \frac{1}{2}x + \frac{1}{6}$ take $\frac{1}{3}x - 1 + \frac{1}{2}x^2$.

24. $\frac{3}{8}x^2 - \frac{2}{3}ax$ take $\frac{1}{3} - \frac{1}{4}x^2 - \frac{5}{6}ax$.

25. $\frac{3}{4}x^2 - \frac{1}{3}xy^2 - y^2$ take $\frac{1}{2}x^2y - \frac{5}{6}y^2 - \frac{1}{3}xy^2$.

26. $\frac{1}{8}a^3 - 2ax^2 - \frac{1}{3}a^2x$ take $\frac{1}{3}a^2x + \frac{1}{4}a^3 - \frac{3}{2}ax^3$.

MISCELLANEOUS EXAMPLES I

1. Simplify (1) $4x - 2x^2 - (2x - 3x^2)$; (2) $3a - 4b - (3b + a) - (5a - 8b)$.
2. To the sum of $2a - 3b - 2c$ and $2b - a + 7c$ add the sum of $a - 4c + 7b$ and $c - 6b$.
3. When $x = 3$, $y = 2$, $z = 0$, find the value of

   (1) $x^2 + \frac{3}{2}y^3 - xyz^3$; (2) $\frac{1}{4}x^3y^4 + \frac{5z^2}{6}$.
4. Define *index*, *coefficient*. In the expressions $4x^2 + 3x, 2x^3 + x^2, x^2 + 7x$, find (1) the sum of the indices, (2) the sum of the coefficients.
5. From $5x^3 + 3x - 1$ take the sum of

   $2x - 5 + 7x^2$ and $3x^2 + 4 - 2x^3 + x$.
6. Subtract $3a - 7a^3 + 5a^2$ from the sum of

   $2 + 8a^2 - a^3$ and $2a^3 - 3a^2 + a - 2$.

– – –

7. Distinguish between *like* and *unlike* terms. Pick out the like terms in the expression

   $a^3 - 3ab + b^2 - 2a^3 - a^2 + 3b^2 + 5ab + 7a^2$.
8. Write down in as many ways as possible the result of adding together x, y and z.
9. Subtract $5x^2 + 3x - 1$ from $2x^3$, and add the result to $3x^2 + 3x - 1$.
10. If the number of rupees I possess is represented by $+ a$, what will $- a$ denote?

11. Write down in algebraical symbols the results diminishing $2a$ by the sum of $3b$ and $5c$.
12. When $x = 1$, $y = 2$, $z = 3$, find the value of the sum of $5x^2, -2x^3z, 3y^4$. Also find the value of $2z^y - 3y^x$.

---

13. Add the sum of $2y - 3y^2$ and $1 - 5y^3$ to the remainder left when $1 - 2y^2 + y$ is subtracted from $5y^3$.
14. Explain clearly why $x - (y - z) = x - y + z$.
15. If $x = 4$, $y = 3$, $z = 2$, $a = 0$, find the value of $3x^2 - 2yz - ax + 5ax^2y$.
16. Simplify $2a - b - (3a - 2b) + (2a - 3b) - (a - 2b)$.
17. Find the algebraical sum of the like terms in the expression $5a^3 - 4a^2b + b^3 + 6a^3b + 7ab^2 - 3a^2b + 4ab^3 + 8a^2b$.
18. A boy works $x + y$ sums, of which only $y - 2z$ are right; how many are wrong?
19. In the expression $3a^3 - 7a^2b + b^4$, point out the highest power, the lowest power, the positive terms, and the coefficient of a^2.
20. Take $x^2 - y^2$ from $3xy - 4y^2$, and add the remainder to the sum of $4xy - x^2 - 3y^2$ and $2x^2 + 6y^2$.
21. If $x = 1, y = 3, z = 5, w = 0$, find the value of $\sqrt{(3xy)} + \sqrt{(5xz)} + \sqrt{(3yw)}$.
22. What is the *degree* of a term in an algebraical expression? In the expression $4x^6 - 3x^5a^2 + a^8$, what is the degree of the negative term?
23. Find the sum of $5a - 7b + c$ and $3b - 9a$, and subtract the result from $c - 4b$.
24. If $x = 3$, $y = 4$, $p = 8, q = 10$, find the value of $xyp + \dfrac{2y}{p - y} + 2a$

---

25. If x represents the date A. D. 10, what will $-3x$ stand for?
26. Add together $3x^2 - 7x + 5$ and $2x^3 + x - 3$, and diminish the result by $3x^2 + 2$.
27. In the expression

$$4a^2b^3 - b^4 + 3a^3b^2 + 5b^5 - ab^3x + 2x^3ab + abx^4 - a^2b^3$$

point out which terms are *like*, and which are homogeneous. What is the degree of the expression?
28. Express in algebraical symbols the excess of the sum of a and b over c diminished by d.
29. A man walks $2a - b$ km due North from a fixed point O, and then walks a distance $3a + 2b$ km due South; what is his final position with regard to O?
30. What expression must be added to $5x^2 - 7x + 2$ to produce $7x^2 - 1$?

5

MULTIPLICATION

[Part of this chapter may be taken at a later stage. See remark on page 35. *The easy graphical work in* Arts. 411-420 *may be studied after* Examples v.b*]*.

28. MULTIPLICATION in its primary sense signifies repeated addition. Thus $3 \times 4 = 3$ taken 4 times $= 3 + 3 + 3 + 3$.

Here the multiplier contains four units, and the number of times we take 3 is the same as the number of units in 4.

Again $a \times b = a$ taken b times $= a + a + a + \ldots$,

the number of terms being b.

Also $3 \times 4 = 4 \times 3$; and so long as a and b denote positive whole numbers, it is easy to shew that $a \times b = b \times a$.

29. When the quantities to be multiplied together are not positive whole numbers, we may define multiplication as *an operation performed on one quantity which when performed on unity produces the other*. For example, to multiply $\frac{4}{5}$ by $\frac{3}{7}$, we perform on $\frac{4}{5}$ that operation which when performed on unity gives $\frac{3}{7}$, that is, we must divide $\frac{4}{5}$ into seven equal parts and take three of them. Now each part will be equal to $\frac{4}{5 \times 7}$, and the result of taking three of such parts is expressed by $\frac{4 \times 3}{5 \times 7}$.

Hence, $\frac{4}{5} \times \frac{3}{7} = \frac{4 \times 3}{5 \times 7}$.

Also, by the last article, $\frac{4 \times 3}{5 \times 7} = \frac{3 \times 4}{7 \times 5} = \frac{3}{7} \times \frac{4}{5}$,

$$\therefore \quad \frac{4}{5} \times \frac{3}{7} = \frac{3}{7} \times \frac{4}{5}.$$

The reasoning is clearly general, and we may now say that $a \times b = b \times a$, where a and b are any positive quantities, integral or fractional.

In the same way it easily follow that

$$abc = a \times b \times c = (a \times b) \times c = (b \times a) \times c = bac$$
$$= b \times (a \times c) = b \times c \times a = bca\,;$$

that is, the factors of a product may be taken in any order. This is the

Commutative Law for Multiplication.

Example. $2a \times 3b \times c = 2 \times 3 \times a \times b \times c = 6abc$.

30. Again, *the factors of a product may be grouped in any way we please.*

Thus $abcd = a \times b \times c \times d = (ab) \times (cd) = a \times (bc) \times d = a \times (bcd)$.

This is the Associative Law of Multiplication.

31. Since, by definition, $a^3 = aaa$, and $a^5 = aaaaa$,

$\therefore\ a^3 \times a^5 = aaa \times aaaaa = aaaaaaaa = a^8 = a^{3+5}$;

that is, the index of a letter in a product is the sum of its indices in the factors of the product. This is the Index Law of Multiplication.

Again, $5a^2 = 5aa$, and $7a^3 = 7aaa$;

$\therefore\ 5a^2 \times 7a^3 = 5 \times 7 \times aaaaa = 35a^5$.

When the expressions to be multiplied together contain powers of different letters, a similar method is used.

Example. $5a^3b^2 \times 8a^2x^3 = 5aaabb \times 8aabxxx = 40a^5b^3x^3$.

NOTE. The beginner must be careful to observe that in this process of multiplication *the indices of one letter cannot combine in any way with those of another.* Thus the expression $40a^5b^3x^3$ admits of no further simplification.

32. Rule. *To multiply two simple expressions together, multiply the coefficients together and prefix their product to the product of the different letters, giving to each letter an index equal to the sum of the indices that letter has in the separate factors.*

The rule may be extended to cases where more than two expressions are to be multiplied' together.

Example 1. Find the product of x^2, x^3, and x^8.

The product $= x^2 \times x^3 \times x^8 = x^{2+3} \times x^8 = x^{2+3+8} = x^{13}$.

The product of three or more expressions is called the continued product.

Example 2. Find the continued product of $5x^2y^3$, $8y^2z^5$ and $3xz^4$.

The product $= 5x^2y^3 \times 8y^2z^5 \times 3xz^4 = 120x^3y^5z^9$.

Multiplication of a Compound Expression by a Simple

Expression 33. By definition,

$$(a+b)m = m + m + m + \ldots \text{ taken } a+b \text{ times}$$

$$= (m + m + m + \ldots \text{ taken } a \text{ times}).$$

together with $(m + m + m + \ldots$ taken b times$)$

$$= am + bm \qquad \ldots(1)$$

Also $(a-b)m = m + m + m + \dots$ taken $a-b$ times

$= (m + m + m + \dots$ taken a times),

diminished by $(m + m + m + \dots$ taken b times)

$$= am - bm \qquad \dots(2)$$

Similarly $(a - b + c)m = am - bm + cm$.

Thus it appears that *the product of a compound expression by a single factor is the algebraic sum of the partial products of each term of the compound expression by that factor.* This is known as the Distributive Law for Multiplication.

NOTE. It should be observed that for the present a, b, c denote positive whole numbers and that a is supposed greater than b.

Examples. $3(2a + 3b - 4c) = 6a + 9b - 12c$.

$$(4x^2 - 7y - 8z^3) \times 3xy^2 = 12x^3y^2 - 21xy^3 - 24xy^2z^3.$$

EXAMPLE V-a

Find the value of

1. $5x^2 \times 7x^5$.

2. $4a^3 \times 5a^8$.

3. $7ab \times 8a^3b^2$.

4. $6xy^2 \times 5x^3$.

5. $8a^3b \times b^5$.

6. $2abc \times 3ac^3$.

7. $2a^3b^3 \times 2a^3b^3$.

8. $5a^2b \times 2a$.

9. $4a^2b^3 \times 7a^5$.

10. $5a^4b^3 \times x^2y^2$.

11. $x^3y^3 \times 6a^2x^4$.

12. $abc \times xyz$.

13. $3a^4b^7x^3 \times 5a^3bx$.

14. $4a^3bx \times 7b^2x^4$.

15. $5a^2x \times 8cx$.

16. $5x^3y^3 \times 6a^3x^3$.

17. $2x^2y \times x^5y^7$.

18. $3a^3x^4y^7 \times a^2x^5y^8$.

Multiplying together:

19. $ab + bc$ and a^3b.

20. $5ab - 7bx$ and $4a^2bx^3$.

21. $5x + 3y$ and $2x^2$.

22. $a^2 + b^2 - c^2$ and a^3b.

23. $bc + ca - ab$ and abc.

24. $5a^2 + 3b^2 - 2c^2$ and $4a^2bc^3$.

25. $5x^2y + xy^2 - 7x^2y^2$ and $3x^3$.

26. $6x^3 - 5x^2y + 7xy^2$ and $8x^2y^3$.

27. $6a^3bc - 7ab^2c^2$ and a^2b^7.

Multiplication of Compound Expressions

34. If in Art. 33 we write $c + d$ for m in (1), we get

$$(a + b)(c + d) = a(c + d) + b(c + d)$$
$$= (c + d)a + (c + d)b \qquad \text{[Art. 29.]}$$
$$= ac + ad + bc + bd \qquad \ldots(3).$$

Again, from (2)

$$(a - b)(c + d) = a(c + d) - b(c + d)$$
$$= (c + d)a - (c + d)b$$
$$= ac + ad - (bc + bd)$$
$$= ac + ad - bc - bd \qquad \ldots(4).$$

Similarly, by writing $c - d$ for m in (1),

$$(a + b)(c - d) = a(c - d) + b(c - d)$$
$$= (c - d)a + (c - d)b$$
$$= ac - ad + bc - bd \qquad \ldots(5).$$

Also, from (2)

$$(a - b)(c - d) = a(c - d) - b(c - d)$$
$$= (c - d)a - (c - d)b$$
$$= ac - ad - (bc - bd)$$
$$= ac - ad - bc + bd \qquad \ldots(6).$$

If we consider each term on the right-hand side of (6), and the way in which it arises, we find that

$$(+a) \times (+c) = +ac.$$
$$(-b) \times (-d) = +bd.$$
$$(-b) \times (+c) = -bc.$$
$$(+a) \times (-d) = -ad.$$

These results enable us to state what is known as the Rule of Signs in multiplication.

Rule of Signs. *The product of two terms with like signs is positive; the product of two terms with unlike signs is negative.*

35. The rule of signs, and especially the use of the negative multiplier, will probably present some difficulty to the beginner. Perhaps the following numerical instances may be useful in illustrating the interpretation that may be given to multiplication by a negative quantity.

To multiply 3 by -4 we must do to 3 what is done to unity to obtain -4. Now -4 means that unity is taken 4 times and the result made negative; therefore $3 \times (-4)$ implies that 3 is to be taken 4 times and the product made negative.

But 3 taken 4 times gives $+12$:

$$\therefore \qquad 3 \times (-4) = -12.$$

Similarly 3×-4 indicates that -3 is to be taken 4 times, and the sign changed; the first operation gives -12, and the second $+12$.

Thus $\qquad (-3) \times (-4) = +12$

Hence, *multiplication by a negative quantity indicates that we are proceed just as if the multiplier were positive, and then change to sign of the product.*

NOTE. An Arithmetical and Symbolical Algebra

36. Arithmetical Algebra is that part of the science which deals solely with symbols and operations arithmetically intelligible. Starting from purely arithmetical definitions, we are enabled to prove certain fundamental laws.

Symbolical Algebra assumes these laws to be true in every case, and thence finds what meaning must be attached to symbols and operations which under unrestricted conditions no longer bear an arithmetical meaning. Thus the results of Arts. 33 and 34 were proved from arithmetical definitions which required the symbols to be positive whole numbers, such that $a > b$ and $c > d$. By the principles of symbolical Algebra we assume these results to be universally true when all restrictions are removed, and accept the interpretation to which we are led thereby.

Henceforth we are able to apply the Law of Distribution and the Rule of Signs without any restriction as to the symbols used. [See Art 33, Note.]

37. To familiarize the beginner with the principles we have just explained we add a few examples in substitutions where some of the symbols denote negative quantities.

Example 1. If $a = -4$, find the value of a^3.

Here $a^3 = (-4)^3 = (-4) \times (-4) = -64$.

By repeated applications of the rule of signs it may easily be shown that any *odd* power of a negative quantity is *negative*, and any *even* power of a negative quantity is positive.

Example 2. If $a = -1, b = 3, c = -2$, find the value of $-3a^4bc^3$.

$$\begin{aligned} \text{Here } -3a^4bc^3 &= -3 \times (-1)^4 \times 3 \times (-2)^3 \\ &= -3 \times (+1) \times 3 \times (-8) \\ &= 72. \text{ We write down at once } (-1)^4 = +1 \text{ and } (-2)^3 = -8. \end{aligned}$$

EXAMPLES V-b

If $a = -2, b = 3, c = -1, x = -5, y = 4$, find the value of

1. $3a^2b$.
2. $8abc^2$.
3. $-5c^3$.
4. $6a^2c^2$.
5. $4c^3y$.
6. $3a^2c$.
7. $-b^2c^2$.
8. $3a^3c^2$.
9. $-7a^3bc$.
10. $-2a^4bx$.
11. $-4a^2c^4$.
12. $3c^3x^3$.
13. $5a^2x^2$.
14. $-7c^4xy$.
15. $-8ax^3$.
16. $4c^5x^3$.
17. $-5a^2b^2c^2$.
18. $-7a^3c^3$.
19. $8c^4x^3$.
20. $7a^5c^4$.

If $a = -4, b = -3, c = -1, f = 0, \ x = 4, y = 1$, find the value of

21. $3a^2 + bx - 4cy$.

22. $2ab^2 - 3bc^2 + 2fx$.

23. $fa^2 - 2b^3 - cx^3$.

24. $3a^2y^3 - 5b^2x - 2c^3$.

25. $2a^3 - 3b^2 + 7cy^4$.

26. $3b^2y^4 - 4b^2f - 6b^4x$.

27. $1\sqrt{(ac)} - 3\sqrt{(xy)} + \sqrt{(b^2c^4)}$.

28. $3\sqrt{(acx)} - 2\sqrt{(b^2y)} - 6\sqrt{c^2y)}$.

29. $7\sqrt{(a^2x)} - 3\sqrt{(b^4c^2)} + 5\sqrt{(f^2x)}$.

30. $3c\sqrt{(3bc)} - 5\sqrt{(4c^2y^3)} - 2cy\sqrt{(3bc^5)}$.

38. The following examples further illustrate the rule of signs and the law of indices.

Example 1. Multiply $4a$ *by* $-3b$.

By the rule of signs the product is negative; also $4a \times 3b = 12ab$;

$\therefore \quad 4a \times (-3b) = -12ab.$

Example 2. Multiply $-5ab^3x$ by $-ab^3x$.

Here the absolute value of the product is $5a^2b^3x^2$, and by the rule of signs the products is positive;

$$(-5ab^3x) \times (-ab^3x) = 5a^2b^6x^2.$$

Example 3. Find the continued product of $3a^2b, -2a^3b^2, -ab^4$.

$3a^2b \times (-2a^3b^2) = -6a^5b^3$,

$(-6a^5b^3) \times (-ab^4) = +6a^6b^7$.

Thus, the complete product is $6a^6b^7$.

This result, however, may be written down at once: for $3a^2b \times 2a^3b^2 \times ab^4 = 6a^6b^7$, and by the rule of signs the required product is positive.

Example 4. Multiply $6a^3 - \frac{5}{3}a^2b - \frac{4}{5}ab^2$ by $-\frac{3}{4}ab^2$.

The product is the algebraical sum of the partial products formed according to the rule enunciated in Art. 33 ; thus

$$\left(6a^3 - \frac{5}{3}a^2b - \frac{4}{5}ab^2\right) \times \left(-\frac{3}{4}ab^2\right) = -\frac{9}{2}a^4b^2 + \frac{5}{4}a^3b^3 + \frac{3}{5}a^2b^4.$$

EXAMPLES V-c

Multiply together:

1. ax and $-3ax$.

2. $-2abx$ and $-7abx$.

3. a^2b and $-ab^2$.

4. $6x^2y$ and $-10xy$.

5. $-abcd$ and $-3a^2b^3c^4d^5$.

6. xyz and $-5x^2y^3z$.

7. $3xy + 4yz$ and $-12xyz$.

8. $ab - bc$ and a^2bc^3.

9. $-x - y - z$ and $-3x$.

10. $a^2 - b^2 + c^2$ and abc.

11. $-ab + bc - ca$ and $-abc$.

12. $-2a^2b - 4ab^2$ and $-7a^2b^2$.

13. $5x^2y - 6xy^2 + 8x^2y^2$ and $3xy$.

14. $-7x^3y - 5xy^3$ and $-8x^3y^3$.

15. $-5xy^2z + 3x^2yz^2 - 8xyz$ and xyz.

16. $4x^2y^2z^2 - 8xyz$ and $-12x^3yz^3$.

17. $-13xy^2 - 15x^2y$ and $-7x^3y^3$.

18. $8xyz - 10x^3yz^3$ and $-xyz$.

19. $abc - a^2bc - ab^2c$ and $-abc$.

20. $-a^2bc + b^2ca - c^2ab$ and $-ab$.

Find the product of

21. $2a - 3b + 4c$ and $-\frac{3}{2}a$.

22. $3x - 2y - 4$ and $-\frac{5}{6}x$.

23. $\frac{2}{3}a - \frac{1}{6}b - c$ and $\frac{3}{8}ax$.

24. $\frac{6}{7}a^2x^2 - \frac{3}{2}ax^3$ and $-\frac{7}{3}a^3x$.

25. $-\frac{5}{3}a^2x^2$ and $-\frac{3}{2}a^2 + ax - \frac{3}{5}x^2$.

26. $-\frac{7}{2}xy$ and $-3x^2 + \frac{2}{7}xy$.

27. $-\frac{3}{2}x^3y^2$ and $-\frac{1}{3}x^2 + 2y^2$.

28. $-\frac{4}{7}x^5y^3$ and $\frac{7}{4}x^2$ and $\frac{7}{4}x^3 - \frac{4}{7}y^3$.

39. The results of Art. 33 may be extended to the case where both of the expressions to be multiplied together contain two or more terms. For instance

$$(a-b+c)m = am - bm + cm\,;$$

replacing m by $x - y$, we have

$$\begin{aligned}(a-b+c)(x-y) &= a(x-y) - b(x-y) + c(x-y)\\ &= (ax-ay) - (bx-by) + (cx-cy)\\ &= ax - ay - bx + by + cx - cy.\end{aligned}$$

We now may state the general rule for multiplying together any two compound expressions.

Rule. *Multiply each term of the first expression by each term of the second. When the terms multiplied together have like sings, prefix to the product the sign +, when unlike prefix –; the algebraical sum of the partial products so formed gives the complete product.* This process is called Distributing the Product.

40. It should be noticed that the product of $a+b$ and $x-y$ is briefly expressed by $(a+b)(x-y)$, in which the brackets indicate that the expression $a+b$ taken as a whole is to be multiplied by the expression $x-y$ taken as a whole. By the above rule, the value of the product is the algebraical sum of the partial products $+ax, +bx, -ay, -by$; the sign of each product being determined by the rule of signs.

Example 1. Multiply $x+8$ by $x+7$.

The product $=(x+8)(x+7)= x^2+8x+7x+56 = x^2+15x+56.$

The operation is more conveniently arranged as follows:

$$\begin{array}{l} x+8 \\ x+7 \\ \hline x^2+8x \\ \qquad +7x+56 \\ \hline x^2+15x+56 \end{array}$$

by addition, $x^2+15x+56$

We begin on the left and work to he right, placing the second result one place to the right, so that like terms may stand in the same vertical column.

Example 2. Multiply $2x-3y$ by $4x-7y$.

$$\begin{array}{l} 2x-3y \\ 4x-7y \\ \hline 8x^2-12xy \\ \qquad -14xy+21y^2 \\ \hline 8x^2-26xy+21y^2. \end{array}$$

by addition, $8x^2-26xy+21y^2.$

EXAMPLES v-d

Find the product of

1. $x+5$ and $x+10$.
2. $x+5$ and $x-5$.
3. $x-7$ and $x-10$.
4. $x-7$ and $x+10$.
5. $x+7$ and $x-10$.
6. $x+7$ and $x+10$.
7. $x+6$ and $x-6$.
8. $x+8$ and $x-4$.
9. $x-12$ and $x-1$.
10. $x+12$ and $x-1$.
11. $x-15$ and $x+15$.
12. $x-15$ and $x-1$.
13. $-x-2$ and $-x-3$.
14. $-x+7$ and $x-7$.
15. $-x+5$ and $-x-5$.
16. $x-13$ and $x+14$.
17. $x-17$ and $x+18$.
18. $x+19$ and $x-20$.
19. $-x-16$ and $-x+16$.
20. $-x+21$ and $x-21$.
21. $2x-3$ and $x+8$.
22. $2x+3$ and $x-8$.

Find the product of

23. $x-5$ and $2x-1$.
24. $2x-5$ and $x-1$.
25. $3x-5$ and $2x+7$.
26. $3x+5$ and $2x-7$.
27. $5x-6$ and $2x+3$.
28. $5x+6$ and $2x-3$.
29. $3x-5y$ and $3x+5y$.
30. $3x-5y$ and $3x-5y$.
31. $a-2b$ and $a+3b$.
32. $a-7b$ and $a+8b$.
33. $3a-6b$ and $a-8b$.
34. $a-9b$ and $a+5b$.
35. $x+a$ and $x-b$.
36. $x-a$ and $x+b$.
37. $x-2a$ and $x+3b$.
38. $ax-by$ and $ax+by$.
39. $xy-ab$ and $xy+ab$.
40. $2pq-3r$ and $2pa+3r$.

[*With the exception of* Art. 44, *the rest of this chapter may be postponed and taken after* (Chapter xiv.)]

***41.** We shall nowgive a few examples of greater difficulty.

Example 1. Find the product of $3x^2-2x-5$ and $2x-5$.

$$\begin{array}{l} 3x^2-2x-5 \\ \underline{2x-5} \\ 6x^3-4x^2-10x \\ \underline{\qquad -15x^2+10x+25} \\ 6x^3-19x^2+25 \end{array}$$

Each term of the first expression is multiplied by $2x$, the first term of the second expression ; then each term of the first expression is multiplied by -5; like terms are placed in the same columns and the results added.

Example 2. Multiplied $a - b + 3c$ by $a + 2b$.

$$\begin{array}{l} a - b + 3c \\ \underline{a + 2b} \\ a^2 - ab + 3ac \\ \qquad 2ab \qquad -2b^2 + 6bc \\ \hline a^2 + ab + 3ac - 2b^2 + 6bc \end{array}$$

***42.** When the coefficients are fractional we use the ordinary process of Multiplication, combining the fractional coefficients by the rules of Arithmetic.

Example. Multiply $\frac{1}{3}a^2 - \frac{1}{2}ab + \frac{2}{3}b^2$ by $\frac{1}{2}a + \frac{1}{3}b$.

$$\begin{array}{l} \frac{1}{3}a^2 - \frac{1}{2}ab + \frac{2}{3}b^2 \\ \frac{1}{2}a + \frac{1}{3}b \\ \hline \frac{1}{6}a^3 - \frac{1}{4}a^2b + \frac{1}{3}ab^2 \\ \qquad + \frac{1}{9}a^2b - \frac{1}{6}ab^2 + \frac{2}{9}b^2 \\ \hline \frac{1}{6}a^3 - \frac{5}{36}a^2b + \frac{1}{6}ab^2 + \frac{2}{9}b^2 \end{array}$$

***43.** If the expressions are not arranged according to powers, ascending, or descending, of some common letter, a rearrangement will be found convenient.

Example 1. Find the product of $2a^2 + 4b^2 - 3ab$ an $3ab - 5a^2 + 4b^2$.

$$\begin{array}{l} 2a^2 - 3ab + 4b^2 \\ \quad -5a^2 + 3ab + 4b^2 \\ \hline -10a^4 + 15a^3b - 20a^2b^2 \\ \qquad + 6a^3b - 9a^2b^2 + 12ab^3 \\ \qquad\qquad 8a^2b^2 - 12ab^3 + 16b^4 \\ \hline -10a^4 + 21a^3b - 21a^2b^2 \quad + 16b^4 \end{array}$$

The rearrangement is not *necessary*, but convenient, because it makes the collection of like terms more easy.

Example 2. Multiply $2xz - z^2 + 2x^2 - 3yz + xy$ by $x - y + 2z$.

$$
\begin{array}{l}
2x^2 + xy + 2xz - 3yz - z^2 \\
\underline{x - y + 2z} \\
2x^3 + x^2y + 2x^2z - 3xyz - xz^2 \\
\quad - 2x^2y \qquad -2xyz \qquad -xy^2 + 3y^2z + yz^2 \\
\hline
\qquad 4x^2z + 2xyz + 4xz^2 \qquad -6yz^2 - 2z^3 \\
2x^3 - x^2y + 6x^2z - 3xyz + 3xz^2 - xy^2 + 3y^2z - 5yz^2 - 2z^3
\end{array}
$$

*EXAMPLES V-e

1. $a + b + c, a + b - c.$

2. $a - 2b + c, a + 2b - c.$

3. $a^2 - ab + b^2, a^2 + ab + b^2.$

4. $x^2 + 3y^2, x + 4y.$

5. $x^3 - 2x^2 + 8, x + 2.$

6. $x^4 - x^2y^2 + y^4, x^2 + y^2.$

7. $x^2 + xy + y^2, x - y.$

8. $a^2 - 2ax + 4x^2, a^2 + 2ax + 4x^2.$

9. $16a^2 + 12ab + 9b^2, 4a - 3b.$

10. $a^2x - ax^2 + x^3 - a^3, x + a.$

11. $x^2 + x - 2, x^2 + x - 6.$

12. $2x^3 - 3x^2 + 2x, 2x^2 + 3x + 2.$

13. $- a^5 + a^4b - a^3b^2, - a - b.$

14. $x^3 - 7x + 5, x^2 - 2x + 3.$

15. $a^3 + 2a^2b + 2ab^2, a^2 - 2ab + 2b^2.$

16. $4x^2 + 6xy + 9y^2, 2x - 3y.$

17. $x^2 - 3xy - y^2, - x^2 + xy + y^2.$

18. $b^2 - a^2b^2 + a^3, a^3 + a^2b^2 + b^2.$

19. $x^2 - 2xy + y^2, x^2 + 2xy + y^2.$

20. $ab + cd + ac + bd, ab + cd + ac - bd.$

21. $- 3a^2b^2 + 4ab^3 + 15a^3b, 5a^2b^2 + ab^3 - 3b^4.$

22. $27x^3 - 36ax^2 + 48a^2x - 64a^3, 3x + 4a.$

23. $a^2 - 5ab - b^2, a^2 + 5ab + b^2.$

24. $x^2 - xy + x + y^2 + y + 1, x + y - 1.$

Multiply together:

25. $a^2 + b^2 + c^3 - bc - ca - ab, a + b + c.$

26. $- x^3y + y^4 + x^2y^2 + x^4 + xy^3, x + y.$

27. $x^{12} - x^9y^2 + x^6y^4 - x^3y^6 + y^8, x^3 + y^2.$

28. $3a^2 + 2a + 2a^3 + 1 + a^4, a^2 - 2a + 1.$

29. $- ax^2 + 3axy^2 - 9ay^4, - ax - 3ay^2.$

30. $- 2x^3y + y^4 + 3x^2y^2 + x^4 - 2xy^3, x^2 + 2xy + y^2.$

31. $\frac{1}{2}a^2 + \frac{1}{3}a + \frac{1}{4}, \frac{1}{2}a - \frac{1}{3}.$

32. $\frac{1}{2}x^2 - 2x + \frac{3}{2}, \frac{1}{2}x + \frac{1}{3}.$

33. $\frac{2}{3}x^2 + xy + \frac{3}{2}y^2, \frac{1}{3}x - \frac{1}{2}y.$

34. $\frac{3}{2}x^2 - ax - \frac{2}{3}a^2, \frac{3}{4}x^2 - \frac{1}{2}ax + \frac{1}{3}a^2.$

35. $\frac{1}{2}x^2 - \frac{2}{3}x - \frac{3}{4}, \frac{1}{2}x^2 + \frac{2}{3}x - \frac{3}{4}.$

36. $\frac{2}{3}ax + \frac{2}{3}x^2 + \frac{1}{3}a^2, \frac{3}{4}a^2 + \frac{3}{2}x^2 - \frac{3}{5}ax.$

44. Products written down by inspection. Although the result of multiplying together two binomial factors, such as $x + 8$ and $x - 7$, can always be obtained by the methods already explained, it is of the utmost importance that the student should soon learn to write down the product rapidly by *inspection*.

This is done by observing in waht way the coefficients of the terms in the product arise, and noticing that they result from the combination of the numerical coefficients in the two binomials which are multiplied together, thus

$$(x + 8)(x + 7) = x^2 + 8x + 7x + 56 = x^2 + 15x + 56.$$

$$(x - 8)(x - 7) = x^2 - 8x - 7x + 56 = x^2 - 15x + 56.$$

$$(x + 8)(x - 7) = x^2 + 8x - 7x - 56 = x^2 + x - 56.$$

$$(x - 8)(x + 7) = x^2 - 8x + 7x - 56 = x^2 - x - 56.$$

In each of these results we notice that:

1. The product consists of three terms.
2. The first term is the product of the first terms of the two binomial expressions.
3. The third term is the product of the second terms of the two binomial expressions.
4. The middle term has for its coefficient in the sum of the numerical quantities (taken with their proper signs) in the second terms of the two binomial expressions.

The intermediate step in the work may be omitted, and the products written down at once, as in the following examples:

$$(x + 2)(x + 3) = x^2 + 5x + 6.$$

$$(x - 3)(x + 4) = x^2 + x - 12.$$

$$(x + 6)(x - 9) = x^2 - 3x - 54.$$

$$(x - 4y)(x - 10y) = x^2 - 14xy + 40y^2.$$

$$(x - 6y)(x + 4y) = x^2 - 2xy - 24y^2.$$

By an easy extension of these principles we may write down the product of *any* two binomials.

Thus $(2x + 3y)(x - y) = 2x^2 + 3xy - + 2xy - 3y^2 = 2x^2 + xy - 3y^2$.

$$(3x - 4y)(2x + y) = 6x^2 - 8xy + 3xy + 3xy - 4y^2 = 6x^2 - 5xy - 4y^2.$$

$$(x + 4)(x - 4) = x^2 + 4x - 4x - 16. = x^2 - 16.$$

$$(2x + 5y)(2x - 5y) = 4x^2 + 10xy - 10xy - 25y^2 = 4x^2 - 25^2.$$

EXAMPLES V-f

Write down the values of the following products:

1. $(x + 8)(x - 5)$.

2. $(x + 6)(x - 1)$.

3. $(x - 3)(x + 10)$.

4. $(x - 1)(x + 5)$.

5. $(x + 7)(x - 9)$.

6. $(x - 10)(x - 8)$.

7. $(x - 4)(x + 11)$.

8. $(x - 2)(x + 4)$.

9. $(x + 2)(x - 2)$.

10. $(a - 1)(a + 1)$.

11. $(a + 9)(a - 5)$.

12. $(a - 3)(a + 12)$.

13. $(a - 8)(a + 4)$.

14. $(a - 8)(a + 8)$.

15. $(a - 6)(a + 13)$.

16. $(a + 3)(a + 3)$.

17. $(a - 11)(a + 11)$.

18. $(a - 8)(a - 8)$.

19. $(x - 3a)(x + 2a)$.

20. $(x + 6a)(x - 5a)$.

21. $(x + 3a)(x - 3a)$.

22. $(x + 4y)(x - 2y)$.

23. $(x + 7y)(x - 7y)$.

24. $(x - 3y)(x - 3y)$.

25. $(a + 3b)(a + 3b)$.

26. $(a - 5b)(a + 10b)$.

27. $(a - 9b)(a - 8b)$.

28. $(2x - 5)(x + 2)$.

29. $(2x - 5)(x - 2)$.

30. $(2x + 3)(x - 3)$.

31. $(3x - 1)(x + 1)$.

32. $(2x + 5)(2x - 3)$.

33. $(3x + 7)(2x - 3)$.

34. $(4x - 3)(2x + 3)$.

35. $(3x + 8)(3x - 8)$.

36. $(2x - 5)(2x - 5)$.

37. $(3x - 2y)(3x + y)$.

38. $(3x + 2y)(3x + 2y)$.

39. $(2x + 7y)(2x - 5y)$.

40. $(5x + 3a)(5x - 3a)$.

41. $(2x - 5a)(x + 5a)$.

42. $(2x + a)(2x + a)$.

Algebra

The Method of Detached Coefficients

45. When two compound expression contain powers of one letter only, the labour of multiplication may be lessened by using detached coefficients, that is by writing down the coefficients only, multiplying them together in the ordinary way, and then inserting the successive power of the letter at the end of the operation. In using this method the expressions must be arranged according to ascending or descending powers of the common letter, and zero coefficients must be used to represent terms corresponding to missing powers of that letters.

Example : Multiply $2x^3 - 5$ by $3x^2 + 4x - 2$.

Here we insert a zero coefficient to may a zero coefficient to represent the power of x which is absent in the multiplicand. In the product the highest power of x is clearly x^5, and the others follow in descending order.

$$\begin{array}{l} 2-4+0-5 \\ \underline{3+4-2} \\ 6-12+0-15 \\ \quad\; 8-16+0-20 \\ \qquad\; -4+8-0+10 \\ \hline 6-4-20-7-20+10 \end{array}$$

Thus the product is $6x^5 - 4x^4 - 20x^3 - 7x^2 - 10x + 10$

The method of detached coefficients may also be used to multiply two compound expressions which are homogeneous and contain powers of two letters.

Example. Multiple $3a^4 + 2a^3b + 4ab^3 + 2b^4$ by $2a^2 - b^2$

We write a zero coefficient to represent the term containing a^2b^2 which is absent in the first expression. Similarly, the term containing ab is represented by a zero coefficient in the second expression.

$$\begin{array}{l} 3+2+0+4+2 \\ \underline{2+0-1} \\ 6+4+0+8+4 \\ \qquad -3-2-0-4-2 \\ \hline 6+4-3+6+4-4-2 \end{array}$$

It is easily seen how the power of a and b arise in the successive terms, and the complete product is

$$6a^6 + 4a^5b - 3a^4b^2 + 6a^3b^3 + 4a^2b^4 - 4ab^5 - 2b^6.$$

NOTE. Beginners should on no account attempt to use detached coefficients until they are well practised in the ordinary full process of multiplication.

6

DIVISION

[*If preferred, the articles in this chapter marked with an asterisk may be postponed and taken after* Chapter XV.]

46. WHEN a quantity a is divided by the quantity b , the quotient is defined to be that which when multiplied by b produces a. This operation of division is denoted by $a \div b$, $\frac{a}{b}$ or a / b; in each of these modes of expression a is called the dividend, and b the divisor.

Division is thus the inverse of multiplication, and $(a \div b) \times b = a$.

This statement may also be expressed verbally as follows :

$$\text{quotient} \times \text{divisor} = \text{dividend}.$$

Since Division is the inverse of multiplication, it follows that the Laws of Commutation, Association, and Distribution, which have been established for multiplication, hold for Division.

47. *The* Rule of Signs *holds for division.*

Thus $$ab \div a = \frac{ab}{a} = \frac{a \times b}{a} = b.$$

$$-ab \div a = \frac{-ab}{a} = \frac{a \times (-b)}{a} = -b.$$

$$ab \div (-a) = \frac{ab}{-a} = \frac{(-a) \times (-b)}{-a} = -b$$

$$-ab + (-a) = \frac{-ab}{-a} = \frac{(-a) \times b}{-a} = b.$$

Hence in division as well as multiplication

like signs produce +,

unlike signs produce –.

Division of Simple Expressions

48. The method is shown in the following examples:

Example 1. Since the product of 4 and x is $4x$, it follows that when $4x$ is divided by x the quotient is 4,

or otherwise, $4x \div x = 4$.

Example 2. Divide $27a^5$ by $9a^3$.

$$\text{The quotient} = \frac{27a^5}{9a^3} = \frac{27aaaaa}{9\,aaa} = 3aa = 3a^2.$$

We remove from the divisor and dividend the factors common to both, just as in arithmetic.

Therefore $\quad 27a^5 \div 9a^3 = 3a^2.$

Example 3. Divide $35a^3b^2c^3$ by $7ab^2c^2$.

The quotient

$$= \frac{35aaa\,.\,bb\,.\,ccc}{7a\,.\,bb\,.\,cc} = 5aa\,.\,c = 5a^2c.$$

We see, in each case, that *the index of any letter in the quotient is the difference of the indices of that letter in the dividend and divisor.* This is called the Index Law for Division.

The rule may now be stated.

Rule. *The index of each letter in the quotient is obtained by subtracting the index of that letter in the divisor from that in the dividend.*

To the result so obtained prefix with its proper sign the quotient of the coefficient of the dividend by that of the divisor.

Example 4. Divide $45a^6b^2x^4$ by $-9a^3bx^2$.

$$\text{The quotient} = (-5) \times a^{6-3}\, b^{2-1}\, x^{4-2} = 5a^3bx^2.$$

Example 5. $-21a^2b^3 \div (-7a^2b^2) = 3b.$

NOTE. If we apply the rule to divide any power of a letter by the same power of the letter we are led to a curious conclusion.

Thus, by the rule $\quad a^3 \div a^3 = a^{3-3} = a^0;$

but also $\quad a^3 \div a^3 = \dfrac{a^3}{a^3} = 1;$

$\therefore \quad a^0 = 1.$

This result will appear somewhat strange to the beginner, but its full significance will be explained in the chapter on the Theory of Indices.

Division of a Compound Expression by a Simple Expression

49. Rule. *To divide a compound expression by factor, divide each term separately by that factor, and algebraic sum of the partial quotients so obtained.*

This follows at once from Art. 33.

Examples.

(1) $(9x - 12y + bz) \div -3 = -3x + 4y - z.$

(2) $(36a^3b^2 - 24a^2b^5 - 20a^4b^2) \div 4a^2b = 9ab - 6b^4 - 5a^2b.$

(3) $(2x^2 - 5xy + \frac{3}{2}x^2y^3) \div -\frac{1}{2}x = -4x + 10y - 3xy^3.$

EXAMPLES VI-a

Divide

1. $3x^3$ by x^2.

2. $27x^4$ by $-9x^3$.

3. $-35x^6$ by $7x^3$.

4. abx^2 by $-ax$.

5. x^3y^3 by x^2y.

6. a^4x^3 by $-a^2x^3$.

7. $4a^2b^2c^3$ by ab^2c^2.

8. $12a^6b^6c^6$ by $-3a^4b^2c$.

9. $-a^5c^9$ by $-ac^3$.

10. $15x^5y^7z^4$ by $5x^2y^2z^2$.

11. $-16x^3y^2$ by $-4xy^2$.

12. $-48a^9$ by $-8a^3$.

13. $35a^{11}$ by $7a^7$.

14. $63a^7b^8c^3$ by $9a^5b^5c^3$.

15. $7a^2bc$ by $-7a^2bc$.

16. $28a^4b^3$ by $-4a^3b$.

17. $16b^2yx^2$ by $-2xy$.

18. $-50y^3x^3$ by $-5x^3y$.

19. $x^2 - 2xy$ by x.

20. $x^3 - 3x^2 + x$ by x.

21. $x^6 - 7x^5 + 4x^4$ by x^2.

22. $10x^7 - 8x^6 + 3x^4$ by x^3.

23. $15x^5 - 25x^4$ by $-5x^3$.

24. $27x^6 - 36x^5$ by $9x^5$.

25. $-24x^6 - 32x^4$ by $-8x^3$.

26. $34x^3y^2 - 51x^2y^3$ by $17xy$.

27. $a^2 - ab - ac$ by $-a$.

28. $a^3 - a^2b - a^2b^2$ by a^2.

29. $3x^3 - 9x^2y - 12xy^2$ by $-3x$.

30. $4x^4y^4 - 8x^3y^4 + 6xy^3$ by $-2xy$.

31. $-3a^2 + \frac{9}{2}ab - 6ac$ by $-\frac{3}{2}a$.

32. $\frac{1}{2}x^5y^2 - 3x^3y^4$ by $-\frac{3}{2}x^3y^2$.

33. $-\frac{5}{2}x^2 + \frac{5}{8}xy + \frac{10}{3}x$ by $-\frac{5}{6}x$.

34. $-2a^5x^3 + \frac{7}{4}a^4x^4$ by $\frac{7}{3}a^3x$.

35. $\frac{1}{4}a^2x - \frac{1}{10}abx - \frac{3}{8}acx$ by $\frac{3}{8}ax$.

Division of Compound Expressions

50. To divide one compound expression by another.

Rule 1. *Arrange divisor and dividend in ascending or descending powers of some common letter.*

2. *Divide the term on the left of the dividend by the term on the left of the divisor, and put the result in the quotient.*

3. *Multiply the* WHOLE *divisor by this quotient, and put the product under the dividend.*
4. *Subtract and bring down from the dividend as many terms as may be necessary.*

   Repeat these operations till all the terms from the dividend are brought down.

Example 1. Divide $x^2 + 11x + 30$ by $x + 6$.

Arrange the work thus :

$$x + 6)x^2 + 11x + 30\,($$

divide x^2, the first term of the dividend, by x, the first term of the divisor; the quotient is x. Multiple the *whole* divisor by x, and put the product $x^2 + 6x$ under the dividend. We then have

$$\begin{array}{l} x + 6)\ x^2 + 11x + 30\,(x \\ \qquad\quad \underline{x^2 + 6x} \end{array}$$

by subtraction, $5x + 30$.

On repeating the process above explained we find that the next term in quotient is $+ 5$.

The entire operation is more compactly written as follows :

$$\begin{array}{l} x + 6)\ x^2 + 11x + 30\,(x + 5 \\ \qquad\quad \underline{x^2 + 6x} \\ \qquad\qquad\quad 5x + 30 \\ \qquad\qquad\quad \underline{5x + 30} \end{array}$$

The reason for the rule is this : the dividend may be divided into as many parts as may be convenient, and the complete quotient is found by taking the sum of all the partial quotients. Thus $x^2 + 11x + 30$ is divided by the above process into two parts, namely $x^2 + 6x$, and $5x + 30$, and each of these is divided by $x + 6$; thus we obtain the complete quotient $x + 5$.

Example 2. Divide $24x^2 - 65xy + 21y^2$ by $8x - 3y$.

$$\begin{array}{l} 8x - 3y)\ 24x^2 - 65xy + 21y^2\,(3x - 7y \\ \qquad\qquad \underline{24x^2 - 9xy} \\ \qquad\qquad\qquad\quad - 56xy + 21y^2 \\ \qquad\qquad\qquad\quad \underline{- 56xy + 21y^2} \end{array}$$

EXAMPLES VI-b

Divide

1. $x^2 + 3x + 2$ by $x + 1$.

2. $x^2 - 7x + 12$ by $x - 3$.

3. $a^2 - 11a + 30$ by $a - 5$.

4. $a^2 - 49a + 600$ by $a - 25$.

5. $3x^2 + 10x + 3$ by $x + 3$.

6. $2x^2 + 11x + 5$ by $2x + 1$.

7. $5x^2 + 11x + 2$ by $x + 2$.

8. $2x^2 + 17x + 21$ by $2x + 3$.

9. $5x^2 + 16x + 3$ by $x + 3$.

10. $3x^2 + 34x + 11$ by $3x + 1$.

11. $4x^2 + 23x + 15$ by $4x + 3$.

12. $6x^2 - 7x - 3$ by $2x - 3$.

13. $3x^2 + x - 14$ by $x - 2$.

14. $3x^2 - x - 14$ by $x + 2$.

15. $6x^2 - 31x + 35$ by $2x - 7$.

16. $4x^2 + x - 14$ by $x + 2$.

17. $12a^2 - 7ax - 12x^2$ by $2a - 4x$.

18. $15a^2 + 17ax - 4x^2$ by $3a + 4x$.

19. $12a^2 - 11ac - 36c^2$ by $4a - 9c$.

20. $9a^2 + 6ac - 35c^2$ by $3a + 7c$.

21. $60x^2 - 4xy - 45y^2$ by $10x - 9y$.

22. $96x^2 - 15y^2 - 4xy$ by $12x - 5y$.

23. $7x^3 + 96x^2 - 28x$ by $7x - 2$.

24. $100x^3 - 3x - 13x^2$ by $3 + 25x$.

25. $27x^3 + 9x^2 - 3x - 10$ by $3x - 2$.

26. $16a^3 - 46a^2 + 39a - 9$ by $8a - 3$.

27. $15 + 3a - 7a^2 - 4a^3$ by $5 - 4a$.

28. $16 - 96x + 216x^2 - 216x^3 + 81x^4$ by $2 - 3x$.

***51.** The process of Art. 50 is applicable to cases in which the divisor consists of more than two terms.

Example 1. Divide

$$6x^5 - x^4 + 4x^3 - 5x^2 - x - 15 \text{ by } 2x^2 - x + 3.$$

$$2x^2 - x + 3)6x^5 - x^4 + 4x^3 - 5x^2 - x - 15(3x^3 + x^2 + 2x - 5$$

$$\underline{6x^5 - 3x^4 + 9x^3}$$

$$2x^4 - 5x^3 - 5x^2$$

$$\underline{2x^4 - x^3 - 3x^2}$$

$$-4x^3 - 8x^2 - x$$

$$\underline{-4x^3 + 2x^2 - 6x}$$

$$-10x^2 + 5x - 15$$

$$\underline{-10x^2 + 5x - 15}$$

Example 2. Divide $2a^3 + 10 - 16a - 39a^2 + 15a^4$ by $2 - 4a - 5a^2$.

Arrange the expressions in *ascending* powers of a and use detached coefficients as in Art. 45.

$$2 - 4 - 5)10 - 16 - 39 + 2 + 15(5 + 2 - 3$$
$$\underline{10 - 20 - 25}$$
$$4 - 14 + 2$$
$$\underline{4 - 8 - 10}$$
$$-6 + 12 + 15$$
$$\underline{-6 + 12 + 15}$$

Thus the quotient is $5 + 2a - 3a^2$.

***52.** We add a few harder cases worked out in full.

Example 1. Divide $x^4 + 4a^4$ by $x^2 + 2xa + 2a^2$.

$$x^2 + 2xa + 2a^2)\ x^4 + 4a^4\ (x^2 - 2xa + 2a^2$$
$$\underline{x^4 + 2x^3a + 2x^2a^2}$$
$$-2x^3a - 2x^2a^2$$
$$\underline{-2x^3a + 4x^2a^2 - 4xa^3}$$
$$2x^2a^2 + 4xa^3 + 4a^4$$
$$\underline{2x^2a^2 + 4xa^3 + 4a^4}$$

Thus the quotient is $x^2 - 2xa + 2a^2$.

Example 2. Divide $a^3 + b^3 + c^3 - 3abc$ by $a + b + c$.

$$a + b + c)\ a^3 - 3abc + b^3 + c^3\ (a^2 - ab - ac + b^2 - bc + c^2$$
$$\underline{a^3 + a^2b + a^2c}$$
$$-a^2b - a^2c - 3abc$$
$$\underline{-a^2b - ab^2 - abc}$$
$$-a^2c + ab^2 - 2abc$$
$$\underline{-a^2c \qquad - abc - ac^2}$$
$$ab^2 - abc + ac^2 + b^3$$
$$\underline{ab^2 \qquad\qquad + b^3 + b^2c}$$
$$-abc + ac^2 \qquad -b^2c$$
$$\underline{-abc \qquad\qquad -b^2c - bc^2}$$
$$ac^2 \quad + bc^2 \quad + c^3$$
$$\underline{ac^2 \quad + bc^2 \quad + c^3}$$

Thus the quotient is $a^2 - ab - ac + b^2 - bc + c^2$.

NOTE. In the above example the dividend and successive remainders are arranged in *discending* powers of a.

The result of this important division will be referred to later.

***53.** When the coefficients are fractional the ordinary process may still be employed.

Example. Divide $\frac{1}{4}x^3 + \frac{1}{72}xy^2 + \frac{1}{12}y^3$ by $\frac{1}{2}x + \frac{1}{3}y$.

$$\frac{1}{2}x + \frac{1}{3}y\Big)\ \frac{1}{4}x^3 + \frac{1}{72}xy^2 + \frac{1}{12}y^3\Big(\frac{1}{2}x^2 - \frac{1}{3}xy + \frac{1}{4}y^2$$

$$\frac{1}{4}x^3 + \frac{1}{6}x^2y$$

$$-\frac{1}{6}x^2y + \frac{1}{72}xy^2$$

$$-\frac{1}{6}x^2y - \frac{1}{9}xy^2$$

$$\frac{1}{8}xy^2 + \frac{1}{12}y^3$$

$$\frac{1}{8}xy^2 + \frac{1}{12}y^3$$

***54.** In the examples given hitherto the divisor has been exactly contained in the dividend. When the division is not exact the work should be carried on until the remainder is of lower dimensions [Art. 24] then the divisor.

EXAMPLES VI-c

[*Examples* 1-20 *will furnish practice in the use of Detached Coefficients as explained in Art.* 51.]

Divide

1. $x^3 - x^2 - 9x - 12$ by $x^2 + 3x + 3$.
2. $2y^3 - 3y^2 - 6y - 1$ by $2y^2 - 5y - 1$.
3. $6m^3 - m^2 - 14m + 3$ by $3m^2 + 4m - 1$.
4. $6a^5 - 13a^4 + 4a^3 + 3a^2$ by $3a^3 - 2a^2 - a$.
5. $x^4 + x^3 + 7x^2 - 6x + 8$ by $x^2 + 2x + 8$.
6. $a^4 - a^3 - 8a^2 + 12a - 9$ by $a^2 + 2a - 3$.
7. $a^4 + 6a^3 + 13a^2 + 12a + 4$ by $a^2 + 3a + 2$.
8. $2x^4 - x^3 + 4x^2 + 7x + 1$ by $x^2 - x + 3$.
9. $x^5 - 5x^4 + 9x^3 - 6x^2 - x + 2$ by $x^2 - 3x + 2$.
10. $x^5 - 4x^4 + 3x^3 + 3x^2 - 3x + 2$ by $x^2 - x - 2$.
11. $30x^4 + 11x^3 - 82x^3 - 5x + 3$ by $2x - 4 + 3x^3$.
12. $30y + 9 - 71y^3 + 28y^4 - 35y^2$ by $4y^2 - 13y + 6$.
13. $6k^5 - 15k^4 + 4k^3 + 7k^2 - 7k + 2$ by $3k^3 - k + 1$.
14. $15 + 2m^4 - 31m + 9m^2 + 4m^3 + m^5$ by $3 - 2m - m^2$.

15. $2x^3 - 8x + x^4 + 12 - 7x^2$ by $x^2 + 2 - 3x$.

16. $x^5 - 2x^4 - 4x^8 + 19x^2$ by $x^3 - 7x + 5$.

17. $192 - x^4 + 128x + 4x^2 - 8x^3$ by $16 - x^2$.

18. $14x^4 + 45x^2y + 78x^2y^2 + 45xy^3 + 14y^4$ by $2x^2 + 5xy + 7y^2$.

19. $x^5 - x^4y + x^3y^2 - x^3 + x^2 - y^3$ by $x^3 - x - y$.

20. $x^5 + x^4y - x^3y^2 + x^3 - 2xy^2 + y^3$ by $x^2 + xy - y^2$.

21. $a^9 - b^9$ by $a^3 - b^3$.

22. $x^9 - y^9$ by $x^2 + xy + y^3$.

23. $x^7 - 2y^{14} - 7x^5y^4 - 7xy^{12} + 14x^3y^8$ by $x - 2y^2$.

24. $a^3 + 3a^2b + b^3 - 1 + 3ab^2$ by $a + b - 1$.

25. $x^8 - y^8$ by $x^3 + x^2y + xy^2 + y^3$.

26. $a^{12} - b^{12}$ by $a^2 - b^2$.

27. $a^{12} + 2a^6b^6 + b^{12}$ by $a^4 + 2a^2b^2 + b^4$.

28. $1 - a^3 - 8x^3 - 6ax$ by $1 - a - 2x$.

Find the quotient of

29. $\frac{1}{8}a^3 - \frac{9}{4}a^2x + \frac{27}{2}ax^2 - 27x^3$ by $\frac{1}{2}a - 3x$.

30. $\frac{1}{27}a^3 - \frac{1}{12}a^2 + \frac{1}{16}a - \frac{1}{64}$ by $\frac{1}{3}a - \frac{1}{4}$.

31. $\frac{3}{4}a^2c^3 + \frac{6}{125}a^5$ by $\frac{1}{5}a^2 + \frac{1}{2}ac$.

32. $\frac{9}{16}a^4 - \frac{3}{4}a^3 - \frac{7}{4}a^2 + \frac{4}{3}a + \frac{16}{9}$ by $\frac{3}{2}a^2 - \frac{8}{3} - a$.

33. $36x^2 + \frac{1}{9}y^2 + \frac{1}{4} - 4xy - 6x + \frac{1}{3}y$ by $6x - \frac{1}{3}y - \frac{1}{2}$.

34. $\frac{8}{27}a^5 - \frac{243}{512}ax^4$ by $\frac{2}{3}a - \frac{3}{4}x$.

55. *The following examples in division may be easily verified; they are of great importance, and should be carefully noticed.

I. $$\begin{cases} \dfrac{x^2 - y^2}{x - y} = x + y, \\[2ex] \dfrac{x^3 - y^3}{x - y} = x^2 + xy + y^2, \\[2ex] \dfrac{x^4 - y^4}{x - y} = x^3 + x^2y + xy^2 + y^3, \end{cases}$$

and so on; the divisor being $x - y$. the terms in the quotient *all positive* and the index in the dividend *either odd or even.*

II. $$\begin{cases} \dfrac{x^3 + y^3}{x + y} = x^2 - xy + y^2, \\ \dfrac{x^5 + y^5}{x + y} = x^4 - x^3y + x^2y^2 - xy^3 + y^4, \\ \dfrac{x^7 + y^7}{x + y} = x^6 - x^5y + x^4y^2 - x^3y^3 + x^2y^4 - xy^5 + y^6, \end{cases}$$

and so on; the divisor being $x + y$, the terms in the quotient *alternately positive and negative*, and the index in the dividend *always odd.*

III. $$\begin{cases} \dfrac{x^2 - y^2}{x + y} = x - y, \\ \dfrac{x^4 - y^4}{x + y} = x^3 - x^2y + xy^2 - y^3, \\ \dfrac{x^4 - y^4}{x + y} = x^5 - x^4y + x^3y^2 - x^2y^3 + xy^4 - y^5, \end{cases}$$

and so on; the divisor being $x + y$, the terms in the quotient *alternately positive and negative*, and the index in the dividend *always even.*

IV. The expressions $x^2 + y^2, x^4 + y^4, x^6 + y^6, \ldots$ (where the index is *even*, and the terms *both positive*) *are never* divisible by
$x + y$ or $x - y$.

All these different cases may be more concisely stated as follows:

(1) $x^n - y^n$ is divisible by $x - y$ if n be any whole number.

(2) $x^n + y^n$ is divisible by $x + y$ if n be any *odd* whole number.

(3) $x^n - y^n$ is divisible by $x + y$ if n be any *even* whole number.

(4) $x^n + y^n$ is never divisible by $x + y$ or $x - y$, when n is an *even* whole number.

7

REMOVAL AND INSERTION OF BRACKETS

56. QUANTITIES are enclosed within brackets to indicate that they must all be operated upon in the same way. Thus in the expression $2a - 3b - (4a - 2b)$ the brackets indicate that the expression $4a - 2b$ *treated as a whole* has to be subtracted from $2a - 3b$. When we wish to enclose within brackets part of an expression already enclosed within brackets it is usual to employ brackets of different forms. The brackets in common use are $()$, $\{\}$, $[]$. Sometimes a line called a vinculum is drawn over the symbols to be connected; thus $a - \overline{b + c}$ is used with the same meaning as $a - (b + c)$, and hence $a - \overline{b + c} = a - b - c$.

Removal of Brackets

57. To remove brackets it is usually best to begin with the inside pair, and in dealing with each pair in succession we apply the rules already given in Arts. 21, 22.

Example 1. Simplify, by removing brackets, the expression

$$a - 2b - [4a - 6b - \{3a - c + (5a - 2b - \overline{3a - c + 2b})\}].$$

Removing the brackets one by one, we have

$$\begin{aligned} & a - 2b - [4a - 6b - \{3a - c + (5a - 2b - 3a + c - 2b)\}] \\ &= a - 2b - [4a - 6b - \{3a - c + 5a - 2b - 3a + c - 2b)\}] \\ &= a - 2b - [4a - 6b + 3a + c - 5a + 2b + 3a - c + 2b] \\ &= a - 2b - 4a + 6b + 3a - c + 5a - 2b - 3a + c - 2b \\ &= 2a, \text{ by collecting like terms.} \end{aligned}$$

Example 2. Simplify the expression

$$-[-2x - \{3y - (2x - 3y) + (3x - 2y)\} + 2x].$$

$$\begin{aligned} \text{The expression} &= -[-2x - \{3y - 2x + 3y + 3x - 2y\} + 2x] \\ &= -[-2x - 3y + 2x - 3y - 3x + 2y + 2x] \\ &= 2x + 3y - 2x + 3y + 3x - 2y - 2x \\ &= x + 4y. \end{aligned}$$

EXAMPLES VII-a

Simplify by removing brackets:

1. $a-(b-c)+a+(b-c)+b-(c+a)$.
2. $a-[b+\{a-(b+a)\}]$.
3. $a-[2a-\{3b-(4c-2a)\}]$.
4. $\{a-(b-c)\}+\{b-(c-a)\}-\{c-(a-b)\}$.
5. $2a-(5b+[3c-a])-(5a-[b+c])$.
6. $-\{-[-(a-\overline{b-c})]\}$.
7. $-[a-\{b-(c-a)\}]-[b-\{c-(a-b)\}]$.
8. $-(-(-(-x)))-(-(-y))$.
9. $-[-\{b+c-a)\}]+[-\{-(c+a-b)\}]$.
10. $-5x-[3y-\{2x-(2y-x)\}]$.
11. $-(-(-a)-(-(-(-x)))$.
12. $3a-[a+b-\{a+b+c-(a+b+c+d)\}]$.
13. $-2a-[3x+\{3c-(4y+3x+2a)\}]$.
14. $3x-[5y-\{6z-(4x-7y)\}]$.
15. $-[5x-(11y-3x)]-[5y-(3x-6y)]$.
16. $-[15x-\{14y-(15z+12y)-(10x-15z)\}]$.
17. $8x-\{16y-[3x-(12y-x)-8y]+x\}$.
18. $-[x-\{z+(x-z)-(z-x)-z\}-x]$.
19. $-[a+\{a-(a-x)-(a+x)-a\}-a]$.
20. $-[a-\{a+(x-a)-(x-a)-a\}-2a]$.

58. A coefficient placed before any bracket indicates that every term of the expression within the bracket is to be multiplied by that coefficient.

NOTE. The line between the numerator and denominator of a fraction is a kind of vinculum. Thus $\frac{x-5}{3}$ is equivalent to $\frac{1}{3}(x-5)$.

Again, an expression of the form $\sqrt{(x+y)}$ is often written $\sqrt{x+y}$, the line above being regarded as a vinculum indicating the square root of the compound expression $x+y$ *taken as a whole.*

Thus $\sqrt{25+144}=\sqrt{169}=13$,

whereas $\sqrt{25}+\sqrt{144}=5+12=17$.

59. Sometimes it is advisable to simplify in the course of the work.

Example. Find the value of

$$84-7[-11x-4\{-17x+3(8-\overline{9-5x})\}].$$

$$\begin{aligned}\text{The expression} &= 84-7[-11x-4\{-17x+3(8-9+5x)\}]\\ &= 84-7[-11x-4\{-17x+3(5x-1)\}]\\ &= 84-7[-11x-4\{-17x+15x-3)\}]\\ &= 84-7[-11x-4\{-2x-3)\}]\\ &= 84-7[-11x+8x+12]\\ &= 84-7[-3x+12]\\ &= 84+21x-84\\ &= 21x.\end{aligned}$$

When the beginner has had a little practice the number of steps may be considerably diminished.

EXAMPLES VII-b

Simplify by removing brackets:

1. $a-[2b+\{3c-3a-(a+b)\}+2a-(b+3c)]$.
2. $a+b-(c+a-[b+c-(a+b-\{c+a-(b+c-a)\})])$.
3. $a-(b-c)-[a-b-c-2\{b+c-3(c-a)-d\}]$.
4. $2x-(3y-4z)-(2x-\{3y+4z)\}-(3y-(4z+2x)\}$.
5. $b+c-(a+b-[c+a-(b+c-\{a+b-(c+a-b)\}])$.
6. $3b-\{5a-[6a+2(10a-b)]\}$.
7. $a-(b-c)-[a-b-c-2\{b+c\}]$.
8. $3a^2-[6a^2-\{8b^2-(9c^2-2a^2)\}]$.
9. $b-(c-a)-[b-a-c-2\{c+a-3(a-b)-d\}]$.
10. $-20(a-d)+3(b-c)-2[b+c+d-3\{c+d-4(d-a)\}]$.
11. $-4(a+d)+24(b-c)-2[c+d+a-3\{d+a-4(b-c)\}]$.
12. $-10(a+b)-[c+a+b-3\{a+2b-(c+a-b)\}]+4c$.
13. $a-2(b-c)-[-\{-(4a-b-c-2\{a+b+c\})\}]$.
14. $8(b-c)-[-\{a-b-3(c-b+a)\}]$.
15. $2(3b-5a)-7[a-6\{2-5(a-b)\}]$.
16. $6\{a-2[b-3(c+d)]\}-4(a-3[b-4(c-d)]\}$.
17. $5\{a-2[a-2(a+a)]\}-4\{a-2[a-2(a+x)]\}$.
18. $-10\{a-6[a-(b-c)]\}+60\{b-(c+a)\}$.
19. $-3\{-2[-4(-a)]\}+5\{-2[-2(-a)]\}$.

20. $-2\{-[-(x-y)]\}+\{-2[-(x-y)]\}$.

21. $\frac{1}{4}\{a-5(b-a)\}-\frac{3}{2}\left\{\frac{1}{3}\left(b-\frac{a}{3}\right)-\frac{2}{9}\left[a-\frac{3}{4}\right]\left(b-\frac{4a}{5}\right)\right\}$.

22. $35\left[\frac{3x-4y}{5}-\frac{1}{10}\left\{3x-\frac{5}{7}(7x-4y)\right\}\right]+8(y-2x)$.

23. $\frac{3}{8}\left\{\frac{4}{3}(a-b)-8(b-c)\right\}-\left\{\frac{b-c}{2}-\frac{c-a}{3}\right\}-\frac{1}{2}\left\{c-a-\frac{2}{3}(a-b)\right\}$.

24. $\frac{1}{2}x-\frac{1}{2}\left(\frac{2}{3}y-\frac{1}{2}z\right)-\left[x-\left\{\frac{1}{2}x-\left(\frac{1}{3}y-\frac{1}{4}z\right)\right\}-\left(\frac{2}{3}y-\frac{1}{2}z\right)\right]$.

Insertion of Brackets

60. The converse operation of inserting brackets is important. The rules for doing this have been enunciated in Arts. 21, 22; for convenience we repeat them.

(1) *Any part of an expression may be enclosed within brackets and the sign + prefixed, the sign of every term within the brackets remaining unaltered.*

(2) *Any part of an expression may be enclosed within brackets and the sign – prefixed, provided the sign of every term within the brackets be changed.*

Examples. $a-b+c-d-e=a-b+(c-d-e)$.

$$a-b+c-d-e=a-(b-c)-(d+e).$$

$$x^2-ax+bx-ab=(x^2-ax)+(bx-ab).$$

$$xy-ax-by+ab=(xy-by)-(ax-ab).$$

61. The terms of an expression can be bracketed in various ways.

Example. The expression $ax-bx+cx-ay+by-cy$

may by written $(ax-bx)+(cx-ay)+(by-cy)$,

or $(ax-bx+cx)-(ay+by+cy)$,

or $(ax-ay)-(bx-by)+(cx-cy)$.

62. Whenever a factor is common to every term within a bracket, it may be removed and placed outside as a multiplier of the expression within the bracket.

Example 1. In the expression

$$ax^3-cx+7-dx^2+bx-c-dx^3+bx^2-2x$$

bracket together the powers of x so as to have ths sign + before each bracket.

The expression $= (ax^3 - dx^3) + (bx^2 - dx^2) + (bx - cx - 2x) + (7 - c)$

$= x^3(a - d) + x^2(b - d) + x(b - c - 2) + (7 - c)$

$= (a - d)x^3 + (b - d)x^2 + (b - c - 2)x + 7 - c.$

In this last result the compound expressions $a - d, b - d, b - c - 2$ are regarded as the coefficients of x^3, x^2, and x respectively.

Example 2. In the expression $-a^2x - 7a + a^2y + 3 - 2x - ab$ bracket together the powers of a so as to have sign $-$ before each bracket.

The expression $= -(a^2x - a^2y) - (7a + ab) - (2x - 3)$

$= -a^2(x - y) - a(7 + b) - (2x + 3)$

$= -(x - y)a^2 - (7 + b)a - (2x - 3).$

EXAMPLES VII-c

In the following expressions bracket the powers of x so that the signs before all the brackets shall be positive:

1. $ax^2 + bx^2 + 5 + 2bx - 5x^2 + 2x^4 - 3x.$

2. $3bx^2 - 7 - 2x + ab + 5ax^3 + cx - 4x^2 - bx^3.$

3. $2 - 7x^3 + 5ax^2 - 2cx + 9ax^3 + 7x - 3x^2.$

4. $2cx^5 - 3abx + 4dx - 3bx^4 - a^2x^5 + x^4.$

In the following expressions bracket the powers of x so that the signs before all the brackets shall be negative.

5. $ax^2 + 5x^3 - a^2x^4 - 2bx^3 - 3x^2 - bx^4.$

6. $7x^3 - 3c^2x - abx^5 + 5ax + 7x^5 - abcx^3.$

7. $ax^2 + a^2x^3 - bx^2 - 5x^2 - cx^3.$

8. $3b^2x^4 - bx - ax^4 - cx^4 - 5c^2x - 7x^4.$

Simplify the following expressions, and in each result re-group the terms according to powers of x:

9. $ax^3 - 2cx - [bx^2 - \{cx - dx - (bx^3 + 3cx^2)\} - (cx^2 - bx)].$

10. $5ax^3 - 7(bx - cx^3) - \{6bx^2 - (3ax^2 + 2ax) - 4cx^3\}.$

11. $ax^2 - 3\{-ax^3 + 3bx - 4\left[\frac{1}{6}cx^3 - \frac{2}{3}(ax - bx^2)\right]\}.$

12. $x^5 - 4bx^4 - \frac{1}{6}\left[12ax - 4\left\{3bx^4 - 9\left(\frac{cx}{2} - bx^5\right) - \frac{3}{2}ax^4\right\}\right].$

13. $x\{x - b - x(a - bx)\} + ax - x\{x - x(ax - b)\}.$

63. In certain cases of addition, multiplication, etc., of expressions which involve literal coefficients, the results may be more conveniently. written by grouping the terms according to powers of some common letter.

Example 1. Add together $ax^3 - 2bx^2 + 3, bx - cx^3 - x^2$ and $x^3 - ax^2 + cx$.

$$\begin{aligned}\text{The sum} &= ax^3 - 2bx^2 + 3 + bx - cx^3 - x^2 + x^3 - ax^2 + cx \\ &= ax^3 - cx^3 + x^3 - ax^2 - 2bx^2 - x^2 + bx + cx + 3 \\ &= (a - c + 1)\,x^3 - (a + 2b + 1)\,x^2 + (b + c)\,x + 3.\end{aligned}$$

Example 2. Multiply $ax^2 - 2bx + 3c$ by $px - q$.

$$\begin{aligned}\text{The product} &= (ax^2 - 2bx + 3c)\,(px - q) \\ &= apx^3 - 2bpx^2 + 3cpx - aqx^2 + 2bqx - 3cq \\ &= apx^3 - (2bp + aq)x^2 + (3cp + 2bq)x - 3cq.\end{aligned}$$

EXAMPLES VII-d

Add together the following expressions, and in each case arrange the result according to powers of x:

1. $ax^3 - 2cx, bx^2 - cx^3, cx^2 - x$.

2. $x^2 - x - 1, ax^2 - bx^3, bx + x^3$.

3. $a^2x^3 - 5x, 2ax^2 - 5ax^3, 2x^3 - bx^2 - ax$.

4. $ax^2 + bx - c, qx - r - px^2, x^2 + 2x + 3$.

5. $px^3 - qx, qx^2 - px, q - x^3, px^2 + qx^3$.

Multiply together the following expression, and in each case arrange the result according to powers of x :

6. $ax^2 + bx + 1$ and $cx + 2$.

7. $cx^2 - 2x + 3$ and $ax - b$.

8. $ax^2 - bx - c$ and $px + q$.

9. $2x^2 - 3x - 1$ and $bx + c$.

10. $ax^2 - 2bx + 3c$ and $x - 1$.

11. $px^2 - 2x - q$ and $ax - 3$.

12. $x^3 + ax^2 - bx - c$ and $x^3 - ax^2 - bx + c$.

13. $ax^3 - x^2 + 3x - b$ and $ax^3 + x^2 + 3x + b$.

14. $x^4 - ax^3 - bx^2 + cx + d$ and $x^4 + ax^3 - bx^2 - cx + d$.

8

SUNOKE EQYATUIBS

64. AN equation is a statement that two algebraical are equal.
Thus (i) $x + 3 + x + 4 = 2x + 7$, (ii) $4x + 2 = 14$ are equations.

The parts of an equation separated by the sign of equality are called members or sides of the equation, and are distinguished as the *right side* and the *left side*.

65. If the two expressions are *always* equal, for *any* values we give to the symbols, the equation is called an identical equation, or briefly an identity, Thus equation (i) above is an *identity*, as a easily seen by collecting the term on the left side.

If two expression are only equal for a particular value or values of the symbols, the equation is called an equation of condition, or more usually an *equation*, simply.

Thus the statement $4x + 2 = 14$ will be found to be true only when $x = 3$.

This, then, is an equation in the ordinary sense of the term, and the value 3 is said to satisfy the equation. The object of the present chapter is to shew how to find the values which satisfy equations of the simpler kinds.

66. The letter whose value it is required to find in any equation is called the unknown quantity. The process of finding its value is called solving the equation. The value so found is called the root or solution of the equation.

67. An equation which, when reduced to a simple form, involves no power of the unknown quantity higher than the first is called a simple equation. It ia usual to denote the unknown quantity by x.

68. The process of solving a simple equation depends only on the following axioms.

1. If to equals we add equals the sums are equal.
2. If from equals we take equals the remainders are equal.
3. If equals are multiplied by equals the products are equal.
4. If equals are divided by equals the quotients are equal.

Example 1. To solve the equation $7x = 14$.

Dividing both sides by 7, (Axiom 4) we get

$$x = 2.$$

Example 2. Solve the equation $\frac{x}{2} = -6$.

Multiplying both sides by 2, (Axiom 3) we get

$$x = -12$$

Example 3. Solve the equation $7x - 2x - x = 10 - 23 - 15$.

By collecting terms on each side, we get

$$4x = -28$$

Dividing by 4, (Axiom 4) we get $x = -7$.

EXAMPLES (Oral)

Find the values which satisfy the following equations.

1. $3x = 18$.

2. $4x = 12$.

3. $6x = 12$.

4. $7x = -7$.

5. $3x = 21$.

6. $11x = 55$.

7. $13x = 39$.

8. $14x = -42$.

9. $7x = -35$.

10. $-5x = 30$.

11. $-2x = -12$

12. $-3x = 21$.

13. $3x = 0$.

14. $-4x = 0$.

15. $2x = 11$.

16. $9x = 15$.

17. $51x = 39$.

18. $3x = -7$.

19. $28x = 35$.

20. $34x = -51$.

21. $\frac{x}{3} = 7$.

22. $\frac{x}{7} = -3$.

23. $-\frac{x}{5} = 4$.

24. $\frac{x}{6} = 0$.

25. $8x + 5x - 3x = 17 - 9 + 33 - 11$.

26. $5x - 7x + 8x = 12 - 5 + 7 + 10$.

27. $-3x - 12x + 5x = 29 - 2 + 6 - 13$.

28. $4x - 15x - 9x + 27x = -28 + 8 - 60 + 17$.

69. In the preceding examples the terms have been so arranged that those involving the unknown quantity have been on one side of the equation and the numerical quantities on the other. We can always arrive at this arrangement by the aid of the axioms.

Example. Solve the equation $3x - 8 = x + 12$.

Substracting x from both sides, we get

$$3x - x - 8 = 12. \qquad \text{[Axiom 2.]}$$

Adding 8 to both sides, we have

$$3x - x = 12 + 8\ ; \qquad \text{[Axiom 1.]}$$

$\therefore$ $2x = 20;$

dividing by 2, $x = 10.$ [Axiom 4.]

70 Beginners should verify, that is, prove the correctness of their solutions by substituting, in both sides, the value obtained for the unknown quantity.

In the last equation $3x - 8 = x + 12$,

if $x = 10,$

the left side $= 3 \times 10 - 8 = 22,$

and the right side $= 10 + 10 = 22.$

Since these two results are equal the solutions is correct.

71. In the following examples some preliminary reduction is necessary.

Example 1. Solve $5(x - 3) - 7(6 - x) = 24 - 3(8 - x) - 3.$

Removing brackets, $5x - 15 - 42 + 7x = 24 - 24 + 3x - 3\ ;$

Collecting terms, $12x - 57 = 3x - 3.$

Subtracting $3x$ from each side, we get

$$9x - 57 = -3 \qquad \text{[Axiom 2.]}$$

Adding 57 to each side, we have

$$9x = 54 \qquad \text{[Axiom 1.]}$$

Dividing by 9. $x = 6$ [Axiom 4.]

[*verification*. When $x = 6$,

the left side $= 5(6 - 3) - 7(6 - 6) = 5 \times 3 - 0 = 15.$

The right side $= 24 - 3\ (8 - 6) - 3 = 24 - 3 \times 2 - 3 = 24 - 9 = 15.$

Thus the solution is correct.]

Example 2. Solve $\frac{4x}{5} - \frac{3}{10} = \frac{x}{5} + \frac{x}{4}.$

Here it is convenient to begin by clearing the equation of fractional coefficients. This can be done by multiplying every term on each side of the equation by the least common multiple of the denominators. [Axiom 3.]

Hence, multiplying throughout by 20,

$$16x - 6 = 4x + 5x.$$

Subtracting $9x$ from each side,

$$7x-6=0.$$

Adding 6 to each side, $7x=6$.

Dividing by 7, $x=\frac{6}{7}$.

Verification. When $x=\frac{6}{7}$.

the left side $=\frac{4}{5}\times\frac{6}{7}-\frac{3}{10}=\frac{48-21}{70}=\frac{27}{10}$.

The right side $=\frac{1}{5}\times\frac{6}{7}+\frac{1}{4}\times\frac{6}{7}=\frac{24+30}{140}=\frac{54}{140}=\frac{27}{90}$.

Thus the solution is correct.

72. The preceding example have been worked out very fully in every detail for the purpose of impressing on beginners the importance of shewing clearly the meaning of every step of their work in solving simple equations.Each step should occupy a separate line, and each successive process should be referred to one of the fundamental axioms, the object in each case being to gradually reduce the equation until it consists of a single term containing x on one side, and a single known term on the other. The required root is then of found by dividing each side by the coefficient of x.

Orderly arrangement should be studied throughout, and in particular, the signs of equality in the several lines should be written nearly in column.

In order to furnish the requisite practice in *method* and *arrangement*, we shall now give an exercise containing easy equations which are free from difficulty in the way of reduction, and which involve little actual work.

EXAMPLES VIII-a

Find the value of x which satisfies each of the following equations, and in each case verify the solution.

1. $7x-4=17$. **2.** $3x-5=0$.

3. $2x+15=23$. **4.** $5x-9=21$.

5. $7x=18-2x$. **6.** $3x=25-2x$.

7. $4x-3=2x+1$. **8.** $5x+2=6x-1$.

9. $3x+2=4x-3$. **10.** $4x-3=3x+4$.

11. $8x-9=33-4x$. **12.** $5x+3=15-x$.

13. $2x+15=27-4x$. **14.** $7x+11=3x+27$.

15. $15-5x=24-8x$. **16.** $9x+21-4x=46$.

17. $5x+7+4x+11+3x=24$. **18.** $0=9-6x-19+10x$.

19. $7-3x=5+4x+11-16x$. **20.** $-3x-5=-7x+1$.

21. $6x + 7 - 19 = 7x + 13 - 3x - 21.$

22. $3x + 4 + 10x - 17 = 14 - 23x + 16 - 7x.$

Solve and verify the following equations:

23. $\frac{x}{3} = \frac{5}{6}.$

24. $\frac{x}{5} = \frac{4}{3}.$

25. $\frac{2x}{3} = \frac{5}{12}.$

26. $\frac{4x}{5} = \frac{7}{15}.$

27. $\frac{7x}{6} = \frac{4}{9}.$

28. $\frac{3x}{8} = \frac{5}{9}.$

29. $\frac{1}{2}x - \frac{1}{4}x = x - 9.$

30. $\frac{x}{3} - \frac{1}{2} = \frac{x}{5} + 1\frac{1}{2}.$

31. $\frac{x}{3} - 2\frac{1}{2} = \frac{4x}{9} - \frac{2x}{3}.$

32. $\frac{1}{8}x + \frac{1}{6}x - x = \frac{5}{6} - \frac{1}{2}x.$

73. After enough practice to enforce the reasons for the several steps, the solutions may be presented in a shorter form.

When any term is brought over from one side of an equation to the other it is said to be transposed.

We shall now shew that any term may be transposed from one side of an equation to the other by simply writing it down on the opposite side *with its sign changed.*

Consider the equation $3x - 8 = x + 12$.

Subtracting x from each side, we get $3x - x - 8 = 12$

Adding 8 to each side, we have $3x - x = 12 + 8$

Thus we see that $+ x$ has been removed from one side, and appears as $-x$ on the other; and -8 has been removed from one side and appears as $+ 8$ on the other.

Similar steps may be employed in all cases.

It appears from this that *we may change the sign of every term in an equation*; for this is equivalent to transposing all the terms, and then making the two sides change places.

Example. Take the equation $-3x - 12 = x - 24$.

Transposing.

$$-x + 24 = 3x + 12,$$

or

$$3x + 12 = -x + 24,$$

which is the original equation with the sign of every term changed.

74. We can now give a general rule for solving any simple equation with one unknown quantity.

Rule. *First, if necessary, clear of fractions; then transpose all the terms containing the unknown quantity to one side of the equation, and the known quanitites to the other. Collect the terms on each side; divide both sides by the coefficient of the unknown quantity and the value required is obtained.*

Example 1. Solve $5x - (4x - 7)(3x - 5) = 6 - 3(4x - 9)(x - 1)$

Here the products $(4x - 7)(3x - 5)$ and $(4x - 9)(x - 1)$ must be multiplied out, or written down by inspection as in Art. 44, before any further reduction can be made.

Forming the products, we have

$$5x - 12x^2 - 41x + 35 = 6 - 3(4x^2 - 13x + 9);$$

and by removing brackets,

$$5x - 12x^2 + 41x - 35 = 6 - 12x^2 + 39x - 27.$$

The term $-12x^2$ may be removed from each side without altering the equality ; thus

$$5x + 41x - 35 = 6 + 39x - 27.$$

Transposing, $5x + 41x - 39x = 6 - 27 + 35;$

collecting terms, $7x = 14; \quad \Rightarrow \quad x = 2.$

NOTE. Since the minus sign before a bracket affects every term within it, in the first line of work we do not remove the brackets until we have formed the products.

Example 2. Solve $7x - 5\{x - [7 - 6(x - 3)]\} = 3x + 1.$

Removing brackets, we have

$$7x - 5(x - [7 - 6x + 18]] = 3x + 1,$$

$$7x - 5[x - 25 + 6x] = 3x + 1,$$

$$7x - 5x + 125 - 30x = 3x + 1;$$

transposing, $7x - 5x - 30x - 3x = 1 - 125;$

collecting terms, $\quad -31x = 124;$

$\therefore \quad x = 4.$

EXAMPLES VIII-b

[*It is recommended that Nos.* 1-16 *of the following examples should be solved in full by reference to the axioms. In the rest of the exercise the solutions may be shortened by transposition of terms.*]

Solve the following equations and verify the solutions in Examples 1 to 20.

1. $3x + 15 = x + 25.$

2. $2x - 3 = 3x - 7.$

3. $3x + 4 = 5(x - 2).$

4. $2x + 3 = 16 - (2x - 3).$

5. $8(x - 1) + 17(x - 3) = 4(4x - 9) + 4.$

6. $15(x - 1) + 4(x + 3) = 2(7 + x).$

7. $5x - 6(x - 5) = 2(x + 5 + (x - 4).$

8. $8(x - 3) - (6 - 2x) = 2(x + 2) - 5(5 - x).$

Solve the following equations:

9. $7(25 - x) - 2x = 2(3x - 25).$

10. $3(169 - x) - (78 + x) = 29x.$

11. $5x - 17 + 3x - 5 = 6x - 7 - 8x + 115.$

12. $7x - 39 - 10x + 15 = 100 - 33x + 26.$

13. $118 - 65x - 123 = 15x + 35 - 120x.$

14. $157 - 21(x + 3) = 163 - 15(2x - 5).$

15. $179 - 18(x - 10) = 158 - 3(x - 17).$

16. $97 - 5(x + 20) = 111 - 8(x + 3).$

17. $x - [3 + \{x - (3 + x)\}] = 5.$

18. $5x - (3x - 7) - [4 - 2x - (6x - 3)] = 10.$

19. $14x - (5x - 9) - \{4 - 3x - (2x - 3)\} = 30.$

20. $25x - 19 - [3 - \{4x - 5\}] = 3x - (6x - 5).$

21. $(x + 1)(2x + 1) = (x + 3)(2x + 3) - 14.$

22. $(x + 1)^2 - (x^2 - 1) = x(2x + 1) - 2(x + 2)(x + 1) + 20.$

23. $2(x + 1)(x + 3) + 8 = (2x + 1)(x + 5).$

24. $6(x^2 - 3x + 2) - 2(x^2 - 1) = 4(x + 1)(x + 2) - 24.$

25. $2(x - 4) - (x^2 + x - 20) = 4x^2 - (5x + 3)(x - 4) - 64.$

26. $(x + 15)(x - 3) - (x^2 - 6x + 9) = 30 - 15(x - 1).$

27. $2x - 5\{3x - 7(4x - 9\} = 66.$

28. $20(2-x)+3(x-7)-2[x+9-3[9-4(2-x)]]=22.$

29. $x+2-[x-8-2\{8-3(5-x)-x\}]=0$.

30. $3(5-6x)-5[x-5\{1-3(x-5)\}]=23.$

31. $(x+1)(2x+3)=2(x+1)^2+8.$

32. $3(x-1)^2-3(x^2-1)=x-15.$

33. $(3x+1)(2x-7)=6(x-3)^2+7.$

34. $x^2-8x+25=x(x-4)-25(x-5)-16.$

35. $x(x+1)+(x+1)(x+2)=(x+2)(x+3)+x(x+4)-9.$

36. $2(x+2)(x-4)=x(2x+1)-21.$

37. $(x+1)^2+2(x+3)^2=3x(x+2)+35.$

38. $4(x+5)^2-(2x+1)^2=3(x-5)+180.$

39. $84+(x+4)(x-3)(x+5)=(x+1)(x+2)(x+3).$

40. $(x+1)(x+2)(x+6)=x^3+9x^2+4(7x-1)$.

75. The following examples illustrate the most useful methods of solving equations with fractional coefficients.

Example 1. Solve $4-\frac{x-9}{8}=\frac{x}{22}-\frac{1}{2}.$

Multiply by 88, the least common multiple of the denominators ;

thus $352-11(x-9)=4x-44$;

removing brackets, $352-11x+99=4x-44$;

transposing, $-11x-4x=-44-352-99$;

collecting terms and changing signs, $15x=495$;

$$x=33$$

NOTE. Here $-\frac{x-9}{8}$ is equivalent to $-\frac{1}{8}(x-9)$, the *vinculum* or line between the numerator and denominator having the same effect as a bracket. [Art. 58].

75. In certain cases it will be found more convenient not to multiply thoughtout by the L.C.M. of the denominators, but to clear of fractions in two or more steps.

Example 2. Solve $\frac{x-4}{3}+\frac{2x-3}{35}=\frac{5x-32}{9}-\frac{x+9}{28}.$

Multiplying throughout by 9, we have

$$3x-12+\frac{18x-27}{35}=5x-32-\frac{9x+81}{28}.$$

transposing, $\frac{18x-27}{35}+\frac{9x+81}{28}=2x-20.$

Now, clear of fractions by multiplying by $5 \times 7 \times 4$ or 140;

thus $72x - 108 + 45x + 405 = 280x - 2800$;

$\therefore \quad 2800 - 108 + 405 = 280x - 72x - 45x;$

$\therefore \quad 3097 = 163x;$

$\therefore \quad x = 19.$

77. To solve equations whose coefficients are decimals, we may express the decimals as vulgar fractions, and proceed as before; but it is often found more simple to work entirely in decimals.

Example 1. Solve $\cdot 6x + \cdot 25 - \frac{1}{9}x = 1\cdot 8 - \cdot 75x - \frac{1}{3}$.

Expressing the decimals as vulgar fractions; we have

$$\frac{2}{3}x + \frac{1}{4} - \frac{1}{9}x = 1\frac{8}{9} - \frac{3}{4}x - \frac{1}{3};$$

clearing of fractions, $24x + 9 - 4x = 68 - 27x - 12$;

transposing, $24x - 4x + 27x = 68 - 12 - 9$,

$$47x = 47$$

$$x = 1$$

Example 2. Solve $\cdot 375x - 1\cdot 875 = \cdot 12x + 1\cdot 185$.

Transposing, $\cdot 375x - \cdot 12x = 1\cdot 185 + 1\cdot 875$;

collecting terms, $(\cdot 375 - \cdot 12)x = 3\cdot 06$,

$$x = \frac{3\cdot 06}{\cdot 255} = 12.$$

EXAMPLES VIII-c

Solve the following equations, and verify Nos. 1-16.

1. $\frac{x}{4} + \frac{x-5}{3} = 10.$

2. $\frac{x-5}{10} + \frac{x+5}{5} = 5.$

3. $\frac{x-2}{2} + \frac{x+10}{9} = 5.$

4. $\frac{x+19}{5} = 3 + \frac{x}{4}.$

5. $\frac{x-4}{7} = \frac{x-10}{5}.$

6. $\frac{x-1}{8} = 1 + \frac{x+1}{18}.$

7. $\frac{4(x+2)}{5} = 7 + \frac{5x}{13}.$

8. $\frac{x+4}{14} + \frac{x-4}{6} = 2.$

9. $\frac{x+20}{9} + \frac{3x}{7} = 6.$

10. $\frac{x-1}{7} + \frac{x-3}{3} + \frac{5}{21} = 0.$

11. $\frac{x+5}{6} - \frac{x+1}{9} = \frac{x+3}{4}.$

12. $\frac{4-5x}{6} - \frac{1-2x}{3} = \frac{13}{42}.$

13. $\dfrac{5(x+5)}{8} - \dfrac{2(x-3)}{7} = 5\dfrac{19}{28}$

14. $\dfrac{4(x+2)}{3} - \dfrac{6(x-7)}{7} = 12.$

15. $1 + \dfrac{x}{2} - \dfrac{2x}{3} = \dfrac{3x}{4} - 4\dfrac{1}{2}.$

16. $\dfrac{x}{2} + \dfrac{x}{3} - \dfrac{x}{4} + \dfrac{x}{5} = 7\dfrac{5}{6}.$

17. $\dfrac{3}{16}(x-1) - \dfrac{5}{12}(x-4) = \dfrac{2}{5}(x-6) + \dfrac{5}{48}.$

18. $x + \dfrac{5}{3}(x-7) - \dfrac{6}{7}(x-8) = 3x - 14\dfrac{1}{3}.$

19. $\dfrac{3x}{4} - \dfrac{6}{17}(x+10) - (x-3) = \dfrac{x-7}{51} - 4\dfrac{3}{4}.$

20. $\dfrac{7x}{5} - \dfrac{1}{14}(x-11) = \dfrac{3}{7}(x-25) + 34.$

21. $3 + \dfrac{x}{4} = \dfrac{1}{2}\left(4 - \dfrac{x}{3}\right) - \dfrac{5}{6} + \dfrac{1}{3}\left(11 - \dfrac{x}{2}\right).$

22. $\dfrac{1}{5}(x-8) + \dfrac{4+x}{4} + \dfrac{x-1}{7} = 7 - \dfrac{23-x}{5}.$

23. $\dfrac{1}{3}\left(\dfrac{x}{4} - 3\right) + \dfrac{5x}{6} - \dfrac{5x}{4} = \dfrac{x-12}{5} - \dfrac{x+3}{3}.$

24. $x - \left(3x - \dfrac{2x-5}{10}\right) = \dfrac{1}{6}(2x-57) - \dfrac{5}{3}.$

25. $\dfrac{x}{4} - \dfrac{x+10}{5} + 4\dfrac{3}{4} = x - 1 - \dfrac{x-2}{3}.$

26. $\cdot 5x - \cdot 3x = \cdot 25x - 1.$

27. $3 + \dfrac{x}{\cdot 5} = 7 - \dfrac{x}{\cdot 2}$

28. $2.25x - \cdot 125 = 3x + 3\cdot 75.$

29. $\cdot 2x - \cdot 16x = \cdot 6 - \cdot 3.$

30. $\cdot 6x - \cdot 7x + \cdot 75x - \cdot 875x + 15 = 0.$

31. $12[3x - \cdot 25(x-4) - \cdot 3(5x+14)] = 47.$

32. $\dfrac{\cdot 25(x-3) + \cdot 3(x-4)}{\cdot 125} = 5x - 19.$

33. $\dfrac{x + \cdot 75}{\cdot 125} - \dfrac{x - \cdot 25}{\cdot 25} = 15.$

34. $\dfrac{5}{6}x + \cdot 25x - \cdot 3x = x - 3.$

35. $\cdot 5x - \cdot 2x = \cdot 3x - 1\cdot 5.$

36. $1.5 = \dfrac{\cdot 36}{2} - \dfrac{\cdot 09x - \cdot 18}{\cdot 9}.$

[*Some of the examples in Miscellaneous Examples II. p.* 88, *will furnish further practice in Simple Equations.*]

78. Before concluding this chapter it will be worth while to draw attention to the following cases which occurs so frequently in solving equations that the beginner should learn to write down the solution at sight.

***Case* I.** Suppose $\frac{7x}{5}=\frac{4}{3}$.

Multiplying both sides by 5, we have

$$\left.\begin{aligned} 7x &= \frac{4\times 5}{3} \\ x &= \frac{4\times 5}{3\times 7} \end{aligned}\right\} \quad \ldots(1)$$

***Case* II.** Suppose $\frac{5}{3x}=\frac{9}{7}$.

Multiplying both sides by $3x$, we have

$$\left.\begin{aligned} 5 &= \frac{9\times 3x}{7} \\ 5\times 7 &= 9\times 3x \\ \frac{5\times 7}{9\times 3} &= x \end{aligned}\right\} \quad \ldots(2)$$

By a careful examination of the results in (1) and (2), the truth of the following principles will be evident:

Any factor of the numerator of one side of an equation may be transferred to the denominator of the other side, and any factor of the denominator of one side may be transferred to the numerator of the other side.

the ready application of these principles will be found very useful.

Example 1. If $\frac{3x}{14}=\frac{9}{35}$.

then $\quad x=\frac{9\times 14}{35\times 3}=1\frac{1}{5}$.

Example 2. If $\frac{2}{x}=-5$,

Then, $\quad \frac{2}{5}=-x;$

$\therefore \quad x=-\frac{2}{5}$.

After a little practice the arithmetic should be performed mentally, and the intermediate steps omitted.

EXAMPLES VIII-d

Write down the values of x which satisfy the following equations:

1. $\frac{2}{x} = \frac{3}{4}$.

2. $\frac{3}{7} = \frac{x}{14}$

3. $\frac{3}{5} = \frac{6}{x}$.

4. $-\frac{x}{3} = 2$.

5. $\frac{x}{17} = \frac{29}{51}$.

6. $\frac{2x}{15} = \frac{8}{45}$.

7. $\frac{3}{2x} = -\frac{1}{8}$.

8. $-\frac{4x}{3} = -\frac{1}{2}$.

9. $\frac{5}{3x} = \frac{25}{27}$.

10. $\frac{5}{2x} = -\frac{10}{3}$.

11. $\frac{13}{21} = \frac{65x}{84}$.

12. $-\frac{7}{2} = \frac{1}{3x}$.

13. $\frac{3}{8} = \frac{x}{4}$.

14. $\frac{8}{21x} = -\frac{4}{7}$.

15. $\frac{36}{35} = \frac{9}{5x}$.

16. $\frac{5}{2} = \frac{15}{2x}$.

17. $\frac{x}{18} = \frac{9}{42}$.

18. $\frac{4}{3x} = \frac{16}{27}$.

19. $\frac{49}{15} = \frac{7}{3x}$.

20. $\frac{56}{15} = \frac{8x}{3}$.

21. $\frac{19x}{7} = \frac{57}{49}$.

9

SYMBOLICAL EXPRESSION

79. IN solving algebraical problems the chief difficulty of the beginner is to express the conditions of the question by means of symbols. A question proposed in algebraical symbols will frequently be found puzzling, when a similar arithmetical question would present no difficulty. Thus, the answer to the question "find a number greater than x by a" may not be self-evident to the beginner, who would of ccurse readily answer an analogous arithmetical question, "find a number greater than 50 by 6." The process of addition which gives the answer in the second case supplies the necessary hint; and, just as the number which is greater than 50 by 6 is 50 + 6, so the number which is greater than x by a is $x + a$.

80. The following examples will perhaps be the best introduction to the subject of this chapter. After the first we leave to the student the choice of arithmetical instances, should be find them necessary.

Example 1. By how much does x exceed 17.

Take a numerical instance; "by how much does 27 exceed 17?" The answer obviously is 10, which is equal to 27 – 17.

Hence the excess of x over 17 is $x - 17$.

Similarly the defect of x from 17 is $17 - x$.

Example 2. If x is one *part* of 45 the other part is $45 - x$.

Example 3. If x is one *factor* of 45 the other factor is $\frac{45}{x}$

Example 4. How far can a man walk in a hours at the rate of 4 km an hour?

In 1 hour he walks 4 km.

In a hours he walks a times as far, that is, $4a$ km.

Example 5. If Rs. 20 is divided equally among y persons, the share of each is the total sum divided by the number of persons, or Rs $\frac{20}{y}$.

Example 6. If 17 be divided by 6 the quotient is 2, and the remainder 5, that is, $\frac{17}{6} = 2 + \frac{5}{6}$.

So, if N be divided by D, and the quotient be Q and the remainder R, we have

$$\frac{N}{D} = Q + \frac{R}{D},$$

or $$N = QD + R.$$

Thus, if the divisor is x, the quotient y, and the remainder z, the dividend is $xy + z$.

Example 7. A and B are playing for money; A begins with Rs p and B with q paise:- after B has won Rs x, how many paise has each? What R has won A has lost,

A has $100(p - x)$ paise,

B has $q + 100x$ paise.

EXAMPLES IX-a

1. What must be added to x to make y?

2. By what must 3 be multiplied to make a?

3. What dividend gives b as the quotient when 5 is the divisor?

4. What is the defect of $2c$ from $3d$?

5. By how much does $3k$ exceed k ?

6. If 100 be divided into two parts and one part be x, what is the other?

7. If a be one factor of b, what is the other?

8. What number is less than 20 by c ?

9. What is the price in paise of Q oranges at 84 paise a dozen?

10. What is the price in rupees of 100 oranges when x cost 25 paise?

11. If the difference of two numbers be 11, and if the smaller be x, what is the greater?

12. If the sum of two numbers be c and one of them is 20, what is the other?

13. What is the excess of 90 over x?

14. By how much does x exceed 30?

15. If 100 contains x five times, what is the value of x?

16. What is the cost in rupees of 200 books at x paise each?

17. In x years a man will be 36 years old, what is his present age?

18. How old will a man be in a years if his present age is x years?

19. If x men take 5 days to reap a field, how long will one man take?

20. What value of x will make $5x$ equal to 20?

21. What is the price in rupees of 1000 apples, when the cost of a score is x paise?

22. How many hours will it take to walk x km at 4 km an hour?

23. How far can I walk in x hours at the rate of y km an hour?

24. In x days a man walks y km, what is his rate per day?

25. How many minutes will it take to walk x km at a km an hour?

26. A train goes x km an hour, how long does it take to go from Bristol to London, a distance of 200 km?

27. How many km is it between two places, if a train travelling p km an hour takes 5 hours to perform the journey?

28. What is the velocity in metres per second of a train which travels 36 km in x hours?

29. A man has a rupees and b 25- paise coins, how many paise has he?

30. If I spend x paise out of a sum of Rs 20, how many paise have I left?

31. Out of a purse containing Rs a and b 50-paise coins a man spends c paise; express in paise the sum left.

32. By how much does $2x - 5$ exceed $x + 1$?

33. What number must be taken from $a - 2b$ to leave $a - 3b$?

34. If a bill is shared equally amongst x persons and each pays Rs 1.40, how many paise does the bill amount to?

35. If I give away c paise out of a purse containing a rupee coins and b 25-paise coins, how many paise have I left?

36. In how many weeks will x horses eat 100 kg of grain if one horse eats y kg a week?

37. If I spend x paise a week, how many rupees do I save out of a yearly income of Rs y?

38. A bookshelf contains x Latin, y Greek, and z English books; if there are 100 books, how many are there in other languages?

39. I have x rupees in my purse, y five-paise coins in one pocket and z paise coins in another; if I give away 25 paise, how many paise have I left?

40. In a class of x boys, y work at Classics, z at Mathematics and the rest are idle: what is the excess of workers over idlers?

41. We subjoin a few harder examples worked out in full.

Example 1. What is the present age of a man who x years hence will be m times as old as his son now aged y years?

In x years the son's age will be $y + x$ years; hence the father's age will be $m(y + x)$ years; therefore *now* the father's age is $m(y + x) - x$ years.

Example 2. Find the simple interest on Rs k in n years at f per cent.

Interest on Rs 100 tor 1 year is Rs f.

$\therefore$ ... Re 1 ... Rs $\frac{f}{100}$,

$\therefore$ ... Rs k... Rs $\frac{kf}{100}$,

$\therefore$ Interest on Rs k for n years is Rs $\frac{nkf}{100}$.

Example 3. A room is x metres long, y dm broad, and a dm high; find how many square metres of'carpet will be required for the floor, and how many square metres of paper for the walls.

(1) The area of the floor is $10xy$ square decimeters;

$\therefore$ the number of square metres of carpet required is $\frac{10xy}{100} = \frac{xy}{10}$

(2) The perimeter of the room is $2(10x + y)$ dm;

$\therefore$ the area of the walls is $2a(10x + y)$ square dm;

$\therefore$ number of equare metres of paper required is $\frac{2a(10x + y)}{100}$.

Example 4. The digits of a number beginning from the left are $a, b, c,$ what is the number?

Here c is the digit in the units' place; b standing in the tens' place represents b tens; similarly a represents a hundreds.

The number is therefore equal to a hundreds + b tens + c units

$$= 100c + 10b + c.$$

If the digits of the number are inverted, a new number is formed which is symbolically expressed by

$$100c + 10b + a.$$

Example 5. What is (1) the sum, (2) the product of three consecutive numbers of which the least is n?

The numbers consecutive to n are $n + 1, n + 2$;

$\therefore$ the sum $= n + (n + 1) + (n + 2)$

$= 3n + 3.$

And the product $= n(n + 1)(n + 2)$

We may remark here that any *even* number may be denoted by $2n$, where n is *any* positive whole number; for this expression is exactly divisible by 2.

Similarly, any odd number may be denoted by $2n+1$; for this expression when divided by 2 leaves remainder 1.

Example 6. How many days will a men take to mow b sq. metres if c boys can mow a sq. metres in b days, and each man's work equals that of n boys?

Since c boys can mow a sq. metres in b days;

$\therefore$ 1 boy.................................. bc days,

$\therefore$ n boys, or 1 man, ... $\frac{bc}{n}$ days,

$\therefore$ a men................................ $\frac{bc}{an}$ days,

$\therefore$ a men .... 1 sqmetres ... $\frac{bc}{a^2n}$ days.

therefore a men can mow b sq. metres in $\frac{bc}{a^2n}$ days.

EXAMPLES IX-b

1. Write down four consecutive numbers of which x is the least.
2. Write down three consecutive numbers of which y is the greatest.
3. Write down five consecutive numbers of which x is the middle one.
4. What is the next even number after $2n$?
5. What is the odd number next before $2x + 1$?
6. Find the sum of three consecutive odd numbers of which the middle one is $2n+1$.
7. A man makes a journey of x km. He travels a km by coach, b by train, and finishes the journey by boat. How far does the boat carry him?
8. A horse eats a kg and a donkey b kg of corn in a week: how many kg will they together consume in n weeks?
9. If a man was x years old 5 years ago, how old will he be y years hence?
10. A boy is x years old, and 5 years hence his age will be half that of his father. How old is the father now?
11. What is the age of man who y years ago was m times as old as a child then aged x years?
12. A's age is double B's, B's is three times C's, and C is x years old: find A's age.
13. What is the interest on Rs 1000 in b years at c per cent?
14. What is the interest on Rs x in a years at 5 per cent?
15. What is the interest on Rs 50 a in a years at a per cent?
16. What is the interest on Rs $24xy$ in x months at y per cent, per annum?
17. A room is x metres in length, and y decimetres in breadth: how many decimetres^2 are there in the area of the floor?

18. A square room measures x decimetres each way: how many square metres of carpet will be required to cover it?
19. A room is p dm long and x metres in width: how many metres of carpet 2 dm wide will be required for the floor?
20. What is the cost in rupees of carpeting a room a metres long, b dm broad, with carpet costing c paise a square metre?
21. How many metres of carpet x cm wide will be required to cover the floor of a room y dm long and z dm broad?
22. A room is a metres long and b metres broad; in the middle there is a carpet c dm square: how many square metres of oil-cloth will be required to cover the rest of the floor?
23. How many km can a person walk in 45 minutes if he walks a km in x hours?
24. How long will it take a person to walk b km if he walks 20 km in c hours?
25. If a train travels a km in b hours, how many metres does it move through in one second?
26. A train is running with a velocity of x dm per second: how many km will it travel in y hours?
27. How long will x men take to mow y sq. metres of corn, if each man mows z sq. metres a day?
28. How many men will be required to do in x hours what y men do in xz hours?
29. What is the rate per cent which will produce Rs y interest from a principal of Rs 1000 in r years?
30. Find in how many years a principal of Rs a will produce Rs p interest at r per cent per annum.

    [*The following examples will assist the student in starting the conditions of a problem in educational form.*]
31. If y is the product of three consecutive number of which the greatest is p, express this fact by an equation.
32. The sum of three consecutive even numbers is equal to x. If the middle number is $2n$ express this by an equation.
33. The product of p and q is equal to five times the excess of a over b; express this by an equation.
34. If x is divided by y, the quotient is equal to 10 more than the sum of m and n; express this in algebraical symbols.
35. A man is x years older than his son, whose present age is a years; five years hence the father's age wiil be twice that of the son; express this in algebraical symbols. If the son is now 15, what is the father's age? If the father is now 53, how old is the son?

36. A has Rs p and B has q paise; A hands Rs x to B and finds that then the has three times as much as B; express this fact by an equation.

37. A man who is p years old has a son whose age is q years; five years ago the father's age was seven times that of his son. Express this in algebraical symbols.

Formulae

82. In Example 6, Art. 80, we proved

$$\frac{N}{D} = Q + \frac{R}{D},$$

a result which gives in a single statement a general relation expressing the connection between a number, its divisor, and resulting quotient and remainder.

This is an example of a very important class of algebraical statements known as *formulae*, the use and application of which we shall now briefly explain.

DEFINITION. A formula is a relation established by reasoning among certain quantities, any one of which may in turn be regarded as the unknown.

Thus in the formula above mentioned, if Q, R, and D are given quantities, we have an equation to find the corresponding value of N. Or, a question may be proposed as follows: "By what must 96 be devided so as to give, a quotient 5, and a remainder 11?" Here we have given $N = 96, Q = 5, R = 11$ and therefore from the formula we obtain

$$\frac{96}{D} = 5 + \frac{11}{D},$$

where $D = 17$, the required divisor.

83. A formula, it must be observed, includes all particular cases in one general statement; and so by the use of a single algebraical formula we are enabled briefly to express a whole class of results in a form at once simple, easily remembered, and easily applied. Experience will convince the student how much of the power and utility of Algebra lies in the ready application of formulae to many kinds of problems.

It would be out of place here to make more than a passing allusion to other branches of Mathematics, or to Physical Science; but on account of the interest and importance of the subject, it may be useful to draw the reader's attention to a few of the more elementary formulae he is likely to meet with in his other studies.

(1) If a triangle on a base b, has a height h, its area A is given by the formula

$$A = \frac{1}{2}hb.$$

(2) If a pyramid of height h stands on a base whose area is a^2, its volume V is given by the formula

$$V = \frac{1}{3}a^2h.$$

In these cases any linear unit, inch, foot,.., being chosen, the superficial and solid units will be respectively the square and cubic inch, foot,...; and in each of these formulae if two of the three quantities be given, the third is easily obtained by Arithmetic.

Example. The Great Pyramid of Egypt stands on a square base eachside of which is 235 metres; and its height is 150 metres. Find the number of cubic metres of stone used in its construction-

From the formula, $V = \frac{1}{3} \times (235)^2 \times 150$

$$= 235 \times 235 \times 50 = 21250.$$

$$= 2761250 \text{ metres}.$$

84. We have in this chapter given several examples involving space, velocity, and time; and all these can be solved without difficulty by common sense reasoning. At the same time we may remark that they are only particular cases of the general formulas $s = vt$, in which s denotes the space described by a body which moves with uniform velocity v for a time.

In this formula, if t denotes the number of seconds the body has been in motion, and v the number of cm. passed over in one second, then s is the space (in cm.) described in t seconds.

Example. If a train has a velocity of 75 dm a second, how long will it take to cross a viaduct which is 300 m in length?

Substituting the values of s and v (expressed in dm) in the formula, we get

$$3000 = 75t,$$

$$t = \frac{3000}{75} = 40$$

Therefore, the time is 40 seconds.

85. Another very interesting case is that of a body falling vertically under the action of gravity.

It is proved in works on Dynamics that if a body fall freely from rest, and if s denote the space (in cm) described in t seconds,

$$s = \frac{1}{2}gt^2.$$

In this formula g denotes the number of cm per second by which the velocity is increased in each successive second in consequence of the earth's attraction, and it is found by experiment that $g = 981$ nearly.

Example 1. A stone dropped from the Clifton suspension bridge takes 4 seconds before it reaches the water. Find the height of the bridge above the river.

From the above formula, $s = \frac{1}{2} \times 981 \times (4)^2$

$$= 7848 \text{ cm}$$

and the height is therefore 7848 cm.

Example 2. How long will it take a stone to reach the bottom of a well 49.05 metres deep?

From the formula, $4905 = \frac{1}{2} \times 981 \times t^2$;

$\therefore$ $t = \frac{4905 \times 2}{981} = 10$

$\therefore$ $t = \sqrt{10} = 3.2$ secs.

Therefore, the time is 3.2 seconds.

EXAMPLES IX-c

1. From the formula for the area of a triangle in Art. 83, find

(i) The area, when the base is 32 dm, and the height 17 dm.

(ii) The base, when the area is 56 sq. dm, and the height 7 dm.

(iii) The height when the area is 5.985 sq. metres, and the base 11.97 m.

2. By means of formula (2) in Art. 83, find

(i) The volume of a pyramid of height 10 metres, on a base whose area is 15 sq. metres.

(ii) The volume of a pyramid of height 6 metres, standing on a square base each of whose sides is $1\frac{1}{2}$ metres.

(iii) The height of a pyramid whose volume is 20 cu. metres and whose base has an area of 12 sq. metres.

3. By means of the formula $s = vt$ (Art. 84), find

(i) How many km a train will run in 84 minutes at 70km per hour.

(ii) How long a train will take to run 56 km at 42 km per hour.

(iii) The velocity in km per hour of a train which travels 5500 m in 5 minutes.

4. By means of the formula $s = \frac{1}{2}gt^2$ (Art. 85g = 981), find

   (i) The height of a flagstaff if a stone dropped from the top takes 3 seconds to reach the ground.

   (ii) How long will it take a stone to drop from a balloon whose height above the ground is 19.62 m.

5. The circumference C of a circle is π times the diameter d; and the area A of a circle is π times the square of the radius r. Express these two results by formulae.

   If $\pi = \frac{22}{7}$, find the circumferences and areas of circles whose radii are $3\frac{1}{2}$ cm and 1.75 dm respectively.

6. The surface S of a sphere of radius r is given by the formula

$$S = 4 \times \frac{22}{7} r^2.$$

   Find (i) the surface of a sphere whose radius is 1.4 cm;

   (ii) the radius of a sphere whose surface is $38\frac{1}{2}$ sq.dm.

7. If a room is x dm long, y dm broad, and z dm high, find formula for

   (i) the perimeter,

   (ii) the area of the floor,

   (iii) the area of the walls.

8. Form the formulae of the last example find the perimeter, area of floor, and area of the walls of a room 6 metres long 4 metres, wide, and 4 metres high.

9. From formula (iii) of Example 7, find the height of a room when the length and breadth are 6.5 metres, 3.5 metres respectively, and the area of the walls is 70 sq. metres.

10. If a parallelogram on a base b has a height h, its area A is given by the formula

$$A = bh.$$

   Find the area of parallelograms in which

   (i) the base = 5.5 cm, and the height = 4 cm;

   (ii) the base = 2.4 dm, and the height = 1.5 dm.

11. The area of a parallelogram is 4.2 sq. cm, and the base is 2.8 cm^2. Find. the height

12. The area of a trapezium is equal to $\frac{1}{2}$ (sum of parallel sides)

$\times$ (distance between them).

Express this in algebraical symbols, and apply the formula to find the area of a trapezium when the parallel sides are 6.5 dm and 7 dm and the distance between them is 4 dm.

13. Use the formula of Art. 80, Ex. 6, to find a number which when divided by 19 gives a quotient 17 and remainder 5.

14. By what number must 566 be divided so as to give a quotient 37 and remainder 11?

15. What is the present age of a man who 5 years hence will be three times as old as his son who is now 15? Verify the answer by substituting in the formula of Art. 81, Ex. 1.

16. In a right-angled triangle if a and b denote the lengths of the sides containing the right angle and c denotes the length of the hypotenuse, it is known that $c^2 = a^2 + b^2$.

By substitution find which of the following sets of numbers can be taken to represent the sides of a right-angled triangle.

(i) 7, 24, 25. (ii) 12, 35, 36. (iii) 1.6, 6.3, 6.5.

17. The rectangle contained by two straight lines, one of which is divided into any number of parts, is equal to the sum of the rectangles contained by the undivided line and the several parts of the divided line.

Prove this by taking algebraical symbols to represent the undivided line and the segments of the divided line.

18. AB is a straight line divided into any two parts at O. Prove algebraically, as in the last example:

(i) $AB^2 = AB \cdot AO + AB \cdot OB$. (ii) $AB \cdot AO = AO^2 + AO \cdot OB$.

Express these two results in a verbal form as in Example 17.

19. Prove algebraically the following theorems:

(i) If a straight line is divided into any two parts, the square on the whole line is equal to the sum of the squares on the two parts together with twice the rectangle contained by the two parts.

(ii) If a straight line is divided into any two parts, the sum of the squares on the whole line and on one of the parts is equal to twice the rectangle contained by the whole and that part, together with the square on the other part.

Express the results of these theorems in a form corresponding to (i) and (ii) of Example 18.

20. With the notation of Example 16, find the value of

(i) c when $a = 15, b = 8$;

(ii) a when $c = 25, b = 7$;

(iii) b when $c = 41, a = 9$;

(iv) a when $c = 6.5, b = 6.3$

21. If $x = 3.1416, l = 2.0125, s = 144.9$, $g = 32.2, m = 18.75, v = 5.6$, find the value of

(i) $\pi\sqrt{\frac{l}{g}}$; (ii) $\sqrt{2gs}$; (iii) $\frac{1}{2}mv^2$.

22. In the formula $F = \frac{mv^2}{gr}$, given $m = 12.075, r = 3, g = 32.2, F = 200$, find v.

23. In the formula $v^2 - u^2 = 2\alpha s$, find the falue α when $r = 50, u = 10, s = 100$.

24. From the formula $s = \frac{n}{2}(a + l)$, find

(i) the value of s, when $n = 20, a = 14, l = 964$;

(ii) the value of a, when $s = 25.2, n = 12, l = 3.2$;

(iii) the value of n, when $s = 46.8, a = .6, l = 7.2$;

(iv) the value of l, when $s = -175.5, a = 13.5, n = 13$.

25. If $y = 4 + \frac{3}{10}x$, find the value of y when x has the values $0, 4, 8, 12, 16, 20$.

There is a wall 20 dm long, whose height at any point x dm from one end is $4 + \frac{3}{10}x$ dm. Draw the wall on a scale of 1 cm to 4 dm, marking on it the height at each end and at intervals of 4 dm.

Further examples on formulae will be found on pages 196-201.

10

PROBLEMS LEADING TO SIMPLE EQUATIONS

86. THE principles of the last chapter may now be employed to solve various problems.

The method of procedure is as follows:

Represent the unknown quantity by a symbol x, and express in symbolical language the conditions of the question; we thus obtain a simple equations which can be solved by the methods already given in Chapter VIII.

Example 1. Find two numbers whose sum is 28, and whose difference is 4.

Let x be the smaller number, then $x + 4$ is the greater.

Their sum is $x + (x + 4)$, which is to be equal to 28.

Hence $x + x + 4 = 28$: ,

$2x = 24$;

$\therefore$ $x = 12$

and $x + 4 = 16$;

so that the numbers are 12 and 16.

The beginner is advised to test his solution by finding whether it satisfies the data of the question or not.

Example 2. Divide 60 into two parts, so that three times the greater may exceed 100 by as much as 8 times the less falls short of 200.

Let x be the greater part, then $60 - x$ is the less.

Three times the greater part is 3x, and its excess? over 100 is

$$3x - 100.$$

Eight times the less is $8(60 - x)$, and its defect from 200 is

$$200 - 8(50 - x).$$

Whence the symbolical statement of the question is

$$3x - 100 = 200 - 8(60 - x);$$

$$3x - 100 = 200 - 480 + 8x,$$

$$480 - 100 - 200 = 8x - 3x,$$

$$5x = 180;$$

$\therefore$ $x = 36$, the greater part,

and $60 - x = 24$, the less.

Example 3. Divide Rs 47 between A, B, C, so that A may have Rs 10 more than B, and B Rs 8 more than C.

Suppose that C has x rupees; then B has $x+8$ rupees, and A has $x+8+10$ rupees,

Hence $x+(x+8)+(x+8+10)=47$;

$$x+x+8+x+8+10=47;$$

$$3x=21;$$

$$\therefore \quad x=21;$$

so that C has Rs 7, B Rs 15, A Rs 25.

Example 4. A person spent Rs 564 in buying geese and ducks; if each geese cost Rs 7, and each duck Rs 3, and if the total number of birds bought was 108: how many of each did he buy?

In questions of this kind it is of essential importance to have all quantities expressed in the same denomination; in the present instance it will be convenient to express the money in rupees.

Let x be the number of geese, then $108-x$ is the number of ducks.

Since each geese costs 7 rupees, x geese cost $7x$ rupees.

And since each duck costs 3 rupees, $108-x$ ducks cost $3(108-8)$ rupees.

Therefore, the amount spent is $7x+3(108-x)$ rupees; but the question states that the amount is also Rs 564.

Hence $7x+3(108-x)=564$;

$$7x+324-3x=564,$$

$$4x=240,$$

$$\therefore x=60, \text{ the number of geese,}$$

and $108-x=48$, the number of ducks.

Example 5. A is twice as old as B, ten years ago he was four times as old: what are their present ages?

Let B's age be x years, then A's age is $2x$ years.

Ten years ago their ages were respectively, $x-10$ and $2x-10$ years, thus we have $2x-10=4(x-10)$

$$2x-10=4x-40.$$

$$2x=30;$$

$$\therefore x=15.$$

so that B is 15 years old, A 32 years.

NOTE. In the above examples the unknown quantity x represents a *number* of pounds, ducks, years, etc.; and the student must be careful to avoid beginning a solution with a supposition of the kind, "let x=A's share" or "let x = the ducks", or any statement so vague and inexact.

EXAMPLES X-a

1. One number exceeds another by 5, and their sum if 29; find them.
2. The difference between two numbers is 8; if 2 be added to the greater the result will be three times the smaller; find the numbers.
3. Find a number such that it excess over 50 may be greater by 11 than its defect from 89.
4. A man walks 10km, then travels a certain distance by train, and then twice as far by coach. If the whole journey is 70 km, how far does he travel by train?
5. What two numbers are those whose sum is 58, and difference 28?
6. If 288 be added to a certain number, the result will be equal to three times he excess of the number over 12: find the number.
7. Twenty-three times a certain number is as much above 14 as 16 is above seven times the number: find it.
8. Divide 105 into two parts, one of which diminished by 20 shall be equal to the other diminished by 15.
9. Find three consecutive numbers whose sum shall equal to 84.
10. The sum of two numbers is 8, and one of them with 22 added to it is five times the other; find the numbers.
11. Find two numbers differing by 10 whose sum if equal to twice their differences.
12. *A* and *B* begin to play each with Rs 60. If they play till *A*'s money is double *B*'s what does *A* win?
13. Find a number such that if 5, 15 and 35 are added to it, the product of the first and third results may be equal to the square of the second.
14. The difference between the squares of two consecutive numbers is 121: find the numbers.
15. The difference of two numbers is 3, and the differences of their squares is 27: find the numbers.
16. Divide Rs 380 between *A*, *B*, and *C* , so that *B* may have Rs 30 more than *A*, and *C* may have Rs 20 more than *B*.
17. A sum of Rs 8.85 is made up of 124 coins which are either 10-paise coins or 5-paise coins; how much are there of each?
18. If silk costs six times as much as linen: and I spend Rs 118 in buying 23 metres of silk and 50 metres of linen: find the cost of each per metre.
19. A father is four times as old as his son; in 24 years he will only be twice as old: find their ages.
20. *A* is 25 years older than *B*, and *A*'s ages is as much above 20 as *B*'s is below 85: find their ages.
21. *A*'s ages is six times *B*'s and fifteen years hence *A* will be three times as old as *B*: find their ages.

22. A sum of Rs 3.75 was paid in 25-, 10-, and 5-paise coins. The number of 10-paise coins was four times the number of 25-paise coins and twice the number of 5-paise coins; how many were there of each?

23. The sum of the ages of *A* and *B* is 30 years, and five years hence *A* will be three times as old as *B*: find their present ages.

24. In a cricket match the byes were double of the wides, and the remainder of the score was greater by three than twelve times the number of byes. If the whole score was 138, how were the runs obtained?

25. The length of a room exceeds its breadth by 3 dm; if the length had been increased by 3cm, and the breadth diminished by 2 dm. the area would not have been altered: find the dimensions.

26. The length of a room exceeds its breadth by 8 dm; if each had been increased by 2 dm, the area would have been increased by 60 square dm: find the original dimensions of the room.

27. We add some problems which lead to equations with fractional coefficients.

Example 1. Find two numbers which differ by 4, and such that one-half of the greater exceeds one-sixth of the less by 8.

Let x be the smaller number, then $x + 4$ is the greater.

One-half of the greater is represented by $\frac{1}{2}(x + 4)$, and one-sixth of the less by $\frac{1}{6}x$.

Hence $$\frac{1}{2}(x+4) - \frac{1}{6}x = 8;$$

multiplying by 6, $$3x + 12 - x = 48;$$

$$\therefore \quad 2x = 36;$$

$$\therefore \quad x = 18, \text{ the less number.}$$

and $$x + 4 = 22, \text{ the greater.}$$

Example 2. *A* has Rs 9, and *B* has Rs 4 and 20 paise; after *B* has won from *A* a certain sum, *A* has then five-sixths of what *B* has: how much did *B* win?

Suppose that *B* wins *x paise*, *A* has then $900 - x$ paise, and *B* has $420 + x$ paise.

Hence $$900 - x = \frac{5}{6}(420 + x);$$

$$5400 - 6x = 2100 + 5x$$

$$11x = 3300;$$

$$x = 300.$$

Therefore *B* wins 300 paise or Rs 3.

EXAMPLES X-b

1. Find a number such that the sum of its sixth and ninth parts may be equal to 15.
2. What is the number whose eighth, sixth, and fourth parts together make up 13?
3. There is a number whose fifth part is less than its fourth part by 3: find it.
4. Find a number such that six-sevenths of it shall exceed four-fifths of it by 2.
5. The fifth, fifteenth, and twenty-fifth parts of a number together make up 23: find the number.
6. Two consecutive numbers are such that one-fourth of the less exceeds one-fifth of the greater by 1: find the numbers.
7. Two numbers differ by 28, and, one is eight-ninths of the other: find them.
8. There are two consecutive numbers such that one-fifth of the greater exceeds one-seventh ofthe less by 3: find them.
9. Find three consecutive numbers such that if they be divided by 10. 17. and 26 respectively, the sum of the quotients will be 10.
10. *A* and *B* begin to play with equal sums, and when *B* has lost five-elevenths of what he had to begin with, *A* has gained Rs 6 more than half of what *B* has left: what had they at first?
11. From a certain number 3 is taken, and the remainder is divided by 4; the quotient is then increased by 4 and divided by 5 and the result is 2: find the number.
12. In a godown one-fifth of the acid is sulphuric and one-third hydrochloric; besides that is contains 15 dozen bottles of nitric and 30 of carbolic: how much sulphuric and hydrochloric does it contain?
13. Two-fifths of *A*'s money is equal to *B*'s, and seven-ninths of *B*'s is equal to *C*'s; in all they have Rs 770: what have they each?
14. *A*, *B*, and *C* have Rs 1285 between them: *A*'s share is greater then five-sixths of *B*'s by Rs 25, and *C*'s is four-fifteenths of *B*'s: *find the share of each.*
15. A man sold a horse for Rs 600 and half as much as he gave for it, and gained thereby Rs. 400: what did he pay for the horse?
16. The width of a room is two-thirds of its length. If the width had been 3 dm more, and the length 3 dm less, the room would have been square: find its dimensions.
17. What is the property of a person whose income is Rs 430, when he has two-thirds of it invested at 4 per cent, one-fourth at 3 per cent, and the remainder at 2 per cent?
18. I bought a certain number of apples at three for 5 paise, and five-sixths of that number at four for 5 paise;. by selling them at eleven for 20 paise, I gained 15 paise: how many apples did I buy?

11

HIGHEST COMMON FACTOR, LOWEST COMMON MULTIPLE OF SIMPLE EXPRESSIONS

Highest Common Factor

88. DEFINITION. The highest common factor of two or more algebraical expressions is the expression of highest dimensions [Art. 24] which divides each of them without remainder.

The abbreviation H.C.F. is sometimes used instead of the words *highest common factor*.

89. In the case of *simple expressions* the highest common factor can be written down by inspection.

Example 1. The highest common factor of a^4, a^3, a^2, a^6 is a^2.

Example 2. The highest common factor of a^3b^4, ab^5c^2, a^2b^7c is ab^4; for a is the highest power of a that will divide a^3, a, a^2; b^4 is the highest power of b that will divide b^4, b^5, b^7; and c is not a *common* factor.

90. If the expressions have numerical coefficients, find by Arithmetic their greatest common measure, and prefix it as a coefficient to the algebraical highest common factor.

Example. The highest common factor of $21a^4x^3y$, $35a^2x^4y$, $28a^3xy^4$ is $7a^2xy$; for it consists of the product of

(1) the greatest common measure of the numerical coefficients;

(2) the highest power of each letter which divides every one of the given expressions.

EXAMPLES XI-a

Find the highest common factor of

1. $4ab^2, 2a^2b$.

2. $3x^2y^2, x^3y^2$.

3. $6xy^2z, 8x^2y^3z^2$.

4. $abc, 2ab^2c$.

5. $5a^3b^3, 15abc^2$.

6. $9x^2y^2z^2, 12xy^3z$.

7. $4a^2b^3c^2, 6a^3b^2c^3$.

8. $7a^2b^4c^5, 14ab^2c^3$.

9. $15x^4y^3z^2, 12x^2yz^2$.

10. $8a^2x, 6abxy, 10abx^3y^2$.

11. $49ax^2, 63ay^2, 56az^2$.

12. $17ab^2c, 34a^2bc, 51abc^2$.

13. $a^3x^2y^2, b^3xy^2, c^3x^2y$.

14. $24a^2b^3c^3, 64a^3b^3c^2, 48a^3b^2c^3$.

15. $25xy^2z, 100x^2yz, 125xy$.

16. $a^2bpxy, b^2qxy, a^3bxr^2$.

17. $15a^5b^3c^7, 60a^3b^7c^6, 25a^4b^5c^2$.

18. $35a^2c^3b, 42a^3cb^2, 30ac^2b^3$.

Lowest Common Multiple

91. DEFINITION. The lowest common multiple of two or more algebraical expressions is the expression of lowest dimensions which is divisible by each of them without remainder.

The abbreviation L.C.M. is sometimes used instead of the words *lowest common multiple.*

92. In the case of *simple expressions* the lowest common multiple can be written down by inspection.

Example 1. The lowest common multiple of a^4, a^3, a^2, a^6 is a^6.

Example 2. The lowest common multiple of a^3b^4, ab^5, a^2b^7 is a^3b^7; for a^3 is the lowest power of a that is divisible by each of the quantities a^3, a, a^2; and b^7 is the lowest power of b that is divisible by each of the quantities b^4, b^5, b^7.

93. If the expressions have numerical coefficients, find by Arithmetic their least common multiple, and prefix it as a coefficient to the algebraical lowest common multiple.

Example . The lowest common multiple of $21a^4x^3y, 35a^2x^4y, 28a^3xy$ is $420a^4x^4y^4$, for it consists of the product of

(i) the least common multiple of the numerical coefficients;

(2) the lowest power of each letter which is divisible by every power of that letter occurring in the given expressions.

EXAMPLES XI-b

Find the lowest common multiple of

1. $abc, 2a^2$.
2. x^3y^2, xyz.
3. $3x^2yz, 4x^3y^3$.
4. $5a^2bc^3, 4ab^2c$.
5. $3a^4b^2c^3, 5a^2b^3c^5$.
6. $12ab, 8xy$.
7. ac, bc, ab.
8. a^2c, bc^2, cb^2.
9. $2ab, 3ab, 4ca$.
10. $2x, 3y, 4z$.
11. $3x^2, 4y^3, 3z^2$.
12. $7a^2, 2ab, 3b^3$.
13. a^2bc, b^2ca, c^2ab.
14. $5a^2c, 6cb^2, 3bc^2$.
15. $2x^2y^3, 3xy, 4x^3y^4$.
16. $7x^4y, 8xy^5, 2x^3y^3$.
17. $35a^2c^3b, 42a^3cb^2, 30ac^2b^3$.
18. $66a^4b^2c^3, 44a^3b^4c^2, 24a^2b^3c^4$.

Find both the highest common factor and the lowest common multiple of

19. $2abc, 3ca, 4bca$.
20. $2xy, 4yz, 6zxy$.
21. $9abc, 3b^2c, cab$.
22. $13a^2bc, 39a^3bc^2$.
23. $17xyz^2, 15x^2y$.
24. $15x^3y^3z, 25xy^3z^2$.
25. $3ab, 2bc, 5cab$.
26. $17m^2n^4p^2, 51m^4p^4$.
27. $x^3y^2, y^2z^4, z^4x^3y^5$.
28. $15p^3q^4, 20m^2p^2q^3, 30mp^3$.
29. $72k^2m^3n^4, 108k^3m^2n^5$.

12

ELEMENTARY FRACTIONS

94. DEFINITION. If a quantity x be divided into b equal parts, and a of these parts be taken, the result is called the *fraction* $\frac{a}{b}$ *of* x. If x be the unit, the fraction $\frac{a}{b}$ of x is called simply "the fraction $\frac{a}{b}$"; so that the *fraction* $\frac{a}{b}$ *represents* a *equal parts,* b *of which make up the unit.*

95. In this chapter we propose to deal only with the easier kinds of fractions, where the numerator and denominator are simple expressions. Their reduction and simplification will be peformed by the usual arithmetical rules. The proofs of these rules will be given in Chapters XIX and XXI.

Rule. To reduce a fraction to its lowest terms : *divide numerator and denominator by every factor which is common to them both, that is by their highest common factor.*

Dividing the numerator and denominator of a fraction by a common factor is called *cancelling* that factor.

Examples.

(1) $\frac{6a^2c}{9ac^2} = \frac{2a}{3c}$.

(2) $\frac{7x^2yz}{28x^3yz^2} = \frac{1}{4xz}$.

(3) $\frac{35a^5b^3c}{7ab^2c} = \frac{5a^4b}{1} = 5a^4b$.

EXAMPLES XII-a

Reduce to lowest term

1. $\frac{3a}{6ab}$.

2. $\frac{4a^2}{16ab}$.

3. $\frac{2xy^2}{5x^2y}$.

4. $\frac{3abc}{15a^2b^2c}$.

5. $\frac{x^2yz^3}{x^3y^2z}$.

6. $\frac{15ab}{25bc}$.

7. $\dfrac{21x^2y^2}{28y^2z^2}$.

8. $\dfrac{8a^2b}{12b^2c}$.

9. $\dfrac{12mn^2p}{15m^2np^2}$.

10. $\dfrac{15m^2p^3}{18n^4p}$.

11. $\dfrac{abc^2}{a^3b^2c}$.

12. $\dfrac{3x^2yz^3}{5xy^4z^2}$.

13. $\dfrac{2xy^3z^4}{4x^2y^2z}$.

14. $\dfrac{5a^3b^2c^4}{15ab^4c}$.

15. $\dfrac{mn^4pq}{m^2n^3p^4}$.

16. $\dfrac{4m^3n^2p^5}{6m^4np^2}$.

17. $\dfrac{15ax^3y^2}{25a^2xy^6}$.

18. $\dfrac{39a^2b^4c^3}{52a^3b^5c^4}$.

19. $\dfrac{38k^2p^3m^4}{57k^3pm^2}$.

20. $\dfrac{46x^3y^4z^5}{69x^2y^3z^4}$.

Multiplication and Division of Fractions

96. Rule. To multiply algebraical fractions : *as in Arithmetic, multiply together all the numerators to form a new numerator and all the denominators to form a new denominator.*

Example 1. $\dfrac{2a}{3b} \times \dfrac{5x^2}{2a^2b} \times \dfrac{3b^2}{2x} = \dfrac{2a \times 5x^2 \times 3b^2}{3b \times 2a^2b \times 2x} = \dfrac{5x}{2a}$.

by cancelling like factors in numerator and denominator.

Example 2. $\dfrac{3a^2b}{5c^2} \times \dfrac{7bc}{3a^3} \times \dfrac{5ca}{7b^2} = 1$,

all the factors cancelling each other.

97. Rule. To divide one fraction by another : *invert the divisor and proceed as in multiplication.*

Example. $\dfrac{7a^3}{4x^3y^2} \times \dfrac{6c^3x}{5ab^2} \div \dfrac{28a^2c^2}{15b^2xy^2} = \dfrac{7a^3}{4x^3y^2} \times \dfrac{6c^3x}{5ab^2} \times \dfrac{15b^2xy^2}{28a^2c^2} = \dfrac{9c}{8x}$, all the other factors cancelling each other.

EXAMPLES XII-b

Simplify the following expressions :

1. $\frac{2ab}{3cd} \times \frac{c^2d^3}{ab^2}$.

2. $\frac{12a^2bc}{8ab^3} \times \frac{24ab^2}{36bc^2}$.

3. $\frac{15xyz^3}{a^2bc} \times \frac{3a^3x}{5yz}$.

4. $\frac{7a^2b^3}{9ax^2y} \times \frac{18x^2c}{15ac^4}$.

5. $\frac{8m^2n^3}{5x^2yz} \times \frac{15xyz^3}{16mn^2}$.

6. $\frac{21k^2p^3}{13mn^2} \times \frac{39n^3m^2}{28p^2k^3}$.

7. $\frac{3a^2b}{4b^3c} \times \frac{2c^2}{8a^3} \div \frac{6ac}{16b^2x}$.

8. $\frac{2x^2y}{3yz} \times \frac{5z^2x}{7xy^2} \div \frac{21x^2y^3z^2}{40xy^2z}$.

9. $\frac{7m^2p}{17x^2y} \times \frac{51y^3z}{21p^2n} \div \frac{m^2x^2}{pyz}$.

10. $\frac{26xk^2p^3}{58mp^4} \times \frac{2xk^3}{13pkm} \div \frac{2x^2k^4}{87m^2p^2}$.

11. $\frac{15b^2}{40c} \times \frac{27c^2}{81d^3} \div \frac{abc}{14d^3}$.

12. $\frac{b^2}{3c} \times \frac{4c^2}{5d^3} \div \frac{16a^2b^2c^2}{15d^5}$.

13. $\frac{8ax^2}{7by} \times \frac{49cy^2}{64dx^3}$.

14. $\frac{15abc}{16xyz} \times \frac{128x^3y^2z^2}{100a^2bc}$.

15. $\frac{45a^2b^3c^4}{27x^4y^3z} \times \frac{243xy^2z^3}{180a^2bc^3}$.

16. $\frac{104xyzk^2p}{28xy^2kp^2} \times \frac{56y^3z^5p}{26y^2z^6k}$.

17. $\frac{m^2}{8n} \times \frac{36p^3q^2}{81mn} \div \frac{15mpx^5}{27n^2x^3y}$.

18. $\frac{a^3}{b^3} \times \frac{xy^2}{ab} \times \frac{pb^2}{ax} \div \frac{ap}{b^2}$.

Reduction to a Common Denominator

98. In order to find the sum or difference of any fractions, we must, as in Arithmetic, first reduce them to a common denominator; and it is most convenient to take the lowest common multiple of the denominators of the given fractions.

Example. Express with lowest common denominator the fractions

$$\frac{a}{3xy}, \frac{b}{6xyz}, \frac{c}{2yz}.$$

The lowest common multiple of the denominators is $6xyz$. Multiplying the numerator of each fraction by the factor which is required to make its denominator $6xyz$, we have the equivalent fractions

$$\frac{2az}{6xyz}, \frac{b}{6xyz}, \frac{3cx}{6xyz}.$$

NOTE. The same result would clearly be obtained by dividing the lowest common denominator by each of the denominators in turn, and multiplying the corresponding numerators by the respective quotients.

EXAMPLES XII-c

Express as equivalent fractions with common denominator :

1. $\frac{2x}{a}, \frac{y}{2a}$.
2. $\frac{4x}{3y}, \frac{y}{x^2}$.
3. $\frac{a}{2b}, \frac{b}{c}$.
4. $\frac{a}{b}, \frac{c}{d}, 2$.
5. $\frac{2a}{b}, \frac{b}{3c}$.
6. $\frac{m}{4n}, \frac{P}{5n}$.
7. $\frac{k}{2x}, \frac{P}{3x}$.
8. $\frac{m}{3x}, \frac{n}{6x}$.
9. $\frac{a}{bc}, \frac{b}{ca}$.
10. $\frac{a}{x}, \frac{b}{x^2}$.
11. $\frac{2}{x}, \frac{3}{y}$.
12. $\frac{x}{y}, \frac{y}{x}, 3x$.
13. $\frac{2x}{3y}, \frac{3y}{2x}$.
14. $\frac{4a}{5b}, \frac{3a}{10c}$.
15. $\frac{3a}{7b}, \frac{5b}{21c}$.
16. $\frac{2}{a}, \frac{b}{3}, \frac{a}{9}$.

Addition and Subtraction of Fractions

Rule. To add or subtract fractions : *express all the fractions with their lowest common denominator; form the algebraical sum of the numerators, and retain the common denominator.*

Example 1. Simplify $\frac{5x}{3} + \frac{3}{4}x - \frac{7x}{6}$.

The least common denominator is 12.

The expression $= \frac{20x + 9x - 14x}{12} = \frac{15x}{12} = \frac{5x}{4}$.

Example 2. Simplify $\frac{3ab}{5x} - \frac{ab}{2x} - \frac{1}{10} \cdot \frac{ab}{x}$.

The expression $= \frac{6ab - 5ab - ab}{10x} = \frac{0}{10x} = 0$.

Example 3. Simplify $\frac{2x}{a^2c^2} - \frac{y}{3ca^3}$

The expression $= \frac{6ax - cy}{3a^3c^2}$, and admits of no further simplification.

NOTE. The beginner must be careful to distinguish between erasing equal terms with different signs, as in Example 2, and cancelling equal factors in the course of multiplication, or in reducing fractions to lowest terms. Moreover, in simplifying fractions he must remember that a factor can only be removed from numerator and denominator when it divides each *taken as a whole.*

Thus, in $\frac{6ax-cy}{3a^3c^2}$, c cannot be cancelled because it only divides cy and not the *whole* numerator. Similarly a cannot be cancelled because it only divides $6ax$ and not the whole numerator. The fraction is therefore in its simplest form.

When no denominator is expressed the denominator 1 may be understood.

Example 4. $3x-\frac{a^2}{4y}=\frac{3x}{1}-\frac{a^2}{4y}-\frac{12xy-a^2}{4y}$.

If a fraction is not in its lowest terms it should be simplified before combining it with other fractions.

Example 5. $\frac{ax}{2}-\frac{x^2y}{3xy}=\frac{ax}{2}-\frac{x}{3}=\frac{3ax-2x}{6}$.

EXAMPLES XII-d

Simplify the following expressions

1. $\frac{x}{2}+\frac{x}{3}$.

2. $\frac{y}{4}-\frac{y}{5}$.

3. $\frac{a}{3}-\frac{a}{4}$.

4. $\frac{2x}{3}-\frac{5}{x}$.

5. $\frac{x}{2}+\frac{y}{5}$.

6. $\frac{a}{4}-\frac{b}{6}$.

7. $\frac{m}{8}-\frac{n}{12}$.

8. $\frac{2m}{15}-\frac{n}{5}$.

9. $\frac{x}{7}-\frac{y}{21}$.

10. $\frac{a}{13}+\frac{b}{39}$.

11. $\frac{p}{16}-\frac{q}{48}$.

12. $\frac{5m}{12}-\frac{n}{36}$.

13. $\frac{2x}{3}+\frac{4x}{5}$.

14. $\frac{5x}{4}-\frac{4x}{5}$.

15. $\frac{5x}{6}-\frac{7x}{12}$.

16. $\frac{2a}{5}-\frac{4b}{15}$.

Simplify the following expressions:

17. $\frac{a}{2}-\frac{a}{3}+\frac{a}{5}$.

18. $\frac{x}{4}-\frac{x}{8}+\frac{x}{12}$.

19. $\frac{x}{3}+\frac{x}{6}-\frac{x}{9}$.

20. $\frac{2x}{3}-\frac{x}{6}+\frac{3x}{4}$.

21. $\frac{5x}{6}-\frac{x}{12}+\frac{x}{9}$.

22. $\frac{7x}{8}+\frac{x}{12}-\frac{x}{4}$.

23. $\frac{x}{a} - \frac{y}{b}$.

24. $\frac{3x^3}{ax^2} + \frac{2y}{3b}$.

25. $a + \frac{b}{c}$.

26. $x = \frac{y^2}{yz}$.

27. $\frac{a^3}{3a^2} - \frac{b^2}{a}$.

28. $a^2 + \frac{b^3}{a}$.

29. $\frac{3x^2}{6x} - \frac{y^2}{x^2}$.

30. $p^3 - \frac{k^5}{p^2}$.

MISCELLANEOUS EXAMPLES II

(*Chiefly on Chapters* I-VIII)

[*The examples marked with an asterisk must be postponed by those who adopt the suggestion printed in italics on papes* 35 *and* 40.]

1. What expression must be added to $4x^3 - 3x^2 + 2$ to produce $4x^3 + 7x - 6$?

2. If $A = 6x - 3y + 2z$, $B = x + y + z$, and $C = 10x + y - 7z$, find the value of $A + 4B - C$.

3. If $x = 3$, $y = 4$, $z = 1$, find the value of $\sqrt{2xy + 4xz} + \sqrt{9y} + \frac{2xyz}{3}$.

4. Simplify by removing brackets:

$$a^2 + 2d^2 - (2e^2 - b^2) - \{(d^2 - c^2 - e^2) + (d^2 - e^2)\}.$$

***5.** Multiply $x^3 + x^2 + 3x + 5$ by $x^2 - x - 2$.

6. Solve the equations :

(1) $3 - 4x = 36x - 17$; (2) $5x - 15 = 17x + 21$.

***7.** Divide $x^4 - 10x^2 + 9$ by $x^2 - 2x - 3$.

8. Simplify $7a - 4b - \{5a - 3[b - 2(a - b)]\}$.

9. In an examination A has $x + y$ marks, B has $2x - 3y$, and C has twice as many as A ; how many marks have A, B, and C together?

10. Find the sum of $1 - 2x + x^2$, $3x - 2x^2$, $5x^2 - 7x - 2$, arranging the result in descending powers of x.

11. Write down the following products:

(1) $(x + 17)(x - 3)$; (2) $(3x - 8)(8x + 3)$.

12. Solve the equations:

(1) $7x - 3 - (7 - 5x) = 3 - 3x - (5x + 8)$;

(2) $(5x + 1)(x - 2) - (4x - 3)(3x - 1) = 10 - (7x + 2)(x + 1)$.

....

13. From the sum of $3ab, -5ab, 2ab, 7ab, -9ab$, subtract the sum of $-8ab, 6ab, -9ab, 10ab$.

14. When $a = 4, b = 3, c = 2$, find the numerical value of

$$\frac{2a + b(2c - a)}{3b - \sqrt{2c^3}}.$$

15. From what expression must $11a^2 - 5ab - 7bc$ be subtracted so as to give for remainder $7b(a + c) + 5a^2$?

***16.** Multiply $x^3 + 6x^2 + 8x - 8$ by $x^2 - 2x + 4$.

17. Simplify $12a - [6a - 2\{3a - 4(b - a)\} - (9a + 8b)]$.

18. Solve the equations:

(1) $3(2x - 1) + 2(3x - 2) + 3 = 4(x - 5)$;

(2) $\frac{1}{3}(x + 1) + \frac{1}{4}(x + 3) = \frac{1}{5}(x + 4) + 16$.

***19.** Divide $3p^5 + 16p^4 - 33p^3 + 14p^2$ by $p^2 + 7p$.

20. Add together

$a + 2b - (2c + d)$, $3a - (b - 2c) + 2d$, and $2a - [b - (2c - 3d)]$.

21. To what expression must $7x^3 - 6x^2 - 5x$ be added so as to make $9x^3 - 6x - 7x^2$?

22. What value of x will make the product of $x + 1$ and $2x + 1$ less than the product of $x + 3$ and $2x + 3$ by 14?

23. When $a = 2, b = 3, c = 1, q = 4, r = 6$, find the value of

$$5a^b c^r - 3^a 2^b + 2^r a^5 - c^b b^q.$$

24. Solve the equation :

$$x - \frac{x - 13}{9} = \frac{6x + 1}{5} + \frac{2}{3}\left(6 - \frac{3x}{2}\right).$$

Show also that $x = 3$ does *not* satisfy the equation.

25. A horse can eat $3m + 2n$ bags of corn in a week; how many weeks will he be in eating $12m^2 - 7mn - 10n^2$ bags?

26. Subtract the sum of

$$2x^3 - 3x + 4 \text{ and } -3x^2 + 2x - 7$$

from $\quad 4x^3 - 3x^2 + x - 6 - [2x^3 - (x - 6).]$

27. Find the value of $a^3 + b^3 + c^3 - 3abc$, when $a = 1, b = 4, c = -5$.

28. Solve the equations:

(1) $\frac{2x}{15} + \frac{x-6}{12} = \frac{3}{10}\left(\frac{x}{2} - 5\right)$;

(2) $\frac{2(x-1)}{5} + \frac{15}{2}\left(1 - \frac{x}{3}\right) + \frac{19}{10} = \frac{9}{5}\left(\frac{x}{6} - \frac{1}{3}\right)$.

29. *Divide $3y^6 - 37y^3 + 35y^2 + 7y^2 + 2$ by $y(y-1)(y+4) - 2$.

30. Divide Rs 1120 between A and B so that for every 25-paise coin that A receives B may receive a 10-paise coin.

....

31. Find the value of

$$(a+b)^2 + (b+c)^2 + (c+a)^2$$

when $a = -1, b = -2, c = 3$.

32. Multiply $(2m^2 + 8)(m + 2)$ by $3m - 6$.

33. Divide the product of

$$x - 2,\ x + 3, \text{ and } 2x - 7$$

by the sum of $3(x^2 - 2x - 2)$ and $5x - x^2 - 15$.

34. A man walks at the rate of a km an hour for p hours; he then rides for q hours at the rate of b km an hour. How far has he travelled, and how long would it have taken to ride the same distance at c km an hour? Also, work out the result supposing $p = 7, q = 3, a = 4, b = 9, c = 11$

35. Solve the equations:

(1) $\frac{3x}{2} - \frac{5}{7} = 21x - \frac{1}{3}\left(2x + 10\frac{3}{14}\right)$;

(2) $3x - 4 - \frac{4(7x-9)}{15} = \frac{4}{5}\left(6 + \frac{x-1}{3}\right)$.

36. An egg-dealer bought a certain number of eggs at 80 paise per score, and five times the number at Rs 3.75 per hundred. He sold the whole at 50 paise per dozen, gaining Rs 16.20 by the transaction. How many eggs did he buy?

13

SIMULTANEOUS EQUATIONS

[*In connection with this chapter the student may read* Chap. XLIV. Arts. 417-424.]

100. CONSIDER the equation $2x + 5y = 23$, which contains *two* unknown quantities.

From this, we get $\quad 5y = 23 - 2x,$

that is, $$y = \frac{23 - 2x}{5} \qquad \ldots(1).$$

From this it appears that for every value we choose to give to x there will be one corresponding value of y. Thus we shall be able to find as many pairs of values as we please which satisfy the given equation.

For instance, if $x = 1$, then from (1) $y = \frac{21}{5}$.

Again, if $x = -2$, then $y = \frac{27}{5}$; and so on.

But if also we have a second equation of the same kind, such as

$$3x + 4y = 24,$$

we have from this $$y = \frac{24 - 3x}{4} \qquad \ldots(2).$$

If now we seek values of x and y which satisfy *both* equations, the values of y in (1) and (2) must be identical.

Therefore $$\frac{23 - 2x}{5} = \frac{24 - 2x}{4}.$$

Multiplying up, $\quad 92 - 8x = 120 - 15x;$

$$\therefore \quad 7x = 28;$$

$$\therefore \quad x = 4.$$

Substituting the value in the first equation, we have

$$8 + 5y = 23;$$

$$\therefore \quad 5y = 15;$$

$$\therefore \text{ and } \quad \left.\begin{array}{l} y = 3, \\ x = 4. \end{array}\right\}$$

Thus, if both equations are to be satisfied by the *same* values of x and y, there is only one solution possible.

101. DEFINITION. When two or more equations are satisfied by the same values of the unknown quantities they are called simultaneous equations.

We proceed to explain the different methods for solvings simultaneous equations. In the present chapter we shall confine our attention to the simpler cases in which the unknown quantities are involved in the first degree.

102. In the example already worked we have used the method of solution which best illustrates the meaning of the term *simultaneous equation*; but in practice it will be found that this is rarely the readiest mode of solution. It must be borne in mind that since the two equations are simultaneously true, *any* equation formed by combining them will be satisfied by the values of x and y which satisfy the original equations. Our object will always be to obtain an equation which involves *one only* of the unknown quantities.

103. The process by which we get rid of either of the unknown quantities is called elimination, and it must be effected in different ways according to the nature of the equations proposed.

Example 1. Solve $3x + 7y = 27$ ...(1).

$5x + 2y = 16$ ... (2).

To eliminate x we multiply (1) by 5 and (2) by 3, so as to make the coefficients of x in both equations equal. This gives

$$15x + 35y = 135,$$

$$15x + 6y = 48:$$

subtracting, $29y = 87$;

$\therefore$ $y = 3,$

To find x, substitute the value of y in *either* of the given equations.

Thus from (1) $3x + 21 = 27$;

$\because$ and $\left.\begin{aligned} x &= 2, \\ y &= 0, \end{aligned}\right\}$

NOTE. When one of the unknowns has been found, it is immaterial which of the equations we use to complete the solution. Thus in the present example, if we substitute 3 for y in (2), we have

$$5x + 6 = 16;$$

$\because$ $x = 2$, as before.

Example 2. Solve $7x + 2y = 47$ ...(1).

$5x - 4y = 1$ ... (2).

Here it will be more convenient to eliminate y.

Multiplying (1) by 2, $14x + 4y = 94$;

and from (2) $5x - 4y = 1$;

adding, $19x = 95$;

$\therefore$ $x = 5$.

Substitute this value in (1),

$\therefore$ $35 + 2y = 47$;

$\therefore$ and $\left.\begin{array}{l} y = 6, \\ x = 5. \end{array}\right\}$

NOTE. *Add* when the coefficients of one unknown are equal and *unlike* in sign; *subtract* when the coefficients are equal and *like* in sign.

Example 3. Solve $2x = 5y + 1$ ...(1),

$24 - 7x = 3y$ ... (2).

Here we can eliminate x by substituting in (2) its value obtained from (1). Thus

$$24 - \frac{7}{2}(5y + 1) = 3y;$$

$\therefore$ $48 - 35y - 7 = 6y$;

$\therefore$ $41 = 41y$;

$\therefore$ $\left.\begin{array}{l} y = 1, \\ x = 3. \end{array}\right\}$ and from (1)

104. Any one of the methods given above will be found sufficient; but there are certain arithmetical artifices which will frequently shorten the work.

Example 1. Solve $171x - 213y = 642$ ... (1),

$114x - 326y = 244$ ... (2).

Noticing that 171 and 114 contain a common factor 57, we shall make the coefficient of x in the two equations equal to the *least common multiple* of 171 and 114 if we multiply (1) by 2 and (2) by 3.

Thus, $342x - 426y = 1284$;

$342x - 978y = 732$;

subtracting, $552y = 552$;

that is, $y = 1$,

and therefore from (1) $x = 5$.

Example 2. Solve $127x + 59y = 1928$ ...(1),

$59x + 127y = 1792$ ... (2).

By addition, $186x + 186y = 3720$;

$\therefore$ $x + y = 20$ ...(3).

Subtracting (2) from (1), $68x - 68y = 136$;

$\therefore$ $x - y = 2$ ...(4).

Thus, by an easy combination of (1) and (2), the problem is reduced to the solution of the equations (3) and (4). From these we obtain by addition $2x = 22$, and by subtraction $2y = 18$.

Therefore $x = 11$, and $y = 9$.

EXAMPLES XIII-a

[Art. 421 *may be read in connection with these Examples.*]

Solve the equations:

1. $3x + 4y = 10$, $4x + y = 9$.

2. $x + 2y = 13$, $3x + y = 14$.

3. $4x + 7y = 29$, $x + 3y = 11$.

4. $2x - y = 9$, $3x - 7y = 19$.

5. $5x + 6y = 17$, $6x + 5y = 16$.

6. $2x + y = 10$, $7x + 8y = 53$.

7. $8x - y = 34$, $x + 8y = 53$.

8. $15x + 7y = 29$, $9x + 15y = 39$.

9. $14x - 3y = 39$, $6x + 17y = 35$.

10. $28x - 23y = 33$, $63x - 25y = 101$.

11. $35x + 17y = 86$, $56x - 13y = 17$.

12. $15x + 77y = 92$, $55x - 33y = 22$.

13. $5x - 7y = 0$, $7x + 5y = 74$.

14. $21x - 50y = 60$, $28x - 27y = 199$.

15. $39x - 8y = 99$, $52x - 15y = 80$.

16. $5x = 7y - 21$, $21x - 9y = 75$.

17. $6y - 5x = 18$, $12x - 9y = 0$.

18. $8x = 5y$, $13x = 8y + 1$.

19. $3x = 7y$, $12y = 5x - 1$.

20. $19x + 17y = 0$, $2x - y = 53$.

21. $93x + 15y = 123$, $15x + 93y = 201$.

105. We add a few cases in which, before proceeding to solve, it will be necessary to simplify the equations.

Example 1. Solve $5(x+2y)-(3x+11y)=14$ ... (1),

$$7x-9y-3(x-4y)=38 \quad \text{... (2).}$$

From (1) $5x+10y-3x-11y=14$;

$\therefore$ $2x-y=14$ ...(3).

From (2) $7x-9y-3x+12y=38$;

$\therefore$ $4x+3y=38$ ...(4).

From (3) $6x-3y=42$.

By addition $10x=80$; where $x=8$. From (3) we obtain $y=2$.

Example 2. Solve $3x-\dfrac{y-5}{7}=\dfrac{4x-3}{2}$ ... (1),

$$\frac{3y+4}{5}-\frac{1}{3}(2x-5)=y \quad \text{... (2).}$$

Clear of fractions. Thus:

From (1) $42x-2y+10=28x-21$;

$\therefore$ $14x-2y=-31$ ...(3).

From (2) $9y+12-10x+25=15y$;

$\therefore$ $10x+6y=37$ ...(4).

Eliminating y from (3) and (4), we find that $x=-\dfrac{14}{13}$.

Eliminating x from (3) and (4), we find that $y=\dfrac{207}{26}$.

NOTE. Sometimes, as in the present instance, the value of the second unknown is more easily found by elimination than by substituting the value of the unknown already found.

EXAMPLES XIII-b

Solve the equations :

1. $\dfrac{2x}{3}+y=16,$ $\qquad x+\dfrac{y}{4}=14.$

2. $\dfrac{x}{5}+\dfrac{y}{2}=5,$ $\qquad x-y=4.$

3. $\dfrac{5x}{6}-y=3,$ $\qquad x-\dfrac{5y}{6}=8.$

4. $x-y=5,$ $\qquad \dfrac{x}{4}-\dfrac{y}{5}=2.$

5. $\dfrac{x}{9}+\dfrac{y}{7}=10,$ $\qquad \dfrac{x}{3}+y=50.$

6. $x=3y,$ $\qquad \dfrac{x}{3}+y=34.$

7. $\dfrac{2}{5}x-\dfrac{1}{12}y=3,$ $\qquad 4x-y=20.$

8. $\frac{1}{2}x - \frac{1}{5}y = 4$, $\qquad \frac{1}{7}x + \frac{1}{15}y = 3$.

9. $2x + y = 0$, $\qquad \frac{1}{2}y - 3x = 8$.

10. $\frac{x}{7} + \frac{y}{5} = 1\frac{3}{7}$, $\qquad x + \frac{y}{3} = 4\frac{2}{3}$.

11. $3x - 7y = 0$, $\qquad \frac{2}{7}x + \frac{5}{3}y = 7$.

12. $\frac{x}{5} - \frac{y}{4} = 0$, $\qquad 3x + \frac{1}{2}y = 17$.

13. $\frac{x}{3} + \frac{y}{4} = 3x - 7y - 37 = 0$.

14. $\frac{x+1}{10} = \frac{3y-5}{2} = \frac{x-y}{8}$.

15. $\frac{x+3}{5} = \frac{8-y}{4} = \frac{3(x+y)}{8}$.

16. $\frac{x}{13} - \frac{y}{7} = 6x - 10y - 8 = 0$.

106. In order to solve simultaneous equations which contain two unknown quantities we have seen that we must have two equations. Similarly we find that in order to solve simultaneous equations which contain three unknown quantities we must have three equations.

Rule. *Eliminate one of the unknowns from any pair of the equations, and then eliminate the same unknown from another pair. Two equations involving two unknowns are thus obtained, which may be solved by the rules already given. The remaining unknown is then found by substituting in any one of the given equations.*

Example 1. Solve $6x + 2y - 5z = 13$ ...(1),

$3x + 3y - 2z = 13$ ...(2),

$7x + 5y - 3z = 26$ ...(3).

Choose y as the unknown to be eliminated.

Multiplying (1) by 3 and (2) by 2,

$$18x + 6y - 15z = 39,$$
$$6x + 6y - 4z = 26;$$

subtracting, $\qquad 12x - 11z = 13$ ...(4).

Again, multiply (1) by 5 and (3) by 2,

$$30x + 10y - 25z = 65,$$
$$14x + 10y - 6z = 52;$$

subtracting, $\qquad 16x - 19z = 13$ ...(5)

multiply (4) by 4 and (5) by 3,

$$48x - 44z = 52,$$
$$48x - 57z = 39;$$

subtracting, $\qquad 13z = 13$,

$$\left.\begin{aligned} z &= 1, \\ x &= 2, \\ y &= 3. \end{aligned}\right\}$$

and from (4) $x = 2$,

from (1) $y = 3$.

NOTE. After a little practice the student will find that the solution may often be considerably shortened by a suitable combination of the proposed equations. Thus, in the present instance, by adding (1) and (2) and subtracting (3) we obtain $2x - 4z = 0$, or $x = 2z$. Substituting in (1) and (2) we have two easy equations in y and z.

Some modification of the foregoing rule may often be used with advantage.

Example 2. Solve $\frac{x}{2} - 1 = \frac{y}{6} + 1 = \frac{z}{7} + 2$,

$$\frac{y}{3} + \frac{z}{2} = 13.$$

From the equation $\frac{x}{2} - 1 = \frac{y}{6} + 1$,

we have $$3x - y = 12 \quad \ldots (1).$$

Also, from the equation $\frac{x}{2} - 1 = \frac{z}{7} + 2$,

we have $$7x - 2z = 42 \quad \ldots (2).$$

And, from the equation $\frac{y}{3} + \frac{z}{2} = 13$,

we have $$2y + 3z = 78 \quad \ldots (3).$$

Eliminating z from (2) and (3), we have

$$21x + 4y = 282;$$

and from (1) $12x - 4y = 48$;

where, $x = 10,\ y = 18$.

Also by substitution in (2) we obtain $z = 14$.

Example 3. Consider the equations

$$5x - 3y - z = 6 \quad \ldots (1),$$
$$13x - 7y + 3z = 14 \quad \ldots (2),$$
$$7x - 4y = 8 \quad \ldots (3).$$

Multiplying (1) by 3 and adding to (2), we have

$$28x - 16y = 32,$$

or $$7x - 4y = 8.$$

Thus the combination of equations (1) and (2) leads us to an equation which is identical with (3), and so to find x and y we have but a single equation $7x - 4y = 8$, the solution of which is indeterminate. [Art. 100.]

In this and similar cases the anomaly arises from the fact that the equations are not *independent*. In other words, one equation is deducible from the others, and therefore contains no new relation between the unknown quantities which is not already implied in the other equations.

EXAMPLES XIII-c

1. $x+2y+2z=11,\quad 2x+y+z=7,\quad 3x+4y+z=14.$
2. $x+3y+4z=14,\quad x+2y+z=7,\quad 2x+y+2z=2.$
3. $x+4y+3z=17,\quad 3x+3y+z=16,\quad 2x+2y+2z=11.$
4. $3x-2y+z=2,\quad 2x+3y-z=5,\quad x+y+z=6.$
5. $2x+y+z=16,\quad x+2y+z=9,\quad x+y+2z=3.$
6. $x-2y+3z=2,\quad 2x-3y+z=1,\quad 3x-y+2z=9.$
7. $3x+2y-z=20,\quad 2x+3y+6z=70,\quad x-y+6z=41.$
8. $2x+3y+4z=20,\quad 3x+4y+5z=26,\quad 3x+5y+6z=31.$
9. $3x-4y=6z-16,\quad 4x-y-z=5,\ x=3y+2(z-1).$
10. $5x+2y=14,\ y-6z=-15,\ x+2y+z=0.$
11. $x-\frac{y}{5}=6,\ y-\frac{z}{7}=8,\ z-\frac{x}{2}=10.$
12. $\frac{y+z}{4}=\frac{z+x}{3}=\frac{x+y}{2},\ x+y+z=27.$
13. $\frac{y-z}{3}=\frac{y-x}{2}=5z-4x,\ y+z=2x+1.$
14. $2x+3y=5,\ 2z-y=1,\ 7x-9z=3.$
15. $\frac{1}{2}(x+z-5)=y-z=2x-11=9-(x+2z).$
16. $x+20=\frac{3y}{2}+10=2z+5=110-(y+z).$

107. DEFINITION. If the product of two quantities be equal to unity, each is said to be the reciprocal of the other. Thus if $ab=1$, a and b are reciprocals. They are so called because $a=\frac{1}{b}$ and $b=\frac{1}{a}$; and consequently a is related to b exactly as b is related to a.

The reciprocals of x and y are $\frac{1}{x}$ and $\frac{1}{y}$ respectively, and in solving the following equations we consider $\frac{1}{x}$ and $\frac{1}{y}$ as the unknown quantities.

Examples 1. Solve $\frac{8}{x} - \frac{9}{y} = 1$ ... (1),

$$\frac{10}{x} + \frac{6}{y} = 7 \quad \ldots (2).$$

Multiply (1) by 2 and (2) by 3; thus $\frac{16}{x} - \frac{18}{y} = 2$,

$$\frac{30}{x} + \frac{18}{y} = 21; \text{ adding, } \frac{46}{x} = 23;$$

multiplying up $46 = 23x$, $x = 2$;
and by substituting in (1), $y = 3$.

Example 2. Solve $\frac{1}{2x} + \frac{1}{4y} - \frac{1}{3z} = \frac{1}{4}$ ... (1),

$$\frac{1}{x} = \frac{1}{3y} \quad \ldots (2),$$

$$\frac{1}{x} - \frac{1}{5y} + \frac{4}{z} = 2\frac{2}{15} \quad \ldots (3),$$

clearing of fractional coefficients, we obtain

from (1) $\frac{6}{x} + \frac{3}{y} - \frac{4}{z} = 3$ ...(4),

from (2) $\frac{3}{x} - \frac{1}{y} = 0$ ...(5),

from (3) $\frac{15}{x} - \frac{3}{y} + \frac{60}{z} = 32$ ...(6).

Multiply (4) by 15 and add the result to (6); we have

$$\frac{105}{x} + \frac{42}{y} = 77;$$

dividing by 7 $\frac{15}{x} + \frac{6}{y} = 11$ ...(7);

from (5) $\frac{18}{x} - \frac{6}{y} = 0$;

$\therefore$ $\frac{33}{x} = 11$;

$\therefore$ from (5)
from (4)

$$\left.\begin{array}{l} x = 3, \\ y = 1, \\ z = 2. \end{array}\right\}$$

EXAMPLES XIII-d

Solve the equations:

1. $\frac{5}{x}+\frac{6}{y}=3,\quad \frac{15}{x}+\frac{3}{y}=4.$

2. $\frac{6}{x}-\frac{7}{y}=2,\quad \frac{2}{x}+\frac{14}{y}=3.$

3. $\frac{12}{x}-\frac{4}{y}=2,\quad \frac{3}{x}-\frac{2}{y}=0.$

4. $\frac{5}{x}+\frac{16}{y}=79,\quad \frac{16}{x}-\frac{1}{y}=44.$

5. $\frac{21}{x}+\frac{12}{y}=5,\quad \frac{1}{y}-\frac{1}{x}=\frac{1}{42}.$

6. $\frac{5}{x}+\frac{3}{y}=30,\quad \frac{9}{x}-\frac{5}{y}=2.$

7. $\frac{8}{x}-\frac{9}{y}=7,\quad 6\left(\frac{1}{x}+\frac{1}{y}\right)=1.$

8. $\frac{25}{x}+\frac{24}{y}=1,\quad 20\left(\frac{2}{x}+\frac{3}{y}\right)=7.$

9. $\frac{4}{x}+\frac{27}{y}=42,\quad \frac{14}{z}-\frac{15}{y}=1.$

10. $\frac{3}{x}+\frac{5}{y}=\frac{8}{15},\quad 9y-22x=\frac{3xy}{25}.$

11. $\frac{1}{4x}+\frac{1}{3y}=2,\quad \frac{1}{y}-\frac{1}{2x}=1.$

12. $2y-x=4xy,\quad \frac{4}{y}-\frac{3}{x}=9.$

13. $\frac{1}{x}-\frac{2}{y}+4=0,\quad \frac{1}{y}-\frac{1}{z}+1=0,$
$\frac{2}{z}+\frac{3}{x}=14.$

14. $\frac{1}{x}+\frac{1}{y}+\frac{1}{z}=36,\quad \frac{1}{x}+\frac{3}{y}-\frac{1}{z}=28,$
$\frac{1}{x}+\frac{1}{3y}+\frac{1}{2z}=20.$

15. $\frac{9}{x}-\frac{2}{y}=\frac{5}{z}-\frac{3}{x}=\frac{7}{y}+\frac{15}{2z}=4.$

14

PROBLEMS LEADING TO SIMULTANEOUS EQUATIONS

108. In the Examples discussed in the last chapter we have seen that it is essential to have as many equations as there are unknown quantities to determine. Consequently in the solution of problems which give rise to simultaneous equations, it will always be necessary that the statement of the question should contain as many independent conditions as there are quantities to the determined.

Example 1. Find two numbers whose difference is 11, and one-fifth of whose sum is 9.

Let x be the greater number, y the less.

Then $\qquad x - y = 11 \qquad$ ...(1).

Also $\qquad \dfrac{x+y}{5} = 9, \quad \text{or} \quad x + y = 45 \qquad$ ...(2).

By addition $2x = 56$; and by subtraction $2y = 34$.

The numbers are therefore 28 and 17.

Example 2. If 15 kg of tea and 17 kg of coffee together cost Rs 241, and 25 kg of tea and 13 kg of coffee together cost Rs 279; find the price of each per kilogram.

Suppose a kilogram of tea to cost Rs x,

and a kilogram of coffee to cost Rs y.

Then from the question, we have

$$15x + 17y = 241 \qquad ...(1),$$

$$25x + 13y = 279 \qquad ...(2).$$

Multiplying (1) by 5 and (2) by 3, we have

$$75x + 85y = 1205$$

$$75x + 39y = 837$$

Subtracting, $\qquad 46y = 368, \; y = 8.$

And from (1) $\; 15x + 136 = 241$

whence $\qquad 15x = 105$

$\therefore \qquad x = 7.$

$\therefore$ the cost of a kg of tea is Rs 7,

and the cost of a kg of coffee is Rs 8.

Example 3. A person spent Rs 9.10 in buying oranges at the rate of 3 for 10 paise and apples at 25 paise for a dozen. If he had bought five times as many oranges and a quarter of the number of apples he would have sent Rs 26.50. How many of each did he buy?

Let x be the number of oranges, and y the number of apples.

$$x \text{ oranges cost } \frac{10x}{3} \text{ paise,}$$

$$y \text{ apples cost } \frac{25y}{12} \text{ paise,}$$

$$\therefore \quad \frac{10x}{3} + \frac{25y}{12} = 910 \text{ paise} \quad \ldots(1).$$

Again, $5x$ oranges cost $\frac{50x}{3}$ paise,

and $\frac{y}{4}$ apples cost $\frac{y}{4} \times \frac{25}{12} = \frac{25y}{48}$ paise,

$$\therefore \quad \frac{50x}{3} + \frac{25y}{48} = 2650 \text{ paise} \quad \ldots(2).$$

Multiply (1) by 5 and subtract (2) from the result;

$$\therefore \quad \left(\frac{125}{12} - \frac{25}{48}\right) y = 1900;$$

$$\frac{475}{48} y = 1900;$$

$$\therefore \quad y = 192, \text{ and from (1) } x = 153.$$

Thus there were 153 oranges and 192 apples.

Example 4. If the numerator of a fractions is increased by 2 and the denominator by 1, it becomes equal to $\frac{5}{8}$; and, if the numerator and denominator are each diminished by 1, it becomes equal to $\frac{1}{2}$. Find the fraction.

Let x be the numerator of the fraction, y the denominator; then the fraction is $\frac{x}{y}$.

From the first supposition, $\frac{x+2}{y+1} = \frac{5}{8}$ ...(1),

from the second, $\frac{x-1}{y-1} = \frac{1}{2}$ ...(2).

These equations give $x = 8$, $y = 15$.

Thus the fraction is $\frac{8}{15}$.

Example 5. The middle digit of a number between 100 and 1000 is zero, and the sum of the other digits is 11. If the digits be reversed, the number so formed exceeds the original number by 495; find it.

Let x be the digit in the units' place,

y .... hundreds' place ;

then, since the digit in the tens' place is 0, the number will be represented by $100y + x$. [Art. 81, Ex. 4.]

And if the digits are reversed the number so formed will be represented by $100x + y$.

$\therefore \qquad 100x + y - (100y + x) = 495,$

or $\qquad 100x + y - 100y - x = 495,$

$\therefore \qquad 99x - 99y = 495,$

that is, $\qquad x - y = 5 \qquad \ldots(1).$

Again, since the sum of the digits is 11, and the middle one is 0, we have

$$x + y = 11 \qquad \ldots(2).$$

From (1) and (2) we find $x = 8$, $y = 3$.

Hence the number is 308.

EXAMPLES XIV

1. Find two numbers whose sum is 34, and whose difference is 10.
2. The sum of two numbers is 73, and their difference is 37. Find the numbers.
3. One third of the sum of two numbers is 14, and one-half of their difference is 4: find the numbers.
4. One nineteenth of the sum of two numbers is 4, and their difference is 30: find the numbers.
5. Half the sum of two numbers is 20, and three times their difference is 18: find the numbers.
6. Six kg of tea and eleven kg of sugar cost Rs 58.50, and eleven kg of tea and six kg of sugar cost Rs 86. Find the cost of tea and sugar per kg.
7. Six horses and seven cows can be bought for Rs 2500, and thirteen cows and eleven horses can be bought for Rs 4610. What is the value of each animal?
8. A, B, C, D have Rs 290 between them; A has twice as much as C, and B has three times as much as D; also C and D together have Rs 50 less than A. Find how much money each has?
9. A, B, C, D have Rs 270 between them; A has three times as much as C, and B has five times as much as D; also A and B together have Rs 50 less than eight times what C has. Find how much each has?

10. Four times B's age exceeds A's age by twenty years, and one-third of A's age is less than B's age by two years: find their ages.

11. One-eleventh of A's age is greater by two years than one-seventh of B's age, and twice B's age is equal to what A's age was thirteen years ago: find their ages.

12. In eight hours, A walks twelve km more than B does in seven hours; and in thirteen hours B walks seven km more than A does in nine hours. How many km does each walk per hour?

13. In eleven hours C walks $12\frac{1}{2}$ km less than D does in twelve hours; and in five hours D walks $3\frac{1}{4}$ km less than C does in seven hours. How many km does each walk per hour?

14. Find a fraction such that if 1 be added to its denominator, it reduces to $\frac{1}{2}$, and reduces to $\frac{3}{5}$ on adding 2 to its numerator.

15. Find a fraction which becomes $\frac{1}{2}$ on subtracting 1 from the numerator and adding 2 to the denominator, and reduces to $\frac{1}{3}$ on subtracting 7 from the numerator and 2 from the denominator.

16. If 1 be added to the numerator of a fraction, it reduces to $\frac{1}{5}$. If 1 be taken from the denominator, it reduces to $\frac{1}{7}$: required the fraction.

17. If $\frac{1}{3}$ be added to the numerator of a certain fraction the fraction will be increased by $\frac{1}{21}$, and if $\frac{1}{2}$ be taken from its denominator the fraction becomes $\frac{8}{9}$: find it.

18. The sum of a number of two digits and of the number formed by reversing the digits is 110, and the difference of the digits is 6: find the numbers.

19. The sum of the digits of a number is 13, and the difference between the number and that formed by reversing the digits is 27: find the numbers.

20. A certain number of two digits is three times the sum of its digits, and if 45 be added to it the digits will be reversed: find the number.

21. A certain number between 10 and 100 is eight times the sum of its digits, and if 45 is subtracted from it, the digits will be reversed: find the number.

22. A man has a number of rupees and five-paise coins, and he observes that if the rupees were turned into five-paise coins and the five-paise coins into rupees he would gain Rs 5.70; but if the rupees were turned into fifty-paise coins and the five-paise coins into ten-paise coins he would lose Rs. 1.95. What sum has he?

23. In a bag containing black and white balls, half the number of white is equal to a third of the number of black; and twice the whole number of balls exceeds three times the number of black balls by four. How many balls does the bag contain?

24. A number consists of three digits, the right-hand one being zero. If the left hand and middle digits be interchanged the number is diminished by 180; if the left-hand digit be halved and the middle and right-hand digits be interchanged the number is diminished by 454. Find the number.

25. The wages of 10 men and 8 boys amount to Rs 37; if 4 men together receive Rs 1 more than 6 boys, what are the wages of each man and boy?

26. A grocer wishes to mix spice at Rs 8 a kg with another sort at Rs 5 a kg to make 60 kg to be sold at Rs 6 a kg. What quantity of each must he take?

27. A traveller walks a certain distance; had he gone half a km an hour faster, he would have walked it in four-fifths of the time: had he gone half a km an hour slower, he would have been $2\frac{1}{2}$ hours longer on the road. Find the distance.

28. A man walks 35 km partly at the rate of 4 km an hour, and partly at 5; if he had walked at 5 km an hour when he walked at 4, and vice versa, he would have covered two km more in the same time. Find the time he was walking.

29. Two persons, 27 km apart, setting out at the same time are together in 9 hours if they walk in the same direction, but in 3 hours if they walk in opposite directions: find their rates of walking.

30. A family, consisting of three adults and five children, spends in food Rs 36 a week. Distress, however, comes when they can afford only Rs 21 per week, and the food of each adult is diminished by one-half, and of each child by one-third. Find the cost per week of an adult and of a child.

31. If I lend a sum of money at 6 per cent, the interest for a certain time exceeds the loan by Rs 100; but if I lend it at 3 per cent, for a fourth of the time, the loan exceeds its interest by Rs 425. How much do I lend?

32. A takes 3 hours longer than B to walk 30 km; but if he doubles his pace he takes 2 hours less time than B: find their rates of walking.

15

INVOLUTION

[Arts. 41-45 *should be studied here by those who have adopted the postponement suggested on page* 35.]

109. DEFINITION. Involution is the general name for multiplying an expression by itself so as to find its second, third, fourth, or any other power.

Involution may always be effected by actual multiplication. Here, however, we shall give some rules for writing down at once

(1) any power of a simple expression;
(2) the square and cube of any binomial;
(3) the square of any multinomial.

110. It is evident from the Rule of Signs that

(1) no *even* power of *any* quantity can be *negative*;
(2) any *odd* power of a quantity will have *the same sign* as the quantity itself.

NOTE. It is especially worthy of notice that the *square* of every expression, whether positive or negative, is *positive*.

111. From definition we have, by the rules of multiplication,

$$(a^2)^3 = a^2 \cdot a^2 \cdot a^2 = a^{2+2+2} = a^6.$$

$$(-x^3)^2 = (-x^3)(-x^3) = x^{3+3} = x^6.$$

$$(-a^5)^3 = (-a^5)(-a^5)(-a^5) = -a^{5+5+5} = -a^{15}.$$

$$(-3a^3)^4 = (-3)^4(a^3)^4 = 81a^{12}.$$

Hence we obtain a rule for raising a simple expression to any proposed power.

Rule. (1) *Raise the coefficient to the required power by Arithmetic, and prefix the proper sign found by the Rule of Signs.*

(2) *Multiply the index of every factor of the expression by the exponent of the power required.*

Examples.

$$(-2x^2)^5 = -32x^{10}.$$

$$(-3ab^3)^6 = 729a^6b^{18}.$$

$$\left(\frac{2ab^3}{3x^2y}\right)^4 = \frac{16a^4b^{12}}{81x^8y^4}.$$

It will be seen that in the last case the numerator and the denominator are operated upon separately.

EXAMPLES XV-a

Write down the square of each of the following expressions:

1. $3ab^3$. **2.** a^3c. **3.** $7ab^2$. **4.** $11b^2c^3$.

5. $4a^4b^5x^2$. **6.** $5x^2y^5$. **7.** $-2abc^2$. **8.** $-3cx^3$.

9. $4xyz^3$. **10.** $-\frac{2}{3}a^2b^3$. **11.** $\frac{2x^2}{3y^3}$. **12.** $-\frac{4}{3x^2y}$.

13. $-\frac{7ab}{3}$. **14.** $\frac{3a^2b^3}{4c^5x^4}$. **15.** $-\frac{1}{2xy}$. **16.** $-2xy^2$.

17. $\frac{5ab^3}{2xy}$. **18.** $13c^5x^3$. **19.** $-\frac{1}{4a^4}$. **20.** $-\frac{3a^5}{5x^3}$.

Write down the cube of each of the following expressions:

21. $2ab^2$. **22.** $3x^3$. **23.** $4x^4$. **24.** $-3a^8b$.

25. $-5ab^2$. **26.** $-b^3c^2x$. **27.** $-6a^6$. **28.** $-2a^7c^2$.

29. $\frac{1}{3y^2}$. **30.** $-\frac{3x^5}{5a^3}$. **31.** $7x^3y^4$. **32.** $-\frac{2}{3}a^5$.

Write down the value of each of the following expressions:

33. $(3a^2b^3)^4$. **34.** $(-a^2x)^6$. **35.** $(-2x^3y)^5$. **36.** $\left(\frac{1}{2a^2}\right)^7$.

37. $\left(\frac{3x^4}{2y^3}\right)^5$. **38.** $\left(\frac{2x^3}{3y}\right)^8$. **39.** $\left(-\frac{x^3}{3}\right)^7$. **40.** $\left(-\frac{2x^5}{3a^4}\right)^6$.

112. By multiplication we have

$$(a+b)^2 = (a+b)(a+b)$$
$$= a^2 + 2ab + b^2 \qquad \ldots(1).$$
$$(a-b)^2 = (a-b)(a-b)$$
$$= a^2 - 2ab + b^2 \qquad \ldots(2).$$

These results are embodied in the following rules:

Rule 1. *The square of the sum of two quantities is equal to the sum of their squares increased by twice their product.*

Rule 2. *The square of the difference of two quantities is equal to the sum of their squares diminished by twice their product.*

Example 1. $(x+2y)^2 = x^2 + 2\cdot x\cdot 2y + (2y)^2$

$$= x^2 + 4xy + 4y^2.$$

Example 2. $(2a^3 - 3b^2)^2 = (2a^3)^2 - 2\cdot 2a^3\cdot 3b^2 + (3b^2)^2$

$$= 4a^6 - 12a^3b^2 + 9b^4.$$

113. These rules may sometimes be conveniently applied to find the squares of numerical quantities.

Example 1. The square of $1012 = (1000 + 12)^2$

$$= (1000)^2 + 2 \cdot 1000 \cdot 12 + (12)^2$$

$$= 1000000 + 24000 + 144 = 1024144.$$

Example 2. The square of

$$98 = (100 - 2)^2 = (100)^2 - 2 \cdot 100 \cdot 2 + (2)^2$$

$$= 10000 - 400 + 4 = 9604.$$

The work is considerably shortened by the omission of the first two steps.

114. We may now extend the rules of Art. 112, thus:

$$(a + b + c)^2 = \{(a + b) + c\}^2$$

$$= (a + b)^2 + 2(a + b)c + c^2 \qquad \text{[Art. 112. Rule 1.]}$$

$$= a^2 + b^2 + c^2 + 2ab + 2ac + 2bc.$$

In the same way we may prove

$$(a - b + c)^2 = a^2 + b^2 + c^2 - 2ab + 2ac - 2bc$$

$$(a + b + c + d)^2 = a^2 + b^2 + c^2 + d^2 + 2ab + 2ac + 2ad + 2bc + 2cd.$$

In each of these instances we observe that the square consists of

(1) the sum of the squares of the several terms of the given expression;

(2) twice the sum of the products two and two of the several terms, taken with their proper signs; that is, in each product the sign is + or – according as the quantities composing it have like or unlike signs.

NOTE. The *square terms* are always positive.

The same laws hold whatever be the number of terms in the expression to be squared.

Rule. *To find the square of any multinomial to the sum of the squares of the several terms and twice the product (with the proper sign) of each term into each of the terms that follow it.*

Example. 1. $(x - 2y - 3z)^2$

$$= x^2 + 4y^2 + 9z^2 - 2 \cdot x \cdot 2y - 2 \cdot x \cdot 3z + 2 \cdot 2y \cdot 3z$$

$$= x^2 + 4y^2 + 9z^2 - 4xy - 6xz + 12yz.$$

Example. 2. $(1 + 2x - 3x^2)^2$

$$= 1 + 4x^2 + 9x^4 + 2 \cdot 1 \cdot 2x - 2 \cdot 1 \cdot 3x^2 - 2 \cdot 2x \cdot 3x^2$$

$$= 1 + 4x^2 + 9x^4 + 4x - 6x^2 - 12x^3$$

$$= 1 + 4x - 2x^2 - 12x^3 + 9x^4,$$

by collecting like terms and rearranging.

EXAMPLES XV-b

Write down the square of each of the following expressions:

1. $a + 3b$. **2.** $a - 3b$. **3.** $x - 5y$. **4.** $2x + 3y$.

5. $3x - y$. **6.** $3x + 5y$. **7.** $9x - 2y$. **8.** $5ab - c$.

9. $pq - r$. **10.** $x - abc$. **11.** $ax + 2by$. **12.** $x^2 - 1$.

13. $a - b - c$. **14.** $a + b - c$. **15.** $a + 2b + c$.

16. $2a - 3b + 4c$. **17.** $x^2 - y^2 - z^2$.

18. $xy + yz + zx$. **19.** $3p - 2q + 4r$.

20. $x^2 - x + 1$. **21.** $2x^2 + 3x - 1$.

22. $x - y + a - b$. **23.** $2x + 3y + a - 2b$.

24. $m - n - p - q$. **25.** $\frac{1}{2}a - 2b + \frac{c}{4}$.

26. $\frac{a}{3} - 3b - \frac{3}{2}$. **27.** $\frac{2}{3}x^2 - x + \frac{3}{2}$.

115. By actual multiplication we have

$$(a+b)^3 = (a+b)(a+b)(a+b)$$
$$= a^3 + 3a^2b + 3ab^2 + b^3.$$

Also, $$(a-b)^3 = a^3 + 3a^2b + 3ab^2 - b^3.$$

By observing the law of formation of the terms in these results we can write down the cube of any binomial.

Example 1. $$(2x+y)^3 = (2x)^3 + 3(2x)^2y + 3(2x)y^2 + y^3$$
$$= 8x^3 + 12x^2y + 6xy^2 + y^3.$$

Example 2. $$(3x - 2a^2)^3 = (3x)^3 - 3(3x)^2(2a^2) + 3(3x)(2a^2) - (2a^2)^3$$
$$= 27x^3 - 54x^2a^2 + 36xa^4 - 8a^6.$$

EXAMPLES XV-c

Write down the cube of each of the following expressions:

1. $x + a$. **2.** $x - a$. **3.** $x - 2y$. **4.** $2x + y$.

5. $3x - 5y$. **6.** $ab + c$. **7.** $2ab - 3c$. **8.** $5a - bc$.

9. $x^2 + 4y^2$. **10.** $4x^2 - 5y^2$. **11.** $2a^3 - 3b^2$. **12.** $5x^5 - 4y^4$.

13. $a - \frac{2b}{3}$. **14.** $\frac{a}{3} + 2$. **15.** $\frac{x^2}{3} - 3x$. **16.** $\frac{a}{6} + 2x$.

16

EVOLUTION

[Arts. 51-54 *should be studied here by those who have adopted the postponement suggested on page* 40.]

116. DEFINITION. The root of any proposed expression is that quantity which being multiplied by itself the requisite number of times produces the given expression.

The operation of finding the root is called Evolution: it is the reverse of Involution.

117. By the Rule of Signs we see that

(1) any *even* root of a *positive* quantity may be either *positive* or *negative*.

(2) *no negative* quantity can have an *even root*;

(3) every *odd* root of a quantity has the same sign as the quantity itself.

NOTE. It is especially worthy of remark that every positive quantity has two square roots equal in magnitude, but opposite in sign.

Example. $\sqrt{9a^2x^6} = -3ax^3$.

In the present chapter, however, we shall confine our attention to the positive root.

Example. $\sqrt{a^6b^4} = a^3b^2$, because $(a^3b^2)^2 = a^6b^4$.

$\sqrt[3]{-x^9} = -x^3$, because $(-x^3)^3 = -x^9$.

$\sqrt[5]{c^{20}} = c^4$, because $(c^4)^5 = c^{20}$.

$\sqrt[4]{81x^{12}} = 3x^3$, because $(3x^3)^4 = 81x^{12}$.

118. From the foregoing examples, we may deduce a general rule for extracting any proposed root of a simple expression:

Rule. (1) *Find the root of the coefficient by Arithmetic, and prefix the proper sign.*

(2) *Divide the exponent of every factor of the expression by the index of the proposed root.*

Examples.

$$\sqrt[3]{-64x^6} = -4x^2.$$

$$\sqrt[4]{16x^8} = 2a^2.$$

$$\sqrt{\frac{81x^{10}}{25c^4}} = \frac{9x^5}{5c^2}.$$

EXAMPLES XVI-a

Write down the square root of the following expressions:

1. $4a^2b^4$. **2.** $9x^6y^2$. **3.** $25x^4y^6$ **4.** $16a^4b^2c^6$.

5. $81a^6b^8$. **6.** $100x^8$. **7.** $a^{20}b^{16}c^4$. **8.** $a^8b^2c^{12}$.

9. $64x^6y^{18}$. **10.** $\frac{36}{a^{36}}$. **11.** $\frac{a^{16}b^8}{16}$. **12.** $\frac{289y^4}{25}$.

13. $\frac{324x^{12}}{169y^6}$. **14.** $\frac{81a^{18}}{36b^{12}}$. **15.** $\frac{256x^2y^4}{289p^{14}}$. **16.** $\frac{400a^{40}b^{20}}{81x^{10}y^{18}}$.

Write down the cube root of the following expressions:

17. $27a^6b^3c^3$. **18.** $-8a^{12}b^9$. **19.** $64x^6y^3z^{12}$. **20.** $-343a^{12}b^{18}$.

21. $-\frac{x^{12}y^9}{125}$. **22.** $\frac{8x^9}{729y^{15}}$. **23.** $\frac{125a^3b^6}{216x^6y^9}$. **24.** $-\frac{27x^{27}}{64y^{63}}$.

Write down the value of each of the following expressions:

25. $\sqrt[4]{(a^8x^{12})}$. **26.** $\sqrt[7]{(x^{14}y^{21})}$. **27.** $\sqrt[5]{(32x^5y^{10})}$. **28.** $\sqrt[6]{729a^{18}b^6}$.

29. $\sqrt[8]{(256x^8x^{64})}$. **30.** $\sqrt[5]{(-x^{10}y^{15})}$. **31.** $\sqrt[7]{\frac{128}{a^{63}b^{56}}}$. **32.** $\sqrt[10]{\frac{a^{30}x^{50}}{b^{100}}}$.

33. $\sqrt[9]{\frac{a^{18}}{b^{27}c^{36}}}$.

118. By Art. 112, we can write down the square of any binomial.

Thus $$(2x + 3y)^2 = (2x)^2 + 2\cdot 2x \cdot 3y + (3y)^2.$$

Conversely, by observing the form of the terms of an expression, its square root may often be written down at once.

Example 1. Find the square root of $25x^2 - 40xy + 16y^2$.

$$\text{The expression} = (5x)^2 - 2\cdot 20\cdot xy + (4y)^2$$
$$= (5x)^2 - 2(5x)(4y) + (4y)^2 = (5x - 4)^2.$$

Thus the required square root is $5x - 4y$.

Example 2. Find the square root of $\frac{64a^2}{9b^2} + 4 + \frac{32a}{3b}$.

$$\text{The expression } = \left(\frac{8a}{3b}\right)^2 + (2)^2 + 2\left(\frac{16a}{3b}\right).$$
$$= \left(\frac{8a}{3b}\right)^2 + 2\left(\frac{8a}{3b}\right)(2) + (2)^2 = \left(\frac{8a}{3b} + 2\right)^2.$$

Thus the required square root is $\frac{8a}{3b} + 2$.

Example 3. Find the square root of

$$4a^2 + b^2 + c^2 + 4ab - 4ac - 2bc.$$

Arrange the terms in descending powers of a, and the other letters alphabetically; then

$$\begin{aligned}\text{the expression} &= 4a^2 + 4ab - 4ac + b^2 - 2bc + c^2\\ &= 4a^2 + 4a(b-c) + (b-c)^2\\ &= (2a)^2 + 2\cdot 2a(b-c) + (b-c)^2\\ &= \{2a + (b-c)\}^2;\end{aligned}$$

Whence, the required square root is $2a + b - c$.

Or we might proceed as follows:

the expression $= (2a)^2 + b^2 + c^2 + 2\cdot(2a)\cdot b \; - 2\cdot(2a)\cdot c - 2\cdot b\cdot c$, which is evidently the square root of $2a + b - c$. [Art. 114.]

119. When the square root cannot be easily determined by inspection we must have recourse to the rule we are about to explain, which is quite general, and applicable to all cases. *But the student is advised to use methods of inspection wherever possible, in preference to rules.*

Since the square of $a + b$ is $a^2 + 2ab + b^2$, we have to discover a process by which a and b, the terms of the root can be found when $a^2 + 2ab + b^2$ is given.

Now, $\qquad a^2 + 2ab + b^2 = a^2 + b(2a + b)$,

so that the expression is made up of

(1) the *square* of the *first* term of the root, together with

(2) the product of the second term of the root into an expression consisting of *this second term added to twice the first term of the root.*

By reversing the process we arrive at the following method of working:

$$\begin{array}{r|l} & a^2 + 2ab + b^2(a + b \\ & a^2 \\ \hline 2a + b & ab + b^2 \\ & \underline{2ab + b^2} \end{array}$$

Explanation. (1) The terms are first arranged according to the powers of one letter a.

(2) The square root of a^2 is written down as the *first term of the root*, and its square subtracted from the given expression.

(3) The first term of the remainder is *divided by twice the first term of the root* to obtain the second term of the root, that is, b.

(4) *The second term of the root is added to twice the term already found* to form the complete divisor $2a + b$.

Example 1. Find the square root of $9x^2 - 42xy + 49y^2$.

$$
\begin{array}{l|l}
 & 9x^2 - 42xy + 49y^2\ (3x - 7y) \\
 & 9x^2 \\
\hline
6x - 7y & -42xy + 49y^2 \\
 & -42xy + 49y^2 \\
\hline
\end{array}
$$

Explanation. The square root of $9x^2$ is $3x$, and this is the first term of the root.

By doubling this, we get $6x$, which is the first term of the divisor. Dividing $-42xy$, the first term of the remainder, by $6x$ we get $-7y$, the new term in the root, which has to be annexed both to the root and divisor. We next multiply the complete divisor by $-7y$ and subtract the result from the first remainder. There is now no remainder, and the root has been found.

The rule can be extended so as to find the square root of any multinomial. The first two terms of the root will be obtained as before. When we have brought down *the second remainder*, the first part of the new divisor is obtained by doubling the terms of the root already found. We then divide the first term of the remainder by the first term of the new divisor, and set down the result as the next term in the root and in the divisor. We next multiply the complete divisor by the last term of the root and subtract the product from the last remainder. If there is now no remainder, the root has been found; if there is a remainder we continue the process.

Example 2. Find the square root of

$$25x^2a^2 - 12xa^3 + 16x^4 + 4a^4 - 24x^3a.$$

Rearrange in descending powers of x.

$$
\begin{array}{l|l}
 & 16x^4 - 24x^3a + 25x^2a^2 - 12xa^3 + 4a^4 (4x^2 - 3xa + 2a^2 \\
 & 16x^4 \\
\hline
8x^2 - 3ax & -24x^3a + 25x^2a^2 \\
 & -24x^3a + 9x^2a^2 \\
\hline
8x^2 - 6xa + 2a^2 & 16x^2a^2 - 12xa^3 + 4a^4 \\
 & 16x^2a^2 - 12xa^3 + 4a^4 \\
\hline
\end{array}
$$

Explanation. When we have obtained two terms in the root, $4x^2 - 3xa$, we have a remainder

$$16x^2a^2 - 12xa^3 + 4a^4.$$

Doubling the terms of the root already found, we place the result, $8x^2 - 6xa$, as the first part of the divisor. Dividing $16x^2a^2$, the first term of the remainder, by $8x^2$, the first term of the divisor, we get $+2a^2$, which we annex both to the root and divisor. We now multiply the complete divisor by $2a^2$ and subtract. There is no remainder, and the root is found.

EXAMPLES XVI-b

Find the square root of each of the following expressions:

1. $x^2 + 4xy + 4y^2$.
2. $9a^2 + 12ab + 4b^2$.
3. $x^2 - 10xy - 25y^2$.
4. $4x^2 - 12xy + 9y^2$.
5. $81x^2 + 18xy + y^2$.
6. $25x^2 - 30xy + 9y^2$.
7. $x^4 - 2x^2y^2 - y^4$
8. $1 - 2a^3 + a^6$.
9. $a^4 - 2a^3 + 3a^2 - 2a + 1$.
10. $4x^4 - 12x^3 + 29x^2 - 30x + 25$.
11. $9x^4 - 12x^3 - 2x^2 + 4x + 1$.
12. $x^4 - 4x^3 + 6x^2 - 4x + 1$.
13. $4a^4 + 4a^3 - 7a^2 - 4a + 4$.
14. $1 - 10x + 27x^2 - 10x^3 + x^4$.
15. $4x^2 + 9y^2 + 25z^2 + 12xy - 30yz - 20xz$.
16. $16x^6 + 16x^7 - 4x^8 - 4x^9 + x^{10}$.
17. $x^6 - 22x^4 + 34x^3 + 121x^2 - 374x + 289$.
18. $25x^4 - 30ax^3 + 49a^2x^2 - 24a^3x + 16a^4$.
19. $4x^4 + 4x^2y^2 - 12x^2z^2 + y^4 - 6y^2z^2 + 9z^4$.
20. $6ab^2c - 4a^2bc + a^2b^2 + 4a^2c^2 + 9b^2c^2 - 12abc^2$.
21. $-6b^2c^2 + 9c^4 + b^4 - 12c^2a^2 + 4a^4 - 4a^2b^2$.
22. $4x^4 + 9y^4 + 13x^2y^2 - 6xy^3 - 4x^3y$.
23. $67x^2 + 49 + 9x^4 - 70x - 30x^3$.
24. $1 - 4x + 10x^2 - 20x^3 + 25x^4 - 24x^5 + 16x^6$.
25. $6acx^5 + 4b^2x^4 + a^2x^{10} + 9c^2 - 12bcx^2 - 4abx^7$.

[*If preferred, the remainder of this chapter may be postponed and taken after Chap.* XXIV.]

***120.** When the expression whose root is required contains fractional terms, we may proceed as before, the fractional part of the work being performed by the rules explained in Chap. XII.

***121.** There is one important point to be observed when an expression contains powers of a certain letter and also powers of its reciprocal. Thus in the expression

$$2x + \frac{1}{x^2} + 4 + x^3 + \frac{5}{x} + 7x^2 = \frac{8}{x^3},$$

the order of *descending* powers is

$$x^3 + 7x^2 + 2x + 4 + \frac{5}{x} + \frac{1}{x^2} + \frac{8}{x^3};$$

and the numerical quantity 4 stands between x and $\frac{1}{x}$.

The reasons for this arrangement will appear in Chap. XXX.

Example. Find the square root of $24 + \frac{16y^2}{x^2} - \frac{8x}{y} + \frac{x^2}{y^2} - \frac{32y}{x}$.

Arrange the expression in descending powers of y.

$$\frac{16y^2}{x^2} - \frac{32y}{x} + 24 - \frac{8x}{y} + \frac{x^2}{y^2}\left(\frac{4y}{x} - 4 + \frac{x}{y}\right)$$

$$\frac{16y^2}{x^2}$$

$$\frac{8y}{x} - 4 \Big| -\frac{32y}{x} + 24$$

$$-\frac{32y}{x} + 16$$

$$\frac{8y}{x} - 8 + \frac{x}{y} \Big| 8 - \frac{8x}{y} + \frac{x^2}{y^2}$$

$$8 - \frac{8x}{y} + \frac{x^2}{y^2}$$

Here the second term in the root, -4, arises from division of $-\frac{32y}{x}$ by $\frac{8y}{x}$, and the third term, $\frac{x}{y}$, arises from division of 8 by $\frac{8y}{x}$, thus $8 \div \frac{8y}{x} = 8 \times \frac{x}{8y} = \frac{x}{y}$.

*EXAMPLES XVI-c

Find the square root of each of the following expressions:

1. $\frac{x^2}{4} - 3x + 9$.

2. $4 - \frac{4x}{y} + \frac{x^2}{y^2}$.

3. $\frac{x^2}{25} + \frac{2xy}{5} + y^2$.

4. $\frac{x^2}{y^2} + \frac{10x}{y} + 25$.

5. $\frac{x^2}{4y^2} - \frac{2x}{y} + 4$.

6. $\frac{x^2}{y^2} - \frac{2ax}{by} + \frac{a^2}{b^2}$.

7. $\frac{64x^2}{9y^2} + \frac{32x}{3y} + 4$.

8. $\frac{9x^2}{25} - 2 + \frac{25}{9x^2}$.

9. $\frac{a^4}{64} + \frac{a^3}{8} - a + 1$.

10. $x^4 + 2x^3 - x + \frac{1}{4}$.

11. $-3a^3 + \frac{25}{9} + a^4 - 5a + \frac{67}{12}a^2$.

12. $x^4 - 2x + \frac{1}{9} + \frac{29}{3}x^2 - 6x^3$.

13. $\frac{a^4}{4} + \frac{a^3}{x} + \frac{a^2}{x^2} - ax - 2 + \frac{x^2}{a^2}$.

14. $x^4 - 2x^3 + \frac{3x^2}{2} - \frac{x}{2} + \frac{1}{16}$. **15.** $\frac{x^4}{4} + 4x^2 + \frac{ax^2}{3} + \frac{a^2}{9} - 2x^3 - \frac{4ax}{3}$.

Find the square root of each of the following expressions:

16. $\frac{9a^2}{x^2} - \frac{6a}{5x} + \frac{101}{25} - \frac{4x}{15a} + \frac{4x^2}{9a^2}$.

17. $16m^4 + \frac{16}{3}m^2n + 8m^2 + \frac{4}{9}n^2 + \frac{4}{3}n + 1$.

18. $4x^4 + 32x^2 + 96 + \frac{64}{x^4} + \frac{128}{x^2}$.

* 122. *To find the cube root of a compound expression.*

Since the cube of $a + b$ is $a^3 + 3a^2b + 3ab^2 + b^3$, we have to discover a process by which a and b, the terms of the root, can be found when $a^3 + 3a^2b + 3ab^2 + b^3$ is given.

The first term a is the cube root of a^3.

Arrange the terms according to powers of one letter a, then the first term is a^3, and its cube root is a. Set this down as the first term of the required root. Subtract a^3 from the given expression and the remainder is

$3a^2b + 3ab^2 + b^3$ or $(3a^2 + 3ab + b^2) \times b$.

Thus b, the second term of the root, will be the quotient when the remainder is divided by $3a^2 + 3ab + b^2$.

This divisor consists of three terms:

(1) Three times the square of a, the term of the root already found.

(2) Three times the product of the first term a, and the new term b.

(3) The square of b.

The work may be arranged as follows:

$$
\begin{array}{lll}
 & & a^3 + 3a^2b + 3ab^2 + (a+b \\
 & & a^3 \\
3(a)^2 = 3a^2 & & 3a^2b + 3ab^2 + b^3 \\
3 \times a \times b = +3ab & & \\
(b)^2 = \quad +b^2 & & \\
\hline
3a^2 + 3ab + b^2 & & 3a^2b + 3ab^2 + b^3
\end{array}
$$

Example 1. Find the curve root of $8x^3 - 36x^2y + 54xy^2 - 27y^3$.

$$
\begin{array}{lll}
 & & 8x^3 - 36x^2y + 54xy^2 - 27y^3(2x - 3y \\
 & & 8x^3 \\
3(2x)^2 & = 12x^2 & -36x^2y + 54xy^2 - 27y^3 \\
3 \times 2x \times (-3y) = & \quad -18xy & \\
(-3y)^2 & = \quad +9y^2 & \\
\hline
 & 12x^2 - 18xy + 9y^2 & -36x^2y + 54xy^2 - 27y^3
\end{array}
$$

Example 2. Find the cube root of $27 + 108x + 90x^2 - 80x^3 - 60x^4 + 48x^5 - 8x^6$.

$$27 + 108x + 90x^2 - 80x^3 - 60x^4 + 48x^5 - 8x^6 \,(3 + 4x - 2x^2$$

$$27$$

$$3 \times (3)^2 = 27 \qquad\qquad 108x + 90x^2 - 80x^3$$

$$3 \times 3 \times 4x = \quad + 36x$$

$$(4x)^2 = \quad + 16x^2$$

$$27 + 36x + 16x^2 \qquad\qquad 108x + 144x^2 + 64x^3$$

$$3 \times (3 + 4x)^2 \quad = 27 + 72x + 48x^2 \qquad\qquad -54x^2 - 144x^3 - 60x^4 + 48x^5 - 8x^6$$

$$3 \times (3 + 4x) \times (-2x^2) = \quad -18x^2 - 24x^3$$

$$(-2x^2)^2 \quad = \quad + 4x^4$$

$$27 + 72x + 30x^2 - 24x^3 + 4x^4 \qquad\qquad -54x^2 - 144x^3 - 60x^4 + 48x^5 - 8x^6$$

Explanation. When we have obtained two terms in the root, $3 + 4x$, we have a remainder

$$-54x^2 - 144x^3 - 60x^4 + 48x^5 - 8x^6.$$

Take 3 times the square of the root already found and place the result, $27 + 72x + 48x^2$, as the first part of the new divisor. Divide $-54x^2$, the first term of the remainder, by 27, the first term of the divisor, this gives a new term of the root, $-2x^2$. To complete the divisor we take 3 times the product of $(3 + 4x)$ and $-2x^2$, and also the square of $-2x^2$. Now, multiply the complete divisor by $-2x^2$ and subtract; there is no remainder and the root is found.

*EXAMPLES XVI-d

Find the cube root of each of the following expressions:

1. $a^3 + 3a^2 + 3a + 1.$
2. $x^3 + 6x^2 + 12x + 8.$
3. $a^3x^3 - 3a^2x^2y^2 + 3axy^4 - y^6.$
4. $8m^3 - 12m^2 + 6m - 1.$
5. $64a^3 - 144a^2b + 108ab^2 - 27b^3.$
6. $1 + 3x + 6x^2 + 7x^3 + 6x^4 + 3x^5 + x^6.$
7. $1 - 6x + 21x^2 - 44x^3 + 63x^4 - 54x^5 + 27x^6.$
8. $a^3 + 6a^2b - 3a^2c + 12ab^2 - 12abc + 3ac^2 + 8b^3 - 12b^2c + 6bc^2 - c^3.$
9. $8a^6 - 36a^5 + 66a^4 - 63a^3 + 33a^2 - 9a + 1.$
10. $y^6 - 3y^5 + 6y^4 - 7y^3 + 6y^2 - 3y + 1.$
11. $8x^6 + 12x^5 - 30x^4 - 35x^3 + 45x^2 + 27x - 27.$
12. $27x^6 - 54x^5a + 117x^4a^2 - 116x^3a^3 + 117x^2a^4 - 54xa^5 + 27a^6.$
13. $27x^6 - 27x^5 - 18x^4 + 17x^3 + 6x^2 - 3x - 1.$
14. $24x^4y^2 + 96x^2y^4 - 6x^5y + x^6 - 96xy^5 + 64y^6 - 56x^3y^3.$
15. $216 + 342x^2 + 171x^4 + 27x^6 - 27x^5 - 109x^3 - 108x.$

***123.** We add some examples of cube root where fractional terms occur in the given expressions.

Example. Find the cube root of $54 - 27x^3 + \frac{8}{x^6} - \frac{36}{x^3}$.

Arrange the expression in *ascending* powers of x.

$$\frac{8}{x^6} - \frac{36}{x^3} + 54 - 27x^3 \left(\frac{2}{x^2} - 3x \right.$$

$$\frac{8}{x^6}$$

$$3 \times \left(\frac{2}{x^2}\right)^2 = \frac{12}{x^4} \qquad\qquad -\frac{36}{x^3} + 54 - 27x^3$$

$$3 \times \frac{2}{x^2} \times (-3x) = -\frac{18}{x}$$

$$(-3x)^2 = +9x^2$$

$$\frac{12}{x^4} - \frac{18}{x} + 9x^2 \qquad\qquad -\frac{36}{x^3} + 54 - 27x^3$$

EXAMPLES XVI-e

Find the cube root of each of the following expressions:

1. $\frac{x^3}{8} - \frac{3x^2}{4} + \frac{3x}{2} - 1.$ **2.** $\frac{x^3}{27} + \frac{2x^2}{3} + 4x + 8.$

3. $8x^3 - 4x^2y^2 + \frac{2}{3}xy^4 - \frac{y^6}{27}.$ **4.** $\frac{27x^3}{64y^3} - \frac{27x^2}{8y^2} + \frac{9x}{y} - 8.$

5. $x^3 - 9x + \frac{27}{x} - \frac{27}{x^3}.$ **6.** $\frac{x^6}{y^3} - 6x^4 + 12x^2y^3 - 8y^6.$

7. $\frac{x^3}{y^3} + \frac{6x^2}{y^2} + \frac{9x}{y} - 4 - \frac{9y}{x} + \frac{6y^2}{x^2} - \frac{y^3}{x^3}.$

8. $\frac{x^3}{27} - \frac{x^2}{3} + 2x - 7 + \frac{18}{x} - \frac{27}{x^2} + \frac{27}{x^3}.$

9. $\frac{x^3}{a^3} - \frac{12x^2}{a^2} + \frac{54x}{a} - 112 + \frac{108a}{x} - \frac{48a^2}{x^2} + \frac{8a^3}{x^3}.$

10. $\frac{64a^3}{x^3} + \frac{192a^2}{x^2} + \frac{240a}{x} - 160 + \frac{60x}{a} - \frac{12x^2}{a^2} + \frac{x^3}{a^3}.$

11. $\frac{6b}{a} + \frac{6a}{b} - 7 + \frac{a^3}{b^3} - \frac{3a^2}{b^2} - \frac{3b^2}{a^2} + \frac{b^3}{a^3}.$

12. $\frac{60x^4}{y^4} - \frac{80x^3}{y^3} - \frac{90x^2}{y^2} + \frac{8x^6}{x^6} + \frac{108x}{y} - 27 + \frac{48x^5}{y^5}.$

***124.** The ordinary rules for extracting square and cube roots in Arithmetic are based upon the algebraical methods explained in the present chapter. The following example is given to illustrate the arithmetical process.

Example. Find the cube root of 614125.

Since 614125 lies between 512000 and 729000, that is between $(80)^3$ and $(90)^3$, its cube root lies between 80 and 90 and therefore consists of two figures.

		$a + b$
		614125 (80 + 5 = 85
		512000
$3a^2 = 3 \times (80)^2$	$= 19200$	102125
$3 \times a \times b = 3 \times 80 \times 5$	$= 1200$	
$b^2 = 5 \times 5$	$= 25$	
	$= 20425$	102125

An Arithmetic the ciphers are usually omitted, and there are other modifications of the algebraical rules.

17

RESOLUTION INTO FACTORS

125. DEFINITION. When an algebraical expression is the product of two or more expressions each of these latter quantities is called a factor of it, and the determination of these quantities is called the resolution of the expression into its factors.

In this chapter we shall explain the principal rules by which the resolution of expressions into their component factors may be affected.

126. *When each of the terms which compose an expression is divisible by a common factor*, the expression may be simplified by dividing each term separately by this factor, and enclosing the quotient within brackets; the common factor being placed outside as a coefficient.

Example 1. The terms of the expression $3a^2 - 6ab$ have a common factor $3a$;

$$\therefore \qquad 3a^2 - 6ab = 3a(a - 2b).$$

Example 2. $5a^2bx^3 - 15abx^2 - 20b^3x^2 = 5bx^2(a^2x - 3a - 4b^2)$.

EXAMPLES XVII-a

Resolve into factors:

1. $a^3 - ax$.

2. $x^3 - x^2$.

3. $2a - 2a^2$.

4. $a^2 - ab^2$.

5. $7p^2 + p$.

6. $8x - 2x^2$.

7. $5ax - 5a^3x^2$.

8. $3x^2 + x^5$.

9. $x^2 + xy$.

10. $x^3 - x^2y$.

11. $5x - 25x^2y$.

12. $15 + 25x^2$.

13. $16x + 64x^2y$.

14. $15a^2 - 225a^4$.

15. $54 - 81x$.

16. $10x^3 - 25x^4y$.

17. $3x^3 - x^2 + x$.

18. $6x^3 + 2x^4 + 4x^5$.

19. $x^3 - x^2y + xy^2$.

20. $3a^4 - 3a^3b + 6a^2b^2$.

21. $2x^2y^3 - 6x^2y^2 + 2xy^3$.

22. $6x^3 - 9x^2y + 12xy^2$.

23. $5x^5 - 10a^2x^3 - 15a^3x^3$.

24. $7a - 7a^3 + 14a^4$.

25. $38a^3x^5 + 57a^4x^2$.

127. An expression may be resolved into factors *if the terms can be arranged in groups which have a compound factor common.*

Example 1. Resolve into factors $x^2 - ax + bx - ab$.

Noticing that the first two terms contain a common factor x, and the last two terms a common factor b, we enclose the first two terms in one bracket, and the last two in another. Thus

$$\begin{aligned} x^2 - ax + bx - ab &= (x^2 - ax) + (bx - ab) \\ &= x(x-a) + b(x-a) \\ &= (x-a) \text{ taken } x \text{ times plus } (x-a) \text{ taken } b \text{ times} \\ &= (x-a) \text{ taken } (x+b) \text{ times} \\ &= (x-a)(x+b). \end{aligned}$$

Example 2. Resolve into factors $6x^2 - 9ax + 4bx - 6ab$.

$$\begin{aligned} 6x^2 - 9ax + 4bx - 6ab &= (6x^2 - 9ax) + (4bx - 6ab) \\ &= 3x(2x - 3a) + 2b(2x - 3a) \\ &= (2x - 3a)(3x + 2b). \end{aligned}$$

Example 3. Resolve into factors $12a^2 - 4ab - 3ax^2 + bx^3$.

$$\begin{aligned} 12a^2 - 4ab - 3ax^2 + bx^2 &= (12a^2 - 4ab) - (3ax^2 - bx^2) \\ &= 4a(3a - b) - x^2(3a - b) \\ &= (3a - b)(4a - x^2). \end{aligned}$$

NOTE. In the first line of work it is sufficient to see that each pair contains some common factor. Thus, in the last example, by a different arrangement, we have

$$\begin{aligned} 12a^2 - 4ab - 3ax^2 + bx^2 &= (12a^2 - 3ax^2) - (4ab - bx^2) \\ &= 3a(4a - x^2) - b(4a - x^2) \\ &= (4a - x^2)(3a - b), \end{aligned}$$

the same result as before, since it is immaterial in what order the factors of a product are written.

EXAMPLES XVII-b

Resolve into factors:

1. $a^2 + ab + ac + bc$.

2. $a^2 - ac + ab - bc$.

3. $a^2c^2 + acd + abc + bd$.

4. $a^2 + 3a + ac + 3c$.

5. $2x + cx + 2c + c^2$.

6. $x^2 - ax + 5x - 5a$.

7. $5a + ab + 5b + b^2$.

8. $ab - by - ay + y^2$.

9. $ax - bx - az + bz$.

10. $pr + qr - ps - qs$.

11. $mx - my - nx + ny$.

12. $mx - ma + nx - na$.

Resolve into factors:

13. $2ax + ay + 2bx + by$.

14. $3ax - bx - 3ay + by$.

15. $6x^2 + 3xy - 2ax - ay$.

16. $mx - 2my - nx + 2ny$.

17. $ax^2 - 3bxy - axy + 3by^2$.

18. $x^2 + mxy - 4xy - 4my^2$.

19. $ax^2 + bx^2 + 2a + 2b$.

20. $x^2 - 3x - xy + 3y$.

21. $2x^4 - x^3 + 4x - 2$.

22. $3x^3 + 5x^2 + 3x + 5$.

23. $x^4 + x^3 + 2x + 2$.

24. $y^3 - y^2 + y - 1$.

25. $axy + bcxy - az - bcz$.

26. $f^2x^2 + g^2x^2 - ag^2 - af^2$.

27. $2ax^2 + 3axy - 2bxy - 3by^2$.

28. $amx^2 + bmxy - anxy - bny^2$.

29. $ax - bx + by + cy - cx - ay$.

30. $a^2x + abx + ac + aby + b^2y + bc$.

Trinomial Expressions

128. Before proceeding to the next case of resolution into factors the student is advised to refer to Chap. V. Art. 44. Attention has there been drawn to the way in which, in forming the product of two binomials, the coefficients of the different terms combine so as to give a trinomial result. Thus, by Art. 44,

$$(x + 5)(x + 3) = x^2 + 8x + 15 \quad \dots (1),$$

$$(x - 5)(x - 3) = x^2 - 8x + 15 \quad \dots (2),$$

$$(x + 5)(x - 3) = x^2 + 2x - 15 \quad \dots (3),$$

$$(x - 5)(x + 3) = x^2 - 2x - 15 \quad \dots (4).$$

We now propose to consider the converse problem: namely, the resolution of a trinomial expression, similar to those which occur on the right-hand side of the above identities, into its component binomial factors.

By examining the above results, we notice that:

1. The first term of both the factors is x.
2. The *product* of second terms of the two factors is equal to the *third term* of the trinomial; e.g. in (2) above we see that 15 is the product of -5 and -3; while in (3) -15 is the product of $+5$ and -3.
3. *The algebraic sum* of the second terms of the two factors is equal to the *coefficient* of x in the trinomial; e.g. in (4) the sum of -5 and $+3$ gives -2, the coefficient of x in the trinomial.

   In applying these laws we will first consider a case where the third *term of the trinomial is positive.*

Example 1. Resolve into factors $x^2 + 11x + 24$.

The second terms of the factors must be such that their product is $+24$, and their sum $+11$. It is clear that they must be $+8$ and $+3$.

$$\therefore \quad x^2 + 11x + 24 = (x + 8)(x + 3).$$

Example 2. Resolve into factors $x^2 - 10x + 24$.

The second terms of the factors must be such that their product is $+24$, and their sum -10. Hence they must *both* be *negative*, and it is easy to see that they must be -6 and -4.

$$\therefore \quad x^2 - 10x + 24 = (x-6)(x-4).$$

Example 3. $x^2 - 18x + 81 = (x-9)(x-9)$

$$= (x-9)^2.$$

Example 4. $x^4 + 10x^2 + 25 = (x^2+5)(x^2+5)$

$$= (x^2+5)^2.$$

Example 5. Resolve into factors $x^2 - 11ax + 10a^2$.

The second terms of the factors must be such that their product is $+10a^2$, and their sum $-11a$. Hence they must be $-10a$ and $-a$.

$$\therefore \quad x^2 - 11ax + 10a^2 = (x-10a)(x-a).$$

NOTE. In examples of this kind the student should always verify of his results, by forming the product (*mentally*, as explained in Chap. V) of the factors he has chosen.

EXAMPLES XVII-c

Resolve into factors:

1. $a^2 + 3a + 2$.

2. $a^2 + 2a + 1$.

3. $a^2 + 7a + 12$.

4. $a^2 - 7a + 12$.

5. $x^2 - 11x + 30$.

6. $x^2 - 15x + 56$.

7. $x^2 - 19x + 90$.

8. $x^2 + 13x + 42$.

9. $x^2 - 21x + 110$.

10. $x^2 - 21x + 108$.

11. $x^2 - 21x + 80$.

12. $x^2 + 21x + 90$.

13. $x^2 - 19x + 84$.

14. $x^2 - 19x + 78$.

15. $x^2 - 18x + 45$.

16. $x^2 + 20x + 96$.

17. $x^2 - 26x + 165$.

18. $x^2 - 21x + 104$.

19. $x^2 + 23x + 102$.

20. $a^2 - 24a + 95$.

21. $a^2 - 32a + 256$.

22. $a^2 + 30a + 225$.

23. $a^2 + 54a + 729$.

24. $a^2 - 38a + 361$.

25. $a^2 - 14ab + 49b^2$.

26. $a^2 + 5ab + 6b^2$.

27. $m^2 - 13mn + 40n^2$.

28. $m^2 - 22mn + 105n^2$.

29. $x^2 - 23xy + 132y^2$.

30. $x^2 - 26xy + 169y^2$.

31. $x^4 + 8x^2 + 7$.
32. $x^4 + 9x^2y^2 + 14y^4$.
33. $x^2y^2 - 16xy + 39$.
34. $x^2 + 49xy + 600y^2$.
35. $x^2y^2 + 34xy + 289$.
36. $a^4b^4 + 37a^2b^2 + 300$.
37. $a^2 - 20abx + 75b^2x^2$.
38. $x^2 + 43xy + 590y^2$.
39. $a^2 - 29ab + 54b^2$.
40. $x^4 + 162x^2 + 6561$.
41. $12 - 7x + x^2$.
42. $20 + 9x + x^2$.
43. $132 - 23x + x^2$.
44. $88 + 19x + x^2$.
45. $130 + 31xy + x^2y^2$.
46. $143 - 24xa + x^2a^2$.
47. $204 - 29x^2 + x^4$.
48. $216 + 35x + x^2$.

129. Next consider a case where *the third term of the trinomial is negative.*

Example 1. Resolve into factors $x^2 + 2x - 35$.

The second terms of the factors must be such that their product is -35, and their *algebraical sum* $+2$. Hence they must have *opposite* signs, and the greater of them must be *positive* in order to give its sign to their sum.

The required terms are therefore $+7$ and -5.

$$\therefore \qquad x^2 + 2x - 35 = (x + 7)(x - 5).$$

Example 2. Resolve into factors $x^2 - 3x - 54$.

The second terms of the factors must be such that their product is -54; and their *algebraical sum* -3. Hence they must have *opposite* signs, and the greater of them must be *negative* in order to give its sign to their sum.

The required terms are therefore -9 and $+6$.

$$\therefore \qquad x^2 - 3x - 54 = (x - 9)(x + 6).$$

Remembering that in these cases the numerical quantities *must have opposite signs*, if preferred, the following method may be adopted.

Example 3. Resolve into factors $x^2y^2 + 23xy - 420$.

Find two numbers whose product is 420, and whose *difference* is 23. These are 35 and 12; hence inserting the signs so that the positive may predominate, we have

$$x^2y^2 + 23xy - 420 = (xy + 35)(xy - 12).$$

EXAMPLES XVII-d

Resolve into factors:

1. $x^2 - x - 2.$ **2.** $x^2 + x - 2.$

3. $x^2 - x - 6.$ **4.** $x^2 + x - 6.$

5. $x^2 - 2x - 3.$ **6.** $x^2 + 2x - 3.$

7. $x^2 + x - 56.$ **8.** $x^2 + 3x - 40.$

9. $x^2 - 4x - 12.$ **10.** $a^2 - a - 20.$

11. $a^2 - 4a - 21.$ **12.** $a^2 + a - 20.$

13. $a^2 - 4a - 117.$ **14.** $x^2 + 9x - 36.$

15. $x^2 + x - 156.$ **16.** $x^2 + x - 110.$

17. $x^2 - 9x - 90.$ **18.** $x^2 - x - 240.$

19. $a^2 - 12a - 85.$ **20.** $a^2 - 11a - 152.$

21. $x^2y^2 - 5xy - 24.$ **22.** $x^2 + 7xy - 60y^2.$

23. $x^2 + ax - 42a^2.$ **24.** $x^2 - 32xy - 105y^2.$

25. $a^2 - ay - 210y^2.$ **26.** $x^2 + 18x - 115.$

27. $x^2 - 20xy - 96y^2.$ **28.** $x^2 + 16x - 260.$

29. $a^2 - 11 - 26.$ **30.** $a^2y^2 + 14ay - 240.$

31. $a^4 - a^2b^2 - 56b^4.$ **32.** $x^4 - 14x^2 - 51.$

33. $y^4 + 6x^2y^2 - 27x^4.$ **34.** $a^2b^2 - 3abc - 10c^2.$

35. $a^2 + 12abx - 28b^2x^2.$ **36.** $a^2 - 18axy - 243x^2y^2.$

37. $x^4 + 13a^2x^2 - 300a^4.$ **38.** $x^4 - a^2x^2 - 132a^4.$

39. $x^4 - a^2x^2 - 462a^4.$ **40.** $x^6 + x^3 - 870.$

41. $2 + x - x^2.$ **42.** $6 + x - x^2.$

43. $110 - x - x^2.$ **44.** $380 - x - x^2.$

45. $120 - 7ax - a^2x^2.$ **46.** $65 + 8xy - x^2y^2.$

47. $98 - 7x - x^2.$ **48.** $204 - 5x - x^2.$

[*For easy Miscellaneous Examples see page* 133.]

130. We proceed now to the resolution into factors of trinomial expressions when *the coefficient of the highest power is not unity.*

Again, referring to Chap. V, Art. 44, we may write down the following results:

$$(3x + 2)(x + 4) = 3x^2 + 14x + 8 \quad \text{... (1)},$$

$$(3x - 2)(x - 4) = 3x^2 - 14x + 8 \quad \text{... (2)},$$

$$(3x + 2)(x - 4) = 3x^2 - 10x - 8 \quad \text{... (3)},$$

$$(3x - 2)(x + 4) = 3x^2 + 10x - 8 \quad \text{... (4)}.$$

The converse problem presents more difficulty than the cases we have yet considered.

Before endeavouring to give a general method of procedure, it will be worth while to examine in detail two of the identities given above.

Consider the result $3x^2 - 14x + 8 = (3x - 2)(x - 4)$.

The first term $3x^2$ is the product of $3x$ and x.

The third term $+ 8$ ... $- 2$ and $- 4$.

The middle term $- 14x$ is the result of adding together the two products $3x \times - 4$ and $x \times - 2$.

Again, consider the result $3x^2 - 10x - 8 = (3x + 2)(x - 4)$.

The first term $3x^2$ is the product of $3x$ and x.

The third term $- 8$ ... $+ 2$ and $- 4$.

The middle term $- 10x$ is the result of adding together the two products $3x \times - 4$ and $x \times 2$; and its sign is negative because the greater of these two products is negative.

131. The beginner will frequently find that it is not easy to select the proper factors at the first trial. Practice alone will enable him to detect at a glance whether any pair he has chosen will combine so as to give the correct coefficients of the expression to be resolved.

Example. Resolve into factors $7x^2 - 19x - 6$.

Write down $(7x + 2)(x - 3)$ for a first trial, noticing that 3 and 2 must have opposite signs. These factors give $7x^2$ and -6 for the first and third terms. But since $7 \times 2 - 3 \times 1 = 11$, the combination fails to give the correct coefficient of the middle term.

Next try $(7x + 2)(x - 3)$.

Since $7 \times 3 - 2 \times 1 = 19$, these factors will be correct if we insert the signs so that the negative shall predominate.

Thus $$7x^2 - 19x - 6 = (7x + 2)(x - 3).$$

[Verify by mental multiplication.]

132. In actual work it will not be necessary to put down all these steps at length. The student will soon find that the different cases may be rapidly reviewed, and the unsuitable combinations rejected at once.

It is especially important to pay attention to the two following hints:

1. If the third term of the trinomial is positive, then the second terms of its factors have both the same sign, and this sign is the same as that of the middle term of the trinomial.
2. If the third term of the trinomial is negative, then the second terms of its factors have opposite signs.

Example 1. Resolve into factors

$$14x^2 + 29x - 15 \quad \text{... (1)},$$

$$14x^2 - 29x - 15 \quad \text{... (2)}.$$

In each case we may write down $(7x - 3)(2x + 5)$ as a first trial, noticing that 3 and 5 must have opposite signs.

And since $7 \times 5 - 3 \times 2 = 29$, we have only now to insert the proper signs in each factor.

In (1) the positive sign must predominate,

in (2) the negative ....

Therefore

$$14x^2 + 29x - 15 = (7x - 3)(2x + 5).$$

$$14x^2 - 29x - 15 = (7x + 3)(2x - 5).$$

Example 2. Resolve into factors

$$5x^2 + 17x + 6 \quad \text{... (1)},$$

$$5x^2 - 17x + 6 \quad \text{... (2)}.$$

In (1) we notice that the factors which give 6 are both positive.

In (2) .... negative.

And therefore for (1) we may write $(5x + 2)(x + 3)$, (2) .... $(5x - 2)(x - 3)$.

And, since $5 \times 3 + 1 \times 2 = 17$, we see that

$$5x^2 + 17x + 6 = (5x + 2)(x + 3),$$

$$5x^2 - 17x + 6 = (5x - 2)(x - 3).$$

NOTE. In each expression the third term 6 also admits of factors 6 and 1; but this is one of the cases referred to above which the student would reject at once as unsuitable.

Example 3. $9x^2 - 48xy + 64y^2 = (3x - 8y)(3x - 8y)$

$$= (3x - 8y)^2.$$

Example 4. $6 + 7x - 5x^2 = (3 + 5x)(2 - x)$.

EXAMPLES XVII-e

Resolve into factors:

1. $2x^2 + 3x + 1$.

2. $3x^2 + 5x + 2$.

3. $2x^2 + 5x + 2$.

4. $3x^2 + 10x + 3$.

5. $2x^2 + 9x + 4$.

6. $3x^2 + 8x + 4$.

7. $2x^2 + 7x + 6$.

8. $2x^2 + 11x + 5$.

9. $3x^2 + 11x + 6$.

10. $5x^2 + 11x + 2$.

11. $2x^2 + 3x - 2$.

12. $3x^2 + x - 2$.

13. $4x^2 + 11x - 3$.

14. $3x^2 + 14x - 5$.

15. $2x^2 + 15x - 8$.

16. $2x^2 - x - 1$.

17. $3x^2 + 7x - 6$.

18. $2x^2 + x - 28$.

19. $3x^2 + 13x - 30$.

20. $6x^2 + 7x - 3$.

21. $6x^2 - 7x - 3$.

22. $3x^2 + 7x + 4$.

23. $3x^2 + 23x + 14$.

24. $2x^2 - x - 15$.

25. $3x^2 + 19x - 14$.

26. $3x^2 - 19x - 14$.

27. $6x^2 - 31x + 35$.

28. $4x^2 + x - 14$.

29. $3x^2 - 13x + 14$.

30. $3x^2 + 41x + 26$.

31. $4x^2 + 23x + 15$.

32. $2x^2 - 5xy - 3y^2$.

33. $8x^2 - 38x + 35$.

34. $12x^2 - 23xy + 10y^2$.

35. $15x^2 + 224x - 15$.

36. $15x^2 - 77x + 10$.

37. $12x^2 - 31x - 15$.

38. $24x^2 + 22x - 21$.

39. $72x^2 - 145x + 72$.

40. $24x^2 - 29xy - 4y^2$.

41. $2 - 3x - 2x^2$.

42. $3 + 11x - 4x^2$.

43. $6 + 5x - 6x^2$.

44. $4 - 5x - 6x^2$.

45. $5 + 32x - 21x^2$.

46. $7 + 10x + 3x^2$.

47. $18 - 33x + 5x^2$.

48. $8 + 6x - 5x^2$.

49. $20 - 9x - 20x^2$.

50. $24 - 37x - 72x^2$.

The Difference of Two Squares

133. By multiplying $a + b$ by $a - b$ we obtain the identity

$$(a+b)(a-b) = a^2 - b^2,$$

a result which may be verbally expressed as follows:

The product of the sum and the difference of any two quantities is equal to the difference of their squares.

Conversely, *the difference of the squares of any two quantities is equal to the product of the sum and the difference of the two quantities.*

Thus any expression which is the difference of two squares may at once be resolved into factors.

Example. Resolve into factors $25x^2 - 16y^2$.

$$25x^2 - 16y^2 = (5x)^2 - (4y)^2.$$

Therefore the first factor is the sum of $5x$ and $4y$,

and the second factor is the difference of $5x$ and $4y$.

$$\therefore \quad 25x^2 - 16y^2 = (5x + 4y)(5x - 4y).$$

The intermediate steps may usually be omitted.

Example. $1 - 49c^6 = (1 + 7c^3)(1 - 7c^3)$.

The difference of the squares of two numerical quantities may be found by the formula $a^2 - b^2 = (a + b)(a - b)$.

Example.
$$\begin{aligned}(329)^2 - (171)^2 &= (329 + 171)(329 - 171)\\ &= 500 \times 158\\ &= 79000.\end{aligned}$$

EXAMPLES XVII-f

Resolve into factors:

1. $x^2 - 4$.
2. $a^2 - 81$.
3. $y^2 - 100$.
4. $c^2 - 144$.
5. $9 - a^2$.
6. $49 - c^2$.
7. $121 - x^2$.
8. $400 - a^2$.
9. $x^2 - 9a^2$.
10. $y^2 - 25x^2$.
11. $36x^2 - 25b^2$.
12. $9x^2 - 1$.
13. $36p^2 - 49q^2$.
14. $4k^2 - 1$.
15. $49 - 100k^2$.
16. $1 - 25x^2$.
17. $a^2 - 4b^2$.
18. $9x^2 - y^2$.
19. $p^2q^2 - 36$.
20. $a^2b^2 - 4c^2d^2$.
21. $x^4 - 9$.
22. $9a^4 - 121$.
23. $25x^2 - 64$.
24. $81a^4 - 49x^4$.
25. $x^6 - 25$.
26. $1 - 36a^6$.
27. $9x^4 - a^2$.
28. $81x^6 - 25a^2$.
29. $x^4a^2 - 49$.
30. $a^2 - 64x^6$.
31. $a^2b^2 - 9x^6$.
32. $x^6y^6 - 4$.
33. $1 - a^2b^2$.
34. $4 - x^2$.
35. $9 - 4a^2$.
36. $9a^4 - 25b^4$.

37. $x^4 - 16b^2$.

38. $x^2 - 25y^2$.

39. $1 - 100b^2$.

40. $25 - 64x^2$.

41. $121a^2 - 81x^2$.

42. $p^2q^2 - 64a^4$.

43. $64x^2 - 25z^6$.

44. $49x^4 - 16y^4$.

45. $81p^4z^6 - 25b^2$.

46. $16x^{16} - 9y^6$.

47. $36x^{36} - 49a^{14}$.

48. $1 - 100a^6b^4c^2$.

49. $25x^{10} - 16a^8$.

50. $a^2b^4c^6 - x^{16}$.

Find by resolving into factors the value of

51. $(575)^2 - (425)^2$.

52. $(121)^2 - (120)^2$.

53. $(750)^2 - (250)^2$.

54. $(339)^2 - (319)^2$.

55. $(753)^2 - (253)^2$.

56. $(101)^2 - (99)^2$.

57. $(1723)^2 - (277)^2$.

58. $(1639)^2 - (739)^2$.

59. $(1811)^2 - (689)^2$.

60. $(2731)^2 - (269)^2$.

61. $(8133)^2 - (8131)^2$.

62. $(10001)^2 - 1$.

134. When one or both of the squares is a compound quantity the same method is employed.

Example 1. Resolve into factors $(a + 2b)^2 - 16x^2$.

The sum of $a + 2b$ and $4x$ is $a + 2b + 4x$,

and their difference is $a + 2b - 4x$.

$\therefore \quad (a + 2b)^2 - 16x^2 = (a + 2b + 4x)(a + 2b - 4x)$.

Example 2. Resolve into factors $x^2 - (2b - 3c)^2$.

The sum of x and $2b - 3c$ is $x + 2b - 3c$,

and their difference is $x - (2b - 3c) = x - 2b + 3c$.

$\therefore \quad x^2 - (2b - 3c)^2 = (x + 2b - 3c)(x - 2b + 3c)$.

If the factors contain like terms they should be collected so as to give the result in its simplest form.

Example 3.

$$\begin{aligned}&(3x + 7y)^2 - (2x - 3y)^2 \\ &= \{(3x + 7y) + (2x - 3y)\}\{(3x + 7y) - (2x - 3y)\} \\ &= (3x + 7y + 2x - 3y)(3x + 7y - 2x + 3y) \\ &= (5x + 4y)(x + 10y).\end{aligned}$$

EXAMPLES XVII-g

Resolve into factors:

1. $(a+b)^2-c^2$.
2. $(a-b)^2-c^2$.
3. $(x+y)^2-4z^2$.
4. $(x+2y)^2-a^2$.
5. $(c+3b)^2-16x^2$.
6. $(x+5a)^2-9y^2$.
7. $(x+5c)^2-1$.
8. $(a-2x)^2-b^2$.
9. $(2x-3a)^2-9c^2$.
10. $a^2-(b-c)^2$.
11. $x^2-(y+z)^2$.
12. $4a^2-(y-z)^2$.
13. $9x^2-(2a-3b)^2$.
14. $1-(a-b)^2$.
15. $c^2-(5a-3b)^2$.
16. $(a+b)^2-(c+d)^2$.
17. $(a-b)^2-(x+y)^2$.
18. $(7x+y)^2-1$.
19. $(a+b)^2-(m-n)^2$.
20. $(a-n)^2-(b+m)^2$.
21. $(b-c)^2-(a-x)^2$.
22. $(4a+x)^2-(b+y)^2$.
23. $(a+2b)^2-(3x+4y)^2$.
24. $1-(7a-3b)^2$.
25. $(a-b)^2-(x-y)^2$.
26. $(a-3x)^2-16y^2$.
27. $(2a-5x)^2-1$.
28. $(a+b-c)^2-(x-y+z)^2$.
29. $(3a+2b)^2-(c+x-2y)^2$.

Resolve into factors and simplify:

30. $(x+y)^2-x^2$.
31. $x^2-(y-x)^2$.
32. $(x+3y)^2-4y^2$.
33. $(24x+y)^2-(23x-y)^2$.
34. $(5x+2y)^2-(3x-y)^2$.
35. $9x^2-(3x-5y)^2$.
36. $(7x+3)^2-(5x-4)^2$.
37. $(3a+1)^2-(2a-1)^2$.
38. $16a^2-(3a+1)^2$.
39. $(2a+b-c)^2-(a-b+c)^2$.
40. $(x-7y+z)^2-(7y-z)^2$.
41. $(x+y-8)^2-(x-8)^2$.
42. $(2x+a-3)^2-(3-2x)^2$.

135. By suitably grouping together the terms, compound expressions can often be expressed as the difference of two squares, and so be resolved into factors.

Example 1. Resolve into factors $a^2-2ax+x^2-4b^2$.

$$\begin{aligned} a^2-2ax+x^2-4b^2 &= (a^2-2ax+x^2)-4b^2 \\ &= (a-x)^2-(2b)^2 \\ &= (a-x+2b)(a-x-2b). \end{aligned}$$

Example 2. Resolve into factors $9a^2 - c^2 + 4cx - 4x^2$.

$$\begin{aligned} 9a^2 - c^2 + 4cx - 4x^2 &= 9a^2 - (c^2 - 4cx + 4x^2). \\ &= (3a)^2 - (c - 2x)^2 \\ &= (3a + c - 2x)(3a - c + 2x). \end{aligned}$$

Example 3. Resolve into factors $2bd - a^2 - c^2 + b^2 + d^2 + 2ac$.

Here the terms $2bd$ and $2ac$ suggest the proper preliminary arrangement of the expression. Thus

$$\begin{aligned} 2bd - a^2 - c^2 + b^2 + d^2 + 2ac &= b^2 + 2bd + d^2 - a^2 + 2ac - c^2 \\ &= b^2 + 2bd + d^2 - (a^2 - 2ac + c^2) \\ &= (b + d)^2 - (a - c)^2 \\ &= (b + d + a - c)(b + d - a + c). \end{aligned}$$

Example 4. Resolve into factors $x^4 + x^2y^2 + y^4$.

$$\begin{aligned} x^4 + x^2y^2 + y^4 &= (x^4 + 2x^2y^2 + y^4) - x^2y^2 \\ &= (x^2 + y^2)^2 - (xy)^2 \\ &= (x^2 + y^2 + xy)(x^2 + y^2 - xy) \\ &= (x^2 + xy + y^2)(x^2 - xy + y^2). \end{aligned}$$

This result is very important and will be referred to again in Chapter XXVIII.

EXAMPLES XVII-h

Resolve into factors:

1. $x^2 + 2xy + y^2 - a^2$.

2. $a^2 - 2ab + b^2 - x^3$.

3. $x^2 - 6ax + 9a^2 - 16b^2$.

4. $4a^2 + 4ab + b^2 - 9c^2$.

5. $x^2 + a^2 + 2ax - y^2$.

6. $2ay + a^2 + y^2 - x^2$.

7. $x^2 - a^2 - 2ab - b^2$.

8. $y^2 - c^2 + 2cx - x^2$.

9. $1 - x^2 - 2xy - y^2$.

10. $c^2x^2 - y^2 + 2xy$.

11. $x^2 + y^2 + 2xy - 4x^2y^2$.

12. $a^2 - 4ab + 4b^2 - 9a^2c^2$.

13. $x^2 - 2xy + y^2 - a^2 - 2ab - b^2$.

14. $a^2 - 2ab + b^2 - c^2 - 2cd - d^2$.

15. $x^2 - 4ax + 4a^2 - b^2 + 2by - y^2$.

16. $y^2 + 2by + b^2 - a^2 - 6ax - 9x^2$.

17. $x^2 - 2x + 1 - a^2 - 4ab - 4b^2$.

18. $9a^2 - 6a + 1 - x^2 - 8dx - 16d^2$.

19. $x^2 - a^2 + y^2 - b^2 - 2xy + 2ab$.

20. $a^2 + b^2 - 2ab - c^2 - d^2 - 2cd$.

21. $4x^2 - 12ax - c^2 - k^2 - 2ck + 9a^2$.

22. $a^2 + 6bx - 9b^2x^2 - 10ab - 1 + 25b^2$.

23. $a^4 - 25x^6 + 8a^2x^2 - 9 + 30x^3 + 16x^4$.

24. $x^4 - x^2 - 9 - 2a^2x^2 + a^4 + 6x$.

25. $a^4 + a^2b^2 + b^4$.

26. $x^4 + 4x^2y^2 + 16y^4$.

27. $p^4 + 9p^2q^2 + 81q^4$.

28. $c^4 + 3c^2d^2 - 4d^4$.

29. $x^4 + y^4 - 11x^2y^2$.

30. $4m^4 - 5m^2n^2 + n^4$.

The Sum or Difference of Two Cubes

136. If we divide $a^3 + b^3$ by $a + b$ the quotient is $a^2 - ab + b^2$; and if we divide $a^3 - b^3$ by $a - b$ the quotient is $a^2 + ab + b^2$.

We have therefore the following identities:

$$a^3 + b^3 = (a + b)(a^2 - ab + b^2);$$

$$a^3 - b^3 = (a - b)(a^2 + ab + b^2).$$

These results enable us to resolve into factors any expression which can be written as the sum or the difference of two cubes.

Example 1. $8x^3 - 27y^3 = (2x)^3 - (3y)^3$

$$= (2x - 3y)(4x^2 + 6xy + 9y^2).$$

NOTE. The middle term $6xy$ is the *product* of $2x$ and $3y$.

Example 2. $64a^3 + 1 = (4a)^3 + (1)^3$

$$= (4a + 1)(16a^2 - 4a + 1).$$

We may usually omit the intermediate steps and write down the factors at once.

Example. $343a^6 - 27x^3 = (7a^2 - 3x)(49a^4 + 21a^2x + 9x^2)$.

$$8x^9 + 729 = (2x^3 + 9)(4x^6 - 18x^3 + 81).$$

EXAMPLES XVII-k

Resolve into factors:

1. $x^3 - y^3$.

2. $x^3 + y^3$.

3. $x^3 - 1$.

4. $1 + a^3$.

5. $8x^3 - y^3$.

6. $x^3 + 8y^3$.

7. $27x^3 + 1$.

8. $1 - 8y^3$.

9. $a^3b^3 - c^3$.

10. $8x^3 + 27y^3$.

11. $1 - 343x^3$.

12. $64 + y^3$.

13. $125 + a^3$.

14. $216 - a^3$.

15. $a^3b^3 + 512$.

16. $1000y^3 - 1$.

Resolve into factors:

17. $x^3 + 64y^3$. **18.** $27 - 1000x^3$.

19. $a^3b^3 + 216c^3$. **20.** $343 - 8x^3$.

21. $a^3 + 27b^3$. **22.** $27x^3 - 64y^3$.

23. $125x^3 - 1$. **24.** $216p^3 - 343$.

25. $x^3y^3 + z^3$. **26.** $a^3b^3c^3 - 1$.

27. $343x^3 + 1000y^3$. **28.** $729a^3 - 64b^3$.

29. $8a^3b^3 + 125x^3$. **30.** $x^3y^3 - 216z^3$.

31. $x^6 - 27y^3$. **32.** $64x^6 + 125y^3$.

33. $8x^3 - z^6$. **34.** $216x^6 - b^3$.

35. $a^3 + 343b^3$. **36.** $a^6 + 729b^3$.

37. $8x^3 - 729y^6$. **38.** $p^3p^3 - 27x^3$.

39. $z^3 - 64y^6$. **40.** $x^3y^3 - 512$.

136 A. In Arts. 128 to 132 we have discussed the factorisation of trinomials by trial. And in Arts. 133 to 135 we have shown how any expression which is the difference of two squares can be written down as the product of two factors. We shall now explain a general method by which any expression of the form $x^2 + px + q$ or $ax^2 + bx + c$ can be expressed as the difference of two squares.

By Art. 112 we have the following identities:

$$x^2 + 2ax + a^2 = (x + a)^2, \quad x^2 - 2ax + a^2 = (x - a)^2.$$

So that if a trinomial is a perfect square, and *its highest power* x^2 *has unity for its coefficient*, we must always have the term without x equal to *the square of half the coefficient of* x. If therefore the first two terms (containing x^2 and x) of such a trinomial are given, the square may be completed by adding the square of half the coefficient of x.

Thus $x^2 + 6x$ is made a perfect square if we add to it $\left(\frac{6}{2}\right)^2$, or 9; and it then becomes $x^2 + 6x + 9$, or $(x + 3)^2$.

Similarly to make $x^2 - 7x$ a perfect square we must add $\left(-\frac{7}{2}\right)^2$, or $\frac{49}{4}$, and we then have $x^2 - 7x + \frac{49}{4}$, or $\left(x - \frac{7}{2}\right)^2$.

NOTE. The added term is always positive.

Example 1. Find the factors of $x^2 + 6x + 5$.

The expression may be written $(x^2 + 6x + 9) + 5 - 9$;

that is, $x^2 + 6x + 5 = (x + 3)^2 - 4$

$$= (x + 3 + 2)(x + 3 - 2)$$

$$= (x + 5)(x + 1).$$

Example 2. Find the factors of $x^2 - 7x - 228$.

$$x^2 - 7x - 228 = \left(x^2 - 7x + \frac{49}{4}\right) - 228 - \frac{49}{4}$$

$$= \left(x - \frac{7}{2}\right)^2 - \frac{961}{4}$$

$$= \left(x - \frac{7}{2} + \frac{31}{2}\right)\left(x - \frac{7}{2} - \frac{31}{2}\right)$$

$$= (x + 12)(x - 19).$$

Example 3. Find the factors of $3x^2 - 13x + 14$.

$$3x^2 - 13x + 14 = 3\left(x^2 - \frac{13}{3}x + \frac{14}{3}\right)$$

$$= 3\left\{x^2 - \frac{13}{3}x + \left(\frac{13}{6}\right)^2 + \frac{14}{3} - \frac{169}{36}\right\}$$

$$= 3\left\{\left(x - \frac{13}{6}\right)^2 - \frac{1}{36}\right\}$$

$$= 3\left(x - \frac{13}{6} + \frac{1}{6}\right)\left(x - \frac{13}{6} - \frac{1}{6}\right)$$

$$= 3\left(x - \frac{7}{3}\right)(x - 2)$$

$$= (3x - 7)(x - 2).$$

As the process of completing the square is quite general and applicable to all cases, it may conveniently be used when factorisation by trial would prove uncertain and tedious. For example, if the factors of $24x^2 + 118x - 247$ were required, it would probably be best to apply the general method at once.

136 B. The following exercise contains easy miscellaneous examples of the different cases explained in this chapter.

EXAMPLES XVII-1 (Miscellaneous)
(*On Arts.* 128, 129)

Resolve into factors:

1. $x^2 - 3x + 2.$ **2.** $a^2 + 7a + 10.$

3. $b^2 + b - 12.$ **4.** $y^2 - 4y - 21.$

5. $c^2 + 12c + 11.$ **6.** $x^2 - 4x - 5.$

7. $n^2 + 12n + 20.$ **8.** $y^2 + 9y - 10.$

9. $p^2 - 2pq - 24q^2.$ **10.** $y^2 + y - 110.$

11. $z^2 - 9z - 90.$ **12.** $k^2 - 14k + 48.$

Resolve into factors:

13. $a^2 + 18a + 81.$ **14.** $b^2 - 24b - 81.$

15. $c^2 + 30c + 81.$ **16.** $x^2 - 14x + 49.$

17. $y^2 + 10yz + 21z^2.$ **18.** $z^2 + 2z - 63.$

19. $n^2 + 11n + 24.$ **20.** $p^2 - 5p - 24.$

21. $l^2 + 9l - 36.$ **22.** $a^2b^2 - 4ab + 4.$

23. $a^2b^2 + 10ab + 16.$ **24.** $b^2 - 4b - 45.$

25. $m^2 + 3m - 88.$ **26.** $n^2 - 12n - 45.$

27. $p^2 + 10p - 39.$ **28.** $x^2y^2 - xy - 72.$

29. $z^2 - z - 20.$ **30.** $x^2 + xy - 56y^2.$

31. $a^2 - 11ab - 26b^2.$ **32.** $a^2b^2 - ab - 56.$

33. $y^4 + y^2 - 156.$ **34.** $z^4 - 7z^2 - 78.$

35. $y^4 - 2y^2 - 35.$ **36.** $x^2 + 6xy - 91y^2.$

(*On Arts.* 125-132)

Resolve into two or more factors:

37. $m^3n^2 - 3m^2n^3.$ **38.** $10x^3 + 25x^4y.$

39. $y^2 - 2y - 15.$ **40.** $(a+b)x + (a+b)y.$

41. $x^2 - xz + xy + yz.$ **42.** $3c^2 + c - 2.$

43. $2b^2 + 11b + 5.$ **44.** $x^2 - 6xy + 9y^2.$

45. $3x^2 - 10x + 3.$ **46.** $c^2d^2 - cd - 2.$

47. $6x^2 + 7x - 3.$ **48.** $4(a-b) - c(a-b).$

49. $a^4 - a^3 + 2a + 2.$ **50.** $2c^3d - 6c^2d^2 + 2c^2d^3.$

51. $x^3y + 2x^2y - 63xy.$ **52.** $6y^2 - 7y - 3.$

53. $4x^2 - 12x + 9$.

54. $3 - 5p - 12p^2$.

55. $16 + 8pq + p^2q^2$.

56. $4z^3 + 5z^2 - 6z$.

57. $a^3 + a^2 - 42a$.

58. $2m^4 - m^3 + 4m - 2$.

59. $a^4 - 3a^3 - a^3b + 3a^2b$.

60. $14 - 5x - x^2$.

61. $17 - 18z + z^2$.

62. $2m^4 - 11m^2 - 21$.

63. $5x^2 + 7xy - 6y^2$.

64. $6m^6 + 17m^3 - 45$.

65. $9m^2 - 24m + 16$.

(*On Arts.* 125-136A)

66. $25 - 81a^2$.

67. $a^4b^4 - 9$.

68. $27 + l^3$.

69. $1 - 64m^3$.

70. $k^4 - 25l^2$.

71. $p^3q^3 - 1$.

72. $8z^3 + 1$.

73. $1 - 64x^2$.

74. $250p^3 + 2$.

75. $100a^2b^4 - 4$.

76. $729 + c^3d^3$.

77. $(a + x)^2 - 1$.

78. $16 - (b - c)^2$.

79. $9x^3 - 4xy^2$.

80. $p^2 - pq - 20q^2$.

81. $l^3 - l^2 - 421$.

82. $a^2b^2c^2 - 81d^2$.

83. $64x^6 - 27y^3$.

84. $x^2 + 2x - 323$.

85. $x^4 - 289$.

86. $l^2 + l - 272$.

87. $1000z^3 - 27$.

88. $a^2 + 10a - 299$.

89. $a^2 - b^2 - 2bc - c^2$.

90. $1 - x^2 + 6xy - 9y^2$.

91. $x^4 + y^4 - 7x^2y^2$.

92. $a^4 + 3a^2 + 4$.

93. $b^2 - 2b - 783$.

137. Miscellaneous cases of resolution into factors.

Example 1. Resolve into factors $16a^4 - 81b^4$.

$$16a^4 - 81b^4 = (4a^2 + 9b^2)(4a^2 - 9b^2)$$
$$= (4a^2 + 9b^2)(2a + 3b)(2a - 3b).$$

Example 2. Resolve into factors $x^6 - y^6$.

$$x^6 - y^6 = (x^3 + y^3)(x^3 - y^3) = (x + y)(x^2 - xy + y^2)(x - y)(x^2 + xy + y^2).$$

NOTE. When an expression can be arranged either as the difference of two squares, or as the difference of two cubes, it will be found simplest to first use the rule for the difference of two squares.

Example 3. Resolve into factors $28x^4y + 64x^3y - 60x^2y$.

$$28x^4y + 64x^3y - 60x^2y = 4x^2y\,(7x^2 + 16x - 15)$$
$$= 4x^2y(7x - 5)\,(x + 3).$$

Example 4. Resolve into factors $x^3p^2 - 8y^3p^2 - 4x^3q^2 + 32y^3q^2$.

$$\text{The expression} = p^2(x^3 - 8y^3) - 4q^2(x^3 - 8y^3)$$
$$= (x^3 - 8y^3)\,(p^2 - 4q^2)$$
$$= (x - 2y)\,(x^2 + 2xy + 4y^2)\,(p + 2q)\,(p - 2q).$$

Example 5. Resolve into factors $4x^2 - 25y^2 + 2x + 5y$.

$$4x^2 - 25y^2 + 2x + 5y = (2x + 5y)\,(2x - 5) + 2x + 5y$$
$$= (2x + 5y)\,(2x - 5y + 1).$$

EXAMPLES XVII-1 (*Continued*)

Resolve into two or more factors:

94. $x^6 - 64$.

95. $729y^6 - 64x^6$.

96. $x^8 - 1$.

97. $729a^7b - ab^7$.

98. $a^8x^6 - 64a^2y^6$.

99. $a^{12} - b^{12}$.

100. $x^4 + 4x^2y^2z^2 + 4y^4z^4$.

101. $a^3b^3 + 512$.

102. $2x^2 + 17x + 35$.

103. $500x^2y - 20y^3$.

104. $(a + b)^4 - 1$.

105. $(c + d)^3 - 1$.

106. $1 - (x - y^3)$.

107. $x^2 - 6x - 247$.

108. $a^2 - 22a - 279$.

109. $250(a - b)^3 + 2$.

110. $(c + d)^3 + (c - d)^3$.

111. $8(x + y)^3 - (2x - y)^3$.

112. $x^2 - 4y^2 + x - 2y$.

113. $a^2 - b^2 + a - b$.

114. $(a + b)^2 + a + b$.

115. $a^3 + b^3 + a + b$.

116. $a^2 - 9b^2 + a + 3b$.

117. $4(x - y)^3 - (x - y)$.

118. $x^4y - x^2y^3 - x^3y^2 + xy^4$.

[Miscellaneous Examples IV., p. 184, *and* Chapter XXVIII *will furnish further practice in Resolution into Factors*].

MISCELLANEOUS EXAMPLES III

1. Subtract $3x^3 - 7x + 1$ from $2x^2 - 5x - 3$, then subtract the difference from zero, and add this last result to $2x^2 - 2x^3 - 4$.
2. Simplify $2\{3a - (4b - 5c)\} + 4\{4a - (5b - 2c)\} + 4\{5a - 3(b - c)\}$.
3. Find the product of $a^3 - 2a^2c + 2ac^2 - c^3$ and $a^3 + 2a^2c + 2ac^2 + c^3$.
4. Solve the equations:

   (1) $\frac{x}{2} + \frac{x}{3} = \frac{x}{4} + 7$; (2) $9x + 5y = 75,\ 7x - 4y = 11$.
5. Find the square root of $8x^4 + 16x^2 + 1 - 8x - 2x^3 + x^6$.
6. Find a number whose third, fourth, sixth, and eighth parts together make up 63.
7. If $a = 4, b = 3, c = 3$, find the value of $\frac{a^2 - b^2}{b + c} + \frac{b^2 - c^2}{c + a} + \frac{c^2 - a^2}{a + b}$.
8. Divide $x^4 + \frac{9}{4}x^3 + \frac{21}{8}x^2 + \frac{33}{16}x + \frac{5}{16}$ by $x^2 + \frac{3x}{2} + \frac{1}{4}$.
9. Add $5x^2 - 6x$ to the excess of 1 over $3x^2 - 5x + 1$.
10. Find the factors of (1) $a^2x^2 - 2ax - 15$; (2) $4m^4 - 81p^2q^2$.
11. Solve the equations:

    (1) $13x + 11y = 18, 11x + 13y = 30$.

    (2) $57x + 52y = 181,\ 76x - 39y = 458$.
12. A train which travels a km in b hours is p times as fast as a coach. If the coach takes m hours to cover the distance between two places, how many km are they apart?
13. Find the continued product of $3x^2 - 2x + 3$, $4x + 5$, $7x - 2$.
14. Solve the equations:

    (1) $\frac{5x}{7} - \frac{4}{5}\left(x - \frac{3}{4}\right) - \frac{2}{21}\left(x + \frac{7}{2}\right) + 1 = 0$;

    (2) $2\left(\frac{5x}{3} - 1\right) + \frac{11}{5}\left(1 + \frac{14x}{33}\right) = \frac{2x + 7}{5} - 7$.
15. Write down the square of $x^2 + 7x - 11$.
16. Resolve into factors:

    (1) $x^2 + 2ax - bx - 2ab$; (2) $x^2 + 10x^2y - 56y^2$.
17. Find the H.C.F. and L.C.M. of $49bc^3, 21a^2b^2, 56ca^3, 63abc^2$.
18. A has Rs. 50, and B has Rs. 6; after B has won from A a certain sum he then has five-ninths of what A has: how much did B win?

19. Simplify $\dfrac{15a^2p^3}{56mk^2} \times \dfrac{49ak^5}{40p^2m^3} \div \dfrac{7a^3k^3}{64m^4}$.

20. Shew that $a(a-1)(a-2)(a-3) = (a^2 - 3a + 1)^2 - 1$.

21. Express by means of symbols:

(1) The excess of m over n is greater than a by c;

(2) Three times the square of ab together with the cube of c is equal to p times the sum of m and n.

22. Solve $\dfrac{x}{4}\left(3 - \dfrac{8}{x}\right) - \dfrac{7}{8}\left(7 - \dfrac{3x}{4}\right) = 15\left(\dfrac{1}{3} - \dfrac{x}{64}\right)$, and show that $x = 2$ does *not* satisfy the equation.

23. Divide the product of $3x^2 - 2xy - y^2$ and $2x - y$ by $x - y$.

24. What is the price of apples per dozen, and of eggs per score, when 60 apples and 100 eggs together cost Rs. 65, and 72 apples cost as much as 270 eggs?

25. Express the product $(2x^2 - 13x + 15)(x^2 - 4x - 5)(2x^2 - x - 3)$ in simple factors, and thence write down its square root as the product of three binomial factors.

26. If $x = 6$, $y = 7$, $z = 8$, find the value of

$$x - (y - z) - 2[x + z - 3\{-2(y-1)\}] + 4\left[\frac{x}{2} - \left(3 - \frac{9}{2}y\right)\right].$$

27. Divide $6x^5 + 57x^4y + 128x^3y^2 - 60x^2y^3 - 130xy^4 + 63y^5$ by $3x^3 + 15x^2y + 7xy^2 - 9y^3$.

28. Solve the equations:
$4x + 2y + z = 14$, $3x - y + 2z = 3$, $x + 7y - z = 23$.

29. Resolve into two or more factors:

(1) $x^3y - 4xy^3$; (2) $2m^4 + m^2n^2 - 3n^4$.

30. In how many days will a men do $\dfrac{1}{m}$th of a piece of work, the whole of which can be done by a men in c days?
If $m = 4$, $a = 24$, $b = 14$, $c = 18$, what is the numerical value of the answer?

18

HIGHEST COMMON FACTOR

138. DEFINITION. The highest common factor of two or more algebraical expressions is the *expression of highest dimensions* which divides each of them without remainder.

NOTE. The term *greatest common measure* is sometimes used instead of *highest common factor*; but, strictly speaking, the term *greatest common measure* ought to be confined to arithmetical quantities; for the highest common factor is not necessarily the greatest common measure in all cases, as will appear later. [Art. 145.]

In Chap. XI we have explained how to write down by inspection the highest common factor of two or more *simple* expressions. An analogous method will enable us readily to find the highest common factor of *compound* expressions which are given as the product of factors, or which can be easily resolved into factors.

Example 1. Find the highest common factor of

$4cx^3$ and $2cx^3 + 4c^2x^2$.

It will be easy to pick out the common factors if the expressions are arranged as follows:

$$4cx^3 = 4cx^3,$$
$$2cx^3 + 4c^2x^2 = 2cx^2(x + 2c);$$

therefore the H.C.F. is $2cx^2$.

Example 2. Find the highest common factor of

$$3a^2 + 9ab,\ a^3 - 9ab^2,\ a^3 + 6a^2b + 9ab^2$$

Resolving each expression into its factors, we have

$$3a^2 + 9ab = 3a(a + 3b),$$
$$a^3 - 9ab^2 = a(a + 3b)(a - 3b),$$
$$a^3 + 6a^2b + 9ab^2 = a(a + 3b)(a + 3b);$$

therefore the H.C.F. is $a(a + 3b)$.

139. When there are two or more expressions containing different powers of the same *compound* factor, the student should be careful to notice that the highest common factor must contain the highest power of the compound factor which is common to all the given expressions.

Example 1. The highest common factor of

$$x(a-x)^2,\ a(a-x)^3, \text{ and } 2ax(a-x)^5 \text{ is } (a-x)^2.$$

Example 2. Find the highest common factor of

$$ax^2 + 2a^2x + a^3,\ 2ax^2 - 4a^2x - 6a^3,\ 3(ax + a^2)^2.$$

Resolving the expressions into factors, we have

$$\begin{aligned} ax^2 + 2a^2x + a^3 &= a(x^2 + 2ax + a^2) \\ &= a(x+a)^2 \qquad \ldots(1), \\ 2ax^2 + 4a^2x - 6a^3 &= 2a(x^2 - 2ax + 3a^2) \\ &= 2a(x+a)(x-3a) \qquad \ldots(2), \\ 3(ax + a^2)^2 &= 3a^2(x+a)^2 \qquad \ldots(3). \end{aligned}$$

Therefore from (1), (2), (3), by inspection, the highest common factor is $a(x + a)$.

EXAMPLES XVIII-a

Find the highest common factor of

1. $a^2 + ab,\ a^2 - b^2.$

2. $(x + y)^2,\ x^2 - y^2.$

3. $2x^2 - 2xy,\ x^3 - x^2y.$

4. $6x^2 - 9xy,\ 4x^2 - 9y^2.$

5. $x^3 + x^3y,\ x^3 + y^3$

6. $a^3b - ab^3,\ a^5b^2 - a^2b^5.$

7. $a^3 - a^2x,\ a^3 - ax^2,\ a^4 - ax^3.$

8. $a^2 - 4x^2,\ a^2 + 2ax.$

9. $a^2bx + ab^2x,\ a^2b - b^3.$

10. $2x^2y - 6xy^2,\ x^2 - 9y^2.$

11. $a^2 - x^2,\ a^2 - ax,\ a^2x - ax^2.$

12. $4x^2 + 2xy,\ 12x^2y - 3y^3.$

13. $20x - 4,\ 50x^2 - 2.$

14. $6bx + 4by,\ 9cx + 6cy.$

15. $x^2 + x,\ (x + 1)^2,\ x^3 + 1.$

16. $xy - y,\ x^4y - xy.$

17. $x^2 - 2xy + y^2,\ (x - y)^3.$

18. $x^3 + a^2x,\ x^4 - a^4.$

19. $x^3 + 8y^3,\ x^2 + xy - 2y^2.$

20. $x^4 - 27a^2x,\ (x - 3a)^2.$

21. $x^2 + 3x + 2,\ x^2 - 4.$

22. $x^2 - x - 20,\ x^2 - 9x + 20.$

23. $x^2 - 18x + 45,\ x^2 - 4.$

24. $2x^2 - 7x + 3,\ 3x^2 - 7x - 6.$

25. $12x^2 + x - 1,\ 15x^2 + 8x + 1.$

26. $2x^2 - x - 1,\ 3x^2 - x - 2.$

27. $c^2x^2 - d^2,\ acx^2 - bcx + adx - bd.$

28. $x^5 - xy^2,\ x^3 + x^2y + xy + y^2.$

29. $a^3x - a^2bx - 6ab^2x,\ a^2bx^2 - 4ab^2x^2 + 3b^3x^2.$

30. $2x^2 + 9x + 4,\ 2x^2 + 11x + 5,\ 2x^2 - 3x - 2.$

31. $3x^4 + 8x^3 + 4x^2,\ 3x^5 + 11x^4 + 6x^3,\ 3x^4 - 16x^3 - 12x^3.$

[*If preferred, the remainder of this chapter may be taken after* Chap. XXV.]

140. The highest commo factor should always be found by inspection if possible, but it may happen that the expressions cannot be readily resolved into factors. In such cases we adopt a method analogous to that used in Arithmetic, for finding the greatest common measure of two or more numbers.

141. We shall now illustrate the algebraical process of finding the highest common factor by examples, postponing for the present the complete proof of the rules we use. But we shall *enunciate* two principles, which the student should bear in mind in reading the examples which follow.

I. *If an expression contains a certain factor, any multiple of the expression is divisible by that factor.*

II. *If two expressions have a common factor, it will divide their sum and their difference; and also the sum and the difference of any multiples of them.*

Example. Find the highest common factor of

$$4x^3-3x^2-24x-9 \text{ and } 8x^3-2x^2-53x-39.$$

x	$4x^3-3x^2-24x-9$	$8x^3-2x^2-53x-39$	2
	$4x^3-5x^2-21x$	$8x^3-6x^2-48x-18$	
$2x$	$2x^2-3x-9$	$4x^2-5x-21$	2
	$2x^2-6x$	$4x^2-6x-18$	
3	$3x-9$	$x-3$	
	$3x-9$		

Therefore the H.C.F. is $x-3$.

Explanation. First arrange the given expressions according to descending or ascending powers of x. The expressions so arranged having their first terms of the same order, we take for divisor that whose highest power has the smaller coefficient. Arrange the work in parallel columns as above. When the first remainder $4x^2-5x-21$ is made the divisor we put the quotient x to the *left* of the dividend. Again, when the second remainder $2x^2-3x-9$ is in turn made the divisor, the quotient 2 is placed to the *right*; and so on. As in Arithmetic, the last divisor $x-3$ is the highest common factor required.

142. This method is only useful to determine the *compound* factor of the highest common factor. Simple factors of the given expressions mast be first removed from them, and the highest common factor of these, if any, must be observed and multiplied into the *compound* factor given by the rule.

Example. Find the highest common factor of

$$24x^4 - 2x^3 - 60x^2 - 32x \text{ and } 18x^4 - 39x^2 - 18x.$$

We have $24x^4 - 2x^3 - 60x^2 - 32x = 2x\,(12x^3 - x^2 - 30x - 16)$,

and $\quad 18x^4 - 6x^3 - 39x^2 - 18x = 3x(6x^3 - 2x^2 - 13x - 6)$.

Also $2x$ and $3x$ have the common factor x. Removing the simple factors $2x$ and $3x$, and *reserving* their common factor x, we continue as in Art. 141.

$$\begin{array}{r|r|r|r}
 & & 12x^3 - x^2 - 30x - 16 & \\
2x & 6x^3 - 2x^2 - 13x - 6 & 12x^3 - 4x^2 - 26x - 12 & 2 \\
 & 6x^3 - 8x^2 - 8x & 3x^2 - 4x - 4 & \\
2 & 6x^2 - 5x - 6 & 3x^2 + 2x & x \\
 & 6x^2 - 8x - 8 & -6x - 4 & \\
 & 3x + 2 & -6x - 4 & -2
\end{array}$$

Therefore the H.C.F. is $x(3x + 2)$.

143. So far the process of Arithmetic has been found exactly applicable to the algebraical expressions we have considered. But in many cases certain modifications of the arithmetical method will be found necessary. These will be more clearly understood if it is remembered that, at every stage of the work, the remainder must contain as a factor of itself the highest common factor we are seeking. [See Art. 141. I & II.]

Example 1. Find the highest common factor of

$$3x^3 - 13x^2 + 23x - 21 \text{ and } 6x^3 + x^2 - - 44x + 21.$$

$$\begin{array}{r|r|l}
3x^3 - 13x^2 + 23x - 21 & 6x^3 + x^2 - 44x + 21 & 2 \\
 & 6x^3 - 26x^2 + 46x - 42 & \\
 & 27 - 90x + 63 &
\end{array}$$

Here on making $27x^2 - 90x + 63$ a divisor, we find that it is not contained in $3x^3 - 13x^2 + 23x - 21$ with an *integral* quotient. But noticing that $27x^2 - 90x + 63$ may be written in the form $9\,(3x^2 - 10x + 7)$, and also bearing in mind that every remainder in the course of the work contains the H.C.F., we conclude that the H.C.F. we are seeking is contained in $9\,(3x^2 - 10x + 7)$. But the two original expressions have no *simple* factors, therefore their H.C.F. can have none. We may therefore *rejected* factor 9 and go on with divisor $3x^2 - 10x + 7$.

Resuming the work, we have

$$
\begin{array}{r|r|r|l}
x & 3x^2 - 13x^2 + 23x - 21 & 3x^2 - 10x + 7 & x \\
 & 3x^3 - 10x^2 + 7x & 3x^2 - 7x & \\
\hline
 & -3x^2 + 16x - 21 & 3x + 7 & 1 \\
-1 & -3x^2 + 10x - 7 & -3x + 7 & \\
\hline
 & 2)\ 6x - 14 & & \\
 & 3x - 7 & & \\
\end{array}
$$

Therefore the H.C.F. is $3x - 7$.

The factor 2 has been removed on the same grounds as the factor 9 above.

Example 2. Find the highest common factor of

$$2x^3 + x^2 - x - 2 \qquad \ldots(1),$$

and

$$3x^3 - 2x^3 + x - 2 \qquad \ldots(2).$$

As the expressions stand we cannot begin to divide one by the other without using a fractional quotient. The difficulty may be obviated by *introducing* a suitable factor, just as in the last case we found it useful to remove a factor when we could no longer proceed with the division in the ordinary way. The given expressions have no common *simple* factor, hence their H.C.F. cannot be affected if we multiply either of them by any simple factor.

Multiply (2) by 2, and use (I) as a divisor:

$$
\begin{array}{r|r|r|l}
 & 2x^3 + x^2 - x - 2 & 6x^3 - 4x^2 + 2x - 4 & 3 \\
 & 7 & 6x^3 + 3x^2 - 3x - 6 & \\
\hline
-2x & 14x^3 + 7x^2 - 7x - 14 & -7x^2 + 5x + 2 & \\
 & 14x^3 - 10x^2 - 4x & 17 & \\
\hline
17x & 17x^2 - 3x - 14 & -119x^2 + 85x + 34 & -7 \\
 & 17x^2 - 17x & -119x^2 + 21x + 98 & \\
\hline
 & 14x - 14 & 64)64x - 64 & \\
14 & 14x - 14 & x - 1 & \\
\end{array}
$$

Therefore the H.C.F. is $x - 1$.

After the first division the factor 7 is introduced because the first remainder $-7x^2 + 5x + 2$ will not divide $2x^3 + x^2 - x - 2$. At the next stage the factor 17 is introduced for a similar reason, and finally the factor 64 is removed as explained in Example 1.

NOTE. Here the highest common factor might have been more easily obtained by arranging the expressions in *ascending* powers of x. In this case it will be found that there is no need to introduce a numerical factor in the course of the work. Detached coefficients, as explained in Art. 45, may also be used with advantage here, and will often effect a considerable saving of labour.

***144.** From the last two examples it appears that we may multiply or divide either of the given expressions, or any of the remainders which occur in the course of the work, by any factor which does not divide both of the given expressions.

***145.** Let the two expressions in Example 2, Art. 143, be written in the form

$$2x^3 + x^2 - x - 2 = (x-1)(2x^2 + 3x + 2),$$

$$3x^3 - 2x^2 + x - 2 = (x-1)(3x^2 + x + 2).$$

Then their highest common factor is $x - 1$, and therefore $2x^2 + 3x + 2$ and $3x^2 + x + 2$ *have no algebraical common divisor.* If, however, we put $x = 6$, then

$$2x^3 + x^2 - x - 2 = 460,$$

and $$3x^3 - 2x^2 + x - 2 = 580;$$

and the greatest common measure of 460 and 580 is 20; whereas 5 is the numerical value of $x - 1$; the algebraical highest common factor. Thus the numerical values of the algebraical highest common factor and of the arithmetical greatest common measure do not in this case agree.

The reason may be explained as follows: when $x = 6$, the expressions $2x^2 + 3x + 2$ and $3x^2 + x + 2$ become equal to 92 and 116 respectively and have a common arithmetical factor 4, whereas the expressions have no algebraical common factor.

It will thus often happen that the highest common factor of two expressions, and their numerical greatest common measure, when the letters have particular values, are not the same; for this reason the term *greatest common measure* is inappropriate when applied to algebraical quantities.

EXAMPLES XVIII-b

Find the highest common factor of the following expressions:

1. $x^3 + 2x^2 - 13x + 10$, $x^3 + x^2 - 10x + 8$.
2. $x^3 - 5x^2 - 99x + 40$, $x^3 - 6x^2 - 86x + 35$.
3. $x^3 + 2x^2 - 8x - 16$, $x^3 + 3x^2 - 8x - 24$.
4. $x^3 + 4x^2 - 5x - 20$, $x^3 + 6x^2 - 5x - 30$.
5. $x^3 - x^2 - 5x - 3$, $x^3 - 4x^2 - 11x - 6$.

Find the highest common factor of the following expressions :

6. $x^3 + 3x^2 - 8x - 24, x^3 + 3x^2 - 3x - 9.$

7. $x^3 - 5a^2x + 7ax^2 - 3x^3, a^3 - 3ax^2 + 2x^3.$

8. $x^4 - 2x^3 - 4x - 7, x^4 + x^3 - 3x^2 - x + 2.$

9. $2x^3 - 5x^2 + 11x + 7, 4x^3 - 11x^2 + 25x + 7.$

10. $2x^3 + 4x^2 - 7x - 14, 6x^3 - 10x^2 - 21x + 35.$

11. $3x^4 - 3x^3 - 2x^2 - x - 1, 9x^4 - 3x^3 - x - 1.$

12. $2x^4 - 2x^3 + x^2 + 3x - 6, 4x^4 - 2x^3 + 3x - 9.$

13. $3x^3 - 3ax^2 + 2a^2x - 2a^3, 3x^3 + 12ax^2 + 2ax^2 + 8a^3.$

14. $2x^3 - 9ax^2 + 9a^2x - 7a^3, 4x^3 - 20ax^2 + 20a^2x - 16a^3.$

15. $10x^3 + 25ax^2 - 5a^3, 4x^3 + 9ax^2 - 2a^2x - a^3.$

16. $6a^3 + 13a^2x - 9ax^2 - 10x^3, 9a^3 + 12a^2x - 11ax^2 - 10x^3.$

17. $24x^4y + 72x^3y^2 - 6x^2y^3 - 90xy^4, 6x^4y^2 + 13x^3y^3 - 4x^2y^4 - 15xy^5.$

18. $4x^5a^2 + 10x^4a^3 - 60x^3a^4 + 54x^2a^5, 24x^5a^3 + 30x^3a^5 - 126x^2a^6.$

19. $4x^5 + 14x^4 + 20x^3 + 70x^2, 8x^7 + 28x^6 - 8x^6 - 12x^4 + 56x^3.$

20. $72x^3 - 12ax^2 + 72a^2x - 420a^3, 18x^3 + 42ax^2 - 282a^2x + 270a^3.$

21. $9x^4 + 2x^2y^2 + y^4, 3x^4 - 8x^3y + 5x^2y^2 - 2xy^3.$

22. $x^5 - x^3 - x + 1, x^7 + x^6 + x^4 + 1.$

23. $1 + x + x^3 - x^5, 1 - x^4 - x^6 + x^7.$

24. $6 - 8a - 32a^2 - 18a^3, 20 - 35a - 95a^2 - 40a^3.$

25. $9x^2 - 15x^3 - 45x^4 - 12x^5, 42x - 49x^2 - 203x^3 - 84x^4.$

26. $3x^5 - 5x^3 + 2, 2x^5 - 5x^2 + 3.$

27. $4x^5 - 6x^3 - 28x, 6x^4 + 10x^3 - 17x^2 - 35x - 14.$

***146.** The statements of Art. 141 may be proved as follows.

I. If F divides A it will also divide mA.

For suppose $A = aF$, then $mA = maF$.

Thus F is a factor of mA.

II. If F divides A and B, then it will divide $mA \pm nB$.

For suppose $A = aF, B = bF$,

then $mA \pm nB = maF \pm nbF$

$$= F(ma \pm nb).$$

Thus F divides $mA \pm nB$.

***147.** We may now enunciate and prove the rule for finding the highest common factor of any two compound algebraical expressions. We suppose that any simple factors are first removed. [See Example, Art. 142.]

Let A and B be the two expressions after the simple factors have been removed. Let them be arranged in descending or ascending powers of some common letter; also let the highest power of that letter in B be not less than the highest power in A

Divide B by A; let p be the quotient, and C the remainder. Suppose C to have a *simple* factor m. Remove this factor, and so obtain a new divisor D. Further, suppose that in order to make A divisible by D it is necessary to multiply A by a *simple* factor n. Let q be the next quotient and E the remainder. Finally, divide D by E; let r be the quotient, and suppose that there is no remainder. Then E will be the H.C.F. required.

The work will stand thus :

$$
\begin{array}{llll}
A)\,B\,(p & & & \\
\;\;\;\underline{pA} & & & \\
m)\,\underline{C} & & & \\
\;\;\;\;D)\,nA\,(q & & & \\
\;\;\;\;\;\;\;\;\underline{qD} & & & \\
\;\;\;\;\;\;\;\;E)\,D\,(r & & & \\
\;\;\;\;\;\;\;\;\;\;\;\;\underline{rE} & & &
\end{array}
$$

First, to show that E is a common factor of A and B.

By examining the steps of the work, it is clear that E divides D, therefore also qD; therefore $qD + E$, therefore nA; therefore A, since n is a *simple* factor.

Again, E divides D, therefore mD, that is, C. And since E divides A and C, it also divides $pA + C$, that is, B. Hence E divide both A and B.

Secondly, to show that E is the *highest* common factor.

If not, let these be a factor X of higher dimensions than E.

Then X divides A and B, therefore $B - pA$, that is, C; therefore D (since m is a *simple* factor); therefore $nA - qD$, that is, E.

Thus X divides E; which is impossible since by hypothesis, X is of higher dimensions than E.

Therefore E is the highest common factor.

***148.** The highest common factor of three expressions A, B, C may be obtained as follows.

First determine F the highest common factor of A and B; next find G the highest common factor of F and C; then G will be the required highest common factor of A, B, C.

For F contains *every* factor which is common to A and B, and G is the highest common factor of F and C. Therefore G it the highest common factor of A, B, C.

19

FRACTIONS

[On first reading the subject, the student may omit the general proofs of the rules given in this chapter.

The articles and examples marked with an asterisk must be omitted by those who adopt the suggestion printed at the top of page 140].

149. In Chapter XII we discussed the simpler kinds of fractions, using the ordinary arithmetical rules. We here propose to give proofs of those rules, and show that they are applicable to algebraical fractions.

DEFINITION. If a quantity x be divided into b equal parts, and a of these parts be taken, the result is called the *fraction* $\frac{a}{b}$ of x. If x be unit, the fraction $\frac{a}{b}$ of x is called simply "the fraction $\frac{a}{b}$"; so that the *fraction* $\frac{a}{b}$ *represents a equal parts, b of which make up the unit.*

NOTE. This definition requires that a and b should be positive whole numbers. In Art. 155 we shall adopt a definition which will enable us to remove this restriction.

150. *To prove* that $\frac{a}{b} = \frac{ma}{mb}$, *where* a, b, m *are positive integers.*

By $\frac{a}{b}$ we mean a equal parts, b of which make up the unit ...(1);

by $\frac{ma}{mb}$..................ma...........mb.........(2).

But b parts in (1) $= mb$ parts in (2);

$\therefore$ 1 part .... $= m$............. .

$\therefore$ a parts ...... $= ma$ ....

this is, $\frac{a}{b} = \frac{ma}{mb}$

Conversely, $\frac{ma}{mb} = \frac{a}{b}$.

Hence, *the value of a fraction is not altered if we multiply or divide the numerator and denominator by the same quantity.*

Reduction to Lowest Terms

151. An algebraical fraction may be changed into an equivalent fraction by dividing numerator and denominator by any common factor; if this factor be the highest common factor the resulting fraction is said to be reduced to its lowest terms.

Example 1. Reduce to lowest terms $\dfrac{24a^3c^2x^2}{18a^3x^2 - 12a^2x^3}$.

The expression $= \dfrac{24a^3c^2x^2}{6a^2x^2(3a-2x)} = \dfrac{4ac^2}{3a-2x}$.

Example 2. Reduce to lowest terms $\dfrac{6x^2 - 8xy}{9xy - 12y^2}$.

The expression $= \dfrac{2x(3x-4y)}{3y(3x-4y)} = \dfrac{2x}{3y}$.

NOTE. The beginner should be careful not be begin cancelling until he has expressed both numerator and denominator in the most convenient form, by resolution into factors where necessary.

EXAMPLES XIX. a

Reduce to lowest terms :

1. $\dfrac{3a^2 - 6ab}{2a^2b - 4ab^2}$.

2. $\dfrac{abx + bx^2}{acx + cx^2}$.

3. $\dfrac{ac}{a^2x^2 - ax}$.

4. $\dfrac{15a^2b^2c}{100(a^2 - a^2b)}$.

5. $\dfrac{4x^2 - 9y^2}{4x^2 + 6xy}$.

6. $\dfrac{20(x^3 - y^2)}{5x^2 + 5xy + 5y^2}$.

7. $\dfrac{x(2a^2 - 3ax)}{a(4a^2x - 9x^3)}$.

8. $\dfrac{x^2 - 2xy^2}{x^4 - 4x^2y^2 + 4y^4}$.

9. $\dfrac{(xy - 3y^2)^2}{x^2y^2 - 27y^5}$.

10. $\dfrac{x^2 - 5x}{x^2 - 4x - 5}$.

11. $\dfrac{3x^2 + 6x}{x^2 + 4x + 4}$.

12. $\dfrac{5a^3b + 10a^2b^2}{3a^2b^2 + 6ab^3}$.

13. $\dfrac{x^3y + 2x^2y + 4xy}{x^3 - 8}$.

14. $\dfrac{3a^4 + 9a^3b + 6a^2b^2}{a^4 + a^3b - 2a^2b^2}$.

15. $\dfrac{x^4 - 14x^2 - 51}{x^4 - 2x^2 - 15}$.

16. $\dfrac{x^2 + xy - 2y^2}{x^3 - y^3}$.

17. $\dfrac{2x^2 + 17x + 21}{3x^2 + 26x + 35}$.

18. $\dfrac{a^2x^2 - 16a^2}{ax^2 + 9ax + 20a}$.

19. $\dfrac{3x^2 + 23x + 14}{3x^2 + 41x + 26}$.

20. $\dfrac{27a + a^4}{18a - 6a^2 + 2a^3}$.

***152.** When the factors of the numerator and denominator cannot be determined by inspection, the fraction may be reduced to its lowest terms by dividing both numerator and denominator by the highest common factor, which may be found by the rules given in Chap. XVIII.

Example. Reduce to lowest terms $\dfrac{3x^3 - 13x^2 + 23x - 21}{15x^3 - 38x^2 - 2x + 21}$.

First Method. The H.C.F. of numerator and denominator is $3x - 7$.

Dividing numerator and denominator by $3x - 7$, we obtain as respective quotients $x^2 - 2x + 3$ and $5x^2 - x - 3$.

Thus

$$\frac{3x^3 - 13x^2 + 23x - 21}{15x^3 - 38x^2 - 2x + 21} = \frac{(3x-7)(x^2 - 2x + 3)}{(3x-7)(5x^2 - x - 3)} = \frac{x^2 - 2x + 3}{5x^2 - x - 3}.$$

This is the simplest solution for the beginner; but in this and similar cases we may often effect the reduction without actually going through the process of finding the highest common factors.

Second Method. By Art. 141, the H.C.F. of numerator and denominator must be a factor of their sum $18x^3 - 51x^2 + 21x$, that is, of $3x(3x - 7)(2x - 1)$. If there be a common divisor it must clearly be $3x - 7$; hence arranging numerator and denominator so as to show $3x - 7$as a factor.

the fraction

$$= \frac{x^2(3x-7) - 2x(3x-7) + 3(3x-7)}{5x^2(3x-7) - x(3x-7) - 3(3x-7)}$$

$$= \frac{(3x-7)(x^2 - 2x + 3)}{(3x-7)(5x^2 - x - 3)}$$

$$= \frac{x^2 - 2x + 3}{5x^2 - x - 3}.$$

***153.** If either numerator or denominator can readily be resolved into factors we may use the following method.

Example. Reduce to lowest terms $\dfrac{x^3 + 3x^2 - 4x}{7x^3 - 18x^2 + 6x + 5}$.

The numerator $= x(x^2 + 3x - 4) = x(x + 4)(x - 1)$.

Of these factors the only one which can be a common divisor is $x-1$. Hence, arranging the denominator,

$$\text{the fraction} = \frac{x(x+4)(x-1)}{7x^2(x-1)-11x(x-1)-5(x-1)}$$

$$= \frac{x(x+4)(x-1)}{(x-1)(7x^2-11x-5)} = \frac{x(x+4)}{7x^2-11x-5}.$$

*EXAMPLES XIX - b

Reduce to lowest terms:

1. $\dfrac{a^3-a^2b-ab^2-2b^3}{a^3+3a^2b+3ab^2+2b^3}$.

2. $\dfrac{x^3-5x^2+7x-3}{x^3-3x+2}$.

3. $\dfrac{a^3+2a^2-13a+10}{a^3+a^2-10a+8}$.

4. $\dfrac{2x^3+5x^2y-30xy^2-27y^3}{4x^3+5xy^2-21y^3}$.

5. $\dfrac{4a^3+12a^2b-ab^2-15b^3}{6a^3+13a^2b-4ab^2-15b^3}$.

6. $\dfrac{1+2x^2+x^3+2x^4}{1+3x^2+2x^3+3x^4}$.

7. $\dfrac{x^2-2x+1}{3x^3+7x-10}$.

8. $\dfrac{3a^3-3a^2b+ab^2-b^3}{4a^2-5ab+b^2}$.

9. $\dfrac{4x^3+3ax^2+a^3}{x^3+ax^3+a^3x+a^4}$.

10. $\dfrac{4x^3-10x^2+4x+2}{3x^4-2x^3-3x+2}$.

11. $\dfrac{16x^4-72x^2a^2+81a^4}{4x^2+12ax+9a^2}$.

12. $\dfrac{6x^3+x^2-5x-2}{6x^3+5x^2-3x-2}$.

13. $\dfrac{5x^3+2x^2-15x-6}{7x^3-4x^2-21x+12}$.

14. $\dfrac{4x^4+11x^2+25}{4x^4-9x^2+30x-25}$.

15. $\dfrac{3x^3-27ax^2+78a^2x-72a^3}{2x^3+10ax^2-4a^2x-48a^3}$.

16. $\dfrac{ax^3-5a^2x^2-99a^3x+40a^4}{x^4-6ax^3-86a^2x^2+35a^3x}$.

Multiplication and Division of Fractions

154. Rule I. To multiply a fraction by an integer: *multiply the numerator by that integer; or, if the denominator be divisible by the integer, divide the denominator by it.*

The rule may be proved as follows :

(1) $\dfrac{a}{b}$ represents a equal parts, b of which make up the unit,;

$\dfrac{ac}{b}$ represents ac equal parts, b of which make up the unit;

and the number of parts taken in the second fraction is c times the number taken in the first :

that is $\qquad \frac{a}{b} \times c = \frac{ac}{b} c.$ [Art.151.]

(2) $\frac{a}{bd} \times d = \frac{ad}{bd}$, by the preceding case, $= \frac{a}{b}$.

155. By the preceding article $\frac{a}{b} \times b = \frac{ab}{b} = a,$

that is, the fraction $\frac{a}{b}$ is that which must be multiplied by b in order to obtain a. But, by Art. 46, the quantity which must be multiplied by b in order to obtain a is the quotient resulting from the division of a by b : we may therefore define a fraction thus :

the fraction $\frac{a}{b}$ is the quotient of a divided by b

156. Rule II. To divided a fraction by an integer: *divide the numerator, if it be divisible, by the integer : or if the numerator be not divisible, multiply the denominator by that integer* :

The rule may be proved as follows :

(1) $\frac{ac}{b}$ represents ac equal parts, b of which make up the unit ;

$\frac{a}{b}$ represents a equal parts, b of which make up the unit.

The number of parts taken in the first fraction is c times the number taken in the second. Therefore the second fraction is the quotient of the first fraction divided by c :

that is $\qquad \frac{ac}{b} \div c = \frac{a}{b}.$

(2) But if the numerator be not divisible by c, we have

$$\frac{a}{b} = \frac{ac}{bc};$$

$\therefore \qquad \frac{a}{b} \div c = \frac{ac}{bc} \div c = \frac{a}{bc}$, by the preceding case.

157. Rule III. To multiply together two or more fractions: *multiply together all the numerators to form a new numerator, and all the denominators to form a new denominator.*

To find the value of $\frac{a}{b} \times \frac{c}{d}$.

Let $\qquad x = \frac{a}{b} \times \frac{c}{d}$

Multiplying each side by $b \times d$, we have

$$x \times b \times d = \frac{a}{b} \times \frac{c}{d} \times b \times d$$

$$= \frac{a}{b} \times b \times \frac{c}{d} \times d \qquad \text{[Art. 29.]}$$

$$= a \times c; \qquad \text{[Art. 154.]}$$

$\therefore$ $$x \times bd = ac.$$

Dividing each side by bd, we have

$$x = \frac{ac}{bd};$$

$\therefore$ $$\frac{a}{b} \times \frac{c}{d} = \frac{ac}{bd}.$$

Similarly $$\frac{a}{b} \times \frac{c}{d} \times \frac{e}{f} = \frac{ace}{bdf};$$

and so for any number of fractions.

158.

Rule IV. To divide one fraction by another : *invert the divisor, and proceed as in multiplication.*

Since division is the inverse of multiplication, we may define the quotient x, when $\frac{a}{b}$ is divided by $\frac{c}{d}$, to be such that

$$x \times \frac{c}{d} = \frac{a}{b}.$$

Multiplying by $\frac{d}{c}$ we have $x \times \frac{c}{d} \times \frac{d}{c} = \frac{a}{b} \times \frac{d}{c}$;

$\therefore$ $$x = \frac{ad}{bc}.$$

Hence $$\frac{a}{b} \div \frac{c}{d} = \frac{ad}{bc} = \frac{a}{b} \times \frac{d}{c}, \qquad \text{[Art. 157.]}$$

which proves the rule.

Example 1. Simplify $\frac{2a^2 + 3a}{4a^3} \times \frac{4a^2 - 6a}{12a + 18}$.

$$\frac{2a^2 + 3a}{4a^3} \times \frac{4a^2 - 6a}{12a + 18} = \frac{a(2a + 3)}{4a^3} \times \frac{2a(2a - 3)}{6(2a + 3)}.$$

$$= \frac{2a - 3}{12a}.$$

by cancelling those factors which are common to both numerator and denominator.

Example 2. Simplify $\dfrac{6x^2 - ax - 2a^2}{ax - a^2} \times \dfrac{x - a}{9x^2 - 4a^2} \div \dfrac{2x + a}{3ax + 2a^2}$.

$$\text{The expression} = \frac{6x^2 - ax - 2a^2}{ax - a^2} \times \frac{x - a}{9x^2 - 4a^2} \times \frac{3ax + 2a^2}{2x + a}$$

$$= \frac{(3x - 2a)(2x + a)}{a(x - a)} \times \frac{x - a}{(3x + 2a)(3x - 2a)} \times \frac{a(3x + 2a)}{2x + a} = 1,$$

since all the factors cancel each other.

EXAMPLES XIX-c

Simplify

1. $\dfrac{14x^2 - 7x}{12x^3 + 24x^2} \div \dfrac{2x - 1}{x^2 + 2x}$.

2. $\dfrac{a^2b^2 + 3ab}{4a^2 - 1} \div \dfrac{ab + 3}{2a + 1}$.

3. $\dfrac{x^2 - 4a^2}{ax + 2a^2} \times \dfrac{2a}{x - 2a}$.

4. $\dfrac{a^2 - 121}{a^2 - 4} \div \dfrac{a + 11}{a + 2}$.

5. $\dfrac{16x^2 - 9a^2}{x^2 - 4} \times \dfrac{x - 2}{4x - 3a}$.

6. $\dfrac{25a^2 - b^2}{9a^2x^2 - 4x^2} \times \dfrac{x(3a + 2)}{5a + b}$.

7. $\dfrac{x^2 + 5x + 6}{x^2 - 1} \times \dfrac{x^2 - 2x - 3}{x^2 - 9}$.

8. $\dfrac{x^2 + 3x + 2}{x^2 + 9x + 20} \times \dfrac{x^2 + 7x + 12}{x^2 + 5x + 6}$.

9. $\dfrac{2x^2 + 5x + 2}{x^2 - 4} \times \dfrac{x^2 + 4x}{2x^2 + 9x + 4}$.

10. $\dfrac{2x^2 + 13x + 15}{4x^2 - 9} \div \dfrac{2x^2 + 11x + 5}{4x^2 - 1}$.

11. $\dfrac{x^2 - 14x - 15}{x^2 - 4x - 45} \div \dfrac{x^2 - 12x - 45}{x^2 - 6x - 27}$.

12. $\dfrac{2x^2 - x - 1}{2x^2 + 5x + 2} \times \dfrac{4x^2 + x - 14}{16x^2 - 49}$.

13. $\dfrac{b^4 - 27b}{2b^2 + 5b} \times \dfrac{4b^2 + 25}{2b^2 - 11b + 15}$.

14. $\dfrac{x^3 - 6x^2 + 36x}{x^2 - 49} \div \dfrac{x^4 + 216x}{x^2 - x - 42}$.

15. $\dfrac{64p^2q^2 - z^4}{x^2 - 4} \times \dfrac{(x - 2)^2}{8pq + z^2} \div \dfrac{x^2 - 4}{(x + 2)^2}$.

16. $\dfrac{x^2 - x - 20}{x^2 - 25} \times \dfrac{x^2 - x - 2}{x^2 + 2x - 8} \div \dfrac{x + 1}{x^2 + 5x}$.

17. $\dfrac{x^2 - 18x + 80}{x^2 - 5x - 50} \times \dfrac{x^2 - 6x - 7}{x^2 - 15x + 56} \times \dfrac{x + 5}{x - 1}$.

18. $\dfrac{x^2 - 8x - 9}{x^2 - 17x + 72} \times \dfrac{x^2 - 25}{x^2 - 1} \div \dfrac{x^2 + 4x - 5}{x^2 - 9x + 8}$.

19. $\dfrac{4x^2 + x - 14}{6xy - 14y} \times \dfrac{4x^2}{x^2 - 4} \times \dfrac{x - 2}{4x - 7} \div \dfrac{2x^2 + 4x}{3x^2 - x - 14}.$

20. $\dfrac{x^2 + x - 2}{x^2 - x - 20} \times \dfrac{x^2 + 5x + 4}{x^2 - x} \div \left(\dfrac{x^2 + 3x + 2}{x^2 - 2x - 15} \times \dfrac{x + 3}{x^2}\right).$

21. $\dfrac{4x^2 - 16x + 15}{2x^2 + 3x + 1} \times \dfrac{x^2 - 6x - 7}{2x^2 - 17x + 21} \times \dfrac{4x^2 - 1}{4x^2 - 20x + 25}.$

22. $\dfrac{x^4 - 8x}{x^2 - 4x - 5} \times \dfrac{x^2 + 2x + 1}{x^3 - x^2 - 2x} \div \dfrac{x^2 + 2x + 4}{x - 5}.$

23. $\dfrac{(a + b)^2 - c^2}{a^2 + ab - ac} \times \dfrac{a}{(a + c)^2 - b^2} \times \dfrac{(a - b)^2 - c^2}{ab - b^2 - bc}.$

24. $\dfrac{a^2 + 2ab + b^2 - c^2}{a^2 - b^2 - c^2 - 2bc} \times \dfrac{a^2 - 2ac + c^2 - b^2}{b^2 - 2bc + c^2 - a^2}.$

25. $\dfrac{x^2 - 64}{x^2 + 24x + 128} \times \dfrac{x^2 + 12x - 64}{x^3 - 64} \div \dfrac{x^2 - 16x + 64}{x^2 + 4x + 16}.$

26. $\dfrac{(a^2 + ax)^3}{a^2 - x^2} \times \dfrac{(a - x)^2}{a^5 + a^2x^3} \times \dfrac{a^2 - ax + x^2}{a^3 + 2a^2x + ax^2}.$

27. $\dfrac{m^3 + 4m^2n + 4mn^2}{3m^2n - 5mn^2 - 2n^3} \times \dfrac{m^2 - 4n^2}{9m^2 - 3mn + n^2} \div \dfrac{(m + 2n)^3}{27m^3 + n^3}.$

28. $\dfrac{1 + 8x^3}{(2 - x)^2} \times \dfrac{4x - x^3}{1 - 4x^2} \div \dfrac{(1 - 2x)^2 + 2x}{2 - 5x + 2x^2}.$

29. $\dfrac{x^2(x - 4)^2}{(x + 4)^2 - 4x} \times \dfrac{64 - x^3}{16 - x^2} \div \dfrac{(x^2 - 4x)^3}{(x + 4)^2}.$

30. $\dfrac{(p + q)^2 - r^2}{(p + q + r)^2} \times \dfrac{p^2 + pq + pr}{(p - r)^2 - q^2} \div \dfrac{p^2 - Pq + \mathrm{Pr}}{(p - q)^2 - r^2}.$

31. $\dfrac{a^4 - x^4}{a^2 - 2ax + x^2} \div \left(\dfrac{a^2x + x^3}{a^3 - x^3} \times \dfrac{a^4 + a^2x^2 + x^4}{a^2x - ax^2 + x^3}\right).$

32. $\dfrac{a^3 + 8a^2b + 15ab^2}{(64a^3 - b^3)(a^3 + b^3)} \times \dfrac{16a^4 - 17a^2b^2 + b^4}{4a^2 + 21ab + 5b^2} \div \dfrac{a^2 + 2ab - 3b^2}{a^3 - a^2b + ab^2}.$

20

LOWEST COMMON MULTIPLE

[*The articles and examples marked with an asterisk must be omitted by those adopt the suggestion printed at the top of page 140.*]

159. DEFINITION. The lowest common multiple of two or more algebraical expressions is the expression of lowest dimensions which is divisible by each of them without remainder.

In Chapter XI we have explained how to write down by inspection the lowest common multiple of two or more *simple* expressions; the lowest common multiple of compound expressions which are given as the product of factors, or which can be easily resolved into factors, can be readily found by a similar method.

Example 1. The lowest common multiple of $6x^2(a-x^2), 8a^3(a-x)^3$ and $12ax(a-x)^5$ is $24a^3x^2(a-x)^5$.

For it consists of the product of

(1) the L.C.M. of the numerical coefficients;

(2) the lower of the each factor which is divisible by every power of that factor occurring in the given expressions.

Example 2. Find the lowest common multiple of

$$3a^2+9ab, 2a^3-18ab^2, a^3+6a^2b+9ab^2.$$

$$3a+9ab=3a(a+3b),$$

$$2a^3-18ab^2=2a(a+3b)(a-3b),$$

$$a^3+6a^2b+9ab^2=a(a+3b)(a+3b)$$

$$=a(a+3b)^2.$$

Therefore the L.C.M. is $6a(a+3b)^2(a-3b)$.

EXAMPLES XX-a

Find the lowest common multiple of

1. $x, x^2+x.$

2. $x^2, x^2-3x.$

3. $3x^2, 4x^2+8x.$

4. $21x^3, 7x^2(x+1).$

5. $x^2-1, x^2+x.$

6. $a^2+ab, ab+b^2.$

7. $4x^2y-y, 2x^2+x.$

8. $6x^2-2x, 9x^2-3x.$

9. $x^2 + 2x, x^2 + 3x + 2.$ **10.** $x^2 - 3x + 2, x^2 - 1.$

11. $x^2 + 4x + 4, x^2 + 5x + 6.$ **12.** $x^2 - 5x + 4, x^2 - 6x + 8.$

13. $x^2 - x - 6, x^2 + x - 2, x^2 - 4x + 3.$

14. $x^2 + x - 20, x^2 - 10x + 24, x^2 - x - 30.$

15. $x^2 + x - 42, x^2 - 11x + 30, x^2 + 2x - 35.$

16. $2x^2 + 3x + 1, 2x^2 + 5x + 2, x^2 + 3x + 2.$

17. $3x^2 + 11x + 6, 3x^2 + 8x + 4, x^2 + 5x + 6.$

18. $5x^2 + 11x + 2, 5x^2 + 16x + 3, x^2 + 5x + 6.$

19. $2x^2 + 3x - 2, 2x^2 + 15x - 8, x^2 + 10x + 16.$

20. $3x^2 - x - 14, 3x^2 - 13x + 14, x^2 - 4.$

21. $12x^2 + 3x - 42, 12x^3 + 30x^2 + 12x, 32x^2 - 40x - 28.$

22. $3x^4 + 26x^3 + 35x^2, 6x^2 + 38x - 28, 27x^3 + 27x^2 - 30x.$

23. $60x^4 + 5x^3 - 5x^2, 60x^2y + 32xy + 4y, 40x^3y - 2x^2y - 2xy.$

24. $8x^2 - 38xy + 35y^2, 4x^2 - xy + 5y^2, 2x^2 - 4xy - 7y^2.$

25. $12x^2 - 23xy + 10y^2, 4x^2 - 9xy + 5y^2, 3x^2 - 5xy + 2y^2.$

26. $6ax^3 + 7a^2x^2 - 3a^3x, 3a^2x^2 + 14a^3x - 5a^4, 6x^2 + 39ax + 45a^2.$

27. $4ax^2y^2 + 11axy^2 - 3ay^2, 3x^3y^3 + 7x^2y^3 - 6xy^3, 24ax^2 - 22ax + 4x.$

28. $(3x - 5x^2)^2, 6 - 7x - 5x^2, 4x + 4x^2 + x^3.$

29. $14a^4(a^3 - b^3), 21a^2b^2(a - b)^3, 6a^3b(a - b)(a^2 - b^2).$

30. $m^4 + m^2n^2 + n^4, m^3n + n^4, (m^3 - mn)^3.$

31. $(2c^2 - 3cd)^2, (4c - 6d)^3, 8c^3 - 27d^3.$

***160.** When the given expressions are such that their factors cannot be determined by inspection, they must be resolved by finding the highest common factor.

Example. Find the lowest common multiple of

$2x^4 + x^3 - 20x^3 - 7x + 24$ and

$2x^4 - 3x^3 - 13x^2 - 7x + 15.$

The highest common factor is $x^2 + 2x - 3.$

By division, we obtain

$$2x^4 + x^3 - 20x^2 - 7x + 24 = (x^2 + 2x - 3)(2x^2 - 3x - 8).$$

$$2x^4 + 3x^3 - 13x^2 - 7x + 15 = (x^2 + 2x - 3)(2x^2 - x - 5).$$

Therefore the L.C.M. is $(x^2 + 2x - 3)(2x^2 - 3x - 8)(2x^2 - x - 5).$

***161.** We may now give the proof of the rule for finding the lowest common multiple of two compound algebraical expressions.

Let A and B be the two expressions, and F their highest common factor. Also suppose that a and b are the respective quotients when A and B are divide by F; then $A = aF, B = bF$. Therefore, since a and b have no common factor, the lowest common multiple of A and B is abF, by inspection.

***162.** There is an important relation between the highest common factor and the lowest common multiple of two expressions which it is desirable to notice.

Let F be the highest common factor, and X the lowest common multiple of A and B. Then, as in the preceding article,

$$A = aF, B = bF,$$

and $$X = abF.$$

Therefore the product $AB = aF \cdot bF$

$$= F.abF$$

$$= FX \qquad ...(1).$$

Hence *the product of two expressions is equal to the product of their highest common factor and lowest common multiple.*

Again, from (1) $X = \dfrac{AB}{F} = \dfrac{A}{F} \times B = \dfrac{B}{F} \times A;$

hence *the lowest common multiple of two expressions may be found by dividing their product by their highest common factor; or by dividing either of them by their highest common factor, and multiplying the quotient by the other.*

***163.** The lowest common multiple of three expressions A, B, C may be obtained as follows.

First, find X the L.C.M. of A and B. Next find Y the L.C.M. of X and C; then Y will be the required L.C.M. of A, B, C.

For Y is the expression of lowest dimensions which is divisible by X and C, and X is the expression of lowest dimensions divisible by A and B. Therefore Y is the expression of lowest dimensions divisible by all three.

EXAMPLES XX-b

1. Find the highest common factor and the lowest common multiple of $x^2 - 5x + 6, x^2 - 4, x^3 - 3x - 2$.
2. Find the lowest common multiple of $ab(x^2 + 1) + x(a^2 + b^2)$ and $ab(x^2 - 1) + x(a^2 - b^2)$.

3. Find the lowest common multiple of
$xy - bx, xy - ay, y^2 - 3by + 2b^2, xy - 2bx - ay + 2ab,$
$xy - bx - ay + ab.$

4. Find the highest common factor and the lowest common multiple of
$x^3 + 2x^2 - 3x, 2x^3 + 5x^2 - 3x.$

5. Find the lowest common multiple of
$1 - x, (1 - x^2)^2, (1 + x)^3.$

6. Find the lowest common multiple of
$$x^2 - 10x + 24, x^2 - 8x + 12, x^2 - 6x + 8.$$

7. Find the highest common factor and the lowest common multiple of
$6x^3 + x^2 - 5x - 2,\ 6x^3 + 5x^2 - 3x - 2.$

8. Find the lowest common multiple of
$$(bc^2 - abc)^2, b^2(ac^2 - a^3), a^2c^2 + 2ac^3 + c^4.$$

9. Find the lowest common multiple of
$$x^3 - y^3, x^3y - y^4,\ y^2(x - y)^2, x^2 + xy + y^2.$$
Also find the highest common factor of the first three expressions.

10. Find the highest common factor of
$$6x^2 - 13x + 6, 2x^2 + 5x - 12, 6x^2 - x - 12.$$
Also show that the lowest common multiple is the product of the three quantities divided by the square of the highest common factor.

11. Find the lowest common multiple of $x^4 + ax^3 + a^3x + a^4$, $x^4 + a^2x^2 + a^4$.

*12. Find the highest common factor and the lowest common multiple of
$3x^3 - 7x^2y + 5xy^2 - y^3,\ x^2y + 3xy^2 - 3x^3 - y^3, 3x^3 + 5x^2y + xy^2 - y^3.$

*13. Find the highest common factor of,
$$4x^3 - 10x^2 + 4x + 2,$$
$$3x^4 - 2x^3 - 3x + 2.$$

14. Find the lowest common multiple of
$a^2 - b^2, a^3 - b^3,$
$a^3 - a^2b - ab^2 - 2b^3.$

15. Find the highest common factor and the lowest common multiple of
$(2x^2 - 3a^2)y + (2a^2 - 3y^2)x,\ (2a^2 + 3y^2)x + (2x^2 + 3a^2)y.$

*16. Find the highest common factor and the lowest common multiple of
$x^3 - 9x^2 + 26x - 24,\ x^3 - 12x^2 + 47x - 60.$

*17. Find the highest common factor of
$x^3 - 15ax^2 + 48a^2x + 64a^3, x^2 - 10ax + 16a^2.$

18. Find the lowest common multiple of
$$21x(xy - y^2)^2, 35(x^4y^2 - x^2y^4), 15y(x^2 + xy)^2.$$

21

ADDITION AND SUBTRACTION OF FRACTIONS

164. HAVING explained the rules for finding the lowest common multiple of any given expressions, we now proceed to show how the addition and subtraction of fractions may be effected.

165. *To prove* $\frac{a}{b} + \frac{c}{d} = \frac{ad + bc}{bd}$.

We have $\frac{a}{b} - \frac{ad}{bd}$, and $\frac{c}{d} = \frac{bc}{bd}$. [Art. 150.]

Thus in each case we divide the unit into bd equal parts, and we take first ad of these parts, and then bc of them; that is, we take $ad + bc$ of the bd parts of the unit; and this is expressed by the fraction $\frac{ad + bc}{bd}$.

$$\therefore \qquad \frac{a}{b} + \frac{c}{d} = \frac{ad + bc}{bd}.$$

Similarly,

$$\frac{a}{b} - \frac{c}{d} = \frac{ad - bc}{bd}.$$

166. Here the fractions have been both expressed with a common denominator bd. But if b and d have a common factor, the product bd is not the lowest common denominator, and the fraction $\frac{ad + bc}{bd}$ will not be in its lowest terms. To avoid working with fractions which are not in their lowest terms, some modification of the above will be necessary. In practice it will be found advisable to take the *lowest* common denominator, which is the lowest common multiple of the denominators of the given fractions.

Rule I. To reduce fractions to their lowest common denominator: *find the L.C.M. of the given denominators, and take it for the common denominator, divide it by the denominator of the first fraction, and multiply the numerator of this fraction by the quotient so obtained; and do the same with all the other given fractions.*

Example. Express with lowest common denominator

$$\frac{5x}{2a(x-a)} \text{ and } \frac{4a}{3x(x^2-a^2)}.$$

The lowest common denominator is $6ax(x-a)(x+a)$.

We must therefore multiple the numerators by $3x(x+a)$ and $2a$ respectively.

Hence the equivalent fractions are

$$\frac{15x^2(x+a)}{6ax(x-a)(x+a)}$$

and $$\frac{8a^2}{6ax(x-a)(x+a)}.$$

167. We may now enunciate the rule for the addition or subtraction of fractions.

Rule II. To add or subtract fractions: *reduce them to the lowest common denominator; find the algebraical sum of the numerators, and retain the common denominator.*

Example 1. Find the value of $\frac{2x+a}{3a}+\frac{5x-4a}{9a}$.

The lowest common denominator is $9a$.

Therefore the expression

$$=\frac{3(2x+a)+5x-4a}{9a}$$

$$=\frac{6x+3a+5x-4a}{9a}=\frac{11x-a}{9a}.$$

Example 2. Find the value of $\frac{x-2y}{xy}+\frac{3y-a}{ay}-\frac{3x-2a}{ax}$.

The lowest common denominator is axy.

Thus the expression

$$=\frac{a(x-2y)+x(3y-a)-y(3x-2a)}{axy}$$

$$=\frac{ax-2ay+3xy-ax-3xy+2ay}{axy}$$

$$=0,$$

since the terms in the numerator destroy each other.

NOTE. To ensure accuracy the beginner is recommended to use brackets as in first line of work above.

EXAMPLES XXI-a

Find the value of

1. $\frac{x-1}{2}+\frac{x+3}{5}+\frac{x+7}{10}$.

2. $\frac{2x-1}{3}+\frac{x-5}{6}+\frac{x-4}{4}$.

3. $\frac{5x-1}{8}-\frac{3x-2}{7}+\frac{x-5}{4}$.

4. $\frac{2x-3}{9}-\frac{x+2}{6}+\frac{5x+8}{12}$.

5. $\frac{x-7}{15}+\frac{x-9}{25}-\frac{x+3}{45}$.

6. $\frac{2x+5}{x}-\frac{x+3}{2x}-\frac{27}{8x^2}$.

7. $\frac{a-b}{ab}+\frac{b-c}{bc}+\frac{c-a}{ca}$.

8. $\frac{a-2b}{2a}-\frac{a-5b}{4a}+\frac{a+7b}{8a}$.

9. $\frac{b+c}{2a}+\frac{c+a}{4b}-\frac{a-b}{3c}$.

10. $\frac{a-x}{x}+\frac{a+x}{x}-\frac{a^2-x^2}{2ax}$.

11. $\frac{x+2}{17x}-\frac{x-5}{34x}+\frac{x+2}{51x}$.

12. $\frac{2a^2-b^2}{a^2}-\frac{b^2-c^2}{b^2}-\frac{c^2-a^2}{c^2}$.

13. $\frac{x-3}{5x}+\frac{x^2-9}{10x^2}-\frac{8-x^3}{15x^3}$.

14. $\frac{2}{xy}-\frac{3y^2-x^2}{xy^3}+\frac{xy+y^2}{x^2y^2}$.

15. $\frac{2x-3y}{xy}+\frac{3x-2z}{xz}+\frac{5}{x}$.

16. $\frac{a^2-bc}{bc}-\frac{ac-b^2}{ac}-\frac{ab-c^2}{ab}$.

Example 3. Simplify $\frac{2x-3a}{x-2a}-\frac{2x-a}{x-a}$.

The lowest common denominator is $(x-2a)(x-a)$.

Hence, multiplying the numerators by $x-a$ and $x-2a$ respectively, we have

$$\text{the expression } = \frac{(2x-3a)(x-a)-(2x-a)(x-2a)}{(x-2a)(x-a)}$$

$$= \frac{2x^2-5ax+3a^2-(2x^2-5ax+2a^2)}{(x-2a)(x-a)}$$

$$= \frac{2x^2-5ax+3a^2-2x^2+5ax-2a^2}{(x-2a)(x-a)}$$

$$= \frac{a^2}{(x-2a)(x-a)}.$$

NOTE. In finding the value of such an expression as $-(2x-a)(x-2a)$, the beginner should first express the product in brackets, and then remove the brackets, as we have done. After a little practice he will be able to take both steps together.

The work will sometimes be shortened by first reducing the fractions to their lowest terms.

Example 4. Simplify $\dfrac{x^2+5xy-4y^2}{x^2-16y^2}-\dfrac{2xy}{2x^2+8xy}$.

$$\text{The expression} = \frac{x^2+5xy-4y^2}{x^2-16y^2}-\frac{y}{x+4y}$$

$$=\frac{x^2+5xy-4y^2-y(x-4y)}{x^2-16y^2}$$

$$=\frac{x^2+5xy-4y^2-xy+4y^2}{x^2-16y^2}$$

$$=\frac{x^2+4xy}{x^2-16y^2}=\frac{x}{x-4y}.$$

EXAMPLES XXI-b

Find the value of

1. $\dfrac{1}{x+2}+\dfrac{1}{x+3}$.

2. $\dfrac{2}{x+3}-\dfrac{1}{x+4}$.

3. $\dfrac{1}{x-5}-\dfrac{1}{x-4}$.

4. $\dfrac{3}{x-6}-\dfrac{1}{x+2}$.

5. $\dfrac{a}{x+a}-\dfrac{b}{x+b}$.

6. $\dfrac{a}{x-a}+\dfrac{b}{x-b}$.

7. $\dfrac{x+3}{x+4}-\dfrac{x+1}{x+2}$.

8. $\dfrac{a+x}{a-x}-\dfrac{a-x}{a+x}$.

9. $\dfrac{x+2}{x-2}-\dfrac{x-2}{x+2}$.

10. $\dfrac{x-4}{x-2}-\dfrac{x-7}{x-5}$.

11. $\dfrac{a}{x-a}-\dfrac{a^2}{x^2-a^2}$

12. $\dfrac{3}{x-3}+\dfrac{2x}{x^2-9}$.

13. $\dfrac{1}{2x-3y}-\dfrac{x+y}{4x^2-9y^2}$.

14. $\dfrac{x+a}{x-2a}-\dfrac{x^2+2a^2}{x^2-4a^2}$.

15. $\dfrac{4a^2+b^2}{4a^2-b^2}-\dfrac{2a-b}{2a+b}$.

16. $\dfrac{2x^2}{x^2-y^2}-\dfrac{2x^2}{x^2+xy}$.

17. $\dfrac{x^2}{x-x^3}-\dfrac{x}{1+x^2}$.

18. $\dfrac{1}{x(x-y)}+\dfrac{1}{y(x+y)}$.

19. $\dfrac{xy}{25x^2-y^2}+\dfrac{2x^2y}{10x^2y+2xy^2}$.

20. $\dfrac{y}{x(x^2-y)^2}+\dfrac{x}{y(x^2+y^2)}$.

21. $\dfrac{x^2-4a^2}{x^2-2ax}-\dfrac{x^2+2ax-8a^2}{x^2-4a^2}$.

22. $\dfrac{x^2+xy+y^2}{x+y}+\dfrac{x^2-xy+y^2}{x-y}$.

23. $\dfrac{1}{a-2x}-\dfrac{(a+2x)^2}{a^3-8x^3}$.

24. $\dfrac{a^3+b^3}{a^2-ab+b^2}-\dfrac{a^3-b^3}{a^2+ab-b^2}$.

25. $\dfrac{3}{x^2-4}+\dfrac{1}{(x-2)^2}$.

26. $\dfrac{1}{a(x^2-a^2)}-\dfrac{1}{x(x+a)^2}$.

168. Some modification of the foregoing general methods may sometimes be used with advantage. The most useful artifices are explained in the examples which follow, but no general rules can be given which will apply to all cases.

Example 1. Simplify $\dfrac{a+3}{a-4}-\dfrac{a+4}{a-3}-\dfrac{8}{a^2-16}$.

Taking the first two fractions together, we have

$$\text{the expression } = \frac{a^2-9-(a^2-16)}{(a-4)(a-3)}-\frac{8}{a^2-16}$$

$$=\frac{7}{(a-4)(a-3)}-\frac{8}{(a+4)(a-4)}$$

$$=\frac{7(a+4)-8(a-3)}{(a+4)(a-4)(a-3)}=\frac{52-a}{(a+4)(a-4)(a-3)}.$$

Example 2. Simplify $\dfrac{1}{2x^2+x-1}+\dfrac{1}{3x^2+4x+1}$.

$$\text{The expression } =\frac{1}{(2x-1)(x+1)}+\frac{1}{(3x+1)(x+1)}$$

$$=\frac{3x+1+2x-1}{(2x-1)(x+1)(3x+1)}=\frac{5x}{(2x-1)(x+1)(3x+1)}.$$

Example 3. Simplify $\dfrac{1}{a-x}-\dfrac{1}{a+x}-\dfrac{2x}{a^2+x^2}-\dfrac{4x^3}{a^4+x^4}$.

Here it should be evident that the first two denominators give L.C.M. a^2-x^2, which readily combines with a^2+x^2 to give L.C.M. a^4-x^4, which again combines with a^4+x^4 to give L.C.M. a^8-x^8.

Hence it will be convenient to proceed as follows:

$$\text{The expression } =\frac{a+x-(a-x)}{a^2-x^2}-\ldots\ldots-\ldots\ldots$$

$$=\frac{2x}{a^2-x^2}-\frac{2x}{a^2+x^2}-\ldots\ldots$$

$$=\frac{4x^3}{a^4-x^4}-\frac{4x^3}{a^4+x^4}=\frac{8x^7}{a^8-x^8}.$$

EXAMPLES XXI-c

Find the value of

1. $\frac{1}{x+y}-\frac{1}{x-y}+\frac{2x}{x^2-y^2}$.

2. $\frac{1}{2x+y}+\frac{1}{2x-1}-\frac{3x}{4x^2-y^2}$.

3. $\frac{5}{1+2x}-\frac{3x}{1-2x}-\frac{4-13x}{1-4x^2}$.

4. $\frac{2a}{2a+3b}+\frac{3b}{2a-3b}-\frac{8b^2}{4a^2-9b^2}$.

5. $\frac{10}{9-a^2}-\frac{2}{3+a}-\frac{1}{3-a}$.

6. $\frac{5x}{6(x^2-1)}-\frac{1}{2(x-1)}+\frac{1}{3(x+1)}$.

7. $\frac{1}{2(a-b)}-\frac{1}{2(a+b)}-\frac{b}{a^2-b^2}$.

8. $\frac{2a}{2a-3}-\frac{5}{6a+9}-\frac{4(3a+2)}{3(4a^2-9)}$.

9. $\frac{3}{x-2}+\frac{2}{3x+6}+\frac{5x}{x^2-4}$.

10. $\frac{x}{x^3+y^3}-\frac{y}{x^3-y^3}+\frac{x^3y+xy^3}{x^6-y^6}$.

11. $\frac{1}{x^2-9x+20}+\frac{1}{x^2-11x+30}$.

12. $\frac{1}{x^2-7x+12}-\frac{1}{x^2-5x+6}$.

13. $\frac{1}{2x^2-x-1}-\frac{3}{2x^2+x-3}$.

14. $\frac{1}{2x^2-x-1}-\frac{3}{6x^2-x-2}$.

15. $\frac{4}{4-7a-2a^2}-\frac{3}{3-a-10a^2}$.

16. $\frac{5}{5+x-18x^2}-\frac{2}{2+5x+2x^4}$.

17. $\frac{1}{x+1}-\frac{1}{(x+1)(x+2)}+\frac{1}{(x+1)(x+2)(x+3)}$.

18. $\frac{5x}{2(x+1)(x-3)}-\frac{15(x-1)}{16(x-3)(x-2)}-\frac{9(x+3)}{16(x+1)(x-2)}$.

19. $\frac{a+3b}{4(a+b)(a+2b)}+\frac{a+2b}{(a+b)(a+3b)}-\frac{a+b}{4(a+2b)(a+3b)}$.

20. $\frac{2}{x^2-3x+2}+\frac{2}{x^2-x-2}-\frac{1}{x^2-1}$.

21. $\frac{x}{x^2+5x+6}+\frac{15}{x^2+9x+14}-\frac{12}{x^2+10x+21}$.

22. $\frac{3}{x^2-1}+\frac{4}{2x+1}+\frac{4x+2}{2x^2+3x+1}$.

23. $\frac{5(2x-3)}{11(6x^2+x-1)}+\frac{7x}{6x^2+7x-3}-\frac{12(3x+1)}{11(4x^2+8x+3)}$.

24. $\frac{x-3}{x+2}-\frac{x-2}{x+3}+\frac{1}{x-1}$.

25. $\frac{x-3}{x-4}-\frac{x+4}{x+3}-\frac{5}{x^2-16}$.

Find the value of

26. $\dfrac{1+2a}{1-2a}-\dfrac{1-2a}{1+2a}-\dfrac{8a}{(1-2a)^2}$.

27. $\dfrac{24x}{9-12x+4x^2}-\dfrac{3+2x}{3-2x}+\dfrac{3-2x}{3+2x}$.

28. $\dfrac{1}{3-x}-\dfrac{1}{3+x}-\dfrac{2x}{9+x^2}$.

29. $\dfrac{1}{2a+3}+\dfrac{1}{2a-3}-\dfrac{4a}{4a^2+9}$.

30. $\dfrac{1}{4(1+x)}+\dfrac{1}{4(1-x)}+\dfrac{1}{2(1+x^2)}$.

31. $\dfrac{3}{8(a-x)}+\dfrac{1}{8(a+x)}-\dfrac{(a-x)}{4(a^2+x^2)}$.

32. $\dfrac{2x}{4+x^2}+\dfrac{1}{2-x}-\dfrac{1}{2+x}$.

33. $\dfrac{5}{3-6x}-\dfrac{5}{3+6x}-\dfrac{x}{2+8x^2}$.

34. $\dfrac{1}{2a-8x}-\dfrac{a}{3a^2+48x^2}+\dfrac{1}{2a+8x}$.

35. $\dfrac{1}{6a^2+54}+\dfrac{1}{3a-9}-\dfrac{a}{3a^2-27}$.

36. $\dfrac{1}{8-8x}-\dfrac{1}{8+8x}+\dfrac{x}{4+4x^2}-\dfrac{x}{2+2x^4}$.

37. $\dfrac{1}{6a-18}-\dfrac{1}{6a+18}-\dfrac{1}{a^2+9}+\dfrac{18}{a^4+81}$.

38. $\dfrac{x+1}{2x^3-4x^2}+\dfrac{x-1}{2x^3+4x^2}-\dfrac{1}{x^2-4}$.

39. $\dfrac{1}{3x^2-4xy+y^2}+\dfrac{1}{x^2-4xy+3y^2}-\dfrac{3}{3x^2-10xy+3y^2}$.

40. $\dfrac{1}{x-1}+\dfrac{2}{x+1}-\dfrac{3x-2}{x^2-1}-\dfrac{1}{(x+1)^2}$.

41. $\dfrac{108-52x}{x(3-x)^2}-\dfrac{4}{3-x}-\dfrac{12}{x}+\left(\dfrac{1+x}{3-x}\right)^2$.

42. $\dfrac{(a+b)^2}{(x-a)(x+a+b)}-\dfrac{a+2b+x}{2(x-a)}+\dfrac{(a+b)x}{x^2+bx-a^2-ab}+\dfrac{1}{2}$.

43. $\dfrac{3(x^2+x-2)}{x^2-x-2}-\dfrac{3(x^2-x-2)}{x^2+x-2}-\dfrac{8x}{x^2-4}$.

169. We have thus far assumed both numerator and denominator to be positive integers, and have shown in Art. 155 that a fraction itself is the quotient resulting from the division of the numerator by denominator. But in algebra division is a process not restricted to positive integers, and we shall extend this definition as follows:

The algebraic fraction $\frac{a}{b}$ *is the quotient resulting from the division of* a *by* b, *where* a *and* b *may have any values whatever.*

170. By the preceding article $\frac{-a}{-b}$ is the quotient resulting from the division of $-a$ by $-b$; and this is obtained by dividing a by b, and, by the rule of signs, prefixing +.

Again, $\frac{-a}{b}$ is the quotient resulting from the division of $-a$ by b; and this is obtained by dividing a by b, and, by the rule of signs, prefixing —

Therefore $\frac{-a}{b} = -\frac{a}{b}$ ...(2)

Likewise $\frac{a}{-b}$ is the quotient resulting from the division of a by $-b$; and this is obtained by dividing a by b, and, by the rule of signs, prefixing–.

Therefore $\frac{a}{-b} = -\frac{a}{b}$ ...(3).

These results may be enunciated as follows:

1. *If the signs of* BOTH *numerator and denominator of a fraction be changed, the sign of the whole fraction will be unchanged.*
2. *If the sign of* EITHER *numerator or denominator alone be changed, the sign of the whole fraction will be changed.*

The principles here involved are so useful in certain cases of reduction of fractions that we quote them in another form, which will sometimes be found more easy of application.

1. *We may change the sign of every team in the numerator and denominator of a fraction without altering its value.*
2. *We may change the sign of a fraction by simply changing the sign of every term in* EITHER *the numerator or denominator.*

Example 1. $\frac{b-a}{y-x} = \frac{-b+a}{-y+x} = \frac{a-b}{x-y}$.

Example 2. $\frac{x-x^2}{2y} = \frac{-x+x^2}{2y} = -\frac{x^2-x}{2y}$.

Example 3. $\frac{3x}{4-x^2} = -\frac{3x}{-4+x^2} = -\frac{3x}{x^2-4}$.

The intermediate step may usually be omitted.

Example 4. Simplify $\dfrac{a}{x+a}+\dfrac{2x}{x-a}+\dfrac{a(3x-a)}{a^2-x^2}$.

Here it is evident that the lowest common denominator of the first two fractions is x^2-a^2, therefore it will be convenient to alter the sign of the denominator in the third fraction.

Thus the expression $=\dfrac{a}{x+a}+\dfrac{2x}{x-a}-\dfrac{a(3x-a)}{x^2-a^2}$

$$=\frac{a(x-a)+2x(x+a)-a(3x-a)}{x^2-a^2}$$

$$=\frac{ax-a^2+2x^2+2ax-3ax+a^2}{x^2-a^2}$$

$$=\frac{2x^2}{x^2-a^2}.$$

Example 5. Simplify $\dfrac{5}{3x-3}+\dfrac{3x-1}{1-x^2}+\dfrac{1}{2x+2}$.

The expression $=\dfrac{5}{3(x-1)}-\dfrac{3x-1}{x^2-1}+\dfrac{1}{2(x+1)}$

$$=\frac{10(x+1)-6(3x-1)+3(x-1)}{6(x^2-1)}$$

$$=\frac{10x+10-18x+6+3x-3}{6(x^2-1)}$$

$$=\frac{13-5x}{6(x^2-1)}.$$

EXAMPLES XXI-d

Simplify

1. $\dfrac{1}{4x-4}-\dfrac{1}{5x+5}+\dfrac{1}{1-x^2}$.

2. $\dfrac{3}{1+a}-\dfrac{2}{1-a}-\dfrac{5a}{a^2-1}$.

3. $\dfrac{x-2a}{x+a}+\dfrac{2(a^2-4ax)}{a^2-x^2}-\dfrac{3a}{x-a}$.

4. $\dfrac{x-a}{x+a}+\dfrac{a^2+3ax}{a^2-x^2}+\dfrac{x+a}{x-a}$.

5. $\dfrac{1}{2x+1}+\dfrac{1}{2x-1}+\dfrac{4x}{1-4x^2}$.

6. $\dfrac{3x}{1-x^2}-\dfrac{2}{x-1}-\dfrac{2}{x+1}$.

7. $\dfrac{2-5x}{x+3}-\dfrac{3+x}{3-x}+\dfrac{2x(2x-11)}{x^2-9}$.

8. $\dfrac{3-2x}{2x+3}-\dfrac{2x+3}{3-2x}+\dfrac{12}{4x^2-9}$.

9. $\dfrac{5}{2b+2}-\dfrac{3}{4b-4}+\dfrac{11}{6-6b^2}$.

10. $\dfrac{1}{6a+6}+\dfrac{1}{6-6a}-\dfrac{1}{3a^2-3}$.

11. $\dfrac{y^2}{x^3 - y^3} + \dfrac{x^3y^3}{y^6 - x^6}$.

12. $\dfrac{x^2 - y^2}{xy} - \dfrac{xy - y^2}{xy - x^2}$.

13. $\dfrac{x^2 + y^2}{x^2 - y^2} + \dfrac{x}{x + y} + \dfrac{y}{y - x}$.

14. $\dfrac{x^2 + 2x + 4}{x + 2} - \dfrac{x^2 - 2x + 4}{2 - x}$.

15. $\dfrac{1}{2a + 5b} + \dfrac{3a}{25b^2 - 4a^2} + \dfrac{1}{2a - 5b}$.

16. $\dfrac{2b - a}{x - b} + \dfrac{3x(a - b)}{b^2 - x^2} + \dfrac{b - 2a}{b + x}$.

17. $\dfrac{ax^2 + b}{2x - 1} + \dfrac{2(bx + ax^2)}{1 - 4x^2} - \dfrac{ax^2 - b}{2x + 1}$.

18. $\dfrac{a + c}{(a - b)(x - a)} + \dfrac{b + c}{(b - a)(x - b)}$.

19. $\dfrac{a - c}{(a - b)(x - a)} - \dfrac{b - c}{(b - a)(b - x)}$.

20. $\dfrac{2a + y}{(x - a)(a - b)} + \dfrac{a + b + y}{(x - b)(b - a)} - \dfrac{x + y - a}{(x - a)(x - b)}$.

21. $\dfrac{1}{(a^2 - b^2)(x^2 + b^2)} + \dfrac{3}{(b^2 - a^2)(x^2 + a^2)} - \dfrac{1}{(x^2 + a^2)(x^2 + b^2)}$.

22. $\dfrac{1}{x + a} + \dfrac{4a}{x^2 - a^2} + \dfrac{1}{a - x} - \dfrac{2a}{x^2 + a^2}$.

23. $\dfrac{3}{x + a} - \dfrac{1}{x + 3a} + \dfrac{3}{a - x} + \dfrac{b}{x - 3a}$.

24. $\dfrac{1}{4a^3(a + x)} - \dfrac{1}{4a^3(x - a)} + \dfrac{1}{2a^2(a^2 + x^2)} - \dfrac{a^4}{a^3 - x^3}$.

25. $\dfrac{x}{x^2 - y^2} - \dfrac{y}{x^2 + y^2} + \dfrac{x^3 + y^3}{y^4 - x^4} + \dfrac{xy}{(x + y)(x^2 + y^2)}$.

26. $\dfrac{b}{a(a^2 - b^2)} + \dfrac{a}{b(a^2 + b^2)} + \dfrac{a^4 + b^4}{ab(b^4 - a^4)} - \dfrac{a^6}{a^8 - b^8}$.

27. $\dfrac{a^2 - 2ax + x^2}{2(a^2 - x^2)} - \dfrac{2ax(a + x)}{(a - x)(a^2 + 2ax + x^2)} - \dfrac{x^2 - a^2}{2(x - a)^2}$.

28. $\dfrac{2}{a + b} - \dfrac{1}{a - b} - \dfrac{3b}{b^2 - a^2} + \dfrac{ab}{a^3 + b^3}$.

29. $\dfrac{3}{8(1 - x)} + \dfrac{1}{8(1 + x)} - \dfrac{1 - x}{4(1 + x^2)} - \dfrac{3}{4(x^2 - 1)}$.

30. $\dfrac{1}{x} + \dfrac{1}{x - 1} + \dfrac{1}{x + 1} + \dfrac{x}{1 - x^2} + \dfrac{3}{x(x^2 - 1)}$.

31. $\dfrac{a^2 + ac}{a^2c - c^3} - \dfrac{a^2 - c^2}{a^2c + 2ac^2 + c^3} + \dfrac{2c}{c^2 - a^2} - \dfrac{3}{a + c}$.

32. $\dfrac{4a + 6b}{a + b} + \dfrac{6a - 4b}{a - b} + \dfrac{4a^2 + 6b^2}{b^2 - a^2} + \dfrac{4b^2 - 6a^2}{a^2 + b^2} - \dfrac{20b^4}{b^4 - a^4}$.

***171.** Consider the expression

$$\frac{1}{(a-b)(a-c)}+\frac{1}{(b-c)(b-a)}+\frac{1}{(c-a)(c-b)}.$$

Here in finding the L.C.M. of the denominators it must be observed that there are not *six* different compound factors to be considered; for three of them differ from the other three only in sign.

Thus
$$(a-c)=-(c-a),$$
$$(b-a)=-(a-b),$$
$$(c-b)=-(b-c).$$

Hence, replacing the second factor in each denominator by its equivalent, we may write the expression in the form

$$-\frac{1}{(a-b)(c-a)}-\frac{1}{(b-c)(a-b)}-\frac{1}{(c-a)(b-c)} \qquad \ldots(1).$$

Now the L.C.M. is $(b-c)(c-a)(a-b)$;

and the expression
$$=\frac{-(b-c)-(c-a)-(a-b)}{(b-c)(c-a)(a-b)}$$
$$=\frac{-b+c-c+a-a+b}{(b-c)(c-a)(a-b)}$$
$$=0.$$

***172.** There is a peculiarity in the arrangement of this example which it is desirable to notice. In the expression (1) the letters occur in what is known as Cyclic Order; that is, b follows a, a follows c, c follows b. Thus if a, b, c are arranged round the circumference of a circle, as in the annexed diagram, if we start from any letter and move round in the direction of the arrows, the other letters follow in cyclic order, namely, abc, bca, cab.

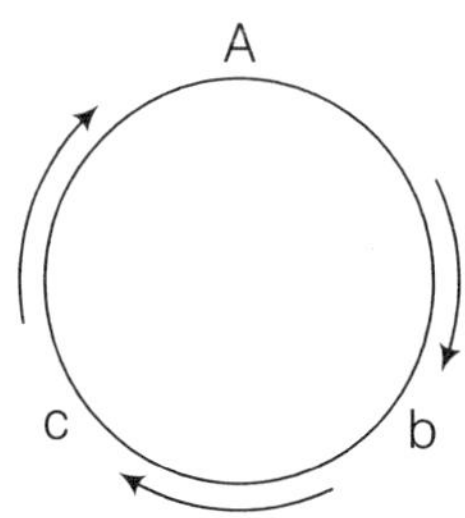

The observance of this principle is especially important in a large class of examples in which the differences of three letters are involved. Thus we are observing cyclic order when we write $b-c$, $c-a$, $a-b$; where as we are violating cyclic order by the use of arrangements such as $b-c$, $a-c$, $a-b$, or $a-c$, $b-a$, $b-c$. It will always be found that the work is rendered shorter and easier by following cyclic order from the beginning and, adhering to it throughout the question.

In the present chapter we shall confine our attention to a few of the simpler cases, resuming the subject in Chapter XXIX.

*EXAMPLES XXI-e

Find the value of

1. $\frac{a}{(a-b)(a-c)}+\frac{b}{(b-c)(b-a)}+\frac{c}{(c-a)(c-b)}$.

2. $\frac{b}{(a-b)(a-c)}+\frac{c}{(b-c)(b-a)}+\frac{a}{(c-a)(c-b)}$.

3. $\frac{z}{(x-y)(x-z)}+\frac{x}{(y-z)(y-x)}+\frac{y}{(z-x)(z-y)}$.

4. $\frac{y+z}{(x-y)(x-z)}+\frac{z+x}{(y-z)(y-x)}+\frac{x+y}{(z-x)(z-y)}$.

5. $\frac{b-c}{(a-b)(a-c)}+\frac{c-a}{(b-c)(b-a)}+\frac{a-b}{(c-a)(c-b)}$.

6. $\frac{x^2yz}{(x-y)(x-z)}+\frac{y^2zx}{(y-z)(y-x)}+\frac{z^2xy}{(z-x)(z-y)}$.

7. $\frac{1+a}{(a-b)(a-c)}+\frac{1+b}{(b-c)(b-a)}+\frac{1+c}{(c-a)(c-b)}$.

8. $\frac{p-a}{(p-q)(p-r)}+\frac{q-a}{(q-r)(q-p)}+\frac{r-a}{(r-p)(r-q)}$.

9. $\frac{p+q-r}{(p-q)(p-r)}+\frac{q+r-p}{(q-r)(q-p)}+\frac{r+p-q}{(r-p)(r-q)}$.

10. $\frac{a^2}{(a^2+b^2)(a^2-c^2)}+\frac{b^2}{(b^2-c^2)(b^2-a^2)}+\frac{c^2}{(c^2-a^2)(c^2-b^2)}$.

11. $\frac{x+y}{(p-q)(p-r)}+\frac{x+y}{(q-r)(q-p)}+\frac{x+y}{(r-p)(r-q)}$.

12. $\frac{q+r}{(x-y)(x-z)}+\frac{r+p}{(y-z)(y-x)}+\frac{p+q}{(z-x)(z-y)}$.

22

MISCELLANEOUS FRACTIONS

[*Examples marked with an asterisk may be taken at a later stage.*]

173. WE now propose to consider some miscellaneous questions involving fractions of a more complicated kind than those already discussed.

In the previous chapters on Fractions, the numerator and denominator have been regarded as integers; but cases frequently occur in which the numerator or denominator of a fraction is itself fractional.

174. DEFINITION. A fraction of which the numerator or denominator is itself a fraction is called a Complex Fraction.

Thus $\dfrac{\frac{a}{b}}{c}$, $\dfrac{a}{\frac{b}{x}}$, $\dfrac{\frac{a}{b}}{\frac{c}{d}}$ are Complex Fractions.

In the last of these types, the outside quantities, a and d, are sometimes referred to as the *extremes*, while the two middle quantities b and c, are called the *means*.

175. Instead of using the horizontal line to separate numerator and denominator, it is sometimes convenient to write complex fractions in the forms

$$a \,/\, \frac{b}{c}, \; \frac{a}{b} \,/\, x, \; \frac{a}{b} \,/\, \frac{c}{d}.$$

176. By definition (Art. 169) $\dfrac{\frac{a}{b}}{\frac{c}{d}}$ is the quotient resulting from the division of $\frac{a}{b}$ by $\frac{c}{d}$; and this by Art. 158 is $\frac{ad}{bc}$;

$$\therefore \qquad \frac{\frac{a}{b}}{\frac{c}{d}} = \frac{ad}{bc}.$$

Simplification of Complex Fractions

177. From the preceding article we deduce an easy method of writing down the simplified form of a complex fraction.

Multiply the extremes for a new numerator, and the means for a new denominator.

Example. $$\frac{\frac{a+x}{b}}{\frac{a^2-x^2}{ab}} = \frac{ab\,(a+x)}{b\,(a^2-x^2)} = \frac{a}{a-x}.$$

by cancelling common factors in numerators and denominators.

178. The student should especially notice the following cases, and should be able to write down the results easily.

$$\frac{1}{\frac{a}{b}} = 1 \div \frac{a}{b} = 1 \times \frac{b}{a} = \frac{b}{a},$$

$$\frac{a}{\frac{1}{b}} = a \div \frac{1}{b} = a \times b = ab,$$

$$\frac{\frac{1}{a}}{\frac{1}{b}} = \frac{1}{a} \div \frac{1}{b} = \frac{1}{a} \times \frac{b}{1} = \frac{b}{a}.$$

179. The following examples illustrate the simplification of complex fractions.

Example 1. $$\frac{\frac{a}{b}+\frac{c}{d}}{\frac{a}{b}-\frac{c}{d}} = \left(\frac{a}{b}+\frac{c}{d}\right) \div \left(\frac{a}{b}-\frac{c}{d}\right)$$

$$= \frac{ad+bc}{bd} \div \frac{ad-bc}{bd}$$

$$= \frac{ad+bc}{bd} \times \frac{bd}{ad-bc} = \frac{ad+bc}{ad-bc}.$$

Or more simply thus:

Multiply the fractions above and below by bd which is the L.C.M. of their denominators.

Then the fraction becomes $\frac{ad+bc}{ad-bc}$, as before.

Example 2. Simplify $\dfrac{x + \dfrac{a^2}{x}}{x - \dfrac{a^4}{x^3}}$.

Here by multiplying above and below by x^3, we have

the fraction $$= \frac{x^4 + a^2x^2}{x^4 - a^4} = \frac{x^2(x^2 + a^2)}{x^4 - a^4} = \frac{x^2}{x^2 - a^2}.$$

Example 3. Simplify $\dfrac{\dfrac{3}{a} + \dfrac{a}{3} - 2}{\dfrac{a}{6} + \dfrac{1}{2} - \dfrac{3}{a}}$.

Here the expression $$= \frac{18 + 2a^2 - 12a}{a^2 + 3a - 18}$$

$$= \frac{2(a^2 - 6a + 9)}{(a + 6)(a - 3)} = \frac{2(a - 3)}{a + 6}$$

Example 4. Simplify $\dfrac{\dfrac{a^2 + b^2}{a^2 - b^2} - \dfrac{a^2 - b^2}{a^2 + b^2}}{\dfrac{a + b}{a - b} - \dfrac{a - b}{a + b}}$

The numerator $$= \frac{(a^2 + b^2)^2 - (a^2 - b^2)^2}{(a^2 + b^2)(a^2 - b^2)} = \frac{4a^2b^2}{(a^2 + b^2)(a^2 - b^2)}.$$

Similarly the denominator $$= \frac{4ab}{(a + b)(a - b)}.$$

Hence the fraction $$= \frac{4a^2b^2}{(a^2 + b^2)(a^2 - b^2)} \div \frac{4ab}{(a + b)(a - b)}$$

$$= \frac{4a^2b^2}{(a^2 + b^2)(a^2 - b^2)} \times \frac{(a + b)(a - b)}{4ab} = \frac{ab}{a^2 + b^2}.$$

NOTE. To ensure accuracy and neatness, when the numerator and denominator are somewhat complicated, the beginner is advised to simplify each separately as in the above example.

180. In the case of fractions like the following, called Continued Fractions, we begin from the lowest fraction and simplify step by step.

Example. Simplify $\dfrac{9x^2 - 64}{x - 1 - \dfrac{1}{1 - \dfrac{x}{4 + x}}}$

$$\text{The expression} = \frac{9x^2 - 64}{x - 1 - \cfrac{1}{\cfrac{4 + x - x}{4 + x}}} = \frac{9x^2 - 64}{x - 1 - \cfrac{4 + x}{4}}$$

$$= \frac{9x^2 - 64}{\cfrac{4x - 4 - (4 + x)}{4}} = \frac{9x^2 - 64}{\cfrac{3x - 8}{4}} = \frac{4(9x^2 - 64)}{3x - 8} = 4(3x + 8).$$

EXAMPLES XXII-a

Find the value of

1. $\dfrac{\frac{m}{n} - \frac{l}{m}}{\frac{a}{m} - \frac{b}{n}}$.

2. $\dfrac{\frac{1}{x} + \frac{1}{y}}{\frac{1}{x} - \frac{1}{y}}$.

3. $\dfrac{a + \frac{b}{d}}{x - \frac{y}{d}}$.

4. $\dfrac{1 + \frac{c}{x}}{\frac{b}{x} - 1}$.

5. $\dfrac{2 + \frac{3a}{4b}}{a + \frac{8b}{3}}$.

6. $\dfrac{3a + \frac{7b}{8c}}{3c + \frac{7b}{8a}}$.

7. $\dfrac{1 - \frac{y^2}{x^2}}{1 + \frac{y^2}{x^2}}$.

8. $\dfrac{1}{a + \frac{b}{c}}$.

9. $\dfrac{a}{b + \frac{c}{d}}$.

10. $\dfrac{x}{x - \frac{m}{n}}$.

11. $\dfrac{\frac{a}{b} + \frac{c}{d}}{\frac{m}{n} + \frac{k}{p}}$.

12. $\dfrac{x - \frac{1}{x}}{1 + \frac{1}{x}}$.

13. $\dfrac{x + 5 + \frac{6}{x}}{1 + \frac{6}{x} + \frac{8}{x^2}}$.

14. $\dfrac{\frac{1}{x} + \frac{2}{x^2} - \frac{3}{x^3}}{\frac{9}{x} - x}$.

15. $\dfrac{2x^2 - x - 6}{\frac{4}{x^2} - 1}$.

Find the value of

16. $\dfrac{2}{1 - x^2} \div \left(\dfrac{1}{1 - x} - \dfrac{1}{1 + x}\right)$.

17. $\left(\dfrac{a^3 - b^3}{a - b} - \dfrac{a^3 + b^3}{a + b}\right) \div \dfrac{4ab}{a^2 - b^2}$.

18. $\left(\dfrac{a^2 - ax + x^2}{a - x} - \dfrac{a^2 + ax + x^2}{a + x}\right) \div \dfrac{x^3}{a^2 - x^2}$.

19. $\left(y + \dfrac{xy}{y - x}\right)\left(y - \dfrac{xy}{x + y}\right) \times \dfrac{y^2 - x^2}{y^2 + x^2}$.

20. $\left(\dfrac{x}{1 + x} + \dfrac{1 - x}{x}\right) \div \left(\dfrac{x}{1 + x} - \dfrac{1 - x}{x}\right)$.

21. $\dfrac{\dfrac{a+b}{a-b}-\dfrac{a-b}{a+b}}{1-\dfrac{a^2+b^2}{(a+b)^2}}$. 22. $\dfrac{\dfrac{a}{x^2}+\dfrac{x}{a^2}}{\dfrac{1}{a^2}-\dfrac{1}{ax}+\dfrac{1}{x^2}}$. 23. $\dfrac{\dfrac{1}{3x-2}-\dfrac{1}{3x+2}}{\dfrac{1}{9-\dfrac{4}{x^2}}}$.

24. $1+\dfrac{x}{1+x+\dfrac{2x^2}{1-x}}$. 25. $\dfrac{1}{a-\dfrac{a^2-1}{a+\dfrac{1}{a-1}}}$. 26. $\dfrac{1}{4x+\dfrac{4x}{1+\dfrac{2(x+y)}{6-x}}}$.

27. $\dfrac{a}{x+\dfrac{m}{y+\dfrac{n}{z}}}$. 28. $\dfrac{1}{1-\dfrac{1+x}{x-\dfrac{1}{x}}}$.

*29. $\dfrac{x-2}{x-2-\dfrac{x}{x-\dfrac{x-1}{x-2}}}$. *30. $\dfrac{1}{x-\dfrac{1}{x+\dfrac{1}{x}}}-\dfrac{1}{x+\dfrac{1}{x-\dfrac{1}{x}}}$.

*31. $\dfrac{\dfrac{a-b}{1+ab}+\dfrac{b-c}{1+bc}}{1-\dfrac{(a-b)(b-c)}{(1+ab)(1+bc)}}$. *32. $\dfrac{1+\dfrac{a-b}{a+b}}{1-\dfrac{a-b}{a+b}}\div\dfrac{1+\dfrac{a^2-b^2}{a^2+b^2}}{1-\dfrac{a^2-b^2}{a^2+b^2}}$.

*33. $\dfrac{a-x}{a^2-ax-\dfrac{(a-x)^2}{1-\dfrac{a}{x}}}$. *34. $\dfrac{\dfrac{2x^2+2x}{x}}{\dfrac{x}{x-2}-1}-\dfrac{3}{2}-\dfrac{\dfrac{3(x-1)}{x}}{\dfrac{x}{4-x}-1}+\dfrac{3}{4}$.

*35. $\dfrac{2-4x}{4x-2-\dfrac{4x}{\dfrac{1}{1+\dfrac{2x-1}{1+\dfrac{1}{4x-1}}}}}$. *36. $\dfrac{x^2}{1-\dfrac{1}{\dfrac{1}{x^2+\dfrac{x}{x+\dfrac{1}{x}}}}}+\dfrac{x^2-2}{1-\dfrac{1}{\dfrac{1}{x^2-\dfrac{x}{x-\dfrac{1}{x}}}}}$.

181. Sometimes it is convenient to express a single fraction as a group of fractions.

Example. $$\frac{5x^2y-10xy^2+15y^3}{10x^2y^2}=\frac{5x^2y}{10x^2y^2}-\frac{10xy^2}{10x^2y^2}+\frac{15y^3}{10x^2y^2}$$
$$=\frac{1}{2y}-\frac{1}{x}+\frac{3y}{2x^2}.$$

182. Since a fraction represents the quotient of the numerator divided by the denominator, we may often express a fraction in an equivalent form, partly integral and partly fractional.

Example 1. $\dfrac{x+7}{x+2} = \dfrac{(x+2)+5}{x+2} = 1 + \dfrac{5}{x+2}.$

Example 2. $\dfrac{3x-2}{x+5} = \dfrac{3(x+5)-15-2}{x+5} = \dfrac{3(x+5)-17}{x+5} = 3 - \dfrac{17}{x+5}.$

In some cases actual division may be advisable.

Example 3. Show that $\dfrac{2x^2-7x-1}{x-3} = 2x - 1 - \dfrac{4}{x-3}.$

By division,

$$
\begin{array}{l}
x-3)\ 2x^2-7x-1\ (2x-1 \\
\quad\quad\ \underline{2x^2-6x} \\
\quad\quad\quad\quad -x-1 \\
\quad\quad\quad\quad \underline{-x+3} \\
\quad\quad\quad\quad -4
\end{array}
$$

Thus the quotient is $2x-1$, and the remainder -4.

Therefore $\dfrac{2x^2-7x-1}{x-3} = 2x - 1 - \dfrac{4}{x-3}.$

183. If the numerator be of lower dimensions than the denominator, we may still perform the division, and express the result in a form which is partly integral and partly fractional.

Example. Prove that $\dfrac{2x}{1+3x^2} = 2x - 6x^3 + 18x^5 - \dfrac{54x^7}{1+3x^2}.$

By division

$$
\begin{array}{l}
1+3x^2)\ 2x\quad (2x-6x^3+18x^5 \\
\quad\quad\quad \underline{2x+6x^3} \\
\quad\quad\quad\quad -6x^3 \\
\quad\quad\quad\quad \underline{-6x^3-18x^5} \\
\quad\quad\quad\quad\quad\quad 18x^5 \\
\quad\quad\quad\quad\quad\quad \underline{18x^5+54x^7} \\
\quad\quad\quad\quad\quad\quad\quad -54x^7
\end{array}
$$

where the result follows.

Here the division may be carried on to any number of terms in the quotient, and we can stop at any term we please by taking for our remainder the fraction whose numerator is the remainder last found, and whose denominator is the divisor.

Thus, if we carried on the quotient to four terms, we should have

$$\frac{2x}{1+3x^2} = 2x - 6x^3 + 18x^5 - 54x^7 + \frac{162x^9}{1+3x^2}.$$

The terms in the quotient may be fractional; thus if x^2 is divided by $x^3 - a^3$, the first four terms of the quotient are $\frac{1}{x} + \frac{a^3}{x^4} + \frac{a^6}{x^7} + \frac{a^9}{x^{10}}$, and the remainder is $\frac{a^{12}}{x^{10}}$.

184. Miscellaneous examples in multiplication and division occur which can be dealt with by the preceding rules for the reduction of fractions.

Example. Multiply $x + 2a - \frac{a^2}{2x+3a}$ by $2x - a - \frac{2a^2}{x+a}$.

$$\text{The product } = \left(x + 2a - \frac{a^2}{2x+3a}\right) \times \left(2x - a - \frac{2a^2}{x+a}\right)$$

$$= \frac{2x^2 + 7ax + 6a^2 - a^2}{2x+3a} \times \frac{2x^2 + ax - a^2 - 2a^2}{x+a}$$

$$= \frac{2x^2 + 7ax + 5a^2}{2x+3a} \times \frac{2x^2 + ax - 3a^2}{x+a}$$

$$= \frac{(2x+5a)(x+a)}{2x+3a} \times \frac{(2x+3a)(x-a)}{x+a} = (2x+5a)(x-a).$$

EXAMPLES XXII-b

Express each of the following fractions as a group of simple fractions in lowest terms:

1. $\frac{3x^2y + xy^2 - y^3}{9xy}$.

2. $\frac{3a^3x - 4a^2x^2 + 6ax^3}{12ax}$.

3. $\frac{a^3 - 3a^2b + 3ab^2 + b^3}{2ab}$.

4. $\frac{a+b+c}{abc}$.

5. $\frac{bc + ca + ab}{abc}$.

6. $\frac{a^3bc - 3ab^3c + 2abc}{6abc}$.

Perform the following divisions, giving the remainder after four terms in the quotient:

7. $x \div (1 + x)$.

8. $a \div (a - b)$.

9. $(1 + x) \div (1 - x)$.

10. $1 \div (1 - x + x^2)$.

11. $x^2 \div (x + 3)$.

12. $1 \div (1 - x)^2$.

13. Show that $\dfrac{a^3 - b^3}{(a - b)^2} = a + 2b + \dfrac{3b^2}{a - b}$.

14. Show that $x^2 - xy + y^2 - \dfrac{2y^3}{x + y} = \dfrac{x^3 - y^3}{x + y}$.

15. Show that $\dfrac{60x^3 - 17x^2 - 4x + 1}{5x^2 + 9x - 2} = 12x - 25 + \dfrac{49}{x + 2}$.

16. Show that $1 + \dfrac{a^2 + b^2 - c^2}{2ab} = \dfrac{(a + b + c)(a + b - c)}{2ab}$.

17. Divide $x + \dfrac{16x - 27}{x^2 - 16}$ by $x - 1 + \dfrac{13}{x + 4}$.

18. Multiply $a^2 - 2ax + 4x^2 - \dfrac{16x^3}{a + 2x}$ by $3 - \dfrac{6x(a + 4x)}{a^2 + 2ax + 4x^2}$.

19. Divide $b^2 + 3b - 2 - \dfrac{12}{b - 3}$ by $3b + 6 - \dfrac{2b^2}{b - 3}$.

20. Divide $a^2 + 9b^2 + \dfrac{65b^4}{a^2 - 9b^2}$ by $a + 3b + \dfrac{13b^2}{a - 3b}$.

21. Multiply $4x^2 + 14x + \dfrac{98x - 27}{2x - 7}$ by $\dfrac{1}{6} - \dfrac{3x + 29}{12x^2 + 18x + 27}$.

185. The following exercise contains miscellaneous examples which illustrate most of the processes connected with fractions.

EXAMPLES XXII-c

Simplify the following fractions :

1. $\dfrac{4a(a^2 - x^2)}{3b(c^2 - x^2)} \div \left[\dfrac{a^2 - ax}{bc + bx} \times \dfrac{a^2 - 2ax + x^2}{c^2 - 2cx + x^2}\right]$.

2. $\dfrac{x(x + a)(x + 2a)}{3a} - \dfrac{x(x + a)(2x + a)}{6a}$.

3. $\dfrac{1}{b}\left(\dfrac{1}{a - b} - \dfrac{1}{a + 2b}\right) - \dfrac{1}{a^2 + ab - 2b^2}$.

4. $\left(\dfrac{x + y}{x - y}\right)^2 - \left(\dfrac{x - y}{x + y}\right)^2$.

5. $\dfrac{2}{x-1}+\dfrac{2}{x+1}-\dfrac{4x}{x^2-x+1}$.

6. $\left(\dfrac{x^2}{1-x^4}+\dfrac{2x^4}{1-x^8}\right)\div\left(\dfrac{x^2+1}{x}\right)^2$.

7. $\dfrac{1}{x}-\dfrac{1}{(x+1)^2}-\dfrac{2}{x+1}+\dfrac{x}{1+x+x^2}$.

8. $\dfrac{1+x^3}{1+2x+2x^2+x^3}$.

9. $\dfrac{2x^3-9x^2+27}{3x^3-81x+162}$.

10. $\dfrac{a}{b}-\dfrac{(a^2-b^2)x}{b^2}+\dfrac{a(a^2-b^2)x^2}{b^2(b+ax)}$.

11. $\left\{\dfrac{x^4-a^4}{x^2-2ax+a^2}\div\dfrac{x^2+ax}{x-a}\right\}\times\dfrac{x^5-a^2x^3}{x^3+a^3}\div\left(\dfrac{x}{a}-\dfrac{a}{x}\right)$.

12. $\dfrac{a^2-x^2}{a^2+ax+x^2}\div\dfrac{\left(1-\dfrac{x}{a}\right)^3\left(1+\dfrac{x}{a}\right)^3}{a^3-x^3}$.

13. $\dfrac{x^4-2x^2+1}{3x^5-10x^3+15x-8}$.

14. $\dfrac{a^3+a(1+a)y+y^2}{a^4-y^2}$.

15. $\dfrac{1}{a}+\dfrac{2}{a+1}+\dfrac{3}{a+2}-\dfrac{\dfrac{4}{a}}{1+\dfrac{1}{a}}$.

16. $\dfrac{x+3}{2x^2+9x+9}+\dfrac{1}{2}\cdot\dfrac{1}{2x-3}-\dfrac{1}{x-\dfrac{9}{4x}}$.

17. $\dfrac{2}{x^3+x^2+x+1}-\dfrac{2}{x^3-x^2+x-1}$.

18. $\dfrac{1-a^2}{(1+ax)^2-(a+x)^2}\div\dfrac{1}{2}\left(\dfrac{1}{1-x}+\dfrac{1}{1+x}\right)$.

19. $\dfrac{2x^3-x^2-2x+1}{x^3-3x+2}$.

20. $\dfrac{x^2-6x+8}{4x^3-21x^2+15x+20}$.

21. $\dfrac{2a}{(x-2a)^2}-\dfrac{x-a}{x^2-5ax+6a^2}+\dfrac{2}{x-3a}$.

22. $\dfrac{1}{2}\left(\dfrac{a^2+x^2}{a^2-x^2}\right)-\dfrac{1}{2}\cdot\dfrac{a+x}{a-x}-\left(\dfrac{a}{a+x}\right)^2$.

23. $\dfrac{x}{2}\left(\dfrac{1}{x-y}-\dfrac{1}{x+y}\right)\times\dfrac{x^2-y^2}{x^2y+xy^2}\div\dfrac{1}{x+y}$.

24. $\dfrac{1}{x+y}\div\left[\dfrac{y}{2}\left(\dfrac{1}{x+y}+\dfrac{1}{x-y}\right)\times\dfrac{x^2-y^2}{x^2y+xy^2}\right]$.

25. $\left(3x-5-\dfrac{2}{x}\right)\left(3x+5-\dfrac{2}{x}\right)\div\left(x-\dfrac{4}{x}\right).$

26. $\left\{\dfrac{2}{x}-\dfrac{1}{a+x}+\dfrac{1}{a-x}\right\}\div\left(\dfrac{a+x}{a-x}-\dfrac{a-x}{a+x}\right).$

27. $\dfrac{1}{2x-1}-\dfrac{2x-\dfrac{1}{2x}}{4x^2-1}.$

28. $\left(b+\dfrac{ab}{b-a}\right)\left(b-\dfrac{ab}{a+b}\right)\left(\dfrac{b^2-a^2}{b^2+a^2}\right).$

29. $\left\{\dfrac{b+\dfrac{a-b}{1+ab}}{1-\dfrac{(a-b)b}{1+ab}}-\dfrac{a-\dfrac{a-b}{1-ab}}{1-\dfrac{a(a-b)}{1-ab}}\right\}\div\left(\dfrac{a}{b}-\dfrac{b}{a}\right).$

30. $\dfrac{\dfrac{x^2+y^2}{y}-x}{\dfrac{1}{y}-\dfrac{1}{x}}\times\dfrac{x^2-y^2}{x^3+y^3}.$

31. $\dfrac{2\left(x^2-\dfrac{1}{4}\right)}{2x+1}+\dfrac{1}{2}.$

32. $\dfrac{a+\dfrac{b-a}{1+ab}}{1-\dfrac{a(b-a)}{1+ab}}\times\dfrac{\dfrac{x+y}{1-xy}-y}{1+\dfrac{y(x+y)}{1-xy}}.$

33. $\dfrac{\dfrac{a+b}{a-b}+\dfrac{a-b}{a+b}}{\dfrac{a-b}{a+b}-\dfrac{a+b}{a-b}}\times\dfrac{ab^3-a^3b}{a^2+b^2}.$

Simplify the following fractions :

34. $\dfrac{(1-x^2)(1-x^3)}{x(1+x)(1-x)^2}-\dfrac{x^3+\dfrac{1}{x^3}}{x^2+\dfrac{1}{x^2}-1}.$

35. $\left\{x^3-\dfrac{1}{x^3}-3\left(x-\dfrac{1}{x}\right)\right\}\div\left(x-\dfrac{1}{x}\right).$

36. $\dfrac{1+\dfrac{1}{m}}{\dfrac{1}{m}}\times\dfrac{\dfrac{1}{m}}{m^2+\dfrac{1}{m}}\div\dfrac{\dfrac{1}{m}}{m-1+\dfrac{1}{m}}.$

37. $\dfrac{\dfrac{x}{y}+\dfrac{y}{x}-1}{\dfrac{x^2}{y^2}+\dfrac{x}{y}+1}\times\dfrac{1+\dfrac{y}{x}}{x-y}\div\dfrac{1+\dfrac{y^3}{x^3}}{\dfrac{x^2}{y}-\dfrac{y^2}{x}}.$

38. $\dfrac{\left(\dfrac{3x+x^3}{1+3x^2}\right)^2-1}{\dfrac{3x^2-x}{3x^3-1}+1} \div \dfrac{\dfrac{9}{x^2}-\dfrac{33-x^2}{3x^2+1}}{\dfrac{3}{x^2}-\dfrac{2(x^2+3)}{(x^3-x)^2}}.$

39. $\dfrac{1}{a^2-2}-\dfrac{2}{a^2-1}+\dfrac{2}{a^2+1}-\dfrac{1}{a^2+2}.$

40. $\dfrac{1}{6m-2n}+\dfrac{1}{3m+2n}-\dfrac{3}{6m+2n}.$

41. $\dfrac{3}{4(1-x)^2}+\dfrac{3}{8(1-x)}+\dfrac{1}{8(1+x)}+\dfrac{x-1}{4(1+x^2)}.$

42. $\dfrac{4}{9(x-2)}+\dfrac{5}{9(x+1)}-\dfrac{1}{3(x+1)^2}-\dfrac{1}{x+2+\dfrac{1}{x}}.$

43. $\left(\dfrac{x^2}{y}+\dfrac{y^2}{x}\right)\left(\dfrac{1}{y^2-x^2}\right)-\dfrac{y}{x^2+xy}+\dfrac{x}{xy-y^2}.$

44. $\dfrac{x^2-(y-z)^2}{(x+z)^2-y^2}+\dfrac{y^2-(z-x)^2}{(x+y)^2-z^2}+\dfrac{z^2-(x-y)^2}{(y+z)^2-x^2}.$

45. $\dfrac{x^2-(y-2z)^2}{(2z+x)^2-y^2}+\dfrac{y^2-(2z-x)^2}{(x+y)^2-4z^2}+\dfrac{4z^2-(x-y)^2}{(y+2z)^2-x^2}.$

46. $\dfrac{(x-y)(y-z)+(y-z)(z-x)+(z-x)(x-y)}{x(z-x)+y(x-y)+z(y-z)}.$

47. $\dfrac{a-b-c}{(a-b)(a-c)}+\dfrac{b-c-a}{(b-c)(b-a)}+\dfrac{c-a-b}{(c-a)(c-b)}.$

48. $\dfrac{c+a}{(a-b)(a-c)}+\dfrac{a+b}{(b-c)(b-a)}+\dfrac{b+c}{(c-a)(c-b)}.$

49. $\dfrac{x^2-(2y-3z)^2}{(3z+x)^2-4y^2}+\dfrac{4y^2-(3z-x)^2}{(x+2y)^2-9z^2}+\dfrac{9z^2-(x-2y)^2}{(2y+3z)^2-x^2}.$

50. $\dfrac{9y^2-(4z-2x)^2}{(2x+3y)^2-16z^2}+\dfrac{16z^2-(2x-3y)^2}{(3y+4z)^2-4x^2}+\dfrac{4x^2-(3y-4z)^2}{(4z+2x)^2-9y^2}.$

51. $\dfrac{\dfrac{1}{x}-\dfrac{x+a}{x^2+a^2}}{\dfrac{1}{a}-\dfrac{a+x}{a^2+x^2}}+\dfrac{\dfrac{1}{x}-\dfrac{x-a}{x^2+a^2}}{\dfrac{1}{a}-\dfrac{a-x}{a^2+x^2}}.$

52. $\dfrac{(x+a)(x+b)-(y+a)(y+b)}{x-y}-\dfrac{(x-a)(y-b)-(x-b)(y-a)}{a-b}.$

53. $\left(\frac{a+x}{a^2-ax+x^2}-\frac{a-x}{a^2+ax+x^2}\right)\div\left(\frac{a^2+x^2}{a^3-x^3}-\frac{a^2-x^2}{a^3+x^3}\right).$

54. $\dfrac{\frac{x-1}{3}+\frac{x-1}{x-2}}{\frac{x+2}{4}+\frac{x+2}{x-3}}\div\dfrac{\frac{x+3}{7}-\frac{x+3}{x+4}}{\frac{x-2}{3}+\frac{x-2}{x-1}}.$

55. $\dfrac{x-2+\frac{6}{x+3}}{x-4+\frac{12}{x+3}}\times\dfrac{\frac{x+3}{4}-\frac{x+3}{x+1}}{\frac{x-3}{7}+\frac{x-3}{x-4}}.$

56. $(x+2)\left\{1+\frac{6(x+2)}{x^2-x-6}\right\}\left\{1-\frac{5(x+1)}{x^2+3x+2}\right\}.$

57. $(1+a)^2\div\left\{1+\dfrac{a}{1-a+\frac{a}{1+a+a^2}}\right\}.$

58. $\dfrac{\{ax^2+(b-c)x-f\}^2-\{ax^2+(b+c)x-f\}^2}{\{ax^2+(b+e)x-f\}^2-\{ax^2+(b-e)x-f\}^2}.$

MISCELLANEOUS EXAMPLES IV

[*The following Examples for revision are arranged in groups under different headings: each group illustrates one or more of the principal rules and processes already discussed and for the most part the Examples present more variety and difficulty than those of the same type which have appeared in previous exercises.*]

Substitution and Brackets

1. Find the value of $\dfrac{a+\sqrt{a^2+b^2}}{a^3-2b(a^2-b^2)}$ when $a=-4, b=-3$.
2. When $a=1,\ b=-1,\ c=2$ evaluate the expression $\sqrt{3a^3(b-c)+3b^3(c-a)+3c^3(a-b)}$.
3. Simplify $a(b-c)^3-a(b-c)(2b^2-bc+2c^2)+(ab+ac)(b^2-c^2)$; and find its value when $a=1, b=2, c=3$.
4. Find the value of $\sqrt[3]{\{5(b^2-c^2)-a^2\}}+\sqrt[4]{3\{a(a^2-c^2)-1\}}$ when $a=4, b=5, c=3$.
5. Find the value of $\sqrt{(x^2+y^2+z)(x-y-3z)}\div\sqrt[3]{xy^3z^2}$ when $x=-1, y=-3, z=1$.

6. When $a=0, b=2, x=1, y=-3, z=5$, find the numerical value of

(1) $(x-y)^3-3a(x-y)^2+3b(x^3-y^3)$;

(2) $(x-a)^3-b^2(x-y+z)+\sqrt{(bx^2-axy+y^2+z^2)}$.

7. If $x=6, y=7, z=8$, find the value of

(1) $x\left\{\frac{x}{7}-\frac{2}{3}\left(\frac{y}{4}+1\right)\right\}-\frac{2}{7}\left\{y(x+1)+\frac{1}{2}(x^2-2y)-\frac{7x}{3}\right\}$;

(2) $x\left\{y\left(z-\frac{1}{z}\right)\right\}-\frac{y}{z}\left\{y-3\left(\frac{x}{3}-xz^2\right)\right\}-2xz\left\{-y\left(1+\frac{y}{2xz^2}\right)\right\}$.

8. Evaluate $\frac{2a-b\{c-a(b-c)\}}{a^2(b+c)+b^2(c+a)}\cdot\sqrt{\frac{a+bc}{b^3+4ac}}$,

when $a=2, b=-1, c=1$.

9. Find the value of

$\frac{a-[b-\{a-(b-c)\}-\sqrt{2a^2+b^2+c^2}]}{\sqrt{c^4+a^2b^2+2a^3c}}$, when $a=-1, b=5, c=3$.

10. When $a=4, b=-2, c=\frac{3}{2}, d=-1$, find the value of

(1) $a^3-b^3-(a-b)^3-11(3b+2c)\left(2c^2-\frac{d^2}{2}\right)$;

(2) $\sqrt[3]{4c^2-a(a-2b-d)}-\sqrt[3]{b^4c+11b^3d^2}$.

11. Find the value of $l-m-3\left[\left\{l-m+lm\left(\frac{1}{l}+\frac{1}{m}\right)\right\}^2-4l^2\right]$ when

$l=\frac{2}{3}, m=-\frac{1}{3}$.

12. When $a=1, b=-\frac{1}{2}, c=0$, evaluate

$$\frac{a-\left[b-c-\left\{2a-2b-\frac{1}{2}(3c-b)\right\}\right]}{a-\cfrac{b}{c-\cfrac{1}{a}}}.$$

13. Simplify

$42\left\{\frac{4x-3y}{6}-\frac{3}{7}\left(x-\frac{4}{3}y\right)\right\}-56\left\{\frac{1}{7}(3x-2y)-\frac{3}{8}\left(\frac{16}{3}x-y\right)\right\}$; and

find its value when $x=\frac{1}{6}, y=-\frac{3}{2}$.

14. If $x = 6, y = 7, z = 8$, find the value of

(1) $\frac{z}{x}\left\{y-\left(2z-\frac{x}{z}\right)\right\}-\frac{y}{z}\left[\frac{z^2}{x}-3\left\{1+\frac{2z^3}{3xy}\right\}+\frac{x}{2}\right]$;

(2) $3y\left\{\frac{2yz}{3}-\left(\frac{y}{5}-1\right)\right\}+\frac{y^2}{5}\left[3-z\left\{10-\frac{x}{2}(y-7)\right\}\right]$.

Resolution into Factors

(*On Arts.* 128-132)

Resolve into two or more factors:

15. $x^2 + 21x + 108$.

16. $a^2 + 6a - 91$.

17. $x^2 - 20xy + 96y^2$.

18. $a^2b^2 - 14ab - 51$.

19. $c^3 + c^2 - 156c$.

20. $m^2n - 6mn^2 + 9n^3$.

21. $p^4 - p^2q^2 - 56q^4$.

22. $d^4 - 4d^2c^2 - 45c^4$.

23. $x^3y - x^2y^2 - 42xy^3$.

24. $m^2 + 28m + 195$.

25. $210 - a - a^2$.

26. $57 + 16pq - p^2q^2$.

27. $x^4 + 27x^2 + 176$.

28. $a^4 + 7a^2 - 98$.

29. $c^2 + 54c + 729$.

30. $72 + xy - x^2y^2$.

31. $a^4 + 9a^2x^2 + 14x^4$.

32. $p^2 - 3pq - 108q^2$.

33. $2a^6 + 2a^3 - 264$.

34. $x^4 - 2x^3 - 63x^2$.

35. $b^2c^2 + 5bc - 84$.

36. $z^2 + 34z + 289$.

37. $a^2 - 22ac + 57c^2$.

38. $y^3z + 6y^2z - 91yz$.

39. $2 + x^3 - 3x^6$.

40. $2a^2b^2 + ab - 15$.

41. $9p^2 - 24p + 16$.

42. $35 + 12mn + m^2n^2$.

43. $119 - 10c - c^2$.

44. $6x^3 - 5x^4 + x^5$.

45. $6m^2 + 7m - 3$.

46. $4a^2 - 8ab - 5b^2$.

47. $6p^2 - 13pq + 2q^2$.

48. $20x^2 - 9xz - 20z^2$.

49. $8x^4 + 2x^2 - 15$.

50. $12y^2 - 30y + 12$.

51. $12(a^2b^2 - 1) + 7ab$.

52. $2(a^4b^2 + 5) - 9a^2b$.

53. $21x^2 + 2y(5x - 8y)$.

54. $3(6m^2 - 5m^2) + 17mn$.

(On Arts. 133-137)

Resolve into two or more factors:

55. $c^2 - a^2 - b^2 + 2ab$.

56. $a^2 + 2bc - b^2 - c^2$.

57. $125x^3 + 27y^3$.

58. $a^3b^3 + 343$.

59. $512b^3 - a^6$.

60. $a^2 - 4(x - y)^2$.

61. $2mn + m^2 - 1 + n^2$.

62. $8c^4 - 2c^2(d + c)^2$.

63. $(a^2b^2 - 1)^2 - x^2 + 2xy - y^3$.

64. $1 - 64m^6$.

65. $p^3 + 1000\,p^3q^3$.

66. $6561 - a^4$.

67. $x^4 - 2x^2 - y^2 - z^2 + 2yz + 1$.

68. $a^2 - 16(b - c)^2$.

69. $c - d - 4(c - d)^3$.

70. $p^2 - 16q^2 + p - 4q$.

71. $2 + 128(a - b)^3$.

72. $x + 3y + x^3 + 27y^3$.

(*Miscellaneous Factors*)

Resolve into two or more factors:

73. $x^3 + x^2y + xy^2 + y^3$.

74. $acx^2 + bcx - adx - bd$.

75. $14 - 5a - a^2$.

76. $98x^4 - 7x^2y^2 - y^4$.

77. $51 - 14a - a^2$.

78. $1 - (m^2 + p^2) - 2mp$.

79. $ab(x^2 + 1) - x(a^2 + b^2)$.

80. $9b^2 - 6bc - 16 + c^2$.

81. $x^2c^3 - c^3 + x^2 - 1$.

82. $3x^2 - 2ab - x(b - 6a)$.

83. $m^3 - n^3 - (x^2 - mn)(m - n)$.

84. $a(b^2 + c^2 - a^2) + b(a^2 + c^2 - b^2)$.

85. $x^7 - x^3 + 8x^4 - 8$.

86. Express in factors the square root of

$$(x^2 + 8x + 7)(2x^2 - x - 3)(2x^2 + 11x - 21)$$

87. Find the expression whose square is $(2x^2 - xy - 15y^2)(4x^2 - 25y^2)(2x^2 - 11xy + 15y^2)$.

Highest Common Factor and Lowest Common Multiple

88. Find the lowest common multiple of $13ab^2(x^3 - 3a^2x + 2a^3)$, $65a^3b(x^2 + ax - 2a^2)$, $25b^3(x^2 - a^2)^2$.

89. Find the highest common factor of $2(x^4 + 9) - 5x^2(x + 1)$, $2x^3(2x - 9) + 81(x - 1)$.

90. Find the expression of lowest dimensions which is divisible by each of the following expressions:
$(2x^4 + 4x^3)(x^2 + 2x - 8)$, $(2x^3 - 4x^2)(x^2 - 2x - 8)$, $(x^2 - 4x)(x^2 + 2x - 8)$.

91. Find the H.C.F. and the L.C.M. of the three expressions $a(a + c) - b(b + c)$, $b(b + a) - c(c + a)$, $c(c + b) - a(a + b)$.

92. Find the divisor of highest dimensions of the expressions $(a + b)(a - b) + c(c - 2a)$, $(a + c)(a - c) + b(b + 2a)$.

93. Find the expression of lowest dimensions such that the L.C.M. of it and $2a^2 - 3ab + b^2$ is

$$2a^4 - 3a^3b - a^2b^2 + 3ab^3 - b^4.$$

94. Show that $x^2 - 4y^2$ is the H.C.F. of the expressions

$$x^4 - 3x^2y^2 - 4y^4, x^6 - 64y^6$$

and $x^5 + 32y^5 - 8x^3y^2 + 2x^4y + 16xy^4 - 16x^2y^3$.

95. Find the lowest common multiple of

$(a-c)^2 - (b-c)^2, a^2 + b^2 - 2ac - 2bc + 2ab, a^4 - b^4$.

96. Show that the lowest common multiple of

$$a(a-b)^2 - ac^2, a^2b - b(b-c)^2,$$

$(a+c)^2c - b^2c$ is $abc\,(a^4 + b^4 + c^4 - 2b^2c^2 - 2c^2a^2 - 2a^2b^2)$.

97. Prove that $x^4 - 15x^3 + 75x^2 - 145x + 84$ and

$x^4 - 17x^3 + 101x^2 - 247x + 210$ have the same H.C.F. and L.C.M as

$x^4 - 13x^3 + 53x^2 - 83x + 42$

and $x^4 - 19x^3 + 131x^2 - 389x + 420$.

Simplification of Fractions

Simplify

98. $\dfrac{1+x+x^2}{1-x^3} + \dfrac{x-x^2}{(1-x)^3}$.

99. $\dfrac{2x-7}{(x-3)^2} - \dfrac{2(x+2)}{x^2-9}$.

100. $\dfrac{1}{2x^2 - \dfrac{1}{2}} + \dfrac{1}{(2x+1)^2}$.

101. $\dfrac{(x+1)^3 - (x-1)^3}{3x^3 + x}$.

102. $\dfrac{1}{(1-x)^2} + \dfrac{2}{1-x^2} + \dfrac{1}{(1+x)^2}$.

103. $\dfrac{(x^3 - 2x)^2 - (x^2-2)^2}{(x-1)(x+1)(xt-2)^2}$.

104. $\dfrac{1}{6x-2} - \dfrac{1}{2\left(x - \dfrac{1}{3}\right)} - \dfrac{1}{1-3x}$.

105. $\dfrac{x}{9} + \dfrac{2}{3} + \dfrac{4}{x-6} - \dfrac{2}{3} \cdot \dfrac{1}{1 - \dfrac{6}{x}}$.

106. $\dfrac{x}{x^2-y^2} - \dfrac{1}{x-y} + \dfrac{1}{x+y} + \dfrac{1}{x} - \dfrac{1}{y} + \dfrac{x^2 - xy + y^2}{xy(x-y)}$.

107. $\left(x - y - \dfrac{4y^2}{x-y}\right)\left(x + y - \dfrac{4x^2}{x+y}\right) \div \left\{3(x+y) - \dfrac{8xy}{x-y}\right\}$.

108. $\dfrac{a^4 + b^4 + ab(a^2+b^2)}{(a+b)^2} - \dfrac{a^4 + b^4 - ab(a^2+b^2)}{(a-b)^2} + \dfrac{12a^2b^2}{(a+b)^2 - (a-b)^2}$.

109. $\dfrac{(ac+bd)^3 - (ad+bc)^3}{(a-b)(c-d)} - \dfrac{(ac+bd)^3 + (ad+bc)^3}{(a+b)(c+d)}$.

110. $\left[\left(\frac{x}{a}\right)^2+\left(\frac{z-x}{b}\right)^2\right]\div\left[\frac{z^2}{a^2+b^2}+\frac{a^2+b^2}{a^2b^2}\left(x-\frac{za^2}{a^2+b^2}\right)^2\right].$

111. $\frac{x^4-(x-1)^2}{(x^2+1)^2-x^2}+\frac{x^2-(x^2-1)^2}{x^2(x+1)^2-1}+\frac{x^2(x-1)^2-1}{x^4-(x+1)^2}.$

112. $\dfrac{\frac{1+x}{1-x}+\frac{4x}{1+x^2}+\frac{8x}{1-x^2}-\frac{1-x}{1+x}}{\frac{1+x^2}{1-x^2}+\frac{4x^2}{1+x^4}-\frac{1-x^2}{1+x^2}}.$

113. $\left\{\dfrac{f}{g-\frac{g^2}{f}}+\dfrac{g}{f-\frac{f^2}{g}}\right\}\times\dfrac{1}{\frac{f^2}{g}-\frac{g^2}{f}}.$

114. $\dfrac{1}{x-\dfrac{2}{x+\frac{1}{2}}}\times\dfrac{1}{2+\frac{1}{x}}\div\dfrac{x}{2x-\frac{x+4}{x+1}}.$

115. $\dfrac{x}{1+\dfrac{x}{1-x+\frac{x}{1+x}}}\div\dfrac{1+x+x^2}{1+3x+3x^2+2x^3}.$

116. $\frac{ab}{a+b}\left(3c+\frac{b}{a}\right)-\frac{b^2}{(a+b)^2}(x^2+b^2)-2a\left(\frac{b}{a+b}\right)^3.$

117. $\dfrac{\frac{(a+b)^2+(a-b)^2}{b-a}-(a+b)}{\frac{1}{b-a}-\frac{1}{a+b}}\div\dfrac{(a+b)^3+(b-a)^3}{(a+b)^2-(a-b)^2}.$

118. $\left\{\frac{c-b}{(a-b)(a-c)}-\frac{c-a}{(b-c)(b-a)}+\frac{b-a}{(c-a)(c-b)}\right\}\div$
$\frac{2(a^2+b^2+c^2-bc-ca-ab)}{(a-b)(b-c)(c-a)}.$

23

HARDER EQUATIONS

186. IN this chapter we propose to give a miscellaneous collection of equations. Some of these will serve as a useful exercise for revision of the methods already explained in previous chapters; but we also add others presenting more difficulty, the solution of which will often be facilitated by some special artifice.

The following examples worked in full will sufficiently illustrate the most useful methods.

Example 1. Solve $\frac{6x-3}{2x+7} = \frac{3x-2}{x+5}$.

Multiplying up, we have

$$(6x-3)(x+5) = (3x-2)(2x+7).$$

$$6x^2 + 27x - 15 = 6x^2 + 17x - 14;$$

$$\therefore \quad 10x = 1;$$

$$\therefore \quad x = \frac{1}{10}.$$

NOTE. By a simple reduction many equations can be brought to the form in which the above equation is given. When this is the case, the necessary simplification is readily completed by "multiplying up" or "multiplying across", as it is sometimes called.

Example 2. Solve $\frac{8x+23}{20} - \frac{5x+2}{3x+4} = \frac{2x+3}{5} - 1$.

Multiply by 20, and we have

$$8x + 23 - \frac{20(5x+2)}{3x+4} = 8x + 12 - 20.$$

By transposition, $31 = \frac{20(5x+2)}{3x+4}$.

Multiplying across, $93x + 124 = 20(5x+2)$.

$$84 = 7x;$$

$$\therefore \quad x = 12.$$

When two or more fractions have the same denominator they should be taken together and simplified.

Example 3. Solve $\dfrac{13-2x}{x+3}+\dfrac{23x+8\frac{1}{3}}{4x+5}=\dfrac{16-\frac{1}{4}x}{x+3}+4.$

By transposition, we have

$$\frac{23x+8\frac{1}{3}}{4x+5}-4=\frac{16-\frac{1}{4}x-13+2x}{x+3}.$$

$$\therefore \qquad \frac{7x-\frac{35}{3}}{4x+5}=\frac{3+\frac{7x}{4}}{x+3}.$$

Multiplying across, we have

$$7x^2-\frac{35x}{3}+21x-35=12x+7x^2+15+\frac{35x}{4}.$$

$$-\frac{137x}{12}=50;$$

$$\therefore \qquad x=-\frac{600}{137}.$$

Example 4. Solve $\dfrac{x-8}{x-10}+\dfrac{x-4}{x-6}=\dfrac{x-5}{x-7}+\dfrac{x-7}{x-9}.$

This equation might be solved by clearing of fractions, but the work would be very laborious. The solution will be much simplified by proceeding as follows:

Transposing, $\dfrac{x-8}{x-10}-\dfrac{x-5}{x-7}=\dfrac{x-7}{x-9}-\dfrac{x-4}{x-6}.$

Simplifying each side *separately*, we have

$$\frac{(x-8)(x-7)-(x-5)(x-10)}{(x-10)(x-7)}=\frac{(x-7)(x-6)-(x-4)(x-9)}{(x-9)(x-6)};$$

$$\therefore \frac{x^2-15x+56-(x^2-15x+50)}{(x-10)(x-7)}=\frac{x^2-13x+42-(x^2-13x+36)}{(x-9)(x-6)};$$

$$\therefore \qquad \frac{6}{(x-10)(x-7)}=\frac{6}{(x-9)(x-6)}.$$

Hence, since the numerators are equal, the denominators must be equal;

that is, $\qquad (x-10)(x-7)=(x-9)(x-6),$

$$x^2-17x+70=x^2-15x+54;$$

$$\therefore \qquad 16=2x;$$

$$\therefore \qquad x=8.$$

The above equation may also be solved very neatly by the following artifice.

The equation may be written in the form

$$\frac{(x-10)+2}{x-10}+\frac{(x-6)+2}{x-6}=\frac{(x-7)+2}{x-7}+\frac{(x-9)+2}{x-9};$$

whence we have

$$1+\frac{2}{x-10}+1+\frac{2}{x-6}=1+\frac{2}{x-7}+1+\frac{2}{x-9};$$

which gives $\dfrac{1}{x-10}+\dfrac{1}{x-6}=\dfrac{1}{x-7}+\dfrac{1}{x-9}.$

Transposing, $\dfrac{1}{x-10}-\dfrac{1}{x-7}=\dfrac{1}{x-9}-\dfrac{1}{x-6};$

$$\therefore \qquad \frac{3}{(x-10)(x-7)}=\frac{3}{(x-9)(x-6)}.$$

and the solution may be completed as before.

Example 5. Solve $\dfrac{5x-64}{x-13}-\dfrac{2x-11}{x-6}=\dfrac{4x-55}{x-14}-\dfrac{x-6}{x-7}.$

We have $5+\dfrac{1}{x-13}-\left(2+\dfrac{1}{x-6}\right)=4+\dfrac{1}{x-14}-\left(1+\dfrac{1}{x-7}\right);$

$$\therefore \qquad \frac{1}{x-13}-\frac{1}{x-6}=\frac{1}{x-14}-\frac{1}{x-7}.$$

The solution may now be completed as before, and we obtain $x=10$.

EXAMPLES XXIII-a

Solve the following:

1. $\dfrac{x+4}{3x-8}=\dfrac{x+5}{3x-7}.$

2. $\dfrac{3x+1}{3(x-2)}=\dfrac{x-2}{x-1}.$

3. $\dfrac{7-5x}{1+x}=\dfrac{11-15x}{1+3x}.$

4. $\dfrac{3(7+6x)}{2+9x}=\dfrac{35+4x}{9+2x}.$

5. $\dfrac{6x+13}{15}=\dfrac{3x+5}{5x-25}=\dfrac{2x}{5}.$

6. $\dfrac{6x+8}{2x+1}-\dfrac{2x+38}{x+12}=1.$

7. $\dfrac{3x-1}{2x-1}-\dfrac{4x-2}{3x-1}=\dfrac{1}{6}.$

8. $\dfrac{x+25}{x-5}=\dfrac{2x+75}{2x-15}.$

9. $\dfrac{x}{x+2}+\dfrac{4}{x+6}=1.$

10. $\dfrac{6x+7}{9x+6}=\dfrac{1}{12}+\dfrac{5x-5}{12x+8}.$

11. $\dfrac{2x-5}{5}+\dfrac{x-3}{2x-15}=\dfrac{4x-3}{10}-1\dfrac{1}{10}.$

12. $\frac{4(x+3)}{9} = \frac{8x+37}{18} - \frac{7x-29}{5x-12}$.

13. $\frac{(2x-1)(3x+8)}{6x(x+4)} - 1 = 0$.

14. $\frac{2x+5}{5x+3} - \frac{2x+1}{5x+2} = 0$.

15. $\frac{4}{x+3} - \frac{2}{x+1} = \frac{5}{2x+6} - \frac{2\frac{1}{2}}{2x+2}$.

16. $\frac{7}{x-4} - \frac{60}{5x-30} = \frac{10\frac{1}{2}}{3x-12} - \frac{8}{x-6}$.

17. $\frac{3}{4-2x} + \frac{30}{8(1-x)} = \frac{3}{2-x} + \frac{5}{2-2x}$.

18. $\frac{25-\frac{x}{3}}{x+1} + \frac{16x+4\frac{1}{5}}{3x+2} = 5 + \frac{23}{x+1}$.

19. $\frac{30+6x}{x+1} + \frac{60+8x}{x+3} = 14 + \frac{48}{x+1}$.

20. $\frac{x}{x-2} - \frac{x+1}{x-1} = \frac{x-8}{x-6} - \frac{x-9}{x-7}$.

21. $\frac{x+5}{x+4} - \frac{x-6}{x-7} = \frac{x-4}{x-5} - \frac{x-15}{x-16}$.

22. $\frac{x-7}{x-9} - \frac{x-9}{x-11} = \frac{x-13}{x-15} - \frac{x-15}{x-17}$.

23. $\frac{x+3}{x+6} - \frac{x+6}{x+9} = \frac{x+2}{x+5} - \frac{x+5}{x+8}$.

24. $\frac{x+2}{x} + \frac{x-7}{x-5} - \frac{x+3}{x+1} = \frac{x-6}{x-4}$.

25. $\frac{4x-17}{x-4} + \frac{10x-13}{2x-3} = \frac{8x-30}{2x-7} + \frac{5x-4}{x-1}$.

26. $\frac{5x-8}{x-2} + \frac{6x-44}{x-7} - \frac{10x-8}{x-1} = \frac{x-8}{x-6}$.

27. $\frac{2x-3}{.3x-.4} = \frac{0.4x-0.6}{0.06x-0.07}$.

28. $\frac{x-2}{0.05} - \frac{x-4}{0.0625} = 56$.

29. $0.083(x-0.625) = 0.09(x-0.59375)$.

30. $(2x+1.5)(3x-2.25) = (2x-1.125)(3x+125)$.

31. $\frac{0.3x-1}{0.5x-.4} = \frac{0.5+1.2x}{2x-0.1}$.

32. $\frac{1-1.4x}{0.2+x} = \frac{7(x-1)}{0.1-0.5x}$.

33. $\frac{(0.3x-2)(0.3x-1)}{0.2x-1} - \frac{1}{6}(0.3x-2) = 0.4x-2$.

Literal Equations

187. In the equations we have discussed hitherto the coefficients have been numerical quantities, but equations often involve *literal* coefficients. [Art. 6.] These are supposed to be known, and will appear in the solution.

Example 1. Solve $(x+a)(x+b)-c(a+c)=(x-c)(x+c)+ab$.

Multiplying out, we have

$$x^2+ax+bx+ab-ac-c^2=x^2-c^2+ab;$$

whence $$ax+bx=ac,$$

$$(a+b)x=ac;$$

$$\therefore \qquad x=\frac{ac}{a+b}.$$

Example 2. Solve $\dfrac{a}{x-a}-\dfrac{b}{x-b}=\dfrac{a-b}{x-c}$.

Simplifying the left side, we have

$$\frac{a(x-b)-b(x-a)}{(x-a)(x-b)}=\frac{a-b}{x-c}.$$

$$\frac{(a-b)x}{(x-a)(x-b)}=\frac{a-b}{x-c};$$

$$\therefore \qquad \frac{x}{(x-a)(x-b)}=\frac{1}{x-c}.$$

Multiplying across, $x^2-cx=x^2-ax-bx+ab$,

$$ax+bx-cx=ab,$$

$$(a+b-c)x=ab;$$

$$\therefore \qquad x=\frac{ab}{a+b-c}.$$

EXAMPLES XXIII-b

Solve the equations:

1. $ax-2b=5bx-3a$.
2. $a^2(x-a)+b^2(x-b)=abx$.
3. $x^2+a^2=(b-x)^2$.
4. $(x-a)(x+b)=(x-a+b)^2$.
5. $a(x-2)+2x=6+a$.
6. $m^2(m-x)-mnx=n^2(n+x)$.
7. $(a+x)(b+x)=x(x-c)$.
8. $(a-b)(x-a)=(a-c)(x-b)$.
9. $\dfrac{2x+3a}{x+a}=\dfrac{2(3x+2a)}{3x+a}$.
10. $\dfrac{2(x-b)}{3x-c}=\dfrac{2x+b}{3(x-c)}$.

11. $\frac{1}{a}-\frac{1}{x}=\frac{1}{x}-\frac{1}{b}$.

12. $\frac{2}{3}\left(\frac{x}{a}+1\right)=\frac{3}{4}\left(\frac{x}{a}-1\right)$.

13. $\frac{a}{x}=c(a-b)+\frac{b}{x}$.

14. $\frac{9a}{b}-\frac{3x}{b}=\frac{4b}{a}-\frac{2x}{a}$.

15. $\frac{x-a}{b-x}=\frac{x-b}{a-x}$.

16. $\frac{x-a}{2}=\frac{(x-b)^2}{2x-a}$.

17. $\frac{1}{4}x(x-a)-\left(\frac{x+a}{2}\right)^2=\frac{2a}{3}\left(x-\frac{a}{2}\right)$.

18. $(a+b)x^2-a(bx+a^2)=bx(x-a)+ax(x-b)$.

19. $b(a+x)-(a+x)(b-x)=x^2+\frac{bc^2}{a}$.

20. $b(a-x)-\frac{a}{b}(b+x)^2+ab\left(\frac{x}{b}+1\right)^2=0$.

21. $x^2+a(2a-x)-\frac{3b^2}{4}=\left(x-\frac{b}{2}\right)^2+a^2$.

22. $(2x-a)\left(x+\frac{2a}{3}\right)=4x\left(\frac{a}{3}-x\right)-\frac{1}{2}(a-4x)(2a+3x)$.

23. $\frac{x-a+b}{x-a}+\frac{x-b}{x-2b}=\frac{x}{x-b}+\frac{x-a}{x-a-b}$.

24. $\left(\frac{x}{a}-3\right)\left(\frac{3x}{a}-1\right)-\frac{1}{a^2}(x-2a)(2x-a)=\left(\frac{x}{a}-1\right)^2-1$.

25. $\frac{b(x+a)}{x^2-b^2}+\frac{2x+3b-a}{x+b}=\frac{2(x^2+bx-b^2)}{x^2-b^2}$.

Example 3. Solve $ax+by=c$ ...(1),

$a'x+b'y=c'$ ...(2).

The notation here first used is one that the student will frequently meet with in the course of his reading. In the first equation we choose certain letters as the coefficients of x and y, and we choose *corresponding letters with accents* to denote corresponding quantities in the second equation. There is no necessary connection between the value of a and a', and they are as different as a and b; but it is often convenient to use the same letter thus slightly varied to mark some common meaning of such letters, and thereby assist the memory. Thus a, a' have a common property as being coefficients of x; b, b' as being coefficients of y.

Sometimes instead of accents letters are used with a *suffix* such as $x_1, a_2, a_3; b_1, b_2, b_3$, etc.

To return to the equations $ax+by=c$ ...(1),

$a'x+b'y=c'$ ...(2).

Multiply (1) by b' and (2) by b. Thus

$$ab'x + bb'y = b'c,$$

$$a'bx + bb'y = bc';$$

by subtraction, $(ab' - a'b)x = b'c - bc'$;

$$\therefore \qquad x = \frac{b'c - bc'}{ab' - a'b} \qquad \text{...(3).}$$

As previously explained in Art. 104, we might obtain y by substituting this value of x in *either* of the equations (1) and (2); but y is more conveniently found by eliminating x, as follows:

Multiplying (1) by a' and (2) by a, we have

$$aa'x + a'by = a'c,$$

$$aa'x + ab'y = ac';$$

by subtraction, $(a'b - ab')y = a'c - ac'$;

$$\therefore \qquad y = \frac{a'c - ac'}{a'b - ab'},$$

or, changing signs in the terms of the denominator so as to have the same denominator as in (3),

$$y = \frac{ac' - a'c}{ab' - a'b} \text{ and } x = \frac{b'c - bc'}{ab' - a'b}.$$

Example 4. Solve $\dfrac{x-a}{c-a} + \dfrac{y-b}{c-b} = 1$ ...(1),

$$\frac{x+a}{c} + \frac{y-a}{a-b} = \frac{a}{c} \qquad \text{...(2).}$$

From (1) by clearing of fractions, we have

$$x(c-b) - a(c-b) + y(c-a) - b(c-a) = (c-a)(c-b),$$

$$x(c-b) + y(c-a) = ac - ab + bc - ab + c^2 - ac - bc + ab,$$

$$x(c-b) + y(c-a) = c^2 - ab \qquad \text{...(3).}$$

Again, from (2), we have

$$x(a-b) + a(a-b) + cy - ca = a(a-b)$$

$$x(a-b) + cy = ac \qquad \text{...(4).}$$

Multiply (3) by c and (4) by $c - a$ and subtract,

$$x\{c(c-b) - (c-a)(a-b)\} = c^3 - abc - ac(c-a),$$

$$x(c^2 - ac + a^2 - ab) = c(c^2 - ab - ac + a^2),$$

$$\therefore \qquad x = c;$$

and therefore from (4) $\quad y = b.$

EXAMPLES XXIII-c

Solve the equations:

1. $ax + by = l,\qquad bx + ay = m.$

2. $lx + my = n,\qquad px + qy = r.$

3. $ax = by,\qquad bx + ay = c.$

4. $ax + by = a^2,\qquad bx + ay = b^2.$

5. $x + ay = a',\qquad ax + a'y = 1.$

6. $px - qy = r,\qquad rx - py = q.$

7. $\frac{x}{a} + \frac{y}{b} = \frac{1}{ab},\qquad \frac{x}{a'} - \frac{y}{b'} = \frac{1}{a'b'}.$

8. $\frac{x}{a} - \frac{y}{b} = 0,\qquad bx + ay = 4ab.$

9. $\frac{3x}{a} + \frac{2y}{b} = 3,\qquad \frac{9x}{a} - \frac{6y}{b} = 3.$

10. $qx - rb = p(a - y),\qquad \frac{qx}{a} + r = p\left(1 + \frac{y}{b}\right).$

11. $\frac{x}{m} + \frac{y}{m'} = 1,\qquad \frac{x}{m'} - \frac{y}{m} = 1.$

12. $px + qy = 0,\qquad lx + my = n.$

13. $(a - b)x = (a + b)y,\qquad x + y = c.$

14. $(a - b)x + (a + b)y = 2a^2 - 2b^2,\qquad (a + b)x - (a - b)y = 4ab.$

15. $\frac{x}{a} + \frac{y}{b} = 1.\qquad \frac{x}{3a} + \frac{y}{6b} = \frac{2}{3}.$

16. $\frac{x}{a} + \frac{y}{b} = 2,\qquad \frac{x}{a'} = \frac{y}{b'}.$

17. $\frac{x}{a} - \frac{y}{b} = 1,\qquad \frac{x}{b} + \frac{y}{a} = \frac{a}{b}.$

18. $\frac{m}{l}x + \frac{l}{m}y = \left(\frac{l}{l} + \frac{1}{m}\right)(m^2 + l^2),$

$(x + y)(m^2 + l^2) = 2(m^3 + l^3) + ml(x + y).$

19. $bx + cy = a + b,$

$ax\left(\frac{1}{a - b} - \frac{1}{a + b}\right) + cy\left(\frac{1}{b - a} - \frac{1}{b + a}\right) = \frac{2a}{a + b}.$

20. $(a - b)x + (a + b)y = 2(a^2 - b^2),\ ax - by = a^2 + b^2.$

21. $x\left(a - b + \frac{ab}{a - b}\right) = y\left(a + b - \frac{ab}{a + b}\right),\ x + y = 2a^3.$

EXAMPLES XXIII-d

1. If $x = \dfrac{a+b}{a-b}$, find (i) a in terms of b and x, (ii) b in terms of a and x.

2. If $a = -\dfrac{bc}{b+c}$, find b in terms of a and c.

3. Make c the subject of the following formulae:

$$b = \frac{a+c}{2}, b = \sqrt{ac}, b = \frac{2ac}{a+c}.$$

4. The area and circumference of a circle are given by $A = \pi r^2, C = 2\pi r$. Find r in terms of A and r in terms of C.

5. The volume and surface of a sphere are given by $V = \frac{4}{3}\pi r^3$, $A = 4\pi r^2$. Find r (i) in terms of V, (ii) in terms of A.

6. The volume and surface of a cylinder are given by $V = \pi r^2 h$, $A = 2\pi r^2 + 2\pi rh$. Find h (i) in terms of V, π, r, (ii) in terms of A, π, r.

7. A method for determining the value of π consists of finding the surface area, radius and height of a cylinder and using the formula $A = 2\pi r^2 + 2\pi rh$. Arrange this formula so that the value of π can be easily calculated.

8. The volume and surface of a cone are given by $V = \frac{1}{3}\pi r^2 h$, $A = \pi r^2 + \pi rs$. Find r in terms of V, π, h and s in terms of A, π, r.

9. In No. 6. find V in terms of r, π, A.

10. The area of a trapezium is A sq. cm when the parallel sides are a cm and b cm in length and the distance between those sides is h cm, where $A = \frac{1}{2}h(a+b)$. Find (i) h in terms of A, a, b, (ii) a in terms of A, h, b.

11. Invent numerical problems in which your answers to Ex. 10 could be used.

12. The number of degrees in the angle of a regular n-sided figure is given by

$$N = 90\left(2 - \frac{4}{n}\right).$$

Find n in terms of N. Hence find the number of sides of a regular polygon if its interior angle is 144°.

13. The period of oscillation of a magnet is given by $t = 2\pi\sqrt{\dfrac{I}{MH}}$. Find I, M, H respectively in terms of the other letters.

14. T and V are connected by the formula $T = \dfrac{76V}{12V + 10.6m}$. Make V the subject of the formula.

15. Find T when $t = 2\pi\sqrt{\frac{la^3}{8T}}$.

16. If $v = k\left(1 - \frac{a}{b}\right)\sqrt{h}$, express a, h in terms of the other letters.

17. The amount at compound interest for n years on Rs. P at r% per annum is given by $A = P\left(1 + \frac{r}{100}\right)^n$. Make P, r respectively the subject of this formula.

18. Given that $x = \frac{3ay - 5bz}{3ay + 5bz}$, make a, b respectively the subject of the formula.

19. If $\frac{a}{b} = k$, express $\frac{4a - 5b}{\sqrt{18a^2 - 4b^2}}$ in terms of k.

20. If $A = \pi r^2, C = 2\pi r$, express (i) A in terms of C, (ii) C in terms of A.

21. If $V = \frac{4}{3}\pi r^3$, $A = 4\pi r^2$, express (i) V in terms of A, (ii) A in terms of V.

22. If $\frac{1}{u} + \frac{1}{v} = \frac{1}{f}$ and $u + v = s$, express s in terms of u and f only, and give the expression for s in terms of v and f only. Show that $s = \frac{uv}{f}$.

23. If $a - b = 5$, express $(a - 4)(a + 3)$ in terms of b.

24. If $a = 1 - \frac{1}{b}$ and $b = 1 + \frac{2}{c}$, express c in terms of b, and prove that $a + b + c = \frac{b^3 + 1}{b(b - 1)}$. (Oxf. Sch. Certif.)

25. Given that $p = \frac{1 + 4q}{q - 4}$, express $p + q$ as a fraction (i) in terms of p only, (ii) in terms of q only.

26. The two expressions $\frac{1}{6}\pi h\{a^2 + b^2 + (a + b)^2\}$ and $\frac{1}{3}\pi\{b^2(h + x) - a^2 x\}$ are found by different methods for the volume of a certain solid. Prove that they are equivalent provided that $\frac{b}{h + x} = \frac{a}{x}$. (Lond. Matric.)

27. The floor of a room is in the form of a rectangle, a dm long and b dm broad, but with one corner rounded off by a quadrant of a circle of radius r dm, r being less than both a and b. Show that the area A square dm is given by

$$A = ab - \left(1 - \frac{1}{4}\pi\right)r^2.$$

Change the subject of this formula so as to have an expression for r. Also, find an expression for b. (Cent. Welsh Bd.)

28. In a form consisting of m boys the average mark was a, and in another form of n boys the average mark was b. What was the average mark for the whole number of boys?

What should have been the average mark in the first form in order to make the average mark for the whole equal to c, the average mark in the second form being unaltered? (Oxf. and Camb. Sch. Certif.)

29. When an article costing Rs. C is sold for Rs. S, a profit of $P\%$ is made. Express each letter in terms of the other two.

30. A man can row upstream at a km an hour and downstream at b km an hour. He rows up to a certain point and then returns to his starting point, and finds that his average speed is s km an hour for the double journey. Express each of the letters in terms of the other two. Find the value of b if $a = 2$ and $s = 3$.

31. Given that $S = \frac{n}{2}\{2a + (n-1)d\}$, find a formula for d in terms of the other letters. If $S = 144a$ and $n = 12$, find the value of d in terms of a.

32. A man has at present a salary of Rs. S. He receives an increase of Rs. I every 2 years. What will be his salary in $2k$ years' time?

How long will he have to wait in order to receive a salary of Rs. T?

33. Plain envelopes cost x paise a dozen. Find a formula giving the cost, C paise, of a packet containing 11 envelopes each bearing a 10 paise stamp.

In a post office a packet of 11 stamped envelopes can be purchased for Rs. 1.21. Using the above formula, find the cost of a dozen plain envelopes.

34. The main petrol tank of a car holds m litres and the reserve tank holds r litres. The car will do x km to the litre. Find the longest journey, J km, which can be made by the car without refilling with petrol.

Find r if $J = 200$, $m = 6$ and $x = 25$.

35. The car mentioned in Ex. 34 starts off with its petrol tanks full and goes at a steady speed of y km an hour. h hours later, it runs completely out of petrol. Find a formula giving h in terms of m, r, x, y.

Find h if $J = 200$ and $y = 40$.

36. A jewel box is a cm long, b cm wide and c cm deep. Find the cost (in Rs.) of covering the outside of the sides and top with silver at Rs. s a square cm.

Find the length of the box if the total cost of covering a box 8 cm wide and 5 cm deep with silver at 30 paise a square cm is Rs. 78.

37. A room p dm long and q dm wide is carpeted so as to leave a border r cm wide between the edge of the carpet and the walls.

Find a formula for the number of square dm in this border; and verify that in the case where $p = 48, q = 36, r = 8$, the formula gives the difference between the areas of the floor and the carpet. (Scot. Leaving.)

38. The Horse Power of a car for taxation purposes is given by the formula $H = \frac{8}{125} nd^2$, where n is the number of cylinders and d cm is the diameter of each cylinder. Find the diameter of each cylinder of a 12 H.P. six-cylinder car.

39. At a cricket match a charge of Re 1 is made for entering the ground and a further charge of Rs. 2 is made for a seat. If N people are admitted to the ground and n people take seats, show that the total amount received, Rs. T, is given by $T = N + 2n$.

Write this formula so that n is the subject. Then find the number of people taking seats if 5000 enter the ground and the total amount received is Rs. 6000.

40. If the same temperature is expressed either by $F°$ Fahrenheit or $C°$ Centigrade we are told that $F - 32 = \frac{9}{5}C$. Verify that this formula holds good if 32° and 212° Fahrenheit are the same respectively as 0° and 100° Centigrade.

41. What Centigrade temperature is the normal temperature of the human body, namely 98.4° Fahrenheit?

42. Find the percentage profit if an article costing Rs. C is sold for Rs. S. Hence find the cost price if an article is sold for Rs. 190 at a gain of 25%.

43. (i) A telephone subscriber has to pay a certain sum Rs. R each quarter for rent and also 5 paise for each call. If a subscriber makes n calls in a given quarter, show that his total bill is B paise where $B = 100R + 5n$.

(ii) If the quarterly rent is Rs. 60 and his quarterly bill is Rs. 100, find how many calls he has made by transforming the formula of part (i) so that n is the subject.

44. In Ex. 43 (i), what is the average cost to the subscriber of each call? Show that if instead of keeping to the present arrangement he paid no rent, but paid p paise for each call, he would gain

$$\text{Rs. } \left\{R - \frac{(p-1)n}{100}\right\} \text{ each quarter.}$$

45. Income Tax is at 25 paise in the rupee. A man has an income of Rs. I. He is allowed Rs. 3600 free of tax, and also does not pay tax on P % of his income which he pays for insurance. Show that he pays Rs. T in tax where $400T = I(100 - P) - 360{,}000$.

46. In Ex. 45, find (*a*) the tax paid by a man who has an income of Rs. 10,000 and pays 20% of his income in insurance.

(b) The percentage of his income paid in insurance by a man having an income of Rs. 10,000 who pays Rs. 1500 in tax.

47. If an object is placed u cm from a spherical mirror of radius r cm and the image is v cm from the mirror, it is known that $\frac{1}{v}+\frac{1}{u}=\frac{2}{r}$. A boy is given a mirror of radius 3 cm for an experiment, and finds that when $u=2, v=5$; when $u=6, v=2$; when $u=4, v=2\frac{1}{2}$. Which of the three sets of results is accurate?

48. From the formula of Ex. 47, find when the image and object are coincident, that is, are at same distance from the mirror.

49. If the pressure of a given mass of gas is equivalent to that of p mm of mercury when its volume is v c.c. and its temperature is $t°$ Centigrade, it is known that $pv=R(t+273)$, where R is constant. Transform this equation to give t in terms of the other letters.

50. Using the formula of Ex. 49, find the volume occupied by a mass of gas at 77°C. If it occupies 200 c.c. at 27°C, the pressure remaining constant.

51. In an election, there are two candidates. The winner's majority is m_1% of the total poll, and m_2% of his own poll. Find what percentage the loser's poll is of the winner's poll, and prove that $(100+m_1)m_2=200m_1$. (Lond. Matric.)

52. If the diameter of the bolt circle in a coupling is D cm and the diameter of the bolts is d cm, we know that $D=hd+k$, and that $D=8\frac{1}{2}$ when $d=2$, $D=17\frac{1}{2}$ when $d=5$. Find the values of h and k, and the diameter of the bolt circle for 3 cm bolts.

53. (i) A man is employed to carry loads a km, returning each time to his starting point. On each journey, he carries a load of L kg. His speed unloaded is a km an hour and his speed loaded is $(a-kL)$ km an hour. Find his average speed, s km an hour.

(ii) Now find L in terms of a, k, s, and k in terms of L, a, s.

(iii) If $a=4$, $k=0.03$, $s=3$, find L.

54. The following formula occurs in connection with dynamos: $W=ab+cb+db^2$. If another value of W, namely W', is given by $W'=ab'+cb'+db'^2$, express d in terms of W, W', b, b'.

55. Two cars travel along a straight road in the same direction. The faster car, going at u km per hour, starts c km behind the slower car which goes at v km per hour. When t minutes have elapsed the cars are d km apart. Find formulae which give d in terms of t, c, u, v in the two cases, (i) when the slower car is in front, (ii) when the faster car is in front. Find, also, expressions for the two times (measured in minutes from the start) at which their distances apart will be D km, D being less than c. (Oxf. and Camb. Sch. Cerlif.)

56. A boy was employed on the understanding that he was to receive p paise for every day he worked and q paise for every day when there was no work for him. After d days, his total earnings amounted to Rs. P. How many days had he worked?

57. A car did a journey in t hours. If the average speed had been l km an hour greater, the journey would have taken v hours less. How long was the journey?

58. A man rented x hectares of land for a certain sum. He worked y hectares himself and let the remainder at Rs. z a hectare more than he paid for it. He found that he received for this portion an amount equal to the rent of the whole. Find the rent of the whole.

59. The circumference of a bogie wheel of a railway engine is x dm. The driving wheel is larger than a bogie wheel, and the number of revolutions each km is N less for the larger wheel than for the smaller. Find by how much the circumference of the larger wheel exceeds that of the smaller.

60. A man bought an article for Rs. C and sold it to a second man at a gain of r%. The purchaser sold it to a third man for Rs. S. Find the second man's percentage profit.

Also find the value of r if the second man's profit was s%.

61. An Education Committee spent Rs. P in one year awarding n scholarships at secondary schools. The school fees of the scholars, amounting to Rs. F, were paid in each case; and in addition some of the scholars received a grant of Rs. a and the remainder a grant of Rs. b. How many received the grant of Rs. a?

62. A fraction is such that if c is added to the numerator and d to the denominator, the value of the fraction becomes $\frac{1}{x}$. If the numerator of the original fraction is doubled and the denominator increased by e, the fraction becomes $\frac{1}{y}$. Find the original fraction.

Confirm your result by putting $c = 1, d = s, x = 3, e = 13, y = 2$.

63. A fast train travelling at x km an hour takes t hours less to travel y km than a slower one takes to travel z km. Find the difference between their speeds.

64. A boy spent Rs. R on rowing, always hiring a boat at b rupees an hour or a better one at c rupees an hour. Had he spent on the first what he actually spent on the second and on the second what he actually spent on the first he would have had a more hours, rowing. For how many hours did he hire the better boat?

Check your result by putting $R = 15, b = 1\frac{1}{2}, c = 2, a = 2$.

24

HARDER PROBLEMS

188. IN previous chapters we have given collections of problems which lead to simple equations. We add here a few examples of some what greater difficulty.

Example 1. A grocer buys 15 lbs. of figs and 28 lbs. of currants for £1. 1*s.* 8*d.*; by selling the figs at a loss of 10 per cent, and the currants at a gain of 30 per cent, he clears 2*s.* 6*d.* On his outlay; how much per pound did he pay for each?

Let x, y denote the number of pence in the price of a pound of figs and currants respectively; then the outlay is

$$15x + 28y \text{ pence.}$$

Therefore $15x + 28y = 260$ ...(1).

The loss upon the figs is $\frac{1}{10} \times 15x$ pence, and the gain upon the currants is $\frac{3}{10} \times 28y$ pence; therefore the total gain is

$$\frac{42y}{5} - \frac{3x}{2} \text{ pence;}$$

$$\therefore \quad \frac{42y}{5} - \frac{3x}{2} = 30 \quad \text{...(2).}$$

From (1) and (2) we find that $x = 8$, and $y = 5$; that is the figs cost 8*d.* a pound, and the currants cost 5*d.* a pound.

Example 2. At what time between 4 and 5 o'clock will the minute hand of a watch be 13 minutes in advance of the hour-hand?

Let x denote the required number of minutes after 4 o'clock; then, as the minute-hand travels twelve times as fast as the hour-hand, the hour-hand will move over $\frac{x}{12}$ minute divisions in x minutes.

At 4 o'clock the minute-hand is 20 divisions behind the hour-hand, and finally the minute-hand is 13 divisions in advance; therefore the minute-hand moves over 20 + 13, or 33 divisions more than the hour-hand.

Hence $$x = \frac{x}{12} + 33, \quad \frac{11}{12}x = 33;$$

$$\therefore \quad x = 36.$$

Thus the time is 36 minutes past 4.

If the question be asked as follows: "At what *times* between 4 and 5 o'clock will there be 13 minutes between the two hands"? we must also take into consideration the case when the minute-hand is 13 divisions *behind* the hour-hand. In this case the minute-hand gains 20—13, or 7 divisions.

Hence $$x = \frac{x}{12} + 7,$$

which gives $$x = 7\frac{7}{11}.$$

Therefore the *times* are $7\frac{7'}{11}$ past 4, and 36′ past 4.

Example 3. Two persons A and B start simultaneously from two places, c km apart, and walk in the same direction. A travels at the rate of p km an hour, and B at the rate of q km; how far will A have walked before he overtakes B? .

Suppose A has walked x km, then B has walked $x - c$ km.

A walking at the rate of p km an hour will travel x km in $\frac{x}{p}$ hours;

and B will travel $x - c$ km in $\frac{x-c}{q}$ hours: these two times being equal,

we have $$\frac{x}{p} = \frac{x-c}{q},$$

$$qx = px - pc;$$

whence $$x = \frac{pc}{p-q}.$$

Therefore A has travelled $\frac{pc}{p-q}$ km.

Example 4. A train travelled a certain distance at a uniform rate. Had the speed been 6 km an hour more, the journey would have occupied 4 hours less; and had the speed been 6 km an hour less, the journey would have occupied 6 hours more. Find the distance.

Let the speed of the train be x km per hour, and let the time occupied be y hours; then the distance traversed will be represented by xy km.

On the first supposition the speed per hour is $x + 6$ km, and the time taken is $y - 4$ hours. In this case the distance traversed will be represented by $(x + 6)(y - 4)$ km.

On the second supposition the distance traversed will be represented by $(x - 6)(y + 6)$ km.

All these expressions for the distance must be equal;

$$\therefore \qquad xy = (x+6)(y-4) = (x-6)(y+6).$$

From these equations we have

$$xy = xy + 6y - 4x - 24,$$

or $6y - 4x = 24$ ...(1).

and $xy = xy - 6y + 6x - 36,$

or $6x - 6y = 36$ ...(2).

From (1) and (2) we obtain $x = 30, y = 24$.

Hence the distance is 720 km.

Example 5. A person invests Rs 3770, partly in 3 per cent. Stock at Rs. 102, and partly in Railway Stock at Rs 84 which pays a dividend of $4\frac{1}{2}$ per cent: if his income from these investments is Rs 136.25 per annum, what sum does he invest in each?

Let x denote the number of pounds invested in 3 per cent, y the number of pounds invested in Railway Stock; then

$$x + y = 3770 \qquad \text{...(1).}$$

The income from 3 per cent. Stock is Rs $\frac{3x}{102}$, or Rs $\frac{x}{34}$; and that from Railway Stock is $\frac{4\frac{1}{2}y}{04}$, or Rs $\frac{3y}{56}$.

Therefore $\frac{x}{34} + \frac{3y}{56} = 136\frac{1}{4}$ ...(2).

From (2) $x + \frac{51}{28}y = 4632\frac{1}{2}$;

therefore by subtracting (1)

$$\frac{23}{28}y = 862\frac{1}{2};$$

whence $y = 28 \times 37\frac{1}{2} = 1050$;

and from (1) $x = 2720$.

Therefore he invests Rs 2720 in 3 per cent. Stock, and Rs 1050 in Railway Stock.

EXAMPLES XXIV

1. A sum of Rs 10 is divided among a number of persons; if the number had been increased by one-fourth each would have received 5 paise less: find the number of persons.
2. I bought a certain number of eggs at four a rupee; I kept one-fifth of them, and sold the rest at three a rupee, and gained a rupee: how many did I buy?

3. I bought a certain number of articles at five for 50 paise; if they had been eleven for one rupee, I should have spent 50 paise less: how many did I buy?

4. A man at a race wins twice as much as he had to begin with, and then loses Rs 20; he then loses four-fifths of what remained, and afterwards wins as much as he had at first: how much had he originally, if he leaves off with Rs 124?

5. I spend Rs 160 in buying 20 metres of calico and 30 metres of silk; the silk costs $\frac{1}{10}$ as many rupees per metre as the calico costs paise per metre: find the price of each.

6. A number of two digits exceeds five times the sum of its digits by 9, and its ten-digit exceeds its unit-digit by 1: find the number.

7. The sum of the digits of a number less than 100 is 6; if the digits be reversed the resulting number will be less by 18 than the original number: find it.

8. A man being asked his age replied, "If you take 2 years from my present age the result will be double my wife's age, and 3 years ago her age was one-third of what mine will be in 12 years". What were their ages?

9. At what time between one and two o'clock are the hands of a watch first at right angles?

10. At what time between 3 and 4 o'clock is the minute-hand one minute ahead of the hour-hand?

11. When are the hands of a clock together between the hours of 6 and 7?

12. It is between 2 and 3 o'clock, and in 10 minutes the minute-hand will be as much before the hour-hand as it is now behind it: what is the time?

13. At an election the majority was 162, which was three-elevenths of the whole number of voters: what was the number of the votes on each side?

14. A certain number of persons paid a bill; if there had been ten more each would have paid Rs 2 less; if there had been 5 less each would have paid Rs 2.50 more: find the number of persons and what each had to pay.

15. A man spends Rs 100 in buying two kinds of silk at Rs 4.50 and Rs 4 a metre; by selling it all at Rs 4.25 a metre he gains 2 per cent; how much of each did he buy?

16. Ten years ago the sum of the ages of two sons was one-third of their father's age: one is two years older than the other, and the present sum of their ages is fourteen years less than their father's age: how old are they?

17. A and B start from the same place walking at different rates; when A has walked 15 km B doubles his pace, and 6 hours later passes A: if A walks at the rate of 5 km an hour, what is B's rate at first?

18. A basket of oranges is emptied by one person taking half of them and one more, a second person taking half of the remainder and one more, and a third person taking half of the remainder and six more. How many did the basket contain at first?

19. A person swimming in a stream which runs $1\frac{1}{2}$ km per hour, finds that it takes him four times as long to swim a km up the stream as it does to swim the same distance down: at what rale does he swim?

20. At what *times* between 7 and 8 o'clock will the hands of a watch be at right angles to each other? When will they be in the same straight line?

21. The denominator of a fraction exceeds the numerator by 4; and if 5 is taken from each, the sum of the reciprocal of the new fraction and four times the original fraction is 5: find the original fraction.

22. Two persons start at noon from towns 60 km apart. One walks at the rate of four km an hour, but stops $2\frac{1}{2}$ hours, on the way; the other walks at the rate of 3 km an hour without stopping. When and where will they meet?

23. A, B, and C travel from the same place at the rates of 4, 5, and 6 km an hour respectively; and B starts 2 hours after A. How long after B must C start in order that they may overtake A at the same instant?

24. A dealer bought a horse, expecting to sell it again at a price that would have given him 10 per cent profit on his purchase; but he had to sell it for Rs 500 less than he expected, and he then found that he [had lost 15 per cent on what it cost him: what did he pay for the horse?

25. A man walking from a town, A, to another, B, at the rate of 4 km an hour, starts one hour before a coach travelling 12 km an hour, and is picked up by the coach. On arriving at B, he finds that his coach journey has lasted 2 hours: find the distance between A and B.

26. What is the property of a person whose income is Rs 1140, when one-twelfth of it is invested at 2 per cent, one-half at 3 per cent, one-third at $4\frac{1}{2}$ per cent and the remainder pays him no dividend?

27. A person spends one-third of his income saves one-fourth, and pays away 5 per cent on the whole as interest at $7\frac{1}{2}$ per cent on debts previously incurred and then has Rs 110 remaining: what was the amount of his debts?

28. Two vessels contain mixtures of sulphuric acid and distilled water; in one there is three times as much acid as water, in the other, five times as much water as acid. Find how much must be drawn off from each to fill a third vessel which holds seven litres, in order that its contents may be half acid and half water.

29. There are two mixtures of sulphuric acid and distilled water, one of which contains twice as much water as acid, and the other three times as much acid as water. How much must there be taken from each to fill a one litre cup, in which the acid and the water shall be equally mixed?

30. Two men set out at the same time to walk, one from A to B, and the other from B to A, a distance of a km. The former walks at the rate of p km, and the latter at the rate of q km an hour: at what distance from A will they meet?

31. A train on the Western line passes from Bombay to Bulsar in 3 hours; a train on the Central line which is 20 km shorter, travelling at a speed which is less by 4 km per hour, passes from one place to the other in 2 hours 52 minutes: find the length of each line.

32. Coffee is bought at Rs 2.4, and chicory at 60 paise per kg; in what proportion must they be mixed, that 10 per cent may be gained by selling the mixture at Rs 2.2 per kg?

33. A man has one kind of coffee at a paise per kg, and another at b paise per kg. How much of each must he take to form a mixture of $a - b$ kg, which he can sell at c paise a kg without loss?

34. A man spends $2.5c$ rupees in buying two kinds of silk at a rupees and b rupees a metre respectively; he could have bought 3 times as much of the first and half as much of the second for the same money, how many metres of each did he buy?

35. A man rides one-third of the distance from A to B at the rate of a km an hour, and the remainder at the rate of $2b$ km an hour. If he had travelled at a uniform rate of $3c$ km an hour, he could have ridden from A to B and back again in the same time. Prove that

$$\frac{2}{c} = \frac{1}{a} + \frac{1}{b}.$$

36. A, B, C are three towns forming a triangle. A man has to walk from one to the next, ride thence to the next, and drive thence to his starting point. He can walk, ride, and drive a km in a, b, c minutes respectively. If he starts from B he takes $a + c - b$ hours, if he starts from C he takes $b + a - c$ hours, and if he starts from A he takes $c + b - a$ hours. Find the length of the circuit.

25

QUADRATIC EQUATIONS

189. SUPPOSE the following problem were proposed for solution : A dealer bought a number of horses for Rs 280. If he had bought four less each would have cost Rs 8 more: How many did he buy?

We should proceed thus :

Let $x =$ the number of horses; then $\frac{280}{x}$ = the number of rupees each cost.

If he had bought 4 less he would have had $x - 4$ horses, and each would have cost $\frac{280}{x-4}$ rupees.

$$\therefore \qquad 8 + \frac{280}{x} = \frac{280}{x-4};$$

Whence $\quad x(x-4) + 35(x-4) = 35x;$

$$\therefore \qquad x^2 - 4x + 35x - 140 = 35x;$$

$$\therefore \qquad x^2 - 4x = 140$$

Here we have an equation which involves the *square* of the unknown quantity; and in order to complete the solution of the problem we must discover a method of solving such equations.

190. DEFINITION. An equation which contains the square of the unknown quantity, but no higher power is called a quadratic equation, or an equation of the second degree.

If the equation contains both the square and the first power of the unknown it is called an *adfected* quadratic; if it contains only the square of the unknown it is said to be a *pure* quadratic.

Thus $2x^2 - 5x = 3$ is an adfected quadratic, and $5x^2 = 20$ is a pure quadratic.

191. A pure quadratic may be considered as a simple equation in which the *square* of the unknown quantity is to be found.

Example. Solve $\frac{9}{x^2 - 27} = \frac{25}{x^2 - 11}$

Multiplying up, $9x^2 - 99 = 25x^2 - 675;$

$$\therefore \qquad 16x^2 = 576;$$

$$\therefore \qquad x^2 = 36;$$

and taking the square root of these equals, we have $x = \pm 6$.

NOTE. We prefix the double sign to the number on the right-hand side for the reason given in Art. 117.

192. In extracting the square root of the two sides of the equation $x^2 = 36$, it might seem that we ought to prefix the double sign to the quantities on both sides, and write $\pm x = \pm 6$. But an examination of the various cases shows this to be unnecessary. For $\pm x = \pm 6$ gives the four cases;

$$+x = +6, +x = -6, -x = +6, -x = -6,$$

and these are all included in the two already given, namely $x = +6$, $x = -6$. Hence, when we extract the square root of the two sides of an equation, it is sufficient to put the double sign before the square root of *one* side.

193. The equation $x^2 = 36$ is an instance of the simplest form of quadratic equations. The equation $(x-3)^2 = 25$ may be solved in a similar way ; for taking the square root of both sides, we have two *simple* equations.

$$x - 3 = \pm 5.$$

Taking the upper sign, $x - 3 = +5$, whence $x = 8$;

taking the lower sign, $x - 3 = -5$, whence $x = -2$.

$\therefore$ The solution is $x = 8$, or -2.

Now the given equation, $(x-3)^2 = 25$

may be written $x^2 - 6x + (3)^2 = 25$

or $x^2 - 6x = 16$.

Hence, by retracing our steps, we learn that the equation

$$x^2 - 6x = 16$$

can be solved by first adding $(3)^2$ or 9 to each side, and then extracting the square root; and the reason why we add 9 to each side is that this quantity added to the left side makes it a *perfect square.*

Now whatever the quantity a may be,

$$x^2 + 2ax + a^2 = (x+a)^2,$$

and $x^2 - 2ax + a^2 = (x-a)^2$;

so that if a trinomial is a perfect square, and *its highest power* x^2, *has unity for its coefficient*, we must always have the term without x equal to the square of half the coefficient of x. If, therefore, the terms in x^2 and x are given, the square may be completed by adding the squre of half the coefficient of x.

NOTE. When an expression is a perfect square, the *square terms* are always *positive*. [Art. 114, Note.] Hence, if necessary, the coefficient of x^2 must be made equal to + 1 before completing the square.

Example 1. solve $x^2 + 14x = 32$.

The square of half 14 is $(7)^2$.

$\therefore \quad x^2 + 14x + (7)^2 = 32 + 49;$

that is, $\quad (x + 7)^2 = 81;$

$\because \quad x + 7 = \pm 9;$

$\therefore \quad x = -7 + 9 \text{ or } -7 - 9;$

$\therefore \quad x = 2 \text{ or } -16.$

Example 2. Solve $7x = x^2 - 8$

Transpose so as to have the terms involving x on one side and the square term positive.

Thus $\quad x^2 - 7x = 8.$

Completing the square, $x^2 - 7x + \left(\frac{7}{2}\right)^2 = 8 + \frac{49}{4};$

that is, $\quad \left(x - \frac{7}{2}\right)^2 = \frac{81}{4};$

$\therefore \quad x - \frac{7}{2} = \pm \frac{9}{2};$

$\therefore \quad x = \frac{7}{2} \pm \frac{9}{2};$

$\therefore \quad x = 8 \text{ or } -1.$

NOTE. We do not work out $\left(\frac{7}{2}\right)^2$ on the left-hand side.

EXAMPLES XXV-a

1. $5(x^2 + 5) = 6x^2$.

2. $3x^2 = 4(x^2 - 4)$.

3. $x^2 + 22x = 75$.

4. $x^2 + 24x = 25$.

5. $x^2 = 10x - 21$.

6. $(9 + x)(9 - x) = 17$.

7. $x^2 + 3x = 18$.

8. $x^2 + 5x = 14$.

9. $x^2 - 5x - 36 = 0$.

10. $x^2 = x + 72$.

11. $x^2 - 341 = 20x$.

12. $9x - x^2 + 220 = 0$.

13. $68 - x^2 = 13x$.

14. $x + 156 = x^2$.

15. $187 = x^2 + 6x$.

16. $23x = 120 + x^2$.

17. $42 + x^2 = 13x.$

18. $22x + 23 - x^2 = 0.$

19. $x^2 - \frac{2}{3}x = 32.$

20. $x^2 + \frac{4}{15}x = \frac{1}{5}.$

21. $x^2 - \frac{7}{6}x - \frac{1}{2} = 0.$

22. $\frac{19}{5}x = \frac{4}{5} - x^2.$

23. $\frac{3}{5}(x + 6)(x - 2) = \frac{2}{3}\left(62\frac{1}{10} + \frac{18x}{5}\right).$

194. We have shown that the square may readily be completed when the coefficient of x^2 is unity. All cases may be reduced to this by dividing the equation throughout by the coefficient of x^2.

Example 1. Solve $32 - 3x^2 = 10x$

Transposing, $3x^2 + 10x = 32.$

Divide throughout by 3, so as to make the coefficient of x^2 unity.

Thus $$x^2 + \frac{10}{3}x = \frac{32}{3};$$

completing the square, $$x^2 + \frac{10}{3}x + \left(\frac{5}{3}\right)^2 = \frac{32}{3} + \frac{25}{9};$$

that is, $$\left(x + \frac{5}{3}\right)^2 = \frac{121}{9}; \qquad \therefore \quad x + \frac{5}{3} = \pm\frac{11}{3};$$

$$\therefore \qquad x = -\frac{5}{3} \pm \frac{11}{3} = 2, \text{ or } -5\frac{1}{3}.$$

NOTE. We do not add $\left(\frac{10}{6}\right)^2$ but $\left(\frac{5}{3}\right)^2$ to the left-hand side.

Example 2. Solve $5x^2 + 11x = 12$

Dividing by 5, $x^2 + \frac{11}{5}x = \frac{12}{5}$

completing the square, $$x^2 + \frac{11}{5}x + \left(\frac{11}{10}\right)^2 = \frac{12}{5} + \frac{121}{100};$$

that is $$\left(x + \frac{11}{10}\right)^2 = \frac{361}{100}$$

$$\therefore \qquad x + \frac{11}{10} = \pm\frac{19}{10};$$

$$\therefore \qquad x = -\frac{11}{10} \pm \frac{19}{10} = \frac{4}{5} \text{ or } -3.$$

195. We see than that the following are the steps required for solving an adfected quadratic equation:

(1) If necessary, simplify the equation so that the terms in x^2 and x are on one side of the equation, and the term without x on the other.

(2) Make the coefficient of x^2 unity and positive by dividing throughout by the coefficient of x^2.

(3) Add to each side of the equation the square of half the coefficient of x.

(4) Take the square root of each side.

(5) Solve the resulting simple equations.

196. In the examples which follow some preliminary reduction and simplification may be necessary.

Example 1. Solve $\frac{3x-2}{2x-3} = \frac{5x}{x+4} - 2$

Simplifying, $\frac{3x-2}{2x-3} = \frac{3x-8}{x+4}$;

multiplying across, $3x^2 + 10x - 8 = 6x^2 - 25x + 24$;

that is, $-3x^2 + 35x = 32$

Dividing by -3, $x^2 - \frac{35}{3}x = -\frac{32}{3}$,

completing the square, $x^2 - \frac{35}{3}x + \left(\frac{35}{6}\right)^2 = \frac{1225}{36} - \frac{32}{3}$;

that is, $\left(x - \frac{35}{6}\right)^2 = \frac{841}{36}$;

$\therefore \quad x - \frac{35}{6} = \pm\frac{29}{6}$;

$\therefore \quad x = 10\frac{2}{3}$, or 1.

Example 2. Solve $7(x+2a)^2 + 3a^2 = 5a(7x+23a)$

Simplifying, $7x^2 + 28ax + 28a^2 + 3a^2 = 35ax + 115a^2$

that is, $7x^2 - 7ax = 84a^2$

Whence $x^2 - ax = 12a^2$;

completing the square, $x^2 - ax + \left(\frac{a}{2}\right)^2 = 12a^2 + \frac{a^2}{4}$;

that is, $\left(x - \frac{a}{2}\right)^2 = \frac{49a^2}{4}$;

$\therefore \quad x - \frac{a}{2} = \pm\frac{7a}{2}$;

$\therefore \quad x = 4a$, or $-3a$.

197. Sometimes there is *only one solution*. Thus if

$$x^2 - 2x + 1 = 0, \text{ then } (x-1)^2 = 0,$$

whence $x = 1$ is the only solution. Nevertheless, in this and similar cases we find it convenient to say that the quadratic has *two equal roots*.

EXAMPLES XXV-b

1. $5x^2 + 14x = 55.$

2. $3x^2 + 121 = 44x.$

3. $25x = 6x^2 + 21.$

4. $8x^2 + x = 30.$

5. $3x^2 + 35 = 22x.$

6. $x + 22 - 6x^2 = 0.$

7. $15 = 17x + 4x^2.$

8. $21 + x = 2x^2.$

9. $9x^2 - 143 - 6x = 0.$

10. $12x^2 = 29x - 14.$

11. $20x^2 = 12 - x.$

12. $19x = 15x - 8x^2.$

13. $21x^2 + 22x + 5 = 0.$

14. $50x^2 - 15x = 27.$

15. $18x^2 - 27x - 26 = 0.$

16. $5x^2 = 8x + 21.$

17. $15x^2 - 2ax = a^2.$

18. $21x^2 = 2ax + 3a^2.$

19. $6x^2 = 11kx + 7k^2.$

20. $12x^2 + 23kx + 10k^2 = 0.$

21. $12x^2 - cx - 20c^2 = 0.$

22. $2(x-3) = 3(x+2)(x-3).$

23. $(x+1)(2x+3) = 4x^2 - 22.$

24. $(3x-5)(2x-5) = x^2 + 2x - 3.$

25. $\dfrac{5x+7}{x-1} = 3x + 2.$

26. $\dfrac{5x-1}{x+1} = \dfrac{3x}{2}.$

27. $\dfrac{3x-8}{x-2} = \dfrac{5x-2}{x+5}.$

28. $\dfrac{3x-1}{4x+7} = 1 - \dfrac{6}{x+7}.$

29. $\dfrac{5x-7}{7x-5} = \dfrac{x-5}{2x-13}.$

30. $\dfrac{x+3}{2x-7} - \dfrac{2x-1}{x-3} = 0$

31. $\dfrac{1}{1+x} - \dfrac{1}{3-x} = \dfrac{6}{35}.$

32. $\dfrac{x+4}{x-4} + \dfrac{x-2}{x-3} = 6\dfrac{1}{3}.$

33. $\dfrac{1}{3-x} - \dfrac{4}{5} = \dfrac{1}{9-2x}.$

34. $\dfrac{4}{x-1} - \dfrac{5}{x+2} = \dfrac{3}{x}.$

35. $\dfrac{5}{x-2} - \dfrac{4}{x} = \dfrac{3}{x+6}.$

36. $\dfrac{x-2}{x-3} + \dfrac{3x-11}{x-4} = \dfrac{4x+13}{x+1}.$

37. $\dfrac{1}{2x-5a} + \dfrac{5}{2x-a} = \dfrac{2}{a}.$

38. $\dfrac{2}{3x-2c} + \dfrac{3}{2x-3c} = \dfrac{7}{2c}.$

39. $\dfrac{a^2b}{x^2} + \left(1 + \dfrac{b}{x}\right)a = 2b + \dfrac{a^2}{x}.$

198. From the preceding examples it appears that after suitable reduction and transposition every quadratic equation can be written in the form

$$ax^2 + bx + c = 0,$$

where a, b, c may have any numerical values whatever. If therefore we can solve this quadratic we can solve any

transposing, $ax^2 + bx = -c$;

dividing by a, $x^2 + \frac{b}{a}x = -\frac{c}{a}$.

Completing the square by adding to each side $\left(\frac{b}{2a}\right)^2$

$$x^2 + \frac{b}{a}x + \left(\frac{b}{2a}\right)^2 = \frac{b^2}{4a^2} - \frac{c}{a};$$

that is,
$$\left(x + \frac{b}{2a}\right)^2 = \frac{b^2 - 4ac}{4a^2};$$

extracting the square root,

$$x + \frac{b}{2a} = \frac{\pm\sqrt{(b^2 - 4ac)}}{2a};$$

$$x = \frac{-b \pm \sqrt{(b^2 - 4ac)}}{2a}.$$

199. Instead of going through the process of completing the square in each particular example, we may now make use of this general formula, adapting it to the case in question by substituting the value of a, b, c.

Example. Solve $5x^2 + 11x - 12 = 0$.

Here $a = 5, b = 11, c = -12$.

$$\therefore \quad x = \frac{-11 \pm \sqrt{(11)^2 - 4.5(-12)}}{10}$$

$$= \frac{-11 \pm \sqrt{361}}{10} = \frac{-11 \pm 19}{10} = \frac{4}{5}, \text{ or } -3.$$

which agrees with the solution of Example 2, Art. 194.

200. In the result $x = \frac{-b \pm \sqrt{(b^2 - 4ac)}}{2a}$,

it must be remembered that the expression $\sqrt{(b^2 - 4ac)}$ is the square root of the compound quantity $b^2 - 4ac$, *taken as a whole*. We cannot simplify the solution unless we know the numerical values of a, b, c. It may sometimes happen that these values do not make $b^2 - 4ac$ a perfect square. In such a case the exact numerical solution of the equation cannot be determined.

Example 1. Solve $5x^2 - 15x + 11 = 0$.

We have $x = \dfrac{15 \pm \sqrt{(-15)^2 - 4.5 \cdot 11}}{2.5} = \dfrac{15 \pm \sqrt{5}}{10}$ ...(1).

Now $\sqrt{5} = 2.236$ approximately.

$\therefore \quad x = \dfrac{15 \pm 2.236}{10} = 1.7236$ or 1.2764.

These solutions are correct only to four places of decimals, and neither of them will be found to *exactly* satisfy the equation.

Unless the *numerical* values of the unknown quantity are required it is usual to leave the roots in the form (1).

Example 2. Solve $x^2 - 3x + 5 = 0$.

We have $x = \dfrac{3 \pm \sqrt{(-3)^2 - 4 \cdot 1 \cdot 5}}{2}$

$= \dfrac{3 \pm \sqrt{9 - 20}}{2} = \dfrac{3 \pm \sqrt{-11}}{2}$.

Now there is no quantity, positive or negative, whose square is negative (Art. 110). Therefore, it is impossible to find any quantity exactly or approximately to represent the square root of -11. Thus there is no real value of x which satisfies the equation. In such a case the roots are said to be *imaginary* or *impossible*. A reference to the general formula of Art. 198 will show that the roots of a quadratic $ax^2 + bx + c = 0$ are always imaginary when $b^2 - 4ac$ is negative.

NOTE. If the equation $x^2 - 3x + 5 = 0$ is treated graphically, as explained in Art. 427, it will be found that the graph never meets the axis of x. In other words there is no numerical value of x which makes the expression $x^2 - 3x + 5$ equal to zero. [Chap. XLIV., Arts. 425—427 *may be read here*.]

201. Solution by Factors. The following method of solution will sometimes be found shorter than either of the methods given.

Consider the equation $x^2 + \dfrac{7}{3}x = 2$.

Clearing the fractions,

$$3x^2 + 7x - 6 = 0 \qquad ...(1);$$

by resolving the left-hand side into factors we have

$$(3x - 2)(x + 3) = 0.$$

Now if *either* of the factors $3x - 2$, $x + 3$ is zero their product is zero. Hence the quadratic equation is satisfied by either of the suppositions.

$$3x - 2 = 0, \text{ or } x + 3 = 0.$$

Thus the roots are $\frac{2}{3}, -3.$

It appears from this that *when a quadratic equation has been simplified and brought to the form of equation* (1), its solution can always be readily obtained if the expression on the left-hand side can be resolved into factors. Each of these factors equated to zero gives a simple equation, and a corresponding root of the quadratic.

Example 1. Solve $2x^2 - ax + 2bx = ab$

Transposing, *so as to have all the terms on one side of the equation,*

We have, $2x^2 - ax + 2bx - ab = 0$

Now $2x^2 - ax + 2bx - ab = x(2x - a) + b(2x - a)$

$= (2x - a)(x + b)$

Therefore, $(2x - a)(x + b) = 0;$

whence $2x - a = 0,$ or $x + b = 0.$

$\therefore \quad x = \frac{a}{2},$ or $-b.$

Example 2. Solve $2(x^2 - 6) = 3(x - 4)$

We have $2x^2 - 12 = 3x - 12;$

that is, $2x^2 = 3x \quad \ldots(1)$

Transposing, $2x^2 - 3x = 0, \; x(2x - 3) = 0$

$\therefore \quad x = 0,$ or $2x - 3 = 0.$

Thus the roots are $0, \frac{3}{2}.$

NOTE. In equation (1) above we might have divided both sides by x and obtained the simple equation $2x = 3$, whence $x = \frac{3}{2}$, which is *one* of the solutions of the given equation. But the student must be particularly careful to notice that whenever an x, or a factor containing x, is removed by division from every term of an equation if must not be neglected, since the equation is satisfied by $x = 0$, which is therefore one of the roots.

202. There are some equations which are not really quadratics, but which may be solved by the methods explained in this chapter.

Example 1. Solve $x^4 - 13x^2 + 36 = 0.$

By resolution into factors, $(x^2 - 9)(x^2 - 4) = 0;$

$\therefore \quad x^2 - 9 = 0,$ or $x^2 - 4 = 0;$

that is, $x^2 = 9$ or $4,$

and $x = \pm 3$ or $\pm 2.$

Example 2. Solve $x^2 + 3x - \frac{20}{x^2 - 3x} = 8.$

While y for $x^2 + 3x$, then we have

$$y - \frac{20}{y} = 8,$$

or $$y^2 - 8y - 20 = 0.$$

From this quadratic $y = 10$, or -2.

Thus we have *two* quadratics to solve, and finally we obtain $x = -5, 2$; or $-1, -2$.

EXAMPLES XXV-c

Solve by Art. 200, and verify graphically by Art. 427:

1. $3x^2 = 15 - 4x.$ **2.** $2x^2 + 7x = 15.$

3. $2x^2 + 7 - 9x = 0.$ **4.** $x^2 = 3x + 5.$

5. $5x^2 + 4 + 21x = 0.$ **6.** $x^2 + 11 = 7x.$

7. $8x^2 = x + 7.$ **8.** $5x^2 = 17x - 10.$

9. $35 + 9x - 2x^2 = 0.$ **10.** $3x^2 = x + 1.$

11. $3x^2 + 5x = 2.$ **12.** $2x^2 + 5x - 33 = 0.$

Solve by resolution into factors:

13. $6x^2 = 7 + x.$ **14.** $21 + 8x^2 = 26x.$

15. $26x - 21 + 11x^2 = 0.$ **16.** $5x^2 + 26x + 24 = 0.$

17. $4x^2 = \frac{4}{15}x + 3.$ **18.** $x^2 - 2 = \frac{23}{12}x.$

19. $7x^2 = 28 - 96x.$ **20.** $96x^2 = 4x + 15.$

21. $25x^2 = 5x + 6.$ **22.** $35 - 4x = 4x^2.$

23. $12x^2 - 11ax = 36a^2.$ **24.** $12x^2 + 36a^2 = 43ax.$

25. $35b^2 = 9x^2 + 6bx.$ **26.** $36x^2 - 35b^2 = 12bx.$

27. $x^2 - 2ax + 4ab = 2bx.$ **28.** $x^2 - 2ax + 8x = 16a.$

29. $3x^2 - 2ax - bx = 0.$ **30.** $ax^2 + 2x = bx.$

Solve as explained in Art. 202:

31. $4 = 5x^2 - x^4.$ **32.** $x^4 + 36 = 13x^2.$

33. $x^6 + 7x^3 = 8.$ **34.** $x^6 - 19x^3 = 216.$

35. $16\left(x^2 + \frac{1}{x^2}\right) = 257.$ **36.** $x^2 + \frac{a^2b^2}{x^2} = a^2 + b^2.$

37. $x^3(19 + x^3) = 216.$ **38.** $(x^2 + 2)^2 + 198 = 29(x^2 + 2).$

39. $x^2 - x + \frac{72}{x^2 - x} = 18.$ **40.** $x(x - 2a) = \frac{8a^4}{x^2 - 2ax} + 7a^2.$

202. The method of solution by factors is applicable to equations of higher degree than the second.

For example, if

$$(x - 2)(x + 1)(x + 2) = 0,$$

the equation must be satisfied by each of the values which satisfy the equations.

$$x - 2 = 0,\ x + 1 = 0,\ x + 2 = 0.$$

Thus the roots are 2, – 1, – 2.

Example. Solve the equation $3x^3 + 5x^2 = 3x + 5.$

Putting the equation in the form

$$3x^3 + 5x^2 - 3x - 5 = 0,$$

we have $x^2(3x + 5) - (3x + 5) = 0;$

or $(x^2 - 1)(3x + 5) = 0$

that is, $(x + 1)(x - 1)(3x + 5) = 0;$

whence $x + 1 = 0,$ or $x - 1 = 0,$ or $3x + 5 = 0..$

Thus the roots are $-1, 1, -\frac{5}{3}.$

NOTE. At the stage marked with an asterisk we might have divided throughout by $3x + 5$, but in so doing the factor must be equated to zero to furnish one root of the equation.

202. If one root of an equation is known, or can be obtained by trial, a corresponding factor of the first degree can be removed. When this is done we have left an equation of lower degree than the original equation.

Example. Solve the equation

$$x^3 - 3x^2 - 6x + 16 = 0.$$

By trial it will be found that the left-hand side vanishes when $x = 2$.

26

SIMULTANEOUS QUADRATIC EQUATIONS

203. WE shall now consider some of the most useful methods of solving simultaneous equations, one or more of which may be of a degree higher than the first; but no fixed rules can be laid down which are applicable to all cases.

Example 1. Solve $x + y = 15$ ...(1),

$xy = 36$ ...(2).

From (1) by squaring, $x^2 + 2xy + y^2 = 225;$

from(2) $4xy = 144;$

by subtraction, $x^2 - 2xy + y^2 = 81;$

by taking the square root, $x - y = \pm 9.$

Combining this with (1) we have to consider the two cases,

$$\left.\begin{array}{l} x + y = 15, \\ x - y = 9. \end{array}\right\} \left.\begin{array}{l} x + y = 15, \\ x - y = -9. \end{array}\right\}$$

from which we find $\left.\begin{array}{l} x = 12, \\ y = 3. \end{array}\right\} \left.\begin{array}{l} x = 3, \\ y = 12. \end{array}\right\}$

Example 2. Solve $x - y = 12$ ...(1),

$xy = 85$ ...(2).

From (1) $x^2 - 2xy + y^2 = 144;$

from (2) $4xy = 340\,;$

by addition, $x^2 + 2xy + y^2 = 484;$

by taking the square root, $x + y = \pm 22\,.$

Combining this with (1) we have the two cases,

$$\left.\begin{array}{l} x + y = 22, \\ x - y = 12. \end{array}\right\} \left.\begin{array}{l} x + y = -22, \\ x - y = 12. \end{array}\right\}$$

whence $\left.\begin{array}{l} x = 17, \\ y = 5. \end{array}\right\} \left.\begin{array}{l} x = -5, \\ y = -17. \end{array}\right\}$ [See Art. 441.]

204. These are the simplest cases that arise, but they are specially important since the solution in a large number of other cases is dependent upon them.

As a rule our object as to solve the proposed equations *symmetrically*, by finding the values of $x + y$ and $x - y$. From the foregoing examples it will be seen that we can always do this as soon as we have obtained the product of the unknowns, and either their sum or their difference.

Example 1. Solve

$$x^2 + y^2 = 74 \qquad \ldots(1),$$
$$xy = 35 \qquad \ldots(2).$$

Multiply (2) by 2; then by addition and subtraction we have

$$x^2 + 2xy + y^2 = 144,$$
$$x^2 - 2xy + y^2 = 4;$$

Whence

$$x + y = \pm 12,$$
$$x - y = \pm 2.$$

We have now four cases to consider; namely,

$$\left.\begin{array}{l} x+y=12, \\ x-y=2. \end{array}\right\} \left.\begin{array}{l} x+y=12, \\ x-y=-2. \end{array}\right\}$$
$$\left.\begin{array}{l} x+y=-12, \\ x-y=2. \end{array}\right\} \left.\begin{array}{l} x+y=-12, \\ x-y=-2. \end{array}\right\}$$

From which the values of x are $7, 5, -5, -7$; [Compare Art. 441.] and the corresponding values of y are $5, 7, -7, -5$.

Example 2. Solve

$$x^2 + y^2 = 185 \qquad \ldots(1),$$
$$x + y = 17 \qquad \ldots(2).$$

By subtracting (1) from the square of (2) we have

$$2xy = 104;$$

$$\therefore \qquad xy = 52 \qquad \ldots(3).$$

Equations (1) and (3) can now be solved by the method of Example 1; and the solution is

$$\left.\begin{array}{l} x = 13, \text{ or } 4, \\ y = 4, \text{ or } 13. \end{array}\right\}$$

EXAMPLES XXVI-a

Solve the following equations:

1. $x + y = 28,$ $\qquad xy = 187.$

2. $x + y = 51,$ $\qquad xy = 518.$

3. $x + y = 74,$ $\qquad xy = 1113.$

4. $x - y = 5,$ $\qquad xy = 126.$

5. $x - y = 8,$ $\qquad xy = 513.$

6. $xy = 1075,$ $\qquad x - y = 18.$

Solve the following equations:

7. $xy = 923$, $\quad x + y = 84$.

8. $x - y = -8$, $\quad xy = 1353$.

9. $x - y = -22$, $\quad xy = 3848$.

10. $xy = -2193$, $\quad x + y = -8$.

11. $x - y = -18$, $\quad xy = 1363$.

12. $xy = -1914$, $\quad x + y = -65$.

13. $x^2 + y^2 = 89$, $\quad xy = 40$.

14. $x^2 + y^2 = 170$, $\quad xy = 13$.

15. $x^2 + y^2 = 65$, $\quad xy = 28$.

16. $x^2 + y^2 = 178$, $\quad x + y = 16$.

17. $x + y = 15$, $\quad x^2 + y^2 = 125$.

18. $x - y = 4$, $\quad x^2 + y^2 = 106$.

19. $x^2 + y^2 = 180$, $\quad x - y = 6$.

20. $x^2 + y^2 = 185$, $\quad x - y = 3$.

21. $x + y = 13$, $\quad x^2 + y^2 = 97$.

22. $x + y = 9$, $\quad x^2 + xy + y^2 = 61$.

23. $x - y = 3$, $\quad x^2 - 3xy + y^2 = -19$.

24. $x^2 - xy + y^2 = 76$, $\quad x + y = 14$.

25. $\frac{1}{10}(x - y) = 1$, $\quad x^2 - 4xy + y^2 = 52$.

26. $\frac{1}{x} + \frac{1}{y} = 2$, $\quad x + y = 2$.

27. $\frac{1}{x} + \frac{1}{y} = \frac{7}{12}$, $\quad xy = 12$.

28. $ax + by = 2$, $\quad abxy = 1$.

29. $x^2 + pxy + y^2 = p + 2$, $\quad qx^2 + xy + qy^2 = 2q + 1$.

205. Any pair of equations of the form

$$x^2 \pm pxy + y^2 = a^2 \qquad \ldots(1),$$

$$x \pm y = b \qquad \ldots(2).$$

where p is any numerical quantity, can be reduced to one of the cases already considered; for by squaring (2) and combining with (1), an equation to find xy is obtained; the solution can then be completed by the aid of equation (2).

Example 1. Solve $x^3 - y^3 = 999$ ...(1),

$$x - y = 3 \qquad ...(2).$$

By division, $x^2 + xy + y^2 = 333$ ...(3);

from (2) $x^2 - 2xy + y^2 = 9;$

by subtraction, $3xy = 324,$

$$xy = 108 \qquad ...(4).$$

From (2) and (4) $\left.\begin{aligned} x &= 12, \text{ or } -9, \\ y &= 9, \text{ or } -12. \end{aligned}\right\}$

Example 2. Solve

$$x^4 + x^2y^2 + y^4 = 2613 \qquad ...(1),$$

$$x^2 + xy + y^2 = 67 \qquad ...(2).$$

Dividing , (1) by (2) $x^2 - xy + y^2 = 39$ ...(3).

From (2) and (3) by addition, $x^2 + y^2 = 53;$

by subtraction, $xy = 14;$

whence $\left.\begin{aligned} x &= \pm 7, \pm 2, \\ y &= \pm 2, \pm 7. \end{aligned}\right\}$ [Art. 204, Ex. 1.]

Example 3. Solve $\dfrac{1}{x} - \dfrac{1}{y} = \dfrac{1}{3}$ ...(1),

$$\frac{1}{x^2} + \frac{1}{y^2} = \frac{5}{9} \qquad ...(2).$$

From (1) by squaring,

$$\frac{1}{x^2} - \frac{2}{xy} + \frac{1}{y^2} = \frac{1}{9};$$

by subtraction, $\dfrac{2}{xy} = \dfrac{4}{9};$

adding to (2), $\dfrac{1}{x^2} + \dfrac{2}{xy} + \dfrac{1}{y^2} = 1;$

$$\therefore \qquad \frac{1}{x} + \frac{1}{y} = \pm 1.$$

Combining with (1), $\dfrac{1}{x} = \dfrac{2}{3},$

or $-\dfrac{1}{3}, \ \dfrac{1}{y} = \dfrac{1}{3}, \text{ or } -\dfrac{2}{3};$

$$\therefore \qquad x = \frac{3}{2},$$

or -3, and $y = 3$, or $-\dfrac{3}{2}.$

EXAMPLES XXVI-b

Solve the equations:

1. $x^3 + y^3 = 407$, $\quad x + y = 11$.
2. $x^3 + y^3 = 637$, $\quad x + y = 13$.
3. $x + y = 23$, $\quad x^3 + y^3 = 3473$.
4. $x^3 - y^3 = 218$, $\quad x - y = 2$.
5. $x - y = 4$, $\quad x^3 - y^3 = 988$.
6. $x^3 - y^3 = 2197$, $\quad x - y = 13$.
7. $x^4 + x^2y^2 + y^4 = 2128$, $\quad x^2 + xy + y^2 = 76$.
8. $x^4 + x^2y^2 + y^4 = 2923$, $\quad x^2 - xy + y^2 = 37$.
9. $x^4 + x^2y^2 + y^4 = 9211$, $\quad x^2 - xy + y^2 = 61$.
10. $x^4 + x^2y^2 + y^4 = 7371$, $\quad x^2 - xy + y^2 = 63$.
11. $\dfrac{1}{x^2} + \dfrac{1}{y^2} = \dfrac{481}{576}$, $\quad \dfrac{1}{x} + \dfrac{1}{y} = \dfrac{29}{24}$.
12. $\dfrac{1}{x^2} + \dfrac{1}{y^2} = \dfrac{61}{900}$, $\quad xy = 30$.
13. $\dfrac{x}{y} + \dfrac{y}{x} = 2\dfrac{1}{2}$, $\quad x + y = 6$.

Solve the equations:

14. $\dfrac{x}{y} + \dfrac{y}{x} = 2\dfrac{16}{21}$, $\quad x - y = 4$.
15. $\dfrac{34}{x^2 + y^2} = \dfrac{15}{xy}$, $\quad x + y = 8$.
16. $x^3 - y^3 = 56$, $\quad x^2 + xy + y^2 = 28$.
17. $4(x^2 + y^2) = 17xy$, $\quad x - y = 6$.
18. $x^3 + y^3 = 126$, $\quad x^2 - xy + y^2 = 21$.
19. $\dfrac{1}{x^3} + \dfrac{1}{y^3} = 1\dfrac{1}{125}$, $\quad \dfrac{1}{x} + \dfrac{1}{y} = 1\dfrac{1}{5}$.
20. $\dfrac{1}{x^3} - \dfrac{1}{y^3} = 91$, $\quad \dfrac{1}{x} - \dfrac{1}{y} = 1$.

206. The following method of solution may always be used when the equations are *of the same degree and homogeneous.* [See Art. 24.]

Example. Solve

$$x^2 + xy + 2y^2 = 74 \qquad \ldots(1),$$

$$2x^2 + 2xy + y^2 = 73 \qquad \ldots(2).$$

Put $y = mx$, and substitute in both equations. Thus

$$x^2(1 + m + 2m^2) = 74 \qquad \ldots(3),$$

and $$x^2(2 + 2m + m^2) = 73 \qquad \ldots(4).$$

By division, $\dfrac{1 + m + 2m^2}{2 + 2m + m^2} = \dfrac{74}{73}$;

$\therefore \quad 73 + 73m + 146m^2 = 148 + 148m + 74m^2;$

$\therefore \quad 72m^2 - 75m - 75 = 0,$

or $\quad 24m^2 - 25m - 25 = 0;$

$\therefore \quad (8m + 5)(3m - 5) = 0;$

$\therefore \quad m = -\dfrac{5}{8}, \text{ or } \dfrac{5}{3}.$

(i) Take $m = -\dfrac{5}{8}$, and substitute in either (3) or (4).

From (3) $x^2\left(1 - \dfrac{5}{8} + \dfrac{50}{64}\right) = 74;$

$\therefore \quad x^2 = \dfrac{64 \times 74}{74} = 64;$

$\therefore \quad x = \pm 8;$

$\therefore \quad y = mx = -\dfrac{5}{8}x = \mp 5.$

(ii) Take $m = \dfrac{5}{3}$; then from (3)

$$x^2\left(1 + \frac{5}{3} + \frac{50}{9}\right) = 74. \quad x^2 = \frac{74 \times 9}{74} = 9;$$

$\therefore \quad x = \pm 3;$

$\therefore \quad y = mx = \dfrac{5}{3}x = \pm 5.$

207. When one of the equations is of the first degree and the other of a higher degree, we may from the simple equation; find the value of one of the unknowns in terms of the other, and substitute in the second equation.

Example. Solve $3x - 4y = 5 \qquad \ldots(1),$

$$3x^2 - xy - 3y^2 = 21 \qquad \ldots(2).$$

From (1) we have $x = \dfrac{5 + 4y}{3}$;

and substituting in (2), $\dfrac{3(5 + 4y)^2}{9} - \dfrac{y(5 + 4y)}{3} - 3y^2 = 21;$

$\therefore \quad 75 + 120y + 48y^2 - 15y - 12y^2 - 27y^2 = 189;$

$$9y^2 + 105y - 114 = 0,$$

$$3y^2 + 35y - 38 = 0;$$

$$\therefore \quad (y - 1)(3y + 38) = 0;$$

$$\therefore \quad y = 1, \text{ or } -\frac{38}{3};$$

and by substituting in (1), $x = 3, \text{or } -\frac{137}{9}$.

208. The examples we have given will be sufficient as a general explanation of the methods to be employed; but in some cases special artifices are necessary.

Example 1. Solve $x^2 + 4xy + 3x = 40 - 6y - 4y^2$ ...(1),

$$2xy - x^2 = 3 \qquad ...(2).$$

From (1) we have

$$x^2 + 4xy + 4y^2 + 3x + 6y = 40;$$

that is, $\quad (x + 2y)^2 + 3(x + 2y) - 40 = 0,$

or $\quad (\overline{x + 2y} + 8)(\overline{x + 2y} - 5) = 0;$

whence $\quad x + 2y = -8, \text{ or } 5.$

(i) Combining $x + 2y = 5$ with (2) we obtain

$$2x^2 - 5x + 3 = 0;$$

whence $x = 1$, or $\frac{3}{2}$; and by substituting in $x + 2y = 5$, $y = 2$, or $\frac{7}{4}$.

(ii) Combining $x + 2y = -8$ with (2) we obtain

$$2x^2 + 8x + 3 = 0;$$

whence $x = \dfrac{-4 \pm \sqrt{10}}{2}$; and $y = \dfrac{-12 \mp \sqrt{10}}{4}$.

Example 2. Solve

$$x^2y^2 - 6x = 34 - 3y \qquad ...(1),$$

$$3xy + y = 2(9 + x) \qquad ...(2).$$

From (1) $\quad x^2y^2 - 6x + 3y = 34;$

from (2) $\quad 9xy - 6x + 3y = 54;$

by subtraction, $\quad x^2y^2 - 9xy + 20 = 0, (xy - 5)(xy - 4) = 0;$

$$\therefore \quad xy = 5, \text{ or } 4.$$

(i) Substituting $xy = 5$ in (2) gives $y - 2x = 3$.

From these equations we obtain

$$\left.\begin{aligned} x &= 1, \text{ or } -\frac{5}{2}, \\ y &= 5, \text{ or } -2. \end{aligned}\right\}$$

(ii) Substituting $xy = 4$ in (2) gives $y - 2x = 6$.

From these equations we obtain and

$$\left.\begin{aligned} x &= \frac{-3 \pm \sqrt{17}}{2}, \\ y &= 3 \pm \sqrt{17}. \end{aligned}\right\}$$

EXAMPLES XXVI-c

Solve the equations:

1. $5x - y = 17$, $\quad xy = 12$.

2. $x^2 + xy = 15$, $\quad y^2 + xy = 10$.

3. $x - y = 10$, $\quad x^2 - 2xy - 3y^2 = 84$.

4. $3x + 2y = 16$, $\quad xy = 10$.

5. $3x - y = 11$, $\quad 3x^2 - y^2 = 47$.

6. $x - 3y = 1$, $\quad x^2 - 2xy + 9y^2 = 17$.

7. $x + 2y = 9$, $\quad 3y^2 - 5x^2 = 43$.

8. $x^2 + y^2 = 5$, $\quad 2xy - y^2 = 3$.

9. $5x + y = 3$, $\quad 2x^2 - 3xy - y^2 = 1$.

10. $3x^2 - 5y^2 = 28$, $\quad 3xy - 4y^2 = 8$.

11. $3x^2 - y^2 = 23$, $\quad 2x^2 - xy = 12$.

12. $x^2 + xy + y^2 = 3\frac{1}{4}$, $\quad 2x^2 - 3xy + 2y^2 = 2\frac{3}{4}$.

13. $x^2 - 3xy + y^2 + 1 = 0$, $\quad 3x^2 - xy + 3y^2 = 13$.

14. $7xy - 8x^2 = 10$, $\quad 8y^2 - 9xy = 18$.

15. $x^2 - 2xy = 21$, $\quad xy + y^2 = 18$.

16. $x^2 + 3xy = 54$, $\quad xy + 4y^2 = 115$.

17. $x^3 + y^3 = 152$, $\quad x^2y + xy^2 = 120$.

18. $x^3 - y^3 = 127$, $\quad x^2y - xy^2 = 42$.

19. $x^3 - y^3 = 208$, $\quad xy(x - y) = 48$.

20. $x^2y^2 + 5xy = 84$, $\quad x + y = 8$.

21. $x^2 + 4y^2 + 80 = 15x + 30y$, $\quad xy = 6$.

22. $9x^2 + y^2 - 63x + 21y + 128 = 0$, $\quad xy = 4$.

27

PROBLEMS LEADING TO QUADRATIC EQUATIONS

209. WE shall now discuss some problems which give rise to quadratic equations.

Example 1. A train travels 300 km at a uniform rate. If the rate had been 5 km an hour more, the journey would have taken two hours less: Find the rate of the train.

Suppose the train travels at the rate of x miles per hour, then the time occupied is $\frac{300}{x}$ hours.

On the other supposition the time is $\frac{300}{x+5}$ hours;

$$\therefore \qquad \frac{300}{x+5} = \frac{300}{x} - 2 \qquad \ldots(1);$$

Whence $\quad x^2 + 5x - 750 = 0, \quad$ or $\quad (x+30)(x-25) = 0,$

$$\therefore \qquad x = 25 \text{ or } -30.$$

Hence the train travels 25 miles per hour, the negative value being inadmissible.

It will frequently happen that the algebraical statement of the question leads to a result which does not apply to the actual problem we are discussing. But such results can sometimes be explained by a suitable modification of the conditions of the question. In the present case we may explain the negative solution as follows. Since the values $x = 25$ and -30 satisfy the equation (1), if we write $-x$ for x the resulting equation,

$$\frac{300}{-x+5} = \frac{300}{-x} - 2 \qquad \ldots(2),$$

will be satisfied by the values $x = -25$ and 30. Now, by changing signs throughout, equation (2) becomes $\frac{300}{x-5} = \frac{300}{x} + 2;$

and this is the algebraical statement of the following question:

A train travels 300 km at a uniform rate; if the rate had been 5 km an hour *less*, the journey would have taken two hours *more*: find the rate of the train. The rase is 30 km an hour.

Example 2. A person is selling a table for Rs 72 finds that his loss percent is one-eighth of the number of rupees that he paid for the table: what was the cost price?

Suppose that the cost price of the table is x rupees then the loss on Rs 100 is Rs $\frac{x}{8}$.

Hence the loss on Rs x is Rs $\left(x \times \frac{x}{800}\right)$, or Rs $\left(\frac{x^2}{800}\right)$ rupees;

$\therefore$ The selling price is Rs $x - \frac{x^2}{800}$

Hence $$x - \frac{x^2}{800} = 72,$$

or $$x^2 - 800x + 57600 = 0;$$

i.e. $$(x-80)(x-720) = 0;$$

$\therefore$ $$x = 80, \text{ or } 720;$$

and each of these values will be found to satisfy the conditions of the problem. Thus, the cost is either Rs 80, or Rs 720.

Example 3. A cistern can be filled by two pipes in $33\frac{1}{3}$ minutes; if the larger pipe takes 15 minutes less than the smaller to fill the cistern, find in what time it will be filled by each pipe singly.

Suppose that the two pipes running singly would fill the cistern in x and $x - 15$ minutes. When running together they will fill $\left(\frac{1}{x} + \frac{1}{x-15}\right)$ of the cistern in one minute. But they fill $\frac{1}{33\frac{1}{3}}$, or $\frac{3}{100}$ of the cistern in one minute.

Hence $$\frac{1}{x} + \frac{1}{x-15} = \frac{3}{100},$$

$$100(2x-15) = 3x(x-15),$$

$$3x^2 - 245x + 1500 = 0,$$

$$(x-75)(3x-20) = 0;$$

$\therefore$ $$x = 75 \text{ or } 6\frac{2}{3}.$$

Thus the smaller pipe takes 75 minutes, the larger 60 minutes. The other solution $6\frac{2}{3}$ is inadmissible.

Example 4. By rowing half the distance and walking the other half, a man can travel 24 km on a river in 5 hours with the stream, and in 7 hours against the stream. If there were no current, the journey would take $5\frac{2}{3}$ hours: Find the rate of his walking, and rowing and the rate of the stream.

Suppose that the man walks x km per hour, rows y km per hour and that the stream flows at the rate of z km per hour.

With the current the man rows $y + z$ km, and against the current $(y - z)$ km per hour.

Hence, we have the following equations:

$$\frac{12}{x} + \frac{12}{y+z} = 5 \qquad \ldots(1)$$

$$\frac{12}{x} + \frac{12}{y-z} = 7 \qquad \ldots(2)$$

$$\frac{12}{x} + \frac{12}{y} = 5\frac{2}{3} \qquad \ldots(3)$$

From (1) and (3) by subtraction, $\frac{1}{y} - \frac{1}{y+z} = \frac{1}{18}$ ...(4)

Similarly, from (2) and (3), $\frac{1}{y-z} - \frac{1}{y} = \frac{1}{9}$ ...(5)

From (4), $18z = y(y + z)$ ...(6)

and from (5), $9z = y(y - z)$ ...(7)

From (6) and (7) by division, $2 = \frac{y+z}{y-z}$;

Whence $y = 3z$;

$\therefore$From (4) $z = 1\frac{1}{2}$, and Hence $y = 4\frac{1}{2}$, $x = 4$

Thus, the rates of walking and rowing are 4 km and $4\frac{1}{2}$ km per hour respectively; and the stream flows at the rate of $1\frac{1}{2}$ km per hour.

EXAMPLES XXVII

1. Find a number whose square diminished by 119 is equal to ten times the excess of the number over 8.
2. A man is five times as old as his son, and the sum of the squares of their ages is to 2106: find their ages.
3. The sum of the reciprocals of two consecutive numbers is $\frac{15}{56}$: find them.
4. Find a number when which increased by 17 is equal to 60 times the reciprocal of the number.
5. Find two numbers whose sum is 9 times their difference, and the difference of whose squares is 81.
6. The sum of a number and its square is nine times the next highest number: find it.
7. If a train travelled 5 km an hour faster it would take one hour less to travel 210 km: what time does it take?
8. Find two numbers the sum of whose squares is 74, and whose sum is 12.
9. The perimeter of a rectangular field is 500 metres and its area is 14400 square: find the length of the sides.
10. The perimeter of one square exceeds that of another by 100 dm; and the area of the larger square exceeds three times the area of the smaller by 325 square dm: find the length of their sides.
11. A cistern can be filled by two pipes running together in $22\frac{1}{2}$ minutes: the larger pipe would fill the cistern in 24 minutes less than the smaller one: find the time taken by each.
12. A man travels 108 km, and finds that he could have made the journey in $4\frac{1}{2}$ hours less had he travelled 2 km an hour faster: at what rate did he travel?
13. I buy a number of cricket balls for Rs 60; had they cost a rupee apiece less, I should have had five more for the money: find the cost of each.
14. A boy was sent out for one rupee's worth of eggs. He broke 5 on his way home, and his master had therefore to pay at the rate of 5 paise more than the market price for 5. How many did the master get for a rupee?
15. What are eggs a dozen when four more in a rupee's worth lowers the price 10 paise per dozen?
16. A lawn 50 dm long and 34 dm broad has a path of uniform width round it: if the area of the path is 540 square dm: find its width.

17. A hall can be paved with 200 square tiles of a certain size; if each tile were 5 cm longer each way it would take 128 tiles: find the length of each tile.

18. In the centre of a square garden there is a square lawn. outside this is a gravel walk 4 dm wide, and then a flower border 6 dm wide. If the flower border and lawn together contain 721 square dm, find the area of the lawn.

19. By lowering the price of apples and selling them ten paise a dozen cheaper, an applewoman finds that she can sell 60 more than she used to do for Rs 6. At what price per dozen did she sell them at first?

20. Two rectangles contain the same area, 480 square metres. The difference of their lengths is 10 metres, and of their breadths 4 metres. Find their sides.

21. There is a number between 10 and 100: when multiplied by the digit on the left the product is 280: if the sum of the digits be multiplied by the same digit the product is 55: required the number.

22. A farmer having sold at Rs 75 a calf which cost him Rs x finds that he has realised x per cent profit on his outlay: find x.

23. A tradesman bought a number of metres of cloth for Rs 50; he kept 5 metres and sold the rest at Re 1 per metre more than he gave, and got Rs 10 more than he originally spent: how many metres did he buy?

24. If a wheel 500 cm in circumference takes $\frac{1}{2}$ second more to revolve, the rate of the carriage per hour will be 3 km less: how fast is the carriage travelling?

25. A broker bought as many railway shares as cost him Rs 1875: he reserved 15, and sold the remainder for Rs 1740, gaining Rs. 4 a share on their cost price. How many shares did he buy?

26. A and B are two stations 300 km apart. Two trains start simultaneously from A and B, each to the opposite station. The train from A reaches B nine hours, the train from B reaches A four hours after they meet: find the rate at which each train travels.

27. A train A starts to go from P to Q, two stations 240 km apart, and travels uniformly. An hour later another train B starts from P, and after travelling for 2 hours, comes to a point that A had passed 45 minutes previously. The pace of B is now increased by 5 km an hour, and it overtakes A just on entering Q. Find the rates at which they started.

28. A cask P is filled with 50 litres of water, and a cask Q with 40 litres of acid; x litres are drawn from each cask mixed and replaced; and the same operation is repeated. Find x when there are $8\frac{7}{8}$ litres of acid in P after the second replacement.

29. Two farmers A and B have 30 cows between them; they sell them at different prices, but each receives the same sum. If A had sold his at B's price, he would have received Rs 3200; and if B had sold his at A's price, he would have received Rs 2450. How many had each?

30. A man arrives at the railway station nearest to his house $1\frac{1}{2}$ hours before the time at which he had ordered his carriage to meet him. He sets out at once to walk at the rate of 4 km an hour, and, meeting his carriage when it had travelled 8 km, reaches home exactly 1 hour earlier than he had originally expected. How far is his home from the station, and at what rate was his carriage driven?

31. P is a point in a line AB of length a. Find AP when $AB \cdot BP = AP^2$. Explain both solutions.

32. If a straight line 6 cm. in length is divided internally so that the rectangle contained by the whole and one part is equal to the square on the other part, find the segments of the line to the nearest millimetre.

33. A line AB is produced to P so that $AB \cdot AP = BP^2$. If $AB = 8$ cm., find the length of AP and BP to the nearest millimetre.

34. If a line AB of any length is divided externally as in the last Example, show that

(i) $AB^2 + AP^2 = 3BP^2$;

(ii) $(AB + AP)^2 = 5BP^2$.

35. A line AB is produced to P so that $BP^2 = 2AB^2$. If $AB = 3.5$ cm., find AP to the nearest millimetre.

36. Find a point P in a straight line AB so that

$AP(AP - BP) = BP^2$.

If $AB = 4.2$ cm., find AP and BP to the nearest millimetre. By substituting these values verify the truth of the given relation.

37. Divide a straight line 13 centimetres long into two parts so that the rectangle contained by them may be equal to 36 square centimetres.

38. Justify the following graphical solution of the previous Example: On AB, a line 13 cm. in length, describe a semicircle. At A draw AP perpendicular to AB and 6 cm. in length; through P draw a line PQR parallel to AB to cut the semicircle in Q and R; draw QX, RY perpendicular to AB. Then AB is divided as required either at X or Y. Verify the algebraical solution of Example 37 by actual measurement.

39. Solve the following equations graphically, taking a centimetres as unit and giving the roots to the nearest millimetre.

(i) $x(7 - x) = 12$; (ii) $x^2 - 11x + 30 = 0$;

(iii) $x^2 - 6x + 4 = 0$; (iv) $x^2 + 13 = 8x$.

28

HARDER FACTORS

210. IN Chapter XVII we have explained several rules for resolving algebraical expressions into factors; in the present chapter we shall continue the subject by discussing cases of greater difficulty.

211. By a slight modification some expressions admit of being written in the form of the difference of two squares, and may than be resolved into factors by the method of Art. 133.

Example 1. Resolve into factors $x^4 + x^2y^2 + y^4$.

$$\begin{aligned} x^4 + x^2y^2 + y^4 &= (x^4 + 2x^2y^2 + y^4) - x^2y^2 \\ &= (x^2 + y^2)^2 - (xy)^2 \\ &= (x^2 + y^2 + xy)(x^2 + y^2 - xy) \\ &= (x^2 + xy + y^2)(x^2 - xy + y^2). \end{aligned}$$

Example 2. Resolve into factors $x^4 - 15x^2y^2 + 9y^4$.

$$\begin{aligned} x^4 - 15x^2y^2 + 9y^4 &= (x^4 - 6x^2y^2 + 9y^4) - 9x^2y^2 \\ &= (x^2 - 3y^2)^2 - (3xy)^2 \\ &= (x^2 - 3y^2 + 3xy)(x^2 - 3y^2 - 3xy). \end{aligned}$$

212. Expressions which can be put into in the form $x^3 \pm \frac{1}{y^3}$ may be separated into factors by the rules for resolving the sum or the difference of two cubes. [Art. 136.]

Example 1. $\frac{8}{a^3} - 27b^6 = \left(\frac{2}{a}\right)^3 - (3b^2)^3 = \left(\frac{2}{a} - 3b^2\right)\left(\frac{4}{a^2} + \frac{6b^2}{a} + 9b^4\right).$

Example 2. Resolve $a^2x^3 - \frac{8a^2}{y^3} - x^3 + \frac{8}{y^3}$ into four factors.

$$\begin{aligned} a^2x^3 - \frac{8a^2}{y^3} - x^3 + \frac{8}{y^3} &= x^3(a^2 - 1) - \frac{1}{y^3}(a^2 - 1) \\ &= (a^2 - 1)\left(x^3 - \frac{8}{y^3}\right) \\ &= (a + 1)(a - 1)\left(x - \frac{2}{y}\right)\left(x^2 + \frac{2x}{y} + \frac{4}{y^2}\right). \end{aligned}$$

Example 3. Resolve $a^9 - 64a^3 - a^6 + 64$ into six factors.

The expression

$$= a^3(a^6 - 64) - (a^6 - 64)$$
$$= (a^6 - 64)(a^3 - 1)$$
$$= (a^3 + 8)(a^3 - 8)(a^3 - 1)$$
$$= (a + 2)(a^2 - 2a + 4)(a - 2)(a^2 + 2a + 4)(a - 1)(a^2 + a + 1).$$

Example 4. $a(a - 1)x^2 - (a - b - 1)xy - b(b + 1)y^2$

$$= \{ax - (b + 1)y\}\{(a - 1)x + by\}.$$

NOTE. In examples of this kind the coefficients of x and y in the binomial factors can usually be guessed at once, and it only remains to verify the coefficient of the middle term.

213. From Example 2, Art. 52, we see that the quotient of $a^3 + b^3 + c^3 - 3abc$ by $a + b + c$ is $a^2 + b^2 + c^2 - bc - ca - ab$.

Thus, $a^3 + b^3 + c^3 - 3abc = (a + b + c)(a^2 + b^2 + c^2 - bc - ca - ab)$ ... (1).

This result is important and should be carefully remembered. We may note that the expression on the left consists of the sum of the cubes of three quantities a, b, c, diminished by 3 times the product abc. Whenever an expression admits of a similar arrangement, the above formula will enable us to resolve it into factors.

Example 1. Resolve into factors $a^3 - b^3 + c^3 + 3abc$.

$$a^3 - b^3 + c^3 + 3abc = a^3 + (-b)^3 + c^3 - 3a(-b)c$$
$$= (a - b + c)(a^2 + b^2 + c^2 + bc - ca + ab),$$

$-b$ taking the place of b in formula (1).

Example 2. $x^3 - 8y^3 - 27 - 18xy = x^3 + (-2y)^3 + (-3)^3 - 3x(-2y)(-3)$

$$= (x - 2y - 3)(x^2 + 4y^2 + 9 - 6y + 3x + 2xy).$$

EXAMPLES XXVIII-a

Resolve into factors :

1. $x^4 + 16x^2 + 256.$

2. $81a^4 + 9a^2b^2 + b^4.$

3. $x^4 + y^4 - 7x^2y^2.$

4. $m^4 + n^4 - 18m^2n^2.$

5. $x^4 - 6x^2y^2 + y^4.$

6. $4x^4 + 9y^4 - 93x^2y^2.$

7. $4m^4 + 9n^4 - 24m^2n^2.$

8. $9x^4 + 4y^4 + 11x^2y^2.$

9. $x^4 - 19x^2y^2 + 25y^4.$

10. $16a^4 + b^4 - 28a^2b^2.$

11. $\dfrac{27}{a^3b^3} - 1.$

12. $216a^3 - \dfrac{b^3}{8}.$

13. $\frac{x^3}{125} + y^3.$ **14.** $\frac{m^3n^3}{729} - 1.$

15. $\frac{a^3b^3}{125} + 1000.$ **16.** $\frac{x^3}{512} - \frac{64}{x^3}.$

Resolve into two or more factors:

17. $x^2y + 3xy^2 - 3x^3 - y^3.$ **18.** $4mn^2 - 20n^3 + 45nm^2 - 9m^3.$

19. $ab(x^2 + 1) + x(a^2 + b^2).$ **20.** $y^2z^2(x^4 - 1) + x^2(y^4 - z^4).$

21. $a^3 + (a + b)ax + bx^2.$ **22.** $pn(m^2 + 1) - m(p^2 + n^2).$

23. $6bx(a^2 + 1) - a(4x^2 + 9b^2).$ **24.** $(2a^2 + 3y^2)x + (2x^2 + 3a^2)y.$

25. $(2x^2 - 3a^2)y + (2a^2 - 3y^2)x.$ **26.** $a(a - 1)x^2 + (2a^2 - 1)x + a(a + 1).$

27. $3x^2 - (4a + 2b)x + a^2 + 2ab.$

28. $2a^2x^2 - 2(3b - 4c)(b - c)y^2 + abxy.$

29. $(a^2 - 3a + 2)x^2 + (2a^2 - 4a + 1)x + a(a - 1).$

30. $a(a + 1)x^2 + (a + b)xy - b(b - 1)y^2.$

31. $b^3 + c^3 - 1 + 3bc.$ **32.** $a^3 + 8c^3 + 1 - 6ac.$

33. $a^3 + b^3 + 8c^3 - 6abc.$ **34.** $a^3 - 27b^3 + c^3 + 9abc.$

35. $a^3 - b^3 - c^3 - 3abc.$ **36.** $8a^3 + 27b^3 + c^3 - 18abc.$

37. Resolve $x^8 + 81x^4 + 6561$ into three factors.

38. Resolve $(a^4 - 2a^2b^2 - b^4)^2 - 4a^4b^4$ into four factors.

39. Resolve $4(ab + cd)^2 - (a^2 + b^2 - c^2 - d^2)^2$ into four factors.

40. Resolve $x^8 - \frac{1}{256}$ into four factors.

41. Resolve $x^{16} - y^{16}$ into five factors.

42. Resolve $x^{18} - y^{18}$ into five factors.

Resolve into four factors :

43. $\frac{a^3}{x^2} - 8x - a^3 + 8x^3.$ **44.** $x^9 + x^3y^6 - 8x^6y^3 - 8y^9.$

45. $x^9 + x^6 + 64x^3 + 64.$ **46.** $4a - 9b + \frac{4b^3}{a^2} - \frac{9a^3}{b^2}.$

47. $\frac{xy^3}{72} - \frac{x^3y^5}{32} - \frac{1}{9x^2} + \frac{y^2}{4}.$ **48.** $x^6 - 25x^2 + 6\frac{1}{4} - \frac{1}{4}x^4.$

Resolve into five factors :

49. $x^7 + x^4 - 16x^3 - 16.$

50. $16x^7 - 81x^3 - 16x^4 + 81.$

214. The actual processes of multiplication and division can often be partially or wholly avoided by a skilful use of factors.

It should be observed that the formulae which the student has seen exemplified in the preceding pages are just as useful in their converse as in their direct application. Thus the formula for resolving into factors the difference of two squares is equally useful as enabling us to write down at once the product of the sum and the difference of two quantities.

Example 1. Multiply $2a + 3b - c$ by $2a - 3b + c$.

These expressions may be arranged thus:

$$2a + (3b - c) \text{ and } 2a - (3b - c).$$

Hence the product $= \{2a + (3b - c)\}\{2a - (3b - c)\}$

$= (2a)^2 - (3b - c)^2$ [Art. 133.]

$= 4a^2 - (9b^2 - 6bc + c^2)$

$= 4a^2 - 9b^2 + 6bc - c^2.$

Example 2. Multiply $(a^2 + a + 1)x - a - 1$ by $(a - 1)x - a^2 + a - 1$.

The product $= \{(a^2 + a + 1)x - (a + 1)\}\{(a - 1)x - (a^2 - a + 1)\}$

$= (a^3 - 1)x^2 - \{(a^4 + a^2 + 1) + (a^2 - 1)\}x + (a^3 + 1)$

$= (a^3 - 1)x^2 - (a^4 + 2a^2)x + a^3 + 1$

$= (a^3 - 1)x^2 - a^2(a^2 + 2)x + a^3 + 1.$

NOTE. The product of $a^2 + a + 1$ and $a^2 - a + 1$ is $a^4 + a^2 + 1$ and should be written down without actual multiplication.

Example 3. Multiply $(3 + x - 2x^2)^2 - (3 - x - 2x^2)^2$ ...(1),

by $(3 + x + 2x^2)^2 - (3 - x - 2x^2)^2$ ...(2)

The expression (1)

$= (3 + x - 2x^2 + 3 - x + 2x^2)(3 + x - 2x^2 - 3 + x - 2x^2)$

$= 6(2x - 4x^2) = 12x(1 - 2x).$

The expression (2)

$= (3 + x + 2x^2 + 3 - x - 2x^2)(3 + x + 2x^2 - 3 + x + 2x^2)$

$= 6(2x + 4x^2) = 12x(1 + 2x).$

Therefore the product

$= 12x(1 - 2x) \times 12x(1 + 2x) = 144x^2(1 - x^2).$

Example 4. Divide the product of $2x^2 + x - 6$ and $6x^2 - 5x + 1$ by $3x^2 + 5x - 2$.

Denoting the division by means of a fraction, the required quotient

$$= \frac{(2x^2 + x - 6)(6x^2 - 5x + 1)}{3x^2 + 5x - 2}$$

$$= \frac{(2x - 3)(x + 2)(3x - 1)(2x - 1)}{(3x - 1)(x + 2)}$$

$$= (2x - 3)(2x - 1).$$

Example 5. Show that $(2x + 3y - z)^3 + (3x + 7y + z)^3$ is divisible by $5(x + 2y)$.

The given expression is of the form $A^3 + B^3$, and therefore has a divisor of the form $A + B$.

Therefore $(2x + 3y - z)^3 + (3x + 7y + z)^3$ is divisible by

$$(2x + 3y - z) + (3x + 7y + z),$$

that is, by $5x + 10y$,

or by $5(x + 2y)$.

Example 6. Find the quotient when $a^3 + 8 - 5b(25b^2 - 6a)$ is divided by $a - 5b + 2$.

The expression $= a^3 + 8 - 125b^3 + 30ab$

$$= a^3 + (-5b)^3 + (2)^3 - 3 \cdot a(-5b)(2)$$

$$= (a - 5b + 2)(a^2 + 25b^2 + 4 + 10b - 2a + 5ab).$$

[Art. 213.]

$\therefore$ the quotient is $a^2 + 25b^2 + 4 + 10b - 2a + 5ab$.

Example 7. If $x + y = a$, and $x - y = b$ show that

$$4(x^4 - 6x^2y^2 + y^4) = 6a^2b^2 - a^4 - b^4.$$

$$x^4 - 6x^2y^2 + y^4 = (x^4 - 2x^2y^2 + y^4) - 4x^2y^2$$

$$= (x^2 - y^2)^2 - \frac{1}{4}(4xy)^2.$$

$$= \{(x + y)(x - y)\}^2 - \frac{1}{4}\{(x + y)^2 - (x - y)^2\}^2$$

$$= (ab)^2 - \frac{1}{4}(a^2 - b^2)^2;$$

$$\therefore \quad 4(x^4 - 6x^2y^2 + y^4) = 4a^2b^2 - (a^2 - b^2)^2 = 6a^2b^2 - a^4 - b^4.$$

EXAMPLES XXVIII-b

Find the product of

1. $2x - 7y + 3z$ and $2x + 7y - 3z$.
2. $3x^2 - 4xy + 7y^2$ and $3x^2 + 4xy + 7y^2$.
3. $5x^2 + 5xy - 9y^2$ and $5x^2 - 5xy - 9y^2$.
4. $7x^2 - 8xy + 3y^2$ and $7x^2 + 8xy - 3y^2$.
5. $x^3 + 2x^2y + 2xy^2 + y^3$ and $x^3 - 2x^2y + 2xy^2 - y^3$.
6. $(x + y)^2 + 2(x + y) + 4$ and $(x + y)^2 - 2(x + y) + 4$.
7. $(1 + x + 2x^2)^2 - (1 - x - 2x^2)^2$ and $(1 + x - 2x^2)^2 - (1 - x + 2x^3)^3$.
8. $(a^2 + 3a - 1)^2 - (a^2 - 3a - 1)^2$ and $(a^2 + a + 1)^2 - (a^2 - a + 1)^2$.
9. $x^3 - 4x^2 + 8x - 8$ and $x^3 + 4x^2 + 8x + 8$.
10. $x^3 - 6ax^2 + 18a^2x - 27a^3$ and $x^3 + 6ax^2 + 18a^2x + 27a^3$.
11. $x - a - \frac{x^2}{a} - \frac{a^2}{x}$ and $x + a + \frac{x^2}{a} - \frac{a^2}{x}$.
12. $(2x^2 + 3x + 1)^2 - (2x^2 - 3x - 1)^2$ and $(x^2 + 6x - 2)^2 - (x^2 - 6x + 2)^2$.

Find the continued product of

13. $x^2 + ax + a^2, x^2 - ax + a^2, x^4 - a^2x^2 + a^4$.
14. $1 - x + x^2, 1 + x + x^2, 1 - x^2 + x^4, 1 - x^4 + x^3$.
15. $(a - x)^3, (a + x)^3, (a^2 + x^2)^3$.
16. $(1 - x^2), (1 + x)^2, (1 + x^2)^2, (1 + x^4)^2$.
17. $x^2 + 4x + 3, x^2 + x - 2, x^2 - 5x + 6$.
18. $x^2 + 2x - 3, x^2 - 5x + 6, x^2 + 3x + 2$.
19. $x + 2, x^2 + 2x + 4, x - 2, x^2 - 2x + 4$.
20. Multiply the square of $a + 3b$ by $a^2 - 6ab + 9b^2$.
21. Multiply $\frac{1}{2}(a - b)^2 + \frac{1}{2}(b - c)^2 + \frac{1}{2}(c - a)^2$ by $a + b + c$.
22. Divide $(4x + 3y - 2z)^2 - (3x - 2y + 3z)^2$ by $x + 5y - 5z$.
23. Divide $x^8 + 16a^4x^4 + 256a^8$ by $x^2 + 2ax + 4a^2$.
24. Divide $(3x + 4y - 2z)^2 - (2x + 3y - 4z)^2$ by $x + y + 2z$.
25. Divide the product of $x^2 + 7x + 10$ and $x + 3$ by $x^2 + 5x + 6$.
26. Divide $2x(x^2 - 1)(x + 2)$ by $x^2 + x - 2$.
27. Divide $5x(x - 11)(x^2 - x - 156)$ by $x^3 + x^2 - 132x$.
28. Divide $x^6 + 19x^3 - 216$ by $(x^2 - 3x + 9)(x - 2)$.

29. Divide $(5x^2 - 3x - 6)^2 - (2x^2 - 7x + 9)^2$ by the product of $3x - 5$ and $x + 3$.

30. Divide $a^9 - b^9$ by the product of $a^2 + ab + b^2$ and $a^6 + a^3b^3 + b^6$.

31. Divide $(x^3 - 3x^2y)^2 - (3xy^2 - y^3)^2$ by $(x - y)^3$.

32. Divide $(x^2 - yz)^3 + 8y^3z^3$ by $x^2 + yz$.

33. Divide $18xy + 1 + 27x^3 - 8y^3$ by $1 + 3x - 2y$.

34. Divide $(2x^2 + 3x - 1)^2 - (x^2 + 4x + 5)^2$ by the product of $3x + 4$ and $x + 2$.

35. Divide the product of $6a^2 - 23a + 20$ and $22a^2 - 81a + 14$ by $33a^2 - 50a + 8$.

36. Divide the product of $x^2 + (a - b)x - ab$ and $x^2 - (a - b)x - ab$ by $x^2 + (a + b)x + ab$.

37. Divide $a^3 - 8y^3 - 9x(3x^2 + 2ay)$ by $a - 3x - 2y$.

38. Divide $27 - 8x^3 - 64y^3 - 72xy$ by $3 - 2(x + 2y)$.

39. Show that $(2x - 3y + 1)^3 - (1 - 3x + 2y)^3$ is divisible by $5(x - y)$.

40. Show that the square of $x + 1$ exactly divides

$$(x^3 + x^2 + 4)^3 - (x^3 - 2x + 3)^3.$$

41. Show that $2b + 2d$ is a factor of the expression

$$(a + b + c + d)^3 - (a - b + c - d)^3.$$

42. Show that $(3x^2 - 7x + 2)^3 - (x^2 - 8x + 8)^3$ is divisible by $2x - 3$ and by $x + 2$.

43. Show that $(7x^2 + 3x - 3)^3 + (5x^2 - 4x - 3)^3$ is divisible by $4x - 3$ and by $3x + 2$.

44. Show that the sum of the cubes of $2x^2 - 5x - 9$ and $x^2 + 6x - 5$ is divisible by the product of $3x + 7$ and $x - 2$.

45. If $x + y = m$ and $x - y = n$, express $x^3 + y^3$ in terms of m and n.

46. If $x + y = m$ and $x - y = n$, show that

$$16(x^4 - 7x^2y^2 + y^4) = (5m^2 - n^2)(5n^2 - m^2).$$

47. Find the value of $x^4 + x^2y^2 + y^4$ when $x + y = 2a$, $x - y = 2b$.

48. If $x + y = 2a$ and $x - y = 2b$ prove that

$$x^4 - 23x^2y^2 + y^4 = (7a^2 - 3b^2)(7b^2 - 3a^2).$$

49. Find the value of $x^4 - 47x^2y^2 + y^4$ in terms of p and q when $x + y = p$ and $x - y = q$.

50. Find the value of $x^4 - 2x^3y + 2xy^3 - y^4$ when $x = a + b$ and $y = a - b$.

29

MISCELLANEOUS THEOREMS AND EXAMPLES

215. EXAMPLES upon the simple rules, e.g. Division, Highest Common Factor, Evolution, etc., frequently occur which cannot be neatly and concisely worked without a ready use of factors and compound expressions. These we have hitherto excluded as unsuitable for the student until he has gained confidence and power by practice. We propose in the present chapter to bring together a miscellaneous collection of examples, for the most part not new in principle, but requiring some skill for their solution. The chapter will be found useful as a revision of the earlier chapters.

Example. Divide

$$ax^4 - (ap - b)x^3 + (aq - bp - c)x^2 + (bq + cp)x - cq \text{ by } ax^2 + bx - c.$$

$$\begin{array}{l|l|l} ax^2 + bx - c & ax^4 - (ap - b)x^3 + (aq - bp - c)x^2 + (bq + cp)x - cq & x^2 - px + q \\ & \underline{ax^4 + bx^3 - cx^2} & \\ & \quad - apx^3 + (aq - bp)x^2 + (bq + cp)x & \\ & \quad \underline{- apx^3 - bpx^2 \qquad + cpx} & \\ & \qquad\qquad aqx^2 + bqx - cq & \\ & \qquad\qquad \underline{aqx^2 + bqx - cq} & \end{array}$$

NOTE. When the coefficients in divisor or dividend are compound quantities it is best to retain them in brackets throughout the work.

216. In the process of finding the highest common factor, by the rules explained in Chap. XVIII, every remainder that occurs in the course of the work contains the factor we are seeking. Hence when any one of the remainders admits of being resolved into factors, we may often shorten the work.

Example 1. Find the H.C.F. of $2x^3 - (4a - 3c)x^2 + 6(b - ac)x + 9bc$ and $2x^3 + (2a + 3c)x^2 + (3ac - 4b)x - 6bc$.

$$\begin{array}{|l|} 2x^3 - (4a - 3c)x^2 + 6(b - ac)x + 9bc \\ 2x^3 + (2a + 3c)x^2 + (3ac - 4b)x - 6bc \end{array}$$

$$\begin{array}{l} 2x^3 - (4a - 3c)x^2 + (6b - 6ac)x + 9bc \\ \hline 6ax^2 + (9ac - 10b)x - 15bc \end{array}$$

Now the remainder $= 6ax^2 + 9acx - 10bx - 15bc$

$= 3ax(2x + 3c) - 5b(2x + 3c)$

$= (2x + 3c)(3ax - 5b)$.

Of these factors, $3ax - 5b$ may clearly be rejected; therefore if there is a common factor it must be $2x + 3c$. And by division, or by the method explained in Art. 152, we find that $2x + 3c$ is a factor of each expression.

Hence the H.C.F. is $2x + 3c$.

Example 2. Find the H.C.F. of $(a^2 - 2a)x^2 + 2(2a - 1)x - a^2 + 1$ and $(a^2 - a - 2)x^2 + (4a + 1)x - a^2 - a$.

Each of these expressions can be resolved into factors as explained in Art. 212, Ex. 4. Thus

$$(a^2 - 2a)x^2 + 2(2a - 1)x - a^2 + 1$$
$$= a(a - 2)x^2 + 2(2a - 1)x - (a + 1)(a - 1)$$
$$= \{(a - 2)x + (a + 1)\}\{ax - (a - 1)\}.$$
$$(a^2 - a - 2)x^2 + (4a + 1)x - a^2 - a$$
$$= (a - 2)(a + 1)x^2 + (4a + 1)x - a(a + 1)$$
$$= \{(a - 2)x + (a + 1)\}\{(a + 1)x - a\}$$

Hence the H.C.F. is $(a - 2)x + a + 1$.

EXAMPLES XXIX-a

Divide

1. $x^3 + (a + b + c)x^2 + (bc + ca + ab)x + abc$ by $x^2 + (a + b)x + ab$.
2. $x^4 - (5 + a)x^3 + (4 + 5a + b)x^2 - (4a + 5b)x + 4b$ by $x^2 - 5x + 4$.
3. $x^3 - (a - b)x^2 - (ab + 2b^2)x + 2ab^2$ by $x - b$.
4. $x^3 - (p^2 + 3q^2)x + 2p^2q - 2q^3$ by $x + p + q$.
5. $x^3 - (3mn + n^2)x + m(m^2 - n^2)$ by $x + m + n$.
6. $a(a - 1)x^2 + (2a^2 - 1)x + a(a + 1)$ by $(a - 1)x + a$.
7. $x^4 + (a + b)x^3 + (a^2 + ab + b^2)x^2 + (a^3 + b^3)x + a^2b^2$ by $x^2 + ax + b^2$.
8. $2l^2x^2 - 2(3m - 4n)(m - n)y^2 + lmxy$ by $lx + 2(m - n)y$.
9. $(a^2 + a - 2)x^2 - (2a + 1)xy - (a^2 + a)y^2$ by $(a - 1)x - ay$.
10. $x^3 - (a - b - 2)x^2 - (ab + 2a - 2b)x - 2ab$ by $(x - a)(x + 2)$.
11. $(x + 1)^8 + 4(x + 1)^6 + 6(x + 1)^4 + 4(x + 1)^2 + 1$ by $x^2 + 2x + 2$.
12. $(m + 1)(bx + an)b^2x^2 - (n + 1)(mbx + a)a^2$ by $bx - a$.

Find the H.C.F. of

13. $(m^2 - 3m + 2)x^2 + (2m^2 - 4m + 1)x + m(m - 1)$ and
$m(m - 1)x^2 + (2m^2 - 1)x + m(m + 1)$.

14. $mpx^3 + (mq - nq)x^2 - (mr + nq)x + nr$ and
$max^3 - (mc + na)x^2 - (mb - nc)x + nb$.

15. $2ap^3 + (3a - 2b)p^2q + (a - 3b)pq^2 - bq^3$ and
$3ap^3 - (a + 3b)p^2q + (2a + b)pq^2 - 2bq^3$.

16. $acx^3 + (bc + ad)x^2 + (bd + ac)x + bc$ and
$2acx^3 + (2bc - ad)x^2 - (3ac + bd)x - 3bc$.

17. $2a^2x^3 - (4b + 3)ax^2 + 2(3b - ac)x + 3c$ and
$2a^2x^3 + (2b - 3)ax^2 - (4ac + 3b)x + 6c$.

18. $2ax^3 + (4a^2 - 1)\ bx^2 - (2ab^2 + 3c)x - 6abc$ and
$ax^3 - (3 - 2a^2)\ bx^2 + (2c - 6ab^2)x + 4abc$.

Find the L.C.M. of

19. $x^4 - px^3 + (q - 1)x^2 + px - q$ and $x^4 - qx^3 + (p - 1)x^3 + qx - p$.

20. $p(p + 1)x^2 + x - p(p - 1)$ and $p(p + 2)x^2 + 2x - p^2 + 1$.

21. $(a^2 - 5a + 6)x^2 + 2(a - 1)x - a(a + 1)$ and
$a(a - 3)x^2 + 12x - (a + 1)(a + 4)$.

217. We add some miscellaneous questions in Evolution.

The *fourth root* of an expression is obtained by extracting the square root of the square root of the expression.

Similarly by successive applications of the rule for finding the square root, we may find the *eighth*, *sixteenth* ... root. The *sixth* root of an expression is found by taking the cube root of the square root, or the square root of the cube root.

Similarly by combining the two processes for extraction of cube and square roots, certain other higher roots may be obtained.

Example 1. Find the fourth root of

$$81x^4 - 216x^3y + 216x^2y^2 - 96xy^3 + 16y^4.$$

Extracting the square root by the rule we obtain $9x^2 - 12xy + 4y^2$, and by *inspection*, the square root of this is $3x - 2y$,
which is the required fourth root.

Example 2. Find the sixth root of

$$\left(x^3 - \frac{1}{x^3}\right)^2 - 6\left(x - \frac{1}{x}\right)\left(x^3 - \frac{1}{x^3}\right) + 9\left(x - \frac{1}{x}\right)^2.$$

By inspection, the square root of this is

$$\left(x^3 - \frac{1}{x^3}\right) - 3\left(x - \frac{1}{x}\right),$$

which may be written $x^3 - 3x + \frac{3}{x} - \frac{1}{x^3}$;

and the cube root of that is $x - \frac{1}{x}$,

which is the required sixth root.

218. In Chap. VI we have given examples of inexact division. In a similar manner when an expression is not an exact square of cube, we may perform the process of evolution, and obtain as many terms of the root as we please.

Example. To find four terms of the square root of $1 + 2x - 2x^2$.

$$1 + 2x - 2x^2 \left(1 + x - \frac{3}{2}x^2 + \frac{3}{2}x^3 \right.$$

$$\begin{array}{ll}
 & 1 \\
2 + x & 2x - 2x^2 \\
 & 2x + x^2 \\
\hline
2 + 2x - \frac{3}{2}x^2 & -3x^2 \\
 & -3x^2 - 3x^3 + \frac{9}{4}x^4 \\
\hline
2 + 2x - 3x^2 + \frac{3}{2}x^3 & 3x^3 - \frac{9}{4}x^4 \\
 & 3x^3 + 3x^4 - \frac{9}{2}x^5 + \frac{9}{4}x^6 \\
\hline
 & -\frac{21}{4}x^4 + \frac{9}{2}x^5 - \frac{9}{4}x^6.
\end{array}$$

Thus the required result is $1 + x - \frac{3}{2}x^2 + \frac{3}{2}x^3$.

***219.** In Art. 124 we pointed out the similarity between the arithmetical and algebraical methods of extracting square and cube roots. We shall now show that in extracting either the square or the cube root of any number, when a certain number of figures have been obtained by the common rule, that number may be nearly doubled by ordinary division.

***220.** *If the square root of a number consists of* $2n + 1$ *figures, when the first* $n + 1$ *of these have been obtained by the ordinary method, the remaining* n *may be obtained by division.*

Let N denote the given number; a the part of the square root already found, that is the first $n + 1$ figures found by the common rule, with n ciphers annexed; x the remaining part of the root.

Then $$\sqrt{N} = a + x;$$

$$\therefore \quad N = a^2 + 2ax + x^2;$$

$$\therefore \quad \frac{N - a^2}{2a} = x + \frac{x^2}{2a} \qquad \ldots(1).$$

Now $N - a^2$ is the remainder after $n + 1$ figures of the root, represented by a, have been found; and $2a$ is the divisor at the same stage of the work. We see from (1) $N - a^2$ divided by $2a$ gives x, the rest of the quotient required, increased by $\frac{x^2}{2a}$. We shall show that $\frac{x^2}{2a}$ is a *proper fraction*, so that by neglecting the remainder arising from the division, we obtain x, the rest of the root.

For x contains n figures, and therefore x^2 contains $2n$ figures at most; also a is a number of $2n + 1$ figures the last n of which are ciphers and thus $2a$ contains $2n + 1$ figures at least; and therefore $\frac{x^2}{2a}$ is a proper fraction.

From the above investigation, by putting $n = 1$, we see that *two* at least of the figures of a square root must have been obtained in order that the method of division, which is employed to obtain the next figure of the square root, may give that figure correctly.

Example. Find the square root of 290 to five places of decimals.

```
       290 (17.02
         1
 27   |190
      |189
       189
3402 | 10000
     |  6804
        3196
```

Here we have obtained four figures in the square root by the ordinary method. Three more may be obtained by division only, using 2×1702, that is 3404, for divisor, and 3196 as remainder.

Thus

```
3404)31960(938
     30636
      13240
      10212
       30280
       27232
        3048
```

And therefore to five places of decimals $\sqrt{290} = 17.02938$.

When the divisor consists of several digits, the method of contracted division may be employed with advantage.

Again, it may be noticed that in obtaining the second figure of the root, the division of 190 by 20 gives 9 for the next figure; this is too great, and the figure 7 has to be obtained tentatively. This is one of the modifications of the algebraical rule to which we referred in Art. 124.

***221.** *If the cube root of a number consists of* $2n + 2$ *figures, when the first* n + 2 *of these have been obtained by the ordinary method, the remaining* n *may be obtained by division.*

Let N denote the given number; a the part of the cube root already found, that is the first $n + 2$ figures found by the common rule, with n ciphers annexed; x the remaining part of the root.

Then $$\sqrt[3]{N} = a + x;$$

$\therefore$ $$N = a^2 + 3a^2x + 3ax^2 + x^3;$$

$\therefore$ $$\frac{N - a^3}{3a^2} = x + \frac{x^2}{a} + \frac{x^3}{3a^2} \qquad \ldots(1).$$

Now $N - a^3$ is the remainder after $n + 2$ figures of the root, represented by a, have been found; and $3a^2$ is the divisor at the same stage of the work. We see from (1) that $N - a^3$ divided by $3a^2$ gives x, the rest of the quotient required, increased by $\frac{x^2}{a} + \frac{x^3}{3a^2}$. We shall show that this expression is a *proper fraction*, so that by neglecting the remainder arising from the division, we obtain x, the rest of the root. By supposition, x is $< 10^n$, and a is $> 10^{2n+1}$;

$\therefore$ $$\frac{x^2}{a} \text{ is } < \frac{10^{2n}}{10^{2n+1}}; \text{ that is, } < \frac{1}{10};$$

and $$\frac{x^3}{3a^2} \text{ is } < \frac{10^{3n}}{3 \times 10^{4n+2}}; \text{ that is , } < \frac{1}{3 \times 10^{n+1}};$$

hence $$\frac{x^2}{a} + \frac{x^3}{3a^2} \text{ is } < \frac{1}{10} + \frac{1}{3 \times 10^{n+1}},$$

and is therefore a proper fraction.

EXAMPLES XXIX-b

Find the fourth roots of the following expressions:

1. $x^4 - 28x^3 + 294x^2 - 1372x + 2401.$

2. $16 - \frac{32}{m} + \frac{24}{m^2} + \frac{8}{m^3} + \frac{1}{m^4}.$

3. $a^4 + 8a^3x + 16x^4 + 32ax^3 + 24a^2x^2.$

4. $1 + 4x + 2x^2 - 8x^3 - 5x^4 + 8x^5 + 2x^6 - 4x^7 + x^8.$

5. $1 + 8x + 20x^2 + 8x^3 - 26x^4 - 8x^5 + 20x^6 - 8x^7 + x^8.$

Find the sixth roots of the following expressions:

6. $1 + 6x + 15x^2 + 20x^3 + 15x^4 + 6x^5 + x^6.$

7. $x^6 - 12ax^5 + 240x^4x^2 - 192a^5x + 60a^2x^4 - 160a^3x^3 + 64a^6.$

8. $a^6 - 18a^5x + 135a^4x^2 - 540a^3x^3 + 1215a^2x^4 - 1458ax^5 + 729x^6.$

Find the eighth roots of the following expressions:

9. $x^8 - 8x^7y + 28x^6y^2 - 56x^5y^3 + 70x^4y^4 - 56x^3y^5 + 18x^2y^6 - 8xy^7 + y^8.$

10. $\{x^4 + 2(p-1)x^3 + (p^2 - 2p - 1)x^2 - 2(p-1)x + 1\}^4.$

Find to four terms the square root of

11. $1 + x.$

12. $1 - 2x.$

13. $4 + 2x.$

14. $1 - x - x^2.$

15. $a^2 - x.$

16. $x^2 + a^2.$

17. $a^4 - 3x^2.$

18. $9a^2 + 12ax.$

Find to three terms the cube root of

19. $x^3 - a^3.$

20. $8 + x.$

21. $\frac{1}{a^3} + 9x.$

22. $1 - 6x + 21x^2.$

23. $27x^6 - 27x^5 - 18x^4.$

24. $64 - 48x + 9x^3.$

Identities and Transformations

***222. DEFINITION.** An identity is an algebraical statement which is true for all values of the letters involved in it.

Examples. $a^3 + b^3 = (a+b)(a^2 - ab + b^2).$

$$x^3 + y^3 + z^3 - 3xyz = (x+y+z)(x^2 + y^2 + z^2 - yz - zx - xy).$$

***223.** An identity asserts that two expressions are always equal; and the proof of this equality is called "proving the identity". The method of procedure is to choose one of the expressions given, and to show by successive transformations that it can be made to assume the form of the other.

Example 1. To prove that

$$bc\ (b-c)+ca\ (c-a)+ab\ (a-b)=-(b-c)(c-a)(a-b).$$

The first side $= bc(b-c)+c^2a-ca^2+a^2b-ab^2$

$$= bc\ (b-c)+a^2(b-c)-a\ (b^2-c^2)$$

$$= (b-c)\{bc+a^2-a\ (b+c)\}$$

$$= (b-c)\{bc+a^2-ab-ac\}$$

$$= (b-c)\{a\ (a-b)-c(a-b)\}$$

$$= (b-c)(a-b)(a-c)$$

$$= -(b-c)(c-a)(a-b),$$

changing the signs of the factor $a-c$, so as to preserve cyclic order.

[Compare Art. 229. Example 3.]

The expression on the left-hand side can be readily put in the following forms:

$a^2(b-c)+b^2(c-a)+c^2(a-b);\ -\{a(b^2-c^2)+b(c^2-a^2)+c(a^2-b^2)\}.$

Hence we have the following results:

$bc\ (b-c)+ca\ (c-a)+ab(a-b)=-(b-c)(c-a)(a-b);$

$a^2(b-c)+b^2(c-a)+c^2(a-b)=-(b-c)(c-a)(a-b);$

$a\ (b^2-c^2)+b(c^2-a^2)+c(a^2-b^2)=(b-c)(c-a)(a-b).$

These identities are of such frequent occurrence that they should be carefully noticed and remembered.

Example 2. If $2s=a+b+c$ prove that

$$\frac{1}{s-a}+\frac{1}{s-b}+\frac{1}{s-c}-\frac{1}{s}=\frac{abc}{s(s-a)(s-b)(s-c)}.$$

The first side $=\left(\dfrac{1}{s-a}+\dfrac{1}{s-b}\right)+\left(\dfrac{1}{s-c}-\dfrac{1}{s}\right)$

$$=\frac{s-b+s-a}{(s-a)(s-b)}+\frac{s-s+c}{s(s-c)}$$

$$=\frac{2s-a-b}{(s-a)(s-b)}+\frac{c}{s(s-c)}$$

$$=\frac{c}{(s-a)\ (s-b)}+\frac{c}{s\ (s-c)}$$

$$=c\left\{\frac{s\ (s-c)+(s-a)(s-b)}{s\ (s-a)(s-b)(s-c)}\right\}$$

$$= \frac{c\{s^2 - cs + s^2 - as - bs + ab\}}{s(s-a)(s-b)(s-c)}$$

$$= \frac{c\{2s^2 - s(a+b+c) + ab\}}{s(s-a)(s-b)(s-c)}$$

$$= \frac{abc}{s(s-a)(s-b)(s-c)},$$

for $\quad s(a+b+c) = s \cdot 2s = 2s^2.$

NOTE. Here $2s$ is a convenient abbreviation of $a+b+c$; and the reduction is much simplified by working in terms of s instead of substituting its value at once. In examples of this kind, as a rule, the student should avoid substituting as long as the work can be carried on in terms of the symbol of abbreviation.

Example 3. If $x^2 + u^2 = 2(xy + yz + zy - y^2 - z^2)$

prove that $\quad x = y = z = u.$

By transposing, we have

$$x^2 - 2xy + y^2 + y^2 - 2yz + z^2 + z^2 - 2zu + u^2 = 0,$$

or $\quad (x-y)^2 + (y-z)^2 + (z-u)^2 = 0.$

Now since the square of any quantity is always positive, each of the expressions $(x-y)^2$, $(y-z)^2$, $(z-u)^2$ is positive. Hence their sum cannot be zero unless each of them be separately equal to zero.

$\therefore \quad x - y = 0,\ y - z = 0,\ z - u = 0;$

or $\quad x = y = z = u.$

NOTE. The student should be careful to notice the difference between the conclusions to be drawn from the two statements

$$(x-a)^2 + (y-b)^2 = 0 \qquad ...(1),$$

and $\quad (x-a)(y-b) = 0 \qquad ...(2).$

From (1) we infer that *both* $x - a = 0$ and $y - b = 0$ *simultaneously*, while from (2) we infer that *either* $x - a = 0$ *or* $y - b = 0$.

*EXAMPLES XXIX-c

Prove the following identities:

1. $b(x^3 + a^3) + ax(x^2 - a^2) + a^3(x+a) = (a+b)(x+a)(x^2 - ax + a^2)$.
2. $(ax+by)^2 + (ay-bx)^2 + c^2x^2 + c^2y^2 = (x^2+y^2)(a^2+b^2+c^2)$.
3. $(x+y)^3 + 3(x+y)^2z + 3(x+y)z^2 + z^3$
   $= (x+z)^3 + 3(x+z)^2y + 3(x+z)y^2 + y^3$.
4. $(a+b+c)(ab+bc+ca) - abc = (a+b)(b+c)(c+a)$.
5. $(a+b+c)^2 - a(b+c-a) - b(a+c-b) - c(a+b-c) = 2(a^2+b^2+c^2)$.

6. $(x-y)^3+(x+y)^3+3(x-y)^2(x+y)+3(x+y)^2(x-y)=8x^3.$

7. $x^2(y-z)+y^2(z-x)+z^2(x-y)+(y-z)(z-x)(z-y)=0.$

8. $a^3(b-c)+b^3(c-a)+c^3(a-b)=-(b-c)(c-a)(a-b)(a+b+c).$

9. If $x+y+z=0$, prove that $x^3+y^3+z^3=3xyz.$

10. Prove that $(b-c)^3+(c-a)^3+(a-b)^3=3\,(b-c)(c-a)(a-b).$

If $2s=a+b+c$, show that

11. $(s-a)^2+(s-b)^2+(s-c)^2+s^2=a^2+b^2+c^2.$

12. $(s-a)^3+(s-b)^3+(s-c)^3+3abc=s^3.$

13. $16s(s-a)(s-b)(s-c)=2b^2c^2+2c^2a^2+2a^2b^2-a^4-b^4-c^4.$

14. $2(s-a)(s-b)(s-c)+a(s-b)(s-c)+b(s-c)(s-a)$

$$+\,c(s-a)(s-b)=abc.$$

If $a+b+c$, show that

15. $(2a-b)^3+(2b-c)^3+(2c-a)^3=3(2a-b)(2b-c)(2c-a).$

16. $\dfrac{a^2}{2a^2+bc}+\dfrac{b^2}{2b^2+ca}+\dfrac{c^2}{2c^2+ab}=1.$

17. Prove that

$$(x+y+z)^3+(x+y-z)^3+(x-y+z)^3+(x-y-z)^3$$
$$=4x(x^2+3y^2+3z^2).$$

18. If $a+b+c=s$, prove that

$$(s+3a)^3-(s-3b)^3-(s-3c)^3-3(s-3a)(s-3b)(s-3c)=0.$$

19. If $X=b+c-2a,\ Y=c+a-2b,\ Z=a+b-2c,$ find the value of $X^3+Y^3+Z^3-3XYZ.$

20. Find the value of $a(a^2+bc)+b(b^2+ac)-c(c^2-ab)$

when $a=.7, b=.08, c=.78.$

21. Prove that $(a-b)^2+(b-c)^2+(c-a)^2$

$$=2\,(c-b)(c-a)+2(b-a)(b-c)+2(a-b)(a-c).$$

22. Prove that $a^2(b^3-c^3)+b^2(c^3-a^3)+c^2(a^3-b^3)$

$$=(a-b)(b-c)(c-a)(ab+bc+ca)$$
$$=a^2(b-c)^3+b^2(c-a)^3+c^2(a-b)^3$$
$$=-\,[a^2b^2(a-b)+b^2c^2(b-c)+c^2a^2(c-a)].$$

23. If $(a+b)^2+(b+c)^2+(c+d)^2=4\,(ab+bc+cd)$, prove that

$$a=b=c=d.$$

24. If $x=a+d,\ y=b+d,\ z=c+d$, prove that

$$x^2+y^2+z^2-yz-zx-xy=a^2+b^2+c^2-bc-ca-ab.$$

25. If $a + b + c = 3$, prove that

$$\frac{1}{b^2 + c^2 - a^2} + \frac{1}{c^2 + a^2 - b^2} + \frac{1}{a^2 + b^2 - c^2} = 0.$$

26. If $a + b + c = 0$, simplify

$$\frac{b+c}{bc}(b^2 + c^2 - a^2) + \frac{c+a}{ca}(c^2 + a^2 - b^2) + \frac{a+b}{ab}(a^2 + b^2 - c^2).$$

27. Prove that the equation

$(x - a)^2 + (y - b)^2 + (a^2 + b^2 - 1)(x^2 + y^2 - 1) = 0$, is equivalent to the equation $(ax + by - 1)^2 + (bx - ay)^2 = 0$;

hence show that the only possible values of x and y are

$$\frac{a}{a^2 + b^2}, \frac{b}{a^2 + b^2}.$$

28. If $2(x^2 + a^2 - ax)(y^2 + b^2 - by) = x^2y^2 + a^2b^2$, show that

$$(x - a)^2(y - b)^2 + (bx - ay)^2 = 0$$

and therefore that $x = a$, $y = b$ are the only possible solutions.

***224.** We shall now give some further examples of fractions to illustrate the advantage of arranging expressions with regard to cyclic order, [Art. 172.]

Example. Find the value of

$$\frac{a}{(a-b)(a-c)(x-a)} + \frac{b}{(b-c)(b-a)(x-b)} + \frac{c}{(c-a)(c-b)(x-c)}.$$

Changing the sign of one factor in each denominator, so as to preserve cyclic order, we get for the lowest common denominator,

$(a - b)(b - c)(c - a)(x - a)(x - b)(x - c)$.

The whole expression has for its numerator or

$$-[a(b-c)(x-b)(x-c) + \ldots + \ldots]$$

or $\quad -[a(b - c)\{x^2 - (b + c)x + bc\} + \ldots + \ldots]$.

Arrange it according to powers of x; thus

coefficient of $x^2 = -\{a(b - c) + b(c - a) + c(a - b)\} = 0$;

coefficient of $x = \{a(b^2 - c^2) + b(c^2 - a^2) + c(a^2 - b^2)\}$

$= (b - c)(c - a)(a - b)$; [Art. 223.]

terms which do not contain x

$$= -\{abc(b - c) + abc(c - a) + abc(a - b)\}$$
$$= -abc\{b - c + c - a + a - b\} = 0.$$

Hence the expression $= \dfrac{(b-c)(c-a)(a-b)x}{(b-c)(c-a)(a-b)(x-a)(x-b)(x-c)}$

$$= \frac{x}{(x-a)(x-b)(x-c)}.$$

NOTE. In examples of this kind the work will be much facilitated if the student accustoms himself to readily writing down the following equivalents:

$$(b-c)+(c-a)+(a-b)=0.$$
$$a(b-c)+b(c-a)+c(a-b)=0.$$
$$a^2(b-c)+b^2(c-a)+c^2(a-b)=-(a-b)(b-c)(c-a).$$
$$bc(b-c)+ca(c-a)+ab(a-b)=-(a-b)(b-c)(c-a).$$
$$a(b^2-c^2)+b(c^2-a^2)+c(a^2-b^2)=(a-b)(b-c)(c-a).$$

Some of the identities in Examples XXIX-c may also be remembered with advantage.

*EXAMPLES XXIX-d

1. $\dfrac{a}{(a-b)(a-c)}+\dfrac{b}{(b-c)(b-a)}+\dfrac{c}{(c-a)(c-b)}.$

2. $\dfrac{bc}{(a-b)(a-c)}+\dfrac{ca}{(b-c)(b-a)}+\dfrac{ab}{(c-a)(c-b)}.$

3. $\dfrac{a^2}{(a-b)(a-c)}+\dfrac{b^2}{(b-c)(b-a)}+\dfrac{c^2}{(c-a)(c-b)}.$

4. $\dfrac{a^3}{(a-b)(a-c)}+\dfrac{b^3}{(b-c)(b-a)}+\dfrac{c^3}{(c-a)(c-b)}.$

5. $\dfrac{a(b+c)}{(a-b)(c-a)}+\dfrac{b(a+c)}{(a-b)(b-c)}+\dfrac{c(a+b)}{(c-a)(b-c)}.$

6. $\dfrac{1}{a(a-b)(a-c)}+\dfrac{1}{b(b-c)(b-a)}+\dfrac{1}{c(c-a)(c-b)}.$

7. $\dfrac{bc}{a(a^2-b^2)(a^2-c^2)}+\dfrac{ca}{b(b^2-c^2)(b^2-a^2)}+\dfrac{ab}{c(c^2-a^2)(c^2-b^2)}.$

8. $\dfrac{(x-b)(x-c)}{(a-b)(a-c)}+\dfrac{(x-c)(x-a)}{(b-c)(b-a)}+\dfrac{(x-a)(x-b)}{(c-a)(c-b)}.$

9. $\dfrac{bc(a+d)}{(a-b)(a-c)}+\dfrac{ca(b+d)}{(b-c)(b-a)}+\dfrac{ab(c+d)}{(c-a)(c-b)}.$

10. $\dfrac{1}{(a-b)(a-c)(x-a)}+\dfrac{1}{(b-c)(b-a)(x-b)}+\dfrac{1}{(c-a)(c-b)(x-c)}.$

11. $\dfrac{a^2}{(a-b)(a-c)(x+a)}+\dfrac{b^2}{(b-c)(b-a)(x+b)}+\dfrac{c^2}{(c-a)(c-b)(x-c)}.$

12. $a^2\dfrac{(a+b)(a+c)}{(a-b)(a-c)}+b^2\dfrac{(b+c)(b+a)}{(b-c)(b-a)}+c^2\dfrac{(c+a)(c+b)}{(c-a)(c-b)}.$

13. $\dfrac{a^3(b-c)+b^3(c-a)+c^3(a-b)}{(b-c)^3+(c-a)^3+(a-b)^3}.$

14. $\dfrac{a^2(b-c)+b^2(c-a)+c^2(a-b)+2(a-b)(b-c)(c-a)}{(b-c)^3+(c-a)^3+(a-b)^3}.$

15. $\dfrac{a^3(b-c)+b^3(c-a)+c^3(a-b)}{a^2(b-c)+b^2(c-a)+c^2(a-b)}$.

16. $\dfrac{a^2(b-c)^3+b^2(c-a)^3+c^2(a-b)^3}{(a-b)(b-c)(c-a)}$.

17. $\dfrac{\frac{1}{a}(b-c)+\frac{1}{b}(c-a)+\frac{1}{c}(a-b)}{\frac{1}{a}\left(\frac{1}{b^2}-\frac{1}{c^2}\right)+\frac{1}{b}\left(\frac{1}{c^2}-\frac{1}{a^2}\right)+\frac{1}{c}\left(\frac{1}{a^2}+\frac{1}{b^2}\right)}$.

18. $\dfrac{a^2\left(\frac{1}{c^2}-\frac{1}{b^2}\right)+b^2\left(\frac{1}{a^2}-\frac{1}{c^2}\right)+c^2\left(\frac{1}{b^2}-\frac{1}{a^2}\right)}{\frac{1}{bc}\left(\frac{1}{c}-\frac{1}{b}\right)+\frac{1}{ca}\left(\frac{1}{a}-\frac{1}{c}\right)+\frac{1}{ab}\left(\frac{1}{b}-\frac{1}{a}\right)}$.

***225.** *To find when* x^3+px^2+qx+r ...(1),

is divisible by x^2+ax+b ...(2).

Divide (1) by (2) in the ordinary way; thus

$$\begin{array}{l|l|l} x^2+ax+b & x^3+px^2+qx+r & x+(p-a) \\ & \underline{x^3+ax^2+bx} & \\ & (p-a)x^2+(q-b)x+r & \\ & \underline{(p-a)x^2+a\,(p-a)\,x+b\,(p-a)} & \\ & \{(q-b)-a\,(p-a)\}\,x+r-b\,(p-a) & \end{array}$$ ...(3).

Now if the remainder is zero the division is exact. This is the case when

$\{(q-b)-a(p-a)\}x+r-b(p-a)=0$, or $x=\dfrac{b(p-a)-r}{q-b-a(p-a)}$.

Hence when x has this value, (1) is divisible by (2).

But if in (3), $q-b-a\,(p-a)=0$, and also $r-b(p-a)=0$, the remainder is equal to zero *whatever value x may have.* Thus x^3+px^2+qx+b is divisible by x^2+ax+b for *all* values of x, provided that $q-b-a(p-a)=0$, and $r-b(p-a)=0$.

***226.** *To find the condition that* x^2+px+q *may be a perfect square.*

Using the ordinary rule for square root, we have

$$\begin{array}{r|l} & x^2+px+q\ \big(\,x+\frac{p}{2} \\ & x^2 \\ \hline 2x+\frac{p}{2} & px+q \\ & \underline{px+\frac{p^2}{4}} \\ & q-\frac{p^2}{4}. \end{array}$$

If therefore $x^2 + px + q$ be a perfect square, the remainder $q - \frac{p^2}{4}$, must be zero.

Hence $q - \frac{p^2}{4} = 0$, or $p^2 = 4q$, is the condition required.

***227.** *To prove that* $x^4 + px^3 + qx^2 + rx + s$ *is a perfect square if*

$$\left(q - \frac{p^2}{4}\right)^2 = 4s \text{ and } r^2 = p^2 s.$$

The square root must clearly be a trinomial expression of the form $x^2 + lx + m$; if therefore we put

$$x^4 + px^3 + qx^2 + rx + s = (x^2 + lx + m)^2,$$

we have, on expanding the right-hand side,

$$x^4 + px^3 + qx^2 + rx + s = x^4 + 2lx^3 + x^2(l^2 + 2m) + 2lmx + m^2.$$

Since this is to be true for all values of x, *we may assume that the coefficients of the like powers of* x *are the same;* hence

$$2l = p,\ l^2 + 2m = q,$$

$$2lm = r,\ m^2 = s.$$

From these equations, by eliminating the unknown quantities l and m, we shall obtain the necessary relations between p, q, r and s.

Thus we have $\quad q - \frac{p^2}{4} = 2m = 2\sqrt{s},$

$$r = 2lm = p\sqrt{s};$$

$$\therefore \quad \left(q - \frac{p^2}{4}\right)^2 = 4s \text{ and } r^2 = p^2 s.$$

NOTE. The method of Art. 226 might have been used here. Also the method of the present article may be used to establish the results of Arts. 225 and 226.

***228.** The proposition in the preceding article has been given to illustrate a useful method, which admits of very wide application. In the course of the proof we assume the truth of an important principle; namely. *If two rational integral expressions involving* x *are identically equal, the coefficients of like powers of* x *in the two expressions are equal.*

[An expression is said to be *rational* when no term contains a square or other root, and it is said to be *integral with respect to* x when the powers of x are all positive integers.]

The demonstration of this principle belongs to a more advanced part of the subject, and could not be discussed completely here.

[*See Higher Algebra*. Art. 3.11.]

The Remainder Theorem

The Remainder Theorem

***229.** *If a rational integral algebraical expression*

$$x^n + p_1x^{n-1} + p_2xs^{n-2} + p_3x^{n-3} + \ldots + p_{n-1}x + p^n.$$

be divided by $x - a$*, the remainder will be*

$$a^n + p_1a^{n-1} + p_2a^{n-2} + p_3a^{n-3} + \ldots + p_{n-1}a + p_n.$$

Divide the given expression by $x - a$ till a remainder is obtained which does not involve x. Let Q be the quotient, and R the remainder; then

$$x^n + p_1x^{n-1} + p_2x^{n-2} + \ldots + p_{n-1}x + p_n = Q(x - n) + R.$$

Since R does not contain x, it will remain unaltered whatever value we give to x.

Put $x = a$, then

$$a^n + p_1a^{n-1} + p_2a^{n-2} + \ldots + p_{n-1}a + p_n = Q \times 0 + R,$$

$$\therefore \quad R = a^n + p_1a^{n-1} + p_2a^{n-2} + \ldots + p_{n-1}a + p_n;$$

which proves the proposition.

From this it appears that when an algebraical expression is divided by $x - a$, the remainder can be obtained at once by writing a in the place of x in the given expression.

Again, the remainder is zero when the given expression is exactly divisible by $x - a$; hence we deduce another important proposition, known as the Factor Theorem.

If a rational integral expression involving x *become equal to* 0 *when a is written for* x*, it will contain* x – a *as a factor.*

Example 1. Resolve into factors $x^3 + 3x^2 - 13x - 15$.

By trial we find that this expression vanishes when $x = 3$; hence $x - 3$ is a factor.

$$\therefore \quad x^3 + 3x^2 - 13x - 15 = x^2(x - 3) + 6x(x - 3) + 5\ (x - 3)$$
$$= (x - 3)(x^2 + 6x + 5)$$
$$= (x - 3)(x + 1)(x + 5).$$

NOTE. The only numerical values that need be substituted for x are the factors of the last term of the expression. Thus, in the present case, by making trial of -5, we should have detected the factor $x + 5$.

Example 2. The remainder when $x^4 - 2x^3 + x - 7$ is divided by $x + 2$ is

$$(-2)^4 - 2\,(-2)^3 + (-2) - 7;$$

that is, $\quad 16 + 16 - 2 - 7$, or 23.

Or the remainder may be found more shortly by substituting $x = -2$ in $[\{(x - 2)x\}x + 1]x - 7$.

Example 3. Find the factors of $bc(b-c)+ca(c-a)+ab(a-b)$.

On trial, this expression vanishes when $b=c$; therefore $b-c$ is a factor. Similarly $c-a$, $a-b$ may be shown to be factors.

$$\therefore \quad bc(b-c)+ca(c-a)+ab(a-b)=M(b-c)(c-a)(a-b) \qquad \dots(1);$$

and since the left-hand member of this identity is only of three dimensions in a, b, c, the factor M must be some numerical quantity independent of a, b, c; its value can therefore be found by giving particular values to a, b, c, or by equating the coefficients of like terms on each side.

Let $a=0, b=1, c=2$, then (1) becomes

$$2(-1)+0+0=M(-1)\times 2\times(-1);$$

whence $M=-1$.

$$\therefore \quad bc(b-c)+ca(c-a)+ab(a-b)=-(b-c)(c-a)(a-b).$$

***230.** We shall now give general proofs of the statements made in Art. 55. We suppose n to be positive and integral.

I. *To prove that* $x^n - y^n$ *is always divisible by* $x-y$.

By the remainder theorem when x^n-y^n is divided by $x-y$ the remainder is y^n-y^n, or 0, that is, x^n-y^n is always divisible by $x-y$.

II. *To prove that* x^n+y^n *is divisible by* $x+y$ *when* n *is odd, but not when* n *is even.*

By the remainder theorem when x^n+y^n is divided by $x+y$ the remainder is $(-y)^n+y^n$.

(1) if n is odd, $(-y)^n+y^n=-y^n+y^n=0$;

(2) if n is even, $(-y)^n+y^n=y^n+y^n=2y^n$;

hence there is a remainder when n is even, but none when n is odd; which proves the proposition.

In like manner it may be proved that x^n-y^n is divisible by $x+y$ when n is even; and x^n+y^n is never divisible by $x-y$.

By going through a few steps of the division, the form of the quotient in each case is easily determined. The results of the present article may be conveniently stated as follows:

(i) For all values of n,

$$x^n-y^n=(x-y)(x^{n-1}+x^{n-2}y+x^{n-3}y^2+\dots+y^{n-1}).$$

(ii) When n is odd,

$$x^n+y^n=(x+y)(x^{n-1}-x^{n-2}y+x^{n-3}y^2-\dots+y^{n-1}).$$

(iii) When n is even,

$$x^n-y^n=(x+y)(x^{n-1}-x^{n-2}y+x^{n-3}y^2-\dots-y^{n-1}).$$

*EXAMPLES XXIX-e

Find the values of x which will make each of the following expressions a perfect square:

1. $x^4 + 6x^3 + 13x^2 + 13x - 1.$

2. $x^4 + 6x^3 + 11x^2 + 3x + 31.$

3. $x^4 - 2ax^3 + (a^2 + 2b)x^2 - 3abx + 2b^2.$

4. $4p^2x^4 - 4pqx^3 + (q^2 + 2p^2)x^2 - 5pqx + \frac{p^2}{2}.$

5. $\frac{a^2x^6}{9} - \frac{abx^4}{2} + \frac{2acx^3}{3} + \frac{9b^2x^2}{16} - \frac{5bcx}{2} + 6c^2.$

6. $x^4 + 2ax^3 + 3a^2x^2 + cx + d.$

7. Find the conditions that $x^4 - ax^3 + bx^2 - cx + 1$ may be a perfect square for all values of x.

Find the values of x which will make each of the following expressions a perfect cube:

8. $8x^3 - 36x^2 + 56x - 39.$

9. $\frac{x^6}{27} - \frac{a^2x^4}{3} + 4a^4x^2 - 28a^6.$

10. $m^3x^6 - 9m^2nx^4 + 39mn^2x^2 - 51n^3.$

11. Find the relation between b and c in order that
$$x^3 + 3ax^2 + bx + c$$
may be a perfect cube for all values of x.

12. Find the conditions that
$$x^6 + 3ax^5 + 3bx^4 + a(6b - 5a^2)x^3 + 3b(b - a^2)x^2 + 3cx + d$$
may be a perfect cube for all values of x.

13. What number must be added to $x^3 + 2x^2$ in order that the expression may be divisible by $x + 4$?

14. If $x + a$ be a common factor of $x^2 + px + q$ and $x^2 + lx + m$, show that $a = \frac{m - q}{l - p}.$

Resolve into factors:

15. $x^3 - 6x^2 + 11x - 6.$

16. $x^3 - 5x^2 - 2x + 24.$

17. $x^3 + 9x^2 + 26x + 24.$

18. $x^3 - x^2 - 41x + 105.$

19. $x^3 - 39x + 70.$

20. $x^3 - 8x^2 - 31x - 22.$

21. $6x^3 + 7x^2 - x - 2.$

22. $6x^3 + x^2 - 19x + 6.$

Write down the quotient in the following cases:

23. $\dfrac{x^7 + y^7}{x + y}$.

24. $\dfrac{x^8 - y^8}{x + y}$.

25. $\dfrac{x^6 - y^6}{x - y}$.

26. $\dfrac{x^9 - y^9}{x - y}$.

Find the square root of

27. $x^4 + (2a - 4)x^3 + (a^2 - 2a + 4)x^2 + (2a^2 - 4a)x + a^2$.

28. $(a + 1)^2 x^4 + (2a^2 + 2a)x^3 + (3a^2 - 4a - 6)x^2 + (2a^2 - 6a)x + a^2 - 6a + 9$.

29. Find what values of m make $3mx^2 + (6m - 12)x + 8$ a perfect square.

30. If $4x^4 + 12x^3y + Px^2y^2 + 6xy^3 + y^4$ is a perfect square, find P.
Without actual division show that

31. $32x^{10} - 33x^5 + 1$ is divisible by $x - 1$.

32. $3x^4 + 5x^3 - 13x^2 - 20x + 4$ ... $x^2 - 4$.

33. $x^4 + 4x^3 - 5x^2 - 36x - 36$ ... $x^2 - x - 6$.

Without actual division find the remainder when

34. $x^5 - 5x^2 + 5$ is divided by $x - 5$.

35. $x^3 - 7x^2a + 8xa^2 + 15a^3$ ... $x + 2a$.

36. If $ax^2 - bx + c$ and $bx^3 - bx + c$ have a common factor, then

$$a^3 - abd + cd^2 = 0.$$

37. If n be any positive integer, prove that $5^{2n} - 1$ is always divisible by 24.

38. Show that $1 - x - x^n + x^{n+1}$ is exactly divisible by
$1 - 2x + x^2$.

39. If $x^3 + px + r$ and $3x^2 + p$ have a common factor, prove that

$$\frac{p^3}{27} + \frac{r^2}{4} = 0.$$

40. Show that if $x^n - py^n + qz^n$ is exactly divisible by

$$x^2 - (ay + bz)x + abyz,$$

then
$$\frac{p}{a^n} + \frac{q}{b^n} + 1 = 0.$$

30

THE THEORY OF INDICES

[*Logarithms* (Chap. XXXIX) *may be taken in connection with this chapter after* Arts. 231-242 *have been read. The articles marked with an asterisk may be postponed on a first reading.*]

231. HITHERTO all the definitions and rules with regard to indices have been based upon the supposition that they were positive integers; for instance

(1) $a^{14} = a \cdot a \cdot a \ldots$ to fourteen factors.

(2) $a^{14} \times a^3 = a^{14+3} = a^{17}$.

(3) $a^{14} \div a^3 = a^{14-3} = a^{11}$.

(4) $(a^{14})^3 = a^{14 \times 3} = a^{42}$.

The object of the present chapter is twofold: first, to give *general* proofs which shall establish the laws of combination in the case of all positive integral indices; secondly, to explain how, in strict accordance with these laws, intelligible meanings may be given to symbols whose indices are fractional, zero, or negative.

We shall begin by proving, directly from the definition of a positive integral index, three important propositions.

232. DEFINITION. When m is a *positive integer*, a^m stands for the product of m factors each equal to a.

233. PROP. I. To prove that $a^m \times a^n = a^{m+n}$, *where* m *and* n *are positive integers.*

By definition, $a^m = a \cdot a \cdot a \ldots$ to m factors;

$$a^n = a \cdot a \cdot a \ldots \text{ to } n \text{ factors};$$

$$\therefore a^m \times a^n = (a \cdot a \cdot a \ldots \text{ to } m \text{ factors}) \times (a \cdot a \cdot a \ldots \text{ to } n \text{ factors})$$

$$= a \cdot a \cdot a \ldots \text{ to } m+n \text{ factors}$$

$$= a^{m+n}, \text{ by definition.}$$

COR. If p is also a positive integer, then $a^m \times a^n \times a^p = a^{m+n+p}$;

and so far any number of factors.

234. PROP. II *To prove that* $a^m \div a^n = a^{m-n}$, *where* m *and* n *are positive integers*, and m > n.

$$a^m \div a^n = \frac{a^m}{a^n} = \frac{a \cdot a \cdot a \ldots \text{to } m \text{ factors}}{a \cdot a \cdot a \ldots \text{to } n \text{ factors}}$$

$$= a \cdot a \cdot a \ldots \text{ to } m-n \text{ factors}$$

$$= a^{m-n}.$$

235. PROP. III. *To prove that* $(a^m)^n = a^{mn}$, *where* m *and* n *are positive integers.*

$$(a^m)^n = a^m \cdot a^m \cdot a^m \ldots \text{ to } n \text{ factors}$$

$$= (a \cdot a \cdot a \ldots \text{ to } m \text{ factors})\,(a \cdot a \cdot a \ldots \text{ to } m \text{ factors})$$

the bracket being repeated n times.

$$= a \cdot a \cdot a \ldots \text{ to } mn \text{ factors}$$

$$= a^{mn}.$$

236. These are the fundamental laws of combination of indices, and they are proved directly from a definition which is intelligible only on the supposition that the indices are *positive* and *integral.*

But it is found convenient to use fractional and negative indices, such as $a^{4/5}, a^{-7}$, or, more generally, $a^{p/q}$, a^{-n}; and these have at present no intelligible meaning. For it is plain that the definition of a^m, [Art. 232], upon which we based the three propositions just proved, is no longer applicable when m is *fractional*, or *negative*.

Now it is important that all indices, whether positive or negative, integral or fractional, should be governed by the same laws. We therefore determine meanings for symbols such as $a^{p/q}, a^{-n}$, in the following way: we assume that they conform to the fundamental law, $a^m \times a^n = a^{m+n}$, and accept the meaning to which this assumption leads us. It will be found that the symbols so interpreted will also obey the other laws enunciated in Props. II and III.

237. *To find a meaning for* $a^{p/q}$, p *and* q *being positive integers.*

Since $a^m \times a^n = a^{m+n}$ is to be true for *all* values of m and n.

by replacing each of the indices m and n by $\frac{p}{q}$, we have

$$a^{p/q} \times a^{p/q} = a^{p/q + p/q} = a^{2p/q}.$$

Similarly, $a^{p/q} \times a^{p/q} \times a^{p/q} = a^{2p/q} \times a^{p/q}$

$$= a^{2p/q + p/q} = a^{3p/q}$$

Proceeding in this way for 4, 5, ... q factors, we have

$a^{p/q} \times a^{p/q} \times a^{p/q} \ldots$ to q factors $= a^{qp/q}$;

that is, $(a^{p/q})^q = a^p$.

Therefore, by taking the qth root,

$$a^{p/q} = \sqrt[q]{a^p},$$

or, in words, $a^{p/q}$ is equal to "the qth root, of a^p".

Examples.

(1) $x^{5/7} = \sqrt[7]{x^5}$.

(2) $a^{1/3} = \sqrt[3]{a}$.

(3) $4^{3/2} = \sqrt{4^3} = \sqrt{64} = 8$.

(4) $a^{2/3} \times a^{5/6} = a^{2/3+5/6} = a^{3/2}$.

(5) $k^{a/2} \times k^{2/3} = a^{a/2+2/3} = k^{3a+4/6}$.

(6) $3a^{2/3}b^{1/2} \times 4a^{1/6}b^{5/6} = 12a^{2/3+1/6}b^{1/2+5/6} = 12a^{5/6}b^{4/3}$.

238. *To find a meaning for* a^0.

Since $a^m \times a^n = a^{m+n}$ is to be true for *all* values of m and n, by replacing the index m by 0, we have

$$a^0 \times a^n = a^{0+n} = a^n;$$

$$\therefore \quad a^0 = \frac{a^n}{a^n}$$

$$= 1.$$

Hence *any quantity* with zero index is equivalent to 1.

Example. $x^{b-c} \times x^{c-b} = x^{b-c+c-b} = x^0 = 1$.

239. *To find a meaning for* a^{-n}.

Since $a^m \times a^n = a^{m+n}$ is to be true for *all* values of m and n, by replacing the index m by $-n$, We have

$$a^{-n} \times a^n = a^{-n+n} = a^0.$$

But $\quad a^0 = 1;$

hence $\quad a^{-n} = \dfrac{1}{a^n},$

and $\quad a^n = \dfrac{1}{a^{-n}}.$

From this it follows that any *factor* may be transferred from the numerator to the denominator of an expression, or vice-versa, by merely changing the sign of the index.

Examples.

(1) $x^{-3} = \dfrac{1}{x^3}$.

(2) $\dfrac{1}{y^{-1/2}} = y^{1/2} = \sqrt{y}$.

(3) $27^{-2/3} = \dfrac{1}{27^{2/3}} = \dfrac{1}{\sqrt[3]{(27)^2}} = \dfrac{1}{\sqrt[3]{3^6}} = \dfrac{1}{3^2} = \dfrac{1}{9}$.

240. *To prove that* $a^m \div a^n = a^{m-n}$ *for all values of* m *and* n.

$$a^m \div a^n = a^m \times \frac{1}{a^n} = a^m \times a^{-n}$$

$= a^{m-n}$, by the fundamental law.

Examples.

(1) $a^3 \div a^5 = a^{3-5} = a^{-2} = \dfrac{1}{a^2}$. (2) $c \div c^{-8/5} = c^{1+8/5} = c^{13/5}$.

(3) $x^{a-b} \div x^{a-c} x^{a-b-(a-c)} = x^{c-b}$.

241. The method of finding a meaning for a symbol, as explained in the preceding articles, deserves careful attention. The usual algebraical process is to make choise of symbols, give them meanings, and then prove the rules for their combination. Here, the process is reversed; the symbols are given, and the law to which they are to conform, and from this the meanings of the symbols are determined.

242. The following examples will illustrate the different principles we have established.

Examples.

(1) $\dfrac{3a^{-2}}{5x^{-1}y} = \dfrac{3x}{5a^2y}$.

(2) $\dfrac{2a^{1/2} \times a^{2/3} \times 6a^{-7/3}}{9a^{-5/3} \times a^{3/2}} = \dfrac{4}{3} a^{1/2+2/3-7/3+5/3-3/2} = \dfrac{4}{3} a^{-1} = \dfrac{4}{3a}$.

(3) $\dfrac{\sqrt{x^3} \times \sqrt[3]{y^2}}{\sqrt[6]{y^{-2}} \times \sqrt[4]{x^6}} = \dfrac{x^{3/2} \times y^{2/3}}{y^{-1/3} \times x^{3/2}} = x^{3/2-2/3} y^{3/2+1/3} = x^0 y = y$.

(4) $2\sqrt{a} + \dfrac{3}{a^{-1/2}} + a^{5/2} = 2a^{1/2} + 3a^{1/2} + a^{5/2}$

$= 5a^{1/2} + a^{5/2} = a^{1/2}(5 + a^2)$.

EXAMPLES XXX-a

Express with positive indices:

1. $2x^{-1/4}$. **2.** $3a^{-2/3}$.

3. $4x^{-2}a^{-3}$. **4.** $3 \div a^{-2}$.

5. $\frac{1}{4a^{-2}}$. **6.** $\frac{1}{5x^{-1/2}}$.

7. $\frac{3a^{-3}x^{2}}{5v^{2}c^{-4}}$. **8.** $\frac{x^{a}y^{-b}}{b^{-a}}$.

9. $2x^{1/2} \times 3x^{-1}$.

Express with positive indices:

10. $1 \div 2a^{-1/2}$. **11.** $xy^{2} \times x^{-1}$.

12. $a^{-2}x^{-1} \div 3x$. **13.** $\frac{1}{\sqrt{x^{3}}}$.

14. $\frac{1}{4\sqrt[5]{x^{-3}}}$. **15.** $\frac{2}{\sqrt{y^{-3}}}$.

16. $\frac{\sqrt[4]{x^{3}}}{\sqrt{x^{-1}}}$. **17.** $a^{-2}x^{-1/2} \div a^{-3}$.

18. $\sqrt[3]{a^{-1}} \div \sqrt[3]{a}$. **19.** $\sqrt[5]{a^{-3}} \div \sqrt[5]{a^{7}}$.

Express with radical signs and positive indices:

20. $x^{3/5}$. **21.** $a^{-1/2}$.

22. $5x^{-1/2}$. **23.** $2a^{-1/x}$.

24. $\frac{1}{2a^{1/3}}$. **25.** $\frac{2}{b^{-3/4}}$.

26. $\frac{c^{-1/3}}{2}$. **27.** $\frac{1}{x^{-1/2}}$.

28. $a^{-1/3} \times 2a^{-1/2}$. **29.** $x^{-2/3} \div 2a^{-1/3}$.

30. $7a^{-1/2} \times 3a^{-1}$. **31.** $\frac{2a^{-2}}{a^{-3/2}}$.

32. $\frac{a^{-1/2}}{3a}$. **33.** $\frac{4x^{-1}}{x^{-1/3}}$.

34. $\frac{\sqrt[3]{x^{-a}}}{\sqrt[3]{x^{2}}}$. **35.** $\sqrt[3]{a^{2}} \times \sqrt[2]{a^{3}}$.

36. $\sqrt[5]{a^{-x}} \div \sqrt[5]{a^{-2x}}$. **37.** $\sqrt[2a]{x} \times \sqrt[a]{x^{2}}$.

38. $\sqrt[q]{x} \div \sqrt[2q]{x^3}$.

39. $\sqrt[3x]{a^3} \div \sqrt[x]{a^2}$.

40. $\sqrt[4]{a^n} \times \sqrt[3]{a^n} \div \sqrt[12]{a^{5n}}$.

Find the value of

41. $16^{3/4}$.

42. $4^{-5/2}$.

43. $125^{5/3}$.

44. $8^{-2/3}$.

45. $36^{-3/2}$.

46. $\dfrac{1}{25^{-2}}$.

47. $243^{2/5}$.

48. $\left(\dfrac{8}{27}\right)^{-1/3}$.

49. $\left(\dfrac{81}{16}\right)^{3/4}$.

50. $\left(\dfrac{32}{243}\right)^{-7/5}$.

243. *To prove that* $(a^m)^n = a^{mn}$ *is universally true for all values of* m *and* n.

Case I. Let n be a *positive integer.*

Now, *whatever be the value of* m

$$(a^m)^n = a^m \cdot a^m \cdot a^m \dots \text{ to } n \text{ factors.}$$
$$= a^{m+m+m+\cdots} \text{ to } n \text{ terms}$$
$$= a^{mn}.$$

Case II. Let m be unrestricted as before, and let n be a *positive fraction.*

Replacing n by $\frac{p}{q}$, where p and q are *positive integers*, we have

$(a^m)^n = (a^m)^{p/q}$.

Now the qth power of $(a^m)^{p/q} = \{(a^m)^{p/q}\}^q$

$$= (a^m)^{p/q \, q}, \qquad \text{[case. I.]}$$
$$= (a^m)^p = a^{mp}. \qquad \text{[case. I.]}$$

Hence by taking the qth root of these equals,

$$(a^m)^{p/q} = \sqrt[q]{a^{mp}} = a^{mp/q}. \qquad \text{[Arit. 237.]}$$

Case III. Let m be unrestricted as before, and let n be *any negative quantity*. Replacing n by $-r$, where r is *positive*, we have

$$(a^m)^n = (a^m)^{-r} \frac{1}{(a^m)^r}, \qquad \text{[Art. 239.]}$$
$$= \frac{1}{a^{mr}}, = a^{-mr} = a^{mn}.$$

Hence, Prop. III. Art. 235, $(a^m)^n = a^{mn}$ has been shown to be universally true.

Examples.

(1) $(b^{2/3})^{6/7} = b^{2/3 \times 6/7} = b^{4/7}$.

(2) $\{(x^{-2})^3\}^{-4} = (x^{-6})^{-4} = x^{24}$.

(3) $(x^{1/a-c})^{a^2-c^2} = x^{1/(a-c)\times(a^2-c^2)} = x^{a+c}$.

244. *To prove that* $(ab)^n = a^n b^n$, *whatever be the value of n;* a and b *being any quantities whatever.*

Case I. Let n be a *positive integer.*

Now $(ab)^n = ab \cdot ab \cdot ab \cdots$ to n factors

$= (a \cdot a \cdot a \cdots$ to n factors$)$ $(b \cdot b \cdot b \cdots$ to n factors$) = a^n b^n$.

Case II. Let n be a *positive fraction*. Replacing n by $\frac{p}{q}$, where p and q are *positive integers*, we have $(ab)^n = (ab)^{p/q}$.

Now the qth power of $(ab)^{p/q} = \{(ab)^{p/q}\}^q$

$= (ab)^p$, [Art. 243.]

$= a^p b^p$

$= (a^{p/q} b^{p/q})^q$ [Case I.]

Taking the qth root, $(ab)^{p/q} = a^{p/q} b^{p/q}$.

Case III. Let n have *any negative value*. Replacing n by $-r$, where r is positive,

$$(ab)^n = (ab)^{-r} = \frac{1}{(ab)^r}$$

$$= \frac{1}{a^r b^r} = a^{-r} b^{-r} = a^n b^n.$$

Hence the proposition is proved universally.

The result we have just proved may be expressed in a verbal form by saying that the index of a product may be *distributed* over its *factors*.

NOTE. An index is not distributive over the *terms* of an expression. Thus $(a^{1/2} + b^{1/2})^2$ is not equal to $a + b$. Again $(a^2 + b^2)^{1/2}$ is equal to $\sqrt{a^2 + b^2}$, and cannot be further simplified.

EXAMPLES.

(1) $(yz)^{a-c}(zx)^c(xy)^{-c} = y^{a-c} z^{a-c} z^c x^c x^{-c} y^{-c} = y^{a-2c} z^a$.

(2) $\{(a-b)^k\}^{-1} \times \{(a+b)^{-k}\}^l = (a-b)^{-kl} \times (a+b)^{-kl}$

$= \{(a-b)(a+b)\}^{-kl}$

$= (a^2 - b^2)^{-kl}$

245. It should be observed that in the proof of Art. 244 the quantities a and b are *wholly unrestricted*, and may themselves involve indices.

EXAMPLES.

(1) $(x^{1/2}y^{-1/2})^{4/3} \div (x^2y^{-1})^{-1/3} = x^{2/3}y^{-2/3} \div x^{-2/3}y^{1/3} = x^{4/3}y^{-1}$.

(2) $$\left(\frac{a^{2/3}\sqrt{b^{-1}}}{b^3\sqrt{a^{-2}}} \div \sqrt{\frac{a\sqrt{b^{-4}}}{b\sqrt{a^{-2}}}}\right)^6 = \left(\frac{a^{2/3}b^{-1/2}}{ba^{-2/3}} \div \sqrt{\frac{ab^{-2}}{ba^{-1}}}\right)^6.$$

$$= (a^{4/3}b^{-3/2} \div \sqrt{a^2b^{-3}})^6$$

$$= (a^{4/3}b^{-3/2} \div ab^{-3/2})^6$$

$$= (a^{1/3})^6 = a^2.$$

EXAMPLES XXX-b

Simplify and express with positive indices:

1. $(\sqrt{a^2b^3})^6$.

2. $(\sqrt[9]{x^{-4}y^3})^{-3}$.

3. $(x^ay^{-b})^3 \times (x^3y^2)^{-a}$.

4. $\left(\dfrac{16x^2}{y^{-2}}\right)^{-1/4}$.

5. $\left(\dfrac{27x^3}{8a^{-3}}\right)^{-2/3}$.

6. $\left(\dfrac{a^{-1/2}}{4c^2}\right)^{-2}$.

7. $\{\sqrt[4]{(x^{-2/3}y^{1/2})^3}\}^{-2/3}$.

8. $\sqrt[4]{x^3\sqrt{x^{-1}}}$.

9. $(4a^{-2} \div 9x^2)^{-1/2}$.

10. $(x \div \sqrt[n]{x^n})$.

11. $(x \times \sqrt[n]{x^{-1/n}})^{n^{2/1-n}}$.

12. $(\sqrt[b]{x^b \div \sqrt[a]{x}})^{-1/1-a}$.

13. $\sqrt{a^{-2}b} \times \sqrt[3]{ab^{-3}}$.

14. $\sqrt[3]{ab^{-1}c^{-2}} \times (a^{-1}b^{-2}c^{-4})^{-1/6}$.

15. $\sqrt[6]{a^{4b}x^6} \times (a^{2/3}x^{-1})^{-b}$.

16. $\sqrt[3]{x^{-1}}\sqrt{y^3} \div \sqrt{y^3\sqrt{x}}$.

17. $(a^{-1/2}\sqrt[3]{x})^{-3} \times \sqrt{x^{-2}\sqrt{a^{-6}}}$.

18. $\sqrt[n]{a^{n+k}b^{2n-k}} \div (a^{1/n}b^{-1/n})^k$.

19. $\sqrt[3]{(a+b)^5} \times (a+b)^{-2/3}$.

20. $\{(x-y)^{-3}\}^n \div \{(x+y)^n\}^3$.

21. $\left(\dfrac{a^{-2}b}{a^3b^{-4}}\right)^{-3} \div \left(\dfrac{ab^{-1}}{a^{-3}b^2}\right)^5$.

22. $\left\{\dfrac{\sqrt[3]{a}}{\sqrt[4]{b^{-1}}} \cdot \left(\dfrac{b^{1/4}}{a^{1/3}}\right)^2 \div \dfrac{a^{-1/2}}{b^{-1/2}}\right\}^6$.

23. $(a^{-1/2}x^{1/2}\sqrt{ax^{-1/3}\sqrt[4]{x^{4/3}}})^{-1/3}$.

24. $\sqrt[4]{(a+b)^6} \times (a^2-b^2)^{-1/2}$.

Simplify and express with positive indices:

25. $\left(\dfrac{a^{-3}}{b^{-2/3}c}\right)^{-3/2} \div \left(\dfrac{\sqrt{a^{-1/2}\cdot\sqrt[6]{b^3}}}{a^2c^{-1}}\right)^{-2}.$

26. $\left(\dfrac{a^{-2/3}x^{1/2}}{x^{-1}a}\right)^2 \div \sqrt[3]{\dfrac{a^{-1}}{x^{-3}}}.$

27. $\left(\sqrt[5]{\dfrac{a^{1/2}x^{-2}}{x^{1/2}a^{-2}}} \times \sqrt[3]{\dfrac{a\sqrt{x}}{x^{-1}\sqrt{a}}}\right)^{-4}.$

28. $\dfrac{\sqrt[3]{(a^3b^3+a^6)}}{\sqrt[3]{(b^6-a^3b^3)^{-1}}}.$

29. $(a^{n^2-1})^{n/n+1} + \dfrac{\sqrt[n]{a^{2n}}}{a}.$

30. $(x^{n/n+1})^{n^2} + \dfrac{\sqrt{x^{2n}}}{x}.$

31. $\left\{\dfrac{a^{p-q}}{\sqrt[q]{a^{q^2-pq}}} \times a^{2(p-q)}\right\}^n.$

32. $(x^{a/b}y^{-1})^b \div \left(\dfrac{x^{a_2-b^2}}{y^{ab+b^2}}\right)^{1/a+b}.$

33. $\left(\dfrac{x^{-2}y^3}{x^3y^{-2}}\right)^{-1/3} \times \left(\dfrac{y^3x^{-3}}{x^3y^{-3}}\right)^{-1}.$

34. $\left(\dfrac{y^{-3}}{x^{2/7}z^{-1}}\right)^{-3/2} \times \left(\dfrac{y^{14/3}x^{-1}}{z^{-21/4}}\right)^{3/7}.$

35. $\dfrac{2^n-(2^{n-1})^n}{2^{n+1}\times 2^{n-1}} \times \dfrac{1}{4^{-n}}.$

36. $\dfrac{2^{n+1}}{(2^n)^{n-1}} \div \dfrac{4^{n+1}}{(2^{n-1})^{n+1}}.$

37. $\dfrac{3.2^n-4.2^{n-2}}{2^n-2^{n-1}}.$

38. $\dfrac{3^{n+4}-6.3^{n+1}}{3^{n+2}\times 7}.$

246. Since the index-laws are universally true, all the ordinary operations of multiplication, division, involotion and evolution are applicable to expressions which contain fractional and negative indices.

247. In Art.121, we pointed our that the descending powers of x are

$$\ldots x^3,\ x^2,\ x,\ 1,\ \frac{1}{x},\ \frac{1}{x^2},\ \frac{1}{x^3},\ \ldots$$

A reason for this may be seen if we write these terms in the form

$$\ldots x^3,\ x^2,\ x^1,\ x^0,\ x^{-1},\ x^{-2},\ x^{-3},\ldots$$

Examples 1. Multiply $3x^{-1/3}+x+2x^{2/3}$ by $x^{1/3}-2$.

Arrange in descending powers of x.

$$x+2x^{2/3}+3x^{-1/3}$$

$$\frac{x^{1/3}-2}{x^{4/3}+2x+3},\ \frac{-2x-4x^{2/3}-6x^{-1/3}}{x^{4/3}-4x^{2/3}+3-6x^{-1/3}}.$$

Example 2. Divide $16a^{-3} - 6a^{-2} + 5a^{-1} + 6$ by $1 + 2a^{-1}$.

$$2a^{-1} + 1)\ 16a^{-3} - 6a^{-2} + 5a^{-1} + 6\ (8a^{-2} - 7a^{-1} + 6$$

$$\underline{16a^{-3} + 8a^{-3}}$$

$$-14a^{-2} + 5a^{-1}$$

$$\underline{-14a^{-2} - 7a^{-1}}$$

$$12a^{-1} + 6$$

$$12a^{-1} + 6$$

Example 3. Find the square root of $\dfrac{4x^2}{y} + \dfrac{\sqrt{x^3}}{y^{-1/2}} - 2x + \dfrac{y}{4} + x^3 - 4\sqrt{(x^5y^{-1})}$.

Getting rid of the radial signs, and arranging in descending powers of x, we have

$$x^3 - 4x^{5/2}y^{-1/2} + 4x^2y^{-1} + x^{3/2}y^{1/2} - 2x + \frac{y}{4}\left(x^{3/2} - 2xy^{-1/2} + \frac{y^{1/2}}{2}\right)$$

$$\underline{x^3}$$

$$2x^{3/2} - 2xy^{-1/2} \quad -4x^{5/2}y^{-1/2} + 4x^2y^{-1}$$

$$\underline{-4x^{5/2}y^{-1/2} + 4x^2y^{-1}}$$

$$2x^{3/2} - 4xy^{-1/2} + \frac{y^{1/2}}{2} \quad x^{3/2}y^{1/2} - 2x + \frac{y}{4}$$

$$\underline{x^{3/2}y^{1/2} - 2x + \frac{y}{4}}$$

Note. In this example it should be observed that the introduction of negative indices enables us to avoid the use of algebraical fractions.

EXAMPLES XXX-c

1. Multiply $3x^{1/3} - 5 + 8x^{-1/3}$ by $4x^{1/3} + 3x^{-1/3}$.
2. Multiply $3a^{3/5} - 4a^{1/5} - a^{-1/5}$ by $3a^{1/5} + a^{-1/5} - 6a^{-3/5}$.
3. Find the product of $c^x + 2c^{-x} - 7$ and $5 - 3c^{-x} + 2c^x$.
4. Find the product of $5 + 2x^{2a} + 3x^{-2a}$ and $4x^a - 3x^{-a}$.
5. Divide $21x + x^{2/3} + x^{1/3} + 1$ by $3x^{1/3} + 1$.
6. Divide $15a - 3a^{1/3} - 2a^{-1/3} + 8a^{-1}$ by $5a^{2/3} + 4$.
7. Divide $16a^{-3} + 6a^{-2} + 5a^{-1} - 6$ by $2a^{-1} - 1$.
8. Divide $5b^{2/3} - 6b^{1/3} - 4b^{-2/3} - 4b^{-1/3} - 5$ by $b^{1/6} - 2b^{-1/6}$.
9. Divide $21a^{3x} + 20 - 27a^x - 26a^{2x}$ by $3a^x - 5$.
10. Divide $8c^{-n} - 8c^n + 5c^{3n} - 3c^{-3n}$ by $5c^n - 3c^{-n}$.

Find the square root of

11. $9x - 12x^{1/2} + 10 - 4x^{-1/2} + x^{-1}$.

12. $25a^{4/3} + 16 - 30a - 24a^{1/3} + 49a^{2/3}$.

13. $4x^{n} + 9x^{-n} + 28 - 24x^{-n/2} - 16x^{n/2}$.

14. $12a^{x} + 4 - 6a^{3x} + a^{4x} + 5a^{2x}$.

15. Multiply $a^{3/2} - 8a^{-3/2} + 4a^{-1/2} - 2a^{1/2}$ by $4a^{-3/2} + a^{1/2} + 4a^{-1/2}$.

16. Multiply $1 - 2\sqrt[3]{x} - 2x^{1/2}$ by $1 - \sqrt[6]{x}$.

Find the square root of

17. Multiply $2\sqrt[3]{a^5} - a^{1/3} - \frac{3}{a}$ by $2a - 3\sqrt[3]{\frac{1}{a}} - a^{-5/3}$.

18. Divide $\sqrt[3]{x^2} + 2x^{1/3} - 16x^{-2/3} - \frac{32}{x}$ by $x^{1/6} + 4x^{-1/6} + \frac{4}{\sqrt{x}}$.

19. Divide $1 - \sqrt{a} - \frac{2}{a^{-1}} + 2a^2$ by $1 - a^{1/2}$.

20. Divide $4\sqrt[3]{x^2} - 8x^{1/3} - 5 + \frac{10}{\sqrt[3]{x}} + 3x^{-2/3}$ by $2x^{5/12-12} - \sqrt[12]{x} - \frac{3}{\sqrt[4]{x}}$.

21. $9x^{-4} - 18x^{3}\sqrt{y} + \frac{15y}{x^2} - 6\sqrt{\left(\frac{y^3}{x^2}\right)} + y^2$.

22. $4\sqrt{x^3} - 12\sqrt[4]{(x^3 y)} + 25\sqrt{y - 24}\;\sqrt[4]{\left(\frac{y^3}{x^3}\right)} + 16x^{-3/2}y$.

23. $81\left(\frac{\sqrt[3]{x^4}}{y^2} + 1\right) + 36\frac{x^{1/3}}{\sqrt{y}}(x^{2/3}y^{-1} - 1) - 158\frac{\sqrt[3]{x^2}}{y}$.

24. $\frac{x^{-2}}{16} + 1 + \frac{9}{\sqrt[3]{y^{-2}}} + \frac{1 - 3\sqrt[3]{y}}{2x} - 6\sqrt[3]{y}$.

248. The following examples will illustrate the formulae of earlier chapters when applied to expression involving fractional and negative indices.

Example 1. $(a^{h/k} - b^{p/q})(a^{-h/k} + b^{-p/q}) = a^{h/k - h/k}$

$$- a^{h/k}b^{p/q} + a^{h/k}b^{-p/q} - b^{p/q - p/q}$$

$$= 1 - a^{-h/k}b^{p/q} + a^{h/k}b^{-p/q} - 1$$

$$= a^{h/k}b^{-p/q} - a^{-h/k}b^{p/q}.$$

Example 2. Multiply $2x^{2p} - x^p + 3$ by $2x^{2p} + x^p - 3$.

$$\text{To product } = \{2x^{2p} - (x^p - 3)\}\{2x^{2p} + (x^p - 3)\}$$
$$= (2x^{2p})^2 - (x^p - 3)^2$$
$$= 4x^{4p} - x^{2p} + 6x^p - 9.$$

Example 3. The square of $3x^{1/2} - 2 - x^{-1/2}$

$$= 9x + 4 + x^{-1} - 2\cdot 3x^{1/2}\cdot 2 - 2\cdot 3x^{1/2}\cdot x^{-1/2} + 2\cdot 3\cdot x^{-1/2}$$
$$= 9x + 4 + x^{-1} - 12x^{1/2} - 6 + 4x^{-1/2}$$
$$= 9x - 12x^{1/2} - 2 + 4x^{-1/2} + x^{-1}$$

by collecting like terms and rearranging.

Example 4. Divide $a^{3n/2} + a^{-3n/2}$ by $a^{n/2} + a^{-n/2}$.

$$\text{The quotient} = (a^{3n/2} + a^{-3n/2}) \div (a^{n+2} + a^{-n/2})$$
$$= \{(a^{n/2})^3 + (a^{-n/2})^3\} \div (a^{n/2} + a^{-n/2})$$
$$= (a^{n/2})^2 - a^{n/2}\cdot a^{-n/2} + (a^{-n/2})^2$$
$$= a^n - 1 + a^{-n}.$$

EXAMPLES XXX-d

Write down the value of

1. $(x^{1/2} - 7)(x^{1/2} + 3)$.

2. $(4x - 5x^{-1})(4x + 3x^{-1})$.

3. $(7x - 9y^{-1})(7x + 9y^{-1})$.

4. $(x^m - y^n)(x^{-m} + y^{-n})$.

5. $(a^x - 2a^{-x})^2$.

6. $(a^x + a^{1/x})^2$.

7. $\left(x^{a/2} - \frac{1}{2}x^{-a}\right)^2$.

8. $(5x^a y^b - 3x^{-a}y^{-b})(4x^a y^b + 5x^{-a}y^{-b})$.

9. $\left(\frac{1}{3}a^{1/3} - a^{-1/3}\right)^2$.

10. $(3x^a y^{-b} + 5x^{-a}y^b)(3x^a y^b - 5x^{-a}y^{-b})$.

11. $\left(a^x - \frac{1}{2} - a^{-x}\right)^2$.

12. $(x^{1/a} - x^{-1/a} + x)^2$.

13. $\{(a+b)^{1/2} + (a-b)^{1/2}\}^2$.

14. $\{(a+b)^{1/2} - (a-b)^{-1/2}\}^2$.

Write down the quotient of

15. $x - 9a$ by $x^{1/2} + 3a^{1/2}$.

16. $x^{3/2} - 27$ by $x^{1/2} - 3$.

17. $a^{2x} - 16$ by $a^x - 4$.

18. $x^{3a} + 8$ by $x^a + 2$.

19. $c^{2x} - c^{-x}$ by $c^x - c^{-x/2}$.

20. $1 - 8a^{-3}$ by $1 - 2a^{-1}$.

21. $a^{4x} - x^6$ by $a^{2x} + x^3$.

22. $x^{-4} - 1$ by $x^{-1} + 1$.

23. $x^{5/3} - 1$ by $x^{1/3} - 1$.

24. $x^{5n} + 32$ by $x^n + 2$.

Find the value of

25. $(x + x^{1/2} - 4)(x + x^{1/2} + 4)$.

26. $(2x^{1/3} + 4 + 3x^{-1/3})(2x^{1/3} + 4 - 3x^{-1/3})$.

27. $(2 - x^{1/3} + x)(2 + x^{1/3} + x)$.

28. $(a^x + 7 + 3a^{-x})(a^x - 7 - 3a^{-x})$.

29. $\dfrac{a^{4/3} - 8a^{1/3}b}{a^{2/3} + 2\sqrt[3]{ab} + 4b^{2/3}}$.

30. $\dfrac{x - 7x^{1/2}}{x - 5\sqrt{x} - 14} \div \left(1 + \dfrac{2}{\sqrt{x}}\right)^{-1}$.

31. $\dfrac{x^{2/3} - 4\sqrt[3]{x^{-2}}}{\sqrt[3]{x^2 + 4 + 4x^{-2/3}}}$.

32. $\dfrac{a^{3/2} + ab}{ab - b^2} - \dfrac{\sqrt{a}}{\sqrt{a} - b}$.

31

ELEMENTARY SURDS

249. DEFINITION. If the root of a quantity cannot be exactly obtained the root is called a surd.

Thus $\sqrt{2}$, $\sqrt[3]{5}$, $\sqrt[5]{a^3}$, $\sqrt{a^2+b^2}$ are surds.

By reference to the preceding chapter it will be seen that these are only cases of fractional indices; for the above quantities might be written

$$2^{1/2}, 5^{1/3}, a^{3/5}, (a^2+b^2)^{1/2}.$$

Since, surds may always be expressed as quantities with fractional indices they are subject to the same laws of combination as other algebraical symbols.

250. A quantity may be expressed in a surd form without really being a surd. Thus $\sqrt[3]{x^6}$ or $x^{6/3}$, though apparently a surd, can be expressed in the equivalent form x^2.

251. A surd is sometimes called an irrational quantity; and quantities which are not surds are for the sake of distinction, termed rational quantities.

252. In the case of numerical surds such as $\sqrt{2}$, $\sqrt[3]{5}$, ..., although the *exact* value can never be found, it can be determined to any degree of accuracy by carrying the process of evolution far enough.

Thus $$\sqrt{5} = 2.236068\ldots;$$

that is $\sqrt{5}$ lies between 2.23606 and 2.23607; and therefore the error in using either of these quantities instead of $\sqrt{5}$ is less than .00001. By taking the root to a greater number of decimal places we can approximate still nearer to the true value.

It thus appears that it will never be *absolutely necessary* to introduce surds into numerical work, which can always be carried on to a certain degree of accuracy; but we shall in the present chapter prove laws for combination of surd quantities which will enable us to work with symbols such as $\sqrt{2}$, $\sqrt[3]{5}$, $\sqrt[4]{a}$, ... with absolute accuracy so long as the symbols are kept in their surd form. Moreover it will be found that even where approximate numerical results are required, the work is considerably simplified and shortened by operating with surd symbols, and afterwards substituting numerical values, if necessary.

253. The *order* of a surd is indicated by the root symbol, or surd index. Thus $\sqrt[3]{x}$, $\sqrt[n]{a}$ are respectively surds of the third and n^{th} orders.

The surds of the most frequent occurrence are those of the second order; they are sometimes called quadratic surds. Thus $\sqrt{3}$, $\sqrt{a}$, $\sqrt{x+y}$ are quadratic surds.

254. It will frequently be found convenient to express a rational quantity in a surd form.

A rational quantity may be expressed in the form of a surd of *any required order* by raising it to the power whose root the surd expresses, and prefixing the radical sign. Thus

$$5 = \sqrt{25} = \sqrt[3]{125} = \sqrt[4]{625} = \sqrt[n]{5n}\ ;$$

$$a + x = \sqrt{(a+x)^2} = \sqrt[6]{(a+x)^6} = \sqrt[n]{(a+x)^n}\ .$$

255. A surd of any order may be transformed into a surd of a different order.

Examples.

1. $\sqrt[3]{2} = 2^{1/3} = 2^{4/12} = \sqrt[12]{2^4}$. **2.** $\sqrt[p]{a} = a^{1/p} = a^{q/pq} = \sqrt[pq]{a^q}$.

256. Surds of different orders may be transformed into surds of the same order. This order may by *any* common multiple of each of the given orders, but it is usually most convenient to choose the *least* common multiple.

Example. Express $\sqrt[4]{a^3}$, $\sqrt[3]{b^2}$, $\sqrt[6]{a^5}$ as surds of the same lowest order.

The least common multiple of 4, 3, 6 is 12; and expressing the given surds as surds of the twelfth order they become $\sqrt[12]{a^9}$, $\sqrt[12]{b^8}$, $\sqrt[12]{a^{10}}$.

257. Surds of different orders may be arranged according to magnitude by transforming them into surds of the same order.

Example. Arrange $\sqrt{3}$, $\sqrt[3]{6}$, $\sqrt[4]{10}$ according to magnitude.

The least common multiple of 2, 3, 4 is 12; and, expressing the given surds of the twelfth order, we have

$$\sqrt{3} = \sqrt[12]{3^6} = \sqrt[12]{729}\ ,$$

$$\sqrt[3]{6} = \sqrt[12]{6^4} = \sqrt[12]{1296}\ ,$$

$$\sqrt[4]{10} = \sqrt[12]{10^3} = \sqrt[12]{1000}\ .$$

Hence arranged in ascending order of magnitude the surds are

$$\sqrt{3}, \sqrt[4]{10}, \sqrt[3]{6}.$$

EXAMPLES XXXI-a

Express as surds of the twelfth order with positive indices:

1. $x^{1/3}$.

2. $a^{-1} \div a^{-1/2}$.

3. $\sqrt[4]{ax^3} \times \sqrt[3]{a^{-1}x^{-2}}$.

4. $\dfrac{1}{a^{-3/4}}$.

5. $\dfrac{1}{\sqrt[8]{a^{-14}}}$.

6. $\sqrt[6]{\dfrac{1}{a^{-2}}}$.

Express as surds of the nth order with positive indices:

7. $\sqrt[3]{x^2}$.

8. x^a.

9. $a^{\frac{1}{2}}$.

10. $\sqrt{a^{-\frac{1}{n}}}$.

11. $\sqrt[3]{x^n y^{\frac{1}{n}}}$.

12. $\dfrac{1}{a^{-1}}$.

13. $\dfrac{x^{-1/2}}{y^2}$.

14. $\dfrac{a^{1/2}}{x^{-n}}$.

Express as surds of the same lowest order:

15. $\sqrt{a}, \sqrt[9]{a^5}$.

16. $\sqrt[5]{a^3}, \sqrt{a}$.

17. $\sqrt[8]{x^3}, \sqrt[9]{x^6}, \sqrt[20]{x^5}$.

18. $\sqrt[16]{x^4}, \sqrt[12]{x^{10}}$.

19. $\sqrt[21]{a^3 b^4}, \sqrt[7]{ab}$.

20. $\sqrt{ax^2}$, $\sqrt[39]{a^9 x^6}$.

21. $\sqrt{5}, \sqrt[3]{11}, \sqrt[6]{13}$.

22. $\sqrt[4]{8}, \sqrt{3}, \sqrt[8]{6}$.

23. $\sqrt[3]{2}, \sqrt[9]{8}, \sqrt[6]{4}$.

258. The root of any expression is equal to the product of the roots of the separate factory of the expression.

For $$\sqrt[n]{ab} = (ab)^{\frac{1}{n}} = a^{1/n} b^{1/n},$$
$$= \sqrt[n]{a} \cdot \sqrt[n]{b}.$$ [Art. 244.]

Similarly, $\sqrt[n]{abc} = \sqrt[n]{a} \cdot \sqrt[n]{b} \cdot \sqrt[n]{c}$;

and so for any number of factors.

Examples.

1. $\sqrt[4]{15} = \sqrt[4]{3} \cdot \sqrt[4]{5}$.

2. $\sqrt[3]{a^6 b} = \sqrt[3]{a^6} \cdot \sqrt[3]{b} = a^2 \sqrt[3]{b}$.

3. $\sqrt{50} = \sqrt{25} \cdot \sqrt{2} = 5\sqrt{2}$.

Hence it appears that a surd may sometimes be expressed as the product of a rational quantity and a surd; when so reduced the surd is said to be in its *simplest form*.

Thus the simplest form of $\sqrt{128}$ is $8\sqrt{2}$.

Conversely, the coefficient of a surd may be brought under the radical sign by first reducing it to the form of a surd, and then multiplying the surds together.

Examples.

1. $7\sqrt{5} = \sqrt{49} \cdot \sqrt{5} = \sqrt{245}$.

2. $a\sqrt[3]{b} = \sqrt[3]{a^8} \cdot \sqrt[3]{b} = \sqrt[3]{a^8 b}$.

When so reduced a surd is said to be an *entire surd*.

259. When surds have, or can be reduced to have, the same irrational factor, they are said to be *like*; otherwise, they are said to be *unlike*.

Thus

$5\sqrt{3},\ 2\sqrt{3}, \frac{1}{5}\sqrt{3}$ are like surds.

But $3\sqrt{2}$ and $2\sqrt{3}$ are unlike surds.

Again, $3\sqrt{20}$, $4\sqrt{5}, \sqrt{\frac{1}{5}}$ are like surds;

for $3\sqrt{20} = 3\sqrt{4} \cdot \sqrt{5} = 3 \cdot 2\sqrt{5} = 6\sqrt{5}$;

and $\sqrt{\frac{1}{5}} = \sqrt{\frac{5}{25}} = \frac{1}{5}\sqrt{5}$.

260. In finding the sum of a number of like surds we reduce them to their simplest form, and prefix to their common irrational part the sum of the coefficients.

Example 1. The sum of $3\sqrt{20}, 4\sqrt{5}, \frac{1}{\sqrt{5}}$

$$= 6\sqrt{5} + 4\sqrt{5} + \frac{1}{5}\sqrt{5}$$

$$= \frac{51}{5}\sqrt{5}.$$

Example 2. The sum of $x\sqrt[3]{8x^3 a} + y\sqrt[3]{-y^3 a} - z\sqrt[3]{z^3 a}$

$$= x \cdot 2x\sqrt[3]{a} + y(-y)\sqrt[3]{a} - z \cdot z\sqrt[3]{a}$$

$$= (2x^2 - y^2 - z^2)\sqrt[3]{a}.$$

261. Unlike surds cannot be collected.

Thus the sum of $5\sqrt{2}, -2\sqrt{3}$, and $\sqrt{6}$ is $5\sqrt{2} - 2\sqrt{3} + \sqrt{6}$, and cannot be further simplified.

EXAMPLES XXXI-b

Express in the simplest form:

1. $\sqrt{288}$. **2.** $\sqrt{147}$. **3.** $\sqrt[3]{256}$. **4.** $\sqrt[3]{432}$.

5. $3\sqrt{150}$. **6.** $2\sqrt{720}$. **7.** $5\sqrt{245}$. **8.** $\sqrt[3]{1029}$.

9. $\sqrt[4]{3125}$. **10.** $\sqrt[3]{-2187}$. **11.** $\sqrt{36a^3}$. **12.** $\sqrt{27a^3b^5}$.

13. $\sqrt[3]{-108x^4y^3}$. **14.** $\sqrt[n]{x^{3n}y^{2n+5}}$. **15.** $\sqrt[p]{x^{a+p}y^{2p}}$.

16. $\sqrt{a^3+2a^2b+ab^2}$. **17.** $\sqrt[3]{8x^4y-24x^3y^2+24x^2y^3-8xy^4}$.

Express as entire surds:

18. $11\sqrt{2}$. **19.** $14\sqrt{5}$.

20. $6\sqrt[3]{4}$. **21.** $5\sqrt[3]{6}$.

22. $\frac{4}{11}\sqrt{\frac{77}{8}}$. **23.** $\frac{3ab}{2c}\sqrt{\frac{20c^2}{9a^2b}}$.

24. $\frac{3x}{y}\sqrt{\frac{a^2y^3}{x^2}}$. **25.** $\frac{a}{x^2}\sqrt{\frac{3x^3}{a}}$.

26. $\frac{2a}{3x}\sqrt[3]{\frac{27x^4}{a^2}}$. **27.** $\frac{2a}{b}\sqrt[4]{\frac{b^4}{8a^3}}$.

28. $a\sqrt[n]{\frac{b^2}{a^{n-2}}}$. **29.** $\frac{a}{b}\sqrt[p]{\frac{b^{p+1}}{a^{p-1}}}$.

30. $\frac{y}{x^n}\sqrt{\frac{x^{2n+1}}{y^3}}$. **31.** $(x+y)\sqrt{\frac{x-y}{x+y}}$.

32. $\frac{ax}{a-x}\sqrt{\frac{a^2-x^2}{a^2x^2}}$.

Find the value of:

33. $3\sqrt{45}-\sqrt{20}+7\sqrt{5}$. **34.** $4\sqrt{63}+5\sqrt{7}-8\sqrt{28}$.

35. $\sqrt{44}-5\sqrt{176}+2|99$. **36.** $2\sqrt{363}-5\sqrt{243}+\sqrt{192}$.

37. $2\sqrt[3]{189}+3\sqrt[3]{875}-7\sqrt[3]{56}$. **38.** $5\sqrt[3]{81}-7\sqrt[3]{192}+4\sqrt[3]{648}$.

39. $3\sqrt[4]{162}-7\sqrt[4]{32}+\sqrt[4]{1250}$. **40.** $5\sqrt[3]{-54}-2\sqrt[3]{-16}+4\sqrt[3]{686}$.

41. $4\sqrt{128}+4\sqrt{75}-5\sqrt{162}$. **42.** $5\sqrt{24}-2\sqrt{54}-\sqrt{6}$.

43. $\sqrt{252}-\sqrt{294}-48\sqrt{\frac{1}{6}}$. **44.** $3\sqrt{147}-\frac{7}{3}\sqrt{\frac{1}{3}}-\sqrt{\frac{1}{27}}$.

262. *To multiply two surds of the same order multiply separately the rational factors and the irrational factors.*

For $a\sqrt[n]{x} \times b\sqrt[n]{y} = ax^{1/n} \times by^{1/n}$

$$= abx^{1/n}y^{1/n}$$

$$ab(xy)^{1/n} = ab\sqrt[n]{xy}.$$

Examples.

1. $5\sqrt{3} \times 3\sqrt{7} = 15\sqrt{21}.$
2. $2\sqrt{x} \times 3\sqrt{x} = 6x.$
3. $\sqrt[4]{a+b} \times \sqrt[4]{a-b} = \sqrt[4]{(a+b)(a-b)} = \sqrt[4]{a^2-b^2}.$

263. If the surds are not in their simplest form, it will save labour to reduce them to this form before multiplication.

Example. The product of $5\sqrt{32}, \sqrt{48}, 2\sqrt{54}$

$$= 5\cdot 4\sqrt{2} \times 4\sqrt{3} \times 2\cdot 3\sqrt{6} = 480\cdot\sqrt{2}\cdot\sqrt{3}\cdot\sqrt{6}$$

$$= 480 \times 6 = 2880.$$

264. *To multiply surds which are not of the same order : reduce them to equivalent surds of the same order, and proceed as before.*

Example. Multiply $5\sqrt[3]{2}$ by $2\sqrt{5}$.

The product $= 5\sqrt[6]{2^2} \times 2\sqrt[6]{5^3} = 10\sqrt[6]{2^2 \times 5^3} = 10\sqrt[6]{500}.$

265. Suppose it is required to find the numerical value of the quotient when $\sqrt{5}$ is divided by $\sqrt{7}$.

At first sight it would seem that we must find the square root of 5, which is 2.236..., and then square root of 7, which is 2.645..., and finally divide 2.236... by 2.645...; three troublesome operations.

But we may avoid much of this labour by multiplying both numerator and denominator by $\sqrt{7}$, so as to make the denominator a rational quantity. Thus

$$\frac{\sqrt{5}}{\sqrt{7}} = \frac{\sqrt{5}}{\sqrt{7}} \times \frac{\sqrt{7}}{\sqrt{7}} = \frac{\sqrt{5\times 7}}{7} = \frac{\sqrt{35}}{7}.$$

Now $\sqrt{35} = 5.916....$

$$\therefore \quad \frac{\sqrt{5}}{\sqrt{7}} = \frac{5.916}{7} = .845.... .$$

266. The great utility of this artifice in calculating the numerical value of surd fractions suggests its convenience in the case of *all* surd fractions, even where numerical values are not required. Thus it is usual to simplify $\dfrac{a\sqrt{b}}{\sqrt{c}}$ as follows:

$$\frac{a\sqrt{b}}{\sqrt{c}}=\frac{a\sqrt{b}\times\sqrt{c}}{\sqrt{c}\times\sqrt{c}}=\frac{a\sqrt{bc}}{c}$$

The process by which surds are removed from the denominator of any fraction is known as rationalising the denominator. It is effected by multiplying both numerator and denominator by any factor which renders the denominator rational. We shall return to this point in Art. 270.

267. The quotient of one surd by another may be found by expressing the result as a fraction, and rationalising the denominator.

Example 1. Divide $4\sqrt{75}$ by $25\sqrt{56}$.

$$\text{The quotient }=\frac{4\sqrt{75}}{25\sqrt{56}}=\frac{4\times5\sqrt{3}}{25\times2\sqrt{14}}=\frac{2\sqrt{3}}{5\sqrt{14}}$$
$$=\frac{2\sqrt{3}\times\sqrt{14}}{5\sqrt{14}\times\sqrt{14}}=\frac{2\sqrt{42}}{5\times14}=\frac{\sqrt{42}}{35}.$$

Example 2. $\dfrac{\sqrt[3]{b}}{\sqrt[3]{c^2}}=\dfrac{\sqrt[3]{b}\times\sqrt[3]{c}}{\sqrt[3]{c^2}\times\sqrt[3]{c}}=\dfrac{\sqrt[3]{bc}}{\sqrt[3]{c^3}}=\dfrac{\sqrt[3]{bc}}{c}.$

EXAMPLES XXXI-c

Find the value of

1. $2\sqrt{14}\times\sqrt{21}.$

2. $3\sqrt{8}\times\sqrt{6}.$

3. $5\sqrt{a}\times2\sqrt{3}.$

4. $2\sqrt{15}\times3\sqrt{5}.$

5. $8\sqrt{12}\times3\sqrt{24}.$

6. $\sqrt[3]{x+2}\times\sqrt[3]{x-2}.$

7. $21\sqrt{384}\div8\sqrt{98}.$

8. $5\sqrt{27}\div3\sqrt{24}.$

9. $-13\sqrt{125}\div5\sqrt{65}.$

10. $\sqrt[3]{168}\times\sqrt[3]{147}.$

11. $5\sqrt[3]{128}\times2\sqrt[3]{432}.$

12. $6\sqrt{14}\div2\sqrt{21}.$

13. $a\sqrt{b^3}\times b^2\sqrt{a}.$

14. $\dfrac{3\sqrt{11}}{2\sqrt{98}}\div\dfrac{5}{7\sqrt{22}}.$

15. $\dfrac{3\sqrt{48}}{5\sqrt{112}}\div\dfrac{6\sqrt{84}}{\sqrt{392}}.$

16. $\dfrac{3}{x}\sqrt{\dfrac{a^2}{x}}\times\dfrac{4}{3}\sqrt{\dfrac{x^3}{2a^4}}.$

17. $\dfrac{3}{a-b}\sqrt{\dfrac{2x}{a-b}}\div\sqrt{\dfrac{18x^3}{(a-b)^5}}.$

Given $\sqrt{2} = 1.41421$, $\sqrt{3} = 1.73205$, $\sqrt{5} = 2.23607$, $\sqrt{6} = 2.44949$, $\sqrt{7} = 2.64575$: find to four places of decimals the numerical value of

18. $\frac{14}{\sqrt{2}}$.

19. $\frac{25}{\sqrt{5}}$.

20. $\frac{10}{\sqrt{7}}$.

21. $\frac{48}{\sqrt{6}}$.

22. $\frac{60}{\sqrt{5}}$.

23. $144 \div \sqrt{6}$.

24. $\sqrt{2} \div \sqrt{3}$.

25. $\frac{1}{2\sqrt{3}}$.

26. $\frac{1}{\sqrt{500}}$.

27. $\frac{4}{\sqrt{243}}$.

28. $\frac{25}{\sqrt{252}}$.

29. $\sqrt{\frac{256}{1575}}$.

268. Hitherto we have confined our attention to simple surds, such as $\sqrt[4]{5}, \sqrt[3]{a}, \sqrt{x+y}$. An expression involving two or more simple surds is called a compound surd; thus $2\sqrt{a} - 3\sqrt{b}$; $\sqrt[3]{a} + \sqrt[4]{b}$ are compound surds.

269. The multiplication of compound surds is performed like the multiplication of compound algebraical expressions.

Example 1. Multiply $2\sqrt{x} - 5$ by $3\sqrt{x}$. The product $= 3\sqrt{x}\,(2\sqrt{x} - 5)$.

$$= 6x - 15\sqrt{x}.$$

Example 2. Multiply $2\sqrt{5} + 3\sqrt{x}$ by $\sqrt{5} - \sqrt{x}$.

$$\begin{aligned}\text{The product } &= (2\sqrt{5} + 3\sqrt{x})(\sqrt{5} - \sqrt{x}) \\ &= 2\sqrt{5}\cdot\sqrt{5} + 3\sqrt{5}\cdot\sqrt{x} - 2\sqrt{5}\cdot\sqrt{x} - 3\sqrt{x}\cdot\sqrt{x} \\ &= 10 - 3x + \sqrt{5x}.\end{aligned}$$

Example 3. Find the square of $2\sqrt{x} + \sqrt{7-4x}$.

$$\begin{aligned}(2\sqrt{x} + \sqrt{7-4x})^2 &= (2\sqrt{x})^2 + (\sqrt{7-4x})^2 + 4\sqrt{x}\cdot\sqrt{7-4x} \\ &= 4x + 7 - 4x + 4\sqrt{7x - 4x^2} \\ &= 7 + 4\sqrt{7x - 4x^2}.\end{aligned}$$

EXAMPLES XXXI-d

Find the value of

1. $(3\sqrt{x} - 5) \times 2\sqrt{x}$.

2. $(\sqrt{x} - \sqrt{a}) \times 2\sqrt{x}$.

3. $(\sqrt{a} + \sqrt{b}) \times \sqrt{ab}$.

4. $(\sqrt{x+y} - 1) \times \sqrt{x+y}$.

5. $(2\sqrt{3} + 3\sqrt{2})^2$.

6. $(\sqrt{7} + 5\sqrt{3})(2\sqrt{7} - 4\sqrt{3})$.

7. $(3\sqrt{5} - 4\sqrt{2})(2\sqrt{5} + 3\sqrt{2})$.

8. $(3\sqrt{a} - 2\sqrt{x})(2\sqrt{a} + 3\sqrt{x})$.

9. $(\sqrt{x} + \sqrt{x-1}) \times \sqrt{x-1}$.

10. $(\sqrt{x+a} - \sqrt{x-a}) \times \sqrt{x+a}$.

11. $(\sqrt{a+x} - 2\sqrt{a})^2$.

12. $(2\sqrt{a} - \sqrt{1+4a})^2$.

13. $(\sqrt{a+x} - \sqrt{a-x})^2$.

14. $(\sqrt{a+x} - 2)(\sqrt{a+x} - 1)$.

15. $(\sqrt{2} + \sqrt{3} - \sqrt{5})(\sqrt{2} + \sqrt{3} + \sqrt{5})$.

16. $(\sqrt{5} + 3\sqrt{2} + \sqrt{7})(\sqrt{5} + 3\sqrt{2} - \sqrt{7})$.

Write down the square of

17. $\sqrt{2x+a} - \sqrt{2x-a}$.

18. $\sqrt{x^2 - 2y^2} + \sqrt{x^2 + 2y^2}$.

19. $\sqrt{m+n} + \sqrt{m-n}$.

20. $3\sqrt{a^2 + b^2} - 2\sqrt{a^2 - b^2}$.

21. $3x\sqrt{2} - 3\sqrt{7 - 2x^2}$.

22. $\sqrt{4x^2 + 1} - \sqrt{4x^2 - 1}$.

270. One case of the multiplication of compound surds deserves careful attention. For if we multiply together the sum and the difference of any two quadratic surds we obtain a rational product.

Examples

(1) $(\sqrt{a} + \sqrt{b})(\sqrt{a} - \sqrt{b}) = (\sqrt{a})^2 - (\sqrt{b})^2 = a - b$.

(2) $(3\sqrt{5} + 4\sqrt{3})(3\sqrt{5} - 4\sqrt{3}) = (3\sqrt{5})^2 - (4\sqrt{3})^2 = 45 - 48 = -3$.

Similarly, $(4 - \sqrt{a+b})(4 + \sqrt{a+b}) = (4)^2 - (\sqrt{a+b})^2 = 16 - a - b$.

271. DEFINITION. When two binomial quadratic surds differ only in the sign which connects their terms they are said to be conjugate.

Thus $3\sqrt{7} + 5\sqrt{11}$ is conjugate to $3\sqrt{7} - 5\sqrt{11}$.

Similarly, $a\sqrt{a^2 - x^2}$ is conjugate to $a + \sqrt{a^2 - x^2}$.

The product of two conjugate surds is rational. [Art. 270.]

Example. $(3\sqrt{a} + \sqrt{x - 9a})(3\sqrt{a} - \sqrt{x - 9a})$

$$= (3\sqrt{a})^2 - (\sqrt{x-9a})^2 = 9a - (x - 9a)$$

$$= 18a - x.$$

272. The only case of the division of compound surds which we shall here consider is that in which the divisor is a binomial quadratic surd. If we express the division by means of a fraction, we can always rationalise the denominator by multiplying numerator and denominator by the surd which is conjugate to the divisor.

Example 1. Divide $4+3\sqrt{2}$ by $5-3\sqrt{2}$.

$$\text{The quotient } = \frac{4+3\sqrt{2}}{5-3\sqrt{2}} = \frac{4+3\sqrt{2}}{5-3\sqrt{2}} \times \frac{5+3\sqrt{2}}{5+3\sqrt{2}}$$

$$= \frac{20+18+12\sqrt{2}+15\sqrt{2}}{25-18} = \frac{38+27\sqrt{2}}{7}.$$

Example 2. Rationalise the denominator of $\dfrac{b^2}{\sqrt{a^2+b^2}+a}$.

$$\text{The expression } = \frac{b^2}{\sqrt{a^2+b^2}+a} \times \frac{\sqrt{a^2+b^2}-a}{\sqrt{a^2+b^2}-a}$$

$$= \frac{b^2\{\sqrt{a^2+b^2}-a\}}{(a^2+b^2)-a^2}$$

$$= \sqrt{a^2+b^2}-a.$$

Example 3. Divide $\dfrac{\sqrt{3}+\sqrt{2}}{2-\sqrt{3}}$ by $\dfrac{7+4\sqrt{3}}{\sqrt{3}-\sqrt{2}}$.

$$\text{The quotient} = \frac{\sqrt{3}+\sqrt{2}}{2-\sqrt{3}} \times \frac{\sqrt{3}-\sqrt{2}}{7+4\sqrt{3}}$$

$$= \frac{(\sqrt{3})^2-\sqrt{(2)^2}}{14-12+8\sqrt{3}-7\sqrt{3}}$$

$$= \frac{1}{2+\sqrt{3}} = 2-\sqrt{3}, \text{ on rationalising}.$$

Example 4. Given $\sqrt{5} = 2.236068$, find the value of $\dfrac{87}{7-2\sqrt{5}}$.

Rationalising the denominator,

$$\frac{87}{7-2\sqrt{5}} = \frac{87(7+2\sqrt{5})}{49-20} = 3(7+2\sqrt{5}) = 34.416408.$$

It will be seen that by rationalising the denominator we have avoided the use of a divisor consisting of 7 figures.

EXAMPLES XXXI-e

Find the value of

1. $(9\sqrt{2}-7)(9\sqrt{2}+7)$.

2. $(3+5\sqrt{7})(3-5\sqrt{7})$.

3. $(5\sqrt{8}-2\sqrt{7})(5\sqrt{8}+2\sqrt{7})$.

4. $(2\sqrt{11}+5\sqrt{2})(2\sqrt{11}-5\sqrt{2})$.

5. $(\sqrt{a}+2\sqrt{b})(\sqrt{a}-2\sqrt{b})$.

6. $(3c-2\sqrt{x})(3c+2\sqrt{x})$.

7. $(\sqrt{a+x}-\sqrt{a})(\sqrt{a+x}+\sqrt{a})$.

8. $(\sqrt{2p+3q}-2\sqrt{q})(\sqrt{2p+3q}+2\sqrt{q})$.

9. $(\sqrt{a+x}+\sqrt{a-x})(\sqrt{a+x}-\sqrt{a-x})$.

10. $(5\sqrt{x^2-3y^2}+7a)(5\sqrt{x^2-3y^2}-7a)$.

11. $29 \div (11+3\sqrt{7})$.

12. $17 \div (3\sqrt{7}+2\sqrt{3})$.

13. $(3\sqrt{2}-1) \div (3\sqrt{2}+1)$.

14. $(2\sqrt{3}+7\sqrt{2}) \div (5\sqrt{3}-4\sqrt{2})$.

15. $(2x-\sqrt{xy}) \div (2\sqrt{xy}-y)$.

16. $(3+\sqrt{5})(5-\sqrt{2}) \div (5-\sqrt{5})$.

17. $\dfrac{\sqrt{a}}{\sqrt{a}-\sqrt{x}} \div \dfrac{\sqrt{a}+\sqrt{x}}{\sqrt{x}}$.

18. $\dfrac{2\sqrt{15}+8}{5+\sqrt{15}} \div \dfrac{8\sqrt{3}-6\sqrt{5}}{5\sqrt{3}-3\sqrt{5}}$.

Rationalise the denominator of

19. $\dfrac{25\sqrt{3}-4\sqrt{2}}{7\sqrt{3}-5\sqrt{2}}$.

20. $\dfrac{10\sqrt{6}-2\sqrt{7}}{3\sqrt{6}+2\sqrt{7}}$.

21. $\dfrac{\sqrt{7}+\sqrt{2}}{9+2\sqrt{14}}$.

22. $\dfrac{2\sqrt{3}+3\sqrt{2}}{5+2\sqrt{6}}$.

23. $\dfrac{y^2}{x+\sqrt{x^2-y^2}}$.

24. $\dfrac{x^2}{\sqrt{x^2+a^2}+a}$.

25. $\dfrac{\sqrt{1+x^2}-\sqrt{1-x^2}}{\sqrt{1+x^2}+\sqrt{1-x^2}}$.

26. $\dfrac{2\sqrt{a+b}+3\sqrt{a-b}}{2\sqrt{a+b}-\sqrt{a-b}}$.

27. $\dfrac{\sqrt{9+x^2}-3}{\sqrt{9+x^2}+3}$.

28. $\dfrac{3+\sqrt{6}}{5\sqrt{3}-2\sqrt{12}-\sqrt{32}+\sqrt{50}}$.

Given $\sqrt{2}=1.41421$, $\sqrt{3}=1.73205$, $\sqrt{5}=2.23607$: find to four places of decimals the value of

29. $\dfrac{1}{2+\sqrt{3}}$.

30. $\dfrac{3+\sqrt{5}}{\sqrt{5}-2}$.

31. $\dfrac{\sqrt{5}+\sqrt{3}}{4+\sqrt{15}}$.

32. $\dfrac{\sqrt{5}-2}{9-4\sqrt{5}}$.

33. $\dfrac{7\sqrt{5}+15}{\sqrt{5}-1} \times \dfrac{\sqrt{5}-2}{3+\sqrt{5}}$.

34. $(2-\sqrt{3})(7-4\sqrt{3}) \div (3\sqrt{3}-5)$.

273. *The square root of a rational quantity cannot be partly rational and partly a quadratic surd.*

If possible let $\sqrt{n} = a + \sqrt{m}$;

then by squaring, $n = a^2 + m + 2a\sqrt{m}$;

$$\therefore \qquad \sqrt{m} = \frac{n - a^2 - m}{2a};$$

that is, a surd is equal to a rational quantity; which is impossible.

274. *If $x + \sqrt{y} = a + \sqrt{b}$, where x and a are both rational and $\sqrt{y}$ and $\sqrt{b}$ are both irrational, then will $x = a$ and $y = b$.*

For if x is not equal to a, let $x = a + m$: then

$$a + m + \sqrt{y} = a + \sqrt{b};$$

that is, $\sqrt{b} = m + \sqrt{y}$;

which is impossible. [Art. 273.]

Therefore $x = a$,

and consequently $y = b$.

If therefore $x + \sqrt{y} = a + \sqrt{b}$,

we must also have $x - \sqrt{y} = a - \sqrt{b}$.

275. It appears from the preceding article that in any equation of the form

$$X + \sqrt{Y} = A + \sqrt{B} \qquad \text{...(1)},$$

we may equate the rational parts on each side, and also the irrational parts; so that the equation (1) is really equivalent to *two* independent equations, $X = A$ and $Y = B$. *But this is only true when $\sqrt{Y}$ and $\sqrt{B}$ are irrational.*

276. If $\sqrt{a + \sqrt{b}} = \sqrt{x} + \sqrt{y}$, *then will* $\sqrt{a - \sqrt{b}} = \sqrt{x} - \sqrt{y}$.

For by squaring, we obtain

$$a + \sqrt{b} = x + 2\sqrt{xy} + y;$$

$$\therefore \qquad a = x + y, \sqrt{b} = 2\sqrt{xy}. \qquad \text{[Art. 275.]}$$

Hence $a - \sqrt{b} = x - 2\sqrt{xy} + y$,

and $\sqrt{a - \sqrt{b}} = \sqrt{x} - \sqrt{y}$.

277. *To find the square root of* $a + \sqrt{b}$.

Suppose $\sqrt{a + \sqrt{b}} = \sqrt{x} + \sqrt{y}$;

then as in the last article,

$$x + y = a \qquad \ldots(1),$$

$$2\sqrt{xy} = \sqrt{b} \qquad \ldots(2).$$

$$\therefore \quad (x - y)^2 = (x + y)^2 - 4xy$$

$$= a^2 - b, \qquad \text{from (1) and (2).}$$

$$\therefore \quad x - y = \sqrt{a^2 - b}.$$

Combining this with (1) we find

$$x = \frac{a + \sqrt{a^2 - b}}{2}, \text{ and } y = \frac{a - \sqrt{a^2 - b}}{2};$$

$$\therefore \quad \sqrt{a + \sqrt{b}} = \sqrt{\frac{a + \sqrt{(a^2 - b)}}{2}} + \sqrt{\frac{a - \sqrt{a^2 - b}}{2}}.$$

278. From the values just found for x and y, it appears that each of them is itself a compound surd unless $a^2 - b$ is a perfect square.

Hence the method of Art. 277 for finding the square root of $a + \sqrt{b}$ is of no practical utility except when $a^2 - b$ is a perfect square.

Example. Find the square root of $16 + 2\sqrt{55}$.

Assume $\sqrt{16 + 2\sqrt{55}} = \sqrt{x} + \sqrt{y}$.

Thus $\quad 16 + 2\sqrt{55} = x + 2\sqrt{xy} + y$.

$$\therefore \quad x + y = 16 \qquad \ldots(1),$$

$$2\sqrt{xy} = 2\sqrt{55} \qquad \ldots(2).$$

$$\therefore \quad (x - y)^2 = (x + y)^2 - 4xy$$

$$= 16^2 - 4 \times 55, \qquad \text{by (1) and (2)}$$

$$= 4 \times 9,$$

$$\therefore \quad x - y = \pm 6. \qquad \ldots(3).$$

From (1) and (3) we obtain
$x = 11$, or 5, and $y = 5$, or 11.
That is, the required square root is $\sqrt{11} + \sqrt{5}$.

In the same way we may show that $\sqrt{16 - 25\sqrt{5}} = \sqrt{11} - \sqrt{5}$.

NOTE. Since every quantity has two square roots equal in magnitude but opposite in sign, strictly speaking we should have
the square root of $16 + 2\sqrt{55} = \pm(\sqrt{11} + \sqrt{5})$, ...
$16 - 2\sqrt{55} = \pm(\sqrt{11} - \sqrt{5})$.

However it is usually sufficient to take the positive value of the square root, so that in assuming $\sqrt{a-\sqrt{b}} = \sqrt{x} - \sqrt{y}$. It is understood that x is greater than y. With this provision it will be unnecessary in any numerical example to use the double sign at the stage of work corresponding to equation (3) of the last example.

279. When the binomial whose square root we are seeking consists of *two* quadratic surds, we proceed as explained in the following example.

Example. Find the square root of $\sqrt{175} - \sqrt{147}$.

Since $\sqrt{175} - \sqrt{147} = \sqrt{7}\,(\sqrt{25} - \sqrt{21}) = \sqrt{7}\,(5 - \sqrt{21})$.

$$\therefore \quad \sqrt{\sqrt{175} - \sqrt{147}} = \sqrt[4]{7} \cdot \sqrt{5 - \sqrt{21}}.$$

And, proceeding as in the last article,

$$\sqrt{5 - \sqrt{21}} = \sqrt{\frac{7}{2}} - \sqrt{\frac{3}{2}};$$

$$\therefore \quad \sqrt{\sqrt{175} - \sqrt{147}} = \sqrt[4]{7}\left(\sqrt{\frac{7}{2}} - \sqrt{\frac{3}{2}}\right).$$

280. The square root of a binomial surd may often be found by inspection.

Example1. Find the square root of $11 + 2\sqrt{30}$.

We have only to find two quantities whose sum is 11, and whose product is 30; thus

$$11 + 2\sqrt{30} = 6 + 5 + 2\sqrt{6 \times 5} = (\sqrt{6} + \sqrt{5})^2.$$

$$\therefore \quad \sqrt{11 + 2\sqrt{30}} = \sqrt{6} + \sqrt{5}.$$

Example 2. Find the square root of $53 - 12\sqrt{10}$.

First write the binomial so that the surd part has a coefficient 2; thus $\quad 53 - 12\sqrt{10} = 53 - 2\sqrt{360}$.

We have now to find two quantities whose sum is 53 and whose product is 360; these are 45 and 8;

hence $\quad 53 - 12\sqrt{10} = 45 + 8 - 2\sqrt{45 \times 8}$;

$$= (\sqrt{45} - \sqrt{8})^2;$$

$$\therefore \quad \sqrt{53 - 12\sqrt{10}} = \sqrt{45} - \sqrt{8};$$

$$= 3\sqrt{5} - \sqrt{22}.$$

EXAMPLES XXXI-f

Find the square root of each of the following binomial surds:

1. $7 - 2\sqrt{10}$.

2. $13 + 2\sqrt{30}$.

3. $8 - 2\sqrt{7}$.

4. $5 + 2\sqrt{6}$.

5. $75 + 12\sqrt{21}$.

6. $18 - 8\sqrt{5}$.

7. $41 - 24\sqrt{2}$.

8. $83 + 12\sqrt{35}$.

9. $47 - 4\sqrt{33}$.

10. $2\frac{1}{4} + \sqrt{5}$.

11. $4\frac{1}{3} - \frac{4}{3}\sqrt{3}$.

12. $16 + 5\sqrt{7}$.

13. $\sqrt{27} + 2\sqrt{6}$.

14. $\sqrt{32} + \sqrt{24}$.

15. $3\sqrt{5} + \sqrt{40}$.

Find the fourth roots of the following binomial surds:

16. $17 + 12\sqrt{2}$.

17. $56 + 24\sqrt{5}$.

18. $\frac{3}{2}\sqrt{5} + 3\frac{1}{2}$.

19. $14 + 8\sqrt{3}$.

20. $49 - 20\sqrt{6}$.

21. $248 + 32\sqrt{60}$.

Find, by inspection, the value of

22. $\sqrt{3 - 2\sqrt{2}}$.

23. $\sqrt{4 + 2\sqrt{3}}$.

24. $\sqrt{6 - 2\sqrt{5}}$.

25. $\sqrt{19 + 8\sqrt{3}}$.

26. $\sqrt{8 + 2\sqrt{15}}$.

27. $\sqrt{9 - 2\sqrt{14}}$.

28. $\sqrt{11 + 4\sqrt{6}}$.

29. $\sqrt{15 - 4\sqrt{14}}$.

30. $\sqrt{29 + 6\sqrt{22}}$.

Equations involving Surds

281. Sometimes equations are proposed in which the unknown quantity appears under the radical sign. Such equations are very varied in character and often require special artifices for their solution. Here, we shall only consider a few of the simpler cases, which can generally be solved by the following method. Bring to one side of the equation a single radical term by itself. On squaring both sides this radical will disappear. By repeating this process any remaining radicals can in turn be removed.

Example 1. Solve $2\sqrt{x} - \sqrt{4x-11} = 1$.

Transposing $2\sqrt{x} - 1 = \sqrt{4x-11}$.

Squaring both sides then

$$4x - 4\sqrt{x} + 1 = 4x - 11,$$

$$4\sqrt{x} = 12, \sqrt{x} = 3;$$

$$\therefore \qquad x = 9.$$

Example 2. Solve $2 + \sqrt[3]{x-5} = 13$.

Transposing $\sqrt[3]{x-5} = 11$.

Here we must *cube* both sides; thus $x - 5 = 1331$;

whence $x = 1336$.

Example 3. Solve $\sqrt{x+5} + \sqrt{3x+4} = \sqrt{12x+1}$.

Squaring both sides,

$$x + 5 + 3x + 4 + 2\sqrt{(x+5)(3x+4)} = 12x + 1.$$

Transposing and dividing by 2,

$$\sqrt{(x+5)(3x+4)} = 4x - 4 \qquad \ldots(1).$$

Squaring

$$(x+5)(3x+4) = 16x^2 - 32x + 16,$$

or $\quad 13x^2 - 51x - 4 = 0,$

$$(x-4)(13x+1) = 0,$$

$$\therefore \qquad x = 4, \text{ or } -\frac{1}{13}.$$

If we proceed to verify the solution by substituting these values in the original equation, it will be found that it is satisfied by $x = 4$, but not by $x = -\frac{1}{13}$. But this latter value will be found on trial to satisfy the given equation if we alter the sign of the second radical, thus

$$\sqrt{x+5} - \sqrt{3x+4} = \sqrt{12x+1}.$$

On squaring this and reducing, we obtain

$$-\sqrt{(x+5)(3x+4)} = 4x - 4 \qquad \ldots(2)$$

and a comparison of (1) and (2) shows that in the next stage of the work *the same quadratic equation is obtained* each case, the roots of which are 4 and $-\frac{1}{13}$, as already found.

From this it appears that when the solution of an equation requires that both sides should be squared, we cannot be certain without trial which of the values found for the unknown quantity will satisfy the original equation.

In order that all the values found by the solution of the equation may be applicable it will be necessary to take into account both signs of the radicals in the given equation.

EXAMPLES XXXI-g

Solve the equations:

1. $\sqrt{x-5}=3.$

2. $\sqrt[3]{4x-7}=5.$

3. $7-\sqrt{x-4}=3.$

4. $13-\sqrt[3]{5x-4}=7.$

5. $\sqrt{5x-1}=2\sqrt{x+3}.$

6. $2\sqrt{3-7x}-3\sqrt{8x-12}=0.$

7. $2\sqrt[3]{5x-35}=5\sqrt[3]{2x-7}.$

8. $\sqrt{9x^2-11x-5}=3x-2.$

9. $\sqrt[4]{2x+11}=\sqrt{5}.$

10. $\sqrt{4x^2-7x+1}=2x-1\frac{4}{5}.$

11. $\sqrt{x+25}=1+\sqrt{x}.$

12. $\sqrt{8x+33}-3=2\sqrt{2x}.$

13. $\sqrt{x+3}+\sqrt{x}=5.$

14. $10-\sqrt{25+9x}=3\sqrt{x}.$

15. $\sqrt{x-4}+3=\sqrt{x+11}.$

16. $\sqrt{9x-8}=3\sqrt{x+4}-2.$

17. $\sqrt{4x+5}-\sqrt{x}=\sqrt{x+3}.$

18. $\sqrt{25x-29}-\sqrt{4x-11}=3\sqrt{x}.$

19. $\sqrt{8x+17}-\sqrt{2x}=\sqrt{2x+9}.$

20. $\sqrt{3x-11}+\sqrt{3x}=\sqrt{12x-23}.$

21. $\sqrt{12x-5}-\sqrt{3x-1}=\sqrt{27x-2}.$

22. $\sqrt{x+3}-\sqrt{x+8}-\sqrt{4x+21}=0.$

23. $\sqrt{x+2}+\sqrt{4x+1}-\sqrt{9x+7}=0.$

24. $\sqrt{x+4ab}=2a+\sqrt{x}.$

25. $\sqrt{x}+\sqrt{4a+x}=2\sqrt{b+x}.$

26. $\sqrt{a-x}+\sqrt{b+x}=\sqrt{a}+\sqrt{b}.$

27. $5\sqrt[3]{70x+29}=9\sqrt[3]{14x-15}.$

28. $\sqrt[3]{x^3-3x^2+7x-11}=x-1.$

29. $\sqrt[3]{8x^3+12x^2+12x-11}=2x+1.$

30. $\sqrt[3]{1+x}+\sqrt[3]{1-x}=\sqrt[3]{2}.$

282. When radicals appear in a fractional form in an equation, we must clear of fractions in the ordinary way, combining the irrational factors by the rules already explained in this chapter.

Example 1. Solve $\dfrac{6\sqrt{x}-11}{3\sqrt{x}}=\dfrac{2\sqrt{x}+1}{\sqrt{x}+6}.$

Multiplying across, we have

$$6x+25\sqrt{x}-66=6x+3\sqrt{x},$$

that is, $$3\sqrt{x}=66,\ 22\sqrt{x}=66,$$

$$\sqrt{x}=3,\ x=9.$$

Example 2. Solve $\sqrt{9+2x}-\sqrt{2x}=\dfrac{5}{\sqrt{9+2x}}$.

Clearing of fractions, $9+2x-\sqrt{2x(9+2x)}=5$,

$$4+2x=\sqrt{2x(9+2x)}.$$

Squaring, $16+16x+4x^2=18x+4x^2$,

$$16=2x;\ x=8.$$

EXAMPLES XXXI-h

Solve the equations:

1. $\dfrac{6\sqrt{x}-21}{3\sqrt{x}-14}=\dfrac{8\sqrt{x}-11}{4\sqrt{x}-13}$.

2. $\dfrac{9\sqrt{x}-23}{3\sqrt{x}-8}=\dfrac{6\sqrt{x}-17}{2\sqrt{x}-6}$.

3. $\dfrac{\sqrt{x}+3}{\sqrt{x}-2}=\dfrac{3\sqrt{x}-5}{3\sqrt{x}-13}$.

4. $2-\dfrac{\sqrt{x}+3}{\sqrt{x+2}}=\dfrac{\sqrt{x}+9}{\sqrt{x+7}}$.

5. $\dfrac{2\sqrt{x}-1}{2\sqrt{x}+\frac{4}{3}}=\dfrac{\sqrt{x}-2}{\sqrt{x}-\frac{4}{3}}$.

6. $\dfrac{6\sqrt{x}-7}{\sqrt{x-1}}-5=\dfrac{7\sqrt{x}-26}{7\sqrt{x}-21}$.

7. $\dfrac{12\sqrt{x}-11}{4\sqrt{x}-4\frac{2}{3}}+\dfrac{6\sqrt{x}+5}{2\sqrt{x}+\frac{2}{3}}$.

8. $\sqrt{1+x}+\sqrt{x}=\dfrac{2}{\sqrt{1+x}}$.

9. $\sqrt{x-1}+\sqrt{x}=\dfrac{2}{\sqrt{x}}$.

10. $\sqrt{x}-\sqrt{x-8}=\dfrac{2}{\sqrt{x-8}}$.

11. $\sqrt{x+5}+\sqrt{x}=\dfrac{10}{\sqrt{x}}$.

12. $2\sqrt{x}-\sqrt{4x-3}=\dfrac{1}{\sqrt{4x-3}}$.

13. $3\sqrt{x}=\dfrac{8}{\sqrt{9x-32}}+\sqrt{9x-32}$.

14. $\sqrt{x}-7=\dfrac{1}{\sqrt{x}+7}$.

15. $(\sqrt{x}+11)(\sqrt{x}-11)+110=0$.

16. $2\sqrt{x}=\dfrac{12-6\sqrt{x}}{2\sqrt{x}-3}$.

17. $3\sqrt{x}-1=\dfrac{5}{3\sqrt{x}+7}+6$.

18. $\dfrac{x-1}{\sqrt{x}-1}=3+\dfrac{\sqrt{x}-1}{2}$.

19. $\dfrac{1}{1-x}+\dfrac{1}{\sqrt{x}+1}+\dfrac{1}{\sqrt{x}-1}=0$.

20. $2=\dfrac{\sqrt{2+x}+\sqrt{2-x}}{\sqrt{2+x}-\sqrt{2-x}}$.

21. $\dfrac{2x-3}{\sqrt{x-2+1}}=2\sqrt{x-2}-1$.

22. $\dfrac{2}{x-6+\sqrt{x}}+\dfrac{1}{\sqrt{x}-2}=\dfrac{4}{\sqrt{x}+3}$.

32

RATIO, PROPORTION AND VARIATION

RATIO

283. DEFINITION. Ratio is the relation which one quantity bears to another of the *same* kind, the comparison being made by considering what multiple, part, or parts, one quantity is of the other.

The ratio of A to B is usually written $A : B$. The quantities A and B are called the *terms* of the ratio. The first term is called the antecedent, the second term the consequent.

284. To find what multiple or part A is of B we divide A by B; hence, the ratio $A : B$ may be measured by the fraction $\frac{A}{B}$, and we shall usually find it convenient to adopt this notation.
In order to compare two quantities they must be expressed in terms of the same unit. Thus the ratio of £2 to 15*s*, is measured by the fraction $\frac{2 \times 20}{15}$ or $\frac{8}{3}$.

NOTE. Since a ratio expresses the *number* of times that one quantity contains another, *every ratio is an abstract quantity.*

285. By Art. 151, $\frac{a}{b} = \frac{ma}{mb}$; and thus the ratio $a : b$ is equal to the ratio $ma : mb$; that is, *the value of a ratio remains unaltered if the antecedent and the consequent are multiplied or divided by the same quantity*.

286. Two or more ratios may be compared by reducing their equivalent fractions to a common denominator. This suppose $a : b$ and $x : y$ are two ratios. Now, $\frac{a}{b} = \frac{ay}{by}$, and $\frac{x}{y} = \frac{bx}{by}$; hence the ratio $a : b$ is greater than, equal to, or less than the ratio $x : y$ according as ay is greater than, equal to, or less than bx.

287. The ratio of two fractions can be expressed as a ratio of two integers. Thus the ratio $\frac{a}{b} : \frac{c}{d}$ is measured by the fraction $\frac{\frac{a}{b}}{\frac{c}{d}}$. or $\frac{ad}{bc}$; and is therefore equivalent to the ratio $ad : bc$.

288. If either, or both, of the terms of a ratio be a surd quantity, then no two integers can be found which will *exactly* measured their ratio. Thus, the ratio $\sqrt{2}:1$ cannot be exactly expressed by any two integers.

289. DEFINITION. If the ratio of any two quantities can be expressed exactly by the ratio of two integers the quantities are said to be commensurable; otherwise, they are said to be incommensurable.

Although we cannot find two integers which will exactly measure the ratio of two incommensurable quantities, we can always find two integers whose ratio differs from that required by as small a quantity as we please.

Thus $$\frac{\sqrt{5}}{4}=\frac{2.236067...}{4}=0.559016...$$

and therefore $$\frac{\sqrt{5}}{4}>\frac{559016}{1000000} \text{ and } <\frac{559017}{1000000},$$

and it is evident that by carrying the decimals further, any degree of approximation may be arrived at.

290. DEFINITION. Ratios are *compounded* by multiplying together the fractions which denote them; or by multiplying together the antecedents for a new antecedent, and the consequents for a new consequent.

Example. Find the ratio compounded of the three ratios

$$2a\cdot 3b, 6ab:5c^2, c:a.$$

$$\text{The required ratio} = \frac{2a}{3b}\times\frac{6ab}{5c^2}\times\frac{c}{a}=\frac{4a}{5c}.$$

291. DEFINITION. When the ratio $a:b$ is compounded with itself the resulting ratio is $a^2:b^2$, and is called the duplicate ratio of $a:b$. Similarly $a^3:b^3$ is called the triplicate ratio of $a:b$. Also, $a^{1/2}:b^{1/2}$ is called the subduplicate ratio of $a:b$.

Examples.

(1) The duplicate ratio of $2a:3b$ is $4a^2:9b^2$.

(2) The subduplicate ratio of $49:25$ is $7:5$.

(3) The triplicate ratio of $2x:1$ is $8x^3:1$.

292. DEFINITION. A ratio is said to be a ratio of *greater inequality*, of *less inequality*, or of *equality*, according as the antecedent is *greater than*, *less than*, or *equal to* consequent.

293. If to each term of the ratio 8 : 3 we add 4, a new ratio 12 : 7 is obtained, and we see that it is less than the former because $\frac{12}{7}$ is clearly less than $\frac{8}{3}$.

This is a particular case of a more general proposition which we shall now prove.

A ratio of greater inequality is diminished, and a ratio of less inequality is increased, by adding the same quantity to both its terms.

Let $\frac{a}{b}$ be the ratio, and let $\frac{a+x}{b+x}$ be the new ratio formed by adding x to both terms.

Now
$$\frac{a}{b}-\frac{a+x}{b+x}=\frac{ax-bx}{b(b+x)}$$
$$=\frac{x(a-b)}{b(b+x)};$$

and $a-b$ is positive or negative according as a is greater or less than b.

Hence if $a>b$, $\frac{a}{b}>\frac{a+x}{b+x}$;

and if $a<b$, $\frac{a}{b}<\frac{a+x}{b+x}$,

which proves the proposition.

Similarly, it can be proved that *a ratio of greater inequality is increased, and a ratio of less inequality is diminished, by taking the same quantity from both its terms.*

294. When two or more ratios are equal, many useful propositions may be proved by introducing a single symbol to denote each of the equal ratios.

The proof of the following important theorem will illustrate the method of procedure.

If
$$\frac{a}{b}=\frac{c}{d}=\frac{e}{f}=\ldots$$

each of these ratios
$$=\left(\frac{pa^n+qc^n+re^n+\ldots}{pb^n+qd^n+rf^n+\ldots}\right)^{1/n}$$

where p, q, r, n *are any quantities whatever.*

Let
$$\frac{a}{b}=\frac{c}{d}=\frac{e}{f}=\ldots=k;$$

then
$$a=bk, c=dk, e=fk\ \ldots;$$

whence $$pa^n = pb^nk^n, qc^n = qd^nk^n, re^n = rf^nk^n, \dots;$$

$$\therefore \quad \frac{pa^n + qc^a + re^n + \dots}{pb^n + qd^n + rf^n + \dots} = \frac{pb^nk^n + qd^nk^n + rf^nk^n + \dots}{pb^n + qd^n + rf^n + \dots}$$

$$\therefore \quad \left(\frac{pa^n + qc^n + re^n + \dots}{pb^n + qd^n + rf^n + \dots}\right)^{1/n} = k = \frac{a}{b} = \frac{c}{d} = \dots$$

By giving different values to p, q, r, n many particular cases of this general proposition may be deduced; or they may be proved independently by using the same method. For instance,

if $\frac{a}{b} = \frac{c}{d} = \frac{e}{f}$, each of these ratios $= \frac{a+c+e}{b+d+f}$; a result which will frequently be found useful.

Example 1. If $\frac{x}{y} = \frac{3}{4}$ find the value of $\frac{5x-3y}{7x+2y}$,

$$\frac{5x-3y}{7x+2y} = \frac{\frac{5x}{y} - 3}{\frac{7x}{y} + 2} = \frac{\frac{15}{4} - 3}{\frac{21}{4} + 2} = \frac{3}{29}.$$

Example 2. Two numbers are in the ratio of $5:8$. If 9 be added to each, they are in the ratio of $8:11$. Find the numbers.

Let the numbers be denoted by $5x$ and $8x$.

Then $$\frac{5x+9}{8x+9} = \frac{8}{11};$$

$$\therefore \quad x = 3.$$

Hence the numbers are 15 and 24.

Example 3. If $A:B$ be in the duplicate ratio of $A + x : B + x$, prove that $x^2 = AB$.

By the given condition, $\left(\frac{A+x}{B+x}\right)^2 = \frac{A}{B}$;

$$\therefore \quad B(A+x)^2 = A(B+x)^2,$$

$$A^2B + 2ABx + Bx^2 = AB^2 + 2ABx + Ax^2,$$

$$x^2(A-B) = AB(A-B);$$

$$\therefore \quad x^2 = AB,$$

since $A - B$ is, by supposition, not zero.

EXAMPLES XXXII-a

Find the ratio compounded of

1. The duplicate ratio of $4:3$, and the ratio $27:8$.
2. The ratio $32:27$, and the triplicate ratio of $3:4$.
3. The subduplicate ratio of $25:36$, and the ratio $6:25$.
4. The ratio $169:200$, and the duplicate ratio of $15:26$.
5. The triplicate ratio of $x:y$, and the ratio $2y^2:3x^2$.
6. The ratio $3a:4b$ and the subduplicate ratio of $b^4:a^4$.
7. If $x:y=5:7$, find the value of $x+y:y-x$.
8. If $\frac{x}{y}=3\frac{1}{3}$, find the value of $\frac{x-3y}{2x-5y}$.
9. If $b:a=2:5$, find the value of $2a-3b:3b-a$.
10. If $\frac{a}{b}=\frac{3}{4}$, and $\frac{x}{y}=\frac{5}{7}$, find the value of $\frac{3ax-by}{4by-7ax}$.
11. If $7x-4y:3x+y=5:13$, find the ratio $x:y$.
12. If $\frac{2a^2-3b^2}{a^2+b^2}=\frac{2}{41}$, find the ratio $a:b$.
13. If $2x:3y$ be in the duplicate ratio of $2x-m:3y-m$, prove that $m^2=6xy$.
14. If $P:Q$ be the subduplicate ratio of $P-x:Q-x$, prove that $x=\frac{PQ}{P+Q}$.
15. If $\frac{a}{b}=\frac{c}{d}=\frac{e}{f}$, prove that each of these ratios is equal to
$$\sqrt[3]{\frac{2a^2c+3c^3e+4e^2c}{2b^2d+3d^3e+4f^2d}}.$$
16. Two members are in the ratio of $3:4$, and if 7 be subtracted from each the remainders are in the ratio of $2:3$. Find them.
17. What number must be taken from each term of the ratio $27:35$ that it may become $2:3$?
18. What number must be added to each term of the ratio $37:29$ that it may become $8:7$?
19. If $\frac{p}{b-c}=\frac{q}{c-a}=\frac{r}{a-b}$, show that $p+q+r=0$.
20. If $\frac{x}{b+c}=\frac{y}{c+a}=\frac{z}{a-b}$, show that $x-y+z=0$.

21. If $\frac{a}{b}=\frac{c}{d}=\frac{e}{f}$, show that the square root of

$$\frac{a^6b-2c^5e+3a^4c^3e^2}{a^7-2d^5f+3b^4cd^2e^2} \text{ is equal to } \frac{ace}{bdf}.$$

22. Prove that the ratio $la+mc+ne : lb+md+nf$ will be equal to each of the ratios $a:b, c:d, e:f$, if these be all equal; and that it will be intermediate in value between the greatest and least of these ratios if they be not all equal.

23. If $\frac{bx-ay}{cy-az}=\frac{cx-az}{by-ax}=\frac{z+y}{x+z}$, then will each of these fractions be equal to $\frac{x}{y}$, unless $b+c=0$

24. If $\frac{2x-3y}{3z+y}=\frac{z-y}{z-x}=\frac{x+3x}{2y-3x}$, prove that each of these ratios is equal to $\frac{x}{y}$; hence show that either $x=y$, or $z=x+y$.

PROPORTION

295. DEFINITION. When two ratios are equal, the four quantities composing them are said to be proportionals. Thus if $\frac{a}{b}=\frac{c}{d}$ then a, b, c, d are proportionals. This is expressed by saying that a is to b as c is to d, and the proportion is written as

$$a:b::c:d; \qquad \text{or} \qquad a:b=c:d.$$

The terms a and d are called the *extremes*, b and c the *means*.

296. *If four quantities are in proportion, the product of the extremes is equal to the product of the means.*

Let a, b, c, d be the proportionals.

Then by definition $\frac{a}{b}=\frac{c}{d}$;

whence, $ad=bc$.

Hence if any three terms of a proportion are given, the fourth may be found. Thus, if a, c, d are given, then $b=\frac{ad}{c}$.

Conversely, if there are any four quantities, a, b, c, a, such that $ad=bc$, then a, b, c, d are proportionals; a and d being the extremes, b and c the means; or vice versa.

297. DEFINITION. Quantities are said to be in continued proportion when the first is to the second, as the second is to the third, as the third to the fourth; and so on. Thus $a, b, c, d, \ldots$ are in continued proportion when

$$\frac{a}{b} = \frac{b}{c} = \frac{c}{d} = \ldots\ldots$$

If three quantities a, b, c are in continued proportion, then

$$a : b = b : c;$$

$$\therefore \quad ac = b^2. \qquad \text{[Art. 296.]}$$

In this case b is said to be a mean proportional between a and c; and c is said to be a third proportional to a and b.

298. *If three quantities are proportionals, the first is to the third in the duplicate ratio of the first to the second.*

Let the three quantities be a, b, c; then $\frac{a}{b} = \frac{b}{c}$.

Now $$\frac{a}{c} = \frac{a}{b} \times \frac{b}{c} = \frac{a}{b} \times \frac{a}{b} = \frac{a^2}{b^2};$$

that is, $$a : c = a^2 : b^2.$$

299. *If* a : b = c : d *and* e : f = g : h *then will*

ae ; bf = cg : dh.

For $$\frac{a}{b} = \frac{c}{d} \text{ and } \frac{e}{f} = \frac{g}{h},$$

$$\therefore \quad \frac{ae}{bf} = \frac{cg}{dh}, \text{ or } ae : bf = cg : dh.$$

COR. If $a : b = c : d$

and $b : x = d : y$

then $a : x = c : y$

This is the theorem known as *ex cequali* in Geometry.

300. If four quantities a, b, c, d, form a proportion, many other proportions may be deduced by the properties of fractions. The results of these operations are very useful, and some of them are often quoted by the annexed names borrowed form Geometry.

(1) If $a : b = c : d$, then $b : a = d : c$. [*Invertendo.*]

For $$\frac{a}{b} = \frac{c}{d}, \text{ therefore } 1 \div \frac{a}{b} = 1 \div \frac{c}{d};$$

that is $$\frac{b}{a} = \frac{d}{c};$$

or $$b : a = d : c.$$

(2) If $a : b = c : d$, then $a : c = c : d$. [*Alternando.*]

For $ad = bc$; therefore $\frac{ad}{cd} = \frac{bc}{cd}$;

that is, $$\frac{a}{c} = \frac{b}{d};$$

or $$a : c = b : d.$$

(3) If $a : b = c : d$, then $a + b : b = c + d : d$. [*Componendo.*]

For $\frac{a}{b} = \frac{c}{d}$; therefore $\frac{a}{b} + 1 = \frac{c}{d} + 1$;

that is, $$\frac{a+b}{b} = \frac{c+d}{d};$$

or $$a + b : b = c + d : d.$$

(4) If $a : b = c : d$, then $a - b : b = c - d : d$. [*Dividendo.*]

For $\frac{a}{b} = \frac{c}{d}$; therefore $\frac{a}{b} - 1 = \frac{c}{d} - 1$;

that is, $$\frac{a-b}{b} = \frac{c-d}{d};$$

or $$a - b : b = c - d : d.$$

(5) If $a : b = c : d$, then $a + b : a - b = c + d : c - d$.

For by (3) $$\frac{a+b}{b} = \frac{c+d}{d};$$

and by (4) $$\frac{a-b}{b} = \frac{c-d}{d};$$

∴ by division, $$\frac{a+b}{a-b} = \frac{c+d}{c-d},$$

or $$a + b : a - b = c + d : c - d.$$

Several other proportions may be proved in a similar way.

301. The results of the preceding article are the algebraical equivalents of some of the propositions in the the fifth book of Euclid, and the student is advised to make himself familiar with them in their verbal form. For example, *dividendo* may be quoted as follows:

When there are four proportionals, the excess of the first above the second is to the second, as the excess of the third above the fourth is to the fourth.

302. We shall now compare the algebraical definition of proportion with that given in Euclid.

In algebraical symbols the definition of Euclid may be stated as follows:

For magnitudes, a, b, c, d, are in proportion when $pc \gtreqless qd$ according as $pa \gtreqless qb$, p and q being *any positive integers whatever.*

I. To deduce the geometrical definition of proportion from the algebraical definition.

Since $\frac{a}{b}=\frac{c}{d}$, by multiplying both sides by $\frac{p}{q}$, we obtain

$$\frac{pa}{qb}=\frac{pc}{qd};$$

hence, from the properties of fractions.

$$pc \gtreqless qd \text{ according as } pa \gtreqless qb,$$

which proves the proposition.

II. To deduce the algebraical definition of proportion from the geometrical definition.

Given that $pc \gtreqless qd$ according as $pa \gtreqless qb$, to prove

$$\frac{a}{b}=\frac{c}{d}.$$

If $\frac{a}{b}$ is not equal to $\frac{c}{d}$, one of them must be the greater. Suppose $\frac{a}{b}>\frac{c}{d}$; then it will be possible to find some fraction $\frac{q}{p}$ which lies between them.

Hence $\qquad \frac{a}{b}>\frac{q}{p}$ ...(1),

and $\qquad \frac{c}{d}<\frac{q}{p}$ ...(2).

From (1) $\qquad pa>qb;$

From (2) $\qquad pc<qd;$

and these contradict the hypothesis.

Therefore $\frac{a}{b}$ and $\frac{c}{d}$ are not unequal; that is $\frac{a}{b}=\frac{c}{d}$; which proves the proposition.

Example 1. If $a:b=c:d=e:f$,

show that $2a^2+3c^2-5e^2 : 2b^2+3d^2-5f^2=ae:bf.$

Let $\qquad \frac{a}{b}=\frac{c}{d}=\frac{e}{f}=k;$

then $\qquad a=bk, c=dk$ and $e=fk;$

$$\therefore \quad \frac{2a^2+3c^2-5e^2}{2b^2+3d^2-5f^2}=\frac{2b^2k^2+3d^2k^2-5f^2k^2}{2b^2+3d^2-5f^2}=k^2=\frac{a}{b}\times\frac{e}{f}=\frac{ae}{bf},$$

or $\quad 2a^2+3c^2-5e^2 : 2b^2+3d^2-5f^2=ae:bf.$

Example 2. Solve the equation $\dfrac{x^2+x-2}{x-2}=\dfrac{4x^2+5x-6}{5x-6}$.

Dividendo, $$\frac{x^2}{x-2}=\frac{4x^2}{5x-6};$$

whence, dividing by x^2, which gives a solution $x=0$, [Art. 20.1.]

$$\frac{1}{x-2}=\frac{4}{5x-6};$$

Hence $x=-2$,

and therefore the roots are $0, -2$.

Example 3. If $(3a+6b+c+2d)(3a-6b-c+2d)$
$$=(3a-6b+c-2d)(3a+6b-c-2d),$$

prove that a, b, c, d are in proportion.

We have $\dfrac{3a+6b+c+2d}{3a-6b+c-2d}=\dfrac{3a+6b-c-2d}{3a-6b-c+2d}$. [Art. 296.]

Componendo and Dividendo,
$$\frac{2(3a+c)}{2(6b+2d)}=\frac{2(3a-c)}{2(6b-2d)}$$

Alternando, $$\frac{3a+c}{3a-c}=\frac{6b+2d}{6b-2d}.$$

Again, Componendo and Dividendo,
$$\frac{6a}{2c}=\frac{12b}{4d};$$

whence $a:b=c:d$.

EXAMPLES XXXII-b

Find a fourth proportional to

1. a, ab, c.

2. $a^2, 2ab, 3b^2$.

3. $x^3, xy, 5x^2y$.

Find a third proportional to

4. a^2b, ab.

5. $x^3, 2x^2$.

6. $3x, 6xy$.

7. $1, x$.

Find a mean proportional between

8. a^2, b^2.

9. $2x^3, 8x$.

10. $12ax^2, 3a^3$.

11. $27a^2b^3, 3b$.

If a, b, c are three proportionals, show that

12. $a : a + b = a - b : a - c$.

13. $(b^2 + bc + c^2)(ac - bc + c^2) = b^4 + ac^3 + c^4$.

If $a : b = c : d$, prove that

14. $ab + cd : ab - cd = a^2 + c^2 : a^2 - c^2$.

15. $a^2 + ac + c^2 : a^2 - ac + c^2 = b^2 + bd + d^2 : b^2 - bd + d^2$.

16. $a : b = \sqrt{3a^2 + 5c^2} : \sqrt{3b^2 + 5d^2}$.

17. $\frac{a}{p} + \frac{b}{q} : a = \frac{c}{p} + \frac{d}{q} : c$.

18. $\frac{b}{a} + \frac{q}{b} : \frac{ab}{a^2 + b^2} = \frac{d}{c} + \frac{c}{d} : \frac{cd}{c^2 + d^2}$.

Solve the equations:

19. $3x - 1 : 6x - 7 = 7x - 10 : 9x + 10$.

20. $x - 12 : y + 3 = 2x - 19 : 5y - 13 = 5 : 14$.

21. $\frac{x^2 - 2x + 3}{2x - 3} = \frac{x^2 - 3x + 5}{3x - 5}$.

22. $\frac{2x - 1}{x^2 + 2x - 1} = \frac{x + 4}{x^2 + x + 4}$.

23. If $(a + b - 3c - 3d)(2a - 2b - c + d)$
$= (2a + 2b - c - d)(a - b - 3c + 3d)$
prove that a, b, c, d are proportionals.

24. If a, b, c, d are in continued proportion, prove that $a : d = a^3 + b^3 + c^3 : b^3 + c^3 + d^3$.

25. If b is a mean proportional between a and c, show that $4a^2 - 9b^2$ is to $4b^2 - 9c^2$ in the duplicate ratio of a to b.

26. If a, b, c, d are in continued proportion, prove that $b + c$ is a mean proportional between $a + b$ and $c + d$.

27. If $a + b : b + c = c + d : d + a$,
prove that $a = c$, or $a + b + c + d = 0$.

28. If $a : b = c : d = e : f$, prove that

(i) $5a - 7c + 3e : 5b - 7d + 3f = c : d$.

(ii) $4a^2 - 5ace + 6e^2f : 4b^2 - 5bde + 6f^3 = ae : bf$.

(iii) $a^2ce : b^2df = 2a^4b^2 + 3a^2e^2 - 5e^4f : 2b^6 + 3b^2f^2 - 5f^5$.

29. If $a : b = x : y$, prove that

(i) $al + xm : bl + ym = ap + xq : bp + yq$.

(ii) $pa^2 + qax + rx^2 : pb^2 + qby + ry^2 = a^2 + x^2 : b^2 + y^2$.

Variation

303. DEFINITION. One quantity A is said to vary directly as another B, when the two quantities depend upon each other in such a manner that if B is changed, A is changed *in the same ratio.*

Note. The word *directly* is often omitted, and A is said to vary as B.

304. For instance : if a train moving at a uniform rate travels 40 kilometres in 60 minutes, it will travel 20 kilometres in 30 minutes, 80 kilometres in 120 minutes, and so no; the distance in each case being increased or diminished in the same ratio as the time. This is expressed by saying that when the velocity is uniform *the distance is proportional to the time,* or more briefly, *the distance varies as the time.*

Again, if we refer to the general formula of Art 84, we find that $\frac{s}{t} = v$ is a relation connecting the space described by a body which moves for a time t with *uniform velocity* v. That is, if $s_1, s_2, s_3 \ldots$ be spaces described in times $t_1, t_2, t_3 \ldots$ respectively, we have

$$\frac{s_1}{t_1} = \frac{s_2}{t_2} = \frac{s_3}{t_3} = \ldots\ldots = v$$

From this it appears that the ratio of any value of s to the corresponding value of t is *constant,* that is, remains the same whatever numerical values s and t may have.

This is an instance of *direct variation,* and s is said to *vary* as t.

305. The symbol $\propto$ is used to denote variation; so that $A \propto B$ is read "A varies as B".

306. *If* A *varies as* B, *then* A *is equal to* B *multiplied by some constant quantity.*

For suppose that $a_1, a_2, a_3 \ldots, b_1, b_2, b_3 \ldots$ are corresponding values of A and B.

Then, by definition, $\frac{A}{a_1} = \frac{B}{b_1}; \frac{A}{a_2} = \frac{B}{b_2}; \frac{A}{a_3} = \frac{B}{b_3}$; and so on.

$\therefore \frac{a_1}{b_1} = \frac{a_2}{b_2} = \frac{a_3}{b_3} = \ldots$, each being equal to $\frac{A}{B}$.

Hence $\frac{\text{any value of } A}{\text{the corresponding value of } B}$ is always the same;

that is, $\frac{A}{B} = m$, where m is constant.

$\therefore \qquad A = mB$.

307. DEFINITION. One quantity A is said to vary inversely as another B when A varies *directly* as the reciprocal of B. [See Art. 107.]

Thus, if A varies inversely as B, $A \frac{m}{B}$, where m is constant.

The following is an illustration of inverse variation: If 6 men do a certain work in 8 hours, 12 men would do the same work in 4 hours, 2 men in 24 hours; and so on. Thus it appears that when the number of men is increased the time is proportionately decreased; and vice versa.

308. DEFINITION. One quantity is said to vary jointly as a number of others when it varies directly as their product.

Thus A varies jointly as B and C when $A = mBC$, where m is constant. For instance, the interest on a sum of money varies jointly as the principal, the time, and the rate per cent.

309. DEFINITION. A is said to vary directly as B and inversely as C when A varies as $\frac{B}{C}$.

310. If A *varies as* B *when* C *is constant, and* A *varies as* C *when* B *is constant, then will* A *vary as* BC *when both* B *and* C *vary.*

The variation of A depends partly on that of B and partly on that of C. Suppose these latter variations to take place separately, each in its turn producing its own effect on A; also let a, b, c be certain simultaneous values of A, B, C.

1. *Let C be constant* while B changes to b ; then A must undergo a partial change and will assume some intermediate value a , where

$$\frac{A}{a'} = \frac{B}{b} \qquad \text{...(1).}$$

2. *Let* B be *constant*, that is, let it retain its value b, while C changes to c; then A must complete its change and pass from its intermediate value a' to its final value a, where

$$\frac{a'}{a} = \frac{C}{c} \qquad \text{...(2).}$$

From (1) and (2) $\frac{A}{a'} \times \frac{a'}{a} = \frac{B}{b} \times \frac{C}{c}$;

that is, $A = \frac{a}{bc} \cdot BC$,

or A varies as BC.

311. The following are illustrations of the theorem proved in the last article.

The amount of work done by a *given number of men* varies directly as the number of days they work, and the amount of work done *in a given time* varies directly as the number of men; therefore when the number of days and the number of men are both variable, the amount of work will vary as the product of the number of men and the number of days.

Again, in Geometry, the area of a triangle varies directly as its base when the height is constant, and directly as the height when the base is constant; and when both the height and base are variable, the area varies as the product of the numbers representing the height and the base.

Example 1. If $A \propto B$ and $C \propto D$, then will $AC \propto BD$.

For, by supposition, $A = mB, C = nD$, where m and n are constants.

Therefore, $AC = mnBD$; and as mn is constant, $AC \propto BD$.

Example 2. If x varies inversely as $y^2 - 1$, and is equal to 24 when $y = 10$; find x when $y = 5$.

By supposition, $x = \frac{m}{y^2 - 1}$, where m is constant.

Putting $x = 24, y = 10$, we obtain $24 = \frac{m}{99}$,

whence $m = 24 \times 99.$ $x = \frac{24 \times 99}{y^2 - 1}$;

hence, putting $y = 5$, we get $x = 99$.

Example 3. The volume of a pyramid varies jointly as its height and the area of its base; and when the area of the base is 60 square dm the height 14 dm and the volume is 280 cubic dm. What is the area of the base of a pyramid whose volume is 390 cubic dm and whose height is 26 dm?

Let V denote the volume, A the area of the base, and h the height; then $V = mAh$, where m is constant.

Substituting the given values of V, A, h, we have

$$280 = m \times 60 \times 14;$$

$$\therefore \quad m = \frac{280}{60 \times 14} = \frac{1}{3}.$$

$$\therefore \quad V = \frac{1}{3} Ah.$$

Also when $V = 390, h = 26$;

$$\therefore \quad 390 = \frac{1}{3} A \times 26;$$

$$\therefore \quad A = 45.$$

Hence the area of the base is 45 square dm.

EXAMPLES XXXII-c

1. If $x \propto y$, and $y = 7$ when $x = 18$, find x when $y = 21$.

2. If $x \propto y$, and $y = 3$ when $x = 2$, find y when $x = 18$.

3. A varies jointly as B and C; and $A = 6$ when $B = 3, C = 2$, find A when $B = 5, C = 7$.

4. A varies jointly as B and C; and $A = 9$ when $B = 5, C = 7$: find B when $A = 54, C = 10$.

5. If $x \propto \frac{1}{y}$, and $y = 4$ when $x = 15$, find y when $x = 6$.

6. If $y \propto \frac{1}{x}$, and $y = 1$ when $x = 1$, find x when $y = 5$.

7. A varies as B directly, and as C inversely; and $A = 10$ when $B = 15, C = 6$; find A when $B = 8, C = 2$.

8. If x varies as y directly, and as z inversely, and $x = 14$ when $y = 10, z = 14$; find z when $x = 49$, $y = 45$.

9. If $x \propto \frac{1}{y}$, and $y \propto \frac{1}{z}$, prove that $z \propto x$.

10. If $a \propto b$, prove that $a^n \propto b^n$.

11. If $x \propto z$ and $y \propto z$, prove that $x^2 - y^2 \propto z^2$.

12. If $3a + 7b \propto 3a + 13b$, and when $a = 5, b = 3$, find the equation between a and b.

13. If $5x - y \propto 10x - 11y$, and when $x = 7, y = 5$, find the equation between x and y.

14. If the cube of x varies as the square of y, and if $x = 3$ when $y = 5$, find the equation between x and y.

15. If the square root of a varies as the cube root of b, and if $a = 4$ when $b = 8$, find the equation between a and b.

16. If y varies inversely as the square of x, and if $y = 8$ when $x = 3$, find x when $= 2$.

17. If $x \propto y + a$, where a is constant, and $x = 15$ when $y = 1$, and $x = 35$ when $y = 5$; find x when $y = 2$.

18. If $a + b \propto a - b$, prove that $a^2 + b^2 \propto ab$; and if $a \propto b$, prove that $a^2 - b^2 \propto ab$.

19. If y be the sum of three quantities which vary as x, x^2, x^3 respectively, and when $x = 1, y = 4$, when $x = 2, y = 8$, and when $x = 3, y = 18$, express y in terms of x.

20. A quantity a varies directly as x and another quantity b varies inversely as x. When $x = 2$, the sum of a and b is 7, and when $x = 3$, the sum is 8. Find the value of $a + b$ when $x = 4$.

21. Given that y is inversely proportional to $ax + 2$, where a is a constant, and that $y = 48$ when $x = 10$, and $y = 30$ when $x = 20$; find a, and write down the definite relation between x and y. (Cent. welsh Bd.)

22. (a) If z varies directly as x and inversely as the square of y, find the percentage increase in z due to an increase in x of 12% and a decrease in y of 20%.

(b) The weight, W, of a body varies jointly as its height, h, and the square of the diameter, d, of its base. Find suitable numbers to fill in the blanks in the following table of values:

W	25		7.2
h	2.5	4	2
d	2	0.6	

(Cent. welsh Bd.)

23. Write as statements of variation of the following quations, in each of which k is a constant:

(i) $y = kx^2z$; (ii) $z = \dfrac{k\,x^2}{y}$; (iii) $x = \dfrac{ky^n}{z^m}$.

24. If p kg weight per sq. dm is the pressure, and v cu. dm the volume of a certain mass of gas, the following table shows values of p and v.

p	15	25	40	50	75
v	600	360	225	180	120

Show that p varies inversely as v.

25. Fill in the following table, if $y \propto x^2$.

x	2	3	4	5	6
y			4.8		

26. Complete the following table, if $y \propto \dfrac{1}{x}$.

x	1	4	5	10	15
y		15			

Try to discover a law connecting y and x consistent with each of the following tables:

27.

x	2	3	7	10
y	.4	.6	1.4	2

28.

x	1	2	3	4
y	12	6	4	3

29.

x	1	2	3	4	5
y	1	3	5	7	9

30. Using a protractor, draw triangles *ABC*, right-angled at *B*, with *AB* 3 cm long and with angle *CAB* $10°, 20°, 30°$, etc., up to $80°$. Show that the length of *CB* is not proportional to the angle *CAB*.

31. Given that the area of a circle varies as the square of its radius, and that the area of a circle is 154 square cm when the radius is 7 cm; find the area of a circle whose radius is 10.5 cm.

32. The area of a circle varies as the square of its diameter; prove that the area of a circle whose diameter is $2\frac{1}{2}$ cm is equal to the sum of the areas of two circles whose diameters are $1\frac{1}{2}$ cm and 2 cm, respectively.

33. The pressure of wind on a plane surface varies jointly as the area of the surface, and the square of the wind's velocity. The pressure on a square cm is $1\frac{5}{9}$ gm when the wind is moving at the rate of 24 km per hour; find the velocity of the wind when the pressure on a square metre is 18 kg.

34. The value of a silver coin varies directly as the square of its diameter, while its thickness remains the same; it also varies directly as its thickness while its diameter remains the same. Two silver coins have their diameters in the ratio of $4:3$. Find the ratio of their thickness if the value of the first be four times that of the second.

35. The volume of a circular cylinder varies as the square of the radius of the base when the height is the same, and as the height when the base is the same. The volume is 88 cubic cm when the height is 7 cm, and the radius of the base is 2 cm; what will be the height of a cylinder on a base of radius 9 cm, when the volume is 396 cubic cm?

36. The altitude of a triangle varies directly as its area and inversely as its base. A triangle, 6 square metres in area, standing on a base of 4 metres, has an altitude of 3 metres: find the altitude of a triangle whose base is 8 metres, and whose area is 12 square metres.

37. The expenses of a school are partly constant and partly vary as the number of boys. The expenses were Rs 10000 for 150 boys and Rs 8400 for 120 boys; what will the expenses be when there are 330 boys? [Compare Art. 442, Ex. 2.]

38. The time of oscillation of a pendulum varies as the square root of the length. The times of oscillation of three pendulums are proportional to a, b, and c. If the second is d cm longer than the first, find the difference in length of the second and third.

39. The electrical resistance of a copper wire of circular cross-section varies as its length and inversely as the square of the thickness. Two copper wires have equal resistance and the length of one is twice that of the other. Show that the one is four times as heavy as the other.

40. The volume of a sphere is known to vary as the cube of its radius, and the surface as the square of its radius. Four spheres A, B, C, D have respective radii 3, 4, 5, 6 cm. Prove that the surface of C is equal to those of A and B together, and that the volume of D is equal to those of A, B and C together.

41. Assume that the rate of consumption of coal by a locomotive varies as the square of the speed and is 1000 kg per hour when the speed is 60 km per hour. If the coal cost the Railway Company Rs 15 per 100 kg and if the other expenses of the train be Rs 12 per hour, find a formula for the cost *in paise per km* when the speed is v km per hour.

42. When a stone is let fall, the time it takes to fall any distance varies as the square root of the distance, and it takes 3 seconds to fall 44.10 metres. How long would it take to fall 122.50 metres?

43. (i) If $\frac{a}{b} = \frac{c}{d} = \frac{e}{f}$, prove that $\left(\frac{a-c}{b-d}\right)^2 = \frac{c^2+e^2}{d^2+f^2}$.

(ii) The distance of the horizon at sea varies as the square root of the height of the eye above sea-level. When the distance is 14.4 km the height of the eye is 18 metres. Find in km the distance when the height of the eye is 8 metres, and find in metres the height of the eye when the distance is 7.2 km.

33

ARITHMETICAL PROGRESSION

312. DEFINITION. Quantities are said to be in Arithmetical Progression when they increase or decrease by a *common difference*.

Thus each of the following series forms an Arithmetical Progression:

$$3, 7, 11, 15, \ldots\ldots$$

$$8, 2, -4, -10, \ldots\ldots$$

$$a, a+d, a+2d, a+3d, \ldots\ldots$$

The common difference is found by subtracting *any* term of the series from that which *follows* it. In the first of the above examples the common difference is 4; in the second it is –6; in the third it is d.

313. If we examine the series $a, a+d, a+2d, a+3d, \ldots\ldots$

we notice that in *any term the coefficient of* d *is always less by one than the number of the term in the series.*

Thus the 3rd term is $a + 2d$;

6th term is $a + 5d$;

20th term is $a + 19d$;

and, generally, the pth term is $a + (p-1)d$.

If n be the number of terms, and if l denote the last, or n^{th} term, we have $l = a + (n-1)d$.

314. *To find the sum of a number of terms in Arithmetical Progression.*

Let a denote the first term, d the common difference, and n the number of terms. Also let l denote the last term, and s the required sum; then

$$s = a + (a+d) + (a+2d) + \ldots + (l-2d) + (l-d) + l;$$

and, by writing the series in the reverse order,

$$s = l + (l-d) + (l-2d) + \ldots + (a+2d) + (a+d) + a.$$

Adding together these two series,

$$2s = (a+l) + (a+l) + (a+l) + \ldots \text{ to } n \text{ terms} = n(a+l),$$

$$\therefore \quad s = \frac{n}{2}(a+l) \qquad \ldots(1);$$

$$\text{and} \quad l = a + (n-1)d \qquad \ldots(2);$$

$$\therefore \quad s = \frac{n}{2}\{2a + (n-1)d\} \qquad \ldots(3).$$

315. In the last article we have three useful formulae (1), (2), (3); in each or these any one of the letters may denote the unknown quantity when the three others are known. [See Art. 82, Chap. IX.] For instance, in (1) if we substitute given values for s, n, l, we obtain an equation for finding a; and similarly in the other formulae. But it is necessary to guard against a too mechanical use of these general formulae, and it will often be found better to solve simple questions by a mental rather than by an actual reference to the requisite formula.

Example 1. Find the 20th and 35th terms of the series

38, 36, 34, ...

Here the common difference is $36-31$, or -2.

$\therefore$ the 20th term $= 38 + 19(-2) = 0$;

and the 35th term $= 38 + 34(-2) = -30$.

Example 2. Find the sum of the series $5\frac{1}{2}, 6\frac{3}{4}, 8, \ldots$ to 17 terms.

Here the common difference is $1\frac{1}{4}$; hence from (3)

$$\text{The sum} \quad = \frac{17}{2}\left\{2 \times \frac{11}{2} + 16 \times 1\frac{1}{4}\right\}$$

$$= \frac{17}{2}(11 + 20) = \frac{17 + 31}{2} = 263\frac{1}{2}.$$

Example 3. The first term of a series is 5, the last 45, and the sum 400. find the number of terms, and the common difference.

If n be the number of terms, then from (1).

$$400 = \frac{n}{2}(5 + 45).$$

whence $n = 16$.

In d be the common difference.

$45 =$ the 16th term $= 5 + 15d$;

whence $d = 2\frac{2}{3}$.

EXAMPLES XXXIII-a

1. Find the 27th and 41st terms in the series 5, 11, 17, ...
2. Find the 13th and 109th terms in the series 71, 70, 69, ...
3. Find the 17th and 54th terms in the series $10, 11\frac{1}{2}, 13, \ldots$.
4. Find the 20th and 13th terms in the series $-3, -2, 1, \ldots$.
5. Find the 90th and 16th terms in the series $-4, 2.5, 9, \ldots$.
6. Find the 37th and 89th terms in the series $-2.8, 0, 2.8, \ldots$.

Find the last term in the following series:

7. 5, 7, 9, ... to 20 terms.

8. 7, 3 −1, ... to 15 terms.

9. $13\frac{1}{2}, 9, 4\frac{1}{2}, \ldots$ to 13 terms.

10. .6, 1.2, 1.8, ... to 12 terms.

11. 2.7, 3.4, 4.1, ... to 11 terms.

12. $x, 2x, 3x, \ldots.$ to 25 terms.

13. $a - d, a + d, a + 3d, \ldots$ to 30 terms.

14. $2a - b, 4a - 3b, 6a - 5b, \ldots$ to 40 terms.

Find the last term and sum of the following series:

15. 14, 64, 114, ... to 20 terms.

16. 1, 1.2, 1.4, ... to 12 terms.

17. 9, 5, 1, ... to 100 terms.

18. $\frac{1}{4}, -\frac{1}{4}, -\frac{3}{4}, \ldots$ to 21 terms.

19. $3\frac{1}{2}, 1, -1\frac{1}{2}, \ldots$ to 19 terms.

20. 64, 96, 128, ... to 16 terms.

Find the sum of the following series:

21. 5, 9, 13, ... to 19 terms.

22. 12, 9, 6, ... to 23 terms.

23. $4, 5\frac{1}{4}, 6\frac{1}{2}, \ldots$ to 37 terms.

24. $10\frac{1}{2}, 9, 7\frac{1}{2}, \ldots$ to 94 terms.

25. −3, 1, 5, ... to 17 terms.

26. $10, 9\frac{2}{3}, 9\frac{1}{3}, \ldots$ to 21 terms.

27. $p, 3p, 5p, \ldots$ to p terms.

28. $3a, a, -a, \ldots$ to a terms.

29. $a, 0, -a, \ldots$ to a terms.

30. $-3q, \ldots -q, q, \ldots$ to p terms.

Find the number of terms and the common difference when

31. The first term is 3, the last term 90, and the sum 1395.

32. The first term is 79, the last term 7, and the sum 1075.

33. The sum is 24, the first term 9, the last term −6.

34. The sum is 714, the first term 1, the last term $58\frac{1}{2}$.

35. The last term is −16, the sum −133, the first term −3.

36. The first term is −75, the sum −740, the last term 1.

37. The first term is a, the last $13a$, and the sum $49a$.

38. The sum is $-320x$, the first term $3x$, the last term $-35x$.

316. If *any two* terms of an Arithmetical Progression be given, the series can be completely determined; for the data furnish *two* simultaneous equations, the solution of which will give the first term, and the common difference

Example. Find the series whose 7th and 51st terms are –3 and –355 respectively.

If a be the first term, and d the common difference,

$$-3 = \text{the } 7^{th} \text{ term}$$

$$= a + 6d;$$

and $$-355 = \text{the } 51^{st} \text{ term}$$

$$= a + 50d;$$

whence, by subtraction, $-352 = 44d$;

$\therefore \quad d = -8$; and consequently $a = 45$.

Hence, the series is 45, 37, 29,.... .

317. DEFINITION. When three quantities are in Arithmetical Progression the middle one is said to be the arithmetic mean of other two.

Thus a is the arithmetic mean between $a - d$ and $a + d$.

318. *To find the arithmetic mean between two given quantities.*

Let a and b be the two quantities; A and arithmetic mean. Then since a, A, b are in A.P. we must have

$$b - A = A - a,$$

each being equal to the common difference:

whence $$A = \frac{a+b}{2}.$$

319. Between two given quantities it is always possible to insert any number of terms such that whole series thus formed shall be in A.P.; and by an extension of the definition in Art. 317, the terms thus inserted are called the *arithmetic means*.

Example. Insert 20 arithmetic means between 4 and 67.
Including the extremes the number of terms will be 22; so that we have to find a series of 22 terms in A.P.; of which 4 is the first and 67 the last.

Let d be the common difference;

then $$67 = \text{the } 22^{nd} \text{ term}$$

$$= 4 + 21d;$$

whence $a = 3$, and the series is 4, 7, 10, ... 61, 64, 67;

and the required means are 7, 10, 13, ... 58, 61, 64.

320. *To insert a given number of arithmetic means between two given quantities.*

Let a and b be the given quantities, n the number of means.

Including the extremes the number of terms will be $n + 2$; so that we have to find a series of $n + 2$ terms in A.P., of which a is the first, and b is the last.

Let d be the common difference;

then $\qquad b = \text{the } (n + 2)^{\text{th}} \text{ term}$

$$= a + (n + 1)d;$$

whence $\qquad d = \dfrac{b - a}{n + 1};$

and the required means are

$$a + \frac{b - a}{n + 1},\ a + \frac{2(b - a)}{n + 1}, \ldots\ldots\ a + \frac{n(b - a)}{n + 1}.$$

Example 1. Find the 30th term of an A.P. of which the first term is 17, and the 100th term -16.

Let d be the common difference,

then $\qquad -16 = \text{the } 100^{\text{th}} \text{ term}$

$$= 17 + 99d;$$

$$\therefore \qquad d = -\frac{1}{3}.$$

The 30th term $\qquad = 17 + 29\left(\dfrac{1}{3}\right)$

$$= 7\frac{1}{3}.$$

Example 2. The sum of three numbers in A.P. is 33, and their product is 722; find them.

Let a be the *middle* number, d the common difference; then the three numbers are $a - d, a, a + d$.

Hence, $a - d + a + a + d = 33$;

whence $a = 11$, and the three numbers are $11 - d, 11, 11 + d$.

$$\therefore \quad 11(11 + d)(11 - d) = 792,$$

$$121 - d^2 = 72,$$

$$d = \pm 7;$$

and the numbers are 4, 11, 18.

Example 3. How many terms of the series 24, 20, 16, ... must be taken that the sum may be 72?

Let the number of terms be n; then, since the common difference is $20 - 24$, or -4, we have form (3), Art. 314,

$$72 = \frac{n}{2}\{2 \times 24 + (n-1)(-4)\}$$

$$= 24n - 2n(n-1);$$

whence $n^2 - 13n + 36 = 0$,

or $(n-4)(n-9) = 0$;

$\therefore$ $n = 4$ or 9.

Both these values satisfy the conditions of the question; for if we write down the first 9 terms, we get 24, 20, 16, 12, 8, 4, 0, -4, -8; and, as the last five terms destroy each other, the sum of 9 terms is the same as that of 4 terms.

Example 4. An A.P. consists of 21 terms; the sum of the three terms in the middle is 129, and of the last three is 237; find the series.

Let a be the first term, and d the common difference. Then

$$237 = \text{the sum of the last three terms}$$

$$= a + 20d + a + 19d + a + 18d$$

$$= 3a + 57d;$$

whence $a + 19d = 79$ ...(1).

Again, the three middle terms are the 10th, 11th, 12th;

hence $129 = \text{the sum of the three middle terms}$

$$= a + 9d + a + 10d + a + 11d$$

$$= 3a + 30d;$$

whence $a + 10d = 43$ ...(2).

Form (1) and (2), we obtain $d = 4$, $a = 3$.

Hence the series is 3, 7, 11, ... 83.

EXAMPLES XXXIII-b

Find the series in which

1. The 27th term is 186, and the 45th term 312.
2. The 5th term is 1, and the 31st term -77.
3. The 15th term is -25, and the 23rd term -41.
4. The 9th term is -11, and the 102nd term $-150\frac{1}{2}$.
5. The 15th term is 25, and the 29th term 46.

6. The 16th term is 214, and the 51st term 739.

7. The 3rd and 7th terms of an A.P. are 7 and 19; find the 15th term.

8. The 54th and 4th terms are -125 and 0; find the 42nd term.

Find the series in which

9. The 31st and 2nd terms are $\frac{1}{2}$ and $7\frac{3}{4}$; find th 59th term.

10. Insert 15 arithmetic means between 71 and 23.

11. Insert 17 arithmetic means between 93 and 69.

12. Insert 14 arithmetic means between $-7\frac{1}{5}$ and $-2\frac{1}{5}$.

13. Insert 16 arithmetic means between 7.2 and -6.4.

14. Insert 36 arithmetic means between $8\frac{1}{2}$ and $2\frac{1}{3}$.

How many terms must be taken of

15. The series 42, 39, 36, ... to make 315?

16. The series $-16, -15, -14$, ... to make -100?

17. The series $15\frac{2}{3}, 15\frac{1}{3}, 15$, ... to make 129?

18. The series $20, 18\frac{3}{4}, 17\frac{1}{2}$, ... to make $162\frac{1}{2}$?

19. The series $-10\frac{1}{2}, -9, -7\frac{1}{2}$, ... to make -42?

20. The series $-6\frac{4}{5}, -6\frac{2}{5}, -6$, ... to make $-52\frac{4}{5}$?

21. The sum of three numbers in A.P. is 39, and their product is 2184; find them.

22. The sum of three numbers in A.P. is 12, and the sum of their squares is 66; find them.

23. The sum of five numbers in A.P. is 75, and the product of the greatest and least is 161; find them.

24. The sum of five numbers in A.P. is 40, and the sum of their squares is 410; find them.

25. The 12th, 85th and last terms of an A.P. are 38, 257, 395 respectively; find the number of terms.

34

GEOMETRICAL PROGRESSION

321. DEFINITION. Quantities are said to be in Geometrical Progression when they increase or decrease by a *constant factor.*

Thus each of the following series forms a Geometrical Progression:

$$3, 6, 12, 24, \ldots$$

$$1, -\frac{1}{3}, \frac{1}{9}, -\frac{1}{27}, \ldots$$

$$a, ar, ar^2, ar^3, \ldots$$

The constant factor is also called the *common ratio,* and it is found by dividing *any* term by that which immediately *precedes* it. In the first of the above examples the common ratio is 2, in the second it is $-\frac{1}{3}$; and in the third it is r.

322. If we examine the series $a, ar, ar^2, ar^3, ar^4, \ldots$

we notice that *in any term the index of* r *is always less by one than the number of the term in the series.*

Thus the 3rd term is ar^2;

the 6th term is ar^5;

the 20th term is ar^{19};

and, generally, the pth term is ar^{p-1}.

If n be the number of terms, and if l denote the last, or nth term,

we have $\quad l = ar^{n-1}$.

Example. Find the 8th term of the series $-\frac{1}{3}, \frac{1}{2}, -\frac{3}{4}, \ldots$

The common ratio is $\frac{1}{2} \div \left(-\frac{1}{3}\right)$, or $-\frac{3}{2}$;

$$\therefore \text{ the 8th term} = -\frac{1}{3} \times \left(-\frac{3}{2}\right)^7$$

$$= -\frac{1}{3} \times -\frac{2187}{128} = \frac{729}{128}.$$

323. DEFINITION. When three quantities are in Geometrical Progression the middle one is called the geometric mean between the other two.

To find the geometric mean between two given quantities.

Let a and b be the two quantities; G the geometric mean. Then since a, G, b are in G.P.,

$$\frac{b}{G} = \frac{G}{a},$$

each being equal to the common ratio;

$$\therefore \qquad G^2 = ab;$$

whence $$G = \sqrt{ab}.$$

324. *To insert a given number of geometric means between two given quantities.*

Let a and b be the given quantities, n the number of means.

In all there will be $n + 2$ terms; so that we have to find a series of $n + 2$ terms in G.P., of which a is the first and b the last.

Let r be the common ratio;

then $$b = (n + 2)\text{ th term}$$
$$= ar^{n+1};$$

$$\therefore \qquad r^{n+1} = \frac{b}{a};$$

$$\therefore \qquad r = \left(\frac{b}{a}\right)^{1/n+1} \qquad \text{...(1).}$$

Hence the required means are $ar, ar^2, \ldots, ar^n$, where r has the value found in (1).

Example. Insert 4 geometric means between 160 and 5.

We have to find 6 terms in G.P. of which 160 is the first, and 5 the sixth.

Let r be the common ratio;

then 5 = the sixth term
$$= 160\, r^5;$$

$$\therefore \qquad r^5 = \frac{1}{32};$$

whence, *by trial*, $r = \dfrac{1}{2}$;

and the means are 80, 40, 20, 10.

325. *To find the sum of a number of terms in Geometrical Progression.*

Let a be the first term, r the common ratio, n the number of terms, and s the sum required. Then

$$s = a + ar + ar^2 + \ldots + ar^{n-2} + ar^{n-1};$$

multiplying every term by r, we have

$$rs = ar + ar^2 + \ldots + ar^{n-2} + ar^{n-1} + ar^n.$$

Hence by subtraction,

$$rs - s = ar^n - a;$$

$$\therefore \quad (r-1)s = a(r^n - 1);$$

$$\therefore \quad s = \frac{a(r^n - 1)}{r - 1} \qquad \ldots(1).$$

Changing the signs in numerator and denominator [Art. 170.]

$$s = \frac{a(1 - r^n)}{1 - r} \qquad \ldots(2).$$

NOTE. It will be found convenient to remember both forms given above for s, using (2) in all cases except when r is *positive and greater than* 1.

Since $ar^{n-1} = l$, the formula (1) may be written

$$s = \frac{rl - a}{r - 1};$$

a form which is sometimes useful.

Example 1. Sum the series 81, 54, 36, ... to 9 terms.

The common ratio $= \frac{54}{81} = \frac{2}{3}$, which is less than 1.

$$\text{hence the sum} = \frac{81\left\{1 - \left(\frac{2}{3}\right)^9\right\}}{1 - \frac{2}{3}}$$

$$= 243\left\{1 - \left(\frac{2}{3}\right)^9\right\}$$

$$= 243 - \frac{512}{81}$$

$$= 236\frac{55}{81}.$$

Example 2. Sum the series $\frac{2}{3}, -1, \frac{3}{2}, \ldots\ldots$ to 7 terms.

The common ratio $= -\frac{3}{2}$; hence by formula (2)

$$\text{the sum} = \frac{\frac{2}{3}\left\{1-\left(-\frac{3}{2}\right)^7\right\}}{2+\frac{3}{2}}$$

$$= \frac{\frac{2}{3}\left\{1+\frac{2187}{128}\right\}}{\frac{5}{2}}$$

$$= \frac{2}{3} \times \frac{2315}{128} \times \frac{2}{5} = \frac{463}{96}.$$

EXAMPLES XXXIV-a

1. Find the 5th and 8th terms of the series 3, 6, 12, ...
2. Find the 10th and 16th terms of the series 256, 128, 64, ...
3. Find the 7th and 11th terms of the series $64, -32, 16, \ldots$.
4. Find the 8th and 12th terms of the series $81, -27, 9, \ldots$.
5. Find the 14th and 7th terms of the series $\frac{1}{64}, \frac{1}{32}, \frac{1}{16}, \ldots$.
6. Find the 4th and 8th terms of the series $.008, .04, .2, \ldots$.

Find the last term in the following series:

7. 2, 4, 8, ... to 9 terms.
8. $2, -6, 18, \ldots$ to 8 terms.
9. $2, 3, 4\frac{1}{2}, \ldots$ to 6 terms.
10. $3, -3^2, 3^3, \ldots$ to $2n$ terms.
11. $x, x^3, x^5, \ldots$ to p terms.
12. $x, 1, \frac{1}{x}, \ldots$ to 30 terms.
13. Insert 3 geometric means between 486 and 6.
14. Insert 4 geometric means between $\frac{1}{8}$ and 128.
15. Insert 6 geometric means between 56 and $-\frac{7}{16}$.

16. Insert 5 geometric means between $\frac{32}{81}$ and $4\frac{1}{2}$.

Find the last term and the sum of the following series:

17. 3, 6, 12, ... to 8 terms.

18. $6, -18, 54, \ldots$ to 6 terms.

19. 64, 32, 16, ... to 10 terms.

20. 8.1, 2.7, .9, ... to 7 terms.

Find the last term and the sum of the following series:

21. $\frac{1}{72}, \frac{1}{24}, \frac{1}{8}, \ldots$ to 8 terms.

22. $4\frac{1}{2}, 1\frac{1}{2}, \frac{1}{2}, \ldots$ to 9 terms.

Find the sum of the series:

23. $3, -1, \frac{1}{3}, \ldots$ to 6 terms.

24. $\frac{1}{2}, \frac{1}{3}, \frac{2}{9}, \ldots$ to 7 terms.

25. $-\frac{2}{5}, \frac{1}{2}, -\frac{5}{8}, \ldots$ to 6 terms.

26. $1, -\frac{1}{2}, \frac{1}{4}, \ldots$ to 12 terms.

27. $9, -6, 4, \ldots$ to 7 terms.

28. $\frac{2}{3}, -\frac{1}{6}, \frac{1}{24}, \ldots$ to 8 terms.

29. $1, 3, 3^2, \ldots$ to p terms.

30. $2, -4, 8, \ldots$ to $2p$ terms.

31. $\frac{1}{\sqrt{3}}, 1, \frac{3}{\sqrt{3}}, \ldots$ to 8 terms.

32. $\sqrt{a}, \sqrt{a^3}, \sqrt{a^5}, \ldots$ to a terms.

33. $\frac{1}{\sqrt{2}}, -2, \frac{8}{\sqrt{2}}, \ldots$ to 7 terms.

34. $\sqrt{2}, \sqrt{6}, 3\sqrt{2}, \ldots$ to 12 terms.

326. Consider the series $1, \frac{1}{2}, \frac{1}{2^2}, \frac{1}{2^3}, \ldots$

$$\text{The sum to } n \text{ terms} = \frac{1 - \frac{1}{2^n}}{1 - \frac{1}{2}}$$

$$= 2\left(1 - \frac{1}{2^n}\right)$$

$$= 2 - \frac{1}{2^{n-1}}.$$

From this result it appears that however many terms be taken the sum of the above series is always less than 2. Also we see that, by making n sufficiently large, we can make the fraction $\frac{1}{2^{n-1}}$ as small as we please. Thus by taking a sufficient number of terms the sum can be made to differ by as little as we please form 2.

In the next article a more general case is discussed.

327. From Art. 325 we have $s = \dfrac{a(1-r^n)}{1-r}$

$$= \frac{a}{1-r} - \frac{ar^n}{1-r}.$$

Suppose r is a proper fraction; then the greater the value of n the smaller is the value of r^n, and consequently of $\dfrac{ar^n}{1-r}$; and therefore by making n sufficiently large, we can make the sum of n terms of the series differ from $\dfrac{a}{1-r}$ by as small a quantity as we please.

This result is usually stated thus: *the sum of an infinite number of terms of a decreasing Geometrical Progression is* $\dfrac{a}{1-r}$; or more briefly, *the sum to infinity is* $\dfrac{a}{1-r}$.

328. Recurring decimals furnish a good illustration of infinite Geometrical Progressions.

Example. Find the value of $.4\dot{2}\dot{3}$.

$$.4\dot{2}\dot{3} = .4232323\ldots$$

$$= \frac{4}{10} + \frac{23}{1000} + \frac{23}{100000} + \ldots$$

$$= \frac{4}{10} + \frac{23}{10^3} + \frac{23}{10^5} + \ldots$$

$$= \frac{4}{10} + \frac{23}{10^3}\left(1 + \frac{1}{10^2} + \frac{1}{10^4} + \ldots\right)$$

$$= \frac{4}{10} + \frac{23}{10^3} \cdot \frac{1}{1 - \frac{1}{10^2}}$$

$$= \frac{4}{10} + \frac{23}{10^3} \cdot \frac{100}{99}$$

$$= \frac{4}{10} + \frac{23}{990}$$

$$= \frac{419}{990},$$

which agrees with the value found by the usual arithmetical rule.

EXAMPLES XXXIV-b

Sum to infinity the following series:

1. 9, 6, 4, ...
2. 12, 6, 3, ...
3. $\frac{1}{3}, \frac{1}{4}, \frac{1}{8}, \ldots.$
4. $\frac{1}{2}, -\frac{1}{4}, \frac{1}{8}, \ldots.$

Sum of infinity the following series.

5. $\frac{1}{3}, \frac{2}{9}, \frac{4}{27}, \ldots.$
6. $\frac{8}{5}, -1, \frac{5}{8}, \ldots\ldots$
7. .9, .03, .001, ...
8. .8, −.4, .2, ...

Find by the method of Art. 328, the value of

9. $.\dot{3}$,
10. $.1\dot{6}$,
11. $.\dot{2}\dot{4}$,
12. $.3\dot{7}\dot{8}$,
13. $.\dot{0}3\dot{7}$.

Find the series in which

14. The 10th term is 320 and the 6th term 20.
15. The 5th term is $\frac{27}{16}$ and the 9th term is $\frac{1}{3}$.
16. The 7th term is 625 and the 4th term -5.
17. The 3rd term is $\frac{9}{16}$ and the 6th term is $-4\frac{1}{2}$.
18. Divide 183 into three parts in G.P. such that the sum of the first and third is $2\frac{1}{20}$ times the second.
19. Show that the product of any odd number of consecutive terms of a G.P. will be equal to the nth power of the middle term, n being the number of terms.
20. The first two terms of an infinite G.P. are together equal to 1, and every term is twice the sum of all the terms which follow. Find the series.

Sum the following series:

21. $y^2 + 2b, y^4 + 4b, y^6 + 6b$, ...to n terms.
22. $\frac{3+2\sqrt{2}}{3-2\sqrt{2}}, 1, \frac{3-2\sqrt{2}}{3+2\sqrt{2}}, \ldots$ to infinity.
23. $\sqrt{\frac{3}{2}}, \frac{1}{3}\sqrt{2}, \frac{2}{9}\sqrt{\frac{2}{3}}, \ldots$ to infinity.
24. $2n - \frac{1}{2}, 4n + \frac{1}{6}, 6n - \frac{1}{18}, \ldots$ to $2n$ terms.

[*Examples for revision will be found in Miscellaneous Examples* V., p. 332.]

35

HARMONICAL PROGRESSION

329. DEFINITION. Three quantities a, b, c are said to be in Harmonical Progression when $\frac{a}{c} = \frac{a-b}{b-c}$.

Any number of quantities are said to be in Harmonical Progression when every three consecutive terms are in Harmonical Progression.

330. *The reciprocals of quantities in Harmonical Progression are in Arithmetical Progression.*

By definition, if a, b, c are in Harmonical Progression, $\frac{a}{c} = \frac{a-b}{b-c}$;

$$\therefore \qquad a(b-c) = c(a-b),$$

dividing every term by abc,

$$\frac{1}{c} - \frac{1}{b} = \frac{1}{b} - \frac{1}{a},$$

which proves the proposition.

331. Harmonical properties are chiefly interesting because of their importance in Geometry and in the Theory of Sound: in Algebra the proposition just proved is the only one of any importance. There is no general formula for the sum of any number of quantities in Harmonical Progression. Questions in H.P. are generally solved by inverting the terms, and making use of the properties of the corresponding A.P.

Example. The 12th term of a H.P. is $\frac{1}{5}$, and the 19th sum is $\frac{3}{22}$: find the series.

Let a be the first term, d the common difference of the corresponding A.P.; then

$$5 = \text{the } 12^{\text{th}} \text{ term}$$

$$= a + 11d;$$

and $\qquad \frac{22}{3} = \text{the } 19^{\text{th}} \text{ term}$

$$= a + 18d;$$

whence $\quad d = \frac{1}{3}, a = \frac{4}{3}.$

Hence the Arithmetical Progression is $\frac{4}{3}, \frac{5}{3}, 2, \frac{7}{3}, \ldots\ldots\ldots\ldots;$

and the Harmonical Progression is $\frac{3}{4}, \frac{3}{5}, \frac{1}{2}, \frac{3}{7}, \ldots\ldots\ldots\ldots.$

332. *To find the harmonic mean between two given quantities.*

Lat a, b the two quantities, H their harmonic mean; then

$\frac{1}{a}, \frac{1}{H}, \frac{1}{b}$ are in A.P.

$$\therefore \qquad \frac{1}{H} - \frac{1}{a} = \frac{1}{b} - \frac{1}{H},$$

$$\frac{2}{H} = \frac{1}{a} + \frac{1}{b},$$

$$H = \frac{2ab}{a+b}.$$

333. If A, G, H be the arithmetic, geometric, and harmonic means between a and b, we have proved

$$A = \frac{a+b}{2} \qquad \ldots(1).$$

$$G = \sqrt{ab} \qquad \ldots.(2).$$

$$H = \frac{2ab}{a+b} \qquad \ldots(3).$$

Therefore $$AH = \frac{a+b}{2} \cdot \frac{2ab}{a+b}$$

$$= ab = G^2;$$

that is, G is the geometric mean between A and H.

334. Miscellaneous questions in the Progressions afford scope for muck skill and ingenuity, the solution being often very neatly effected by some special artifice. The student will find the following hints useful:

1. If the same quantity be added to, or subtracted from, all the terms of an A.P., the resulting terms will form an A.P. with the same common difference as before. [Art. 312.]
2. If all the terms of an A.P. be multiplied or divided by the same quantity, the resulting terms form an A.P., but with a new common difference, [Art. 312.]
3. If all the terms of a G.P. be multiplied or divided by the same quantity, the resulting terms form an G.P., with the same common ratio as before, [Art. 322.]

4. If $a, b, c, d, ...$ be in G.P., they are also in *continued proportion,* since, by definition.

$$\frac{a}{b} = \frac{b}{c} = \frac{c}{d} = ... = \frac{1}{r}.$$

Conversely, a series of quantities in continued proportion may be represented by $x, xr, xr^2, ...$.

Example 1. Find three quantities in G.P. such that their product is 343, and their sum is $30\frac{1}{3}$.

Let $\frac{a}{r}$, a, ar be the three quantities;

then we have $\quad \frac{a}{r} \times a \times ar = 343 \qquad ...(1),$

and $\quad a\left(\frac{1}{r} + 1 + r\right) = \frac{91}{3} \qquad ...(2).$

From (1) $\quad a^3 = 343, \; a = 7;$

$\therefore$ from (2) $\quad 7(1 + r + r^2) = \frac{91}{3} r.$

Whence we obtain $\quad r = 3, \text{ or } \frac{1}{3},$

and the numbers are $\frac{7}{3}, 7, 21.$

Example 2. If a, b, c be in H.P., prove that $\frac{a}{b+c}, \frac{b}{c+a}, \frac{c}{a+b}$ are also in H.P.

Since $\frac{1}{a}, \frac{1}{b}, \frac{1}{c}$ are in A.P., $\frac{a+b+c}{a}, \frac{a+b+c}{b}, \frac{a+b+c}{c}$ are in A.P.;

$\therefore \quad 1 + \frac{b+c}{a}, 1 + \frac{a+c}{b}, 1 + \frac{a+b}{c}$ are in A.P. ;

$\therefore \quad \frac{b+c}{a}, \frac{a+c}{b}, \frac{a+b}{c}$ are in A.P. ;

$\therefore \quad \frac{a}{b+c}, \frac{b}{c+a}, \frac{c}{a+b}$ are in H.P.

Example 3. The nth term of an A.P. is $\frac{n}{5} + 2$, find the sum of 49 terms.

Let a be the first term, and l the last; then by putting $n = 1$, and $n = 49$ respectively, we obtain

$$a = \frac{1}{5} + 2, \; l = \frac{49}{5} + 2;$$

$$\therefore \qquad s = \frac{n}{2}(a + l) = \frac{49}{2}\left(\frac{50}{5} + 4\right)$$

$$= \frac{49}{2} \times 14 = 343.$$

Example 4. If a, b, c, d, e be in G.P., prove that $b + d$ is the geometric mean between $a + c$ and $c + e$.

Since a, b, c, d, e are in continued proportion, $\frac{a}{b} = \frac{b}{c} = \frac{c}{d} = \frac{d}{e}$;

$\therefore$ each ratio $= \frac{a+c}{b+d} = \frac{b+d}{c+e}$. [Art. 294.]

Whence $(b + d)^2 = (a + c)(c + e)$.

EXAMPLES XXXV-a

1. Find the 6th term of the series, 4, 2, $1\frac{1}{3}$, … .

2. Find the 21st term of the series $2\frac{1}{2}, 1\frac{12}{13}, 1\frac{9}{16}$, … .

3. Find the 8th term of the series $1\frac{1}{3}, 1\frac{11}{17}, 2\frac{2}{13}$, … .

4. Find the nth term of the series 3, $1\frac{1}{2}$, 1, … .

Find the series in which

5. The 15th term is $\frac{1}{25}$, and the 23rd term is $\frac{1}{41}$.

6. The 2nd term is 2, and the 31st term is $\frac{4}{31}$.

7. The 39th term is $\frac{1}{11}$, and the 54th term is $\frac{1}{26}$.

Find the harmonic mean between

8. 2 and 4.

9. 1 and 13.

10. $\frac{1}{4}$ and $\frac{1}{10}$.

11. $\frac{1}{a}$ and $\frac{1}{b}$.

12. $\frac{1}{x+y}$ and $\frac{1}{x-y}$.

13. $x + y$ and $x - y$.

14. Insert two harmonic means between 4 and 12.

15. Insert three harmonic means between $2\frac{2}{5}$ and 12.

16. Insert four harmonic means between 1 and 6.

17. If G be the geometric mean between two quantities A and B, show that the ratio of the arithmetic and harmonic means of A and G is equal to the ratio of the arithmetic and harmonic means of G and B.

18. To each of three consecutive terms of a G.P. the second of the three is added. Show that the three resulting quantities are in H.P.

Sum the following series:

19. $1 + 1\frac{3}{4} + 3\frac{1}{16} + \ldots\ldots$ to 6 terms.

20. $1 + 1\frac{3}{4} + 2\frac{1}{2} + \ldots\ldots\ldots$ to 6 terms.

21. $(2a + x) + 3a + (4a - x) + \ldots\ldots\ldots$ to p terms.

22. $1\frac{4}{5} - 1\frac{1}{5} + \frac{4}{5} - \ldots\ldots$ to 8 terms.

23. $1\frac{4}{5} + 1\frac{1}{5} + \frac{3}{5} + \ldots\ldots$ to 12 terms.

24. If $x - a$, $y - a$, and $z - a$ be in G.P., prove that $2(y - a)$ is the harmonic mean between $y - x$ and $y - z$;

25. If a, b, c, d be in A.P., a, e, f, d in G.P., a, g, h, d in H.P. respectively; prove that $ad = ef = bh = cg$.

26. If $a^2,\ b^2,\ c^2$ be in A.P., prove that $b + c, c + a, a + b$ are in H.P.

27. If a, b, c be in A.P., and α, β, γ in H.P., show that $\frac{a + c}{b\beta} = \frac{\alpha + \gamma}{\alpha\gamma}$.

28. If a be the arithmetic mean between b and c, and b the geometric mean between a and c, prove that c will be the harmonic mean between a and b.

29. If $\frac{a + b}{2}, b, \frac{b + c}{2}$ be in H.P., then a, b, c are in G.P.

30. If a, b, c, d, e be in G.P., prove that $c(a + 2c + e) = (b + d)^2$.

31. If a, b, c, d .... be a series of quantities in G.P., show that the reciprocals of $a^2 - b^2, b^2 - c^2, c^2 - d^2$; .... are also in G.P.; and find the sum of n terms of this latter series in terms of a and b.

32. If a, b, c be in A.P., and b, c, d in H.P., then $a, \frac{c^2}{d}, c$ are in H.P., and $b, \frac{ad}{b}, d$ are also in H.P.

33. If g be the geometric and a the arithmetic mean between m and n, and if k^2 be the arithmetic mean between m^2 and n^2, prove that a^2 is the arithmetic mean between g^2 and k^2.

34. If a, b, c, d be in G.P., prove that $(b - c)^2 = ac + bd - 2ad$.

35. If a, b, c, d be in G.P., prove that

$$(a+d)(a-b)^2 : a(a-c)(a-d) = a-b+c : a+b+c.$$

36. If a, b, c be in H.P., prove that $\frac{1}{a}+\frac{1}{b+c}, \frac{1}{b}+\frac{1}{c+a}, \frac{1}{c}+\frac{1}{a+b}$ are also in H.P.

37. In an infinite G.P., find r when each term is equal to half the sum of the following terms.

38. Find the sum of n terms of a series in which the first term $= x+\frac{1}{2x}$, and the nth $= nx+\frac{1}{2^n x}$.

39. Find the sum of the first $2n$ terms of the series $2+3+5+6+8+9+.....$

EXAMPLES XXXV-b

1. In an A.P. the ratio of the 3rd term to the 6th is $9:4$ and the sum of the first 5 terms is 60. Find the sum of the first 10 terms.

2. If b is the arithmetic mean between a and c, prove that $b^2(a+c)$ is the arithmetic mean between $a^2(b+c)$ and $c^2(a+b)$. (Lond. Matric.)

3. In an Arithmetic Progression the first term is a and the common difference is $2a$. Show that the sum of $2n$ terms is always equal to four times the sum of n terms. Conversely, show that if the sum of $2n$ terms is equal to four times the sum of n terms, then the first term is equal to half the common difference. (Lond. Matric.)

4. (i) Prove that the sum of any number of terms of the progression 4, 12, 20, 28 .... is a perfect square.

(ii) The sum of the rth and $(r+1)$th terms in this progression is equal to the sum of the first 16 terms. Find r. (Oxf. Sch. Certif.)

5. If $(y+z)^{-1}, (z+x)^{-1}, (x+y)^{-1}$, are in arithmetic progression, prove that x^2, y^2, z^2 are also in A.P. (Oxf. Sch. Certif.)

6. Find the sum of all the numbers between 100 and 1000 which are divisible by 14. (Camb. Sch. Certif.)

7. The sum of four numbers in arithmetical progression is 26. The sum of the squares of the first and last numbers is greater by 16 than the sum of the squares of the second and third, find the numbers.

(Camb. Sch. Certif.)

8. Find the sum of all the whole numbers less than 1000 whose unit digit is 7.

9. Find the sum of all the even numbers from 14 to 84 inclusive, excluding multiples of 3.

10. Find the sum of the first n whole numbers.

Show that this sum, of the sum of the next n whole numbers, and again the sum, the next n, are themselves three numbers in arithmetical progression. (Scot. Certif.)

11. A child wishes to build up a triangular pile of toy bricks so as to have 1 brick in the top row, 2 in the second, 3 in the third, and so on. If he has 100 bricks, how many rows can be complete and how many bricks has he left? (Oxf. and Camb. Sch. Certif.)

12. In a game a basket and 16 potatoes are placed in line at equal intervals of 6 feet. How long will a competitor take to bring the potatoes one by one into the basket, if he starts from the basket and runs at an average speed of 12 feet a second?

13. Timber is piled on a road at intervals of a quarter of a km. It is collected by a lorry which starts from a depot 1 km from the nearest pile, visits the piles in order and returns to the depot each time.

If the speed of the lorry is 15 km per hour, find a formula for the time in minutes occupied by n double journeys. If it takes 25 minutes to load a pile of timber on to the lorry and 15 minutes to unload it, what is the greatest number of piles that can be removed in a day of 8 working hours? (Lond. Matric.)

14. In a geometrical progression show that, if each term be subtracted from the succeeding, the successive differences are also in geometrical progression.

If this second progression is 2, 6, 18, etc. show that the nth term of the first progression is 3^{n-1} and find its sum to n terms. (Scot. Certif.)

15. A Geometrical Progression whose common ratio is r consists of $2n$ terms. Show that the sum of the n even terms is r times the sum of the n odd terms. (Oxf. Sch. Certif.)

16. Show that three numbers cannot be both in Arithmetic Progression and in Geometric Progression unless they are all equal.

The first, second and fourth terms of an A.P. themselves form three successive terms of a G.P. Show that, if the common difference is not zero, it is equal to the first term. (Lond. Matric.)

17. An A.P. and a G.P. are added together; the sum of their first terms is 2, of their second terms 1, and of their third terms $\frac{1}{4}$. If their first terms are equal, find the common difference and the common ratio, and show that three are two values for each. (Camb. Sch. Certif.)

18. The first three of the four numbers, 10, x, y, 4, are in arithmetical progression and the last there are in geometrical progression. Find x and y. (Oxf. Sch. Certif.)

19. Show that the series $\frac{3}{4}, \frac{10}{11}, 1\frac{1}{10}, 1\frac{1}{3}$, etc., is neither an A.P. nor a G.P., and find a formula for its nth term.

20. A man divided some money in G.P. between his four sons so that the eldest received Rs 1000 and the youngest Rs 512. How much money did he divide between them?

21. The population of a village at the end of consecutive decades was 2173, 2281, 2395, 2514. Show that the population was increasing approximately in G.P.

22. A bouncing tennis ball rebounds each time to a height one-half the height of the previous bounce. If it is dropped from height of 10 dm, find (*a*) the total distance it has travelled when it hits the ground for the 10th time, and (*b*) the total distance it travels before coming to rest.

MISCELLANEOUS EXAMPLES V
(*Chiefly on Chapters* XXXII – XXXV)

1. Simplify $\frac{(a^2b^3)^{1/6}\, b^{-2}c^{1/3}}{a^{2/3}b^{-5/4}c^{1/4}}$, and find its value when $a = b, b = 3$, and $c = 432$.

2. Show that the ratio $x + y : x - y$ is increased by subtracting y from each term, except when x lies between y and $2y$.

3. If $\frac{a}{b} = \frac{c}{d}$, show that

(1) $\frac{2a + 3b}{3a - 7b} = \frac{2c + 3d}{3c - 7d}$;

(2) $\frac{a^2 - c^2}{b^2 - d^2} = \frac{(a + 2c)(a + 3c)}{(b + 2d)(b + 3d)}$.

4. If $\frac{x}{b - c} = \frac{y}{c - a} = \frac{z}{a - b}$, prove that

(1) $x + y + z = 0$; (2) $(b + c)\,x + (c + a)\,y + (a + b)z = 0$.

5. If $\frac{x}{1} = \frac{y}{2} = \frac{z}{3}$, prove that $\sqrt{5x^2 + 8y^2 + 7z^2} = 5y$.

6. If y is the sum of two numbers, of which the first varies directly and the second inversely as x, and if $y = 7$, when $x = 2$, and $y = -1$, when $x = 1$, show that $y = 5x - \frac{6}{x}$.

7. Simplify $\sqrt{45} + \sqrt{8} - \sqrt{80} + \sqrt{18} + \sqrt{7 - \sqrt{40}}$.

8. If $3x + 10$ has to $9x + 4$ the duplicate ratio of 5 to 7, find x.

9. If $\frac{a}{b} = \frac{c}{d} = \frac{e}{f}$, prove that each ratio is equal to

(1) $\sqrt[3]{\frac{4ac^2 - 3ce^3 + 2ace}{4bd^2 - 3cf^3 + 2bdf}}$;

(2) $\sqrt[5]{\frac{6a^2c^2e - c^4ef + 7ac^5}{6b^2d^2f - d^4f^2 + 7ad^5}}$.

10. The sides of a triangle are as $1 : 1\frac{1}{2} : 1\frac{3}{4}$, and the perimeter is 221 metres; find the sides.

11. If $3a + 5b : 3a - 5b = 3c + 5d : 3c - 5d$, prove that $a : b = c : d$.

12. Reduce to their simplest forms:

(1) $\frac{x^{a+b}}{x^{a-b}} + \frac{x^{a-b}}{x^{a+b}}$;

(2) $\frac{(a+b)^{3/2}}{(a-b)^{1/2}} \times \sqrt{a^2 - b^2}$.

13. When $x = -\frac{3a}{4}$, find the value of

$$\frac{x^2 + ax + a^2}{x^3 - a^3} - \frac{x^2 - ax + a^2}{x^3 + a^3}.$$

14. Simplify

(1) $\left\{\frac{a^{-1}b^3}{3\sqrt{a}}\right\}^{5/4} \div \sqrt[6]{\frac{a^2\sqrt{b}}{b^2}}$;

(2) $\frac{2^{n+4} - 2 \times 2^n}{2^{n+2} \times 4}$.

15. Find the ratio compounded of the ratios

$$\frac{x - y}{a + b} : \frac{x^3 - y^3}{a^2 - b^2} \text{ and } \frac{x^2 + xy + y^2}{a^2 - b^2} : \frac{x^2 - y^2}{(a + b)^2}.$$

16. If a, b, c be three proportionals, prove that

(1) $a(a + b) : b(b - a) = b(b + c) : c(c - b)$;

(2) $(a + b + c)(b^2 - bc + c^2) = c(a^2 + b^2 + c^2)$.

17. If $a : b : c = xy : x^2 : yz$, prove that $x : y : z = ab : a^2 : bc$.

18. If $p : q$ be the duplicate ratio of $p - r : q - r$, prove that r is a mean proportional between p and q.

19. If $a:b=c:d$, prove that

(1) $a+c:a+b+c+d=a:a+b$;

(2) $(a-b)-(c-d)=\dfrac{(a-b)(b-d)}{b}$.

20. Show that any ratio is made more nearly equal to unity by adding the same quantity to each of its terms.

21. If x varies as $y+z$, and z varies as x; and if $x=2$ when $y=4$, find the value of y when $x=1$.

22. If $2x+3y:2x-3y=2a^2+3b^2:2a^2-3b^2$, then x has to y the duplicate ratio of a to b.

23. Find an A.P. of seven terms whose sum is 28 and common difference 3.

24. The sum of 10 terms of an A.P. is 145, and the sum of its fourth and ninth terms is five times the third terms determine the series.

25. Find the value of $\sqrt{19+4\sqrt{21}}+\sqrt{7}-\sqrt{12}-\sqrt{29-2\sqrt{28}}$.

26. Sum to 10 terms each of the series

(1) $5+10+15+20+\ldots$;

(2) $5-10+20-40+\ldots$.

27. If $\dfrac{p}{bz-cy}=\dfrac{-q}{cx+az}=\dfrac{-r}{ay+bx}$, show that $ap+bq-cr=0$, and $xp-yq+zr=0$.

28. The sum of five numbers in arithmetical progression is 10, and the sum of their squares is 60; find the numbers.

29. Find the sum of n terms of the progression $3+2\dfrac{1}{2}+2\dfrac{1}{12}+\ldots$

30. Find the ninth term of the harmonic series whose first and third terms are 3 and 2 respectively.

31. Simplify $\dfrac{(a-b)^{1/3}.\sqrt[3]{a^2+2ab+b^2}}{\sqrt[3]{a^2-b^2}\times(a+b)^{-2/3}}$.

32. Sum to n terms $\dfrac{3}{2}+\dfrac{9}{2}+\dfrac{15}{2}+\dfrac{21}{2}+\ldots$,

and find five consecutive terms of this progression whose sum is $187\dfrac{1}{2}$.

33. The 8th term of an Arithmetical Progression is double the 13th term; show that the 2nd term is double the 10th term.

34. Sum the following series:

(1) $(a-2x)+2(a+x)+3(a+2x)+\ldots$ to 18 terms.

(2) $3\dfrac{77}{81}-5\dfrac{25}{27}+8\dfrac{8}{9}-\ldots$ to 7 terms.

35. Show that the sum of $2n$ terms of the series

$$1-\frac{1}{3}-\frac{1}{9}+\frac{1}{27}+\frac{1}{81}-\frac{1}{243}-\frac{1}{729}+\frac{1}{2187}+\ldots \text{ is } \frac{3}{5}\{1-(-1)^n3^{-2n}\}.$$

36. If $\frac{1}{b-a}, \frac{1}{2b}, \frac{1}{b-c}$, are in A.P., then a, b, c are in G.P.

37. The last term of an A.P. is ten times the first, and the last but one is equal to the sum of the 4th and 5th. Find the number of the terms, and show that the common difference is equal to the first term.

38. Sum to $2n$ terms each of the series

(1) $1-3+9-27+\ldots$;

(2) $1-3+5-7+\ldots\ldots$,

and write down the last term of each series.

39. Find two numbers whose arithmetic mean exceeds their geometric mean by 2, and whose harmonic mean is one-fifth of the larger number.

40. Find an infinite geometrical progression, whose first term is 1, and in which each term is twice the sum of all the terms that follow it.

41. The arithmetic mean between two numbers is to the geometric mean as 5 to 4, and the difference of their geometric and harmonic means is $\frac{4}{5}$; find the numbers.

42. If x, y, z be in G.P., prove that $x^2y^2z^2(x^{-3}+y^{-3}+z^{-3}) = x^3+y^3+z^3$.

36

THEORY OF QUADRATIC EQUATIONS

335. IN Chapter XXV it was shown that after suitable reduction every quadratic equation may be written in the form

$$ax^2 + bx + c = 0 \qquad \ldots(1),$$

and that the solution of the equation is

$$x = \frac{-b \pm \sqrt{b^2 - 4ac}}{2a} \qquad \ldots(2).$$

We shall now prove some important propositions connected with the roots and coefficients of all equations of which (1) is the type.

336. *A quadratic equation cannot have more than two roots.*

For, if possible, let the equation $ax^2 + bx + c = 0$ have three *different* roots α, β, γ. Then since each of these values must satisfy the equation, we have

$$a\alpha^2 + b\alpha + c = 0 \qquad \ldots(1),$$

$$a\beta^2 + b\beta + c = 0 \qquad \ldots(2),$$

$$a\gamma^2 + b\gamma + c = 0 \qquad \ldots(3).$$

From (1) and (2), by subtraction.

$$a(\alpha^2 - \beta^2) + b(\alpha - \beta) = 0;$$

divide out by $\alpha - \beta$ which, by hypothesis, is not zero; then

$$a(\alpha + \beta) + b = 0.$$

Similarly from (2) and (3)

$$a(\beta + \gamma) + b = 0;$$

$\therefore$ by subtraction $\qquad a(\alpha - \gamma) = 0;$

which is impossible, since, by hypothesis, a is not zero, and α is not equal to γ. Hence there cannot be three different roots.

337. The terms 'unreal', 'imaginary', and 'impossible' are all used in the same sense: namely, to denote expressions which involve the square root of a negative quantity, it is important that the student should clearly distinguish between the terms *real* and *rational*, *imaginary* and *irrational*. Thus $2\sqrt{5}$ or $5, 3\frac{1}{2}, -\frac{5}{6}$ are rational and real; $\sqrt{7}$ is irrational but real; while $\sqrt{-7}$ is irrational and also imaginary.

338. In Art. 335 if the two roots in (2) are denoted by α and β, we have

$$\alpha = \frac{-b+\sqrt{b^2-4ac}}{2a}, \beta = \frac{-b-\sqrt{b^2-4ac}}{2a}.$$

(1) If $b^2 - 4ac$, the quantity under the radical, is positive, α and β are real and unequal.

(2) If $b^2 - 4ac$ is zero, α and β are real and equal, each reducing in this case to $-\dfrac{b}{2a}$.

(3) If $b^2 - 4ac$ is negative, α and β are imaginary and unequal.

(4) If $b^2 - 4ac$ is a perfect square, α and β are rational and unequal.

By applying these tests the nature of the roots of any quadratic may be determined without solving the equation.

Example 1. Show that the equation $2x^2 - 6x + 7 = 0$ cannot be satisfied by any real values of x.

Here $\quad a = 2, b = -6, c = 7$; so that

$$b^2 - 4ac = (-6)^2 - 4\cdot 2\cdot 7 = -20.$$

Therefore the roots are imaginary.

NOTE. If the equation is solved graphically as in Art. 427, it will be found that the graph does not cut the axis of x. Thus there are no real values of x which make $2x^2 - 6x + 7$ equal to zero.

Example 2. For what value of k will the equation $3x^2 - 6x + k = 0$ have equal roots?

The condition for equal roots gives $(-6)^2 - 4\cdot 3\cdot k = 0$,

whence $\quad k = 3$.

Example 3. Show that the roots of the equation

$$x^2 - 2px + p^2 - q^2 + 2qr - r^2 = 0 \text{ are rational.}$$

The roots will be rational provided $(-2p)^2 - 4(p^2 - q^2 + 2qr - r^2)$ is a perfect square. But this expression reduces to $4(q^2 - 2qr + r^2)$, or $4(q-r)^2$. Hence the roots are rational.

339. Since $\alpha = \dfrac{-b+\sqrt{b^2-4ac}}{2a}, \beta = \dfrac{-b-\sqrt{b^2-4ac}}{2a}$,

we have by addition $\alpha + \beta = \dfrac{-b+\sqrt{b^2-4ac} - b - \sqrt{b^2-4ac}}{2a}$

$$= -\frac{2b}{2a} + -\frac{b}{a} \qquad \ldots(1);$$

and by multiplication we have

$$\alpha\beta = \frac{(-b+\sqrt{b^2-4ac})(-b-\sqrt{b^2-4ac})}{4a^2}$$

$$= \frac{(-b)^2-(b^2-4ac)}{4a^2}$$

$$= \frac{4ac}{4a^2} = \frac{c}{a} \qquad \ldots(2)$$

By writing the equation in the form

$$x^2 + \frac{b}{a}x + \frac{c}{a} = 0,$$

these results may also be expressed as follows:

In a quadratic equation *where the coefficient of the first term is unity.*

(i) the sum of the roots is equal to the coefficient of x with its sign changed;

(ii) the product of the roots is equal to the third term.

NOTE. In any equation the term which does not contain the unknown quantity is frequently called *the absolute term*.

340. Since $-\frac{b}{a} = \alpha + \beta$, and $\frac{c}{a} = \alpha\beta$,

the equation $x^2 + \frac{b}{a}x + \frac{c}{a}$ may be written

$$x^2 - (\alpha+\beta)x + \alpha\beta = 0 \qquad \ldots(1).$$

Hence any quadratic may also be expressed in the form

$$x^2 - (\text{sum of roots})\,x + \text{product of roots} = 0 \qquad \ldots.(2).$$

Again, from (1) we have

$$(x-\alpha)(x-\beta) = 0 \qquad \ldots(3).$$

We may now easily form an equation with given roots.

Example 1. Form the equation whose roots are 3 and -2.

The equation is $(x-3)(x+2) = 0,$

or $x^2 - x - 6 = 0.$

Example 2. Form the equation whose roots are $\frac{3}{7}$ and $-\frac{4}{5}$.

The equation is $\left(x - \frac{3}{7}\right)\left(x + \frac{4}{5}\right) = 0;$

that is, $(7x-3)(5x+4) = 0,$

or $35x^2 + 13x - 12 = 0.$

When the roots are irrational it is easier to use the following method:

Example 3. Form the equation whose roots are $2+\sqrt{3}$ and $2-\sqrt{3}$.

We have sum of root s $= 4$,

product of roots $= 1$;

$\therefore$ the equation is $x^2 - 4x + 1 = 0$,

by using formula (2) of the present article.

341. The results of Art. 339 are most important, and they are generally sufficient to solve problems connected with the roots of quadratics. In such questions *the roots should never be considered singly*, but use should be made of the relations obtained by writing down the sum of the roots, and their product, in terms of the coefficient of the equation.

Example 1. If α and β are the roots of $x^2 - px + q = 0$, find the value of (1) $\alpha^2+\beta^2$, (2) $\alpha^3+\beta^3$.

We have $\alpha+\beta = p$, $\alpha\beta = q$.

$$\therefore \quad \alpha^2+\beta^2 = (\alpha+\beta)^2 - 2\alpha\beta$$

$$= p^2 - 2q.$$

Again,

$$\alpha^3+\beta^3 = (\alpha+\beta)(\alpha^2+\beta^2-\alpha\beta)$$

$$= p\{(\alpha+\beta)^2 - 3\alpha\beta\} = p(p^2-3q).$$

Example 2. If α, β are the roots of the equation $lx^2+mx+n=0$, find the equation whose roots are $\frac{\alpha}{\beta}, \frac{\beta}{\alpha}$.

We have sum of roots $= \frac{\alpha}{\beta}+\frac{\beta}{\alpha} = \frac{\alpha^2+\beta^2}{\alpha\beta}$,

product of roots $= \frac{\alpha}{\beta}\cdot\frac{\beta}{\alpha} = 1$;

$\therefore$ by Art. 340 the required equation is

$$x^2 - \left(\frac{\alpha^2+\beta^2}{\alpha\beta}\right)x + 1 = 0,$$

or

$$\alpha\beta x^2 - (\alpha^2+\beta^2)x + \alpha\beta = 0.$$

As in the last example $\alpha^2+\beta^2 = \frac{m^2-2nl}{l^2}$, and $\alpha\beta = \frac{n}{l}$.

$\therefore$ the equation is

$$\frac{n}{l}x^2 - \frac{m^2-2nl}{l^2}x + \frac{n}{l} = 0,$$

or

$$nlx^2 - (m^2-2nl)x + nl = 0.$$

Example 3. Find the condition that the roots of the equation $ax^2 + bx + c = 0$ should be (1) equal in magnitude and opposite in sign, (2) reciprocals.

The roots will be equal in magnitude and opposite in sign if their sum is zero; therefore $-\frac{b}{a} = 0$, or $b = 0$.

Again, the roots will be reciprocals when their product is unity; therefore $\frac{c}{a} = 1$, or $c = a$.

Example 4. Find the relation which must subsist between the coefficients of the equation $px^2 + qx + r = 0$, when one root is three times the other.

We have $$\alpha + \beta = -\frac{q}{p}, \quad \alpha\beta = \frac{r}{p};$$

but since $\alpha = 3\beta$, we obtain by substitution

$$4\beta = -\frac{q}{p}, \quad 3\beta^2 = \frac{r}{p}.$$

From the first of these equations $\beta^2 = \frac{q^2}{16p^2}$, and from the second

$$\beta^2 = \frac{r}{3p}.$$

$$\therefore \qquad \frac{q^2}{16p^2} = \frac{r}{3p},$$

or $$3q^2 = 16pr,$$

which is the required condition.

342. The following example illustrates a useful application of the results proved in Art. 338.

Example. If x is a real quantity, prove that the expression $\frac{x^2 + 2x - 11}{2(x-3)}$ can have all numerical values except such as lie between 2 and 6.

Let the given expression be represented by y, so that

$$\frac{x^2 + 2x - 11}{2(x-3)} = y;$$

then multiplying up and transposing, we have

$$x^2 + 2x(1 - y) + 6y - 11 = 0.$$

This is a quadratic equation, and if x is to have real values $4(1-y)^2 - 4(6y-11)$ must be positive; or simplifying and dividing by 4, $y^2 - 8y + 12$ must be positive; that is, $(y-6)(y-2)$ must be positive. Hence the factors of this product must be both positive, or both negative. In the former case y is greater than 6; in the latter y is less than 2. Therefore y cannot lie between 2 and 6, but may have any other value.

In this example it will be noticed that the *expression* $y^2 - 8y + 12$ is positive so long as y does not lie between the roots of the corresponding quadratic *equation* $y^2 - 8y + 12 = 0$. This is a particular case of the general proposition investigated in the next article.

343. *For all real values of* x *the expression* $ax^2 + bx + c$ *has the same sign as,* a *except when the roots of the equation* $ax^2 + bx + c = 0$ *are real and unequal, and* x *lies between them.*

CASE I. Suppose that the roots of the equation $ax^2 + bx + c = 0$ are real; denote them by α and β, and let α be the greater.

Then $ax^2 + bx + c = a\left(x^2 + \frac{b}{a}x + \frac{c}{a}\right)$

$$= a\{x^2 - (\alpha + \beta)x + \alpha\beta\} \qquad \text{[Art. 339.]}$$

$$= a(x-\alpha)(x-\beta).$$

Now if x is greater than α or less than β, the factors $x - \alpha$, $x - \beta$ are either both positive or both negative; therefore the expression $(x-\alpha)(x-\beta)$ is positive, and $ax^2 + bx + c$ has the same sign as a. But if x lies between α and β, the expression

$$(x-\alpha)(x-\beta)$$

is negative, and the sign of $ax^2 + bx + c$ is opposite to that of a.

CASE II. If α and β are equal, then

$$ax^2 + bx + c = a(x-\alpha)^2,$$

and $(x-\alpha)^2$ is positive for all real values of x; hence $ax^2 + bx + c$ has the same size as a.

CASE III. Suppose that the equation $ax^2 + bx + c = 0$ has imaginary roots; then

$$ax^2 + bx + c = a\left\{x^2 + \frac{b}{a}x + \frac{c}{a}\right\}$$

$$= a\left\{\left(x + \frac{b}{2a}\right)^2 + \frac{4ac - b^2}{4a^2}\right\};$$

but since $b^2 - 4ac$ is negative [Art. 338], the expression

$$\left(x + \frac{b}{2a}\right)^2 + \frac{4ac - b^2}{4a^2}$$

is positive for all real values of x; therefore $ax^2 + bx + c$ has the same sign as a. [*Arts.* 426, 427 *and* 439, Ex. 2, *may be read here.*]

EXAMPLES XXXVI

Find (without actual solution) the nature of the roots of the following equations:

1. $x^2 + x - 870 = 0$.

2. $8 + 6x = 5x^2$.

3. $\frac{1}{2}x^2 = 14 - 3x^2$.

4. $x^2 + 7 = 4x$.

5. $2x = x^2 + 5$.

6. $(x + 2)^2 = 4x + 15$.

From the equations whose roots are

7. $5, -3$.

8. $-9, -11$.

9. $a + b, a - b$.

10. $\frac{3}{2}, \frac{5}{6}$.

11. $\frac{2}{3}a, -\frac{4}{5}a$.

12. $0, \frac{7}{8}$.

13. If the equation $x^2 + 2(1 + k)x + k^2 = 0$ has equal roots, what is the value of k?

14. (i) One root of $6x^2 - 13x + a = 0$ is $1\frac{1}{2}$. Find a.

(ii) One root of $6x^2 + ax - 5 = 0$ is $1\frac{2}{3}$. Find a.

(iii) One root of $ax^2 + x - 3 = 0$ is $-1\frac{1}{2}$. Find a.

15. Show that $x = 1 - \frac{b}{a}$ satisfies the equation

$a(a + b)x^2 - b(a - b)x = (a - b)^2$, and find the other value of x.

(Oxf. Sch. Certif.)

16. Prove that the equation $3mx^2 - (2m + 3n)x + 2n = 0$ has rational roots.

17. Without solving the equation $3x^2 - 4x - 1 = 0$, find the sum, the difference, and the sum of the squares of the roots.

18. Show that the roots of $a(x^2 - 1) = (b - c)x$ are always real.

19. Find the greatest value of k for which $2x^2 - 5x + k = 0$ has real roots.

20. Find for what range of values of k the equation $5x^2 + kx + 5 = 0$ has real roots?

21. For what range of values of k will $kx^2 + 7x - 3 = 0$ have imaginary roots?

22. Find the factors of $12 + x - x^2$, and state between what limits x must lie, if the expression is positive. (Lond. Matric.)

23. Prove that the roots of the quadratic equation $x^2 - 4x + 3 + a(3x - 1) = 0$ are real for all values of a except those lying between $\frac{2}{9}$ and 2. (Oxf. Sch. Certif.)

Form the equations whose roots are

24. $3 + \sqrt{5}, 3 - \sqrt{5}$.

25. $-2 + \sqrt{3}, -2 - \sqrt{3}$.

26. $-\frac{a}{5}, \frac{b}{6}$.

27. $\frac{1}{2}(4 \pm \sqrt{7})$.

28. $\frac{a+b}{a-b}, \frac{a-b}{a+b}$.

29. $\frac{a}{2b}, \frac{b}{2a}$.

If α, β are the roots of the equation $px^2 + qx + r = 0$, find the values of

30. $\alpha^2 + \beta^2$.

31. $(\alpha - \beta)^2$.

32. $\alpha^2\beta + \alpha\beta^2$.

33. $\alpha^4 + \beta^4$.

34. $\alpha^5\beta^2 + \alpha^2\beta^5$.

35. $\frac{\alpha^2}{\beta} + \frac{\beta^2}{\alpha}$.

36. $\frac{1}{\alpha^3} + \frac{1}{\beta^3}$.

37. $\alpha^5 + \beta^5$.

38. $\left(\alpha + \frac{2}{\beta}\right)\left(\beta + \frac{2}{\alpha}\right)$.

39. If α, β are the roots of $x^2 + ax + b = 0$ and α^2, β^2 are the roots of $x^2 + Ax + B = 0$, prove that $A = 2b - a^2, B = b^2$.

40. If α, β are the roots of $x^2 - px + q = 0$, and α^3, β^3 the roots of $x^2 - Px + Q = 0$, find P and Q in terms of p and q.

41. If α, β are the roots of $x^2 - ax + b = 0$, find the equation whose roots are

(i) $\alpha + 1, \beta + 1$,
(ii) $\alpha - 2, \beta - 2$,
(iii) $3\alpha, 3\beta$,
(iv) $\frac{\alpha}{4}, \frac{\beta}{4}$,
(v) $\sqrt{\alpha}, \sqrt{\beta}$,
(vi) α^2, β^2,
(vii) $\frac{\alpha}{\beta^2}, \frac{\beta}{\alpha^2}$,
(viii) $\alpha + 2\beta, \beta + 2\alpha$,
(ix) $\alpha^2 + \beta, \beta^2 + \alpha$,
(x) $\frac{\alpha}{2} - 2\beta, \frac{\beta}{2} - 2\alpha$.

42. The roots of the equation $5x^2 - 20x + 12 = 0$ are α and β. Factorise the expression $\alpha^3 + \beta^3$, and hence find its numerical value without solving the equation. (Cent. Welsh Bd.)

43. The roots of $x^2 + px + q = 0$ are double the roots of $x^2 - (b + c)\,x + bc = 0$.

Express p and q in terms of b and c. (Cent. Welsh Bd.)

44. Find the value of p, and the roots of the equation $2x^2 - 33x + p = 0$, given that one root is ten times the other. (Cent. Welsh Bd.)

45. If α, β are the roots of $ax^2 + bx - a = 0$, prove that $(a\alpha + b)(a\beta + b) = -a^2$,

and find the equation whose roots are $a\alpha + b, a\beta + b$.

46. If $x^2 + px + q = 0$ and $x^2 + mx + n = 0$ have a root in common, show that this root is the square root of $(pn - qm)/(m - p)$.

(Oxf. Sch. Certif.)

47. If a, p are the roots of $x^2 - 100x + 2491 = 0$, and a, q are the roots of $x^2 + 50x - 4559 = 0$, find *without solving* these equations the values of $p - q$ and $\frac{p}{q}$. (Joint Matric. Bd.)

48. Show that, if the sum of two quantities is a and their product is b, they must be the roots of the equation $x^2 - ax + b = 0$.

Hence, or otherwise, find the lengths of the sides of a rectangle whose perimeter is 52 inches and whose area is 168 square inches.

(Lond. Matric.)

49. If α, β are the roots of $x^2 + px + q = 0$, find the condition that

(i) $\alpha = \beta$, (ii) $\alpha = \frac{1}{\beta}$,

(iii) $\alpha = 2\beta$, (iv) $\alpha - \beta = 2$,

(v) $\alpha + \beta = 7$, (vi) $\frac{1}{\alpha} + \frac{1}{\beta} = 2$.

50. If α, β are the roots of $x^2 + px + q = 0$, find the value of $\alpha^2 + \beta^2$ without solving the equation, and form the equation whose roots are α^2 and β^2, expressing the coefficients in terms of p and q.

Hence, or otherwise, show that each root of the equation $x^2 + x + 1 = 0$ is the square of the other root. (Oxf. Sch. Certif.)

51. Form an equation whose roots shall be the cubes of the roots of the equation $2x\,(x - a) = a^2$.

52. Prove that the roots of the equation $(a + b)\,x^2 - (a + b + c)\,x + \frac{c}{2} = 0$ are always real.

53. Show that $(a+b+c)\,x^2-2\,(a+b)\,x+(a+b-c)=0$ has rational roots.

54. Form an equation whose roots shall be the arithmetic and harmonic means between the roots of $x^2-px+q=0$.

55. In the equation $px^2+qx+r=0$ the roots are in the ratio of l to m, prove that $(l^2+m^2)\,pr+lm\,(2pr-q^2)=0$.

56. Prove for the equation $ax^2+bx+c=0$, which has real roots, that if a, b, c have the same sign, both roots are negative; that if a and c have different signs, one root is positive and one negative; and that if a and c differ in sign from b, both roots are positive.

57. Solve the equation $ax^2+bx+c=0$ by substituting $x=y-\dfrac{b}{2a}$.

58. Solve $\dfrac{2x^2-6x+9}{(x-2)^2}=y$ as a quadratic in x. From your result find the smallest possible value of y if x is real. (Oxf. Sch. Certif.)

59. Show that, if x is real, the value of the expression $\dfrac{x^2-3x+2}{2x}$ cannot lie between $\sqrt{2}-\dfrac{3}{2}$ and $-\sqrt{2}-\dfrac{3}{2}$. (Cent. Welsh Bd.)

60. Find the maximum and minimum values of $\dfrac{10x}{(x-1)\,(x-4)}$.

(Camb. Sch. Certif.)

61. Show that if x is real the expression $\dfrac{x^2-15}{2x-8}$ cannot lie between 3 and 5.

62. If x is real, prove that $\dfrac{3x^2+2}{x^2-2x-1}$ can have all values except such as lie between 2 and $-\dfrac{3}{2}$.

37

PERMUTATIONS AND COMBINATIONS

EACH of the *arrangements* which-can be made by taking some or all of a number of things is called a permutation.

Each of the *groups or selections* which can be made by taking some or all of a number of things is called a combination.

Thus the *permutations* which can be made by taking the letters a, b, c, d two at a time are twelve in number; namely,

ab, ac, ad, bc, bd. cd,

ba, ca, da, cb, db, dc,

each of these presenting a different *arrangement* of two letters.

The *combinations* which can be made by taking the letters a, b, c, d two at a time are six in number: namely,

ab, ac, ad, bc, bd, cd;

each of these presenting a different *selection of two letters.*

From this it appears that in forming *combinations* we are only concerned with the number of things each selection contains; whereas in forming *permutations* we have also to consider the order of the things which make up each arrangement; for instance, if from four letters *a, b, c, d* we make a selection of three, such as *abc*, this single combination admits of being arranged in the following ways:

bc, acb, bca, bac, cab, cba

and so gives rise to six different permutations.

345. Before discussing the general propositions of this chapter the following important principle should be carefully noticed.

If one operation can be performed in m ways, and (where it has been performed in any one of these ways) a second operation can then be performed in n ways; the number of ways of performing the two operations will be m × m.

If the first operation be performed in *any one way*, we can associate with only this any of the n ways of performing the second operation; and thus we shall have n ways of performing the two operations without considering more than *one* way of performing the first; and so, corresponding to each of the m ways of performing the first operation, we shall have n ways of performing the two; hence altogether the number of ways in which the two operations can be performed is represented by the product $m \times n$.

Example. There are 10 steamers plying between Liverpool and Dublin; in how many ways can a man go from Liverpool to Dublin and return by a different steamer?

There are *ten* ways of making the first passage; and with each of these there is a choice of *nine* ways of returning (since the man is not to come back by the same steamer); hence the number of ways of making the two journeys is 10×9, or 90.

This principle might easily be extended to the case in which there are more than two operations each of which can be performed in a give a number of ways.

346. *To find the number of permutations of* n *dissimilar things taken* r *at a time.*

This is the same thing as finding the number of ways in which we can fill up r places when we have n different things at our disposal.

The first place may be filled up in n ways, for any one of the n things may be taken; when it has been filled up in any one of these ways, the second place can then be filled up in $n-1$ ways; and since each way of filling up the first place can be associated with each way of filling up the second, the number of ways in which the first two places can be filled up is given by the product $n(n-1)$. And when the first two places have been filled up in any way, the third place can be filled up in $n-2$ ways. And reasoning as before, the number of ways in which three places can be filled up is $n(n-1)(n-2)$.

Proceeding thus, and noticing that a new factor is introduced with each new place filled up, and that at any stage the number of factors is the same as the number of places filled up, we shall have the number of ways in which r places can be filled up equal to

$n(n-1)(n-2)\ldots$ to r factors;

and the rth factor is $n-(r-1)$, or $n-r+1$.

Therefore the number of permutations of n things taken r at a time is

$n(n-1)(n-2)\ldots(n-r+1)$.

COR. The number of permutations of n things taken all at a time is

$n(n-1)(n-2)\ldots$ to n factors,

or $n(n-1)(n-2)\ldots 3 \cdot 2 \cdot 1$.

It is usual to denote this product by the symbol $\underline{n|}$, which is read "factorial n" Also the symbol $n!$ is sometimes used for n.

347. We shall in future denote the number of permutations of n things taken r at a time by the symbol ^nP_r, so that

$$^nP_r = n(n-1)(n-2)\ldots(n-r+1);$$

also $$^nP_n = \underline{n|}$$

In working numerical examples it is useful to notice that the suffix in the symbol ^nP_r always denotes the number of factors in the formula we are using.

Example 1. Four persons enter a railway carriage in which there are six seats; in how many ways can they take their places?

The first person may seat himself in 6 ways; and then the second person in 5; the third in 4; and the fourth in 3; and since each of these ways may be associated with each of the others, the required answer is $6 \times 5 \times 4 \times 3$, or 360.

Example 2. How many different numbers can be formed by using six out of the nine digits 1, 2, 3, ... 9?

Here we have 9 different things and we have to find the number of permutations of them taken 6 at a time;

$$\therefore \text{the required result} = {}^9P_6$$

$$= 9 \times 8 \times 7 \times 6 \times 5 \times 4$$

$$= 00480.$$

348. *To find the number of combinations of* n *dissimilar things taken* r *at a time.*

Let ^nC_r denote the required number of combinations.

Then each of these combinations consists of a group of r dissimilar things which can be arranged among themselves in $\underline{|r}$ ways, [Art. 346. Cor.]

Hence $^nC_r \times \underline{|r}$ is equal to the number of *arrangements* of n things taken r at a time; that is,

$$^nC_r \times \underline{|r} = {}^nP_r = n(n-1)(n-2)\ldots(n-r+1);$$

$$^nC_r = \frac{n(n-1)(n-2)\ldots(n-r+1)}{\underline{|r}}.$$

COR. This formula for ^nC_r may also be written in a different form; for if we multiply the numerator and the denominator by $\underline{|n-r}$ we obtain

$$\frac{n(n-1)(n-2)\ldots(n-r+1) \times \underline{|n-r}}{\underline{|r}\,\underline{|n-r}},$$

or

$$\frac{\underline{|n}}{\underline{|r}\,\underline{|n-r}};$$

since $n(n-1)(n-2)\ldots(n-r+1) \times \underline{|r}\; n-r = \underline{|n}$

Example. From 12 books in how many ways can a selection of 5 be made, (1) when one specified book is always included, (2) when one specified book is always excluded?

(1) Since the specified book is to be included in every selection, we have only to choose 4 out of the remaining 11.

Hence, the number of ways $= {}^{11}C_4 \dfrac{11 \times 10 \times 9 \times 8}{1 \times 2 \times 3 \times 4} = 330.$

(2) Since the specified book is always to be excluded, we have to select the 5 books out of the remaining 11 .
Hence, the number of ways

$$= {}^{11}C_5 = \frac{11 \times 10 \times 9 \times 8 \times 7}{1 \times 2 \times 3 \times 4 \times 5} = 462 .$$

349. *The number of combinations of* n *things* r *at* a *time is equal to the number of combinations of things* n – r *at* a *time.*

In making all the possible combinations of n things, to each group of r things we select, there is left a corresponding group of $n-r$ things; that is, the number of combinations of n things r at a time is the same as the number of combinations of n things $n-r$ at a time;

$$\therefore \qquad {}^nC_r = {}^nC_{n-r}.$$

This result is frequently useful in enabling us to abridge arithmetical work.

Example. Out of 14 men in how many ways can an eleven be chosen?
The required number = ${}^{14}C_{11}$

$${}^{14}C_3 = \frac{14 \times 13 \times 12}{1 \times 2 \times 3} = 364.$$

If we had made use of the formula ${}^{14}C_{11}$, we should have had to reduce an expression whose numerator and denominator each contained 11 factors.

350. In the examples which follow it is important to notice that the formula for *permutations* should not be used until the suitable *selections* required by the question have been made.

Example 1. From 7 Englishmen and 4 Americans a committee of 6 is to be formed: in how many ways can this be done, (1) when the committee contains exactly 2 Americans, (2) at least 2 Americans?

(1) The number of ways in which the Americans can be chosen is ${}^4C_2$; and the number of ways in which the Englishmen can be chosen is ${}^7C_4$. Each of the first groups can be associated with each of the second; hence.
the required number of ways $= {}^4C_2 \times {}^7C_4$

$$= \frac{\lfloor 4}{\lfloor 2 \lfloor 2} \times \frac{\lfloor 7}{\lfloor 4 \lfloor 3} = \frac{\lfloor 7}{\lfloor 2 \lfloor 2 \lfloor 3} = 210$$

2. We shall exhaust all the suitable combinations by forming all the groups containing 2 Americans and 4 Englishmen; then 3 Americans and 3 Englishmen; and lastly 4 Americans and 2 Englishmen.

The *sum* of the three resulιs will give the answer. Hence the required number of ways

$$^4C_2 \times {}^7C_4 + {}^4C_3 + {}^7C_3 + {}^4C_4 \times {}^7C_3$$

$$= \frac{\lfloor 4}{\lfloor 2 \lfloor 2} \times \frac{\lfloor 7}{\lfloor 4 \lfloor 3} + \frac{\lfloor 4}{\lfloor 3} \times \frac{\lfloor 7}{\lfloor 3 \lfloor 4} + 1 \times \frac{\lfloor 7}{\lfloor 2 \lfloor 5}$$

$$= 210 + 140 + 21 = 3/1.$$

In this example we have only to make use of the suitable formulae for *combinations*, for we are not concerned with the possible arrangements of the members of the committee among themselves.

Example 2. Out of 7 consonants and 4 vowels, how many words can be made each containing 3 consoonants and 2 vowels?

The number of ways of chosing the 2 three consonants is $^7C_3$, and the number of ways of choosing the 2 vowels is $^4C_2$ and since each of the first groups can be associated with each of the second, the number of combined groups, each containing 3 consonants and 2 vowels, is $^7C_3 \times {}^4C_2$.

Further, each of these groups contains 5 letters, which may be arranged among themselves in $\lfloor 5$ ways. Hence

the required number of words

$$= \frac{\lfloor 7}{\lfloor 3 \lfloor 4} \times \frac{\lfloor 4}{\lfloor 2 \lfloor 2} \times \lfloor 5$$

$$= 5 \times 7! = 25200.$$

EXAMPLES XXXVII-a

1. Find the value of $^5P_4$, $^7P_6$, $^8C_5$, $^{25}C_{23}$.
2. How many different arrangements can be made by taking
   (1) five,
   (2) all of the letters of the word *soldiers*?
3. If $^nC_{23}$ $^{n-1}C_4 = 8:5$, find n.
4. How many different selections of four coins can be made from a bag containing a Re 1 coin, and one each of 50 -; 25-; 10-;5-;2- and 1-paise coins?
5. How many numbers between 3000 and 4000 can be made with the digits 9. 3, 4, 6?
6. In how many ways can the letters of the word *volume* be arranged if the vowels can only occupy the even places?
7. If the number of permutations of n things four at a time is fourteen times the number of permutations of $n-2$ things three at a time, find n.

8. From 5 masters and 10 boys how many committees can be selected containing 3 masters and 6 boys?
9. If ${}^{20}C_r = {}^{20}C_{r-10}$ and ${}^{r}C_{12} = {}^{18}C_r$.
10. Out of the twenty-six letters of the alphabet in how many ways can a word be made consisting of five different letters, two of which must be a and c?
11. How many words can be formed by taking 3 consonants and 2 vowels from an alphabet containing 21 consonants and 5 vowels?
12. A railway carriage will accommodate 5 passengers on each side: in how many ways can 10 persons take their seats when two of them decline to face the engine, and a third cannot travel backwards?

351. Hitherto, in the formulae we have proved, the things have been regarded as *unlike*. Before considering cases in which some one or more sets of things may be *like*, if is necessary to point out exactly in what sense the words *like* and *unlike* are used. When we speak of things beings *dissimilar*, '*different*, *unlike*, we imply that the things are *visibly unlike*, so as to be easily distinguishable from each other. On the other hand we shall always use the term *like* things to denote such as are alike to the eye and cannot be distinguished from each other. For instance, in Ex. 2, Art. 350, the consonants and the vowels may be said each to consist of a group of things united by a common characteristic, and thus in a certain sense to be of the same kind; but they cannot be regarded as like things, because there is an individuality existing among the things of each group which makes them easily distinguishable from each other. Hence, in the final stage of the example we considered each group to consist of five *dissimilar* things and therefore capable of 5 arrangements among themselves. [Art. 346, Cor.]

352. *To find the number of ways in which* n *things are may be arranged among themselves, them all at a time, when* p *of* q *of; them exactly alike of one kind,* q *of them exactly alike of another kind,* r *of them exactly alike of a third kind, and the rest all different.*

Let there be n, letters; suppose p them to be a, q of them to be b, r of them to be c, and the rest to be unlike.

Let x be the required number of permutations; then if p letters a were replaced by p unlike letters different from any of the rest, from *any one* of the x permutation, without altering the position of any of the remaining letters, we could form $\underline{|p}$ new permutations. Hence *if* this change were made in each of the x permutations, we should obtain $x \times \underline{|p}$ permutations.

Similarly, if the q letters b were replaced by q unlike letters, the number of permutations would be $x \times \underline{|p} \times \underline{|q}$.

In like manner, by replacing the r letters c by r unlike letters, we should finally obtain $x \times \underline{|p} \times \underline{|q} \times \underline{|r}$ permutations.

But the things are now all different, and therefore admit of $\underline{|n}$ permutations among themselves. Hence

$$x \times \underline{|p} \times \underline{|q} \times \underline{|r} = \underline{|n};$$

That is,
$$x = \frac{\underline{|n}}{\underline{|p}\,\underline{|q}\,\underline{|r}}$$

which is the required number of permutations.

Any case in which the things are not all different may be treated similarly.

Example 1. How many different permutations can be made out of the letters of the word *assassination* taken all together?

We have here 13 letters of which 4 are s, 3 are a, 2 are i and 2 are n. Hence the number of permutations

$$= \frac{\underline{|13}}{\underline{|4}\,\underline{|3}\,\underline{|2}\,\underline{|2}}$$

$$= 13 \cdot 11 \cdot 10 \cdot 9 \cdot 8 \cdot 7 \cdot 3 \cdot 5$$

$$= 1001 \times 10800 = 10810800.$$

Example 2. How many numbers can be formed with the digits 1, 2, 3, 4, 3, 2, 1, so that the odd digits always occupy the odd places?

The odd digits 1, 3, 3, 1 can be arranged in their four places in

$$\frac{\underline{|4}}{\underline{|2}\,\underline{|2}} \text{ ways} \qquad \text{...(1).}$$

The even digits 2, 4, 2 can be arranged in their three places in

$$\frac{\underline{|3}}{\underline{|2}} \text{ ways} \qquad \text{... (2).}$$

Each of the ways in (1) can be associated with each of the ways n (2).

Hence, the required number $= \dfrac{\underline{|4}}{\underline{|2} \times \underline{|2}} \times \dfrac{\underline{|3}}{\underline{|2}} = 6 \times 3 = 18.$

353. *To find the number of permutations of* n *things* r *at a time, when each thing may be repeated once, twice, ...up to* r *times in any arrangement,*

Hence, we have to consider the number of ways in which r places can be filled up when we have n different things at our disposal, each of the n things being used as often as we please in any arrangement.

The first place may be filled up in n ways, and, when it has been filled up in any one way, the second place may also be filled up in n ways, since we are not precluded from using the same thing again. Therefore the number of ways in which the first two places can be filled up is $n \times n$ or n^2.

The third place can also be filled up in n ways, and therefore the first three places in n^3 ways.

Proceeding in this manner, and noticing that at any stage the index of n is always the same as the number of places filled up, we shall have the number of ways in which the r places can be filled up equal to n^r.

Example. In how many ways can 5 prizes be given away to 4 boys, when each boy is eligible for all the prizes?

Any one of the prizes can be given in 4 ways, and then any one of the remaining prizes can also be given in 4 ways, since it may be obtained by the boy who has already received a prize. Thus two prizes can be given away in 4^2 ways, three prizes in 4^3 ways, and so on. Hence, the 5 prizes can be given away in 4^5, or 1024 ways.

354. *To find for what value of* r *the number of combinations of* n *things* r *at a time is greatest.*

Since $${}^nC_r = \frac{n(n-1)(n-2)\ldots(n-r+2)(n-r+1)}{1\cdot 2\cdot 3\ldots(r-1)r}$$

and $${}^nC_r = \frac{n(n-1)(n-2)\ldots(n-r+2)}{1\cdot 2\cdot 3\ldots(r-1),}$$

$$\therefore \quad {}^nC_r = {}^nC_{r-1} \times \frac{n-r+1}{r}.$$

The multiplying factor $= \frac{n-r+1}{r}$ may be written $= \frac{n+1}{r} - 1$, which shows that it decreases as r increases. Hence as r receives the values 1, 2, 3,.... in succession, ${}^nC_r$, is continually increased, until $\frac{n+1}{r} - 1$ becomes equal to 1 or less than 1.

Now $\frac{n+1}{r} - 1 > 1$, so long as $= \frac{n+1}{r} > 2$; that is, $= \frac{n+1}{2} > r$.

We have to choose the greatest value of r consistent with this inequality.

(1) Let n be even, and equal to $2m$; then $\frac{n+1}{2} = \frac{2m+1}{2} = m + \frac{1}{2}$;

and for all values of r up to m inclusive this is greater than r. Hence by putting $r = m = \frac{n}{2}$, we find that the greatest number of combinations is ${}^nC_{\frac{n}{2}}$.

(2) Let n be odd and equal to $2m + 1$; then $\frac{n+1}{2} = \frac{2m+2}{2} = m + 1$; and for all values of r up to m inclusive this is greater than r; but when $r = m + 1$ the multiplying factor becomes equal to 1, and ${}^nC_{m+1} = {}^nC_m$; that is, ${}^nC_{\frac{n+1}{2}} = {}^nC_{\frac{n-1}{2}}$;

and therefore the number of combinations is greatest when the things are taken $\frac{n+1}{2}$, or $\frac{n-1}{2}$ at a time; the result being the same in the two cases.

EXAMPLES XXXVII-b

1. Find the number of permutations which can be made from all the letters of the words,

   (1) *irresisitible,* (2) *phenomenon,*

   (3) *tittle-tattle.*

2. How many different numbers can be formed by using the seven digits 2, 3, 4, 3, 3, 1, 2? How many with the digit 2, 3, 4, 3, 3, 0, 2?

3. How many words can be formed from the letters of the word *Simoom,* so that vowels and consonants occur alternately in each word?

4. A telegraph has 5 arms and each arm has four distinct.positions, including the position of rest: find the total number of signals that can be made.

5. In how many ways can n things be given to m persons, when there is no restriction as to the number of things each may receive?

6. How many different arrangements can be made out of the letters of the expression $a^5b^3c^6$ when written at full length.

7. There are four copies each of 3 different volumes; find the number of ways in which they can be arranged on one shelf ?

8. In how many ways can 6 persons form a ring? Find the number of ways in which 4 gentlemen and 4 ladies can sit at a round table so that no two gentlemen sit together.

9. In how many ways can a word of 4 letters be made out of the letters, *a, b, e, c, d, o,* when there is no restriction as to the number of times a letter is repeated in each word?

10. How many arrangements can be made out of the letters of the word *Toulouse,* so that the consonants occupy the first, fourth, and seventh places?

11. A boat's crew consists of eight men, of whom one can only row on bow side and one only on stroke side: in how many ways can the crew be arranged?

12. Show that ${}^{n+1}C_r = {}^nC_r + {}^nC_{r-1}$.

13. A cricket eleven has to be chosen from 13 men of whom only 4 can bowl: in how many ways can the team be made up so as to include *at least* 2 bowlers?

14. In how many ways can n men be arranged in a row if two specified men are neither of them to be at either extremity of the row?

15. In a box there are eight balls, of which three are white (and indistinguishable) and five are of other colours, all different. Prove that the number of ways of taking three balls at a single draw from the box is 26. (Scot. Certif.)

16. In how many ways may 5 red, 7 green, 4 blue and 8 yellow books be arranged on a shelf so that all books of the same colour are grouped together?

If the red and green groups must not be adjacent, how many arrangements are possible? (Lond. Matric.)

17. Find the number of ways in which 8 different things, can be divided into two groups of 4 each.

How many numbers are there which consist of 4 digits, of which 3 are alike and different from the remaining digit?

(Camb. Sch. Certif.)

18. Five straight lines are drawn in one plane so that each line cuts all the others and all such points of intersection are distinct points. How many points of intersection are there and how many triangles are formed? Give your reasoning, for preference in a form which could be used for any number of lines.

(Lond. Matric.)

19. (i) Determine *from first principles in* how many ways a party of ten may take their seats in a railway carriage compartment which accommodates five on each side.

(ii) In how many ways can the ten passengers take their seats if two particular passengers A and B are always to sit directly opposite each other? (Scot. Certif.).

20. In how many ways can a committee of 11 men, of whom 4 must be British, 4 French, and 3 German, be chosen from a group consisting of 5 men of each nationality? (Camb. Sch. Certif.)

21. Find the number of permutations all together of n things of which p are alike and the rest all different.

In how many ways can 9 balls, of which 7 are white and 2 are black, be arranged in a row (a) when they are subject to no restriction, and (b) when they are subject to the restriction that the two black balls must not be next to each other?

(Camb. Sch. Certif.)

22. Prove from first principles that the number of combinations of n things taken r at a time is equal to the number taken $(n—r)$ at a time; and that each of these is equal to $\dfrac{n!}{r!(n-r)!}$

Out of 12 privates and 4 corporals, in how many ways can a squad of four privates and a corporal be chosen, and how many of these squads will contain a given private? (Sect. Ccrtif.)

23. In how many different ways can three prizes, one of Rs 30, one of Rs 5, and of Rs 2.5, be allotted to three boys out of a class of 17? If the prizes were of equal value, Rs 12.5 each, in how many ways could they be awarded? (Oxf. Sch. Certif.)

24. If you have one white, two blue, and three red flags, find how many different signals you can make, each containing four flags arranged one above the other. (Oxf. Sch. Certif.)

25. In how many ways can $a + b + c$ different books be made up into three parcels, the first containing a, the next b and the next c books? (Scot. Certif.)

26. In how many ways can eight articles be arranged in a row so that three particular ones come together in each arrangement?

In how many ways can they be arranged so that two particular ones do not come together?

27. Each of three dice has its six faces numbered respectively 1 2, 3, 4, 5, 6, but the dice themselves are of different colours. If the three are thrown simultaneously out of a dice-box, in how many ways can they fall?

In how many of these ways will two of the dice show the same number and the third a different number? (Lond. Matric.)

28. A man has 8 bachelor friends, and he wishes to invite 4 of them to dine with him on successive evenings as long as he can have a different selection each time. For how many evenings is it possible to continue these parties, and how often will each of the 8 friends from one of the party?

29. Twenty-two men arrange to play a cricket match. If two of the men are brothers, show that the number of ways in which the teams can be made up so that the brothers do not play on the same side is $2\lfloor 19 \div \lfloor 10 \lfloor 9$.

30. Eight oarsmen and two coxswains are to make up two crews of four oarsmen and one coxswain each. It is found that three men can row on bow side only and two on stroke side only; the rest can row on either side. In how many ways can the crews be made up if their order of rowing in the boats is important, but if the boats are identical?

31. In such a card game as bridge, where 13 cards are dealt to each of 4 persons, in how many different ways can a hand be dealt?

In how many ways can 52 cards be divided into 4 packs of 13 cards each?

32. Solve the following equations for n:

(i) ${}^nC_5 = {}^nC_4$, (ii) ${}^nC_2 = 36$,

(iii) ${}^{n+1}C_3 = 2\,{}^nC_2$.

38

BINOMIAL THEOREM

355. IT may be shown by actual multiplication that

$$(x+a)(x+b)(x+c)(x+d)$$
$$= x^4 + (a+b+c+d)x^3 + (ab+ac+ad+bc+bd+cd)x^2$$
$$+ (abc+abd+acd+bcd)x + abcd \quad \ldots (1)$$

We may, however, write down this result by inspection; for the complete product consists of the sum of a number of partial products each of which is formed by multiplying together four letters, *one* being taken from *each* of the four factors. If we examine the way in which the various partial products are formed, we see that

(1) the term x^4 is formed by taking the letter x out of *each* of the factors.

(2) the terms involving x^3 are formed by taking the letter x out of *any three* factors, in every way possible, and *one* of the letters a, b, c, d out of the remaining factor.

(3) the terms involving x^2 are formed by taking the letter x out of *any two* factors, in every way possible, and *two* of the letters a, b, c, d out of the remaining factors.

(4) the terms involving x are formed by taking the letter x out of *any one* factor, and *three* of the letters a, b, c, d out of the remaining factors.

(5) the term independent of x is the product of all the letters a, b, c, d.

Example. Find the value of $(x-2)(x+3)(x-5)(x+9)$.

The product

$$= x^4 + (-2+3-5+9)x^3 + (-6+10-18-15+27-45)x^2$$
$$+ (30-54+90-135)x + 270$$
$$= x^4 + 5x^3 - 47x^2 - 69x + 270.$$

356. If in equation (1) of the proceding article we suppose $b = c = d = a$, we obtain

$$(x+a)^4 = x^4 + 4ax^3 + 6a^2x^2 + 4a^3x + a^4.$$

We shall now employ the same method to prove a formula known as the Binomial Theorem, by which any binomial of the form $x + a$ can be raised to any assigned positive integral power.

357. *To find the expansion of* $(x + a)^n$ *when* n *is a positive integer.*

Consider the expression $(x + a)(x + b)(x + c) \dots (x + k)$,

the number of factors being n.

The expansion of this expression is the continued product of the n factors, $x + a$, $x + b$, $x + c$, ... $x + k$, and every term in the expansion is of n dimensions, being a product formed by multiplying together n letters, *one* taken from each of these n factors.

The highest power of x is x^n, and is formed by taking the letter x from *each* of the n factors.

The terms involving x^{n-1} are formed by taking the letter x from *any* $n - 1$ of the factors, and *one* of the letters $a, b, c, \dots k$ from the remaining factor, thus the coefficient of x^{n-1} in the final product is the sum of the letters a, b, c, ..., k, denote it by S_1. The terms involving x^{n-2} are formed by taking the letter x from *any* $n - 2$ of the factors, and *two* of the letters a, b, c, ..., k from the two remaining factors; thus the coefficient of x^{n-r} in the final product is the sum of the products of the letters $a, b, c, \dots k$ taken two at a time; denote by S_2.

And, generally, the terms involving x^{n-r} are formed by taking the letter x from *any* $n - r$ of the factors, and r of the letters $a, b, c, \dots k$ from the r remaining factors; thus the coefficient of x^{n-r} in the final product is the sum of the products of the letters $a, b, c, \dots k$ taken r at a time; denote it by S_r.

The last term in the product is $abc \dots k$; denote it by S_n.

Hence $(x + a)(x + b)(x + c) \dots (x + k)$

$$= x^n + S_1 x^{n-1} + S_2 x^{n-2} + \dots + S_r x^{n-r} + \dots + S_{n-1} x + S_n.$$

In S_1 the *number of terms is* n; S_2 *the number of terms* is the *same* as the number of combinations of n things 2 at a time; that is ${}^nC_2$; in S_3 *the number of terms is* ${}^nC_3$; and so on.

Now suppose $b, c, \dots k$, each equal to a; then S_1 becomes ${}^nC_1 a$; S_2 becomes ${}^nC_2 a^2$; S_2 becomes ${}^nC_3 a^3$; and so on; thus

$$(x + a)^n = x^n + {}^nC_1 a x^{n-1} + {}^nC_2 a^2 x^{n-2} + {}^nC_3 a^3 x^{n-3} + \dots + {}^nC_n a^n,$$

Substituting for ${}^nC_1$, ${}^nC_2$, ... we obtain

$$(x + a)^n = x^n + nax^{n-1} + \frac{n(n-1)}{1.2} a^2 x^{n-2}$$

$$+ \frac{n(n-1)(n-2)}{1 \cdot 2 \cdot 3}$$

$$a^3 x^{n-3} + \dots + a^n,$$

the series containing $n + 1$ terms.

This is the *Binomial Theorem*, and the expression on the right is said to be the expansion of $(x + a)^n$.

358. The coefficient in the expansion of $(x + a)^n$ are very conveniently expressed by the symbols ${}^nC_1$, ${}^nC_2$, ${}^nC_3, \ldots {}^nC_n$. We shall, however, sometimes further abbreviate them by omitting n, and writing $C_1, C_2, C_3, \ldots C_n$. With this notation we have

$$(x + a)^n = x^n + C_1 a x^{n-1} + C_2 a^2 x^{n-2} + C_3 a^3 x^{n-3} + \ldots + C_n a^n.$$

If we write $-a$ in the place of a, we obtain

$$\begin{aligned}(x - a)^n &= x^n + C_1(-a)x^{n-1} + C_2(-a)^2 x^{n-2} \\ &\qquad + C_3(-a)^3 x^{n-3} + \ldots + C_n(-a) \\ &= x^n - C_1 a x^{n-1} + C_2 a^2 x^{n-2} - C_3 a^3 x^{n-3} + \ldots + (-1)^n C_n a^n.\end{aligned}$$

Thus the terms in the expansion of $(x + a)^n$ and $(x - a)^n$ are *numerically* the some, but in $(x - a)^n$ they are alternately positive and negative, and the last term is positive or negative according as n is even or odd.

Example 1. Find the expansion of $(x + y)^6$.

By the formula, the expansion

$$\begin{aligned}&= x^6 + {}^6C_1 x^5 y + {}^6C_2 x^4 y^2 + {}^6C_3 x^3 y^3 + {}^6C_4 x^3 y^4 + {}^6C_5 x y^5 + {}^6C_6 y^6 \\ &= x^6 + 6x^5 y + 15x^4 y^2 + 20x^3 y^3 + 15x^2 y^4 + 6xy^5 + y^6,\end{aligned}$$

on calculating the values of ${}^6C_1$, ${}^6C_2$, ${}^6C_3, \ldots$

Example 2. Find the expansion of $(a - 2x)^7$.

$$(a-2x)^7 = a^7 - {}^7C_1 a^6(2x) + {}^7C_2 a^5(2x)^2 - {}^7C_3\, a^4(2x)^3 + \ldots \text{to 8 terms.}$$

Now remembering that ${}^nC_r = {}^nC_{n-r}$, after calculating the coefficients up to ${}^7C_3$, the rest may be written down at once; for ${}^7C_4 = {}^7C_3$; ${}^7C_5 = {}^7C_2$; and so on. Hence

$$\begin{aligned}(a - 2x)^7 &= a^7 - 7a^6(2x) + \frac{7 \cdot 6}{1 \cdot 2} a^5(2x)^2 - \frac{7 \cdot 6 \cdot 5}{1 \cdot 2 \cdot 3} a^4(2x)^3 + \ldots \\ &= a^7 - 7a^6(2x) + 21a^5(2x)^2 - 35a^4(2x)^3 + 35a^3(2x)^4 \\ &\qquad - 21a^2(2x)^5 + 7a(2x)^6 - (2x)^7 \\ &= a^7 - 14a^6 x + 84a^5 x^2 - 280a^4 x^3 + 560a^3 x^4 \\ &\qquad - 672a^2 x^5 + 448a x^6 - 128x^7.\end{aligned}$$

359. In the expansion of $(x + a)^n$, the coefficient of the second term is ${}^nC_1$; of the third term is ${}^nC_2$; of the fourth term is ${}^nC_3$; and so on; *the suffix in each term being one less than the number of the term to which it applies;* hence ${}^nC_r$ is the coefficient of the $(r + 1)$th term. This is called the general term, because by giving to r different numerical values any of the coefficient may be found from ^nC_r; and by giving to x and a their appropriate indices any assigned term may be obtained. Thus the $(r + 1)$th term may be written

$$^nC_r x^{n-r} a^r, \text{ or } \frac{n(n-1)(n-2)\ldots(n-r+1)}{\underline{|r}} x^{n-r} a^r.$$

In applying this formula to any particular case, it should be observed that *the index of* a *is the same as the suffix of* C, *and that the sum of the indices of* x *and* a *is* n.

Example 1. Find the fifth term of $(a + 2x^3)^{17}$.

$$\text{The required term} = {}^{17}C_4 a^{13} (2x^3)^4$$
$$= \frac{17 \cdot 16 \cdot 15 \cdot 14}{1 \cdot 2 \cdot 3 \cdot 4} \times 16a^{13}x^{12}$$
$$= 38080a^{13}x^{12}.$$

Example 2. Find the fourteenth term of $(3 - a)^{15}$.

$$\text{The required term form} = {}^{15}C_13(3)^2(-a)^{13}$$
$$= {}^{15}C_2 \times (-9a^{13}) \qquad \text{[Art. 349.]}$$
$$= -945a^{13}.$$

360. The simplest form of the binomial theorem is the expansion of $(1 + x)^n$. This is obtained from the general formula of Art. 357, by writing 1 in the place of x, and x in the place of a.

$$\text{Thus } (1 + x)^n = 1 + {}^nC_1 x + {}^nC_2 x^2 + \ldots + {}^nC_r x^r + \ldots + {}^nC_n x^n$$
$$= 1 + nx + \frac{n(n-1)}{1 \cdot 2} x^2 + \ldots + x^n;$$

the general term being $\dfrac{n(n-1)(n-2)\ldots(n-r+1)}{\underline{|r}} x^r.$

361. The expansion of a binomial may always be made to depend upon the case in which the first term is unity; thus

$$(x + y)^n = \left\{ x \left(1 + \frac{y}{x} \right) \right\}^n$$
$$= x^n (1 + z)^n, \text{ where } z = \frac{y}{x}.$$

Example. Find the coefficient of x^{16} in the expansion of $(x^2 - 2x)^{10}$.

$$\text{We have} \qquad (x^2 - 2x)^{10} = x^{20} \left(1 - \frac{2}{x} \right)^{10};$$

and, since x^{20} multiplies every term in the expansion of $\left(1-\frac{2}{x}\right)^{10}$, we have in this expansion to seek the coefficient of the term which contains $\frac{1}{x^4}$.

Hence the required coefficient $= {}^{10}C_4(-2)^4$

$$= \frac{10 \cdot 9 \cdot 8 \cdot 7}{1 \cdot 2 \cdot 3 \cdot 4} \times 16 = 3360.$$

EXAMPLES XXXVIII-a

Expand the following binomials:

1. $(x+2)^4$.

2. $(x+3)^5$.

3. $(a+x)^7$.

4. $(a-x)^5$.

5. $(1-2y)^5$.

6. $\left(2x+\frac{y}{2}\right)^4$.

7. $\left(2-\frac{x}{2}\right)^6$.

8. $\left(a-\frac{3}{b}\right)^7$.

9. $\left(ax+\frac{y}{a}\right)^9$.

Write down and simplify:

10. The 4th term of $(1+x)^{12}$.

11. The 6th term of $(2-y)^8$.

12. The 5th term of $(a-5b)^7$.

13. The 15th term of $(2x-1)^{17}$.

14. The 7th term of $\left(1-\frac{1}{x}\right)^{10}$.

15. The 6th term of $\left(3x-\frac{a}{2}\right)^9$.

16. The middle term of $\left(\frac{2}{3}z-\frac{3}{2z}\right)^6$.

17. The 23rd term of $\left(x^5-\frac{5}{x}\right)^7$.

18. The 10th term of $(x^3\ 1)^{15}$.

19. Find the value of $(x-\sqrt{3})^4+(x+\sqrt{3})^4$.

20. Expand $(\sqrt{1-x^2}+1)^5-(\sqrt{1-x^2}-1)^5$.

21. Find the coefficient of x^{12} in $(x^2+2x)^{10}$.

22. Find the coefficient of x in $\left(x^2-\frac{a}{2x}\right)^{14}$.

23. Find the term independent of x in $\left(2x^2-\frac{1}{x}\right)^{12}$.

24. Find the coefficient of x^{-26} in $\left(\frac{x^2}{3}-\frac{2}{x^3}\right)^{15}$.

362. *In the expansion of* $(1 + x)_n$ *the coefficients of terms equidistant from the beginning and end are equal.*

The coefficient of the $(r + 1)$ th term from the beginning is ${}^nC_r$.

The $(r + 1)$ th term from the end has $n + 1 - (r + 1)$, or $n - r$ terms before it; therefore counting from the beginning it is the $(n - r + 1)$ th term, and its coefficient is ${}^nC_{n-r}$, which has been shown to be equal to ${}^nC_r$. [Art. 349.] Hence the proposition follows.

363. *To find the greatest coefficient in the expansion of* $(1 + x)_n$.

The coefficient of the general term of $(1 + x)^n$ is ${}^nC_r$; and we have only to find for what value of r this is greatest. By Art. 354, when n is even, the greatest coefficient is $\frac{{}^nC_n}{2}$; when n is odd, it ${}^nC_{\frac{n-1}{2}}$, or ${}^nC_{\frac{n+1}{2}}$; these two coefficients being equal.

364. *To find the greatest term in the expansion of* $(x + a)^n$.

We have $$(x + a)^n = x^n\left(1 + \frac{a}{x}\right)^n;$$

therefore, since x^n multiplies every term in $\left(1 + \frac{a}{x}\right)^n$, it will be sufficient to find the greatest term in this latter expansion.

Let the rth and $(r + 1)$ th be any two consecutive terms. The $(r + 1)$ th term is obtained by multiplying the rth term by $\frac{n - r + 1}{r} \cdot \frac{a}{x}$; that is, by $\left(\frac{n+1}{r} - \frac{a}{x}\right)$. [Art. 359.]

The factor $\frac{n+1}{r} - 1$ decreases as r increases; hence the $(r + 1)$ th term is not always greater than the rth term, but only until $\left(\frac{n+1}{r} - 1\right)\frac{a}{x}$ becomes equal to 1, or less than 1.

Now $$\left(\frac{n+1}{r} - 1\right)\frac{a}{x} > 1, \text{ so long as } \frac{n+1}{r} - 1 > \frac{x}{a};$$

that is, $$\frac{n+1}{r} > \frac{x}{a} + 1, \text{ or } \frac{(n+1)a}{x+a} > r \qquad \ldots (1).$$

If $\frac{(n+1)a}{x+a}$ be an integer, denote it by p; then if $r = p$ the multiplying factor becomes 1, and the $(p + 1)$ th term is equal to the pth; and these are greater than any other term.

If $\frac{(n+1)a}{x+a}$ be not an integer, denote its integral part by q; then the greatest value of r consistent with (1) is q; hence the $(q+1)$ th term is the greatest.

Since we are only concerned with the *numerically greatest term*, the investigation will be the same for $(x-a)^n$, therefore in any numerical example it is unnecessary to consider the sign of the second term of the binomial. Also it will be found best to work each example independently of the general formula.

Example. Find the greatest term in the expansion of $(1+4x)^8$, when x has the value $\frac{1}{3}$.

Denote the rth and $(r+1)$ th terms by T_r and T_{r+1} respectively; then

$$T_{r+1} = \frac{8-r+1}{r} \cdot 4x \times T_r = \frac{9-r}{r} \times \frac{4}{3} T_r \times;$$

hence $T_{r+1} > T_r$, so long as $\frac{9-r}{r} \times \frac{4}{3} > 1$;

that is, $36 - 4r > 3r$, or $36 > 7r$.

The greatest value of r consistent with this is 5; hence the greatest term is the sixth, and its value

$$= {}^8C_5 \times \left(\frac{4}{3}\right)^5 = {}^8C_3 \times \left(\frac{4}{3}\right)^5 = \frac{57344}{243}.$$

365. *To find the sum of the coefficients in the expansion of* $(1+x)^n$.

In the identity $(1+x)^n = 1 + C_1x + C_2x^2 + C_3x^3 + \ldots + C_nx^n$, put $x = 1$; thus

$$2^n = 1 + C_1 + C_2 + C_3 + \ldots + C_n$$
$$= \text{sum of the coefficients.}$$

COR. $C_1 + C_2 + C_3 + \ldots + C^n = 2^n - 1$;

that is, the total number of combinations of n things *taking some or all of them at a time is* $2^n - 1$.

366. *To prove that in the expansion of* $(1+x)^n$, *the sum of the coefficients of the odd terms is equal to the sum of the coefficients of the even terms.*

In the identity $(1+x)^n = 1 + C_1x + C_2x^2 + C_3x^3 + \ldots + C_nx^n$, put $x = -1$; thus

$$0 = 1 - C_1 + C_2 - C_3 + C_4 - C_5 + \ldots;$$

$$\therefore \quad 1 + C_2 + C_4 + \ldots = C_1 + C_3 + C_5 + \ldots$$

367. The binomial theorem may also be applied to expand expressions which contain more than two terms.

Example. Find the expansion of $(x^2 + 2x - 1)^3$.

Regarding $2x - 1$ as a single term, the expansion

$$= (x^2)^3 + 3(x^2)^2(2x-1) + 3x^2(2x-1)^2 + (2x-1)^3$$

$$= x^6 + 6x^5 + 9x^4 - 4x^3 - 9x^2 + 6x - 1, \text{ on reduction.}$$

368. For a full discussion of the Binomial Theorem when the index is not restricted to positive integral values the student is referred to the *Higher Algebra*, Chap. XIV. It is there shown that when x is less than unity, the formula.

$$(1+x)^n = 1 + nx + \frac{n(n-1)}{1\cdot 2}x^2 + \frac{n(n-1)(n-2)}{1\cdot 2\cdot 3}x^3 + \ldots$$

is true for any value of n.

When n is negative or fractional the number of terms in the expansion is unlimited, but in any particular case we may write down as many terms as we please, or we may find the coefficient of any assigned term.

Example 1. Expand $(1 + x)^{-3}$ to four terms.?

$$(1+x)^{-3} = 1 + (-3)x + \frac{(-3)(-3-1)}{1\cdot 2}x^2 + \frac{(-3)(-3-1)(-3-2)}{1\cdot 2\cdot 3}x^3$$

$$= 1 - 3x + \frac{3\cdot 4}{1\cdot 2}x^2 - \frac{3\cdot 4\cdot 5}{1\cdot 2\cdot 3}x^3 + \ldots$$

$$= 1 + 3x + 6x^2 - 10x^3 + \ldots$$

Example 2. Expand $(4 + 3x)^{3/2}$ to four terms.

$$(4+3x)^{3/2} = 4^{3/2}\left(1 + \frac{3x}{4}\right)^{3/2} = 8\left(1 + \frac{3x}{4}\right)^{3/2}$$

$$= 8\left[1 + \frac{3}{2}\cdot\frac{3x}{4} + \frac{\frac{3}{2}\left(\frac{3}{2}-1\right)}{1\cdot 2}\left(\frac{3x}{4}\right)^2 + \frac{\frac{3}{2}\left(\frac{3}{2}-1\right)\left(\frac{3}{2}-2\right)}{1\cdot 2\cdot 3}\left(\frac{3x}{4}\right) + \ldots\right]$$

$$= 8\left[1 + \frac{3}{2}\cdot\frac{3x}{4} + \frac{3}{8}\cdot\frac{9x^2}{16} - \frac{1}{16}\cdot\frac{27x^3}{64} + \ldots\right]$$

$$= 8 + 9x + \frac{27}{16}x^2 - \frac{27}{128}x^3 + \ldots.$$

369. In finding the general term we must now use the formula

$$\frac{n(n-1)(n-2)\ldots(n-r+1)}{\underline{|r}}x^r$$

written in full; for the symbol ${}^nC_r$ cannot be employed when n is fractional or negative.

Example 1. Find the general term in the expansion of $(1 + x)^{1/2}$.

$$\text{The } (r+1)\text{ th term } = \frac{\frac{1}{2}\left(\frac{1}{2}-1\right)\left(\frac{1}{2}-2\right)\ldots\left(\frac{1}{2}-r+1\right)}{\underline{|r}} x^r$$

$$= \frac{1(-1)(-3)(-5)\ldots(-2r+3)}{2^r \underline{|r}} x^r.$$

The number of factors in the numerator is r, and $r - 1$ of these are negative; therefore, by taking -1 out of each of the negative factors, we may write the above expression

$$(-1)^{r-1} \frac{1 \cdot 3 \cdot 5 \ldots (2r-3)}{2^r \underline{|r}} x^r.$$

Example 2. Find the general term in the expansion of $(1 - x)^{-3}$.

$$\text{The } (r+1)\text{ th term} = \frac{(-3)(-4)(-5)\ldots(-3-r+1)}{\underline{|r}} (-x)^r$$

$$= (-1)^r \frac{3 \cdot 4 \cdot 5 \ldots (r+2)}{\underline{|r}} (-1)^r x^r$$

$$= (-1)^{2r} \frac{3 \cdot 4 \cdot 5 \ldots (r+2)}{1 \cdot 2 \cdot 3 \ldots r} x^r = \frac{(r+1)(r+2)}{1 \cdot 2} x^r,$$

by removing the factors from the numerator and denominator.

370. The following example illustrates a useful application of the Binomial Theorem.

Example. Find the cube root of 126 to five places of decimals,

$$(126)^{1/3} = (5^3 + 1)^{1/3} = 5\left(1 + \frac{1}{5^3}\right)^{1/3}$$

$$= 5\left(1 + \frac{1}{3}\cdot\frac{1}{5^3} - \frac{1}{9}\cdot\frac{1}{5^6} + \frac{5}{81}\cdot\frac{1}{5^9} - \ldots\right)$$

$$= 5 + \frac{1}{3}\cdot\frac{1}{5^2} - \frac{1}{9}\cdot\frac{1}{5^5} + \frac{1}{81}\cdot\frac{1}{5^7} - \ldots$$

$$= 5 + \frac{1}{3}\cdot\frac{2^2}{10^2} - \frac{1}{9}\cdot\frac{2^5}{10^5} + \frac{1}{81}\cdot\frac{2^7}{10^7} - \ldots$$

$$= 5 + \frac{.04}{3} - \frac{.00032}{9} + \frac{.0000128}{81} - \ldots$$

$$= 5 + .013333\ldots - .000035\ldots + \ldots$$

$$= 5.01329, \text{ to five places of decimals.}$$

EXAMPLES XXXVIII-b

In the following expansions find which is the greatest term:

1. $(x+y)^{17}$ when $x=4, y=3$.

2. $(x-y)^{28}$ when $x=9, y=4$.

3. $(1+x)^4$ when $x=\frac{2}{3}$.

4. $(a-4b)^{15}$ when $a=12, b=2$.

5. $(7x+2y)^{30}$ when $x=8, y=14$.

6. $(2x+3)^n$ when $x=\frac{5}{2}, n=15$.

7. In the expansion of $(1+x)^{25}$ the coefficients of the $(2r+1)$ th and $(r+5)$ th terms are equal; find r.

8. Find n when the coefficients of the 16th and 26th terms of $(1+x)^n$ are equal.

9. Find the relation between r and n in order that the coefficients of the $(r+3)$th and $(2r-3)$ th terms of $(1+x)^{3n}$ may be equal.

10. Find the coefficient of x^m in the expansion of $\left(x^2+\frac{1}{x}\right)^{2m}$.

11. Find the middle term of $(1+x)^{2n}$ in its simplest form.

12. Find the sum of the coefficients of $(x+y)^{16}$.

13. Find the sum of the coefficients of $(3x+y)^9$.

14. Find the rth term from the beginning and the rth term from the end of $(a+2x)^n$.

15. Expand $(a^2+2a+1)^2$ and $(x^2-4x+2)^3$.

Expand to 4 terms the following expressions:

16. $(1+x)^{1/3}$.

17. $(1+x)^{3/4}$.

18. $(1+x)^{2/5}$.

19. $(1+3x)^{-2}$.

20. $(1-x^2)^{-3}$.

21. $(1+3x)^{-4}$.

22. $(2+x)^{-3}$.

23. $(1+2x)^{-1/2}$.

24. $(a-2x)^{-3/2}$.

Write down and simplify:

25. The 5th term and the 10th term of $(1+x)^{-3/2}$.

26. The 3rd term and the 11th term of $(1+2x)^{11/2}$.

27. The 4th term and the $(r+1)$ th term of $(1+x)^{-2}$.

28. The 7th term and the $(r+1)$ th term of $(1-x)^{1/2}$.

29. The $(r+1)$th term of $(a-bx)^{-1}$, and of $(1-nx)^{1/n}$.

Find to four places of decimals the value of

30. $\sqrt[3]{122}$.

31. $\sqrt{620}$.

32. $\sqrt[5]{31}$.

33. $1 \div \sqrt{99}$.

39

LOGARITHMS

371. DEFINITION. The logarithm of any number to a given base is the index of the power to which the base must be raised in order to equal the given number. Thus if $a^x = N$, x is called the logarithm of N to the base a.

Examples.

(1) Since $3^4 = 81$, the logarithm of 81 to base 3 is 4.

(2) Since $10^1 = 10, 10^2 = 100, 10^3 = 1000, \ldots\ldots$

the natural numbers 1, 2, 3, ... are respectively the logarithms of 10, 100, 1000, ... to base 10.

372. The logarithm of N to base a is usually written $\log_a N$, so that the same meaning is expressed by the two equations

$$a^x = N; \; x = \log_a N.$$

Example. Find the logarithm of $32\sqrt[5]{4}$ to base $2\sqrt{2}$.

Let x be the required logarithm; then,

by definition,

$$(2\sqrt{2})^x = 32\sqrt[5]{4};$$

$$\therefore \quad (2 \cdot 2^{1/2})x = 2^5 \cdot 2^{3/2};$$

$$\therefore \quad 2^{3/2x} = 2^{5+2/5};$$

hence, by equating the indices,

$$\frac{3}{2}x = \frac{27}{5};$$

$$\therefore \quad x = \frac{18}{5} = 3 \cdot 6.$$

373. When it is understood that a particular system of logarithms is in use, the suffix denoting the base is omitted. Thus in arithmetical calculations in which 10 is the base, we usually write $\log 2, \log 3, \ldots$ instead of $\log_{10} 2, \log_{10} 3, \ldots$.

Logarithms to the base 10 are known as Common Logarithms; this system was first introduced in 1615 by Briggs, a contemporary of Napier. The inventor of Logarithms. Before discussing the properties of common logarithms we shall prove some general propositions which are true for all logarithms independently of any particular base.

374. *The logarithm of* 1 *is* 0.

For $a^0 = 1$ for all values of a; therefore $\log 1 = 0$, whatever the base may be.

375. *The logarithm of the base itself is* 1.

For $a^1 = a$; therefore $\log_a a = 1$.

376. *To find the logarithm of a product.*

Let MN be the product; let a be the base of the system and suppose

$$M = a^x, N = a^y;$$

so that $\quad x = \log_a M, \ y = \log_a N.$

Thus the product $\quad MN = a^x \times a^y = a^{x+y}$:

whence, by definition, $\log_a MN = x + y$

$$= \log_a M + \log_a N$$

Similarly, $\quad \log_a MNP = \log_a M + \log_a N + \log_a P;$

and so on for any number of factors.

Example. $\quad \log 42 = \log(2 \times 3 \times 7) = \log 2 + \log 3 + \log 7.$

377. *To find the logarithm of a fraction.*

Let $\frac{M}{N}$ be the fraction, and suppose

$$M = a^x, N = a^y;$$

so that $\quad x = \log_a M, \ y = \log_a N.$

Thus the fraction $\quad \frac{M}{N} = \frac{a^x}{a^y} = a^{x-y};$

whence, by definition, $\log_a \frac{M}{N} = x - y = \log_a M - \log_a N.$

Example. $\log\left(2\frac{1}{7}\right) = \log\frac{15}{7} = \log 15 - \log 7$

$$= \log(3 \times 5) - \log 7 = \log 3 + \log 5 - \log 7.$$

378. *To find the logarithm of a number raised to any power, integral or fractional.*

Let $\log_a(M^P)$ be required, and suppose

$$M = a^x, \text{ so that } x = \log_a M;$$

then $\quad M^p = (a^x)^p = a^{px};$

whence, by definition, $\log_a (M^p) = px$;

that is, $$\log_a (M^p) = p \log_a M.$$

Similarly, $$\log_a (M^{1/r}) = \frac{1}{r} \log_a M.$$

Example. Express the logarithm of $\frac{\sqrt{a^3}}{c^5 b^2}$ in terms of $\log a$, $\log b$, and $\log c$.

$$\log \frac{\sqrt{a^3}}{c^5 b^2} = \log \frac{a^{3/2}}{c^5 b^2} = \log a^{3/2} - \log (c^5 b^2)$$

$$= \frac{3}{2} \log a - (\log c^5 + \log b^2) = \frac{3}{2} \log a - 5 \log c - 2 \log b.$$

Common Logarithms

379. From the equation $10^x = N$, it is evident that common logarithms will not in general be integral, and that they will not always be positive.

For instance, $3154 > 10^3$ and $< 10^4$;

$\therefore$ $\log 3154 = 3 +$ a fraction.

Again, $.06 > 10^{-2}$ and $< 10^{-1}$;

$\therefore$ $\log .06 = -2 +$ a fraction.

380. DEFINITION. The integral part of a logarithm is called the characteristic, and the fractional part when expressed as a decimal is called the mantissa.

381. The characteristic of the logarithm of any number to base 10 can be written down by inspection, as we shall now show.

(i) *To determine the characteristic of the logarithm of any number greater than unity.*

It is clear that a number with two digits in its integral part lies between 10^1 and 10^2; a number with three digits in its integral part lies between 10^2 and 10^3; and so on. Hence a number with n digits in its integral part lies between 10^{n-1} and 10^n.

Let N be a number whose integral part contains n digits; then

$$N = 10\,(n - 1) + \text{a fraction};$$

$$\therefore \quad \log N = (n - 1) + \text{a fraction}.$$

Hence the characteristic is $n - 1$; that is, *the characteristic of the logarithm of a number greater than unity is less by one than the number of digits in its integral part, and is positive.*

Example. The characteristics of log 314, log 87.263, log 2.78, log 3500 are respectively 2, 1, 0, 3.

(ii) *To determine the characteristic of the logarithm of a number less than unity.*

A decimal with one cipher immediately after the decimal point, such as .0324, being greater than .01 and less than .1, lies between 10^{-2} and 10^{-1}; a number with two ciphers after the decimal point lies between 10^{-3} and 10^{-2}; and so on. Hence a decimal fraction with n ciphers immediately after the decimal point lies between $10^{-(n+1)}$ and 10^{-n},

Let D be a decimal beginning with n ciphers; then

$$D = 10^{-(n+1)} + \text{a fraction};$$

$$\therefore \qquad \log D = -(n+1) + \text{a fraction}.$$

Hence the characteristic is $-(n + 1)$; this is, *the characteristic of the logarithm of a number less than one is negative and one more than the number of ciphers immediately after the decimal point.*

Example. The characteristics of

$$\log .4, \log .3748, \log .000135, \log .08$$

$\therefore$ are respectively $-1, -1, -4, -2$.

382. *The mantissae are the same for the logarithms of all numbers which have the same significant digits.*

For if any two numbers have the same sequence of digits, differing only in the position of the decimal point, one must be equal to the other multiplied or divided by some integral power of 10. Hence their logarithms must *differ by an integer.* In other words, their decimal parts or mantissae are the same.

Examples.

(i) $\log 32700 = \log (3.27 \times 10^4) = \log 3.27 + \log 10^4$
$= \log 3.27 + 4.$

(ii) $\log .0327 = \log (3.27 \times 10^{-2}) = \log 3.27 + \log 10^{-2}$
$= \log 3.27 - 2.$

(iii) $\log .000327 = \log (3.27 \times 10^{-4}) = \log 3.27 + \log 10^{-4}$
$= \log 3.27 - 4.$

Thus, log 32700 , log .0327 , log .000327 differ from log 3.27 only in the *integral* part; that is the mantissa is the same in each case.

NOTE. The characteristics of the logarithms are 4, –2, –4 respectively. The foregoing examples so that by introducing a suitable integral power of 10, all numbers can be expressed in one standard form in which *the decimal point always stands after the first significant digit,* and the characteristics are given by the powers of 10, without using the rules of Art. 381.

383. The logarithms of all integers from 1 to 20000 have been found and tabulated. In Chambers' Mathematical Tables they are given to seven places of decimals, but for many practical purposes sufficient accuracy is secured by using four-figure logarithms (available for all numbers from 1 ot 9999), such as are contained in the Tables given on pages 382 to 385.

384. Advantages of Common Logarithms. It will now be seen that it is unnecessary to tabulate the characteristics, since they can always be written down by inspection [Art. 381.] Also the Tables need only contain the mantissa of the logarithms of integers [Art. 382].

In order to secure these advantages it is convenient *always to keep the mantissa positive,* and it is usual to write the minus sign over a negative characteristic and not before it, so as to indicate that the characteristic alone is negative. Thus $\bar{4}.30103$, which is the logarithm of .0002, is equivalent to $-4+.30103$, and must be distinguished from -4.30103, in which both the integer and the decimal are negative.

385. In the course of work we sometimes have to deal with a logarithm which is wholly negative. In such a case an arithmetical artifice is necessary in order to write the logarithm with mantissa positive. Thus a result such as -3.69897 may be transformed by subtracting 1 from the integral part and adding 1 to the decimal part.

Thus $\qquad -3.69897 = -3-1+(1-.69897) = -4+.30103 = \bar{4}.30103.$

Example 1. Required the logarithm of .0002432.

In the Tables we find that 3859636 is the mantissa of log 2432 (the decimal point as well as the characteristic being omitted); and, by Art. 382, the characteristic of the logarithm of the given number is -4;

$$\therefore \qquad \log .0002432 = \bar{4}.3859636 .$$

Example 2. Find the value of $\sqrt[5]{.00000615}$, given

$$\log 165 = 2.2175 \text{ , } \log 6974 = 3.8435$$

Let x denote the value required; then

$$\log x = \log(.00000165)^{1/5}$$

$$= \frac{1}{5}\log\,(.00000165) = \frac{1}{5}\,(\bar{6}.2175);$$

the *mantissa* of log .00000165 being the same as that of log 165. and the *characteristic* being prefixed by the rule.

Now $\qquad \frac{1}{5}(\bar{6}.2175) = \frac{1}{5}(\overline{10}+4.2175) = \bar{2}.8435$

and .8435 is the mantissa of log 6974; hence x is a number consisting of these same digits but with one cipher after the decimal point

[Art. 382.]

Thus $x = .06974.$

386. It is sometimes necessary to transform logarithms from one base to another.

Suppose for example that the logarithms of all numbers to base a are known and tabulated, it is required to find the logarithms to base b.

Let N be any number whose logarithm to base b is required.

Let $\qquad y = \log_b N$, so that $b^y = N$;

$\therefore \qquad \log_a (a^y) = \log_a N$;

that is, $\qquad y \log_a b = \log_a N$;

$\therefore \qquad y = \dfrac{1}{\log_a b} \times \log_a N$

or $\qquad \log_b N = \dfrac{1}{\log_{ab}} \times \log_a N \qquad \ldots(1).$

Now since N and b are given, $\log_a N$ and $\log_a b$ are known from the Tables, and thus $\log_b N$ may be found.

Hence it appears that to transform logarithms from base a to base b we have only to multiply them all by $\dfrac{1}{\log_a b}$; this is a constant quantity and is given by the Tables, it is known as the *modulus*.

COR. If in equation. (1) we put a for N, we obtain

$$\log_b a = \frac{1}{\log_a b} \times \log_a a = \frac{1}{\log_a b};$$

$$\therefore \qquad \log_b a \times \log_a b = 1.$$

387. In the following examples all necessary logarithms will be given. The use of four-figure Tables will be explained in a future section.

Example 1. Given $\log 3 = .4771213$, find $\log \{(2.7)^3 \times (.81)^{4/5} \div (90)^{3/4}\}$

The required value $= 3 \log \dfrac{27}{10} + \dfrac{4}{5} \log \dfrac{81}{100} - \dfrac{5}{4} \log 90$

$$= 3 (\log 3^3 - 1) + \frac{4}{5} (\log 3^4 - 2) - \frac{5}{4} (\log 3^2 + 1)$$

$$= \left(9 + \frac{16}{5} - \frac{5}{2}\right) \log 3 - \left(3 + \frac{8}{5} + \frac{5}{4}\right)$$

$$= \frac{97}{10} \log 3 - 5\frac{17}{20} = 4.6280766 - 5.85$$

$$= 2.7780766.$$

Obs. The student should notice that the logarithm of 5 and its powers can always be obtained from log 2; thus

$$\log 5 = \log \frac{10}{2} = \log 10 - \log 2 = 1 - \log 2.$$

Example 2. Find the number of digits in 875^{16}, given

$$\log 2 = .301\ ,\ \log 7 = .845.$$

$$\log (875^{16}) = 16 \log (7 \times 125) = 16 (\log 7 + 3 \log 5)$$
$$= 16 (\log 7 + 3 - 3 \log 2) = 16 \times 2.942$$
$$= 47.072;$$

hence the number of digits is 48. [Art. 381.]

Example 3. Given $\log 2 = .301$ and $\log 3 = .477$, find two places of decimals the value of x from the equation

$$6^{3-4x} \cdot 4^{x+5} = 8.$$

Taking logarithms of both sides, we have

$$(3 - 4x) \log 6 + (x + 5) \log 4 = \log 8;$$

$$\therefore \quad (3 - 4x) (\log 2 + \log 3) + (x + 5) 2\log 2 = 3 \log 2;$$

$$\therefore \quad x (- 4\log 2 - 4\log 3 + 2 \log 2)$$
$$= 3 \log 2 - 3 \log 2 - 3 \log 3 - 10 \log 2;$$

$$\therefore \quad x = \frac{10 \log 2 + 3 \log 3}{2 \log 2 + 4 \log 3} = \frac{4.44}{2.51} = 1.77...$$

EXAMPLES XXXIX-a

1. Find the logarithms of $\sqrt{32}$ and .03125 to base $\sqrt[3]{2}$, and 100 and .00001 to base .01.

2. Find the value of $\log_4 512$, $\log_5 .0016$, $\log_{81} \frac{1}{27}$, $\log_{49} 343$.

3. Write down the numbers whose logarithms

to base	25,	3,	.02,	1,	–4,	1.7,	1000
are	$\frac{1}{2}$,	–2,	– 3.5,	–1,	2,	$-\frac{2}{3}$ respectively.	

Simplify the expressions:

4. $\log \frac{(ab^2c^4)^{1/6}}{\sqrt[9]{a^{-3}b^3c^6}}$.

5. $\log \left\{ \left(\frac{x^4 y^{-3}}{x^{-1} y^2} \right)^{-3} \div \left(\frac{x^{-2} y^3}{xy^{-1}} \right)^5 \right\}$.

6. Find by inspection the characteristics of the logarithms of 3174, 625.7, 3.502, .4, .374, .000135, 23.22065.

7. The mantissa of log 37203 is .5705780: write down the logarithms of 37.203, .000037203, 372030000.

8. The logarithm of 7623 is 3.8821259: write down the numbers whose logarithms are .8821259, 6.8821259, 7.8821259.

Given $\log 2 = .3010300$, $\log 3 = .4771213$, $\log 7 = .8450980$, find the value of

9. $\log 729$.

10. $\log 8400$.

11. $\log .256$.

12. $\log 5.832$.

13. $\log \sqrt[3]{392}$.

14. $\log .3048$.

15. Show that $\log \frac{11}{15} + \log \frac{490}{297} - 2 \log \frac{7}{9} = \log 2$.

16. Find to six decimal places the value of $\log \frac{225}{224} - 2 \log \frac{20}{189} + \log \frac{512}{81}$.

17. Simplify $\log \{(10.8)^{1/2} \times (.24)^{5/8} \div (90)^{-2}\}$, and find its numerical value.

18. Find the value of

$\log (\sqrt[3]{126} \cdot \sqrt{108} \div \sqrt[6]{1008} \cdot \sqrt[2]{162})$.

19. Find the value of $\log \sqrt[5]{\frac{588 \times 768}{686 \times 972}}$.

20. Find the number of digits in 42^{42}.

21. Show that $\left(\frac{81}{80}\right)^{1000}$ is greater than 100000.

22. How many ciphers are there between the decimal point and the first significant digit in $\left(\frac{2}{3}\right)^{1000}$?

23. Find the value of $\sqrt[5]{.01008}$, having given

$\log 398742 = 5.6006921$.

24. Find the seventh root of .00792, having given

$\log 11 = 1.0413927$ and $\log 500.977 = 2.6998179$.

25. Find the value of $2 \log \frac{75}{49} + \log \frac{135}{32} - 3 \log \frac{45}{28}$. Find the numerical value of x in the following equations, using the values of log 2 and log 3 given in Ex. 3 of Art. 387.

26. $3^{x+2} = 405$.

27. $10^{5-3x} = 2^{7-2x}$.

28. $5^{x-3} = 8$.

29. $12^{3x-4} \cdot 18^{7-2x} = 1458$.

Use of Four-Figure Tables

387 A. *To find the logarithm of a given number from the Tables.*

Example 1. Find log 38, log 380, log .0038.

We first find the number 38 in the left-hand column on page 382. Opposite to this we find the digits 5798. This, with the decimal point prefixed, is the mantissa for the logarithm of all numbers whose significant digits are 38. Hence, prefixing the characteristics we have

$$\log 38 = 1.5798, \log 380 = 2.5798, \log .0038 = 3.5798.$$

Example 2. Find log 3.86, log .0386, log 386000.

The same line as before will give the mantissa of the logarithms of all numbers which begin with 38. From this line we choose the mantissa which stands in the column headed 6. This gives .5866 as the mantissa for all numbers whose significant digits are 386. Hence, prefixing the characteristics, we have

$$\log 3.86 = .5866, \log .0386 = 2.5866, \log 386000 = 5.5866.$$

387 B. Similarly the logarithm of any number consisting of not more than 3 significant digits can be obtained directly from the Tables. When the number has 4 significant digits, use is made of the principle that when the difference between two numbers is small compared with either of them, the difference between their logarithms is very nearly proportional to the difference between the numbers. It would be out of place to attempt any demonstration of the principle here. It will be sufficient to point out that differences in the logarithms corresponding to small differences in the numbers have been calculated, and are printed ready for use in the *difference columns* at the right-hand of the Tables. The way in which these differences are used is shown in the following example.

Example. Find

(i) log 3.864. (ii) log .003868.

Here, as before, we can find the mantissa for the sequence of digits 386. This has to be *corrected* by the addition of the figures which stand underneath 4 and 8 respectively in the difference columns.

(i) $\log 3.86 = .5866$
diff. for 4 $\quad 5$
$\therefore \log 3.864 = .5871$

(ii) $\log .00386 = \bar{3}.5866$
diff. for 8 $\quad 9$
$\therefore \log .003868 = \bar{3}.5875$

NOTE. After a little practice the necessary 'correction' from the difference columns can be performed mentally.

387 C. The number corresponding to a given logarithm is called its antilogarithm. Thus in the last example 3.864 and .003868 are respectively the numbers whose logarithms are .5871 and 3.5875.

Hence antilog .5871 = 3.864; antilog 3.5875 = .003868.

387 D. *To find the antilogarithm of a given logarithm.*

In using the tables of antilogarithms on pages 383, 384, it is important to remember that we are seeking *numbers* corresponding to *given logarithms.* Thus in the left-hand column we have the first two digits of the given *mantissae,* with the decimal point prefixed. The characteristics of the given logarithms will fix the position of the decimal point in the numbers taken from the Tables.

Example. Find the antilogarithm of (i) 1.583; (ii) $\bar{2}.8249$.

(i) We first find .58 in the left-hand column and pass along the horizontal line and take the number in the vertical column headed by 3. Thus .583 is the mantissa of the logarithm of a number whose significant digits are 3828.

Hence antilog $1.583 = 38.28$.

(ii) antilog $\bar{2}.824 = .06668$

diff. for 9 $\underline{\quad 14}$

$\therefore$ antilog $\bar{2}.8249 = .06682$

Here corresponding to the first 3 digits of the mantissa we find the sequence of digits 6668, and the decimal point is inserted in the position corresponding to the characteristic $\bar{2}$. To the number so found we add 14 from the difference column headed 9, placing it under the fourth digit of the given mantissa.

387 E. The following examples illustrate the use of logarithms in abbreviating arithmetical calculations.

Example 1. Find the value of $\dfrac{3.274 \times .0059}{14.83 \times .077}$ to four significant digits.

By Art. 377, log *fraction* = log *numerator*– log *denominator.*

Numerator		Denominator
$\log 3.27 = .5145$		$\log 14.8 = 1.1703$
diff. for 4	5	diff. for 3 $\quad$ 9
$\log .0059$	$= \bar{3}.7709$	$\log .077 = \bar{2}.8865$
log *numerator*	$= \bar{2}.2859$	log *denominator* $= 0.577$
	$\bar{2}.2859$	antilog $\bar{2}.228 = .01690$
subtract	$\underline{0.0577}$	diff. for 2 $\quad \underline{1}$
log *fraction*	$= 2.2282$	antilog $2.2282 = 0.01691$

Thus $\dfrac{3.274 \times .0059}{14.83 \times .077} = .01691.$

Example 2. Find the value of $(1.05)^{17}$ to four significant digits.

$$\log (1\cdot05)^{17} = 17 \log 1\cdot05 \qquad \text{[Art. 378]}$$
$$= \cdot0212 \times 17, \text{ from the Tables,}$$
$$= \cdot3604.$$

And $\quad$ antilog $\cdot3604 = 2\cdot293$;

thus $\quad (1\cdot05)^{17} = 2\cdot293.$

NOTE. Since $\cdot0212$ is only the approximate logarithm of $1\cdot05$, the error (which may be in excess or defect) is increased when we multiply by 17. Hence there is a corresponding error in the final result. By using seven-figure logarithms it can be shown that to four decimal figures the correct result is $2\cdot2922$.

Example 3. Find a mean proportional between 27.23 and 3.276.

Let x denote the mean proportional; then

$$x = \sqrt{27\cdot23 \times 3\cdot276}; \qquad \text{[Art. 297]}$$

$$\therefore \quad \log x = \frac{1}{2}(\log 27\cdot23 + \log 3\cdot276).$$

From the Tables,

$\log 27\cdot23 = 1\cdot4351$	antilog $\cdot975 = 9\cdot441$
$\log 3\cdot276 = \cdot5153$	diff for 2 $\quad$ 4
2 $\quad 1\cdot9504$	antilog $\cdot9752 = 9\cdot445$
$\log x = \cdot9752$	

$\because \quad x = 9.445.$

EXAMPLES XXXIX-b

[*For Logarithms and Antilogarithms see pages* 382 *to* 385.]

Find the values of the following products to four significant figures :

1. $1927 \times .2501$.

2. $175.6 \times .2632$.

3. $.0035 \times 39.87$.

4. $.231 \times 2.394 \times 0.157$.

5. $5.2 \times 3.81 \times 17.31$.

6. $7.302 \times .7302 \times .007302$.

7. $23 \times 1.7 \times 3.35 \times 0.62$.

Divide

8. $2\cdot803$ by $\cdot0634$.

9. $16\cdot83$ by $24\cdot76$.

10. $30\cdot56$ by $4\cdot105$.

11. $\cdot01254$ by $\cdot4105$.

12. 2417 by 719.

13. 2391 by 3072.

Evaluate the following expressions to four significant figures:

14. $\dfrac{2\cdot38\times3\cdot901}{4\cdot83}$.

15. $\dfrac{14\cdot72\times38\cdot05}{387\cdot9}$.

16. $\dfrac{925\cdot9\times1\cdot597}{74\cdot03}$.

17. $\dfrac{15\cdot38\times\cdot0137}{276\times\cdot0038}$.

18. $(\cdot097)^4$.

19. $(1\cdot73)^{11}$.

20. $\sqrt{\cdot51}$.

21. $\sqrt{8\dfrac{1}{2}}$.

22. $\sqrt[7]{127}$.

23. $\sqrt[5]{27\cdot2}$.

24. $\sqrt[11]{1772}$.

25. $\sqrt[13]{27\cdot82}$.

26. Find a mean proportional between $2\cdot87$ and $30\cdot08$; and a third proportional to $\cdot0238$ and $7\cdot805$.

Evaluate

27. $\sqrt[3]{\left(\dfrac{294\times125}{42\times32}\right)^2}$.

28. $\dfrac{\left(330\times\dfrac{1}{49}\right)^4}{\sqrt[3]{22\times70}}$.

29. Find the value of $\sqrt{\dfrac{\cdot678\times9\cdot01}{0\cdot0234}}$ to the nearest integer.

30. Find a mean proportional between $\sqrt[3]{347\cdot3}$ and $\sqrt[5]{256\cdot4}$.

31. Find a fourth proportional to $\sqrt[3]{32\cdot78}$, $\sqrt[5]{357\cdot8}$, $\sqrt[4]{7836}$.

[*Before attempting the following Examples the student should read* Arts. 403-405.]

32. Find to the nearest rupee the amount of Rs 350 in 25 years at 3 p.c. Compound Interest.

33. Find to the nearest rupee the Present Value of Rs 1000 due to 17 years hence at 4 p.c. Compound Interest.

34. Find in how many years Rs 1130 will amount to Rs 3000 at 5 p.c. Compound Interest.

35. If a paise is put out at Compound Interest for 1000 years at 5 p.c., how many digits will be required to express the amount in rupees?

36. A train starts with velocity $\cdot001$ metre per second, and at the end of each second its velocity is greater by one-third than at the end of the preceding second; find to two places of decimals the rate of the train in km per hour at the end of 25 seconds.

40

SCALES OF NOTATION

388. THE ordinary numbers with which we are acquainted in Arithmetic are expressed by means of multiples of powers of 10; for instance

$$25 = 2 \times 10 + 5;$$

$$4705 = 4 \times 10^3 + 7 \times 10^2 + 0 \times 10 + 5.$$

This method of representing numbers is called the common or denary scale of notation, and ten is said to be the radix of the scale. The symbols employed in this system of notation are the nine digits and zero.

In like manner any number other than ten may be taken as the radix of a scale of notation; thus if 7 is the radix, a number expressed by 2453 represents $2 \times 7^3 + 4 \times 7^2 + 5 \times 7 + 3$; and in this scale no digit higher than 6 can occur.

389. The names Binary, Ternary, Quatenary, Quinary, Senary, Septenary, Octenary, Nonary, Denary, Undenary and Duodenary are used to denote the scales corresponding to the values *two, three,... twelve* of the radix.

In the undenary, duodenary, scales we shall require symbols to represent the digits which are greater than nine. It is unusual to consider any scale higher than that with radix twelve; when necessary we shall employ the symbols t, e, T as digits to denote 'ten', 'eleven' and 'twelve'.

It is especially worthy of notice that in every scale 10 is the symbol not for 'ten', but for the radix itself.

390. The ordinary operations of Arithmetic may be performed in any scale; but, bearing in mind that the successive powers of the radix are no longer powers of ten, in determining the *carrying figures* we must not divided by ten, but by the radix of the scale in question.

Example 1. In the scale of eight subtract 371532 from 530225, and multiply the difference by 7.

$$\begin{array}{r} 530225 \\ \underline{371532} \\ 136473 \end{array} \qquad \begin{array}{r} 136473 \\ \underline{\qquad 7} \\ 1226235 \end{array}$$

Explanation. After the first figure of the subtraction, since we cannot take 3 from 2 we add 8; thus we have to take 3 from ten, which leaves 7; than 6 from ten, which leaves 4; then 2 from eight, which leaves 6; and so on.

Again, in multiplying by 7, we have

$3 \times 7 =$ twenty-one $= 2 \times 8 + 5$;

we therefore put down 5 and carry 2.

Next $7 \times 7 + 2 =$ fifty-one $= 6 \times 8 + 3$;

put down 3 and carry 6; and so on.

Example 2. Divide 15 *et* 20 by 9 in the scale of twelve.

9)15 *et* 20

1*ee*96 ... 6.

Explanation. Since $15 = 1 \times T + 5 =$ seventeen $= 1 \times 9 + 8$, we put down 1 and carry 8.

Also $8 \times T + e =$ one hundred and seven $= e \times 9 + 8$;

we therefore put down *e* and carry 8; and so on.

391. *To express a given integral number in any proposed scale.*

Let N be the given number, and r the radix of the proposed scale.

Let $a_0, a_1, a_2, \ldots a_n$ be the required digits by which N is to be expressed, beginning with that in the unit's place; then

$$N = a_n r^n + a_{n-1} r^{n-1} + \ldots + a_2 r^2 + a_1 r + a_0.$$

We have now to find the values of $a_0, a_1, a_2, \ldots a_n$.

Divide N by r, then the remainder is a_0 and the quotient is

$$a_n r^{n-1} + a_{n-1} r^{n-2} + \ldots + a_2 r + a_1.$$

If this quotient is divided by r, the remainder is a_1;

if the next quotient $\ldots a_2$;

and so on, until there is no further quotient.

Thus all the required digits $a_0, a_1, a_2, \ldots a_n$ are determined by successive divisions by the radix of the proposed scale.

Example 1. Express the denary number 5213 in the scale of seven.

7)5213

7)744...5

7)106...2

7)15...1

2...1

Thus $5213 = 2 \times 7^4 + 1 \times 7^3 + 1 \times 7^2 + 2 \times 7 + 5$;

and the number required is 21125.

Example 2. Transform 21125 from scale seven to scale eleven.

e)21125

e)1244...*t*

e)61 ...0

3...*t*

therefore the required number is 3*t*0*t*.

Explanation. In the first line of work

$$21 = 2 \times 7 + 1 = \text{fifteen} = 1 \times e + 4;$$

therefore on dividing by e we put down 1 and carry 4.

Next $4 \times 7 + 1 = \text{twenty-nine} = 2 \times e + 7;$

therefore we put down 2 and carry 7; and so on.

392. Hitherto we have only discussed whole numbers; but fractions may also be expressed in any scale of notation; thus

$$\cdot 25 \text{ in scale ten denotes } \frac{2}{10} + \frac{5}{10^2};$$

$$\cdot 25 \text{ in scale six denotes } \frac{2}{6} + \frac{5}{6^2};$$

$$\cdot 25 \text{ in scale } r \text{ denotes } \frac{2}{r} + \frac{5}{r^2}.$$

Fractions thus expressed in a form analogous to that of ordinary decimal fractions are called radix-fractions, and the point is called the radix-point. The general type of such fractions in scale r is

$$\frac{b_1}{r} + \frac{b_2}{r^2} + \frac{b_3}{r^3} + \dots;$$

where $b_1, b_2, b_3, \dots$ are integers, all less than r, of which any one or more may be zero.

393. *To express a given radix-fraction in any proposed scale.*

Let F be the given fraction, and r the radix of the scale.

Let $b_1, b_2, b_3, \dots$ be the required digits beginning from the left;

then $$F = \frac{b_1}{r} + \frac{b_2}{r^2} + \frac{b_3}{r^3} + \dots.$$

We have now to find the values of $b_1, b_2, b_3, \dots$.

Multiply both sides of the equation by r, then

$$rF = b_1 + \frac{b_2}{r} + \frac{b_3}{r^2} + \dots.$$

Hence b_1 is equal to the integral part of rF ; and, if we denote the fractional part by F_1.

We have $$F_1 = \frac{b_2}{r} + \frac{b_3}{r^2} + \dots.$$

Multiply again by r ; then b_2 is the integral part of rF_1. Similarly by successive multiplications by r, each of the digits may be found, and the fraction expressed in the proposed scale.

Example 1. Express $\frac{7}{8}$ as a radix-fraction in scale six.

$$\frac{7}{8} \times 6 = \frac{7 \times 3}{4} = 5 + \frac{1}{4};$$

$$\frac{1}{4} \times 6 = \frac{1 \times 3}{2} = 1 + \frac{1}{2};$$

$$\frac{1}{2} \times 6 = 3.$$

$\therefore$ the required fraction $= \frac{5}{6} + \frac{1}{6^2} + \frac{3}{6^3} = .513.$

Example 2. Transform 1606.7 from scale eight to scale five. Treating the integral and the fractional parts separately, we have

$$\begin{array}{rr} 5\underline{)1606} & .7 \\ 5\underline{)264}...2 & \underline{5} \\ 5\underline{)44}...0 & 4.3 \\ 5\underline{)7}...1 & \underline{5} \\ 1...2 & 1.7 \end{array}$$

After this the digits in the fractional part recur; hence the required number is 12102.41.

Example 3. In what scale is the septenary number 2403 represented by 735?.

Let r be the radix of the scale required; then

$$7r^2 + 3r + 5 = 2 \times 7^3 + 4 \times 7^2 + 3 = 885;$$

that is, $\quad 7r^2 + 3r - 880 = 0$; whence $r = 11$ or $-\frac{80}{7}$.

Thus the scale is the undenary.

394. *In any scale of notation of which the radix is* r, *the sum of the digits of any whole number divided by* r – 1 *will leave the same remainder as the whole number divided by* r – 1.

Let N denote the number; $a_0, a_1, a_2, \ldots a_n$ the digits beginning with that in the unit's place, and S the sum of the digits, then

$$N = a_0 + a_1 r + a_2 r^2 + \ldots + a_{n-1} r^{n-1} + a_n r^n,$$

$$S = a_0 + a_1 + a_2 + \ldots + a_{n-1} + a_n.$$

$$\therefore \quad N - S = a_1(r-1) + a_2(r^2 - 1) + \ldots + a_{n-1}(r^{n-1} - 1) + a_n(r^n - 1).$$

Now every term on the right-hand side is divisible by $r - 1$;

$$\therefore \quad \frac{N-S}{r-1} = \text{an integer} = I \text{ suppose};$$

that is, $\quad \frac{N}{r-1} = I + \frac{S}{r-1}$ which proves the proposition.

Hence a number in scale r will be divisible by $r-1$ when the sum of its digits is divisible by $r-1$. For example, in the ordinary scale a number is divisible by 9 when the sum of its digits is divisible by 9.

EXAMPLES XL

1. Add together 352, 21435, 3505, 35 in the scale of six.

2. From 35260013 take 7471235 in the scale of eight.

3. Multiply 31044 by 4302 in the quinary scale.

4. Find the product of the undenary numbers $9t83$ and $3t7$.

5. Divide 31664435 by 6541 in the scale of seven.

6. Find the square of 3024 in the quinary scale.

7. Express 75013 in the nonary, and 5210 in the quaternary scale.

8. Transform 987504 to the scale of twelve.

9. Express the octenary number 76543 in the denary scale.

10. Transform 54321 from scale six to scale seven.

11. Express the duodenary number *te* in the binary scale.

12. Express a thousand and one in powers of two, and one hundred thousand in powers of eleven.

13. Express the sum of the septenary numbers 532, 2106, 3261, 53 in the undenary scale; also express the difference of the ternary numbers 2021121 and 1221212 in the same scale, and find the product of the two results.

14. Find the difference between 53774 in the scale of 8 and 32875 in the scale of 9, expressing the result in the denary scale.

15. Express 131.890625 in scale eight.

16. Transform 1001.12211 from the ternary to the nonary scale.

17. Express the octenary fraction ·2037 in the scale of 4.

18. Express $\frac{27}{32}$ and $\frac{500}{729}$ as radix fractions in scale 6.

19. Reduce the undenary fraction $\frac{587}{749}$ to its lowest terms.

20. In what scale is a hundred denoted by 400?

21. In what scale is 647 the square of 25?

22. In what scale are the numbers denoted by 432, 565, 708 in arithmetical progression?

23. In what scale are the numbers denoted by 22, 2.6, 34 in geometrical progression?

24. Find the square root of 443001 in the scale of 5; 2434524 in the scale of 7; and $t985679$ in the scale of eleven.

41

EXPONENTIAL AND LOGARITHMIC SERIES

395. THE advantages of common logarithms have been explained in Art. 383, and in practice no other system is used. But in the first place these logarithms are calculated to another base and then transformed to the base 10.

In the present chapter we shall prove certain formulae known as the Exponential and Logarithmic Series, and give a brief explanation of the way in which they are used in constructing a table of logarithms.

396. *To expand* a^x *in ascending powers of* x.

By the Binomial Theorem, if $n > 1$, $\left(1+\dfrac{1}{n}\right)^{ax}$

$$= 1 + nx \cdot \frac{1}{n} + \frac{nx(nx-1)}{\underline{|2}} \cdot \frac{1}{n^2} + \frac{nx(nx-1)(nx-2)}{\underline{|3}} \cdot \frac{1}{n^3} + \dots$$

$$= 1 + x + \frac{x\left(x-\dfrac{1}{n}\right)}{\underline{|2}} + \frac{x\left(x-\dfrac{1}{n}\right)\left(x-\dfrac{2}{n}\right)}{\underline{|3}} + \qquad \dots(1).$$

By putting $x = 1$, we obtain

$$\left(1+\frac{1}{n}\right)^n = 1 + 1 + \frac{1-\dfrac{1}{n}}{\underline{|2}} + \frac{\left(1-\dfrac{1}{n}\right)\left(1-\dfrac{2}{n}\right)}{\underline{|3}} + \qquad \dots(2).$$

But $$\left(1+\frac{1}{n}\right)^{nx} = \left\{\left(1+\frac{1}{n}\right)^n\right\}^x;$$

hence, the series (1) is the xth power of the series (2); that is,

$$1 + x + \frac{x\left(x-\dfrac{1}{n}\right)}{\underline{|2}} + \frac{x\left(x-\dfrac{1}{n}\right)\left(x-\dfrac{2}{n}\right)}{\underline{|3}} + \dots$$

$$= \left\{1 + 1 + \frac{1-\dfrac{1}{n}}{\underline{|2}} + \frac{\left(1-\dfrac{1}{n}\right)\left(1-\dfrac{2}{n}\right)}{\underline{|3}} + \dots\right\}^x;$$

and this is true however great n may be. If therefore n be indefinitely increased we have

$$1 + x + \frac{x^2}{\lfloor 2} + \frac{x^3}{\lfloor 3} + \dots = \left(1 + 1 + \frac{1}{\lfloor 2} + \frac{1}{\lfloor 3} + \dots\right)^x$$

The series $1 + 1 + \frac{1}{\lfloor 2} + \frac{1}{\lfloor 3} + \frac{1}{\lfloor 4} + \dots$

is usually denoted by e . hence

$$e^x = 1 + x + \frac{x^2}{\lfloor 2} + \frac{x^3}{\lfloor 3} + \frac{x^4}{\lfloor 4} + \dots$$

Write cx for x, then

$$e^{cx} = 1 + cx + \frac{c^2x^2}{\lfloor 2} + \frac{c^3x^3}{\lfloor 3} + \dots$$

Now let $e^c = a$, so that $c = \log_e a$; by substituting for c we obtain

$$a^x = 1 + x\log_e a + \frac{x^2(\log_e a)^2}{\lfloor 2} + \frac{x^3(\log_e a)^3}{\lfloor 3} + \dots$$

This is the *Exponential Theorem.*

397. The series $1 + 1 + \frac{1}{\lfloor 2} + \frac{1}{\lfloor 3} + \frac{1}{\lfloor 4} + \dots,$

which we have denoted by e, is very important as it is the base to which logarithms are first calculated. Logarithms to this base are known as the Napierian system, so named after Napier their inventor. They are also called *natural* logarithms from the fact that they are the first logarithms which naturally come into consideration in algebraical investigations.

When logarithms are used in theoretical work it is to be remembered that the base e is always understood, just as in arithmetical work the base 10 is invariably employed.

From the series the approximate value of e can be determined to any required degree of accuracy; to 10 places of decimals it is found to be 2.7182818284.

Example 1. Find the sum of the infinite series $1 + \frac{1}{\lfloor 2} + \frac{1}{\lfloor 4} + \frac{1}{\lfloor 6} + \dots.$

We have $\quad e = 1 + 1 + \frac{1}{\lfloor 2} + \frac{1}{\lfloor 3} + \frac{1}{\lfloor 4} + ..;$

and by putting $x = -1$ in the series for e^x, we obtain

$$e^{-1} = 1 - 1 + \frac{1}{\lfloor 2} - \frac{1}{\lfloor 3} + \frac{1}{\lfloor 4} - \dots.$$

$$\therefore \qquad e + e^{-1} = 2\left(1 + \frac{1}{\lfloor 2} + \frac{1}{\lfloor 4} + \frac{1}{\lfloor 6} + \dots\right);$$

hence the sum of the series is $\frac{1}{2}(e + e^{-1})$.

Example 2. Find the coefficient of x^r in the expansion of $\dfrac{a-bx}{e^x}$.

$$\frac{a-bx}{e^x} = (a-bx)e^{-x}$$

$$= (a-bx)\left\{1 - x + \frac{x^2}{\lfloor 2} - \frac{x^3}{\lfloor 3} + \ldots + \frac{(-1)^r x^r}{\lfloor r} + \ldots\right\}.$$

The coefficient required $= \dfrac{(-1)^r}{\lfloor r} \cdot a - \dfrac{(-1)^{r-1}}{\lfloor r-1} \cdot b$

$$= \frac{(-1)^r}{r}(a + rb).$$

398. *To expand* $\log_e(1+x)$ *in ascending powers of* x.

From Art. 396,

$$a^y = 1 + y\log_e a + \frac{y^2(\log_e a)^2}{\lfloor 2} + \frac{y^3(\log_e a)^3}{\lfloor 3} + \ldots\ldots$$

In this series write $1 + x$ for a; thus $(1 + x)^y$

$$1 + y\log_e(1+x) + \frac{y^2}{\lfloor 2}\{\log_e(1+x)\}^2 + \frac{y^3}{\lfloor 3}\{\log_e(1+x)\}^3 + \qquad \ldots(1)$$

Also by the Binomial Theorem, when $x < 1$ we have

$$(1+x)^y = 1 + yx + \frac{y(y-1)}{\lfloor 2}x^2 + \frac{y(y-1)(y-2)}{\lfloor 3}x^3 + \qquad \ldots(2)$$

Now in (2) the coefficient of y is

$$x + \frac{(-1)}{1\cdot 2}x^2 + \frac{(-1)(1-2)}{1\cdot 2\cdot 3}x^3 + \frac{(-1)(-2)(-3)}{1\cdot 2\cdot 3\cdot 4}x^4 + \ldots;$$

that is, $\qquad x - \dfrac{x^2}{2} + \dfrac{x^3}{3} - \dfrac{x^4}{4} + \ldots.$

Equate this to the coefficient of y in (1); thus we have

$$\log_e(1+x) = x - \frac{x^2}{2} + \frac{x^3}{3} - \frac{x^4}{4} + \ldots.$$

This is known as the *Logarithmic Series.*

399. Except when x is very small the series for $\log_e(1+x)$ is of little use for numerical calculations. We can, however, deduce from it other series by the aid of which Tables of Logarithms may be constructed.

400. In Art. 398 we have proved that

$$\log_e(1+x) = x - \frac{x^2}{2} + \frac{x^3}{3} - \ldots;$$

replacing x by $-x$, we have

$$\log_e(1-x) = -x - \frac{x^2}{2} - \frac{x^3}{3} - \ldots$$

By subtraction,

$$\log_e \frac{1+x}{1-x} = 2\left(x + \frac{x^3}{3} + \frac{x^5}{5} + \dots\right).$$

Put $\frac{1+x}{1-x} = \frac{n+1}{n}$, so that $x = \frac{1}{2n+1}$; we thus obtain

$$\log_e (n+1) - \log_e n = 2\left\{\frac{1}{2n+1} + \frac{1}{3(2n+1)^3} + \frac{1}{5(2n+1)^5} + \dots\right\}.$$

From this formula by putting $n = 1$ we can obtain $\log_e 2$. Again, by putting $n = 2$ we obtain $\log_e 3 - \log_e 2$; whence $\log_e 3$ is found, and therefore also $\log_e 9$ is known.

Now by putting $n = 9$ we obtain $\log_e 10 - \log_e 9$; thus the value of $\log_e 10$ is found to be $2 \cdot 30258509\dots$.

To convert Napierian logarithms into logarithms to base 10 we multiply by $\frac{1}{\log_e 10}$, which is the *modulus* [Art. 386] of the common system, and its value is $\frac{1}{2 \cdot 302585509..}$, or $\cdot 43429448\dots$; we shall denote this modulus by μ.

By multiplying the last series throughout by μ we obtain a formula adapted to the calculation of common logarithms. Thus

$$\mu \log_e (n+1) - \mu \log_e n = 2\mu\left\{\frac{1}{2n+1} + \frac{1}{3(2n+1)^3} + \frac{1}{5(2n+1)^5} + \dots\right\};$$

that is, $$\log_{10} (n+1) - \log_{10} n = 2\left\{\frac{\mu}{2n+1} + \frac{\mu}{3(2n+1)^3} + \frac{\mu}{5(2n+1)^5} + \dots\right\}.$$

From this result we see that if the logarithm of one of two consecutive numbers be known, the logarithm of the other may be found, and thus a table of logarithms can be constructed.

EXAMPLES XLI

1. Show that

(1) $e^{-2} = 1 - \frac{2^3}{\lfloor 3} + \frac{2^4}{\lfloor 4} - \frac{2^5}{\lfloor 5} + \dots .$

(2) $\frac{e^2 - 1}{2e} = 1 + \frac{1}{\lfloor 3} + \frac{1}{\lfloor 5} + \frac{1}{\lfloor 7} + \dots .$

2. Expand $\log \sqrt{1+x}$ in ascending power of x.

3. Prove that $\log_e 2 = \frac{1}{2} + \frac{1}{12} + \frac{1}{30} + \frac{1}{56} + \dots .$

4. Show that $\log_{10}\left(\frac{1}{1-x}\right) = \frac{1}{\log_e 10}\left(x + \frac{x^2}{2} + \frac{x^3}{3} + \dots\right)$.

5. Prove that $\log \frac{1+x}{1-3x} = 4x + 4x^2 + \frac{28}{3}x^3 + 20x^4 + \dots$.

6. Show that if $x > 1, \log\sqrt{x^2-1} = \log x - \frac{1}{2x^2} - \frac{1}{4x^4} - \frac{1}{6x^6} - \dots$.

7. Show that $\log\sqrt{\frac{1+x}{1-x}} - \log\sqrt{\frac{1-x}{1+x}} = 2\left(x + \frac{x^3}{3} + \frac{x^5}{5} + \dots\right)$.

8. If $a = b - \frac{b^2}{2} + \frac{b^3}{3} - \frac{b^4}{4} + \dots,$

express b in ascending powers of a.

9. Calculate the value of $\sqrt{e}$ to 4 places of decimals.

10. Prove that

$$\log_e(1 + x - 2x^2) = x - \frac{5x^2}{2} + \frac{7x^3}{3} - \frac{17x^4}{4} + \dots,$$

and find the general term of the series.

11. Prove that $e^{-1} = 2\left(\frac{1}{\lfloor 3} + \frac{2}{\lfloor 5} = \frac{3}{\lfloor 7} + \dots\right)$.

12. Prove that $\log_e 3 = 1 + \frac{1}{3\cdot 2^2} + \frac{1}{5\cdot 2^4} + \frac{1}{7\cdot 2^6} + \dots$.

13. Show that

$$\log_e(1 - 3x + 2x^2)^{-1} = 3x + \frac{5x^2}{2} + 3x^3 + \frac{17x^4}{4} + \dots$$

and find the general term of the series.

14. Prove that the expansion of $\log_e(1 - x + x^2)$ is

$$-x + \frac{x^2}{2} + \frac{2x^3}{3} + \frac{x^4}{4} - \frac{x^5}{5} - \frac{x^6}{3} - \dots\dots$$

15. If $x > 1$, prove that

$$\frac{1}{x} + \frac{1}{2x^2} + \frac{1}{3x^3} + \dots = \frac{1}{x-1} - \frac{1}{2(x-1)^2} + \frac{1}{3(x-1)^3} - \dots.$$

42

MISCELLANEOUS EQUATIONS

401. MANY kinds of miscellaneous equations may be solved by the ordinary rules for quadratic equations as explained in Art. 202; but others require some special artifice for their solution. This will be illustrated in the present chapter.

Example 1. Solve $\dfrac{x^2-6}{x}+\dfrac{5x}{x^2-6}=6.$

Write $\quad y$ for $\dfrac{x^2-6}{x}$; thus

$$y+\frac{5}{y}=6, \text{ or } y^2-6y+5=0;$$

whence $\quad y=5$, or 1.

$$\therefore \quad \frac{x^2-6}{x}=5, \text{ or } \frac{x^2-6}{x}=1;$$

that is, $\quad x^2-5x-6=0$, or $x^2-x-6=0$.

Thus $\quad x=6,-1$; or $x=3,-2$.

Example 2. Solve $3^{2x+3}-55=28(3^x-2)$.

This equation may be written $3^3\cdot 3^{2x}-28\cdot 3^x+1=0$.

By writing y for 3^x, we obtain

$$27y^2-28y-1=0; \text{ that is, } (27y-1)(y-1)=0;$$

whence $\quad y=\dfrac{1}{27}$, or 1.

Thus $\quad 3^x=\dfrac{1}{27}=3^{-3}$, or $3^x=1=3^0$,

and therefore $\quad x=-3$, or 0.

Example 3. Solve $2x^x-3\sqrt{2x^2-7x+7}=7x-3$.

On transposition, $(2x^2-7x)-3\sqrt{2x^2-7x+7}=-3$.

By putting $\sqrt{2x^2-7x+7}=y$, so that $2x^2-7x+7=y^2$, we obtain

$$(y^2-7)-3y=-3, \text{ or } y^2-3y-4=0;$$

Whence $\quad y=4$, or -1.

Thus $\sqrt{2x^2 - 7x + 7} = 4$, or $\sqrt{2x^2 - 7x + 7} = -1$;

that is, $2x^2 - 7x - 9 = 0$, or $2x^2 - 7x + 6 = 0$.

From the first of these quadratics we obtain $x = \frac{9}{2}$, or -1, and from the second $x = 2$, or $\frac{3}{2}$.

It should be noticed that in this solution we have tacitly assumed y to be the *positive* value of the expression $\sqrt{2x^2 - 7x + 7}$, so that the roots obtained from the solutions of $\sqrt{2x^2 - 7x + 7} = -1$ will only satisfy the original equation in the modified form obtained by changing the sign of the radical.

Thus $x = \frac{9}{2}$, or -1 satisfies $2x^2 - 3\sqrt{2x^2 - 7x + 7} = 7x - 3$,

and $x = 2$, or $\frac{3}{2}$ satisfies $2x^2 + 3\sqrt{2x^2 - 7x + 7} = 7x - 3$.

EXAMPLES XLII-a

Solve the following equations :

1. $x^2 + x + 1 = \dfrac{42}{x^2 + x}$.

2. $\dfrac{x}{x^2 - 1} + \dfrac{x^2 - 1}{x} = 2\dfrac{1}{6}$.

3. $\left(x + \dfrac{1}{x}\right)^2 - 4\left(x + \dfrac{1}{x}\right) = 5$.

4. $8x^6 + 65x^3 + 8 = 0$.

5. $\dfrac{x + 8}{x + 12} + \dfrac{5}{x + 4} = \dfrac{3x + 14}{3x + 8}$.

6. $4^x + 8 = 9 \cdot 2^x$.

7. $\dfrac{3x - 6}{5 - x} + \dfrac{11 - 2x}{10 - 4x} = 3\dfrac{1}{2}$.

8. $3\sqrt{x} - 3x^{-1/2} = 8$.

9. $\left(x - \dfrac{6}{x}\right)^2 + x - \dfrac{24}{x} = 5$.

10. $27x^{\frac{3}{2}} - 1 = 26x^{\frac{3}{4}}$.

11. $7\sqrt{x - 8} - \sqrt{21x + 12} = 2\sqrt{3}$.

12. $4^{2x + 1} + 16 = 65 \cdot 4^x$.

13. $x + 2 = \sqrt{4 + x\sqrt{8 - x}}$.

14. $3^{x/2} + 3^{-x/2} = 2$.

15. $2x^2 - 2x + 2\sqrt{2x^2 - 7x + 6} = 5x - 6$.

16. $x^2 + 6\sqrt{x^2 - 2x + 5} = 11 + 2x$.

17. $2\sqrt{x^2 - 6x + 2} + 4x + 1 = x^2 - 2x$.

18. $\sqrt{4x^2 + 2x + 7} = 12x^2 + 6x - 119$.

19. $3x(3-x) = 11 - 4\sqrt{x^2 - 3x + 5}$.

20. $x^2 - x + 3\sqrt{2x^2 - 3x + 2} = \frac{x}{2} + 7$.

21. $\sqrt{\frac{2-x}{3x}} - \sqrt{\frac{3x}{2-x}} = \frac{3}{2}$.

22. $\sqrt{\frac{a}{x}} - \sqrt{\frac{x}{a}} = \frac{a^2 - 1}{a}$.

23. $(a-b)x^2 + (b-c)x + c - a = 0$.

24. $a(b-c)x^2 + b(c-a)x + c(a-b) = 0$.

25. $\sqrt{a-x} + \sqrt{b-x} = \sqrt{a+b-2x}$.

26. $\frac{1}{a-x} + \frac{1}{b-x} = \frac{1}{a-c} + \frac{1}{b-c}$.

27. $\sqrt{x-p} + \sqrt{x-q} = \frac{p}{\sqrt{x-q}} = \frac{q}{\sqrt{x-p}}$.

28. $\sqrt{(x-2)(x-3)} + 5\sqrt{\frac{x-2}{x-3}} = \sqrt{x^2 + 6x + 8}$.

29. $\sqrt{x^2 + 4x - 4} + \sqrt{x^2 + 4x - 10} = 6$.

30. $\sqrt[3]{x-a} - \sqrt[3]{x-b} = \sqrt[3]{b-a}$.

402. No general methods can be given for the solution of simultaneous equations containing two or more unknowns. The simpler cases have been considered in Chapter XXVI; The following examples illustrate useful artifices to be employed in special cases.

Example 1. Solve $\quad x + y = 4 \quad$ ...(1),

$$(x^2 + y^2)(x^3 + y^3) = 280 \qquad ...(2).$$

We have $\quad x^2 + y^2 = (x+y)^2 - 2xy = 16 - 2xy$;

and $\quad x^3 + y^3 = (x+y)^3 - 3xy(x+y) = 64 - 12xy$.

Bn substituting in (2), we obtain

$$(16 - 2xy)(64 - 12xy) = 280; \text{ that is, } 3x^2y^2 - 40xy + 93 = 0;$$

hence $\quad xy = 3, \text{ or } \frac{31}{3}$.

Thus $\left.\begin{array}{r} x + y = 4 \\ xy = 3 \end{array}\right\}$, whence we obtain $\left.\begin{array}{r} x = 3, \text{ or } 1 \\ y = 1, \text{ or } 3 \end{array}\right\}$;

or, $\left.\begin{array}{r} x + y = 4 \\ xy = \frac{31}{3} \end{array}\right\}$, whence, $\left.\begin{array}{r} x = 2 \pm \sqrt{-\frac{19}{3}} \\ y = 2 \pm \sqrt{-\frac{19}{3}} \end{array}\right\}$.

Example 2. Solve $x^2y^2z = 225$, $xy^2z^2 = 75$, $x^2yz^2 = 45$.

By multiplying the three equations together, we have

$$x^5y^5z^5 = 225 \times 75 \times 45 = 5^5 \times 3^5;$$

whence $\qquad xyz = 5 \times 3 = 15.$

By squaring this equation and dividing by each of the given equations in succession, we obtain

$$z = 1,\ x = 3,\ y = 5$$

Example 3. Solve the equations

$$x^2 + xy + xz = 48,\ xy + y^2 + yz = 12,\ xz + yz + z^2 = 84.$$

These equations may be written

$$x(x + y + z) = 48,\ y(x + y + z) = 12,\ z(x + y + z) = 84.$$

By addition, $(x + y + z)(x + y + z) = 144;$

whence $x + y + z = \pm 12.$

On dividing each of the given equations in turn by this last equation, we obtain

$$x = \pm 4,\ y = \pm 1,\ z = \pm 7.$$

It is clear that the root must be taken either all positively or all negatively.

Example 4. Solve $x + y - z = 14$ ...(1),

$$y^2 + z^2 - x^2 = 46 \qquad ...(2),$$

$$yz = 9 \qquad ...(3),$$

From (2) and (3), $(y - z)^2 - x^2 = 28.$

Put u for $y - z$; then this equation becomes

$$u^2 - x^2 = 28.$$

Also from (1), $\qquad u + x = 14;$

by division, $\qquad n - x = 2;$

whence $\qquad x = 6$, and $u = 8.$

Thus $y - z = 8$, and $yz = 9$; whence, $y = 9$, or -1 ; $z = 1$, or -9; and the solution is $x = 6,\ y = 9,\ z = 1$; or $x = 6,\ y = -1,\ z = -9.$

EXAMPLES XLII-b

1. $3x - 2y = 11,\ 9x^2 - 4y^2 = 209.$ **2.** $x^3 + y^3 = 91,\ x^2y + xy^2 = 84.$

3. $x^3 - y^3 = 335,\ x^2y - xy^2 = 70.$

4. $x^2 + xy + y^2 = 84,\ x + \sqrt{xy} + y = 14.$

5. $x^2 + xy + y^2 = 189,\ x - \sqrt{xy} + y = 9.$

6. $\dfrac{3}{x^2} - \dfrac{1}{xy} - \dfrac{2}{y^2} = \dfrac{2}{9},\ \dfrac{3}{x} + \dfrac{2}{y} = \dfrac{4}{3}.$

7. $\dfrac{2}{x^2} - \dfrac{3}{xy} - \dfrac{2}{y^2} = 17,\ \dfrac{1}{x} - \dfrac{2}{y} = 1.$ **8.** $x^2y + y^2x = 20,\ \dfrac{1}{x} + \dfrac{1}{y} = \dfrac{5}{4}.$

9. $x^2 - 7xy + 4y^2 = 34, \dfrac{2x+y}{x-3y} - \dfrac{x-3y}{2x+y} = 2\dfrac{2}{3}$.

10. $x^2 - xy + x = 35, xy - y^2 + y = 15$.

11. $(x+y)^2 + 3(x-y) = 30, xy + 3(x-y) = 11$.

12. $(x-y)^2 = 3 - 2x - 2y, y(x-y+1) = x(y-x+1)$.

13. $x^2 + 1 = 81(y^2 + y), x^2 + x = 9(y^3 + 1)$.

14. Find the rational roots of

(1) $\left.\begin{array}{c} x+y=5 \\ (x^2+y^2)(x^3+y^3)=455 \end{array}\right\}$, (2) $\left.\begin{array}{c} x-y=2 \\ (x^2+y^2)(x^3-y^3)=260 \end{array}\right\}$.

15. $\sqrt{\dfrac{x}{y}} + \sqrt{\dfrac{y}{x}} = 4\dfrac{1}{4}, \dfrac{x}{\sqrt{y}} + \dfrac{y}{\sqrt{x}} = 16\dfrac{1}{4}$.

16. $\sqrt{\dfrac{x+y}{x-y}} + \sqrt{\dfrac{x-y}{x+y}} = \dfrac{34}{15}, \dfrac{x+y}{\sqrt{x-y}} + \dfrac{x-y}{\sqrt{x+y}} = \dfrac{152}{15}$.

17. $x^2yz = 72, xy^2z = 48, xyz^2 = 96$.

18. $xyz = 30, xyz = 120, xzu = 20, yzu = 24$.

19. $yz + zx = 13, zx + xy = 25, xy + yz = 20$.

20. $y(x+z) = 112, z(x+y) = 132, x(y+z) = 90$.

21. $(x+a)(y-b) = 2, (y-b)(z+c) = 3, (z+c)(x+a) = 6$.

22. $(x+y)(x+z) = 63, (y+z)(y+x) = 42, (z+x)(z+y) = 54$.

23. $x^2 - xy - xz = 14, xy - y^2 - yz = 6, xz - yz - z^2 = 4$.

24. $x(3z - 2y) = 42, y(x - 2z) = 4, z(x + 5y) + 34 = 0$.

25. $xy + x + y = 11, yz + y + z = 3, zx + z + x = 2$.

26. $(x+y)^2 - z^2 = 65, x^2 - (y+z)^2 = 13, x + y - z = 5$.

27. $z + x = 9xyz, x + y = 5xyz, y + z = 8xyz$.

28. $x^2 + y^2 + z^2 = 84, x + y + z = 14, xy = z^2$.

29. $x + y - z = 1, x^2 - y^2 + z^2 = 15, xy = 12$.

30. $y + z - x = 9, x^2 - y^2 - z^2 = 15, yz = 3$.

31. $x^2 + y^2 + z^2 = 133, y + z - x = 7, yz = x^2$.

32. $3^x = 9^{y-1}, 16^{3-x} = 8^{y-2}$.

33. $2^{y-1} = 16^{x-1}, 3^{1/x} = 9^{2/x}, \sqrt[x]{2^{y-3}} = \sqrt[2x]{8^{x-2}}$.

34. $x^2 - (y-z)^2 = a^2, y^2 - (z-x)^2 = b^2, z^2 - (x-y)^2 = c^2$.

43

INTEREST AND ANNUITIES

403. QUESTIONS involving Simple Interest are easily solved by the ordinary rules of Arithmetic; but in Compound Interest the calculations are often extremely laborious. We shall now show how these arithmetical calculations may be simplified by the aid of logarithms. Instead of taking as the rate of interest the interest on Rs 100 for one year, it will be found more convenient to take the interest on Re 1 for one year. If this be denoted by Rs r, and the amount of Re 1 for 1 year by Rs R, we have $R = 1 + r$.

404. *To find the interest and amount of a given sum in a given time at compound interest.*

Let P denote the principal, R the amount of Re 1 in one year, n the number of years, I the interest, and M the amount.

The amount of P at the end of the first year is PR; and, since this is the principal for the second year, the amount at the end of the second year is $PR \times R$ or PR^2. Similarly the amount at the end of the third year is PR^3, and so on; hence, the amount in n years is PR^n; that is,

$$M = PR^n;$$

and therefore

$$I = P(R^n - 1).$$

Example. Find the amount of Rs 100 in a hundred years, allowing compound interest at the rate of 5 per cent, payable quarterly; having given

$$\log 2 = .3010300, \log 3 = .4771213, \log 14.3906 = 1.15808.$$

The amount of Re 1 in a quarter of a year is Rs $\left(1 + \frac{1}{4}\cdot\frac{5}{100}\right)$ or Rs $\frac{81}{80}$.

The number of payments is 400. If M be the amount, we have

$$M = 100\left(\frac{81}{80}\right)^{400};$$

$$\therefore \quad \log M = \log 100 + 400(\log 81 - \log 80)$$

$$= 2 + 400(4\log 3 - 1 - 3\log 2)$$

$$= 2 + 400(.0053952) = 4.15808;$$

whence $\quad M = 14390.6.$

Thus the amount is Rs 14390.6 .

NOTE. At simple interest the amount is Rs 600.

405. *To find the present value and discount of a given sum due in a given time, allowing compound interest.*

Let P be the given sum, V the present value, D the discount, R the amount of £ 1 for one year, n the number of years.

Since V is the sum which, put out to interest at the present time, will in n years amount to P, we have

$$P = VR^n ;$$

$$\therefore \quad V = PR^{-n} ,$$

and $$D = P - V = P(1 - R^{-n}) .$$

Annuities

406. An annuity is a fixed sum paid periodically under certain stated conditions; the payment may be made either once a year or at more frequent intervals. Unless it is otherwise stated we shall suppose the payments annual.

407. *To find the amount of an annuity left unpaid for a given number of years allowing compound interest.*

Let A be the annuity, R the amount of Rs 1 for one year, n the number of years, M the amount.

At the end of the first year A is due, and the amount of this sum in the remaining $n-1$ years is AR^{n-1}; at the end of the second year another A is due, and the amount of this sum in the remaining $n-2$ years is AR^{n-2}; and so on.

$$\therefore \quad M = AR^{n-1} + AR^{n-2} + \ldots + AR^2 + AR + A$$

$$= A(1 + R + R^2 + \ldots \text{ to } n \text{ terms})$$

$$= A\,\frac{R^n - 1}{R - 1}.$$

408. *To find the presesnt value of an annuity to continue for a given number of years allowing compound interest.*

Let A be the annuity, R the amount of Re 1 in one year, n the number of years, [V the required] required present value.

The present value of A due in 1 year is AR^{-1} ;

the present value of A due in 2 years is AR^{-2} ;

the present value of A due in 3 years is AR^{-3}; and so on . [Art. 405.]

Now V is the sum of the present values of the different payments ;

$$V = AR^{-1} = AR^{-2} + AR^{-3} + \ldots\ldots \text{ to } n \text{ terms}$$

$$= AR^{-1}\,\frac{1 - R^{-n}}{1 - R^{-1}} = A\,\frac{1 - R^{-n}}{1 - R}.$$

NOTE. This result may also be obtained by dividing the value of M, given in Art. 407, by R^n. [Art. 404.]

COR. If we make n infinite we obtain for the present value of a perpetual annuity $V = \frac{A}{R-1} = \frac{A}{r}$.

409. If mA is the present value of an annuity A, the annuity is said to be worth m years' purchase.

In the case of a perpetual annuity $mA = \frac{A}{r}$; hence,

$$m = \frac{1}{r} \quad \frac{100}{\text{rate per cent}};$$

that is, the number of years' purchase of a perpetual annuity is obtained by dividing 100 by the rate per cent.

A good test of the credit of a Government is furnished by the number of years' purchase of its Stocks ; thus the $2\frac{1}{2}$ p.c. Consols at $92\frac{1}{2}$ are worth 37 years' purchase; Russian 4 p.c. Stock at 96 is worth 24 years' purchase ; while Austrian 5 p.c Stock at 80 is only worth 16 years' purchase.

410. A freehold estate is an estate which yields a perpetual annuity called the *rent;* and thus the value of the estate is equal to the present value of a prepetual annuity equal to the rent.

It follows from Art. 409 that if we know the number of years' purchase that a tenant pays in order to buy his farm, we obtain the rate per cent at which interest is reckoned by dividing 100 by the number of years' purchase.

EXAMPLES XLIII

[*The Examples marked* may be solved directly by use of the Tables.*]

1. If in the year 1600 a sum of Rs 1000 had been left to accumulate for 300 years, find its amount in the year 1900, reckoning compound interest at 4 per cent per annum. Given,

$$\log 104 = 2.017033 \text{ and } \log 12885.5 = 4.10999.$$

***2.** Find in how many years a sum of money will amount to one hundred times its value at $5\frac{1}{2}$ per cent per annum compound interest. Given $\log 1055 = 3.023$.

3. Find the present value of Rs 6000 due in 20 years, allowing compound interest at 8 per cent per annum. Given

$$\log 2 = .30103,$$
$$\log 3 = .47712,$$
and
$$\log 12875 = 4.10975.$$

4. Find at what rate per cent per annum Rs 1200 will amount to Rs 20000 in 15 years at compound interest. Given

$$\log 2 = .30103, \log 3 = .47712, \text{ and } \log 12063 = 4.08145.$$

5. Find the amount of an annuity of Rs 100 in 15 years, allowing compound interest at 4 per cent per annum. Given

$$\log = 1.04 = .01703, \text{ and } \log 180075 = 5.25545.$$

6. A freehold estate worth Rs 280 a year is sold for Rs 7000; find the rate of interest.

*7. If a perpetual annuity is worth 40 years' purchase, find what an annuity of Rs 3000 will amount to in 10 years at the same rate of interest. Given $\log 10.25 = 1.01072$, and $\log 1280 = 3.1072$.

8. Find the present value of an annuity of Rs 900 to continue for 20 years at $4\frac{1}{2}$ per cent compound interest. Given

$$\log 1.045 = .01912, \text{ and } \log 41458 = 4.6176.$$

9. A man borrows Rs 20000 at 5 per cent compound interest. If the principal and interest are to be paid by 20 equal annual instalments, find the amount of each of these; having given,

$$\log 105 = 2.0212, \text{ and } \log 3767 = 3.576.$$

10. A man has a capital of Rs 100000, for which he receives interest at $3\frac{1}{2}$ per cent; if he spends Rs 7000 a year, find in what time he will be ruined. Given

$$\log 2 = .301, \log 3 = .477, \text{ and } \log 23 = 1.362.$$

44

GRAPHICAL REPRESENTATION OF FUNCTIONS

A considerable portion of this chapter may be taken at an early stage. For example, Arts. 411 — 416 *may be read as soon as the student has had sufficient practice in substitutions involving negative quantities. Arts.* 417—424 *may be read in connection with Easy Simultaneous Equations. With the exception of a few articles the rest of the chapter should be postponed until the student is acquainted with quadratic equations.*

411. DEFINITION. Any expression which involves a variable quantity x, and whose value is dependent on that of x, is called a function of x.

Thus $3x + 8, 2x^2 + 6x - 7, x^4 - 3x^3 + x^2 - 9$ are functions of x of the first, second, and fourth degree respectively. [Art. 24.]

412. The symbol $f(x)$ is often used to briefly denote a function of x. If $y = f(x)$, by substituting a succession of numerical values for x we can obtain a corresponding succession of values for y which stands for the value of the function. Hence in this connection it is sometimes convenient to call x the independent variable, and y the dependent variable.

413. Consider the function $x(9 - x^2)$, and let its value to represented by y.

Then, when $x = 0$, $y = 0 \times 9 = 0$,

" $x = 1$, $y = 1 \times 8 = 8$,

" $x = 2$, $y = 2 \times 5 = 10$,

" $x = 3$, $y = 3 \times 0 = 0$,

" $x = 4$, $y = 4 \times (-7) = -28$,

and so on

By proceeding in this way we can find as many values of the function as we please. But we are often not so much concerned with the actual values which a function assumes for different values of the variable as with *the way in which the value of the function changes*. These variations can be very conveniently represented by a graphical method which we shall now explain.

414. Two straight lines XOX', YOY' are taken interesting at right angles in O, thus dividing the plane of the paper into four spaces XOY, YOX', $X'OY'$, $Y'OX$, which are known as the first, second, third, and fourth quadrants respectively.

The lines $X'OX$, YOY' are usually drawn horizontally and vertically; they are taken as lines of reference and are known as the axis of x and y respectively. The point O is called the origin. Values of x are measured from O along the axis of x, according to some convenient scale of measurement, and are called abscissae, *positive* values being drawn to the *right* of O along OX, and *negative* values of the *left* of O along OX.

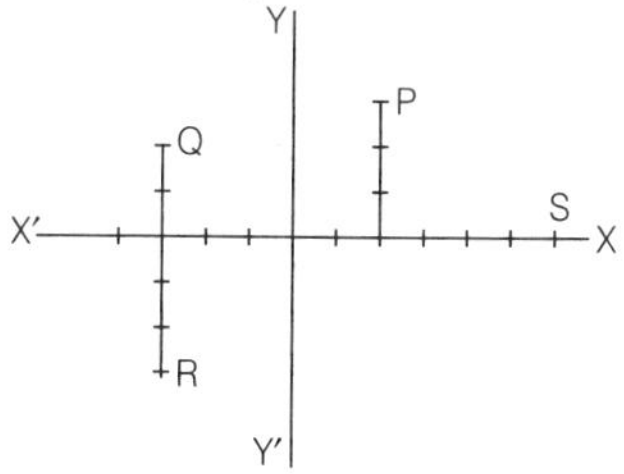

Fig. 1.

Values of y are drawn (on the same scale) parallel to the axis of y, from the ends of the corresponding abscissae, and are called ordinates. These are *positive when* drawn *above* $X'X$, *negative* when drawn *below* $X'X$.

415. The abcissa and ordinate of a point taken together are known as its coordinates. A point whose coordinates are x and y is briefly spoken of as "the point (x, y)".

The coordinates of a point completely determine its position in the plane. Thus if we wish to mark the point (2, 3), we take $x = 2$ units measured to the right of O, $y = 3$ units measured perpendicular to the x-axis and above it. The resulting point P is in the first quadrant. The point $(-3, 2)$ is found by taking $x = 3$ units to the left of O, and $y = 2$ units above the x-axis. The resulting point Q is in the second quadrant. Similarly the points $(-3, -4)$, $(5, -5)$ are represented by R and S in Fig. 1, in the third and fourth quadrants respectively.

The process of marking the position of a point in reference to the coordinate axes is known as plotting the point.

416. In practice it is convenient to use squared paper; that is, paper ruled into small squares by two sets of equidistant parallel straight lines, the one set being horizontal and the other vertical. After selecting two of the intersecting lines as axes (and slightly thickening them to aid the eye) one or more of the divisions may be chosen as our unit, and points may be readily plotted when their coordinates are known. Conversely, if the position of a point in any of the quadrants is marked, its coordinates can be measured by the divisions on the paper.

In the following pages we have used paper ruled to tenths of a cm, but a larger scale will sometimes be more convenient. See Art. 436.

Example. Plot the points (5, 2), (–3, 2), (–3, – 4), (5, – 4) on squared paper. Find the area of the figure determined by these points, assuming the divisions on the paper to be tends of a cm.

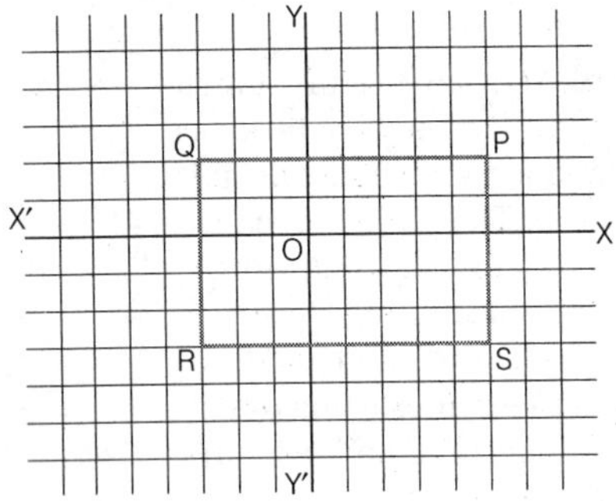

Taking the points in the order given, it is easily seen that they are represented by P, Q, R, S in Fig. 2, and that they form a rectangle which contains 48 squares. Each of these is *one-hundredth* part of a *square* cm. Thus the area of the rectangle is 48 of a square cm.

EXAMPLES XLIV-a

[*The following examples are intended to be done mainly by actual measurement on squared paper; where possible, they should also be verified by calculation.*]

Plot the following pairs of points and draw the line which joins them:

1. (3, 0), (0, 6). **2.** (– 2, 0), (0, – 8).

3. (3, – 8), (–2, 6). **4.** (5, 5), (– 2, – 2)

5. (– 2, 6), (1, – 3). **6.** (4, 5), (– 1, 5).

7. Plot the points (3, 3), (– 3, 3), (– 3, – 3), (3, – 3) and find the number of squares contained by the figure determined by these points.

8. Plot the point (4, 0), (0, 4), (– 4, 0), (0, – 4) and find the number of units of area in the resulting figure.

9. Plot the points (0, 0), (0, 10), (5, 5), and find the number of units of area in the triangle.

10. Show that the triangle whose vertices are (0, 0), (0, 6), (4, 3) contains 12 units of area. Show also that the points (0, 0), (0, 6), (4, 8) determine a triangle of the same area.

11. Plot the points (5, 6), (–5, 6), (5, – 6), (– 5, – 6). If one millimetre is taken as unit, find the area of the figure in square centimetres.

12. Plot the points (1, 3), (–3, – 9), and show that they lie on a line passing through the origin. Name the coordinates of other points on this line.

13. Plot the eight points (0, 5), (3, 4), (5, 0), (4, –3), (– 5, 0), (0, – 5), (– 4, 3), (–4, – 3), and show that they are all equidistant from the origin.

14. Plot the two following series of points:

(i) $(5, 0), (5, 2), (5, 5), (5, -1), (5, -4)$;

(ii) $(-4, 8), (-1, 8), (0, 8), (3, 8), (6, 8)$.

Show that they lie on two lines respectively parallel to the axis of y, and the axis of x. Find the coordinates of the point in which they intersect.

15. Plot the points $(13, 0), (0, -13), (12, 5), (-12, 5), (-13, 0), (-5, -12), (5, -12)$. Find their locus, (i) by measurement, (ii) by calculation.

16. Plot the points $(2, 2), (-3, -3), (4, 4), (-5, -5)$, showing that they all lie on a certain line through the origin. Conversely, show that for *every* point on this line the abscissa and ordinaie are equal.

Graph of a Function

417. Let $f(x)$ represent a function of x, and let its value be denoted by y. If we give to x a series of numerical values we get a corresponding series of values for y. If these are set off as abscissae and ordinates respectively, we plot a succession of points. If *all* such points were plotted we should arrive at a line, straight or curved, which is known as the graph of the *function* $f(x)$, or the graph of the *equation* $y = f(x)$. The variation of the function for different values of the variable x is exhibited by the variation of the ordinates as we pass from point to point.

In practice a few points carefully plotted will usually enable us to draw the graph with sufficient accuracy.

418. The student who has worked inteligently through the preceding examples will have acquired for himself some useful preliminary notions which will be of service in the examples on simple graphs which we are about to give. In particular, before preceding further he should satisfy himself with regard to the following statements:

(i) The coordinates of the origin are $(0, 0)$.

(ii) The abscissa of every point on the axis of y is 0.

(iii) The ordinate of every point on the axis of x is 0.

(iv) The graph of all points which have the same abscissa is a line parallel to the axis of y. (*e.g.* $x = 2$.)

(v) The graph of all points which have the same ordinate is a line parallel to the axis of x. (e.g. $y = 5$.)

(vi) The distance of any point $P(x, y)$ from the origin is given by

$$OP^2 = x^2 + y^2.$$

Example 1. Plot the graph of $y = x$.

When $x = 0$, $y = 0$; thus the origin is one point on the graph.

Also, when $x = 1, 2, 3, \ldots -1, -2, -3, \ldots,$

$$y = 1, 2, 3, \ldots -1, -2, -3, \ldots$$

Thus the graph passes through O, and represents a series of points each of which has its ordinate equal to its abscissa, and is clearly represented by POP' in Fig. 3.

Example 2. Plot the graph of $y = x + 3$.

Arrange the values of x and y as follows:

x	3	2	1	0	-1	-2	-3	...
y	6	5	4	3	2	1	0	...

By joining these points we obtain a line MN parallel to that in Example 1.

The results printed in larger and deeper type should be specially noted and compared with the graph. They show that the distance ON, OM, (usually called the *intercepts on the axes*) are obtained by separately putting $x = 0$, $y = 0$ in the equation of the graph.

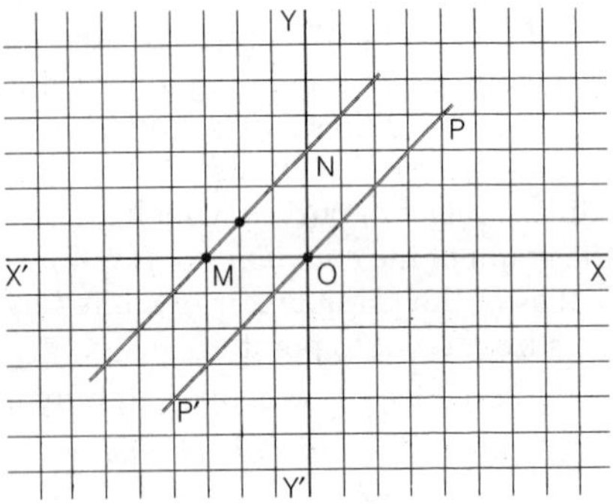

Fig. 3.

NOTE. By observing that in Example 2 each ordinate is 3 units greater than the corresponding ordinate in Example 1, the graph of $y = x + 3$ may be obtained from that of $y = x$ by simply producing each ordinate 3 units in the positive direction.

In like manner the equations

$$y = x + 5, \quad y = x - 5$$

represent two parallel lines on opposite sides of $y = x$ and equidistant from it, as the student may easily verify for himself.

Example 3. Plot the graphs represented by the following equations:

(i) $y = 2x$; (ii) $y = 2x + 4$; (iii) $y = 2x - 5$.

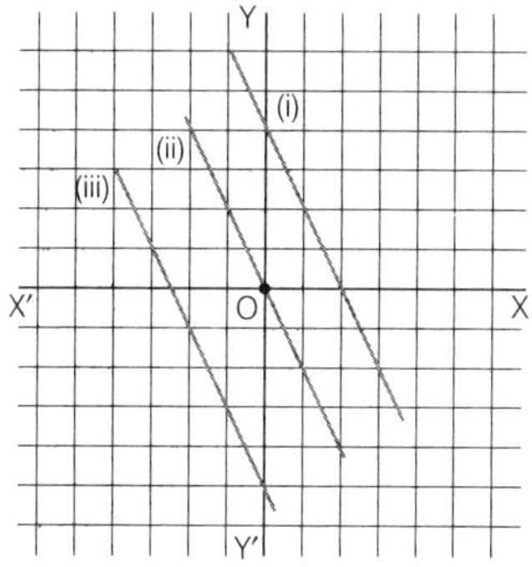

Fig. 4.

Here we only give the diagram which the student should verify in detail for himself, following the method explained in the two preceding examples.

EXAMPLES XLIV-b

[*In the following examples Nos.* 1—18 *are arranged in groups of three; each group should be represented on the same diagram so as to exhibit clearly the position of the three groups relatively to each other.*]

Plot the graphs represented by the following equations:

1. $y = 5x$.
2. $y = 5x - 4$.
3. $y = 5x + 6$.
4. $y = -3x$.
5. $y = -3x + 3$.
6. $y = -3x - 2$.
7. $y + x = 0$.
8. $y + x = 8$.
9. $y + 4 = x$.
10. $4x = 3y$.
11. $3y = 4x + 6$.
12. $4y + 3x = 8$.
13. $x - 5 = 0$.
14. $y - 6 = 0$.
15. $5y = 6x$.
16. $3x + 4y = 10$.
17. $4x + y = 9$.
18. $5x - 2y = 8$.

19. Show by careful drawing that the three last graphs have a common point whose coordinates are 2, 1.

20. Show by careful drawing that the equations

$$x + y = 10, \quad y = x - 4$$

represent two straight lines at right angles.

21. Draw on the same axes the graphs of $x = 5$, $x = 9$, $y = 3$, $y = 11$. Find the number of units of area enclosed by these lines.
22. Taking 1 cm as the unit of length, find the area included between the graphs of $x = 7$, $x = -3$, $y = -2$, $y = 8$.
23. Find the area included by the graphs of
$$y = x + 6, \quad y = x - 6, \quad y = -x + 6, \quad y = -x - 6.$$
24. With one millimetre as linear unit, find a square centimetres the area of the figure enclosed by the graphs of
$$y = 2x + 8, \qquad y = 2x - 8, \qquad y = -2x + 8, \qquad y = -2x - 8.$$

419. The student should now be prepared for the following statements:

(i) For all numerical values of a the equation $y = ax$ represents a straight line through the origin.

(ii) For all numerical values of a are b the equation $y = ax + b$ represents a line parallel to $y = ax$, and cutting off an intercept b from the axis of y.

420. Conversely, since every equation involving x and y only in the first degree can be reduced to one of the forms $y = ax$, $y = ax + b$, it follows that *every simple equation connecting two variables represents a straight line.* For this reason an expression of the form $ax + b$ is said to be a linear function of x, and an equation such as $y = ax + b$, or $ax + by + c = 0$, is said to be a linear equation.

Example. Show that the points $(3, -4)$, $(9, 4)$, $(12, 8)$ lie on a straight line, and find its equation.

Assume $y = ax + b$ as the equation of the line. If it passes through the first two points given, their coordinates must satisfy the above equation. Hence

$$-4 = 3a + b, \qquad 4 = 9a + b.$$

These equations give $a = \frac{4}{3}$, $b = -8$.

Hence
$$y = \frac{4}{3}x - 8, \quad \text{or} \quad 4x - 3y = 24,$$

is the equation of the line passing through the first two points. Since $x = 12$, $y = 8$ satisfies this equation, the line also passes through (12.8). This example may be verfied graphically by plotting the line which joins *any two* of the points and showing that it passes through the third.

Application to Simultaneous Equations

421. It was shown in Art. 100 that in the case of a simple equation between x and y, it is possible to find as many pairs of values of x and y as we please which satisfy the given equation. We now see that this is equivalent to saying that we may find as many points as we please on any given straight line. If, however, we have two simultaneous equations between x and y, there can only be one pair of values which will satisfy both equations. This is equivalent to saying that two straight lines can have only one common point.

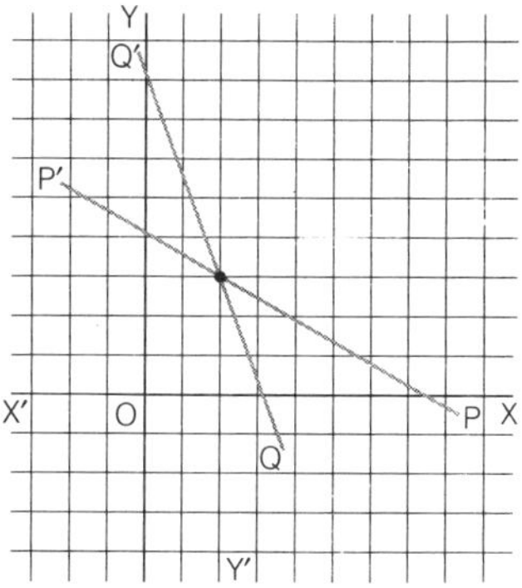

Fig. 5.

Example. Solve graphically the equations:

$$3x + 7y = 27, \quad 5x + 2y = 16.$$

If carefully plotted it will be found that these two equations represent the lines in the annexed diagram. On measuring the coordinates of the point at which they intersect it will be found that $x = 2$, $y = 3$, thus verifying the solution given in Art. 103, Ex. 1.

422. It will now be seen that the process of solving two simultaneous equations is equivalent to finding the coordinates of the point (or points) at which their graphs meet.

423. Since a straight line can always be drawn by joining *any* two points on it, in solving *linear* simultaneous equations graphically, it is only necessary to plot two points on each line. The points where the lines meet the axes will usually be the most convenient to select.

424. Two simultaneous equations lead to no finite solution if they are inconsistent with each other. For example, the equations

$$x + 3y = 2, \qquad 3x + 9y = 8$$

are inconsistent, for the second equation can be written $x + 3y = 2\frac{2}{3}$, which is clearly inconsistent with $x + 3y = 2$. The graphs of these two equations will be found to be two parallel straight lines which have no finite point of intersection.

Again, two simultaneous equations must be independent. The equations

$$4x + 3y = 1, \qquad 16x + 12y = 4$$

are not independent, for the second can be deduced from the first by multiplying throughout by 4. Thus *any pair of values* which will satisfy one equation will satisfy the other. Graphically these two equations represent two coincident straight lines which of course have an unlimited number of common points.

EXAMPLES XLIV-c

Solve the following equations, in each case verifying the solution graphically:

1. $y = 2x + 3$, $y + x = 6$.
2. $y = 3x + 4$, $y = x + 8$.
3. $y = 4x$, $2x + y = 18$.
4. $2x - y = 8$, $4x + 3y = 6$.
5. $3x + 2y = 16$, $5x - 3y = 14$.
6. $6y - 5x = 18$, $4x = 3y$.
7. $2x + y = 0$, $y = \frac{4}{3}(x + 5)$.
8. $2x - y = 3$, $3x - 5y = 15$.
9. $2y = 5x + 15$, $3y - 4x = 12$.
10. Prove by graphical representation that the three points $(3, 0), (2, 7), (4, -7)$ lie on a straight line. Where does this line cut the axis of y?
11. Prove that the three points $(1, 1), (-3, 4), (5, -2)$ lie on a straight line. Find its equation. Draw the graph of this equation, showing that it passes through the given points.
12. Show that the three points $(3, 2), (8, 8), (-2, -4)$ lie on a straight line. Prove algebraically and graphically that it cuts the axis of x at a distance $1\frac{1}{2}$ from the origin.

425. We shall now give some graphs of functions of higher degree than the first.

Example 1. Plot the graph of $2y = x^2$.

Corresponding values of x and y may be tabulated as follows.

x	...	3	2.5	2	1.5	1	0	−1	−2	−3	...
y	...	4.5	3.125	2	1.125	.5	0	.5	2	4.5	...

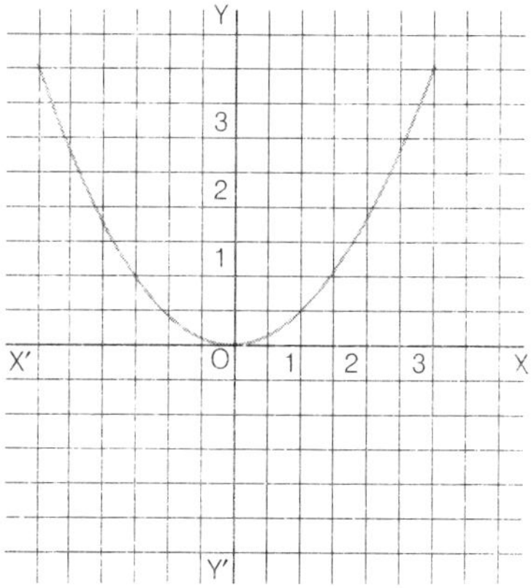

Fig. 6.

Here, in order to obtain a figure on a sufficiently large scale, it will be found convenient to take two divisions on the paper for our unit. If the above points are plotted and connected by a line drawn freehand, we shall obtain the curve shown in Fig. 6. This curve is called a parabola.

There are two facts to be specially noted in this example.

(i) Since from the equation we have $x = \pm\sqrt{2y}$, it follows that for every value of the ordinate we have two values of the abscissa, *equal in magnitude and opposite in sign*. Hence the graph is symmetrical with respect to the axis of *y*; so that after plotting with care enough points to determine the form of the graph in the first quadrant, its form in the second quadrant can be inferred without actually plotting any points in this quadrant. At the same time, in this and similar cases beginners are recommended to plot a few points in each quadrant through which the graph passes.

(ii) We observe that all the plotted points lie above the axis of *x*. This is evident from the equation; for since x^2 must be positive for all values of *x*, every ordinate obtained from the equation $y = \frac{x^2}{2}$ must be positive.

In like manner the student may show that the graph of $2y = -x^2$ is a curve similar in every respect to that in Fig. 6, but lying entirely below the axis of *x*.

NOTE. Some further remarks on the graph of this and the next example will be found in Art. 431.

Example 2. Find the graph of $y = 2x + \frac{x^2}{4}$.

Here the following arrangement will be found convenient:

x	3	2	1	0	−1	−2	−3	−4	−5	−6	−7	−8
$2x$	6	4	2	0	−2	−4	−6	−8	−10	−12	−14	−16
$\frac{x^2}{4}$	2.25	1	.25	0	.25	1	2.25	4	6.25	9	12.25	16
y	8.25	5	2.25	0	−1.75	−3	−3.75	−4	−3.75	−3	−1.75	0

From the form of the equation it is evident that every positive value of x will yield a positive value of y, and that as x increases y also increases. Hence the portion of the curve in the first quadrant lies as in Fig. 7, and can be extended indefinitely in this quadrant. In the present case only two or three positive values of x and y need be plotted, but more attention must be paid to the results arising out of negative values of x.

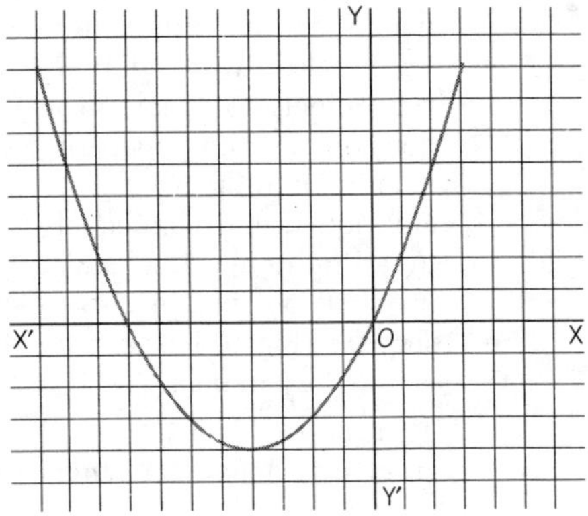

Fig. 7.

When $y = 0$, we have $\frac{x^2}{4} + 2x = 0$; thus the two values of x in the graph which correspond to $y = 0$ furnish the roots of the equation

$$\frac{x^2}{4} + 2x = 0.$$

426. If $f(x)$ represents a function of x, an approximate solution of the equation $f(x) = 0$ may be obtained by plotting the graph of $y = f(x)$, and then measuring the intercepts made on the axis of x. These intercepts are values of x which make y equal to zero, and are therefore roots of $f(x) = 0$.

427. If $f(x)$ gradually increases till it reaches a value a, which is algebraically greater than neighbouring values on either side, a is said to be a maximum value of $f(x)$.

If $f(x)$ gradually decreases till it reaches a value b, which is algebraically less than neighbouring values on either side, b is said to be a minimum value of $f(x)$.

When $y = f(x)$ is treated graphically, it is now evident that maximun and minimum values of $f(x)$ occur at points where the ordinates are algebraically greatest and least in the immediate vicinity of such points.

Example. Solve the equation $x^2 - 7x + 11 = 0$ graphically, and find the minimum value of the function $x^2 - 7x + 11$.

Put $y = x^2 - 7x + 11$, and find the graph of this equation.

x	0	1	2	3	3.5	4	5	6	7
y	11	5	1	– 1	– 1.25	–1	1	5	11

The values of x which make the function $x^2 - 7x + 11$ vanish are those which correspond to $y = 0$. By careful measurement it will be found that the intercepts OM and ON are approximately equal to 2.38 and 4.62.

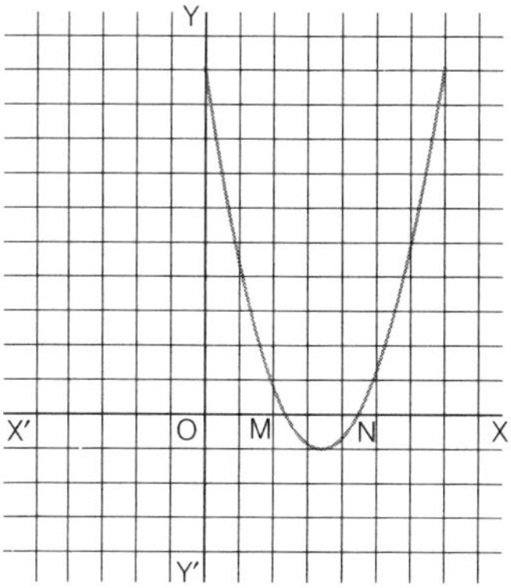

Fig. 8.

The algebraical solution of

$$x^2 - 7x + 11 = 0$$

gives $x = \frac{1}{2}(7 \pm \sqrt{5})$.

If we take 2.236 as the approximate value of $\sqrt{5}$ the values of x will be found to agree with those obtained from the graph.

Again, $x^2 - 7x + 11 = \left(x - \frac{7}{2}\right)^2 - \frac{5}{4}$. Now $\left(x - \frac{7}{2}\right)^2$ must be positive for all real values of x except $x = \frac{7}{2}$, in which case it vanishes, and the value of the function reduces to $-\frac{5}{4}$, which is the least value it can have.

The graph shows that when $x = 3.5$, $y = -1.25x$, and that this is the algebraically least ordinate in the plotted curve.

428. The following example shows that points selected for graphical representation must sometimes be restricted within certain limits.

Example. Find the graph of $x^2 + y^2 = 36$.

The equation may be written in either of the following forms :

(i) $y = \pm\sqrt{36 - x^2}$; (ii) $x = \pm\sqrt{36 - y^2}$.

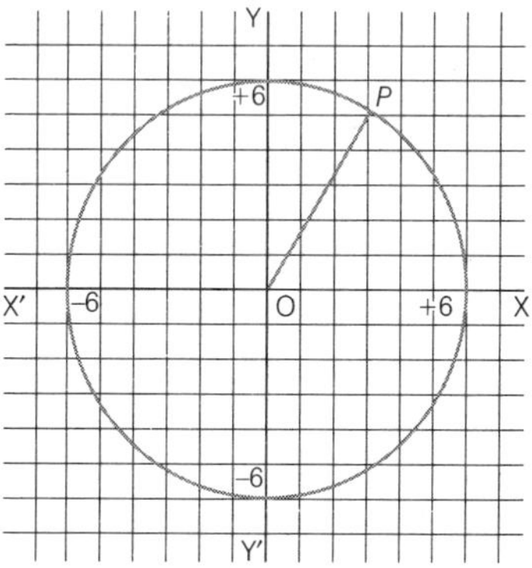

Fig. 9.

In order that y may be a real quantity we see from (i) that $36 - x^2$ must be positive. Thus x can only have values between -6 and $+6$. Similarly from (ii) it is evident that y must also lie between -6 and $+6$. Between these limits it will be found that all plotted points will lie at a distance 6 from the origin. Hence the graph is a circle whose centre is O and whose radius is 6.

This is otherwise evident, for the distance of any point $P(x, y)$ from the origin is given by $OP\sqrt{x^2 + y^2}$. [Art. 418.] Hence the equation $x^2 + y^2 = 36$ asserts that the graph consists of a series of points all of which are at a distance 6 from the origin.

Note. To plot the curve from equation (ii), we should select a succession of values for y and then find corresponding values of x. In other words we make y the *independent* and x the *dependent* variable. The student should be prepared to do this in some of the examples which follow.

EXAMPLES XLIV-d

1. Draw the graphs of $y = x^2$, and $x = y^2$, and show that they have only one common chord. Find its equation.

2. From the graphs, and also by calculation, show that $y = \frac{x^2}{8}$ cuts $x = -y^2$ in only two points and find their coordinates.

3. Draw the graphs of

(i) $y^2 = -4x$; (ii) $y = 2x - \frac{x^2}{4}$; (iii) $y = \frac{x^2}{4} + x - 2$.

4. Draw the graph of $y = x + x^2$. Show also that it may be deduced from that of $y = x^2$, obtained in Example 1.

5. Show (i) graphically; (ii) algebraically, that the line $y = 2x - 3$ meets the curve $y = \frac{x^2}{4} + x - 2$ in one point only. Find its coordinates.

6. Find graphically the roots of the following equations to 2 places of decimals:

(i) $\frac{x^2}{4} + x - 2 = 0$; (ii) $x^2 - 2x = 4$; (iii) $4x^2 - 16x + 9 = 0$;

and verify the solutions algebraically.

7. Find the minimum value of $x^2 - 2x - 4$, and the maximum value of $5 + 4x - 2x^2$.

8. Draw the graph of $y = (x - 1)(x - 2)$ and find the minimum value of $(x - 1)(x - 2)$. Measure, as accurately as you can, the values of x for which $(x - 1)(x - 2)$ is equal to 5 and 9 respectively. Verify algebraically.

9. Solve the simultaneous equations

$x^2 + y^2 = 100, \ x + y = 14;$

and verify the solution by plotting the graphs of the equations and measuring the coordinates of their common points.

10. Plot the graphs of $x^2 + y^2 = 25$, $3x + 4y = 25$, and examine their relation to each other where they intersect. Verify the result algebraically.

429. Infinite and zero values. Consider the fraction $\frac{a}{x}$ in which the numerator a has a certain *fixed value*, and the denominator is a *quantity subject to change*; then it is clear that the smaller x becomes the larger does the value of the fraction $\frac{a}{x}$ become. For instance

$$\frac{a}{\frac{1}{10}} = 10a, \qquad \frac{a}{\frac{1}{1000}} = 1000a,$$

$$\frac{a}{\frac{1}{1000000}} = 1000000a.$$

By making the denominator x sufficiently small the value of the fraction $\frac{a}{x}$ can be made as large as we please; that is, if x is made *less than any quantity that can be named,* the value of $\frac{a}{x}$ will become *greater than quantity that can be named.*

A quantity less than any assignable quantity is called zero and is denoted by the symbol 0.

A quantity greater than any assignable quantity is called infinity and denoted by the symbol ∞.

We may now say briefly

when $x = 0$, *the value of* $\frac{a}{x}$ *is* ∞.

Again, if x is a quantity which gradually increases and finally becomes *greater than any assignable quantity* the fraction becomes *smaller than any assignable quantity.* Or more briefly,

when $x = \infty$, *the value of* $\frac{a}{x}$ *is* 0.

430. It should be observed that when the symbols for zero and infinity are used in the sense above explained, they are subject to the rules of signs which affect other algebraical symbols. Thus we shall find it convenient to use a concise statement such as "when $x = +0$, $y = +\infty$" to indicate that when a *very small and positive value* is given to x, the corresponding value of *y is very large and positive.*

431. If we now return to the examples worked out in Art. 425, in Example 1, we see that when $x = \pm\infty$, $y = \pm\infty$; hence the curve extends upwards to infinity in both the first and second quadrants. In Example 2, when $x = +\infty$, $y = +\infty$. Again y is negative between the values 0 and -8 of x. For all negative values of x numerically greater than 8, y is positive, and when $x = -\infty$, $y = +\infty$. Hence the curve extends to infinity in both the first and second quadrants.

The student should now examine tha nature of the graphs in Examples. XLIV-d, when x and y are infinite.

Example. Find the graph of $xy = 4$.

The equation may be written in the form

$$y = \frac{4}{x},$$

from which it appears that when $x = 0$, $y = \infty$, and when $x = \infty$, $y = 0$. Also y is positive when x is positive, and negative when x is negative. Hence the graph must lie entirely in the first and third quadrants.

It will be convenient in this case to take the positive and negative values of the variables separately.

(1) *positive values:*

x	0	1	2	3	4	5	6	...	∞
y	∞	4	2	$1\frac{1}{8}$	1	.8	$\frac{2}{3}$	...	0

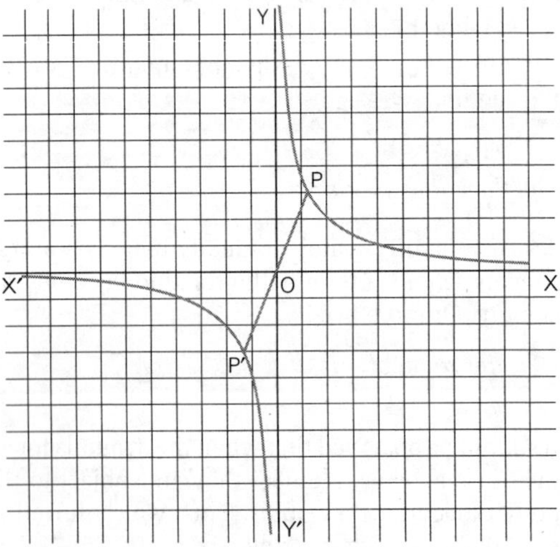

Fig. 10.

Graphically these values show that as we recede further and further from the origin on the x-axis in the positive direction, the values of y are positive and become smaller and smaller. That is, the graph is continually approaching the x-axis in such a way that by taking a sufficiently great positive value of x we obtain a point on the graph as near as we please to the x-axis but never actually reaching it until $x = \infty$. Similarly, as x becomes smaller and smaller the graph approaches more and more nearly to the positive end of the y-axis, never actually reaching it as long as x has any finite positive value, however small.

(2) *Negative values :*

x	-0	-1	-2	-3	-4	-5	...	$-\infty$
y	$-\infty$	-4	-2	$-1\frac{1}{3}$	-1	$-.8$	...	-0

The portion of the graph obtained from these values is in the third quadrant as shown in Fig. 10, and exactly similar to the portion already traced in the first quadrant. It should be noticed that as x passes from $+0$ to -0 the value of y changes from $+\infty$ to $-\infty$. Thus the graph, which in the first quadrant has run away to an infinite distance on the positive side of the y-axis, reappears in the third quadrant coming from an infinite distance on the negative side of that axis. Similar remarks apply to the graph in its relation to the x-axis.

432. When a curve continually approaches more and more nearly to a line without actually meeting it until an infinite distance is reached, such a line is said to be an asymptote the curve. In the above case each of the axes is an asymptote.

433. Every equation of the form $y = \frac{c}{x}$, or $xy = c$, where c is constant, will give a graph similar to that exhibited in the example of Art. 431. The resulting curve is known as a rectangular hyperbola, and has many interesting properties. In particular we may mention that from the form of the equation it is evident that for every point (x, y) on the curve there is a corresponding point $(-x, -y)$ which satisfies the equation. Graphically this amounts to saying that any line through the origin meeting the two branches of the curve in P and P' is bisected at O.

434. In the simpler cases of graphs, sufficient accuracy can usually be obtained by plotting a few points, and there is little difficulty in selecting points with suitable coordinates. But in other cases, and especially when the graph has infinite branches, more care is needed. The most important things to observe are (1) the values for which the function $f(x)$ becomes zero or infinite; and (2) the values which the function assumes for zero and infinite values of x. In other words, we determine the *general character* of the curve in the neighbourhood of the origin, the axes, and infinity. Greater accuracy of detail can then be secured by plotting points at discretion. The selection of such points will usually be suggested by the earlier stages of our work.

The existence of symmetry about either of the axes should also be noted. When an equation contains no *odd* powers of x, the graph is symmetrical with regard to the axis of y. Similarly the absence of odd powers of y indicates symmetry about the axis of x. Compare Art. 425, Ex. 1.

Example. Draw the graph of $y = \dfrac{2x+7}{x-4}$. [See fig. on next page.]

We have $y = \dfrac{2x+7}{x-4} = \dfrac{2+\dfrac{7}{x}}{1-\dfrac{4}{x}}$, the latter form being convenient for infinite values of x.

(i) $\left.\begin{array}{lll} \text{When} & y = 0, & x = -\dfrac{7}{2}, \\ \quad ,, & y = \infty, & x = 4; \end{array}\right\}$

$\therefore$ the curve cuts the axis of x at a distance -3.5 from the origin, and meets the line $x = 4$ at an infinite distance.

If x is positive and very little greater than 4, y is very great and positive. If x is positive and very little less than 4, y is very great and negative. Thus the infinite points on the graph near to the line $x = 4$ have positive ordinates to the right, and negative ordinates to the left of this line.

(ii) $\left.\begin{array}{lll} \text{When} & x = 0, & y = -1.75, \\ \quad ,, & x = \infty, & y = 2; \end{array}\right\}$

$\therefore$ the curve cuts the axis of y at a distance -1.75 from the origin, and meets the line $y = 2$ at an infinite distance.

By taking positive values of y very little greater and very little less than 2, it appears that the curve lies above the line $y = 2$ when $x = +\infty$, and below this line when $x = -\infty$.

The general character of the curve is now determined : the lines $PO'P'$ $(x = 4)$ and $QO'Q'$ $(y = 2)$ are asymptotes; the two branches of the curve lie in the compartments $PO'Q'$, $P'O'Q'$, and the lower branch cuts the axes at distances -3.5 and -1.75 from the origin.

To examine the lower branch in detail values of x may be selected between $-\infty$ and -3.5 and between -3.5 and 4.

x	$-\infty$	...	-16	-8	-6	-3.5	-1	0	2	3	...	4
y	2	...	1.25	.75	.5	0	-1	-1.75	-5.5	-13	...	$-\infty$

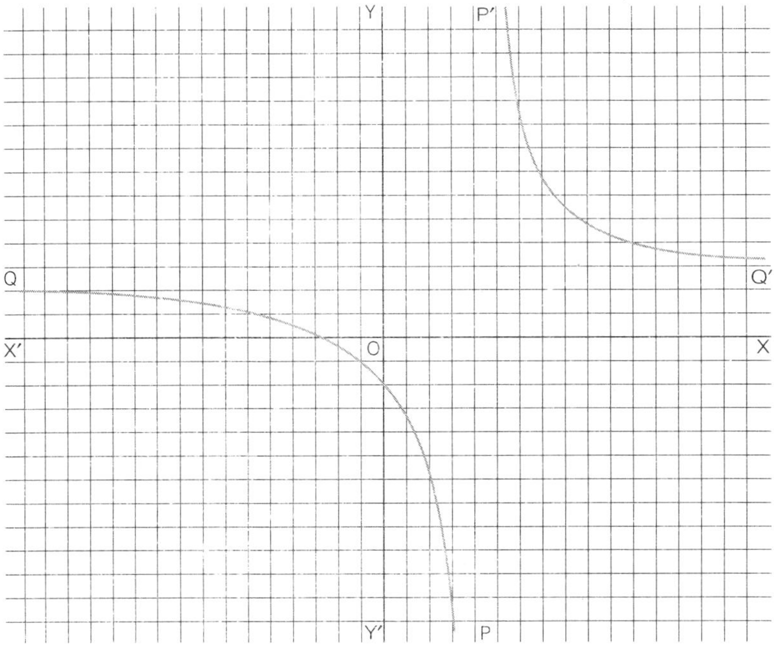

Fig. 11.

The upper branch may now be dealt with in me same way, selecting values of x between 4 and ∞. The graph will be found to be as represented in Fig. 11.

435. When the equation of a curve contains the square or higher power of y, the calculation of the values of y corresponding to selected values of x will have to be obtained by evolution, or else by the aid of logarithms. We give one example to illustrate the way in which a table of four-figure logarithms may be employed in such cases.

Example. Draw the graph of $y^3 = x(9 - x^2)$.

For the sake of brevity we shall confine our attention to that part of the curve which lies to the right of the axis of y, leaving the other half to be traced in like manner by the student.

When $x = 0$, $y = 0$; therefore the curve passes through the origin. Again, y is positive for all values of x between 0 and 3, and vanishes when $x = 3$; for values of x greater than 3, y is negative and continually increases numerically.

x	0	1	2	3	4	5	6	...
x^2	0	1	4	9	16	25	36	...
$9 - x^2$	9	8	5	0	-7	-16	-27	...
y^3	0	8	10	0	-28	-80	-162	...
$\log y^3$			1		*1.4472	1.9031	*2.2095	...
$\log y$			.3333		.4824	.6344	.7365	...
y	0	2	2.15	0	-3.04	-4.31	-5.45	...

These points will be sufficient to give a rough approximation to the curve. For greater accuracy a few intermediate values such as $x = 1.5, 2.5, 3.5 \ldots$ should be taken, and the resulting curve will be as in Fig. 12, in which we have taken *two-tenths of an inch as our linear unit.*

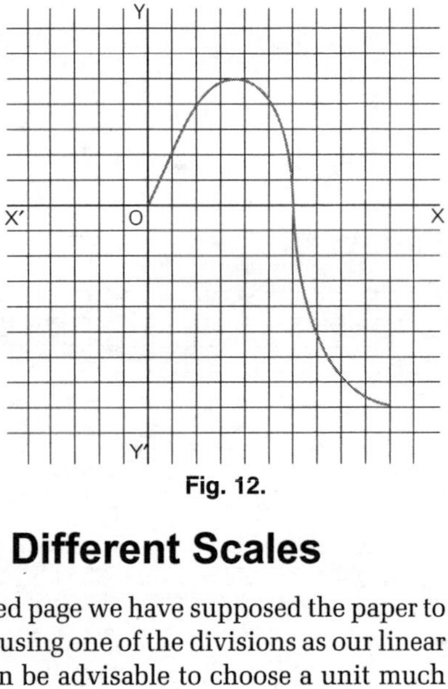

Fig. 12.

Measurement on Different Scales

436. For convenience on the printed page we have supposed the paper to be ruled to tenths of an inch, generally using one of the divisions as our linear unit. In practice, however, it will often be advisable to choose a unit much larger than this in order to get a satisfactory graph.

For the sake of simplicity we have hitherto measured abscissae and ordinates on the same scale, but there is no necessity for so doing, and it will often be found convenient to measure the variables on different scales suggested by the particular conditions of the question.

As an illustration let us take the graph of $y = \frac{x^2}{2}$, given in Art.

*In taking logarithms of the successive values of y^3, the negative sign is disregarded, but care must be taken to insert the proper signs in the last line which gives the successive values of y.

425. If with the same unit as before we plot the graph of $y = x^2$, it will be found to be a curve similar to that drawn on page 415, but elongated in the direction of the axis of y. In fact, it will be the same as if the former graph were stretched to twice its length in the direction of the y-axis.

437. Any equation of the form $y = ax^2$, where a is constant, will represent a parabola elongated more or less according to the value of a; and the larger the value of a the more rapidly will y increase in comparison with x. We might have very large ordinates corresponding to very small abscissae, and the graph might prove quite unsuitable for practical applications. In such a case the inconvenience is obviated by measuring the values of y on a considerably smaller scale than those of x.

Speaking generally, whenever one variable increases much more rapidly than the other, a small unit should be chosen for the rapidly increasing variable and a large one for the other. Further modifications will be suggested in the examples which follow.

438. On the opposite page we give for comparison the graphs of $y = x^2$ (Fig. 13), and $y = 8x^2$ (Fig. 14).

In Fig. 13 the unit for x is twice as great as that for y.

In Fig. 14 the x-unit is ten times the y-unit.

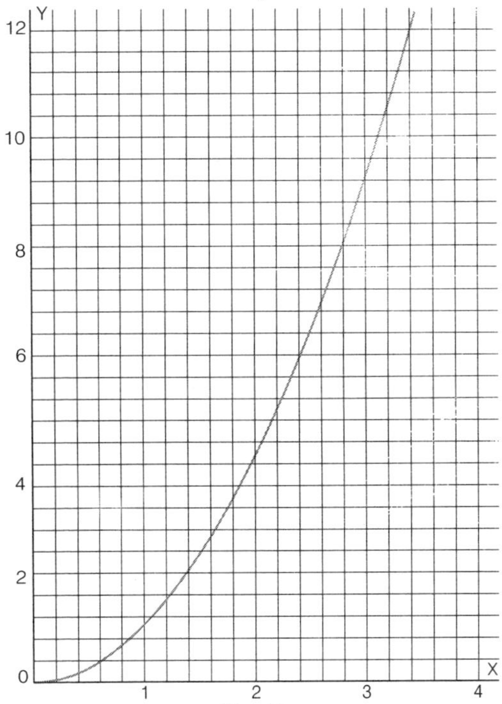

Fig. 13

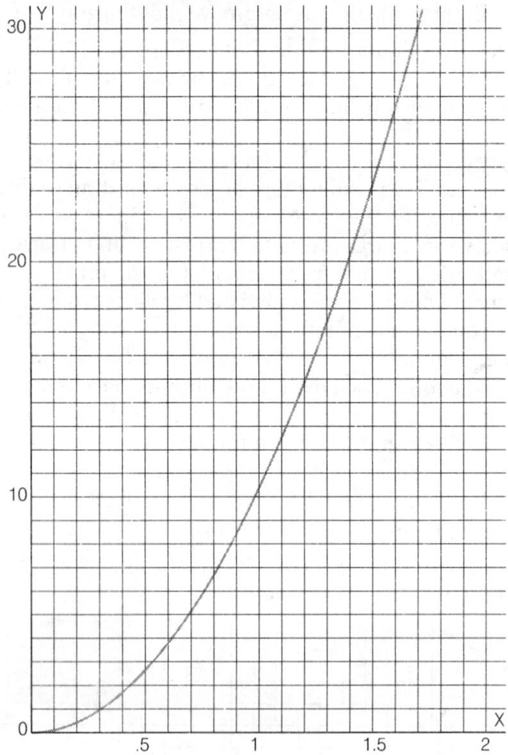

Fig. 14.

It will be useful practice for the student to plot other similar graphs on the same or a larger scale. For example, in Fig. 14 the graphs of $y = 16x^2$ and $y = 2x^2$ may be drawn and compared with that of $y = 8x^2$.

EXAMPLES XLIV-e

1. Plot the graph of $y = x^3$. Show that it consists of a continuous curve lying in the first and third quadrants, crossing the axis of x at the origin. Deduce the graphs of

(i) $y = -x^3$; (ii) $y = \frac{1}{2}x^3$.

2. Plot the graph of $y = x - x^3$. Verify it from the graphs of $y = x$ and $y = x^3$.

3. Plot the graph of $y = \frac{1}{x^2}$, showing that it consists of two branches lying entirely in the first and second quadrants. Examine and compare the nature and position of the graph as it approaches the axes.

4. Disuss the general character of the graph of $y = \frac{a}{x^2}$ where a has some constant integral value. Distinguish between two cases in which a has numerical values, equal in magnitude but opposite in sign.

5. Plot the graphs of

(i) $y = 1 + \frac{1}{x}$, (ii) $y = 2 + \frac{10}{x^2}$.

Verify by deducing them from the graphs of $y = \frac{1}{x}$, and $y = \frac{10}{x^2}$.

6. Plot the graph of $y = x^3 - 3x$. Examine the character of the curve at the points $(1, -2), (-1, 2)$, and show graphically that the roots of the equation $x^3 - 3x = 0$ are approximately -1.732, 0 and 1.732.

7. Solve the equations: $3x + 2y = 16$, $xy = 10$, and verify the solution by finding the coordinates of the points where their graphs intersect.

8. Plot the graphs of (i) $y = \frac{15 - x^2}{x}$, (ii) $x = \frac{10 - y^2}{y}$

and thus verify the algebraical solution of the equations $x^2 + xy = 15$, $y^2 + xy = 10$.

9. Trace the curve whose equation is $y = \frac{x}{2 - x}$, showing that it has two branches, one lying in the first and third quadrants, and the other entirely in the fourth. Find the equations of its asymptotes.

Plot the graphs of

10. $y = \frac{1 + x}{1 - x}$.

11. $y = \frac{1 + x^2}{1 - x}$.

12. $y = \frac{x^2 - 15}{x - 4}$.

13. $y = \frac{(x - 1)(x - 2)}{x - 3}$.

14. $y = \frac{x^2 + x + 1}{x^2 - x + 1}$.

15. $y = \frac{x^2 + 5x + 6}{x^2 + 1}$.

16. $y = x^3 - 6x^2 + 11x - 6$.

17. $10y = x^3 - 5x^2 + x - 5$.

18. $y = \frac{20}{x^2 + 2}$.

19. $y = \frac{40x}{x^2 + 10}$.

20. $y = \frac{x(8 - x)}{x + 5}$.

21. $y = \frac{(x - 2)(x - 3)}{x - 5}$.

22. $y = \frac{(x - 1)(x - 2)(x + 1)}{4}$.

23. $y^2 = x^2 - 5x + 4$.

24. $4y^2 = x^2(5 - x)$.

25. $y^2 = \frac{x(3 - x)(x - 8)}{x^2 + 5}$.

26. $y^2 = \dfrac{(x+7)(x-4)(x-10)}{x^2+5}$. 27. $y^2 = \dfrac{x^2(49-x^2)}{50}$.

28. $y^2 = \dfrac{(81-x^2)(x^2-4)}{100}$. 29. $5y^3 = x(x^2-64)$.

30. $5y^3 = x^2(36-x^2)$.

31. Plot the graphs of $y = x^3$, and of $y = 2x^2 + x - 2$. Hence find the roots of the equation $x^3 - 2x^2 - x + 2 = 0$.

32. Find graphically the roots of the equation
$x^3 - 4x^2 - 5x + 14 = 0$ to three significant figures.

439. Besides the instances already given there are several of the ordinary processes of Arithmetic and Algebra which lend themselves readily to graphical illustration.

For example, the graph of $y = x^2$ may be used to furnish numerical square roots. For since $x = \sqrt{y}$, each ordinate and corresponding abscissa give a number and its square root. Similarly cube roots may be found from the graph of $y = x^3$.

Example 1. Find graphically the cube root of 10 to 3 places of decimals.

The required root is clearly a little greater than 2. Hence it will be enough to plot the graph of $y = x^3$ taking $x = 2.1, 2.2...$. The corresponding ordinates are 9.26, 10.65, ...

When $x = 2$, $y = 8$. Take the axes through this point and let the units for x and y be 20 cm and 1 cm respectively. On this scale the portion of the graph differs but little from a straight line, and yields results to a high degree of accuracy.

When $y = 10$, the measured value of x will be found to be 2.154.

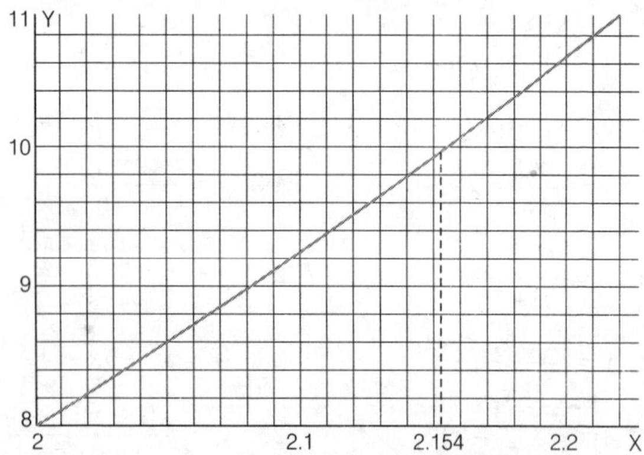

Fig. 15.

Example 2. Show graphically that the expression $4x^2 + 4x - 3$ is negative for all real values of x between .5 and – 1.5, and positive for all real values of x outside these limits. [Fig. 16.]

Put $y = 4x^2 + 4x - 3$, and proceed as in the example given in Art. 427, taking the unit for x four times as great as that for y. It will be found that the graph cuts the axis of x at points whose abscissae are .5 and – 1.5; and that it lies below the axis of x between these points. That is, the value of y is negative so long as x lies between .5 and – 1.5, and positive for all other values of x.

Or we may proceed as follows:

Put $y_1 = 4x^2$, and $y_2 = -4x + 3$, and plot the graphs of these two equations. At their points of intersection $y_1 = y_2$, and the values of x we have

$$4x^2 = -4x + 3, \text{ or } 4x^2 + 4x - 3 = 0.$$

Thus the roots of the equation $4x^2 + 4x - 3 = 0$ are furnished by the abscissae of the common points of the graphs of $4x^2$ and $- 4x + 3$.

Again, between the values .5 and – 1.5 for x it will be found graphically that y_1 is less than y_2, hence $y_1 - y_2$, or $4x^2 + 4x - 3$ is negative.

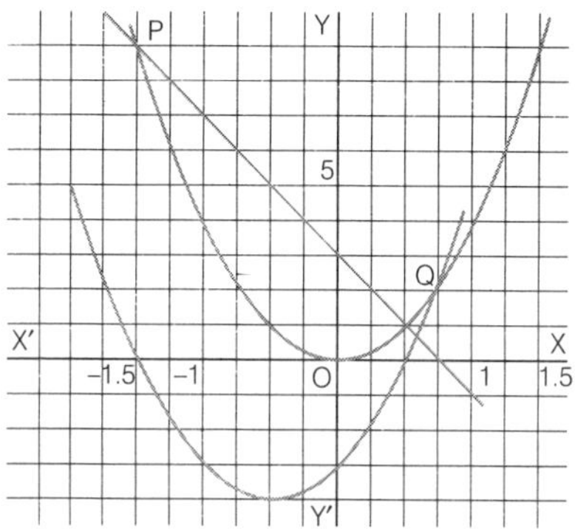

Fig. 16.

Both solutions are here exhibited.

The upper curve is the graph of $y = 4x^2$; PQ is the graph of $y = -4x + 3$; and the lower curve is the graph of $y = 4x^2 + 4x - 3$.

440. Of the two methods in the last example the first is the more direct and instructive; but the second has this advantage:

If a number of equations of the form $x^2 = px + q$ have to be solved graphically, $y = x^2$ can be plotted once for all on a convenient scale, and $y = px + q$ can then be readily drawn for different values of p and q.

Equations of higher degree may be treated similarly.

For Example, the solution of such equations as

$$x^3 = px + q, \text{ or } x^3 = ax^2 + bx + c$$

can be made to depend on the intersection of $y = x^3$ with other graphs.

Example. Find the real roots of the equations

(i) $x^3 - 2.5x - 3 = 0$; (ii) $x^3 - 3x + 2 = 0$

Here, we have to find the points of intersection of

(i) $y = x^3$ $y = 2.5x + 3$

(ii) $y = x^3$ $y = 3x - 2$

Plot the graphs of these equations, choosing the unit for x five times as great as that for y.

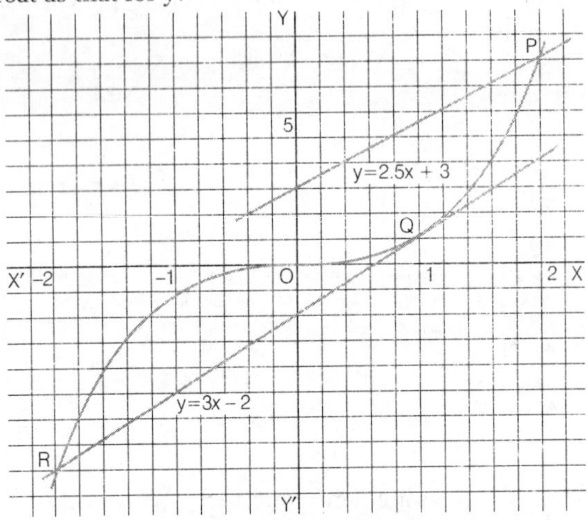

Fig. 17.

It will be seen that $y = 2.5x + 3$ meets $y = x^3$ only at the point for which $x = 2$. Thus 2 is the only real root of equation (i).

Again $y = 3x - 2$ *touches* $y = x^3$ at the point for which $x = 1$, and cuts it where $x = -2$.

Corresponding to the former point the equation $x^3 - 3x + 2 = 0$ has two equal roots. Thus the roots of (ii) are 1, 1, – 2.

441. In Art. 421 we have given the graphical solution of two *linear* simultaneous equations. As the principle is the same for equations of any degree, the few examples of this kind on pages 419, 428 have been given without special explanation. It may, however, be instructive here to show the graphical solution of some of the equations discussed in Chap. XXVI.

Example. Solve the following equations graphically:

(i) $\left.\begin{aligned} x - y &= 2 \\ xy &= 35 \end{aligned}\right\}$ (Compare Art. 203, Ex 2.)

(ii) $\left.\begin{aligned} x^2 + y^2 &= 74 \\ xy &= 35 \end{aligned}\right\}$ (Compare Art. 204, Ex. 1.)

Here, $xy = 35$ is represented by a rectangular hyperbola [art. 431]; $x - y = 2$ is the line QS, and $s^2 + y^2 = 74$ is represented by the circle.

The roots of (i) are the coordinates of Q and S; that is

$x = 7$, $y = 5$; or $x = -5$, $y - 7$.

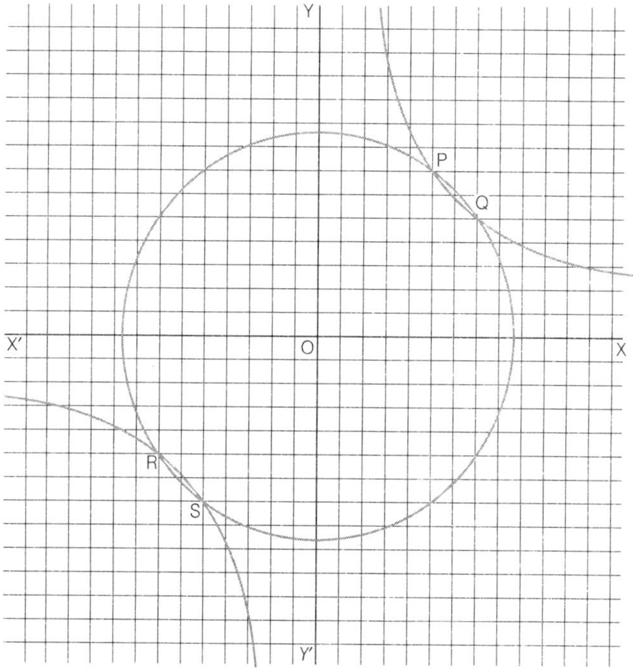

Fig. 18.

The roots of (ii) are the coordinates of P, Q, R and S; that is, $x = 5$, $y = 7$; $x = 7$, $y = 5$; $x = -7$;$y = -5$ $x = -5$, $y = -7$.

EXAMPLES XLIV-f

1. Draw the graph of $y = x^2$ on a scale twice as large as that in Fig · 13, and employ it to find the squares of .72, 1.7, 3.4; and the square roots of 7.56. 5.29, 9.61.

2. Draw the graph of $y = \sqrt{x}$, taking the unit of y five times as great as that for x.
By means of this curve check the values of the square roots found in Example 1.

3. From the graph of $v = x^3$ (on the scale of the diagram of Art. 439) find the values of $\sqrt[3]{9}$ ana $\sqrt[3]{9.8}$ to 4 significant figures.

4. A boy who was ignorant of the rule for cube root required the value of $\sqrt[3]{14.71}$ He plotted the graph of $y = x^3$, using for x the values 2.2, 2.3, 2.4, 2.5, and found 2.45 as the value of the cube root. Verify this process in detail. From the same graph find the, value of $\sqrt[3]{13.8}$

5. Find the graphically the values of x for which the expression $x^2 - 2x - 8$ vanishes. Show that for values of x between these limits the expression is negative and for all other values positive. Find the least value of the expression.

6. Form the graph in the preceeding example show that for any value of a greater than 1 the equation $x^2 - 2x + a = 0$ cannot have real roots.

7. Show graphically that the expression $x^2 - 4x + 7$ is positive for all real values of x.

8. On the same axes draw the graphs of
$y = x^2$, $y = x + 6$, $y = x - 6$, $y = -x + 6$, $y = -x - 6$.
Hence, discuss the roots of the four equations:
$x^2 - x - 6 = 0$, $x^2 - x + 6 = 0$, $x^2 + x - 6 = 0$, $x^2 + x + 6 = 0$

9. If x is real, prove graphically that $5 - 4x - x^2$ is not greater than 9; and that $4x^2 - 4x + 3$ is not less than 2. Between what values of x is the first expression positive?

10. Solve the equation $x^3 = 3x^2 + 6x - 8$ graphically, and show that the function $x^3 - 3x^2 - 6x + 8$ is positive for all values of x between -2 and 1, and negative for all values of x between 1 and 4.

11. Show graphically that the equation $x^3 + px + q = 0$ has only one real root when p is positive.

12. Trace the curve whose equation is $y = 2^x$. Find the approximate values of $2^{4.75}$ and 2^{525}. Express 12 as a power of 2 approximately. Prove also that $\log_2 26.9 + \log_2 38 = 10$.

13. By repeated evolution find the values of $10^{1/2}$, $10^{1/4}$, $10^{1/8}$, $10^{1/16}$. By multiplication find the values of $10^{3/16}$, $10^{5/16}$, $10^{6/16}$, $10^{7/16}$, $10^{9/16}$. Use these values to plot a portion of the curve $y = 10^x$ on a large scale. Find correct to three places of decimals the values of log 3, log 1.68, log 2.24, log 34.3. Also by choosing numerical values for a and b, verify the laws

$$\log ab = \log a + \log b;$$

$$\log \frac{a}{b} = \log a - \log b.$$

[By using paper ruled to tenths of an inch, if 10 in, and 1 in. be taken as units for x and y respectively, a diagonal scale will give values of x correct to three decimal places and values of y correct to two.]

14. Calculate the values of $x(9 - x)^2$ for the values 0, 1, 2, 3, ... 9 of x. Draw the graph of $x(9 - x)^2$ from $x = 0$ to $x = 9$.

If a very thin elastic rod, 9 cm in length, fixed at one end, swings like a pendulum, the expression $x\,(9 - x)^2$ measures the tendency of the rod to break at a place x cm from the point of suspension, from the graph find where the rod is most likely to break.

15. If a man spends ₹ 48 a year on tea whatever the price of tea is, what amounts will be receive when the price is 4, 4.5, 5, 6,8 rupees a kilo respectively? Give your results to the nearest $\frac{1}{10}$ kilo. Draw a curve to the scale of 1 kilo to the cm and Re 1 to - the cm, to show the number of kilos that he would receive at intermediate prices.

16. The reciprocal of a number is multiplied by 2.25 and the product is added to the number. Find graphically what the number must be if the resulting expression has the least possible value.

17. Show graphically that the expression $4x^2 + 2x - 8.75$ is positive for all real values of x except such as lie between 1.25 and −1.75. For what value of x is the expression a minimum?

18. Find graphically the real roots of the equations:

(i) $x^3 + x - 2 = 0$ (ii) $x^3 - 7x + 6 = 0$

19. Draw the graphs of $x + y = 9\frac{1}{2}$, $xy = 12$, $x^2 - y^2 = 32$

on the same axes. Hence find the solutions of the following pairs on simultaneous equations:

(i) $\left.\begin{aligned} x + y^2 &= 9\frac{1}{2} \\ xy &= 12 \end{aligned}\right\}$ (ii) $\left.\begin{aligned} x^2 - y^2 &= 32 \\ x + y &= 9\frac{1}{2} \end{aligned}\right\}$ (iii) $\left.\begin{aligned} x^2 - y^2 &= 32 \\ xy &= 12 \end{aligned}\right\}$

20. Draw the graphs of $y = x^3$ and $y = 3x^2 - 4$ on the same axes, and find the roots of the equation $x^3 - 3x^2 + 4 = 0$.

Show that the expression $x^3 - 3x^2 + 4$ is negative for values of x less than -1, and positive for all other values of x.

21. From a graphical consideration of the following pairs of simultaneous equations:

(i) $\left.\begin{aligned} x^2 + y^2 &= a \\ xy &= b \end{aligned}\right\}$ (ii) $\left.\begin{aligned} x + y &= a \\ xy &= b \end{aligned}\right\}$,

explain why (i) has either *four* solutions or none, while (ii) has *two* solutions or none.

22. Draw the graphs of $y = x^3$ and $y = x^2 + 3x - 3$ on the same axes. Hence, find the roots of the equation $x^3 - x^2 - 3x + 3 = 0$ to three places of decimals, and discuss the sign of the expression $x^3 - x^2 - 3x + 3$ for different values of x.

Practical Applications

442. In all the cases hitherto considered the equation of the curve has been given, and its graph has been drawn by first selecting values of x and y which satisfy the equation, and then drawing a line so as to pass through the plotted points.

We thus determine accurately the position of as many points as we please, and the process employed assures us that they all lie on the graph we are seeking. We could obtain the same result without knowing the equation of the curve provided that we were furnished with a sufficient number of corresponding values of the variables *accurately calculated.*

Sometimes from the nature of the case the form of the equation which connects two variables is known. For example, if a quantity y is directly proportional to another quantity x it is evident that we may put $y = ax$, where a is some constant quantity.

Hence, in all cases of direct proportionality between two quantities the graph which exhibits their variations is a straight line through the origin. Also since two points arc sufficient to determine a straight line, it follows that in the cases under consideration we only require to know the position of one point besides the origin, and this will be furnished by any pair of simultaneous values of the variables.

Example 1. Given that 5.5 kilograms are roughly equal to 12.125 pounds, show graphically how to express any number of pounds in kilograms. Express $7\frac{1}{2}$ lbs. in kilograms, and $4\frac{1}{4}$ kilograms in pounds.

Here, measuring pounds horizontally and kilograms vertically, the required graph is obtained at once by joining the origin to the point whose coordinates are 12.125 and 5.5.

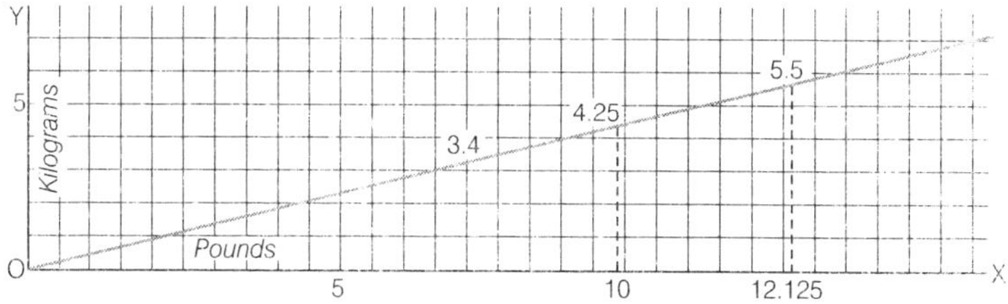

Fig. 19.

By measurement it will be found that $7\frac{1}{2}$ lb = 3.4 kilograms, and $4\frac{1}{2}$ kilograms = 9.37 lb.

Example 2. The expenses of a school are partly constant and partly proportional to the number of boys. The expenses were ₹ 6500 for 105 boys, and ₹ 7420 for 128. Draw a graph to represent the expenses for any number of boys; find the expenses for 115 boys, and the number of boys that can be maintained at a cost of ₹ 7100.

If the expenses for x boys are represented by ₹ y, it is evident that x and y satisfy a linear equation $y = ax + b$, where a and b are constant. Hence, the graph is a straight line.

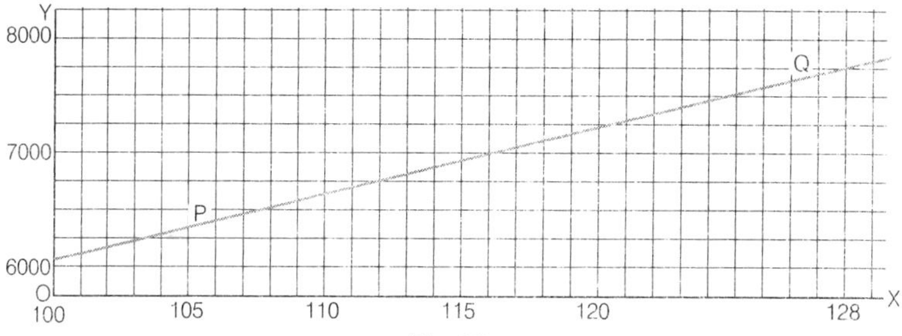

Fig. 20.

As the numbers are large, it will be convenient if we begin measuring ordinates at 6000, and abscissae at 100. This enables us to bring the requisite portion of the graph into a smaller compass. The points P and Q are determined by the data of the question, and the line PQ is the graph required. By measurement we find that when $x = 115$, $y = 6900$; and that when $y = 7100$, $x = 120$. Thus the required answers are ₹ 6900, and 120 boys.

442. Sometimes corresponding values of two variables are obtained by observation or experiment. In such cases the data cannot be regarded as free from error; the position of the plotted points cannot be absolutely relied on; and we cannot correct irregularities in the graph by plotting other points selected at discretion.

All we can do is to draw a curve to lie as evenly as possible among the plotted points, passing through some perhaps, and with the rest fairly distributed on either side of the curve. As an aid to drawing an even continuous curve a thin piece of wood or other flexible material may be bent into the requisite curve, and held in position while the line is drawn.

When the plotted points lie approximately on a straight line, the simplest plan is to use a piece of tracing paper or celluloid on which a straight line has been drawn. When this has been placed in the right position the extremities can be marked on the squared paper, and joining these points the approximate graph is obtained.

Example 1. The following table gives statistics of the population of certain country, where P is the number of millions at the beginning **F** each of the years specified.

One of "Brook's Flexible Curves" will be found very useful.

Year	1830	1835	1840	1850	1860	1865	1870	1870	1880
P	20	2.21	23.5	29.0	29.0	34.2	38.2	41.0	49.4

Let t be the time in the years from 1830. Plot the values of P vertically and those of t horizontally and exhibit the relation between P and t by a simple curve passing fairly evenly among the plotted points. Find what the population was at the beginning of the years 1848 and 1875.

The graph is given in Fig. 21 on the opposite page. The populations in 1848 and 1875, at the points A and B respectively, will be found to be 27.8 millions and 45.3 millions.

Example 2. Corresponding values of x and y are given in the following table:

x	1	4	6.8	8	9.5	12	14.4
y	4	8	12.2	13	15.3	20	24.8

Supposing these values to involve errors of observation, draw the, graph approximately and determine the most probable equation between x and y. [See Fig, 22 on p. 440.]

After carefully plotting the given points we see that a straight line can be drawn passing through three of them and lying evenly among the others. This is the required graph. Assuming $y = ax + b$ for its equation, we find the values of a and b by selecting two pairs of simultaneous values of x and y.

Thus, substituting $x = 4$, $y = 8$, and $x = 12$, $y = 20$ in the equation, we obtain $a = 1.5$, $b = 2$. Thus the equation of the graph is $y = 1.5x + 2$.

444. In the last example as the graph is linear it can be produced to any extent within the limits of the paper, and so any value of one of the variables being determined, the corresponding value of the other can be read off. When large values' are in question this method is not only inconvenient but unsafe, owing to the fact that any divergence from accuracy in the portion of the graph drawn is increased when the curve is produced beyond the limits of the plotted points. The following example illustrates the method of procedure in such cases.

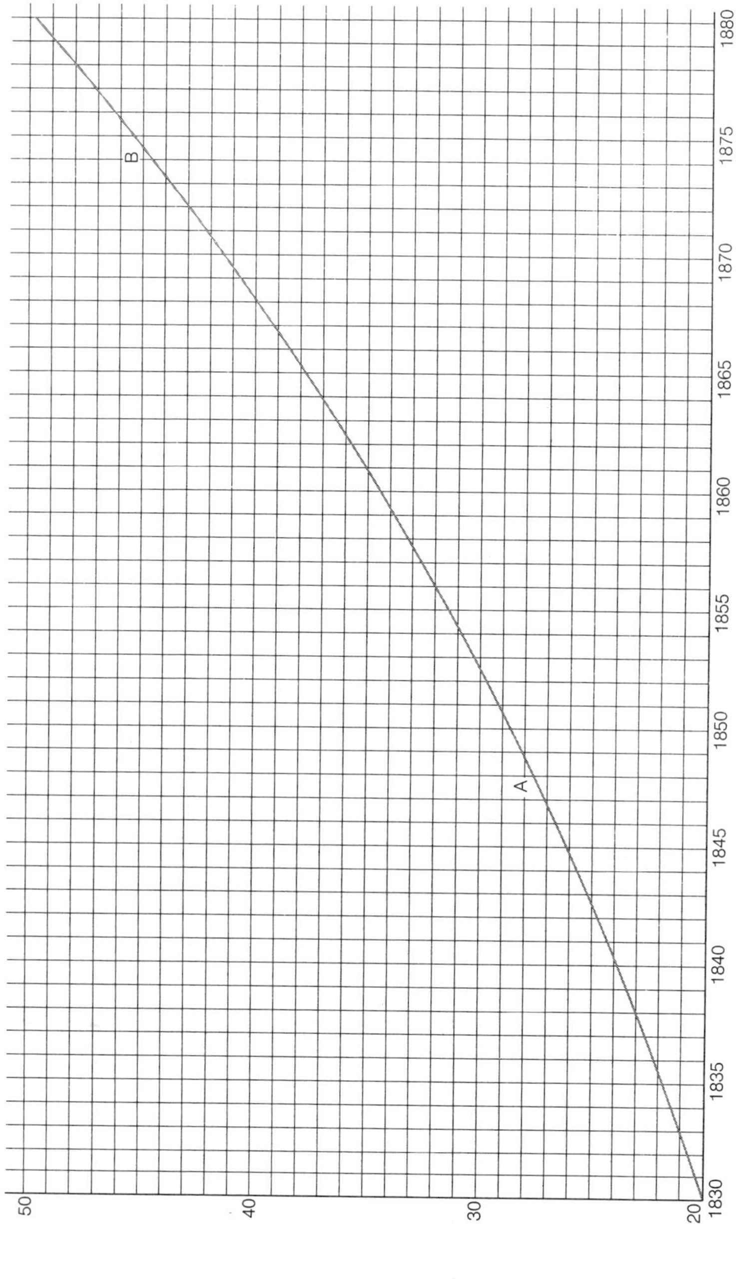

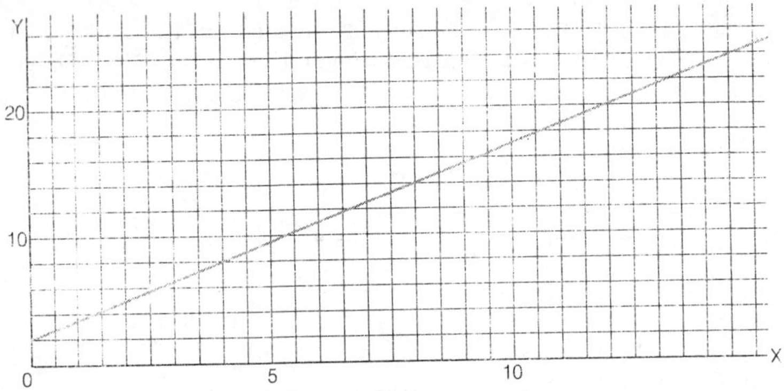

Fig. 22.

Example. In a certain machine P is the force in kg required to raise a weight of W kg. The following corresponding values of P and W were obtained experimentally:

P	3.08	3.9	6.8	8.8	9.2	11*	13.3
W	21	36.25	66.2	87.5	103.75	122	152.5

By plotting these values on squared paper draw the graph connecting P and W, and read off the value of P when $W = 70$. Also determine a linear law connecting P and W; find the force necessary to raise a weight of 310 kg, and also the weight which could be raised by a force of 180.6kg.

As the page is too small to exhibit the graphical work on a convenient scale we shall merely indicate the steps of the solution, which is similar in detail to that of the last example.

Plot the values of P vertically and the values of W horizontally. It will be found that a straight line can be drawn through the points corresponding to the results marked with an asterisk, and lying evenly among the other points. From this graph we find that when $W = 70$, $P = 7$.

Assume $P = aW + b$, and substitute for P and W from the values corresponding to the two points through which the line passes. By solving the resulting equations we obtain $a = .08$, $b = 1.4$. Thus the linear equation connecting P and W is $P = .08W + 1.4$.

This is called the Law of Machine. From this equation, when $W = 310$, $P = 26.2$, and when $P = 180.6$, $W = 2240$.

Thus a force of 26.2 kg will raise a weight of 310 kg; and when a force of 180.6 kg is applied the weight raised is 2240kg.

NOTE. The equation of the graph is not only useful for determining results difficult to obtain graphically, but it can always be used to check results found by measurement.

445. The example in the last article is a simple illustration of a method of procedure which is common in the laboratory or workshop, the object being to determine the law connecting two variables when a certain number of simultaneous values have been determined by experiment or observation.

Though we can always draw a graph to lie fairly among the plotted points corresponding to the observed values, unless the graph is a straight line it may be difficult to find its equation except by some indirect method.

For example, suppose x and y are quantities which satisfy an equation of the form $xy = ax + by$, and that this law has to be discovered.

By writing the equation in the form $\frac{a}{y} + \frac{b}{x} = 1$,

or $\quad au + bv = 1$

where $u = \frac{1}{y}$, $v = \frac{1}{x}$, it is clear that u, v satisfy the equation of a straight line. In other words, if we were to plot the points corresponding to the reciprocals of the given values, their linear connection would be at once apparent. Hence, the values of a and b could be found as in previous examples, and the required law in the form $xy = ax + by$ could be determined.

Again, suppose x and y satisfy an equation of the form $x^n y = c$, where n and c are constants. By taking logarithms, we have $n \log x + \log y = \log c$.

The form of this equation shows that $\log x$ and $\log y$ satisfy the equation to a straight line, If, therefore, the values of $\log x$ and $\log y$ are plotted, a linear graph can be drawn, and the constants n and c can be found as before.

Example, The weight, y grammes, necessary to produce a given deflection in the middle of a beam supported at two points, x centimetres apart, is determined experimentally for a number of values of x with results given in the following table:

x	50	60	70	80	90	100
y	270	150	160	60	47	32

Assuming that x and y are connected by the equation $x^n y = c$ find n and c.

From pages 382, 383 we obtain the annexed values of $\log x$ and $\log y$ corresponding to the observed values of x and y.

By plotting these we obtain the graph given in Fig. 23, and its equation is of the form $n \log x + \log y = \log c$.

$\log x$	$\log y$
1.699	2.431
1.778	2.176
1.845	2.000
1.903	1.778
1.954	1.672
2.000	1.519

To obtain n and c, *choose two extreme points through which the line passes.* It will be found that when

$$\log x = 1.642, \log y = 2.6$$

$$\log x = 2.1, \quad \log y = 1.21 \text{ and when}$$

Substituting these values, we have

$$2.6 + n \times 1.642 = \log c \ldots\ldots\ldots\ldots \qquad \ldots\text{(i)}$$

$$1.21 + n \times 2.1 = \log c \ldots\ldots\ldots\ldots \qquad \ldots\text{(ii)}$$

$$1.39 - 0.458\, n = 0;$$

whence $n = 3.04$.

$\therefore$ from (ii) $\log c = 6.38 + 1.21 = 7.59$;

$\therefore$ $c = 39 \times 10^6$, from the tables.

Thus the required equation is $x^3 y = 39 \times 10^6$.

The student should work through this example in detail on a larger scale. The adjoining figure was drawn on paper ruled to half centimetre and then reduced to a quarter the original scale.

EXAMPLES XLIV-g

1. Given that 6.01 yards $= 5.5$ metres, draw the graph showing the equivalent of any number of yards when expressed in metres. Show that 22.2 yards $= 20.3$ metres approximately.

2. Draw a graph showing the relation between equal weights in grains and grams, having given that 18.1 grains $= 11.7$ grams.

Express (i) 3.5 grams in grains.

(ii) 3.09 grains as a decimal of a gram.

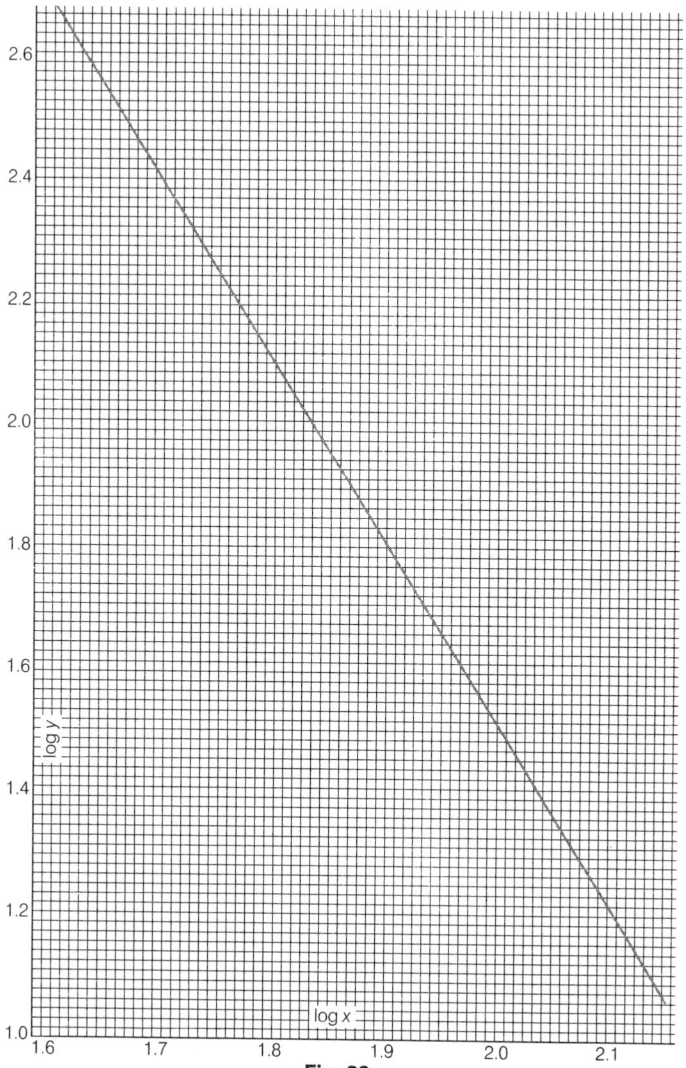

Fig. 23.

3. If 3.26 inches are equivalent to 8.28 centimetres, show how to determine graphically the number of inches corresponding to a given number of centimetres. Obtain the number of inches in a metre, and the number of centimetres in a yard. What is the equation of the graph.

4. The following table gives approximately the circumferences of circles corresponding to different radii:

C	15.7	20.1	31.4	44	52
r	2.5	3.2	5	7	8.3

Plot the values on squared paper, and from the graph determine the diameter of a circle whose circumference is 12.1 cm and the circumference of a circle whose radius is 2.8 cm.

5. For a given temperature, C degrees on a Centigrade are equal to F degrees on a Fahrenheit thermometer. The following table gives a series of corresponding values of F and C.

C	−10	−5	0	5	10	15	25	40
F	14	23	32	41	50	59	77	104

Draw a graph to show the Fahrenheit reading corresponding to a given Centigrade temperature, and find the Fahrenheit readings corresponding to 12.5° C and 31° C.

By observing the form of the graph find the algebraical relation between F and C.

6. For a certain book it costs a publisher ₹ 1000 to prepare the type and Re 1 to print each copy. Find an expression for the total "cost in rupees of x copies. Make a diagram on a scale of 1 cm to 1000 copies, and 1 cm to ₹ 1000 to show the total cost of any number of copies up to 5000. Read off the cost of 2500 copies, and the number of copies costing ₹ 5250.

7. At different ages the mean after-lifetime ("expectation of life") of males, calculated on the death rates of 1871-1880, was given by the following table :

Age	6	10	14	18	22	26	27
Expectation	50.38	47.60	44.26	40.96	37.89	34.96	34.24

Draw a graph to show the expectation of any male between the ages of 6 and 27, and from it determine the expectation of persons aged 12 and 20.

8. In a Mutual Assurance Society the premium (₹ P) to insure ₹ 100 at different ages is given approximately by the following table :

Age	20	22	25	30	35	40	45	50	55
P	1.8	1.9	2.0	2.3	2.3	2.7	3.6	4.4	5.5

Illustrate the same statistics graphically, and estimate to the nearest onee-tenth of a rupee the premiums for persons aged 34 and 43.

9. If W is the weight in gm required to stretch an elastic string till its length is l cm, plot the following values of W and l:

W	2.5	3.75	6.25	7.5	10	11.25
l	8.5	8.7	9.1	9.3	9.7	9.9

From the graph determine the unstretched length of the string, and the weight the string will support when its length is 12 cm.

10. In the following table P and A (expressed in hundreds of rupees) represent the Principal and corresponding Amount for 1 year at 3 per cent simple interest.

P	2.3	2.7	3.0	3.5	3.9	5.2	7.5
A	2.369	2.781	3.090	3.605	4.017	5.356	7.828

Plot the values of P and A on a large scale, and from the graph determine the Principal which will amount to (i) ₹ 329.60 ; (ii) ₹ 597.40.

11. The highest and lowest marks gained in an examination are 297 and 132 respectively. These have to be reduced in such a way that the maximum for the paper (200) shall be given to the first candidate, and that there shall be a range of 150 marks between the first and last. Find the equation between x, the actual marks gained, and y, the corresponding marks when reduced.

Draw the graph of this equation, and read off the marks which should be given to candidates who gained 200, 262, 163 marks in the examination.

12. A body starting with an initial velocity, and subject to an acceleration in the direction of motion, has a velocity of v cm per second after t seconds. If corresponding values of v and t are given by the annexed table,

v	9	13	17	21	25	29	33	37	41	45
t	1	2	3	4	5	6	7	8	9	10

plot the graph exhibiting the velocity at any given time. Find from it (i) the initial velocity, (ii) the time which has elapsed when the velocity is 28 cm per second. Also find the equation between v and t.

13. The connection between the areas of equilateral triangles and their bases (in corresponding units) is given by the following table :

Area	.43	1.73	3.90	6.93	10.82	15.59
Base	1	2	3	4	5	6

Illustrate these results graphically, and determine the area of an equilateral triangle on a base of 2.4 cm.

14. A body falling freely under gravity drops s metres in t seconds from the time of starting. If corresponding values of s and t at intervals of half a second are as follows:

t	.5	1	1.5	2	2.5	3	3.5	4
s	1.22	4.87	10.96	19.48	30.48	43.84	58.8	77.92

draw the curve connecting s and t, and find from it

(i) the distance through which the body has fallen after 1.8 seconds.

(ii) the depth of a well if a stone takes 3.16 seconds to reach the bottom.

15. A body is projected with a given velocity at a given angle to the horizon, and the height in metres reached after t seconds is given by the equation $h = 19.48t - 4.87t^2$. Find the values of h at intervals of $\frac{1}{4}$th of a second and draw the path described by the body. Find the maximum value of h, and the time after projection before the body reaches the ground.

16. The keeper of a hotel finds that when he has G guests a day his total daily profit is P rupees. If the following numbers are averages obtained by comparison of many days' accounts determine a simple relation between P and G.

G	21	27	29	32	35
P	–1.8	2	3.2	4.5	6.6

For what number of guests would he just have no profit?

17. A man wishes to place in his catalogue a list of a certain class of fishing rods varying from 3 to 5 metres in length. Four sizes have been made at prices given in the following table :

3 metres	4 metres	4.5 metres	5 metres
Rs 15	Rs 22	Rs 31	Rs 38

Draw a graph to exhibit prices for rods of intermediate lengths, and from it determine the probable prices for rods of 4.1 metres and 4.7 metres.

18. The following table gives the sun's position at 7 a.m. on different dates:

Mar. 28	Ap. 3	Ap. 20	May 8	May 27	June 22	July 18	Aug. 5	Aug. 25
80° E.	82° E .	85° E.	89° E.	92° E.	95° E.	94° E.	91° E.	85° E.

Show these results graphically, and estimate approximately the sun's position at the same hour on June 8th.

19. At a given temperature p kg per square inch represents the pressure of a gas which occupies a volume of v cubic cm. Draw a curve connecting p and v from the following table of corresponding values :

P	36	30	25.7	22.5	20	18	16.4	15
V	5	6	7	8	9	10	11	12

20. Plot on squared paper the following measured values of x and y, and determine the most probable equation between x and y:

x	3	5	8.3	11	13	15.5	18.6	23	28
y	2	2.2	3.4	3.8	4	4.6	5.4	6.2	7.25

21. Corresponding values of x and y are given in the following table :

x	1	3.1	6	9.5	12.5	16	19	23
y	2	2.8	4.2	5.3	6.6	8.3	9	10.8

Supposing these values to involve errors of observation, draw the graph approximately, and determine the most probable equation between x and y. Find the correct value of y when $x = 19$, and the correct value of x when $y = 2.8$.

22. The following corresponding values of x and y were obtained experimentally:

x	0.5	1.7	3.0	4.7	5.7	7.1	8.7	9.9	10.6	11.8
y	148	186	265	326	388	436	529	562	611	652

It is known that they are connected by an equation of the form $y = ax + b$, but the values of x and y involve errors of measurement. Find the most probable values of a and b, and estimate the error in the measured value of y when $x = 9.9$.

23. In a certain machine P is the force in kg required to raise a weight of W kg. The following corresponding values of P and W were obtained experimentally:

P	2.8	3.7	4.8	5.5	6.5	7.3	8	9.5	10.4	11.75
W	20	25	31.7	35.6	45	52.4	57.5	65	71	82.5

Draw the graph connecting P and W, and read off the value of P when $W = 60$. Also determine the law of the machine, and find from it the weight which could be raised by a force of 31.7 kg.

24. The following values of x and y, some of which are slightly inaccurate, are connected by an equation of the form $y = ax^2 + b$.

x	1	1.6	3	3.7	4	5	.7	6	6.3	7
y	3.25	4	5	6.5	7.4	9.25	10.5	11.6	14	15.25

By plotting these values draw the graph, and find the most probable values of a and b.

Find the true of x when $y = 4$, and the true value of y when $x = 6$.

25. The following table gives corresponding values of two variables x and y:

x	2.75	3	3.2	3.5	4.3	4.5	5.3	6	7	8	10
y	11	9.8	8	6.5	6.1	5.4	5	4.3	4.1	4	3.9

These values involve errors of observation, but the true values are known to satisfy an equation of the form $xy = ax + by$. Draw the graph by plotting the points determined by the above table, and find the most probable values of a and b. Find the correct values of y corresponding to $x = 3.5$ and $x = 7$.

26. Observed values of x and y are given as follows:

x	100	90	70	60	50	40
y	30	31.08	33.5	35.56	37.8	40.7

Assuming that x and y are connected by an equation of the form $xy^n = c$, find n and c.

27. The following values of x and y involve errors of observation:

x	66.83	63.10	58.88	51.52	48.53	44.16	40.36
y	144.5	158.5	177.8	208.9	236.0	264.9	309.0

If x and y satisfy an equation of the form $xy^n = c$, find n and c.

Miscellaneous Applications of Linear Graphs

446. When two quantities x and y are so related that a change in one produces a proportional change in the other, their variations can always be expressed by an equation of the form $y = ax$, where a is some constant quantity.

Hence in all such cases the graph which exhibits their variations is a straight line through the origin, so that in order to draw 'the graph it is only necessary to know the position of one other point on it.

Such examples as deal with work and time, distance and time (when the speed is uniform), quantity and cost of material, principal and simple interest at a given rate per cent, may all be illustrated by linear graphs through the origin.

EXAMPLE 1. *At 8 a.m. A starts from P to ride to Q which is 48 km distant. At the same time B sets out from Q to meet A. If A rides at 8 km an hour, and rests half an hour at the end of every hour, while B walks uniformly at 4 km an hour, find graphically*

(i) *the time and place of meeting;*

(ii) *the distance between* A *and* B *at 11 a.m.;*

(iii) *at what time they are 14 km apart.*

In Fig. 24, on the back page, let the position of P be chosen as origin; let time be measured horizontally from 8 a.m. (2 cm to 1 hour), and let distance be measured vertically (1 cm to 10 km).

In 1 hr A rides 8 km; therefore the point D (1,8) marks his position at 9 a.m. In the next half-hour he makes no advance towards Q; therefore the corresponding portion of the graph is DE. The details of A's motion may now be completed by the broken line PDEFGHKX.

On the vertical axis mark PQ to represent 48 km and mark the hours on the horizontal line through Q. At 9 a.m. B has walked 4 km towards P. Measuring a distance to represent 4 km *downwards* we get the point R, and QR produced is the graph of B's motion. It cuts A's graph at X. Hence the point of meeting is X, which is 28 km from P, and the time is 1 p.m. The distance between A and B at any time is shown by the difference of the ordinates. Thus at 11 a.m. their distance apart is MG, which represents 20 km.

Lastly, NT represents 14 km; thus A and B are 14 km apart at 11.30 a.m.

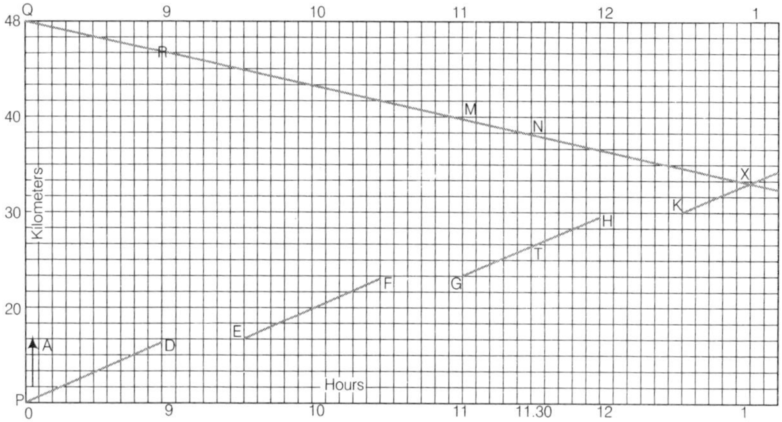

Fig. 24

EXAMPLE 2. A, B, and C run a race of 300 metres. A and C start from scratch, and A covers the distance in 40 seconds, beating C by 60 metres. B, with 12 metres start, beats A by 4 seconds. Supposing the rates of running in each case to be uniform, find graphically the relative positions of the runners when B passes the winning post. Find also by how many yards B is ahead of A when the latter has run three-fourths of the course.

In Fig. 25 let time be measured horizontally (1 cm to 10 seconds), and distance vertically (1 cm to 30 metres). O is the starting point for A and C; take OP equal to 0.4 cm, representing 12 metres, on the vertical axis; then P is B's starting point.

A's graph is drawn by joining O to the point which marks 40 seconds. From this point measure a vertical distance of 2 cm downwards to Q. Then since 1 cm represents 30 metres, Q is C's position when A is at the winning post, and OQ is C's graph.

Along the time-axis take 3.6 cm to R, representing 36 seconds; then PR is B's graph.

Through R draw a vertical line to meet the graphs of A and C in S and T respectively. Then S and T mark the positions of A and C when B passes the winning post.

By inspection RS and ST represent 30 and 54 metres respectively. Thus B is 30 metres ahead of A, and A is 54 met res ahead of C.

Again, since A runs three-fourths of the course in 30 seconds, the difference of the corresponding ordinates of A's and B's graphs after 30 seconds will give the distance between A and B. By measurement we find VW = .9 cm, which represents 27 metres.

The student is recommended to draw a figure for himself on a scale twice as large as that given in Fig. 25.

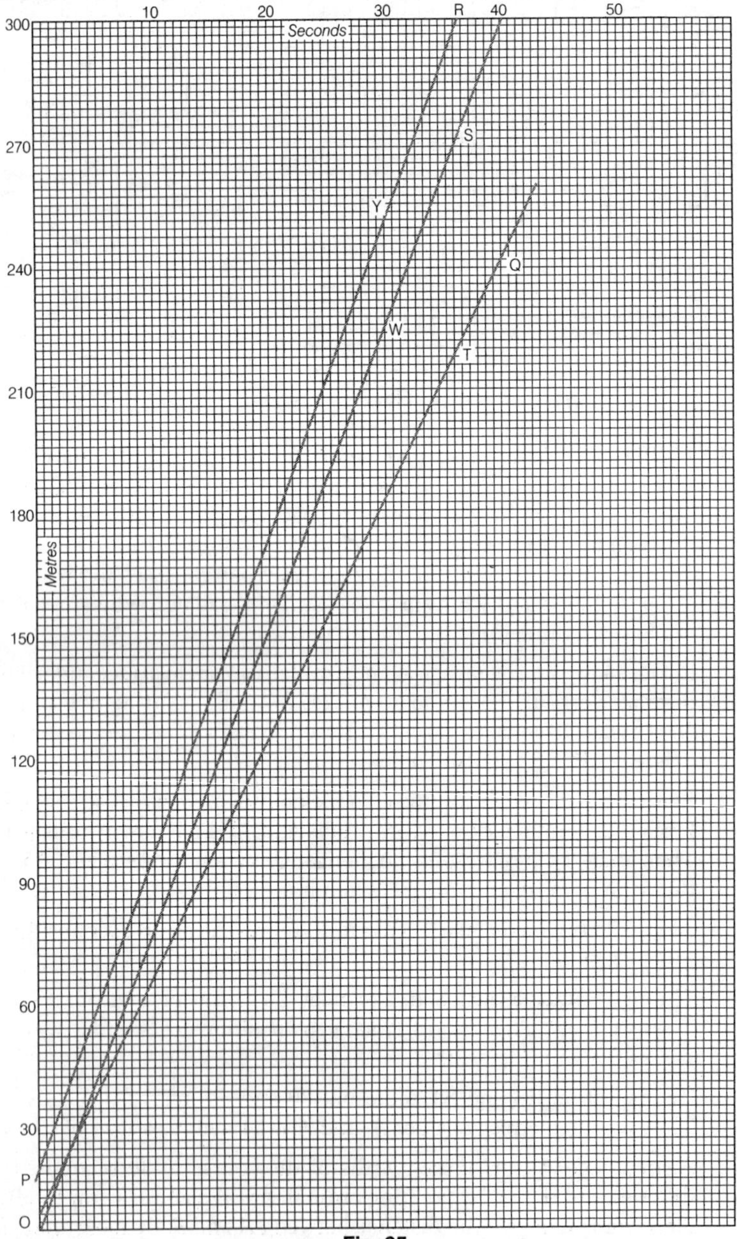

Fig. 25

447. When a variable quantity y is partly constant and partly proportional to a variable quantity x, the algebraical relation between x and y is of the form $y = ax + b$, where a and b are constant.

The corresponding graph will therefore be a straight line; and since a straight line is completely determined when the positions of two points are known, it follows that, in all problems which can be illustrated by linear graphs, it is sufficient if the data furnish for each graph two independent pairs of simultaneous values of the variable quantities.

Some easy examples of this kind have already been given on page 437 and in Examples XLIV-g. We shall now work out two more examples.

EXAMPLE 1. *In a certain establishment the clerks are paid an initial salary per month for the first year, and this is annually increased by a fixed amount, the initial salary and the increment being different in different departments. A receives* Rs 130 *in his* 10th *year, and* Rs 220 *in his* 19th. *B, in another department, receives* Rs 140 *in his* 5th *year and* Rs 180 *in his* 13th. *Draw graphs to show their salaries in different years. In what year do they receive equal salaries? Also find in what year A earns the same salary as that received by B for his* 21st *year.*

In Fig. 26 let each horizontal division represent 1 year; and let the salaries be measured vertically, beginning at 130, with 1 division to represent Rs 2.

If the salary at the end of x years is denoted by Rs y, it is evident that in each case we have a relation of the form $y = ax + b$, where a and b are constant. Thus the variations of time and salary may be represented by linear graphs.

Since no increment is received for the first year, $x = 9$, when $y = 130$ and $x = 18$, when $y = 220$. Thus the points P and Q are determined, and by joining them we have the graph for A's salary. Similarly, the graph for B's salary is found by joining P' (4,140) and Q (12, 180).

These lines have the same ordinate and abscissa at L, where $x = 16$, $y = 200$. Thus A and B have the same salary when each have served 16 years, that is in their 17th year. Again B's salary at the end of 20 years is given by the ordinate of M, which is the same as that of Q which represents A's salary after 18 years.

Thus A's salary for his 19th year is equal B's salary for his 21st year.

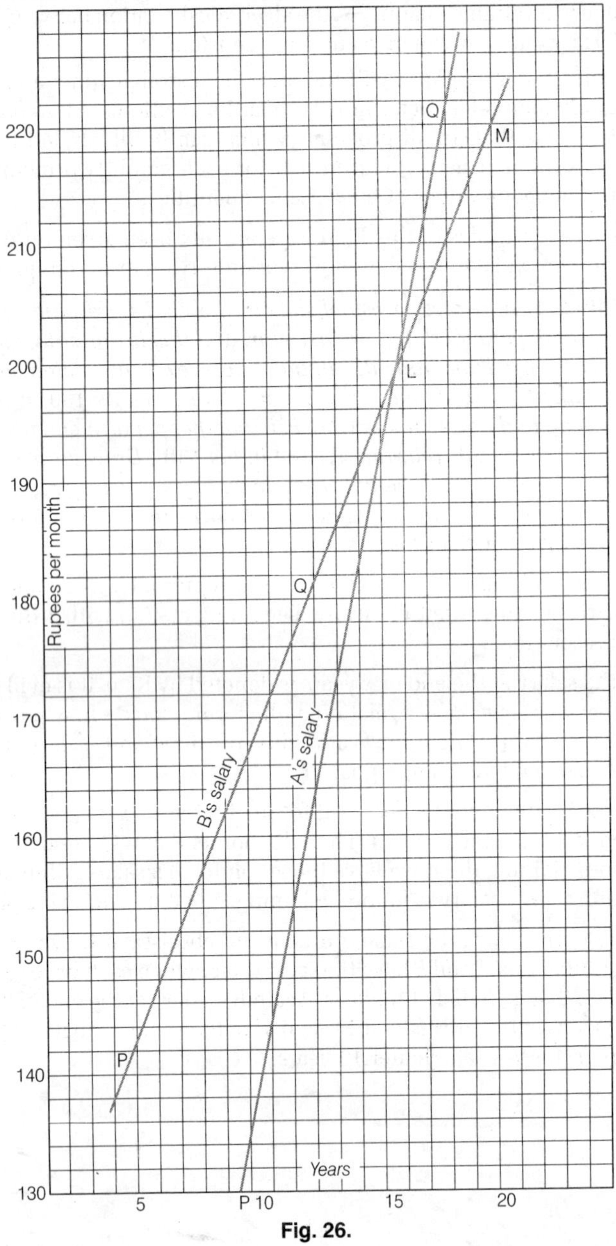

Fig. 26.

EXAMPLE 2. *Two sums of money are put out at simple interest at different rates per cent. In the first case the Amounts at the end of* 6 *years and* 15 *years are* Rs 260 *and* Rs 350 *respectively. In the second case the Amounts for* 5 *years and* 20 *years are* Rs 330 *and* Rs 420. *Draw graphs from which the Amounts may be read off for any year, and find the year in which the Principal with accrued Interest will amount to the same in the two cases. Also from the graphs read off the value of each principal.*

When a sum of money is at simple interest for any number of years, we have

Amount = Principal + Interest,

where 'Principal' is constant, and 'Interest' varies with the number of years. Hence the variations of Amount and Time may be represented by a linear graph in which x is taken to denote the number of years, and y the number of pounds in the corresponding Amount.

Here, as the diagram is inconveniently large we shall merely indicate the steps of the solution, which is similar in detail to that of the last example. The student should draw his own diagram.

Measure time horizontally (1 cm to 10 years), and Amount vertically (1 cm to Rs 40) beginning at Rs 260.

The first graph is the line joining L (6, 260) and M (15, 350). The second graph is the line joining **L′** (5, 330) and **M** (20, 420). In each of these lines the ordinate of any point gives the Amount for the number of years given by the corresponding abscissa.

LM, **L′M′** intersect at a point **P** where $x = 25$, $y = 450$. Thus, each Principal with its Interest amounts to £ 450 in 25 years.

When $x = 0$ there is no Interest; thus the Principals will be obtained by reading off the values of the intercepts made by the two graphs on the y-axis. These are Rs 200 and Rs 300 respectively.

NOTE. To obtain the result $y = 200$ it will be necessary to continue the y-axis downwards sufficiently far to show this ordinate.

EXAMPLES XLIV-h

1. At noon A starts to walk at 6 km an hour, and at 1.30 p.m. B follows on horseback at 8 km an hour. When will B overtake A?

Also find

(i) when A is 5 km ahead of B;

(ii) when A is 3 km behind B.

[Take 1 cm horizontally to represent 1 hour, and 1 cm vertically to represent 10 km.

2. By measuring time along OX (1 cm for 1 hour) and distance along OY (1 cm for 10 km) show how to draw lines.

(i) from O to indicate distance travelled towards Y at 12 km an hour :

(ii) from Y to indicate distance travelled towards O at 9 km an hour.

If these are the rates of two men who ride towards each other from two places 60 km apart, starting at noon, find from the graphs when they are first 18 km from each other. Also find (to the nearest minute) their time of meeting.

3. Two bicyclists ride to meet each other from two places 95 km apart. *A* starts at 8 a.m. at 10 km an hour, and *B* starts at 9.30 a.m. at 15 km an hour. Find graphically when and where they meet, and at what times they are $37\frac{1}{2}$ km apart.

4. *A* and *B* start at the same time from London to Blisworth, *A* walking 4 km an hour, *B* riding 9 km an hour. *B* reaches Blisworth in 4 hours, and immediately rides back to London. After 2 hours rest he starts again for Blisworth at the same rate. How far from London will he overtake *A*, who has in the meantime rested $6\frac{1}{4}$ hours?

5. At what distance from London, and at what time, will a train which leaves London for Rugby at 2.33 p.m., and goes at the rate of 56 km an hour, meet a train which leaves Rugby at 1.45 p.m. and goes at the rate of 40 km an hour, the distance between London and Rugby being 128 km?

Also find at what times the trains are 38.4 km apart, and how far apart they are at 4.9 p.m.

6. *A*, *B* and *C* set out to walk from Bath to Bristol at 5, 6, and 4 km an hour respectively. *C* starts 3 minutes before, and *B* 7 minutes after *A*. Draw graphs to show (i) when and where *A* overtakes *C*; (ii) when and where *B* overtakes *A* ; (iii) *C*'s position relative to the others after he has walked 45 minutes.

[Take 1 cm horizontally to represent 10 minutes, and 1 cm to the km vertically.]

7. X and Y are two towns 35 km apart. At 8.30 p.m. *A* starts to walk from X to Y at 4 km at hour; after walking 8 km he rests for half an hour and then completes his journey on horseback at 10 km an hour. At 9.48 a.m. *B* starts to walk from Y to X at 3 km an hour ; find when and where *A* and *B* meet. Also find at what times they are $6\frac{1}{2}$ km apart.

8. A can beat B by 20 metres in 120, and B can beat C by 10 metres in 50. Supposing their rates of running to be uniform, find graphically how much start A can give C in 120 metres so as to run a dead heat with him. If A, B, and C start together, where are A and C when B has run 80 metres?

9. A, B, and C run a race of 200 metres. A gives B a start of 8 metres, and C starts some seconds after A. A runs the distance in 25 seconds and beats C by 40 metres. B beats A by 1 second, and when he has been running 15 seconds, he is 48 metres ahead of C. Find graphically how many seconds C starts after A. Show also from the graphs that if the three runners started level they would run a dead heat.

[Take 1 cm to 40 metres, and 1 cm to 10 seconds.]

10. A cyclist has to ride 75 km. He rides for a time at 9 km an hour and then alters his speed to 15 km an hour covering the distance in 7 hours. At what time did he change his speed?

11. A and B ride to meet each other from two towns X and Y which are 60 km apart. starts at 1 p.m., and B starts 36 minutes later. If they meet at 4 p.m., and A gets to Y at 6 p.m., find the. time when B gets to X. Also find the times when they are 22 km apart. When A is half-way between X and Y, where is B ?

12. The distance from town A to B is 119 km; if I were to set out at noon to cycle from A, riding 26 km the first hour and decreasing my pace by 3 km each successive hour; find graphically how long it would take me to reach B. Also find approximately the time at which I should reach C, which is 48 km from B.

13. At 8 a.m. A begins a ride on a cycle at 20 km an hour, and an hour and a half later B, starting from the same point, follows on his bicycle at 10 km an hour. After riding 36 km. A rests for 1 hr 24 min, then rides back at 9 km an hour. Find graphically when and where he meets B. Also find (i) at what time the riders were 21 km apart, (ii) how far B will have ridden by the time A gets back to his starting point.

14. I row against a stream flowing $1\frac{1}{2}$ km an hour to a certain point, and then turn back, stopping two km short of the place whence 1 originally started. If the whole time occupied in rowing is 2 hrs 10 mins and my uniform speed in still water is $4\frac{1}{2}$ km an hour, find graphically how far upstream I went. [Take 3 cm horizontally to represent 1 hour, and 1 cm to 1 km vertically.]

15. One train leaves Bristol at 3 p.m. and reaches London at 6 p.m.; a second train leaves London at 1.30 p.m. and arrives at Bristol at 6 p.m.; if both trains are supposed to travel uniformly, at what time will they meet? Show from a graph that the time does not depend upon the distance between London and Bristol.

16. At 7.40 a.m. the ordinary train starts from Norwich and reaches London at 11.40 a.m.; the express starting from London at 9 a.m. arrives at Norwich at 11.40 a.m.; if both trains travel uniformly, find when they meet. Show, as in Ex. 15, that the time is independent of the distance between London and Norwich, and verify this conclusion by solving an algebraical equation.

17. A boy starts from home and walks to school at the rate of 10 metres in 3 seconds, and is 20 seconds too soon. The next day he walks at the rate of 40 metres in 17 seconds, and is half a minute late. Find graphically the distance to the school, and show that he would have been just in time if he had walked at the rate of 20 metres in 7 seconds.

18. The annual expenses of a Convalescent Home are partly constant and partly proportional to the number of inmates. The expenses were Rs 3840 for 12 patients and Rs 4320 for 16. Draw a graph to show the expenses for any number of patients, and find from it the cost of maintaining 15.

In a rival establishment the expenses were Rs 3750 for 5, and Rs 4450 for 15 patients. Find graphically for what number of patients the cost would be the same in the two cases.

19. A body is moving in a straight line with varying velocity. The velocity at any instant is made up of the constant velocity with which it was projected (measured in decimetres per second) diminished by a retardation of a constant number of decimetres per second in every second. After 4 seconds the velocity was 320, and after 13 seconds it was 140. Draw a graph to show the velocity at any time while the body is in motion.

A second body projected at the same time under similar conditions has a velocity of 450 after 5 seconds, and a velocity of 150 after 15 seconds. Show graphically that they will both come to rest at the same time. Also find at what time the second body is moving 100 decimetres per second faster than the first, and determine from the graphs the . velocity of projection in each case.

20. To provide for his two infant sons, a man left by his will two sums of money as separate investments at different rates of interest, on the condition that the principal sums with simple interest were to be paid over to his sons when the amounts were the same. After 5 years the first sum amounted to Rs 4510, and after 15 years to Rs 5330. After 10 years the second sum amounted to Rs 4320, and after 20 years to Rs 5440. Draw graphs from which the amounts may be read off for any year, and find after how many years the sons were entitled to receive their legacies. Also determine from the graphs what the original sums were at the father's death.

21. In a certain examination the highest and lowest marks gained in a Latin paper were 153 and 51. These have to be reduced so that the maximum (120) is given to the first candidate, and the minimum (30) to the lowest. This is done by reducing all the marks in a certain ratio, and then increasing or diminishing them all by the same number. In a Greek paper the highest and lowest marks were 161 and 56; after a similar adjustment these become 100 and 40 respectively. Draw graphs from which all the reduced marks may be read off, and find the marks which should be finally given ro a candidate who scored 102 in Latin and 126 in Greek.

Show also that it is possible in one case for a candidate to receive equal marks in the two subjects both before and after reduction. What are the original and reduced marks in this case?

Miscellaneous Graphs

1. Plot the graphs of

   $2y = 3(x - 4), 3y = 1 - 5x,$

   obtaining at least five points on each graph. Find the coordinates of the point where they meet.

2. Draw the graphs represented by $y = 5 - 3x,\ y = \frac{1}{3}(x + 5)$

   and find the coordinates of their point of intersection.

3. By finding the intercepts on the axes draw the graphs of

   (i) $15x + 20y = 6;$ (ii) $12x + 21y = 14.$

   In (i) take 2 cm for unit, and in (ii) take 1 cm as unit. In each case explain why the unit is convenient.

4. Solve $y = 10x + 8, 7x + y = 25$ graphically. Unit for x, 2 cm; for y, .5 of a cm.]

5. From the graph of the expression $11x + 6$, find its value when $x = 1.8$. Also find the value of x which will make the expression equal to 20.

6. With the same units as in Ex. 4 draw the graph of the function $\frac{36 - 5x}{3}$.

   From the graph find the value of the function when $x = 1.8$; also find for what value of x the function becomes equal to 8.

7. Show that the straight lines given by the equations

$$9y = 5x + 65,$$
$$5x + 2y + 10 = 0,$$
$$x + 3y = 11,$$

   meet in a point. Find its coordinates.

8. Draw the triangle whose sides are given by the equations

   $3y - x = 9,\ x + 7y = 11,\ 3x + y = 13;$

   and find the coordinates of its vertices.

9. Show graphically that the values of x and y which satisfy the equations $5x = 2y - 18, 5y = 6 - 7x$ also satisfy the equation $x + y = 2$.

10. Draw the graphs of

(i) $y = x^2$, (ii) $y = 8x^2$.

In (i) take 1 cm as unit for x, 0.5 can as unit for y.

In (ii) ...... 2cm ...... x, 0.2cm ...... y.

11. On the same scale as in Ex. 10 (ii) draw the graph of $y = 16x^2$. Show that it may also be simply deduced from the graph of Ex. 10(ii).

12. Plot the graph of $y = x^2$, taking 2 cm as unit on both axes, and using the following values of x.

$-0.4, -0.3, -0.2, -0.1, 0, 0.1, 0.2, 0.3, 0.4$

13. Draw the graph of $x = y^2$, from $y = 0$ to $y = 5$, and hence find the square roots of 7 and 3.6.

[Take 0.5 cm as unit for x, 2 cm as unit for y.]

14. Draw the graph of $y = 5 + x - x^2$ for values of x from −2 to +3, and from the figure obtain approximate values for the roots of the equation $5 + x - x^2 = 0$.

[Take 2 cm as unit for x, 0.5 cm as unit for y]

15. Draw the graphs of

(i) $5x + 6y = 60$, (ii) $6y - x = 24$, (iii) $2x - y = 7$;

and show that they represent three lines which meet in a point.

16. If 1 kg of coffee costs Rs 9.50, draw a graph to give the price of any number of kg. Read off the price (to the nearest penny) of 13 kg, 660 g, 1.4kg.

17. If 60 eggs cost Rs 2, find graphically how many can be bought for Rs 1.25, and the cost of 26 eggs to the nearest paise.

18. If 1 quintal of sugar costs Rs 1 30, draw a graph to find the price of any number of kg. Find the cost of 26 kg. How many kg can be brought for Rs 7.80?

19. Solve the following equations graphically:

(i) $x^2 + y^2 = 53$, $y - x = 5$;

(ii) $x^2 + y^2 = 100$, $x + y = 14$;

(iii) $x^2 + y^2 = 34$, $2x + y = 11$;

(iv) $x^2 + y^2 = 36$, $4x + 3y = 12$.

[Approximate roots to be given to one place of decimals.]

20. Solve the equation $3 + 6x = x^2$ graphically, and find the maximum value of the expression $3 + 6x - x^2$.

21. A basket of 96 oranges is bought for Rs 19.20. Draw a graph to show the price of any other number. How many could be bought for Rs 4.60? Find the price (to the nearest paise) which must be paid for 36 and for 78 oranges respectively.

22. If the wages for a day's work of 8 hours are Rs 4.50, draw a graph to show the wages for any fraction of a day, and find (to the nearest paise) what ought to be paid to men who work $2\frac{1}{2}$, $3\frac{1}{2}$, $6\frac{1}{2}$ hours respectively. How many hours' work might be expected for ₹ 2.8?

    [Take 1 inch to represent 1 hour, and one-tenth of an inch to represent 1 paise.]

23. Draw the graphs of x^2 and $3x + 1$. By means of them find approximate values for the roots of $x^2 - 3x - 1 = 0$.

24. If 24 men can reap a field of 29 hectares in a given time, find roughly by means of a graph the number of hectares which could be reaped in the same time by 15, 33, and 42 men respectively.

25. The highest marks gained in an examination were 136, and these are to be raised so that the maximum is 200. Show how this may be done by means of a graph, and read off, to the nearest integer, the final marks of candidates who scored 61 and 49 respectively.

26. Draw a graph which will give the square roots of all numbers between 25 and 36, to three places of decimals.

    [Plot the graph of $y = x^2$, beginning at the point (5, 25) with 10 cm and 0.5 cm as units for x and y respectively.]

27. I want a ready way of finding approximately 0.866 of any number up to 10. Justify the following construction. Join the origin to a point **P** whose coordinates are 10 and 8.66 (2 cm being taken as a unit); then the ordinate of any point on OP is 0.866 of the corresponding abscissa. Read off from the diagram,

    0.866 of 3, 0.866 of 6.5, 0.866 of 4.8, and $\frac{1}{0.866}$ of 5.

28. *A* starts from London at noon at 8 km an hour; two hours later *B* starts, riding at 12 km an hour. Find graphically at what time and at what distance from London *B* overtakes *A*. At what times will *A* and *B* be 8 km apart? If *C* rides after *B*, starting at 3 p.m. at 15 km an hour, find from the graphs

    (i) the distances between *A*, *B*, and *C* at 5 p.m.;

    (ii) the time when *C* is 8 km behind *B*.

29. If O and Y represent two towns 45 km apart, and if A walks from Y to O at 6 km an hour while B walks from O to Y at 4 km an hour, both starting at noon, find graphically their time and place of meeting. Also read off from the graphs

(i) the times when they are 15 km apart;
(ii) B's distance from Y at 6.15 p.m.

30. At 8 a.m. A starts from P to ride to Q which is 48 km distant. At the same time B sets from Q to meet A. If A rides at 8 km an hour, and rests half an hour at the end of every hour, while B walks uniformly at 4 km an hour, find graphically

(i) the time and place of meeting;
(ii) the distance between A and B at 11 a.m.
(iii) at what time they are 14 km apart.

31. The following table gives statistics of the population of a certain country, where P is the number of millions at the beginning of each of the years specified:

Year	1830	1835	1840	1845	1850	1855	1860
P	20	22	24.5	28	31	36	41

Let t be the time in years from 1830. Plot the values of P vertically and those of t horizontally and show the relation between P and t by a simple curve passing fairly evenly among the plotted points. Find what the population was at the beginning of the years 1847 and 1858.

32. The monthly salary of a clerk is increased each year by a fixed sum. After six years' service his salary is raised to Rs 128, and after 15 years to Rs 200. Draw a graph from which his salary may be read off for any year, and determine from it

(i) his initial monthly salary,
(ii) the salary he should receive per month for his 21st year.

33. Draw the graphs of $y = x^2$ and $2y = x + 3$ on the same diagram. Deduce the roots of the equation $2x^2 - x - 3 = 0$.

34. Taking 2 cm as unit, plot the graph of $y = x^3 - 3x$, taking the following values of x: $0, \pm.2, \pm.4, \pm.6, \pm.8, \pm 1, \pm 1.2, \pm 1.4, \pm 1.6, \pm 1.8, \pm 2$.
Find the turning points, and the value of the maximum or minimum ordinates between the limits given.

35. From the graph in Ex. 34 find to two places of decimals the roots of $x^3 - 3x = 0$.

36. Solve the following pairs of equations graphically:

(i) $x + y = 15$, $xy = 36$; (ii) $x - y = 3$, $xy = 18$; (iii) $x^2 + y^2 = 13$, $xy = 6$.

37. An India-rubber cord was loaded with weights, and a measurement of its length was taken for each load as tabulated. Plot a graph to show the relation between the length of the cord and the loads.

Load in kg	10	12	17	21	23	25
Length in centimetres	36.4	37.7	40.5	43.0	44.3	45.4

What was the length of the cord unloaded?

38. A manufacturer has priced a certain set of lathes; the largest sells at Rs 1/60, and the smallest at Rs 400. He wishes to increase his prices so that the largest will sell at Rs 2000 and the smallest at Rs 500. By means of a graph find an algebraical relation between the new price (P) and the old price (Q), and find to the nearest 10 rupees the new prices of lathes originally priced at Rs 1500, at Rs 1255, and at Rs 780.

39. The mean temperature of the first day of each month, on an average of 50 years, bad the following values:

Jan.	1, 37°;	May	1, 50°;	Sept.	1, 59°;
Feb.	1, 38°;	June	1, 57°;	Oct.	1, 54°;
Mar.	1,40°;	July	1, 62°;	Nov.	1, 46°;
April	1, 45°;	Aug.	1, 62°;	Dec.	1, 41°;

Represent these variations bymeans of a smooth curve.

[The difference of length of different months may be neglected.]

40. The price in paise of a dekagramme of silver on January 1st in each of the ten years 1891-1900 was

75, 67, 60, 49, 50, 52, 47, 48, 45, 47.

Draw a smooth curve showing its value approximately at any time during these ten years.

41. A manufacturer wishes to stock a certain article in many sizes; at present he has five sizes made at the prices given below:

Length in cm	20	27	33	45	54
Price in rupees	11	14.5	20	35	48.5

Draw a graph to show suitable prices for intermediate sizes, and find what the prices should be when the lengths are 30 cm and 46 cm.

42. A party of tourists set up for a station 3 km distant and go at the rate of 3 km an hour. After going half a km one of them has to return to the starting point; at what rate must he now walk in order to reach the station at the same time as the others?

43. A motor car on its way to Bristol overtakes a cyclist at 9 a.m. the car reaches Bristol at 10.30 and after waiting 1 hour returns, meeting the cyclist at noon. Supposing the speeds of car and cyclist to be uniform, find when the cyclist will reach Bristol. Also compare the speeds of the car and cyclist.

44. Two trains start at the same time, one from Liverpool to Manchester, and the other in the opposite direction, and running steadily complete the journey in 42 min and 56 min respectively. How long is it from the moment of starting before they meet?

45. The table below shows the distances from Bombay of certain stations, and the times of two trains, one up and one down. Supposing each run to be made at constant speed, show by a graph the distance of each train from Bombay at any time, using 1 cm to represent 20 km and 3 cm to represent in hour.

Distance (in km)

Station	Down train (↓)	Up train (↑)
0 Bombay,	depart 6.40 a.m.	arrive 10.00 am
30 Borivali,	arrive 7.30 a.m. depart 7.40 a.m.	not stopping
120 Dahami Rd,	arrive 8.40 a.m. depart 8.50 a.m.	depart 8.10 a.m. arrive 8.00 a.m.
200 Bulsar,	not stopping	depart 7.00 a.m. arrive 6.50 a.m.
260 Surat,	arrive 11.30 a.m.	depart 6.00 a.m.

At what point do they pass one another, and how far is each from Bombay at 9.30 a.m.? Which of the three runs by the Bombay to Surat train is the fastest?

MISCELLANEOUS EXAMPLES VI

(*Additional Examples on formulae are marked by asterisks.*)

1. Simplify $b - \{b - (a + b) - [b - (b - \overline{a - b})] + 2a\}$.

2. Find the sum of

$$a + b - 2(c + d), b + c - 3(d + a), \text{ and } c + d - 4(a + b).$$

3. Multiply $\frac{1}{2}x + \frac{2}{3}y$ by $x - \frac{1}{3}y$.

4. If $x = 6$, $y = 4$, $z = 3$, find the value of $\sqrt[3]{2x + 3y + z}$.

5. Find the square of $2 - 3x + x^2$.

6. Solve $\frac{x+3}{x-1}+\frac{x-4}{x-6}=2$.

7. Find the H.C.F. of a^3-2a-4 and a^3-a^2-4.

8. Simplify $\frac{2a}{a+b}+\frac{2b}{a-b}-\frac{a^2+b^2}{a^2-b^2}$.

9. Solve $\left.\begin{array}{l}\frac{3}{5}x+\frac{y}{4}=13\\ \frac{1}{3}x-\frac{y}{8}=3\end{array}\right\}$.

10. Two digits, which form a number, change place when 18 is added to the number, and the sum of the two numbers thus formed is 44. find the digits.

11. If $a=1, b=-2, c=3, d=-4$, find the value of $\frac{a^2b^2+b^2c+d(a-b)}{10a-(c+b)^2}$.

12. Subtract $-x^2+y^2-z^2$ from the sum of

$$\frac{1}{3}x^2+\frac{1}{4}y^2, \frac{1}{5}y^2+\frac{1}{3}x^2, \text{ and } \frac{1}{3}z^2-\frac{1}{4}x^2.$$

13. Write down the cube of $x+8y$.

14. Simplify $\frac{x^2+xy}{x^2+y^2}\times\frac{x^4-y^4}{xy-y^2}\times\frac{y}{x}$.

15. Solve $\frac{3}{5}(2x-7)-\frac{2}{3}(x-8)=\frac{4x+1}{15}+4$.

16. Find the H.C.F and L.C.M of

$$x^4+x^3+2x-4 \text{ and } x^3+3x^2-4.$$

17. Find the square root of $4a^4+9(1-2a)+3a^2(7-4a)$.

18. Solve $\left.\begin{array}{l}y=\frac{x+a}{2}+\frac{b}{3}\\ x=\frac{y+b}{2}+\frac{a}{3}\end{array}\right\}$

19. Simplify $\left(\frac{a}{x+a}-\frac{x}{x-a}\right)\div\frac{x^2+a^2}{x^2+ax}$.

***19a.** If $k=\frac{20ab}{4a+5b}$, find (i) a in terms of b and k, (ii) b in terms of a and k. Find also the value of $\sqrt{\frac{k-4a}{k-5b}}$ in terms of a and b.

20. When 1 is added to the numerator and denominator of a certain fraction the result is equal to $\frac{3}{2}$; and when 1 is subtracted from its numerator and denominator the result is equal to 2: find the fraction.

21. Show that the sum of $12a + 6b - c, -7a - b + c$, and $a + b + 6c$, is six times the sum of $25a + 13b - 8c, -13a - 13b - c$, and $-11a + b + 10c$.

22. Divide $x^2 - xy + \frac{3}{16}y^2$ by $x - \frac{1}{4}y$.

23. Add together $18\left\{\frac{2x}{9} - \frac{1}{6}\left(\frac{2y}{3} + z\right)\right\}$,

$$24\left(\frac{3x}{8} - \frac{2y-3z}{12}\right), \text{ and } 30\left\{\frac{7z}{15} - \frac{4}{5}(2x - y)\right\}$$

24. Find the factors of

(1) $10x^2 + 79x - 8$. (2) $729x^6 - y^6$.

25. Solve $\frac{2x-1}{5} + \frac{5x+3}{17} = 3 - \frac{4x-118}{11}$.

26. Find the value of $(5a - 3b)(a - b) - b\{3a - c(4a - b) - b^2(a + c)\}$.

when $a = 0, b = -1, c = \frac{1}{2}$.

27. Find the H.C.F. of $7x^3 - 10x^2 - 7x + 10$ and $2x^3 - x^2 - 2x + 1$.

28. Simplify $\frac{x^2 - 7xy + 12y^2}{x^2 + 5xy + 6y^2} \div \frac{x^2 - 5xy + 4y^2}{x^2 + xy - 2y^2}$.

29. Solve $\left.\begin{aligned} 3abx + y &= 9b \\ 4abx + 3y &= 17b \end{aligned}\right\}$.

***29a.** If x and y are connected by the formula $y = mx + c$, find m and c if $x = 5$ when $y = 10$ and if an increase of 1 in the value of x leads to an increase of 3 in the value of y.

30. Find the two times between 7 and 8 o'clock when the hands of a watch was separated by 15 minutes.

31. If $a = 1, b = -2, c = 3, d = -4$, find the value of

$$\sqrt{d^2 - 4b + a^2} - \sqrt{c^3 + b^3 + a + d}.$$

32. Multiply the product of $\frac{1}{4}x^2 - \frac{1}{2}xy + y^2$ and $\frac{1}{2}x + y$ by $x^3 - 8y^3$.

33. Simplify by removing brackets

$$a^4 - \{4a^3 - (6a^2 - 4a + 1)\} - [-2 - \{a^4 - (-4a^3 - \overline{6a^2 - 4a})3 - (8a - 1)\}].$$

34. Find the remainder when $5x^4 - 7x^3 + 3x^2 - x + 8$ is divided by $x - 4$.

35. Simplify $\dfrac{x^2 + y^2}{x^2 - xy} \times \dfrac{xy - y^2}{x^4 - y^4} \times \dfrac{x}{y}$.

36. Solve $\left.\begin{array}{r} \dfrac{x - 11}{3} + y = 18 \\ 2x + \dfrac{y - 13}{4} = 29 \end{array}\right\}$.

37. Find the square root of $4x^6 - 12x^4 + 28x^3 + 9x^2 - 42x + 49$.

38. Solve $.006x - .491 + .723x = -.005$.

39. Find the L.C.M. of $x^3 + y^3$, $3x^2 + 2xy - y^2$, and $x^3 - x^2y + xy^2$.

*__39a.__ A man's total income is Rs x. On the first Rs 1000 of this he pays no tax. He is also allowed one sixth of his total income free of tax. On the remainder he pays income tax at 12 paise in the rupee. Show that his total tax Rs T is given by

$$T = \frac{x}{10} - 120$$

Transform this formula so that x is the subject, and hence find his income if he pays Rs 247.50 in tax.

40. A bill of Rs 25.25 is paid with 50-paise coins and 25-paise coins, and twice the number of 50-paise coins exceeds three times the number of 25-paise coins by 17; how many of each are used?

41. Simplify
$(a + b + c)^2 - (a - b - c)^2 + (a + b - c)^2 - (-a + b + c)^2$.

42. Find the remainder when $a^4 - 3a^3b + 2a^2b^2 - b^4$ is divided by $a^2 - ab + 2b^2$.

43. If $a = 0, b = 1, c = -2, d = 3$, find the value of

$(3abc - 2bcd)\sqrt[3]{a^3bc - c^3bd + 3}$.

44. Find an expression which will divide both $4x^2 + 3x - 10$ and $4x^3 + 7x^2 - 3x - 15$ without remainder.

45. Simplify $\dfrac{a + \dfrac{ab}{a - b}}{a^2 - \dfrac{2a^2b^2}{a^2 + b^2}} \times \dfrac{\dfrac{1}{a^2} - \dfrac{1}{b^2}}{\dfrac{1}{a} - \dfrac{1}{b}}$.

46. Find the cube root of $8x^3 - 2x^2y + \dfrac{xy^2}{6} - \dfrac{y^3}{216}$.

47. Solve $\left.\begin{array}{l}9x + 8y = 43xy\\ 8x + 9y = 42xy\end{array}\right\}$.

48. Simplify $\dfrac{3}{x-4} - \dfrac{2}{x-5} - \dfrac{x-7}{(x-2)(x-3)}$.

49. Find the L.C.M. of $8x^3 + 38x^2 + 59x + 30$

and $6x^3 - 13x^2 - 13x + 30$.

50. A boy spent half of his money in one shop, one–third of the remainder in a second, and one–fifth of what he had left in a third. He had one rupee at last: how much had he at first?

51. Find the remainder when $x^7 - 10x^6 + 8x^5 - 7x^3 + 3x - 11$ is divided by $x^2 - 5x + 4$.

52. Simplify $4\left\{a - \dfrac{3}{2}\left(b - \dfrac{4c}{3}\right)\right\}\left\{\dfrac{1}{2}(2a - b) + 2(b - c)\right\}$.

53. If $a = \dfrac{25}{16}, b = 1, c = \dfrac{3}{4}$, prove that $(a - \sqrt{b})(\sqrt{a+b})\sqrt{a-b} = \dfrac{3c^4}{\sqrt{a-c^2}}$.

54. Find the L.C.M. of $x^2 - 7x + 12, 3x^2 - 6x - 9$, and $2x^2 - 6x - 8$.

55. Find the sum of the squares of $ax + by, bx - ay, ay + bx, by - ax$; and express the result in factors.

56. Solve $\dfrac{x}{6} + \dfrac{y}{4} = \dfrac{3x - 5z}{4} = \dfrac{z}{8} + \dfrac{7y}{16} = 1$.

57. Simplify $\dfrac{a^3 + b^3}{a^4 - b^4} - \dfrac{a + b}{a^2 - b^2} - \dfrac{1}{2}\left\{\dfrac{a - b}{a^2 + b^2} - \dfrac{1}{a - b}\right\}$.

58. Solve $x - \left(3x - \dfrac{2x + 5}{10}\right) = \dfrac{1}{6}(2x + 67) + \dfrac{5}{3}\left(1 + \dfrac{x}{5}\right)$.

59. Add together the following fractions:

$$\frac{2}{x^2 + xy + y^2}, \frac{-4x}{x^3 - y^3}, \frac{x^2}{y^2(x - y)^2}, \frac{-x^2}{x^3y - y^4}.$$

***59a.** A closed rectangular case measures inside a cm long, b cm wide, and c cm deep. Write down the cost, in rupees, of lining this case at p paise per square cm.

How many kg of sugar, weighing q gm per cubic cm, will the case hold? (Oxf. Sch. Certif.)

60. A man agreed to work for 30 days, on condition that for every day's work he should receive Rs 2, and that for every day's absence from work he should forfeit 90 paise; at the end of the time he received Rs 42.60: how many days did he work?

61. Divide $\frac{3x^5}{4} + 27 - \frac{43x^2}{4} - 4x^4 + \frac{77x^3}{8} - \frac{33x}{4}$ by $\frac{x^2}{2} + 3 - x$.

62. Find the value of $\frac{4y}{5}(y - x) - 35\left[\frac{3x - 4y}{5} - \frac{1}{10}\left\{3x - \frac{5}{7}(7x - 4y)\right\}\right]$

when $x = -\frac{1}{2}$ and $y = 2$.

63. Simplify $\frac{10x - 11}{3(x^2 - 1)} - \frac{10x - 1}{3(x^2 + x + 1)} + \frac{x^2 - 2x + 5}{(x^6 - 1)(x + 1)}$.

64. Find the cube root of $\frac{a^3c^3}{b^3}x^6 - \frac{3a^2c}{b}x^5 + \frac{3ab}{c}x^4 - \frac{b^3}{c^3}x^3$.

65. Solve $\frac{4x - 17}{x - 4} + \frac{10x - 13}{2x - 3} = \frac{8x - 30}{2x - 7} + \frac{5x - 4}{x - 1}$.

66. Find the factors of

(1) $x^3 + 5x^2 + x + 5$. (2) $x^2 - 2xy - 323y^2$.

67. Solve
$$\left.\begin{aligned} \frac{1}{3}(x + y) + 2z &= 21 \\ 3x - \frac{1}{2}(y + z) &= 65 \\ x + \frac{1}{2}(x + y - z) &= 38 \end{aligned}\right\}.$$

68. Simplify $\frac{x + 2y}{\frac{2}{7}x - y} - \frac{3x^2 + 63xy + 70y^2}{2x^2 + 3xy - 35y^2}$.

69. Find the square root of $-(3b - 2c - 2a)^3\{2(a + c) - 3b\}$.

***69a.** Express y in terms of x, given that
$$y = \frac{4z^2}{1 + 3z}$$
and $x = 2z - 1$.

Find the values of x and z when $y = 1$.

(Oxf. and Camb. Sch. Certif.)

70. The united ages of a man and his wife are six times the united ages of their children. Two years ago their united ages were ten times the united ages of their children, and six years hence their united ages will be three times the united ages of the children. How many children have they?

71. Find the sum of

$$x^2 - 3xy - \frac{2}{3}y^2,\ 2y^2 - \frac{2}{3}y^3 + z^2,\ xy - \frac{1}{3}y^2 + y^3, \text{ and } 2xy - \frac{1}{3}y^3.$$

72. From $\{(a+b)(a-x) - (a-b)(b-x)\}$ subtract $(a+b)^2 - 2bx$.

73. If $a = 5, b = 4, c = 3$, find the value of

$$\sqrt[3]{6abc + (b+c)^3 + (c+a)^3 + (a+b)^3 - (a+b+c)^3}.$$

74. Find the factors of

(1) $3x^3 + 6x^2 - 189x$. (2) $a^2 + 2ab + b^2 + a + b$.

75. Solve $\left.\begin{array}{r} px = qy \\ (p+q)x - (q-p)y = r \end{array}\right\}$.

76. Simplify $\dfrac{x + \dfrac{y}{2}}{2x^2 + xy + \dfrac{y^2}{2}} - \dfrac{x^2 - \dfrac{y^2}{2}}{4\left(x^3 - \dfrac{y^3}{8}\right)}$.

77. Solve $\dfrac{x-7}{x+7} + \dfrac{1}{2(x+7)} = \dfrac{2x-15}{2x-6}$.

78. Reduce $\dfrac{x^4 - x^2 - 2x + 2}{2x^3 - x - 1}$ to its lowest terms.

79. Add together the fractions:

$$\frac{1}{2x^2 - 4x + 2},\ \frac{1}{2x^2 + 4x + 2}, \text{ and } \frac{1}{1 - x^2}.$$

*__79a.__ The cost in rupees (C) of a telephone per year is given by the formula $C = A + nk$, where n is the number of calls made and A and k are constants. The cost is Rs 399 for 1200 calls and Rs 474 for 1500 calls. Find A and k, and the cost of 800 calls.

A certain subscriber calculates that the average cost to him per call has been 40 paise. How many calls has he made?

80. A number consists of three digits, the right-hand one being zero. If the left-hand and middle digits be interchanged the number is diminished by 180; if the left-hand digit be halved, and the middle and right-hand digit be interchanged, the number is diminished by 336: find the number.

81. Divide $1 - 5x + \dfrac{152}{15}x^3 - \dfrac{106}{225}x^4 - \dfrac{28}{9}x^5$ by $1 - x - \dfrac{14}{15}x^2$.

82. If $p = 1, q = \frac{1}{2}$, find the value of

$$\frac{(p^2 + q^2) - (p - q)\sqrt{p^2 + 2pq + q^2}}{2p + q - \{p - (q - p)\}}.$$

83. Multiply $\frac{3x^3}{2} - 5x^2 + \frac{x}{4} + 9$ by $\frac{x^2}{2} - x + 3$.

84. Find the L.C.M. of

$(a^2b - 2ab^2)^2$, $2a^2 - 3ab - 2b^2$, and $2(2a^2 + ab)^2$.

85. Solve $\frac{2x + 3}{x + 1} = \frac{4x + 5}{4x + 4} + \frac{3x + 3}{3x + 1}$.

86. Reduce $\frac{5x^3 - 14x^2 + 16}{3x^3 - 2x^2 + 16x - 48}$ to its lowest terms.

87. Find the square root of $4a^4 + 9\left(a^2 + \frac{1}{a^2}\right) + 12a(a^2 + 1) + 18$.

88. Solve $\left.\begin{aligned} \frac{x}{2a} + \frac{y}{3b} &= a + b \\ \frac{3x}{a} - \frac{2y}{b} &= 6(b - a) \end{aligned}\right\}$.

89. Multiply $3x + 4y + \frac{11xy}{x - \frac{3}{2}y}$ by $10x - 3y - \frac{11xy}{\frac{x}{4} + y}$.

***89a.** If a body is thrown straight up in the air, the force acting on it, F kg wt, is given by the formula $F = kv^2 + w$, where v metres a second is the velocity, and k and w are constants. It is found that the force is 80 kg wt when the velocity is 10 m a sec and is 230 kg wt when the velocity is 20 m a sec. Find k and w, and find the velocity when the force is 48 kg wt.

90. A bag contained Rs10 in 10-paise coins and 25-paise coins; after seventeen 10-paise coins and six 25-paise coins were taken out, thrice as many 25-paise coins as 10-paise coins were left: find the number of each coin.

91. Find the value of $5(a - b) - 2\{3a - (a + b)\} + 7\{(a - 2b) - (5a - 2b)\}$,

when $a = -\frac{1}{9}b$.

92. Divide $3x^4 - 5x^3 + 7x^2 - 11x - 13$ by $3x - 2$.

93. Find the L.C.M. of

$15(p^3 + q^3)$, $5(p^2 - pq + q^2)$, $4(p^2 + pq + q^2)$, and $6(p^2 - q^2)$.

94. Resolve into factors:

(1) $a^3 - 8b^{15}$. (2) $-x^2 + 2x - 1 + x^4$.

95. Solve $\dfrac{x+a}{x+b} = \dfrac{x+3a}{x+a+b}$.

96. Simplify

(1) $\dfrac{35a^2b^2c^2 - 49b^3c^3}{65a^5bc - 91a^3b^2c^2}$. (2) $\dfrac{y^4 - 7y^3 + 8y^2 - 12y}{2y^2 - 2y - 60}$.

97. Solve $7x - 9y + 4z = 16$

$$\left.\frac{x+y}{3} = \frac{x+y+z}{2}\right\}. \qquad 2x - 3y + 4z - 5 = 0$$

98. Simplify $\dfrac{y^2 - \dfrac{2y}{y-1}}{y^2 - \dfrac{2y}{y+1}} \div \left(\dfrac{y^2 - 5y - 6}{y^2 - 6y + 5} \times \dfrac{y-2}{y+2}\right)$.

99. Find the square root of $\dfrac{4a^2 - 12ab - 6bc + 4ac + 9b^2 + c^2}{4a^2 + 9c^2 - 12ac}$.

***99a.** An isosceles triangle has a base of length $2a$ and its height is h. On each side of the triangle a square is drawn external to the triangle. Prove that the area of the complete figure thus formed is $6a^2 + 2h^2 + ah$.

If this area is 28 square cm and if the base of the triangle is of length 4 cm, find the value of h. (Lond. Matric.)

100. The express leaves Bristol at 3 p.m. and reaches London at 6; the ordinary train leaves London at 1.30 p.m. and arrives at Bristol at 6. If both trains travel uniformly, find the time when they will meet.

101. Solve (1) $.\dot{6}\,x + .75x - .1\dot{6} = x - .58\dot{3}\,x + 5$.

(2) $\dfrac{37}{x^2 - 5x + 6} + \dfrac{4}{x-2} = \dfrac{7}{3-x}$.

102. Simplify (1) $\dfrac{a+x}{a^2 + ax + x^2} + \dfrac{a-x}{a^2 - ax + x^2} + \dfrac{2x^3}{a^4 + a^2x^2 + x^4}$.

(2) $(1+x)^2 \div \left\{1 + \dfrac{x}{1 - x + \dfrac{x}{1 + x + x^2}}\right\}$.

103. Find the square root of $a^6 + \frac{1}{a^6} - 6\left(a^4 + \frac{1}{a^4}\right) + 15\left(a^2 + \frac{1}{a^2}\right) - 20$; also the cube root of the result.

104. Divide $1 - 2x$ by $1 + 3x$ to 4 terms.

105. I bought a horse and carriage for Rs 750; I sold the horse at a gain of 5 per cent, and the carriage at a gain of 20 per cent, making on the whole a gain of 16 per cent. Find the original cost of the horse.

106. Find the divisor when $(4a^2 + 7ab + 5b^2)^2$ is the dividend, $8(a + 2b)^2$ the quotient, and $b^2(9a + 11b)^2$ the remainder.

107. Solve (1) $5x(x - 3) = 2(x - 7)$.

$$(2)\ \frac{1}{(x-1)(x-2)} + 6 = \frac{3}{x-2} + \frac{2}{x-1}.$$

108. If $x = a + b + \frac{(a-b)^2}{4(a+b)}$, and $y = \frac{a+b}{4} + \frac{ab}{a+b}$,

prove that $(x - a)^2 - (y - b)^2 = b^2$.

109. Find the square root of

$$49x^4 + \frac{1051x^2}{25} - \frac{14x^3}{5} - \frac{6x}{5} + 9.$$

***109a.** The surface area of a circular cone is given by $A = \pi r^2 + \pi rs$, where s cm is the slant height, r cm is the radius of the base and π is the number $\frac{22}{7}$. Find the radius of the base if a cone of surface area $93\frac{1}{2}$ sq cm has a slant height of 5 cm.

110. Solve $\frac{a+x}{a^2+ax+x^2} + \frac{a-x}{a^2-ax+x^2} = \frac{3a}{x(a^4+a^2x^2+x^4)}$.

111. Subtract $\frac{x+3}{x^2+x-12}$ from $\frac{x+4}{x^2-x-12}$,

and divide the difference by $1 + \frac{2(x^2-12)}{x^2+7x+12}$.

112. Find the H.C.F. and L.C.M. of

$2x^2 + (6a - 10b)x - 30ab$ and $3x^2 - (9a + 15b)x + 45ab$.

113. Solve (1) $2cx^2 - abx + 2abd = 4cdx$.

$$(2)\ \frac{x}{2(x+3)} - 2\frac{5}{24} = \frac{x^2}{x^2-9} - \frac{8x-1}{4(x-3)}.$$

114. If $a = 1, b = 2, c = 3, d = 4$, find the value of

$$\frac{a^b + b^c + c^a}{b^a + c^b + d^c + (a+b)(b+c)} + 3(a^c + b^b + c^c)\left(\frac{1}{a} + \frac{1}{b} + \frac{1}{c}\right).$$

115. I rode one-third of a journey at 10 km an hour, one-third more at 9, and the rest at 8 km an hour; if I had ridden half the journey at 10, and the other half at 8 km per hour, I should have been half a minute longer on the way: what distance did I ride?

116. The product of two factors is $(3x + 2y)^3 - (2x + 3y)^3$, and one of the factors is $x - y$; find the other factor.

117. If $a + b = 1$, prove that $(a^2 - b^2)^2 = a^3 + b^3 - ab$.

118. Resolve into factors:

(1) $x^3 + y^3 + 3xy(x + y)$.   (2) $m^3 - n^3 - m(m^2 - n^2) + n(m - n)^2$.

119. Solve (1) $\left.\begin{array}{r} x^3 - y^3 = 28 \\ x^2 + xy + y^2 = 7 \end{array}\right\}$.

(2) $\left.\begin{array}{r} x^2 - 6xy + 11y^2 = 9 \\ x - 3y = 1 \end{array}\right\}$.

120. Find the square root of

$$(a - b)^4 - 2(a^2 + b^2)(a - b)^2 + 2(a^4 + b^4).$$

121. Simplify the fractions:

(1) $\dfrac{1}{a^2 - \dfrac{a^3 - 1}{a + \dfrac{1}{a+1}}}$.   (2) $\dfrac{\left(1 + \dfrac{1}{x}\right) \times \left(1 - \dfrac{1}{x}\right)^2}{x - \dfrac{1}{x}}$.

122. Find the H.C.F. of

$$a^2b + b^2c - abc - ab^2 \text{ and } ax^2 + ab - a^2 - bx^2.$$

***122a.** x and y are connected by the equation $y = ax^2 + b$, and it is known that $y = 10$ when $x = 2$, and $y = 1$ when $x = -1$, find the value of y when $x = -\frac{1}{2}$.

Also find what values of x make x and y equal.

123. A constituency has two-thirds of its number Conservatives: in an election 25 refused to vote, and 60 went over to the Liberals; the voters were now equal. How many voters were there altogether?

124. Solve (1) $\dfrac{x^2}{a+b}+(a-b)=\dfrac{2ax}{a+b}$.

(2) $\dfrac{3}{x}+\dfrac{2}{y}=6\left(\dfrac{1}{y}-\dfrac{1}{2x}\right)=2$.

125. Simplify (1) $\left(1+\dfrac{y^2+z^2-x^2}{2yz}\right)\div\left(1-\dfrac{x^2+y^2-z^2}{2xy}\right)$.

(2) $\dfrac{(x+1)^3-(x-1)^3}{(x+1)^4-(x-1)^4}$.

126. Divide $x^4+(a-1)x^3-(2a+1)\,x^2+(a^2+4a-5)\,x+3a+6$

by $x^2-3x+a+2$.

127. Resolve into factors:

(1) $x^2+5xy-24y^2+x-3y$. (2) $x^3-\dfrac{4}{x}$.

128. Find the square root of p^2-3q to three terms.

129. Solve (1) $\dfrac{x-5}{x-6}-\dfrac{x-6}{x-7}=\dfrac{x-1}{x-2}-\dfrac{x-2}{x-3}$.

(2) $ax+1=by+1=ay+bx$.

130. Find the H.C.F. of $3x^2+(4a-2b)\,x-2ab+a^2$ and $x^3+(2a-b)\,x^2-(2ab-a^2)x-a^2b$.

131. Simplify

(1) $\dfrac{(x^a)^3}{x^{b+c}}\times\dfrac{(x^b)^3}{x^{c+a}}\times\dfrac{(x^c)^3}{x^{a+b}}$.

(2) $x^{1/2}y^{1/3}\left(\dfrac{y^{1/4}}{x^{1/6}}\right)^2\div\dfrac{y^{-1/4}}{x^{1/4}}$.

***131a.** Prior to the last match of the cricket season two bowlers, A and B, have each taken x wickets and a total of $20y$ runs has been scored off each of them. In the last match, A takes 1 wicket for y runs and B takes 9 wickets for z runs. After the last match the averages of the two bowlers are still equal, *i.e.* the ratio of total runs scored off the bowler to the total number of wickets he has taken is the same for A and B. Express the ratio of z to y in terms of x.

Show that $z=3y$ if $x=83$, and also show that, if x exceeds 83, then z is less than $3y$. (Oxf. and Camb. Sch. Certif.)

132. At a cricket match the contractor provided dinner for 24 persons, and fixed the price so as to gain $12\frac{1}{2}$ per cent upon his outlay. Three of the cricketers being absent, the remaining 21 paid the fixed price for their dinner, and the contractor lost 1 rupee: what was the charge for the dinner?

133. Prove that $x(y+2)+\frac{x}{y}+\frac{y}{x}$ is equal to a, if

$$x=\frac{y}{y+1} \text{ and } y=\frac{a-2}{2}.$$

134. Find the cube root of

$$x^3-12x^2+54x-112+\frac{108}{x}-\frac{48}{x^2}+\frac{8}{x^3}.$$

135. Find the H.C.F. and L.C.M. of

$$x^3+2ax^2+a^2x+2a^3 \text{ and } x^3-2ax^2+a^2x-2a^3.$$

136. Simplify

(1) $42\left\{\frac{4x-3y}{6}-\frac{3x-4y}{7}\right\}-56\left\{\frac{3x-2y}{7}-\frac{2x-3y}{8}\right\}.$

(2) $\frac{4b+a}{3b+a}+\frac{a-4b}{a-3b}+\frac{a^2-3b^2}{a^2-9b^2}.$

137. Resolve $4a^2(x^3+18ab^2)-(32a^5+9b^2x^3)$ into four factors.

138. Solve (1) $5\sqrt{3x}-1=\sqrt{75x-29}.$

(2) $\frac{xy}{x+y}=70, \frac{xz}{x+z}=84, \frac{yz}{y+z}=140.$

139. Show that the difference between

$\frac{x}{x-a}+\frac{x}{x-b}+\frac{x}{x-c}$ and $\frac{a}{x-a}+\frac{b}{x-b}+\frac{c}{x-c}$ is the same whatever value x may have.

***140.** Multiply $x^{3/2}+2y^{3/2}+3z^{3/2}$ by $x^{3/2}-2y^{3/2}-3z^{3/2}$.

140a. The sum of the first n whole numbers is given by the formula $S=\frac{1}{2}n(n+1)$. Find the value of n if the sum of the first n whole numbers is 120.

141. Walking $4\frac{1}{4}$ km an hour, I start $1\frac{1}{2}$ hours after a friend whose pace is 3 km an hour: how long shall I been overtaking him?

142. Express in the simplest form:

(1) $(8^{2/3} + 4^{3/2}) \times 16^{-3/4}$. (2) $\dfrac{\left\{9^n \cdot 3^2 \times \dfrac{1}{3^{-n}}\right\} - 27^n}{3^{3n} \times 9}$.

143. Find the square root of

$$\frac{x}{y} + \frac{y}{x} + 3 - 2\sqrt{\frac{x}{y}} - 2\sqrt{\frac{y}{x}}.$$

144. Simplify

(1) $\left(\dfrac{x}{x-1} - \dfrac{1}{x+1}\right) \cdot \dfrac{x^3 - 1}{x^6 + 1} \cdot \dfrac{(x-1)^2 (x+1)^2 + x^2}{x^4 + x^2 + 1}$.

(2) $\left\{\dfrac{a^4 - y^4}{a^2 - 2ay + y^2} \div \dfrac{a^2 + ay}{a - y}\right\} \times \left\{\dfrac{a^5 - a^3y^2}{a^3 + y^3} \div \dfrac{a^4 - 2a^3y + a^2y^2}{a^2 - ay + y^2}\right\}$.

145. Find the value of

(1) $\sqrt{8} + \sqrt{50} - \sqrt{18} + \sqrt{48}$.

(2) $\sqrt{35 + 14\sqrt{6}}$.

146. Solve (1) $\dfrac{x-b}{x-a} - \dfrac{x-a}{x-b} = \dfrac{2(a-b)}{x-(a+b)}$.

(2) $\left.\begin{aligned} 2x + 3y &= 1\frac{1}{2} \\ 4x + 9xy + 9y^2 &= 11 \end{aligned}\right\}$.

147. Show that $\dfrac{(a+b)^3 - c^3}{(a+b) - c} + \dfrac{(b+c)^3 - a^3}{b+c-a} + \dfrac{(c+a)^3 - b^3}{c+a-b}$ is equal to $2(a+b+c)^2 + a^2 + b^2 + c^2$.

148. Divide

$a - x + 4a^{1/4}x^{3/4} - 4a^{1/2}x^{1/2}$ by $a^{1/2} + 2a^{1/4}x^{1/4} - x^{1/2}$.

149. Find the square root of

$(a-1)^4 + 2(a^4 + 1) - 2(a^2 + 1)(a-1)^2$.

***149a.** The area of the surface of a right circular cylinder of height h and diameter d is $\dfrac{22}{7} d\left(h + \dfrac{d}{2}\right)$. Find to the nearest millimetre the diameter of a cylinder whose height is 3 metres and whose surface is 20 square metres in area. (Lond. Matric.)

150. How much are pears a gross when 120 more for Rs 12 lowers the price 10 paise a score?

151. Show that if a number of two digits is six times the sum of its digits, the number formed by interchanging the digits is five times their sum.

152. Find the value of

$$\frac{1}{(a-b)(b-c)} - \frac{1}{(b-c)(a-c)} - \frac{1}{(c-a)(b-a)}.$$

153. Multiply

$$3 + 5x - \frac{12 + 41x + 36x^2}{4 + 7x} \text{ by } 5 - 2x + \frac{26x - 8x^2 - 14}{3 - 4x}.$$

154. If $x - \frac{1}{x} = 1$, prove that $x^2 + \frac{1}{x^2} = 3$, and $x^3 - \frac{1}{x^3} = 4$.

155. Solve (1) $\frac{3x}{11} + \frac{23}{x+4} = \frac{1}{3}(x + 5)$.

(2) $\left.\begin{aligned} 2x^2 - 3y^2 &= 23 \\ 2xy - 3y^2 &= 3 \end{aligned}\right\}$.

156. Simplify

(1) $1\frac{8}{5}\sqrt{20} - 3\sqrt{5} - \sqrt{\frac{1}{5}}$. (2) $\frac{\sqrt{x}}{y^{-1/3}}\left(\frac{\sqrt[4]{y}}{x^{1/6}}\right) \div \frac{y^{-1/4}}{x^{1/4}}$.

157. Find the H.C.F. of $(p^2 - 1)x^2 + (3p - 1)x - p(p - 1)$ and $p(p + 1)x^2 - (p^2 - 2p - 1)x - (p - 1)$.

158. Reduce to its simplest form: $\frac{ax + \frac{a}{y}}{x - \frac{1}{y}} \times \frac{x^2 + \frac{1}{y^2}}{bx^2 - \frac{b}{y^2}} \times \frac{\frac{1}{5}(xy - 1)^2}{\frac{1}{3}(x^4y^4 - 1)}$.

159. Find the square root of

(1) $1 - 2^{2n+1} + 4^{2n}$. (2) $9^n - 2.6^n + 4^n$.

160. A clock gains 4 minutes a day. What time should it indicate at 6 o'clock in the morning, in order that it may be right at 7.15 p.m. on the same day?

161. If $x = 2 + \sqrt{2}$, find the value of $x^2 + \frac{4}{x^2}$.

162. Solve

(1) $\frac{\sqrt{x} + a}{\sqrt{x} - b} = \frac{\sqrt{x} - a}{\sqrt{x}}$. (2) $\frac{\sqrt{1+x} + \sqrt{1-x}}{\sqrt{1+x} - \sqrt{1-x}} = 3$.

163. Simplify

$$\frac{a^2}{(b-a)(c-a)} + \frac{b^2}{(c-b)(a-b)} + \frac{c^2}{(a-c)(b-c)}.$$

164. Find the product of $\frac{1}{5}\sqrt{5}$, $\frac{1}{2}\sqrt[3]{2}, \sqrt[6]{80}, \sqrt[3]{5}$, and divide $\frac{8-4\sqrt{5}}{\sqrt{5}+1}$ by $\frac{3\sqrt{5}-7}{5+\sqrt{7}}$.

165. Resolve $9x^6y^2 - 576y^2 - 4x^8 + 256x^2$ into six factors.

166. Simplify (1) $\dfrac{1-\dfrac{a^2}{(x+a)^2}}{(x+a)(x-a)} \div \dfrac{x(x+2a)}{(x^2-a^2)(x+a)^2}$.\

(2) $\dfrac{6x^2y^2}{m+n} \div \left[\dfrac{3(m-n)x}{7(r+s)} \div \left\{\dfrac{4(r-s)}{21xy^2} \div \dfrac{r^2-s^2}{4(m^2-n^2)}\right\}\right]$.

167. Simplify

(1) $\left(a^{1+\frac{q}{p}}\right)^{\frac{p}{p+q}} \div \sqrt[p]{\dfrac{a^{2p}}{(a^{-1})^{-p}}}$.

(2) $\sqrt{14-\sqrt{132}}$.

168. Find the H.C.F. and L.C.M. of

$20x^4 + x^2 - 1, 25x^4 + 5x^3 - x - 1, 25x^4 - 10x^2 + 1$.

169. Solve

(1) $a + x + \sqrt{2ax + x^2} = b$.

(2) $x + 9\dfrac{5}{8} + \dfrac{1}{\dfrac{x}{7} + \dfrac{11}{8}} = 8$.

170. The price of photographs is raised Rs 3 per dozen, and customers consequently receive seven less than before for Rs 21: what were the prices charged?

171. If $\left(a + \dfrac{1}{a}\right)^2 = 3$, prove that $a^3 + \dfrac{1}{a^3} = 0$.

172. Find the value of

$$\frac{x+2a}{2b-x} + \frac{x-2a}{2b+x} + \frac{4ab}{x^2-4b^2}, \text{ when } x = \frac{ab}{a+b}.$$

173. Reduce to fractions in their lowest terms:

(1) $\left(\frac{1}{x}+\frac{1}{y}+\frac{1}{z}\right)\div\left(\frac{x+y+z}{x^2+y^2+z^2-xy-yz-zx}-\frac{1}{x+y+z}\right)+1.$

(2) $\left(1-\frac{56}{x+4}+\frac{42}{x+3}\right)\left(1+\frac{56}{x-4}-\frac{42}{x-3}\right).$

174. Express as a whole number:

$(27)^{2/3}+(16)^{3/4}-\frac{2}{(8)^{-2/3}}+\frac{\sqrt[5]{2}}{(4)^{-2/5}}.$

175. Simplify

(1) $\frac{n}{1-x^n}+\frac{n}{1-x^{-n}}.$

(2) $\sqrt[4]{97-56\sqrt{3}}.$

176. Solve

(1) $\frac{x-4a}{x-3a}+\frac{x-5a}{x-4a}=\frac{x+6a}{x-4a}+\frac{x+5a}{x-3a}.$

(2) $\left.\begin{aligned}3x^2+xy+3y^2&=8\frac{1}{4}\\ 8x^2-3xy+8y^2&=17\frac{3}{4}\end{aligned}\right\}.$

177. Find the square root of $\frac{a^2x^2+2ab^2x^3+b^4x^4}{a^{2m}+2a^mx^n+x^{2n}}.$

178. Simplify

(1) $\frac{b}{\sqrt{a}}\times\sqrt[3]{ac}\times\frac{\sqrt[4]{c^3}}{\sqrt{b}}\times\frac{\sqrt{b^{-1}}}{a^{-1/6}}.$

(2) $\left\{\frac{(9^{n+1/4})\times\sqrt{3.3^n}}{3\sqrt{3^{-n}}}\right\}^{1/n}$

179. A boat's crew can now 12 km an hour in still water; what is the speed of a river's current if it takes them 2 hours and 40 minutes to row 12 km up and 12 km down?

180. If $a = x^2 - yz, b = y^2 - zx, c = z^2 - xy$, prove that

$a^2 - bc = x(ax + by + cz).$

181. Find a quantity such that when it is subtracted from each of the quantities a, b, c, the remainders are in continued proportion.

182. Simplify

(1) $\left(x+y-\dfrac{1}{x+y-\dfrac{xy}{x+y}}\right)\times\dfrac{x^3-y^3}{x^2-y^2}$.

(2) $\dfrac{2(7x-4)}{6x^2-7x+2}+\dfrac{x-10}{6x^2-x-2}-\dfrac{2(4x-1)}{4x^2-1}$.

183. Find the sixth root of

$729-2916x^2+4860x^4-4320x^6+2160x^8-576x^{10}+64x^{12}$.

184. Simplify

(1) $\dfrac{1}{x+\sqrt{x^2-1}}+\dfrac{1}{x-\sqrt{x^2-1}}$.

(2) $\sqrt[4]{16}+\sqrt[3]{81}-\sqrt[3]{-512}+\sqrt[3]{192}-7\sqrt[6]{9}$.

185. Solve

(1) $\dfrac{5}{6-\dfrac{5}{6-\dfrac{5}{6-x}}}=x$.

(2) $\left.\begin{array}{r} x^2y^2+192=28xy \\ x+y=8 \end{array}\right\}$.

186. Simplify $\dfrac{b-c}{a^2-(b-c)^2}+\dfrac{c-a}{b^2-(c-a)^2}+\dfrac{a-b}{c^2-(a-b)^2}$.

187. Solve

(1) $x-15\dfrac{3}{4}+\dfrac{5}{x-15\dfrac{3}{4}}=6$.

(2) $2(x+y^{-1})=3(x^{-1}-y)=4$.

188. If $xy=ab(a+b)$ and $x^2-xy+y^2=a^3+b^3$. prove that

$\left(\dfrac{x}{a}-\dfrac{y}{b}\right)\left(\dfrac{x}{b}-\dfrac{y}{a}\right)=0$.

189. Find the H.C.F. of

$(2a^2-3a-2)\,x^2+(a^2+7a+2)\,x-a^2-2a$

and $(4a^2+4a+1)\,x^2-(4a^2+2a)\,x+a^2$.

190. Multiply $\sqrt{2x}+\sqrt{2(2x-1)}-\dfrac{1}{\sqrt{2x}}$ by $\dfrac{1}{\sqrt{2x}}+\sqrt{2(2x-1)}-\sqrt{2x}$.

191. Divide $a^4b^2 + b^4c^2 + c^4a^2 - a^2b^4 - b^2c^4 - c^2a^4$

by $a^2b + b^2c + c^2a - ab^2 - bc^2 - ca^2$.

192. Simplify

(1) $\dfrac{7}{2(x+1)} - \dfrac{1}{6(x-1)} - \dfrac{10x-1}{3(x^2+x+1)}$.

(2) $\left\{\dfrac{\sqrt{x+a}}{\sqrt{x-a}} - \dfrac{\sqrt{x-a}}{\sqrt{x+a}}\right\} \times \dfrac{\sqrt{x^3-a^3}}{\sqrt{(x+a)^2-ax}}$.

193. If p be the difference between any quantity and its reciprocal, q the difference between the square of the same quantity and the square of its reciprocal, show that $p^2(p^2+4) = q^2$.

194. A man started for a walk when the hands of his watch were coincident between three and four o'clock. When he finished, the hands were again coincident between five and six o'clock. What was the time when he started, and how long did he walk?

195. If n be an integer, show that $7^{2n+1} + 1$ is always divisible by 8.

196. Simplify $\dfrac{\left(p+\dfrac{1}{q}\right)^p \left(p-\dfrac{1}{q}\right)^q}{\left(q+\dfrac{1}{p}\right)^p \left(q-\dfrac{1}{p}\right)^q}$.

*__196a.__ Write the formula $S = \dfrac{n}{2}\{2a + \overline{n-1}d\}$ as a quadratic equation for n.

Find the number of terms of the series 2 + 5 + 8 + ... which add up to 155.

197. Find the value of

(1) $\dfrac{7+3\sqrt{5}}{7-\sqrt{35}} + \dfrac{7-3\sqrt{5}}{7+3\sqrt{5}}$.

(2) $\dfrac{\sqrt{1+x}+\sqrt{1-x}}{\sqrt{1+x}-\sqrt{1-x}}$ when $x = \dfrac{2b}{b^2+1}$.

198. If $a+b+c+d = 2s$, prove that

$4(ab+cd)^2 - (a^2+b^2-c^2-d^2)^2 = 16(s-a)(s-b)(s-c)(s-d)$.

199. A man buys a number of articles for Rs 10 and sells for Rs 10.80 all but two at 10 paise a piece more than they cost: how many did he buy?

200. Find the square root of

$2(81x^4 + y^4) - 2(9x^2+y^2)(3x-y)^2 + (3x-y)^4$.

201. If $x : a :: y : b :: z : c$, prove that

$$(bc + ca + ab)^2(x^2 + y^2 + z^2) = (bz + cx + ay)^2(a^2 + b^2 + c^2).$$

202. If a man saves ₹ 10 more than he did the previous year, and if he saved ₹ 20 the first year, in how many years will his savings amount to ₹ 1700?

203. Given that 4 is a root of the quadratic $x^2 - 5x + q = 0$, find the value of q and the other root.

204. A person having 7 km to walk increases his speed one km an hour after the first km, and finds that he is half an hour less on the road than he would have been had he not altered his rate. How long did he take?

205. If $(a + b + c)x = (-a + b + c)y = (a - b + c)z = (a + b - c)w$, show that $\frac{1}{y} + \frac{1}{x} + \frac{1}{\omega} = \frac{1}{x}$.

206. Find a Geometrical Progression of which the sum of the first two terms is $2\frac{3}{3}$, and the sum to infinity $4\frac{1}{6}$.

207. Simplify $\dfrac{\left(1 + \dfrac{x}{y}\right)^m \left(1 - \dfrac{y}{x}\right)^n}{\left(1 + \dfrac{y}{x}\right)^n \left(1 - \dfrac{x}{y}\right)^m}$.

208. A man has a stable containing 10 stalls; in how many ways could he stable 5 horses?

209. In boring a well 100 metres deep the cost is Rs 2 for the first metre and an additional 10 paise for each subsequent metre: what is the cost of boring the last metre, and also of boring the entire well?

210. If α, β are the roots of $x^2 + px + q = 0$, show that p, q are the roots of the equation

$$x^2 + (\alpha + \beta - \alpha\beta)x - \alpha\beta(\alpha + \beta) = 0.$$

211. Multiply together the duodenary numbers *tete* and *ete*.

212. If $\frac{x + z}{y} = \frac{z}{x} = \frac{x}{z - y}$; determine the ratios $x : y : z$.

213. If a, b, c are in H.P. show that

$$\left(\frac{3}{a} + \frac{3}{b} - \frac{2}{c}\right)\left(\frac{3}{c} + \frac{3}{b} - \frac{2}{a}\right) + \frac{9}{b^2} = \frac{25}{ac}.$$

214. Find the number of permutations which can be made from all the letters of the words

(1) *Consequences,* (2) *Acarnania.*

215. Expand by the Binomial Theorem $(2a - 3x)^5$; and find the numerically greatest term in the expansion of $(1 + x)^n$, if $x = \frac{3}{5}$, and $n = 7$.

216. When $x = \frac{\sqrt{3}}{4}$, find the value of $\frac{1 + 2x}{1 + \sqrt{1 + 2x}} + \frac{1 - 2x}{1 - \sqrt{1 - 2x}}$.

217. Simplify $\frac{x^2 - bc}{(a - b)(a - c)} + \frac{x^2 - ca}{(b - c)(b - a)} + \frac{x^2 - ab}{(c - a)(c - b)}$.

218. Solve the equations;

(1) $(x^2 - 5x + 2)^2 = x^2 - 5x + 22$.

(2) $\left(x^2 + \frac{1}{x^2}\right)^2 + 4\left(x^2 + \frac{1}{x^2}\right) = 12$.

219. Prove that

$$(y - z)^3 + (x - y)^3 + 3(x - y)(x - z)(y - z) = (x - z)^3.$$

220. Out of 16 consonants and 5 vowels, how many words can be formed each containing 4 consonants and 2 vowels?

221. If $b - a$ is a harmonic mean between $c - a$ and $d - a$, show that $d - c$ is a harmonic mean between $a - c$ and $b - c$.

222. In how many ways may 2 red balls, 3 black, 1 white, 2 blue be selected from 4 red, 6 black, 2 white and 5 blue; and in how many ways may they be arranged?

223. The sum of a certain number of terms of an arithmetical series is 36, and the first and last of these terms are 1 and 11 respectively: find the number of terms, and the common difference of the series.

224. Expand by the Binomial Theorem:

(1) $\left(2 - \frac{3a}{4}\right)^5$; (2) $\left(1 - \frac{2}{3}x\right)^{3/2}$ to 5 terms.

225. In what scale is the denary number 418 represented by 1534?

226. Simplify $\frac{\sqrt{10}}{3\sqrt{27}} \times \frac{15\sqrt{21}}{4\sqrt{15}} \div \frac{5\sqrt{14}}{7\sqrt{48}}$ and find the value of $\frac{1}{3\sqrt{5} - 6}$, given that $\sqrt{5} = 2.236$.

227. By the Binomial Theorem find the cube root of 128 to six places of decimals.

228. There are 9 books of which 4 are Greek, 3 are Latin, and 2 are English; in how many ways could a selection be made so as to include at least one of each language?

229. Simplify

(1) $\dfrac{\sqrt{45x^3} - \sqrt{80x^3} + \sqrt{5a^2x}}{a - x}$;

(2) $\left\{\dfrac{x^{1/2} + x^{-1/2}}{x^2 - x + 1} - \dfrac{x^{1/2} - x^{-1/2}}{x^2 + x + 1}\right\} \div \left\{\dfrac{x^{1/2} + 2x^{-1/2}}{x^3 - 1} - \dfrac{x^{1/2} - 2x^{-1/2}}{x^3 + 1}\right\}$.

230. From the quadratic equation whose roots are $5 \pm \sqrt{6}$. If the roots of $x^2 - px + q = 0$ are two consecutive integers, prove that $p^2 - 4q - 1 = 0$.

231. Subtract 4.72473 from 7.641 in the scale of eight, and find the square root of $t08404$ in the scale of twelve.

232. Find $\log_{16} 128$, $\log_4 \sqrt{128}$, $\log_2 \frac{1}{4}$; and having given $\log 2 = .3010300$ and $\log 3 = .4771213$, find the logarithm of .00001728.

233. A and B start from the same point, B five days after A; A travels 1 km the first day, 2 km the second, 3 km the third, and so on; B travels 12 km a day. When will they be together? Explain the double answer.

234. Solve the equations:

(1) $2^x = 8^{y+1}, 9^y = 3^{x-9}$;

(2) $z^x = y^{2x}, 2^z = 2 \times 4^x, x + y + z = 16$.

235. The sum of the first 10 terms of an arithmetical series is to the sum of the first 5 terms as 13 is to 4. Find the ratio of the first term to the common difference.

236. Find the greatest term in the expansion of $(1 - x)^{-4/8}$ when $x = \dfrac{12}{13}$.

237. Five gentlemen and one lady wish to enter an omnibus in which there are only three vacant places; in how many ways can these places be occupied (1) when there is no restriction, (2) when one of the places is to be occupied by the lady?

238. Given $\log 2 = .301030$, $\log 3 = .477121$, and $\log 7 = .845098$, find the logarithms of .005, 6.3, and $\left(\dfrac{49}{216}\right)^{1/3}$.

Find x from the equation $18^{8-4x} = (54\sqrt{2})^{3x-2}$.

239. If P and Q vary respectively as $y^{1/2}$ and $y^{1/3}$ when z is constant, and as $z^{1/2}$ and $z^{1/3}$ when y is constant, and if $x = P + Q$, find the equation between, x, y, z; it being known that when $y = z = 64$, $x = 12$; and that when $y = 4z = 16$, $x = 2$.

240. Simplify

$$\log\frac{133}{65} + 2\log\frac{13}{7} - \log\frac{143}{90} + \log\frac{77}{171}$$

241. If the number of permutations of n things 4 at a time is to the number of combinations of $2n$ things 3 at a time as 22 to 3, find n.

242. If $\frac{1}{a} + \frac{1}{c} = \frac{1}{2b - a} + \frac{1}{2b - c}$, prove that $2b$ s either the arithmetic mean between $2a$ and $2c$, or the harmonic mean between a and c.

243. If ${}^nC_r$ denote the number of combinations of n things takne r together, prove that

$${}^{n+2}C_{r+1} = {}^nC_{r+1} + {}^nC_{r-1} + (2 \times {}^nC_r);$$

244. Find (1) the characteristic of log 54 to base 3;

(2) $\log_{10}(.0125)^{1/3}$; (3) the number of digits in 3^{45}

Given $\log_{10} 2 = .30103$, $\log_{10} 3 = .47712$.

245. Write down the $(r+1)^{\text{th}}$ term of $(2ax^2 - x^3)^{5/3}$, and express it in its simplest form.

246. A a meeting of a Debating Society there were 9 speakers; 5 spoke for the Government, and 4 for the Opposition. In how many ways could the speeches have been made, if a member of the Government always speaks first, and the speeches are alternately for the Government ann the Oppositions?

247. From the quadratic equation whose roots are

$$a + b + \sqrt{a^2 + b^2} \text{ and } \frac{2}{a + b + \sqrt{a^2 + b^2}}$$

248. A point moves with a speed which is different in different kilometres, but invariable in the same kilometre, and its speed in and kilometre varies inversely as the number of kilometres travelled before it commences this kilometre. If the second kilometre be described in 2 hours, find the time taken to describe the nth kilometre.

ANSWERS

I-a. Page 3

1. 70. **2.** 125. **3.** 105. **4.** 343. **5.** 30. **6.** 32. **7.** 12.
8. 70. **9.** 6. **10.** 108. **11.** 7. **12.** 144. **13.** 48. **14.** 189.
15. 200. **16.** 27. **17.** 1000. **18.** 3. **19.** 1. **20.** 567. **21.** 4.
22. 125. **23.** 81. **24.** 1. **25.** 243. **26.** 512. **27.** 5. **28.** 4096.
29. 64. **30.** 90. **31.** 24. **32.** 2. **33.** 81. **34.** 64. **35.** 8.
36. 2401. **37.** 56. **38.** 3. **39.** 48. **40.** 16.

I-b. Page 4

1. 700. **2.** 686. **3.** 96. **4.** 135. **5.** 15. **6.** 60. **7.** 162.
8. 0. **9.** 0. **10.** 3000. **11.** 98. **12.** 225. **13.** 3. **14.** 1.
15. $5\frac{1}{3}$. **16.** 2. **17.** 36. **18.** 160. **19.** $1\frac{1}{8}$. **20.** 40. **21.** 0.
22. 72. **23.** 2048. **24.** 81. **25.** $11\frac{1}{4}$. **26.** $13\frac{1}{2}$. **27.** $\frac{1}{64}$. **28.** $3\frac{3}{3}$.

I-c. Page 5

1. 4. **2.** 6. **3.** 8. **4.** 36. **5.** 3. **6.** 8. **7.** 8.
8. 0. **9.** 32. **10.** 60. **11.** 0. **12.** 16. **13.** $2\frac{2}{3}$. **14.** $3\frac{1}{3}$.
15. $1\frac{1}{7}$. **16.** 0. **17.** $\frac{2}{3}$. **18.** $2\frac{2}{3}$. **19.** 0. **20.** 3. **21.** 8.

I-d. Page 8

1. 19. **2.** 0. **3.** 7. **4.** 11. **5.** 21. **6.** 6. **7.** 18.
8. 36. **9.** 6. **10.** 14. **11.** 85. **12.** 96. **13.** 36. **14.** 0.
15. 0. **16.** 12. **17.** 24. **18.** 43. **19.** 4. **20.** 8. **21.** 12.
22. 0. **23.** 1. **24.** 6000. **25.** 17. **26.** 16. **27.** 18.
28. 9. **29.** $3\frac{1}{2}$. **30.** 49. **31.** $\frac{1}{4}$. **32.** $\frac{3}{16}$. **33.** 0. **34.** $1\frac{5}{6}$.

I-e. Page 8

1. 20, 2, 2, 12, 30. **2.** 3, 5. 25, 8, 11. 25, 15. **3.** 6.
4. 4.48, 17.76, 27.52, 40. **6.** 504. **8.** The first by 24.
10. 21, 0. **12.** 0.196.

II-a. Page 12

1. – £.12. **2.** 4, – 2. **3.** 20. **4.** – 6°.
5. – 3 feet. **6.** 24. –4. **7.** *A*, *C*, *B* with + 4, 0, – 2 points.

II-b. Page 14

1. $47a$. **2.** $24x$. **3.** $39b$. **4.** $151c$.
5. $-26x$. **6.** $-40b$. **7.** $-17y$. **8.** $-66c$.
9. $-20b$. **10.** $2x$. **11.** 0. **12.** $-16f$.

13. $-s$. **14.** $7y$. **15.** 0. **16.** $2ab$.
17. x^2. **18.** $-14a^2x$. **19.** $-21a^2$. **20.** $-16x^2$.
21. 0. **22.** $-19x^4$. **23.** $-43abcd$. **24.** $\frac{11}{6}x$.
25. $\frac{8}{5}a$. **26.** $-3b$. **27.** $-x^2$. **28.** $-\frac{5}{6}ab$.
29. $\frac{5}{4}x$. **30.** $-5x^2$.

III-a. Page 18

1. 0. **2.** $4a + 4b + 4c$. **3.** 0.
4. $4x + 4y + 4z$. **5.** $3a + 5b - 2c$. **6.** $b - c$.
7. $39a - 5b + 4c$. **8.** $5c$. **9.** $3ax - 3by + 3cz$.
10. $22p - 18q - 20r$. **11.** ab. **12.** $-20ab + ca$.
13. $5ab + bc$. **14.** $pq + qr + rp$. **15.** $6x$.
16. $20a$. **17.** $2xy + 2zx$. **18.** $14ab - 11bc$.
19. $13z$. **20.** $a + b + c$.

III-b. Page 19

1. abc. **2.** $x^2 + xy + y^2$. **3.** $a^2 + 3ab - 2b^2$.
4. $yz + zx + xy$. **5.** $3x^2 + 2xy - y^2$. **6.** $-2x^3 + x^2 + 4x + 2$.
7. $x^2 + 7x$. **8.** $15x^2 - 32x - 18$. **9.** $15x^3 - 4x^2 + 3x - 1$.
10. $a^3 + b^3 + c^3$. **11.** $a^3 + b^3 + c^3 + d^3$. **12.** $x^3 + x^2 + x + 3$.
13. $9a^3 - 3a^2$. **14.** $3x^3 - 2y^2 - 2xy - 4yz - 3xz$.
15. $-x^3 + x^2 + 2y^2 + y$. **16.** $3x^2y + xy^2$. **17.** $2a^2b$.
18. $x^5 - x^4y - y^5$. **19.** $a^3 + b^3 + c^3 - 3abc$.
20. $x^2 + x^2y + 7xy^2 + 3y^2$. **21.** $\frac{1}{4}a - \frac{2}{3}b$.
22. $-3a - \frac{1}{2}b$. **23.** $-\frac{7}{3}a + \frac{2}{3}b - \frac{1}{2}c$.
24. $\frac{3}{8}a - \frac{4}{5}b - \frac{15}{4}c$. **25.** $\frac{1}{3}x^2 - \frac{4}{3}xy + \frac{1}{2}y^2$.
26. $\frac{5}{6}a^2 + \frac{3}{5}ab - \frac{1}{6}b^2$. **27.** $\frac{3}{8}x^2 - \frac{2}{5}xy - \frac{1}{2}y^2$.
28. $-\frac{1}{4}x^3 + \frac{3}{8}ax^2 + \frac{5}{8}a^2x$. **29.** $-\frac{1}{4}x^2 - xy + \frac{3}{5}y^2$.
30. $-a^3 - \frac{1}{2}a^2b + \frac{1}{4}ab^2 + b^3$.

IV-a. Page 22

1. $-2a-2c.$ **2.** $3a-5b-4c.$ **3.** $13x+18y-19z.$

4. $-5a+30b-4c.$ **5.** $11x+13y-16z.$ **6.** $12ab-10bc-10cd.$

7. $21a-13b-33c.$ **8.** $11x+26y+22z.$ **9.** $2ac+2bd.$

10. $2ab-2cd+2ac-2bd.$

11. $-cd-ac-bd.$ **12.** $2xy.$ **13.** $-3x^3-x^2-2x+1.$

14. $-12x^2y+21xy^2+15xyz.$ **15.** $\frac{1}{6}a-\frac{3}{2}b+\frac{5}{6}c.$

16. $\frac{1}{4}x+\frac{3}{2}y-\frac{2}{3}z.$ **17.** $-\frac{5}{2}a-\frac{10}{3}b+\frac{1}{2}c.$

18. $x-y+\frac{1}{5}z.$ **19.** $-\frac{4}{3}x-\frac{4}{3}z.$ **20.** $-\frac{5}{6}x+\frac{13}{6}y.$

IV-b. Page 23

1. $7xy-7yz+18xz.$ **2.** $-12x^2y^2+8x^3y+21xy^3.$

3. $-12+9ab+6a^2b^2.$ **4.** $-2a^2bc+6b^2ca+5c^2ab.$

5. $-12a^2b+15ab^2-5cd.$ **6.** $-16x^2y+10xy^2-2x^2y^2.$

7. $20a^2b^2+16a^2b.$ **8.** $9x^2-9x+9.$

9. $x^3+3x^2+5x+7.$ **10.** $-17a^2x^2+13x^2+20.$

11. $2x^2-2x.$ **12.** $6x^2y+2y^3.$

13. $a^3-c^3-abc.$ **14.** $3x^3+10x^2y-10xy^2.$

15. $4x^4-5x^3-2x^2-x+2.$ **16.** $-4a^3+4b^3-2c^3+10abc.$

17. $-x^5+2x^4+x^3-x^2+2x-2.$ **18.** $4a^5-7a^4-5a^3+9a^2-a-7.$

19. $-5a^2b-14ab^2+a^3b^3+b^4.$ **20.** $-a^3+22a^2b-16ab^2+2b^3.$

21. $2x^2-\frac{4}{3}xy-\frac{1}{2}y^2.$ **22.** $\frac{4}{3}a^2-\frac{7}{2}a-\frac{1}{2}.$

23. $-\frac{1}{6}x^2-\frac{5}{6}x+\frac{7}{6}.$ **24.** $\frac{5}{8}x^2+\frac{1}{6}ax-\frac{1}{3}.$

25. $\frac{3}{4}x^3-\frac{1}{2}x^2y-\frac{1}{6}y^2.$ **26.** $-\frac{1}{8}a^3-\frac{2}{3}a^2x-\frac{1}{2}ax^2.$

Miscellaneous Examples I. Page 24

1. (1) $2x+x^2$; (2) $-3a+b.$ **2.** $2a+2c.$

3. (1) 21; (2) 108. **4.** (1) 11; (2) 18. **5.** $7x^3-10x^2.$

6. $8a^3-2a.$ **9.** $2x^3-2x^2.$ **11.** $2a-(3b+5c).$

12. 47; 12. **13.** $-y^2+y.$ **15.** 36.

16. 0. **17.** $a^2b.$ **18.** $x+2z.$

20. $7xy.$ **21.** 8. **23.** $4a.$

24. 118. **25.** 30 B.C. **26.** $2x^3-2x.$

28. $a+b-(c-d).$ **29.** $a+3b$ km south of O. **30.** $2x^2+7x-3.$

V-a. Page 28

1. $35x^7$. **2.** $20a^{11}$. **3.** $56a^4b^3$. **4.** $30x^4y^2$.
5. $8a^3b^6$. **6.** $6a^2bc^4$. **7.** $4a^6b^6$. **8.** $10a^3b$.
9. $28a^7b^3$. **10.** $5a^4b^3x^2y^2$. **11.** $6a^2x^7y^3$. **12.** $abcxyz$.
13. $15a^7b^8x^4$. **14.** $28a^3b^3x^5$. **15.** $40a^2cx^2$. **16.** $30x^3x^6y^3$.
17. $2x^7y^8$. **18.** $3a^5x^9y^{16}$. **19.** $a^4b^2 + a^3b^2c$.
20. $20a^3b^2x^3 - 28a^2b^2x^4$. **21.** $10x^3 + 6x^2y$.
22. $a^5b + a^3b^3 - a^3bc^2$. **23.** $ab^2c^2 + a^2bc - a^2b^2c$.
24. $20a^4bc^3 + 12a^2b^3c^3 - 8a^2bc^5$. **25.** $15x^5y + 3x^4y^2 - 21x^5y^2$.
26. $48x^5y^3 - 40x^4y^4 + 56x^3y^5$. **27.** $6a^5b^3c - 7a^3b^4c^2$.

V-b. Page 31

1. 36. **2.** –48. **3.** 5. **4.** 24.
5. –16. **6.** –12. **7.** –9. **8.** –24.
9. –168. **10.** 480. **11.** –16. **12.** 375.
13. 500. **14.** 140. **15.** –2000. **16.** 500.
17. –180. **18.** –56. **19.** –1000. **20.** –224.
21. 40. **22.** –63. **23.** 118. **24.** –130.
25. –54. **26.** 3. **27.** 1. **28.** 0.
29. 29. **30.** –13.

V-c. Page 32

1. $-3a^2x^2$. **2.** $14a^2b^2x^2$. **3.** $-a^3b^3$. **4.** $-60x^3y^2$.
5. $3a^3b^4c^5d^6$. **6.** $-5x^3y^4z^2$. **7.** $-36x^2y^2z - 48xy^2z^2$.
8. $a^3b^2c^3 - a^2b^2c^4$. **9.** $3x^2 + 3xy + 3xz$.
10. $a^3bc - ab^3c + abc^3$. **11.** $a^2b^2c - ab^2c^2 + a^2bc^2$.
12. $14a^4b^3 - 28a^3b^4$. **13.** $15x^3y^2 - 18x^2y^3 + 24x^3y^3$.
14. $56x^6y^4 + 40x^4y^6$. **15.** $-5x^2y^3z^2 + 3x^2y^2z^3 - 8x^3y^2z^2$.
16. $-48x^5y^3z^5 + 96x^4y^2z^4$. **17.** $91x^4y^5 + 105x^5y^4$.
18. $-8x^2y^2z^2 + 10x^4y^2z^4$. **19.** $-a^2b^2c^2 + a^3b^2c^2 + a^2b^3c^2$.
20. $a^3b^2c - a^2b^3c + a^2b^2c^2$. **21.** $-3a^2 + \frac{9}{2}ab - 6ac$.
22. $-\frac{5}{2}x^2 + \frac{5}{3}xy + \frac{10}{3}x$. **23.** $\frac{1}{4}a^2x - \frac{1}{16}abx - \frac{3}{8}acx$.
24. $-2a^5x^2 + \frac{7}{2}a^4x^4$. **25.** $\frac{5}{2}a^4x^2 - \frac{5}{3}a^3x^3 + a^2x^4$.
26. $\frac{21}{2}x^3y - x^2y^2$. **27.** $\frac{1}{2}x^5y^2 - 3x^3y^4$.
28. $-x^8y^3 + \frac{16}{49}x^5y^6$.

V-d. Page 34

1. $x^2 + 15x + 50.$ **2.** $x^2 - 25.$ **3.** $x^2 - 17x + 70.$

4. $x^2 + 3x - 70.$ **5.** $x^2 - 3x - 70.$ **6.** $x^2 + 17x + 70.$

7. $x^2 - 36.$ **8.** $x^2 + 4x - 32.$ **9.** $x^2 - 13x + 12.$

10. $x^2 + 11x - 12.$ **11.** $x^2 - 225.$ **12.** $-x^2 + 18x - 45.$

13. $x^2 + 5x + 6.$ **14.** $-x^2 + 14x - 49.$

15. $x^2 - 25.$ **16.** $x^2 + x - 182.$ **17.** $x^2 + x - 306.$

18. $x^2 - x - 380.$ **19.** $x^2 - 256.$ **20.** $-x^2 + 42x - 441.$

21. $2x^2 + 13x - 24.$ **22.** $2x^2 - 13x - 24.$ **23.** $2x^2 - 11x + 5.$

24. $2x^2 - 7x + 5.$ **25.** $6x^2 + 11x - 35.$

26. $6x^2 - 11x - 35.$ **27.** $10x^2 + 3x - 18.$

28. $10x^2 - 3x - 18.$ **29.** $9x^2 - 25y^2.$ **30.** $9x^2 - 30xy + 25y^2.$

31. $a^2 + ac - 6b^2.$ **32.** $a^2 + ab - 56b^2.$

33. $3a^2 - 30ab + 48b^2.$ **34.** $a^2 - 4ab - 45b^2.$

35. $x^2 + ax - bx - ab.$ **36.** $x^2 - ax + bx - ab.$

37. $x^2 - 2ax + 3bx - 6ab.$

38. $a^2x^2 - b^2y^2.$ **39.** $x^2y^2 - a^2b^2.$ **40.** $4p^2q^2 - 9r^2.$

V-e. Page 36

1. $a^2 + 2ab + b^2 - c^2.$ **2.** $a^2 - 4b^2 + 4bc - c^2.$

3. $a^4 + a^2b^2 + b^4.$ **4.** $x^3 + 4x^2y + 3xy^2 + 12y^3.$

5. $x^4 - 4x^2 + 8x + 16.$ **6.** $x^6 + y^6.$ **7.** $x^3 - y^3.$

8. $a^4 + 4a^2x^2 + 16x^4.$ **9.** $64a^3 - 27b^3.$ **10.** $x^4 - a^4.$

11. $x^4 + 2x^3 - 7x^2 - 8x + 12.$ **12.** $4x^5 - x^3 + 4x.$

13. $a^6 + a^3b^3.$ **14.** $x^5 - 2x^4 - 4x^3 + 19x^2 - 31x + 15.$

15. $a^5 + 4ab^4.$ **16.** $8x^3 - 27y^3.$

17. $-x^4 + 4x^3y - x^2y^2 - 4xy^3 - y^4.$ **18.** $a^6 - a^4b^4 + 2a^3b^3 + b^6.$

19. $x^4 - 2x^2y^2 + y^4.$ **20.** $a^2b^2 + c^2d^2 - a^2c^2 - b^2d^2.$

21. $75a^5b^3 - 28a^3b^5 + 13a^2b^6 - 12ab^7.$ **22.** $81x^4 - 256a^4.$

23. $a^4 - 25a^2b^2 - 10ab^3 - b^4.$ **24.** $x^3 + 3xy + y^3 - 1.$

25. $a^3 + b^3 + c^3 - 3abc.$ **26.** $x^5 + y^5.$

27. $x^{15} + y^{10}.$ **28.** $a^6 - 2a^3 + 1.$

29. $a^2x^3 + 27a^2y^6.$ **30.** $x^6 + 2x^3y^3 + y^6.$

31. $\frac{1}{4}a^3 + \frac{1}{72}a - \frac{1}{12}.$ **32.** $\frac{1}{4}x^3 - \frac{5}{6}x^2 + \frac{1}{12}x + \frac{1}{2}.$

33. $\frac{2}{9}x^3 - \frac{3}{4}y^3.$ **34.** $\frac{9}{8}x^4 - \frac{3}{2}ax^3 + \frac{1}{2}a^2x^2 - \frac{2}{9}a^4.$

35. $\frac{1}{4}x^4 - \frac{43}{36}x^2 + \frac{9}{16}$. **36.** $\frac{1}{4}a^4 + x^4$.

V-f. Page 38

1. $x^2 + 3x - 40$. **2.** $x^2 + 5x - 6$. **3.** $x^2 + 7x - 30$.
4. $x^2 + 4x + 5$. **5.** $x^2 - 2x - 63$. **6.** $x^2 - 18x + 80$.
7. $x^2 + 7x - 44$. **8.** $x^2 + 2x - 8$. **9.** $x^2 - 4$.
10. $a^2 - 1$. **11.** $a^2 + 4a - 45$. **12.** $a^2 + 9a - 36$.
13. $a^2 - 4a - 32$. **14.** $a^2 - 64$. **15.** $a^2 + 7a - 78$.
16. $a^2 + 6a + 9$. **17.** $a^2 - 121$. **18.** $a^2 - 16a + 64$.
19. $x^2 - ax - 6a^2$. **20.** $x^2 + ax - 30a^2$. **21.** $x^2 - 9a^2$.
22. $x^2 + 2xy - 8y^2$. **23.** $x^2 - 49y^2$. **24.** $x^2 - 6xy + 9y^2$.
25. $a^2 + 6ab + 9b^2$. **26.** $a^2 + 5ab - 50b^2$. **27.** $a^2 - 17ab + 72b^2$.
28. $2x^2 - x - 10$. **29.** $2x^2 - 9x + 10$. **30.** $2x^2 - 3x - 9$.
31. $3x^2 + 2x - 1$. **32.** $4x^2 + 8x - 5$. **33.** $6x^2 + 5x - 21$.
34. $8x^2 + 6x - 9$. **35.** $9x^2 - 64$. **36.** $4x^2 - 20x + 25$.
37. $9x^2 - 3xy - 2y^2$. **38.** $9x^2 + 12xy + 4y^2$. **39.** $4x^2 + 4xy - 35y^2$.
40. $25x^2 - 9a^2$. **41.** $2x^2 + 5ax - 25a^2$. **42.** $4x^2 + 4ax + a^2$.

VI-a. Page 42

1. $3x$. **2.** $-3x$. **3.** $-5x^3$. **4.** $-bx$.
5. xy^2. **6.** $-a^2$. **7.** $4ac$. **8.** $4a^2b^4c^5$.
9. a^4c^6. **10.** $3x^3y^5z^3$. **11.** $4x^2$. **12.** $6a^6$.
13. $5a^4$. **14.** $7a^2b^2$. **15.** -1. **16.** $-7ab^2$.
17. $-8b^2x$. **18.** $10y^2$. **19.** $x - 2y$.
20. $x^2 - 3x + 1$. **21.** $x^4 - 7x^3 + 4x^2$. **22.** $10x^4 - 8x^3 + 3x$.
23. $-3x^2 + 5x$. **24.** $3x - 4$. **25.** $3x^3 + 4x$.
26. $2x^2y - 3xy^2$. **27.** $-a + b + c$. **28.** $a - b - b^2$.
29. $-x^2 + 3xy + 4y^2$. **30.** $-2x^3y^3 + 4x^2y - 3y^2$. **31.** $2a - 3b + 4c$.
32. $-\frac{1}{3}x^2 + 2y^2$. **33.** $3x - 2y - 4$. **34.** $-\frac{6}{7}a^2x^2 + \frac{3}{2}ax^3$.
35. $\frac{2}{3}a - \frac{1}{6}b - c$.

VI-b. Page 44

1. $x + 2$. **2.** $x - 4$. **3.** $a - 6$. **4.** $a - 24$.
5. $3x + 1$. **6.** $x + 5$. **7.** $5x + 1$. **8.** $x + 7$.
9. $5x + 1$. **10.** $x + 11$. **11.** $x + 5$. **12.** $3x + 1$.
13. $3x + 7$. **14.** $3x - 7$. **15.** $3x - 5$. **16.** $4x - 7$.
17. $4a + 3x$. **18.** $5a - x$. **19.** $3a + 4c$. **20.** $3a - 5c$.

21. $6x + 5y$. **22.** $8x + 3y$. **23.** $x^2 + 14x$. **24.** $4x^2 - x$.
25. $9x^2 + 9x + 5$. **26.** $2a^2 - 5a + 3$. **27.** $3 + 3a + a^2$.
28. $8 - 36x + 54x^2 - 27x^3$.

VI-c. Page 46

1. $x - 4$. **2.** $y + 1$. **3.** $2m - 3$. **4.** $2a^2 - 3a$.
5. $x^2 - x + 1$. **6.** $a^2 - 3a + 1$; rem. $a - 6$. **7.** $a^2 + 3a + 2$.
8. $2x^2 + x - 1$; rem. $3x + 4$. **9.** $x^3 - 2x^2 + x + 1$.
10. $x^3 - 3x^2 + 2x - 1$. **11.** $10x^3 - 3x - 12$; rem. $7x - 45$.
12. $7y^2 + 5y - 3$; rem. $-39y + 27$. **13.** $2k^2 - 5k + 2$.
14. $5 - 7m - m^3$. **15.** $x^2 + 5x + 6$.
16. $x^2 - 2x + 3$; rem. $31x - 15$. **17.** $12 + 8x + x^2$. **18.** $7x^2 + 5xy + 2y^2$.
19. $x^2 - xy + y^2$; rem. x^2. **20.** $x^3 + x - y$.
21. $a^6 + a^3b^3 + b^6$. **22.** $x^7 - x^6y + x^4y^3 - x^3y^4 + xy^6 - y^7$.
23. $x^6 + 2x^5y^2 - 3x^4y^4 - 6x^3y^6 + 2x^2y^8 + 4xy^{10} - y^{12}$.
24. $a^2 + 2ab + b^2 + a + b + 1$. **25.** $x^5 - x^4y + xy^4 - y^5$.
26. $a^{10} + a^8b^2 + a^6b^4 + a^4b^6 + a^2b^8 + b^{10}$.
27. $a^8 - 2a^6b^2 + 3a^4b^4 - 2a^2b^6 + b^8$. **28.** $1 + a + a^2 + 2x - 2ax + 4x^2$.
29. $\frac{1}{4}a^2 - 3ax + 9x^2$. **30.** $\frac{1}{9}a^2 - \frac{1}{6}a + \frac{1}{16}$.
31. $\frac{6}{25}a^3 - \frac{3}{5}a^2c + \frac{3}{2}ac^2$. **32.** $\frac{3}{8}a^2 - \frac{1}{4}a - \frac{2}{3}$.
33. $6x - \frac{1}{3}y - \frac{1}{2}$. **34.** $\frac{4}{9}a^4 + \frac{1}{2}a^3x + \frac{9}{16}a^2x^2 + \frac{81}{128}ax^3$.

VII-a. Page 50

1. $a + b - c$. **2.** a. **3.** $a + 3b - 4c$. **4.** $3a - b - c$.
5. $-2a - 4b - 2c$. **6.** $-a + b - c$. **7.** $b - a$. **8.** $x - y$.
9. $2a - 2b$. **10.** $-2x - 5y$. **11.** $x - a$. **12.** $2a - b - d$.
13. $-3c + 4y$. **14.** $-x + 2y + 6z$. **15.** $-5x$. **16.** $-25x + 2y$.
17. $11x - 36y$. **18.** $2x - 2z$. **19.** $2a$. **20.** a.

VII-b. Page 51

1. $5a$. **2.** a. **3.** $6a + 2b - 2c - 2d$.
4. $2x - 3y + 12z$. **5.** b. **6.** $21a + b$.
7. $2b + 4c$. **8.** $-a^2 + 8b^2 - 9c^2$. **9.** $-2a + 6b + 2c - 2d$.
10. $4a + b + c$. **11.** $-50c$. **12.** $-11a - 2b$.
13. $-a + b + 5c$. **14.** $-2a + 10b - 11c$.

15. $-227a+216b+84$. **16.** $2a-12c+84d$.

17. $3a+4x$. **18.** $-10a$. **19.** $4a$.

20. 0. **21.** $\frac{11}{5}a-2b$. **22.** $12x-30y$.

23. $a-\frac{13}{3}b+\frac{10}{3}c$. **24.** 0.

VII-c. Page 53

1. $(a+2)x^4+(b-5)x^2+(2b-3)x+5$.
2. $(5a-b)x^3+(3b-4)x^2+(c-2)x+ab-7$.
3. $(9a-7)x^3+(5a-3)x^2+(7-2c)x+2$.
4. $(2c-a^2)x^5+(1-3b)x^4+(4d-3ab)x$.
5. $-(a^2+b)x^4-(2b-5)x^3-(3-a)x^2$.
6. $-(ab-7)x^5-(abc-7)x^3-(3c^2-5a)x$.
7. $-(c-a^2)x^3-(b+5-a)x^2$.
8. $-(a+c+7-3b^2)x^4-(b+5c^2)x$.
9. $(a-b)x^3-(b+2c)x^2-(b+c+d)x$.
10. $(5a+4c)x^3+(3a-6b+7c)x^2+(2a-7b)x$.
11. $(3a+2c)x^3+(a+8b)x^2-(8a+9b)x$.
12. $(6b+1)x^5-(a+2b)x^4-(2a+3c)x$.
13. $(a+b)x^3-(a+b)x^2+(a-b)x$.

VIII-d. Page 54

1. $(a-c)x^3+(b+c)x^2-(2c+1)x$.
2. $(1-b)x^3+(a+1)x^2+(b-1)x-1$.
3. $(a^2-5a`+2)x^3+(2a-b)x^2-(a+5)x$.
4. $(a-p+1)x^2+(b+q+2)x-c-r+3$.
5. $(p+q-1)x^3+(p+q)x^2-(p+q)x+q$.
6. $acx^3+(2a+bc)x^2+(2b+c)x+2$.
7. $acx^3-(2a+bc)x^2+(3a+2b)x-3b$.
8. $apx^3+(aq-bq)x^2-(bq+cp)x-cq$.
9. $2bx^3-(3b-2c)x^2-(b+3c)x-c$.
10. $ax^3-(a+2b)x^2+(2b+3c)x-3c$.
11. $apx^3-(2a+3p)x^2+(6-aq)x+3q$.
12. $x^6-(a^2+2b)x^4+(2ac+b^2)x^2-c^2$.
13. $a^2x^6+(6a-1)x^4+(9-2b)x^2-b^2$.
14. $x^8-(a^2+2b)x^6+(2ac+b^2+2d)x^4-(2bd+c^2)x^2+d^2$.

VIII-a. Page 58

1. 3. **2.** 5. **3.** 4. **4.** 6. **5.** 2. **6.** 5. **7.** 2.
8. 3. **9.** 5. **10.** 7. **11.** $3\frac{1}{2}$. **12.** 2. **13.** 2. **14.** 4.
15. 3. **16.** 5. **17.** $\frac{1}{2}$. **18.** $2\frac{1}{2}$. **19.** 1. **20.** $1\frac{1}{2}$. **21.** 2.
22. 1. **23.** $2\frac{1}{2}$. **24.** $6\frac{2}{3}$. **25.** $\frac{5}{8}$. **26.** $\frac{7}{12}$. **27.** $\frac{8}{21}$.
28. $1\frac{13}{27}$. **29.** 12. **30.** 15. **31.** $4\frac{1}{2}$. **32.** -4.

VIII-b. Page 61

1. 5. **2.** 4. **3.** 7. **4.** 4. **5.** 3. **6.** 1. **7.** 5.
8. 3. **9.** 15. **10.** 13. **11.** 13. **12.** 5. **13.** 1. **14.** 16.
15. 10. **16.** 30. **17.** 5. **18.** 1. **19.** 2. **20.** 1. **21.** 1.
22. 2. **23.** 3. **24.** 1. **25.** 4. **26.** 3. **27.** 3. **28.** 3.
29. 1. **30.** 4. **31.** 7. **32.** 3. **33.** 4. **34.** 4. **35.** 1.
36. 1. **37.** 2. **38.** 2. **39.** 1. **40.** 2.

VIII-c. Page 63

1. 20. **2.** 15. **3.** 8. **4.** 16. **5.** 25. **6.** 17. **7.** 13.
8. 10. **9.** 7. **10.** 4. **11.** $-\frac{1}{7}$. **12.** $\frac{1}{7}$. **13.** 5. **14.** 7.
15. 6. **16.** 10. **17.** 6. **18.** 8. **19.** 7. **20.** 25. **21.** $3\frac{1}{7}$.
22. 8. **23.** 12. **24.** 5. **25.** 5. **26.** 12. **27.** $\frac{4}{7}$. **28.** $5\frac{1}{8}$.
29. 8. **30.** $66\frac{8}{3}$. **31.** 7. **32.** 7. **33.** 2. **34.** 12. **35.** 27.
36. 5.

VIII-d. Page 66

1. $2\frac{2}{3}$. **2.** 6. **3.** 10. **4.** -6. **5.** $9\frac{2}{3}$. **6.** $1\frac{1}{3}$. **7.** -12.
8. $\frac{3}{8}$. **9.** $1\frac{4}{5}$. **10.** $-\frac{3}{4}$. **11.** $\frac{4}{5}$. **12.** $-\frac{2}{21}$. **13.** $1\frac{1}{2}$. **14.** $-\frac{2}{3}$.
15. $1\frac{3}{4}$. **16.** 12. **17.** $3\frac{5}{7}$. **18.** $2\frac{1}{4}$. **19.** $\frac{5}{7}$. **20.** $1\frac{2}{5}$. **21.** $\frac{3}{7}$.

IX-a. Page 68

1. $y - x$. **2.** $\frac{a}{3}$. **3.** $5b$. **4.** $3d - 2c$.
5. $2k$. **6.** $100 - x$. **7.** $\frac{b}{a}$. **8.** $20 - c$.
9. $7a$. **10.** $\frac{25}{x}$. **11.** $x + 11$. **12.** $c - 20$.

13. $90 - x$. **14.** $x - 30$. **15.** 20. **16.** $2x$.

17. $36 - x$. **18.** $x + a$. **19.** $5x$ days. **20.** 4.

21. $\frac{x}{2}$. **22.** $\frac{x}{4}$. **23.** xy km. **24.** $\frac{y}{x}$ km.

25. $\frac{60x}{a}$. **26.** $\frac{200}{x}$ hours. **27.** $5p$. **28.** $\frac{10}{x}$.

29. $100a + 25b$. **30.** $2000 - x$. **31.** $100a + 50b - c$.

32. $x - 6$. **33.** b. **34.** $140x$.

35. $100a + 25b - c$. **36.** $\frac{100}{xy}$. **37.** $y - \frac{52x}{100}$.

38. $100 - x - y - z$. **39.** $100x + 5y + z - 25$. **40.** $2y + 2z - x$.

IX-b. Page 71

1. $x, x + 1, x + 2, x + 3$. **2.** $y - 2, y - 1, y$.

3. $x - 2, x - 1, x + 1, x + 2$. **4.** $2n + 2$.

5. $2x - 1$. **6.** $6n + 3$.

7. $x - a - b$ km. **8.** $n(a + b)$.

9. $x + y + 5$. **10.** $2x + 5$.

11. $mx + y$. **12.** $6x$. **13.** Rs. $10bc$. **14.** Rs. $\frac{ax}{20}$.

15. Rs. $\frac{a^3}{2}$. **16.** Rs. $\frac{x^2y^2}{50}$. **17.** $10xy$. **18.** $\frac{x^2}{100}$.

19. $\frac{px}{2}$. **20.** $\frac{abc}{1000}$. **21.** $\frac{yz}{x}$. **22.** $ab - \frac{c^2}{100}$.

23. $\frac{3a}{4x}$. **24.** $\frac{bc}{20}$ hours. **25.** $\frac{5a}{18b}$. **26.** $\frac{9xy}{25}$.

27. $\frac{y}{xy}$ days. **28.** yz. **29.** $\frac{y}{10r}$. **30.** $\frac{100p}{ar}$.

31. $p(p-1)(p-2) = y$. **32.** $6n = x$. **33.** $pq = 5(a - b)$.

34. $\frac{x}{y} = m + n + 10$. **35.** $a + x + 5 = 2(a + 5)$; 35; 24.

36. $100(p - x) = 3(q + 100x)$. **37.** $p - 5 = 7(q - 5)$.

IX. c. Page 75

1. (i) 272 sq dm; (ii) 16 dm; (iii) 10 metres.

2. (i) 50 cu. metres; (ii) $4\frac{1}{2}$ cu. metres; (iii) 5 metres.

3. (i) 98; (ii) 1 hr. 20 min; (iii) 66.

4. (i) 44. 15 metres; (ii) 2 sec.

5. 22 cm, 38.5 sq. cm; 11 dm, 9.625 sq; dm.

6. (i) 24.64 sq. cm; (ii) 1.75 dm.

7. (i) $2(x + y)$ dm; (ii) xy sq. dm; (iii) $2z(x + y)$ sq. dm.
8. 20 metres; 24 sq. metres; 80 sq. metres.
9. 3.5 metres.
10. 22 sq. cm; (ii) 3.6 sq. dm.

11. 1.5 cm. **12.** 27 sq. dm. **13.** 328.
14. 15. **15.** 55. **16.** (i) and (iii).
20. (i) 17; (ii) 24; (iii) 40; (iv) 1.6. **21.** (i) .7854; (ii) 96.6; (iii) 294.
22. 40. **23.** 12.
24. (i) 9780; (ii) 1; (iv) – 40.5. **25.** $4, 5\frac{1}{5}, 6\frac{2}{5}, 7\frac{3}{5}, 8\frac{4}{5}, 10$.

X-a. Page 81

1. 17, 12. **2.** 13, 5. **3.** 75. **4.** 20 km.
5. 15, 43. **6.** 162. **7.** 1. **8.** 50, 55.
9. 27, 28, 29. **10.** 3, 5. **11.** 15, 5. **12.** ₹ 20.
13. 5. **14.** 60, 61. **15.** 6, 3.
16. *A* Rs 100, *B* Rs 130, *C* Rs 150.
17. 53 10-paise coins, 71 5-paise coins
18. Silk Rs 6, Linen Rs 1.
19. 48, 12.
20. 65, 40
21. 60, 10.
22. 20 10-paise coins, 5 25-paise coins, 10 5-paise coins.
23. 25, 5.
24. 123 runs, 10 byes, 5 wides.
25. 15 dm, 12 dm.
26. 18 dm, 10 dm.

X-b. Page 83

1. 54. **2.** 24. **3.** 60. **4.** 35.
5. 75. **6.** 24, 25. **7.** 224, 252. **8.** 49, 50.
9. 50, 51, 52. **10.** Rs 32. **11.** 27.
12. 90 sulphuric, 150 hydrochloric. **13.** *A* ₹ 450, *B* ₹ 180, *C* ₹140.
14. *A* ₹ 525, *B* ₹ 600, *C* ₹ 160. **15.** ₹ 400.
16. 12 dm, 18 dm. **17.** ₹ 12000. **18.** 44.

XI-a. Page 85

1. $2ab$. **2.** x^2y^2. **3.** $2xy^2z$. **4.** abc.
5. $5ab$. **6.** $3xy^2z$. **7.** $2a^2b^2c^2$. **8.** $7ab^2c^3$.
9. $3x^2yz^2$. **10.** $2ax$. **11.** $7a$. **12.** $17abc$.
13. xy. **14.** $8a^2b^2c^2$. **15.** $25xy$. **16.** bx.
17. $5a^3b^3c^2$. **18.** abc.

XI-b. Page 86

In examples 19-29 the H.C.F. stands first, the L.C.M. second.

1. $2a^2bc$. **2.** x^3y^2z. **3.** $12x^3y^3z$.

4. $20a^2b^2c^3$. **5.** $15a^4b^3c^5$. **6.** $24abxy$. **7.** abc.

8. $a^2b^2c^2$. **9.** $12abc$. **10.** $12xyz$. **11.** $12x^2y^2z^2$.

12. $42a^2b^3$. **13.** $a^2b^2c^2$. **14.** $30a^2b^2c^2$. **15.** $12x^3y^4$.

16. $56x^4y^5$. **17.** $210a^3b^3c^3$. **18.** $264a^4b^4c^4$. **19.** $ac, 12abc$.

20. $2y, 12xyz$. **21.** $bc, 9ab^2c$.

22. $13a^2bc, 39a^3bc^2$. **23.** $17xy, 51x^2yz^2$.

24. $5xy^3z, 75x^3y^3z^2$. **25.** $b, 30abc$.

26. $17m^2p^2, 51m^4n^4p^4$. **27.** $y^2, x^3y^5z^4$.

28. $5p^2, 60m^2p^3q^4$. **29.** $36k^2m^2n^4, 216k^3m^3n^5$.

XII-a. Page 87

1. $\frac{1}{2b}$. **2.** $\frac{a}{4b}$. **3.** $\frac{2y}{5x}$. **4.** $\frac{1}{5ab}$.

5. $\frac{z^2}{xy}$. **6.** $\frac{3a}{5c}$. **7.** $\frac{3x^2}{4z^2}$. **8.** $\frac{2a^2}{3bc}$.

9. $\frac{4n}{5mp}$. **10.** $\frac{5m^2p^2}{6n^4}$. **11.** $\frac{c}{a^2b}$. **12.** $\frac{3xz}{5y^3}$.

13. $\frac{yz^3}{2x}$. **14.** $\frac{a^2c^3}{3b^2}$. **15.** $\frac{nq}{mp^3}$. **16.** $\frac{2np^3}{3m}$.

17. $\frac{3x^2}{5ay^4}$. **18.** $\frac{3}{4abc}$. **19.** $\frac{2p^2m^2}{3k}$. **20.** $\frac{2xyz}{3}$.

XII-b. Page 89

1. $\frac{2cd^2}{3b}$. **2.** $\frac{a^2}{bc}$. **3.** $\frac{9ax^2z^2}{bc}$. **4.** $\frac{14b^3}{15c^3y}$.

5. $\frac{3mnz^2}{2x}$. **6.** $\frac{9mnp}{4k}$. **7.** $\frac{x}{2a^2}$. **8.** $\frac{400x}{441y^3}$.

9. $\frac{y^3z^2}{nx^4}$. **10.** 3. **11.** $\frac{7b}{4a}$. **12.** $\frac{d^2}{4a^2c}$.

13. $\frac{7acy}{8bdx}$. **14.** $\frac{6x^2yz}{5a}$. **15.** $\frac{9b^2cz^2}{4x^3y}$. **16.** 8.

17. $\frac{p^2q^2y}{10x^2}$. **18.** y^2.

XII-c. Page 90

1. $\frac{4x, y}{2a}$. **2.** $\frac{4x^3, 3y^2}{3x^2y}$. **3.** $\frac{ac, 2b^2}{2bc}$. **4.** $\frac{ad, bc, 2bd}{bd}$.

5. $\frac{6ac, b^2}{3bc}$. **6.** $\frac{5m, 4p}{20n}$. **7.** $\frac{3k, 2p}{6x}$. **8.** $\frac{2m, n}{6x}$.

9. $\frac{a^2, b^2}{abc}$. **10.** $\frac{ax, b}{x^2}$. **11.** $\frac{2y, 3x}{xy}$.

12. $\frac{x^2, y^2, 3x^2y}{xy}$. **13.** $\frac{4x^2, 9y^2}{6xy}$. **14.** $\frac{8ac, 3ab}{10bc}$.

15. $\frac{9ac, 5b^2}{21bc}$. **16.** $\frac{18, 3ab, a^2}{9a}$.

XII-d. Page 91

1. $\frac{5x}{6}$. **2.** $\frac{y}{20}$. **3.** $\frac{a}{12}$. **4.** $\frac{2x^2 - 15}{3x}$.

5. $\frac{5x + 2y}{10}$. **6.** $\frac{3a - 2b}{12}$. **7.** $\frac{3m - 2n}{24}$. **8.** $\frac{2m - 3n}{15}$.

9. $\frac{3x - y}{21}$. **10.** $\frac{3a + b}{39}$. **11.** $\frac{3p - q}{48}$. **12.** $\frac{15m - n}{36}$.

13. $\frac{22x}{15}$. **14.** $\frac{9x}{20}$. **15.** $\frac{x}{4}$. **16.** $\frac{6a - 4b}{15}$.

17. $\frac{11a}{30}$. **18.** $\frac{5x}{24}$. **19.** $\frac{7x}{18}$. **20.** $\frac{5x}{4}$.

21. $\frac{31x}{36}$. **22.** $\frac{17x}{24}$. **23.** $\frac{bx - ay}{ab}$. **24.** $\frac{9bx + 2ay}{3ab}$.

25. $\frac{ac + b}{c}$. **26.** $\frac{xz - y}{z}$. **27.** $\frac{a^2 - 3b^2}{3a}$. **28.** $\frac{a^3 + b^3}{a}$.

29. $\frac{x^3 - 2y^3}{2x^2}$. **30.** $\frac{p^5 - k^5}{p^2}$.

Miscellaneous Examples II. Page 92

1. $3x^2 + 7x - 8$. **2.** $13z$. **3.** 20.

4. $a^2 + b^2 + c^2$. **5.** $x^5 - 11x - 10$. **6.** (1) $\frac{1}{2}$; (2) -3.

7. $x^2 + 2x - 3$. **8.** $-4a + 5b$. **9.** $5x$.

10. $4x^2 - 6x - 1$. **11.** (1) $x^2 + 14x - 51$; (2) $24x^2 - 55x - 24$.

12. (1) $\frac{1}{4}$; (2) 1. **13.** $-ab$. **14.** $\frac{8}{5}$.

15. $16a^2 + 2ab$. **16.** $x^5 - 4x^4 + 48x - 32$.

17. $29a$. **18.** (1) -2; (2) 41. **19.** $3p^3 - 5p^2 + 2p$.

20. $6a + 2c - 2d$. **21.** $2x^3 - x^2 - x$. **22.** 1.
23. 1935. **24.** 4. **25.** $4m - 5n$.
26. $3x - 9$. **27.** 0. **28.** (1) – 15; (2) 4.
29. $3y^3 - 9y^2 + 2y - 1$. **30.** A Rs 800. B ₹ 320.
31. 14. **32.** $6m^2 - 96$. **33.** $x - 2$.
34. $ap + bq$ km; $\frac{ap + bq}{c}$ hours, Numerically, 55 km; 5 hours.
35. (1) $\frac{1}{7}$; (2) $7\frac{1}{13}$. **36.** 4320.

XIII-a. Page 98

1. $x = 2, y = 1$. **2.** $x = 3, y = 5$. **3.** $x = 2, y = 3$.
4. $x = 4, y = -1$. **5.** $x = 1, y = 2$. **6.** $x = 3, y = 4$.
7. $x = 5, y = 6$. **8.** $x = 1, y = 2$. **9.** $x = 3, y = 1$.
10. $x = 2, y = 1$. **11.** $x = 1, y = 3$. **12.** $x = 1, y = 1$.
13. $x = 7, y = 5$. **14.** $x = 10, y = 3$. **15.** $x = 5, y = 12$.
16. $x = 7, y = 8$. **17.** $x = 6, y = 8$. **18.** $x = 5, y = 8$.
19. $x = -7, y = -3$. **20.** $x = 17, y = -19$. **21.** $x = 1, y = 2$.

XIII-b. Page 99

1. $x = 12, y = 8$. **2.** $x = 10, y = 6$. **3.** $x = 18, y = 12$.
4. $x = 20, y = 15$. **5.** $x = 45, y = 35$. **6.** $x = 51, y = 17$.
7. $x = 20, y = 60$. **8.** $x = 14, y = 15$. **9.** $x = -2, y = 4$.
10. $x = 3, y = 5$. **11.** $x = 7, y = 3$. **12.** $x = 5, y = 4$.
13. $x = 3, y = -4$. **14.** $x = 19, y = 3$. **15.** $x = 12, y = -4$.
16. $x = 13, y = 7$.

XIII-c. Page 102

1. $x = 1, y = 2, z = 3$. **2.** $x = -2, y = 4, z = 1$.
3. $x = 2, y = 3, z = 1$. **4.** $x = 1, y = 2, z = 3$.
5. $x = 9, y = 2, z = -4$. **6.** $x = 3, y = 2, z = 1$.
7. $x = 5, y = 6, z = 7$. **8.** $x = 1, y = 2, z = 3$.
9. $x = 2, y = -2, z = 5$. **10.** $x = 4, y = -3, z = 2$.
11. $x = 8, y = 10, z = 14$. **12.** $x = 3, y = 9, z = 15$.
13. $x = 6, y = 8, z = 5$. **14.** $x = \frac{3}{2}, y = \frac{2}{3}, z = \frac{5}{6}$.
15. $x = 6, y = 2, z = 1$. **16.** $x = 35, y = 30, z = 25$.

XIII-d. Page 104

1. $x = 5, y = 3.$ **2.** $x = 2, y = 7.$ **3.** $x = 3, y = 2.$

4. $x = \frac{1}{3}, y = \frac{1}{4}.$ **5.** $x = 7, y = 6.$ **6.** $x = \frac{1}{3}, y = \frac{1}{5}.$

7. $x = 2, y = -3.$ **8.** $x = -5, y = 4.$ **9.** $x = \frac{2}{2}, y = \frac{3}{4}.$

10. $x = 9, y = 25.$ **11.** $x = \frac{1}{4}, y = \frac{1}{3}.$ **12.** $x = \frac{1}{5}, y = \frac{1}{6}.$

13. $x = \frac{1}{2}, y = \frac{1}{3}, z = \frac{1}{4}.$ **14.** $x = \frac{1}{8}, y = \frac{1}{12}, z = \frac{1}{16}.$

15. $x = 3, y = -2, z = 1.$

XIV. Page 107

1. 22, 12. **2.** 55, 18. **3.** 25, 17. **4.** 53, 23.

5. 23, 17.

6. Tea Rs 7, Sugar Rs 1.50. **7.** Horse Rs 230, Cow Rs 160.

8. *A* Rs 140, *B* Rs 60, *C* Rs 70, *D* Rs 20.

9. *A* Rs 99, *B* Rs 115, *C* Rs 33, *D* Rs 23. **10.** *A* 36 years, *B* 14 years.

11. *A* 55 years, *B* 21 years. **12.** *A* 5 km, *B* 4 km.

13. $C\ 3\frac{1}{2}$ km, $D\ 4\frac{1}{4}$ km. **14.** $\frac{13}{25}.$

15. $\frac{15}{26}.$ **16.** $\frac{2}{15}.$ **17.** $\frac{3}{14}.$

18. 28, 82. **19.** 85, 58. **20.** 27. **21.** 72.

22. Rs 5.55. **23.** 8 white, 12 black. **24.** 860.

25. Man Rs 2.50, Boy Rs 1.50. **26.** 20 kg, 40 kg.

27. 15 km. **28.** 8 hours. **29.** 6 km. 3 km an hour

30. Rs. 6, Rs. 3.60. **31.** Rs. 500. **32.** 3 km, $4\frac{2}{7}$ km an hour.

XV-a. Page 111

1. $9a^2b^6.$ **2.** $a^6c^2.$ **3.** $49a^2b^4.$ **4.** $121b^4c^6.$

5. $16a^8b^{10}x^4.$ **6.** $25x^4y^{10}.$ **7.** $4a^2b^2c^4.$ **8.** $9c^2x^6.$

9. $16x^2y^2z^6.$ **10.** $\frac{4}{9}a^4b^6.$ **11.** $\frac{4x^4}{9y^6}.$ **12.** $\frac{16}{9x^4y^2}.$

13. $\frac{49a^2b^2}{9}.$ **14.** $\frac{9a^4b^6}{16c^{10}x^8}.$ **15.** $\frac{1}{4x^2y^2}.$ **16.** $4x^2y^4.$

17. $\frac{25a^2b^6}{4x^2y^2}.$ **18.** $169c^{10}x^6.$ **19.** $\frac{1}{16a^8}.$ **20.** $\frac{9a^{10}}{25x^6}.$

21. $8a^3b^6.$ **22.** $27x^9.$ **23.** $64x^{12}.$ **24.** $-27a^9b^3.$

25. $-125a^3b^6.$ **26.** $-b^9c^6x^3.$ **27.** $-216\ a^{18}.$ **28.** $-8a^{21}c^6.$

29. $\frac{1}{27y^6}$. **30.** $-\frac{27x^{15}}{125a^9}$. **31.** $343x^9y^{12}$. **32.** $-\frac{8}{27}a^{15}$.

33. $81a^8b^{12}$. **34.** $a^{12}x^6$. **35.** $-32x^{15}y^5$. **36.** $\frac{1}{128a^{14}}$.

37. $\frac{243x^{20}}{32y^{15}}$. **38.** $\frac{256x^{24}}{6561y^3}$. **39.** $-\frac{x^{21}}{2187}$. **40.** $\frac{64x^{30}}{729a^{34}}$.

XV-b. Page 113

1. $a^2 + 6ab + 9b^2$. **2.** $a^2 - 6ab + 9b^2$.

3. $x^2 - 10xy + 25y^2$. **4.** $4x^2 + 12xy + 9y^2$.

5. $9x^2 - 6xy + y^2$. **6.** $9x^2 + 30xy + 25y^2$.

7. $81x^2 - 36xy + 4y^2$. **8.** $25a^2b^2 - 10abc + c^2$.

9. $p^2q^2 - 2pqr + r^2$. **10.** $x^2 - 2abcx + a^2b^2c^2$.

11. $a^2x^2 + 4abxy + 4b^2y^2$. **12.** $x^4 - 2x^2 + 1$.

13. $a^2 + b^2 + c^2 - 2ab - 2ac + 2bc$.

14. $a^2 + b^2 + c^2 + 2ab - 2ac - 2bc$.

15. $a^2 + 4b^2 + c^2 + 4ab + 2ac + 4bc$.

16. $4a^2 + 9b^2 + 16c^2 - 12ab + 16ac - 24bc$.

17. $x^4 + y^4 + z^4 - 2x^2y^2 - 2x^2z^2 + 2y^2z^2$.

18. $x^2y^2 + y^2z^2 + z^2x^2 + 2xy^2z + 2x^2yz + 2xyz^2$.

19. $9p^2 + 4q^2 + 16r^2 - 12pq + 24pr - 16qr$.

20. $x^4 - 2x^3 + 3x^2 - 2x + 1$. **21.** $4x^4 + 12x^3 + 5x^2 - 6x + 1$.

22. $x^2 + y^2 + a^2 + b^2 - 2xy + 2ax - 2bx - 2ay + 2by - 2ab$.

23. $4x^2 + 9y^2 + a^2 + 4b^2 + 12xy + 4ax - 8bx + 6ay - 12by - 4cb$.

24. $m^2 + n^2 + p^2 + q^2 - 2mn - 2mp - 2mq + 2np + 2nq + 2pq$.

25. $\frac{a^2}{4} + 4b^2 + \frac{c^2}{16} - 2ab + \frac{ac}{4} - bc$. **26.** $\frac{a^2}{9} + 9b^2 + \frac{9}{4} - 2ab - a + 9b$.

27. $\frac{4x^4}{9} - \frac{4x^3}{3} + 3x^2 - 3x + \frac{9}{4}$.

XV-c. Page 113

1. $x^3 + 3ax^2 + 3a^2x + a^3$. **2.** $x^3 - 3ax^2 + 3a^2x - a^3$.

3. $x^3 - 6x^2y + 12xy^2 - 8y^3$. **4.** $8x^3 + 12x^2y + 6xy^2 + y^3$.

5. $27x^3 - 135x^2y + 225xy^2 - 125y^3$. **6.** $a^3b^3 + 3a^2b^2c + 3abc^3 + c^3$.

7. $8a^3b^3 - 36a^2b^2c + 54abc^2 - 27c^3$.

8. $125a^3 - 75a^2bc + 15ab^2c^2 - b^3c^3$.

9. $x^6 + 12x^4y^2 + 48x^2y^4 + 64y^6$.

10. $64x^6 - 240x^4y^2 + 300x^2y^4 - 125y^6$.

11. $8a^9 - 36a^6c^2 + 54a^3b^4 - 27b^6$.

12. $125x^{25} - 300x^{10}y^4 + 240x^5y^8 - 64y^{12}$.

13. $a^3 - 2a^2b + \frac{4}{3}ab^2 - \frac{8}{27}b^3$.

14. $\frac{1}{27}a^3 + \frac{2}{3}a^2 + 4a + 8$.

15. $\frac{1}{27}x^6 - x^5 + 9x^4 - 27x^3$.

16. $\frac{1}{216}a^3 + \frac{1}{6}a^2x + 2ax^2 + 8x^3$.

XVI-a. Page 115

1. $2ab^2$. 2. $3x^3y$. 3. $5x^2y^3$. 4. $4a^2bc^3$.

5. $9a^3b^4$. 6. $10x^4$. 7. $a^{10}b^8c^2$. 8. a^4bc^6.

9. $8x^3y^9$. 10. $\frac{6}{a^{18}}$. 11. $\frac{a^8b^4}{4}$. 12. $\frac{17y^2}{5}$.

13. $\frac{18x^6}{13y^3}$. 14. $\frac{9a^9}{6b^6}$. 15. $\frac{16xy^2}{17p^7}$. 16. $\frac{20a^{20}b^{10}}{9x^5y^9}$.

17. $3a^2bc$. 18. $-2a^4b^3$. 19. $4x^2yz^4$. 20. $-7a^4b^6$.

21. $\frac{x^4y^3}{5}$. 22. $\frac{2x^3}{9y^5}$. 23. $\frac{5ab^2}{6x^2y^3}$. 24. $\frac{3x^9}{4y^{21}}$.

25. a^2x^3. 26. x^2y^3. 27. $2xy^2$. 28. $3a^3b$.

29. $2ax^8$. 30. $-x^2y^2$. 31. $\frac{2}{a^9b^8}$. 32. $\frac{a^3x^5}{b^{10}}$.

33. $\frac{a^2}{b^3c^4}$.

XVI-b. Page 118

1. $x + 2y$. 2. $3a + 2b$. 3. $x - 5y$. 4. $2x - 3y$.

5. $9x + y$. 6. $5x - 3y$. 7. $x^2 - y^2$. 8. $1 - a^3$.

9. $a^2 - a + 1$. 10. $2x^2 - 3x + 5$. 11. $3x^2 - 2x - 1$.

12. $x^2 - 2x + 1$. 13. $2a^2 + a - 2$. 14. $1 - 5x + x^2$.

15. $2x + 3y - 5z$. 16. $4x^3 + 2x^4 - x^5$. 17. $x^3 - 11x + 17$.

18. $5x^2 - 3ax + 4a^2$. 19. $2x^2 + y^2 - 3z^2$. 20. $ab - 2ac + 3bc$.

21. $2a^2 + b^2 - 3c^2$. 22. $2x^2 - xy + 3y^2$. 23. $3x^2 - 5x + 7$.

24. $1 - 2x + 3x^2 - 4x^3$. 25. $ax^5 - 2bx^2 + 3c$.

XVI-d. Page 119

1. $\frac{x}{2} - 3$. 2. $2 - \frac{x}{y}$. 3. $\frac{x}{5} + y$. 4. $\frac{x}{y} + 5$.

5. $\frac{x}{2y} - 2$. 6. $\frac{x}{y} - \frac{a}{b}$. 7. $\frac{8x}{3y} + 2$. 8. $\frac{3x}{5} - \frac{5}{3x}$.

9. $\frac{a^2}{8} + \frac{a}{2} - 1$. 10. $x^2 + x - \frac{1}{2}$. 11. $a^2 - \frac{3}{2}a + \frac{5}{3}$.

12. $x^2 - 3x + \frac{1}{3}$. 13. $\frac{a^2}{2} + \frac{a}{x} - \frac{x}{a}$. 14. $x^2 - x + \frac{1}{4}$.

15. $\frac{x^2}{2} - 2x + \frac{a}{3}$. 16. $\frac{3a}{x} - \frac{1}{5} + \frac{2x}{3a}$. 17. $4m^2 + \frac{2}{3}a + 1$.

18. $2x^2 + 8 + \frac{8}{x^2}$.

XVI-d. Page 122

1. $a + 1$. 2. $x + 2$. 3. $ax - y^2$. 4. $2m - 1$.

5. $4a - 3b$. 6. $1 + x + x^2$. 7. $1 - 2x + 3x^2$. 8. $a + 2b - c$.

9. $2a^2 - 3a + 1$. 10. $y^2 - y + 1$. 11. $2x^2 + x - 3$.

12. $3x^2 - 2xa + 3a^2$. 13. $3x^2 - x - 1$. 14. $x^2 - 2xy + 4y^2$.

15. $3x^2 - x + 6$.

XVI-e. Page 123

1. $\frac{x}{2} - 1$. 2. $\frac{x}{3} + 2$. 3. $2x - \frac{y^2}{3}$. 4. $\frac{3x}{4y} - 2$. 5. $x - \frac{3}{x}$.

6. $\frac{x^2}{y} - 2y^2$. 7. $\frac{x}{y} + 2 - \frac{y}{x}$. 8. $\frac{x}{3} - 1 + \frac{3}{x}$. 9. $\frac{x}{a} - 4 + \frac{2a}{x}$.

10. $\frac{4a}{x} - 4 + \frac{x}{a}$. 11. $\frac{a}{b} - 1 + \frac{b}{a}$. 12. $\frac{2x^2}{y^2} + \frac{4x}{y} - 3$.

XVII-a. Page 124

1. $a(a^2 - x)$. 2. $x^2(x - 1)$. 3. $2a(1 - a)$. 4. $a(a - b^2)$.

5. $p(7p + 1)$. 6. $2x(4 - x)$. 7. $5ax(1 - a^2x)$. 8. $x^2(3 + x^3)$.

9. $x(x + y)$. 10. $x^2(x - y)$. 11. $5x(1 - 5xy)$. 12. $5(3 + 5x^2)$.

13. $16x(1 + 4xy)$. 14. $15a^2(1 - 15a^2)$. 15. $27(2 - 3x)$.

16. $5x^3(2 - 5xy)$. 17. $x(3x^2 - x + 1)$. 18. $2x^3(3 + x + 2x^2)$.

19. $x(x^2 - xy + y^2)$. 20. $3a^2(a^2 - ab + 2b^2)$. 21. $2xy^2(xy - 3x + y)$.

22. $3x(2x^2 - 3xy + 4y^2)$. 23. $5x^3(x^2 - 2a^2 - 3a^3)$.

24. $7a(1 - a^2 + 2a^3)$. 25. $19a^3x^2(2x^3 + 3a)$.

XVII-b. Page 125

1. $(a + b)(a + c)$. 2. $(a - c)(a + b)$. 3. $(ac + d)(ac + b)$.

4. $(a + 3)(a + c)$. 5. $(2 + c)(x + c)$. 6. $(x - a)(x + 5)$.

7. $(5 + b)(a + b)$. 8. $(a - y)(b - y)$. 9. $(a - b)(x - z)$.

10. $(p + q)(r - s)$. 11. $(x - y)(m - n)$. 12. $(x - a)(m + n)$.

13. $(2x + y)(a + b)$. 14. $(3a - b)(x - y)$. 15. $(2x + y)(3x - a)$.

16. $(x-2y)(m-n)$. **17.** $(ax-3by)(x-y)$. **18.** $(x+my)(x-4y)$.
19. $(a+b)(x^2+2)$. **20.** $(x-3)(x-y)$. **21.** $(2x-1)(x^3+2)$.
22. $(3x+5)(x^2+1)$. **23.** $(x+1)(x^3+2)$. **24.** $(y-1)(y^2+1)$.
25. $(a+bc)(xy-z)$. **26.** $(f^2+g^2)(x^2-a)$. **27.** $(2x+3y)(ax-by)$.
28. $(ax+by)(mx-ny)$. **29.** $(a-b-c)(x-y)$.
30. $(a+b)(ax+by+c)$.

XVII-c. Page 127

1. $(a+1)(a+2)$. **2.** $(a+1)(a+1)$. **3.** $(a+3)(a+4)$.
4. $(a-4)(a-3)$. **5.** $(x-5)(x-6)$. **6.** $(x-7)(x-8)$.
7. $(x-9)(x-10)$. **8.** $(x+6)(x+7)$. **9.** $(x-10)(x-11)$.
10. $(x-9)(x-12)$. **11.** $(x-5)(x-16)$. **12.** $(x+6)(x+15)$.
13. $(x-7)(x-12)$. **14.** $(x-6)(x-13)$. **15.** $(x-3)(x-15)$.
16. $(x+8)(x+12)$. **17.** $(x-11)(x-15)$. **18.** $(x-13)(x-8)$.
19. $(x+17)(x+6)$. **20.** $(a-19)(a-5)$. **21.** $(a-16)(a-16)$.
22. $(a+15)(a+15)$. **23.** $(a+27)(a+27)$. **24.** $(a-19)(a-19)$.
25. $(a-7b)(a-7b)$. **26.** $(a+2b)(a+3b)$. **27.** $(m-5n)(m-8n)$.
28. $(m-7n)(m-15n)$. **29.** $(x-11y)(x-12y)$. **30.** $(x-13y)(x-13y)$.
31. $(x^2+1)(x^2+7)$. **32.** $(x^2+2y^2)(x^2+7y^2)$. **33.** $(xy-3)(xy-13)$.
34. $(x+24y)(x+25y)$. **35.** $(xy+17)(xy+17)$.
36. $(a^2b^2+25)(a^2b^2+12)$. **37.** $(a-5bx)(a-15bx)$.
38. $(x+13y)(x+30y)$. **39.** $(a-2b)(a-27b)$. **40.** $(x^2+81)(x^2+81)$.
41. $(4-x)(3-x)$. **42.** $(5+x)(4+x)$. **43.** $(12-x)(11-x)$.
44. $(8+x)(11+x)$. **45.** $(26+xy)(5+xy)$. **46.** $(13-xa)(11-xa)$.
47. $(17-x^2)(12-x^2)$. **48.** $(27+x)(8+x)$.

XVII-d. Page 129

1. $(x+1)(x-2)$. **2.** $(x+2)(x-1)$. **3.** $(x+2)(x-3)$.
4. $(x+3)(x-2)$. **5.** $(x+1)(x-3)$. **6.** $(x+3)(x-1)$.
7. $(x+8)(x-7)$. **8.** $(x+8)(x-5)$. **9.** $(x+2)(x-6)$.
10. $(a+4)(a-5)$. **11.** $(a+3)(a-7)$. **12.** $(a+5)(a-4)$.
13. $(a+9)(a-13)$. **14.** $(x+12)(x-3)$. **15.** $(x+13)(x-12)$.
16. $(x+11)(x-10)$. **17.** $(x+6)(x-15)$. **18.** $(x+15)(x-16)$.
19. $(a+5)(a-17)$. **20.** $(a+8)(a-19)$. **21.** $(xy+3)(xy-8)$.
22. $(x+12y)(x-5y)$. **23.** $(x+7a)(x-6a)$. **24.** $(x+3y)(x-35y)$.
25. $(a+14y)(a-15y)$. **26.** $(x+23)(x-5)$. **27.** $(x+4y)(x-24y)$.
28. $(x+26)(x-10)$. **29.** $(a+2)(a-13)$. **30.** $(ay+24)(ay-10)$.

31. $(a^2 + 7b^2)(a^2 - 8b^2)$. **32.** $(x^2 + 3)(x^3 - 17)$.
33. $(y^2 + 9x^2)(y^2 - 3x^2)$. **34.** $(ab + 2c)(ab - 5c)$.
35. $(a + 14bx)(a - 2bx)$. **36.** $(a + 9xy)(a - 27xy)$.
37. $(x^2 + 25a^2)(x^2 - 12a^2)$. **38.** $(x^2 + 11a^2)(x^2 - 12a^2)$.
39. $(x^2 + 21a^2)(x^2 - 22a^2)$. **40.** $(x^3 + 30)(x^3 - 29)$.
41. $(1 + x)(2 - x)$. **42.** $(2 + x)(3 - x)$. **43.** $(11 + x)(10 - x)$.
44. $(20 + x)(19 - x)$. **45.** $(15 + ax)(8 - ax)$. **46.** $(5 + xy)(13 - xy)$.
47. $(14 + x)(7 - x)$. **48.** $(17 + x)(12 - x)$.

XVII-e. Page 131

1. $(x + 1)(2x + 1)$. **2.** $(x + 1)(3x + 2)$. **3.** $(x + 2)(2x + 1)$.
4. $(x + 3)(3x + 1)$. **5.** $(x + 4)(2x + 1)$. **6.** $(x + 2)(3x + 2)$.
7. $(x + 2)(2x + 3)$. **8.** $(x + 5)(2x + 1)$. **9.** $(x + 3)(3x + 2)$.
10. $(x + 2)(5x + 1)$. **11.** $(x + 2)(2x - 1)$. **12.** $(x + 1)(3x - 2)$.
13. $(x + 3)(4x - 1)$. **14.** $(x + 5)(3x - 1)$. **15.** $(x + 8)(2x - 1)$.
16. $(2x + 1)(x - 1)$. **17.** $(x + 3)(3x - 2)$. **18.** $(x + 4)(2x - 7)$.
19. $(x + 6)(3x - 5)$. **20.** $(2x + 3)(3x - 1)$. **21.** $(3x + 1)(2x - 3)$
22. $(3x + 4)(x + 1)$. **23.** $(x + 7)(3x + 2)$. **24.** $(2x + 5)(x - 3)$.
25. $(x + 7)(3x - 2)$. **26.** $(x - 7)(3x + 2)$. **27.** $(3x - 5)(2x - 7)$.
28. $(4x - 7)(x + 2)$. **29.** $(x - 2)(3x - 7)$. **30.** $(x + 13)(3x + 2)$.
31. $(x + 5)(4x + 3)$. **32.** $(2x + y)(x - 3y)$. **33.** $(2x - 7)(4x - 5)$.
34. $(3x - 2y)(4x - 5y)$. **35.** $(15x - 1)(x + 15)$. **36.** $(15x - 2)(x - 5)$.
37. $(12x + 5)(x - 3)$. **38.** $(12x - 7)(2x + 3)$. **39.** $(8x - 9)(9x - 8)$.
40. $(8x + y)(3x - 4y)$. **41.** $(2 + x)(1 - 2x)$. **42.** $(3 - x)(1 + 4x)$.
43. $(2 + 3x)(3 - 2x)$. **44.** $(4 + 3x)(1 - 2x)$. **45.** $(1 + 7x)(5 - 3x)$
46. $(7 + 3x)(1 + x)$. **47.** $(6 - x)(3 - 5x)$. **48.** $(4 + 5x)(2 - x)$.
49. $(5 + 4x)(4 - 5x)$. **50.** $(8 - 9x)(3 + 8x)$.

XVII-f. Page 133

1. $(x + 2)(x - 2)$. **2.** $(a + 9)(a - 9)$. **3.** $(y + 10)(y - 10)$.
4. $(c + 12)(c - 12)$. **5.** $(3 + a)(3 - a)$. **6.** $(7 + c)(7 - c)$.
7. $(11 + x)(11 - x)$. **8.** $(20 + a)(20 - a)$. **9.** $(x + 3a)(x - 3a)$.
10. $(y + 5x)(y - 5x)$. **11.** $(6x + 5b)(6x - 5b)$. **12.** $(3x + 1)(3x - 1)$.
13. $(6p + 7q)(6p - 7q)$. **14.** $(2k + 1)(2k - 1)$. **15.** $(7 + 10k)(7 - 10k)$.
16. $(1 + 5x)(1 - 5x)$. **17.** $(a + 2b)(a - 2b)$. **18.** $(3x + y)(3x - y)$.
19. $(pq + 6)(pq - 6)$. **20.** $(ab + 2cd)(ab - 2cd)$. **21.** $(x^2 + 3)(x^2 - 3)$.
22. $(3a^2 + 11)(3a^2 - 11)$. **23.** $(5x + 8)(5x - 8)$.

24. $(9a^2 + 7x^2)(9a^2 - 7x^2)$.
25. $(x^3 + 5)(x^3 - 5)$.
26. $(1 + 6a^3)(1 - 6a^3)$.
27. $(3x^2 + a)(3x^2 - a)$.
28. $(9x^3 + 5a)(9x^3 - 5a)$.
29. $(x^2a + 7)(x^2a - 7)$.
30. $(a + 8x^3)(a - 8x^3)$.
31. $(ab + 3x^3)(ab - 3x^3)$.
32. $(x^2y^2 + 2)(x^2y^2 - 2)$.
33. $(1 + ab)(1 - ab)$.
34. $(2 + x)(2 - x)$.
35. $(3 + 2a)(3 - 2a)$.
36. $(3a^2 + 5b^2)(3a^2 - 5b^2)$.
37. $(x^2 + 4b)(x^2 - 4b)$.
38. $(x + 5y)(x - 5y)$.
39. $(1 + 10b)(1 - 10b)$.
40. $(5 + 8x)(5 - 8x)$.
41. $(11a + 9x)(11a - 9x)$.
42. $(pq + 8a^2)(pq - 8a^2)$.
43. $(8x + 5z^3)(8x - 5z^3)$.
44. $(7x^2 + 4y^2)(7x^2 - 4y^2)$.
45. $(9p^2z^3 + 5b)(9p^2z^3 - 5b)$.
46. $(4x^8 + 3y^3)(4x^8 - 3y^3)$.
47. $(6x^{18} + 7a^7)(6x^{18} - 7a^7)$.
48. $(1 + 10a^3b^2c)(1 - 10a^3b^2c)$.
49. $(5x^5 + 4a^4)(5x^5 - 4a^4)$.
50. $(ab^2c^3 + x^8)(ab^2c^3 - x^8)$.
51. $1000 \times 150 = 150000$.
52. $241 \times 1 = 241$.
53. $1000 \times 500 = 500000$.
54. $658 \times 20 = 13160$.
55. $1006 \times 500 = 503000$.
56. $200 \times 2 = 400$.
57. $2000 \times 1446 = 2892000$.
58. $2378 \times 900 = 2140200$.
59. $2500 \times 1122 = 2805000$.
60. $3000 \times 2462 = 7386000$.
61. $16264 \times 2 = 32528$.
62. $10002 \times 10000 = 100020000$.

XVII-g. Page 135

1. $(a + b + c)(a + b - c)$.
2. $(a - b + c)(a - b - c)$.
3. $(x + y + 2z)(x + y - 2z)$.
4. $(x + 2y + a)(x + 2y - a)$.
5. $(a + 3b + 4x)(a + 3b - 4x)$.
6. $(x + 5a + 3y)(x + 5a - 3y)$.
7. $(x + 5c + 1)(x + 5c - 1)$.
8. $(a - 2x + b)(a - 2x - b)$.
9. $(2x - 3a + 3c)(2x - 3a - 3c)$.
10. $(a + b - c)(a - b + c)$.
11. $(x + y + z)(x - y - z)$.
12. $(2a + y - z)(2a - y + z)$.
13. $(3x + 2a - 3b)(3x - 2a + 3b)$.
14. $(1 + a - b)(1 - a + b)$.
15. $(c + 5a - 3b)(c - 5a + 3b)$.
16. $(a + b + c + d)(a + b - c - d)$.
17. $(a - b + x + y)(a - b - x - y)$.
18. $(7x + y + 1)(7x + y - 1)$.
19. $(a + b + m - n)(a + b - m + n)$.
20. $(a - n + b + m)(a - n - b - m)$.
21. $(b - c + a - x)(b - c - a + x)$.
22. $(4a + x + b + y)(4a + x - b - y)$.
23. $(a + 2b + 3x + 4y)(a + 2b - 3x - 4y)$.
24. $(1 + 7a - 3b)(1 - 7a + 3b)$.
25. $(a - b + x - y)(a - b - x + y)$.

26. $(a-3x+4y)(a-3x-4y)$. **27.** $(2a-5x+1)(2a-5x-1)$.

28. $(a+b-c+x-y+z)(a+b-c-x+y-z)$.

29. $(3a+2b+c+x-2y)(3a+2b-c-x+2y)$.

30. $y(2x+y)$. **31.** $y(2x-y)$. **32.** $(x+5y)(x+y)$.

33. $47x(x+2y)$. **34.** $(8x+y)(2x+3y)$.

35. $5y(6x-5y)$. **36.** $(12x-1)(2x+7)$.

37. $5a(a+2)$. **38.** $(7a+1)(a-1)$.

39. $3a(a+2b-2c)$. **40.** $x(x-14y+2z)$.

41. $y(2x+y-16)$. **42.** $a(4x+a-6)$.

XVII-h. Page 136

1. $(x+y+a)(x+y-a)$. **2.** $(a-b+x)(a-b-x)$.

3. $(x-3a+4b)(x-3a-4b)$. **4.** $(2a+b+3c)(2a+b-3c)$.

5. $(x+a+y)(x+a-y)$. **6.** $(a+y+x)(a+y-x)$.

7. $(x+a+b)(x-a-b)$. **8.** $(y+c+x)(y-c+x)$.

9. $(1+x+y)(1-x-y)$. **10.** $(c+x-y)(c-x+y)$.

11. $(x+y+2xy)(x+y-2xy)$. **12.** $(a-2b+3ac)(a-2b-3ac)$.

13. $(x+y+a+b)(x+y-a-b)$. **14.** $(a-b-c+d)(a-b-c-d)$.

15. $(x-2a+b-y)(x-2a-b+y)$.

16. $(y+b+a+3x)(y+c-a-3x)$.

17. $(x-1+a+2b)(x-1-a-2b)$.

18. $(3a-1+x+4d)(3a-1-x-4d)$.

19. $(x-y+a-b)(x-y-a+b)$.

20. $(a-b+c+d)(a-b-c-d)$.

21. $(2x-3a+c+k)(2x-3a-c-k)$.

22. $(a-5b+3bx-1)(a-5b-3bx+1)$.

23. $(a^2+4x^2+5x^3-3)(a^2+4x^2-5x^3+3)$.

24. $(x^2-a^2+x-3)(x^2-a^2-x+3)$.

25. $(a^2+ab+b^2)(a^2-ab+b^2)$.

26. $(x^2+2xy+4y^2)(x^2-2xy+4y^2)$.

27. $(p^2+3pq+9q^2)(p^2-3pq+9q^2)$.

28. $(c^2+cd+2d^2)(c^2-cd+2d^2)$.

29. $(x^2+3xy-y^2)(x^2-3xy-y^2)$.

30. $(2m^2+3mn+n^2)(2m^2-3mn+n^2)$, or $(4m^2-n^2)(m^2-n^2)$.

XVII-k Page 137

1. $(x - y)(x^2 + xy + y^2)$. **2.** $(x + y)(x^2 - xy + y^2)$.

3. $(x - 1)(x^2 + x + 1)$. **4.** $(1 + a)(1 - a + a^2)$.

5. $(2x - y)(4x^2 + 2xy + y^2)$. **6.** $(x + 2y)(x^2 - 2xy + 4y^2)$.

7. $(3x + 1)(9x^2 - 3x + 1)$. **8.** $(1 - 2y)(1 + 2y + 4y^2)$.

9. $(ab - c)(a^2b^2 + abc + c^2)$. **10.** $(2x + 3y)(4x^2 - 6xy + 9y^2)$.

11. $(1 - 7x)(1 + 7x + 49x^2)$. **12.** $(4 + y)(16 - 4y + y^2)$.

13. $(5 + a)(25 - 5a + a^2)$. **14.** $(6 - a)(36 + 6a + a^2)$.

15. $(ab + 8)(a^2b^2 - 8ab + 64)$. **16.** $(10y - 1)(100y^2 + 10y + 1)$.

17. $(x + 4y)(x^2 - 4xy + 16y^2)$. **18.** $(3 - 10x)(9 + 30x + 100x^2)$.

19. $(ab + 6c)(a^2b^2 - 6abc + 36c^2)$.

20. $(7 - 2x)(49 + 14x + 4x^2)$. **21.** $(a + 3b)(a^2 - 3ab + 9b^2)$.

22. $(3x - 4y)(9x^2 + 12xy + 16y^2)$. **23.** $(5x - 1)(25x^2 + 5x + 1)$.

24. $(6p - 7)(36p^2 + 42p + 49)$. **25.** $(xy + z)(x^2y^2 - xyz + z^2)$.

26. $(abc - 1)(a^2b^2c^2 + abc + 1)$. **27.** $(7x + 10y)(49x^2 - 70xy + 100y^2)$.

28. $(9a - 4b)(81a^2 + 36ab + 16b^2)$.

29. $(2ab + 5x)(4a^2b^2 - 10abx + 25x^2)$.

30. $(xy - 6z)(x^2y^2 + 6xyz + 36z^2)$.

31. $(x^2 - 3y)(x^4 + 3x^2y + 9y^2)$. **32.** $(4x^2 + 5y)(16x^4 - 20x^2y + 25y^2)$.

33. $(2x - z^2)(4x^2 + 2xz^2 + z^4)$. **34.** $(6x^2 - b)(36x^4 + 6x^2b + b^2)$.

35. $(a + 7b)(a^2 - 7ab + 49b^2)$. **36.** $(a^2 + 9b)(a^4 - 9a^2b + 81b^2)$.

37. $(2x - 9y^2)(4x^2 + 18xy^2 + 81y^4)$.

38. $(pq - 3x)(p^2q^2 + 3pqx + 9x^2)$.

39. $(z - 4y^2)(z^2 + 4xy^2 + 16y^4)$.

40. $(xy - 8)(x^2y^2 + 8xy + 64)$.

XVII-l Page 142

1. $(x - 1)(x - 2)$. **2.** $(a + 2)(a + 5)$.

3. $(b + 4)(b - 3)$. **4.** $(y - 7)(y + 3)$.

5. $(c + 1)(c + 11)$. **6.** $(x - 5)(x + 1)$.

7. $(n + 2)(n + 10)$. **8.** $(y + 10)(y - 1)$.

9. $(p - 6q)(p + 4q)$. **10.** $(y + 11)(y - 10)$.

11. $(z - 15)(z + 6)$. **12.** $(k - 6)(k - 8)$.

13. $(a + 9)(a + 9)$. **14.** $(b - 27)(b + 3)$.

15. $(c + 27)(c + 3)$. **16.** $(x - 7)(x - 7)$.

17. $(y + 7z)(y + 3z)$. **18.** $(z + 9)(z - 7)$.

19. $(n+8)(n+3)$.
20. $(p-8)(p+3)$.
21. $(l+12)(l-3)$.
22. $(ab-2)(ab-2)$.
23. $(ab+8)(ab+2)$.
24. $(b-9)(b+5)$.
25. $(m+11)(m-8)$.
26. $(n-15)(n+3)$.
27. $(p+13)(p-3)$.
28. $(xy-9)(xy+8)$.
29. $(z-5)(z+4)$.
30. $(x+8y)(x-7y)$.
31. $(a-13b)(a+2b)$.
32. $(ab-8)(ab+7)$.
33. $(y^2+13)(y^2-12)$.
34. $(z^2-13)(z^2+6)$.
35. $(y^2+5)(y^2-7)$.
36. $(x+13y)(x-7y)$.
37. $m^2n^2(m-3n)$.
38. $5x^3(2+5xy)$.
39. $(y-5)(y+3)$.
40. $(a+b)(x+y)$.
41. $(x+y)(x-z)$.
42. $(3c-2)(c+1)$.
43. $(2b+1)(b+5)$.
44. $(x-3y)(x-3y)$.
45. $(3x-1)(x-3)$.
46. $(cd+1)(cd-2)$.
47. $(2x+3)(3x-1)$.
48. $(a-b)(4-c)$.
49. $(a^2+2)(a+1)$.
50. $2c^2d\,(c-3d+d^2)$.
51. $xy(x+9)(x-7)$.
52. $(2y-3)(3y+1)$.
53. $(2x-3)(2x-3)$.
54. $(3+4p)(1-3p)$.
55. $(4+pq)(4+pq)$.
56. $z(4z-3)(z+2)$.
57. $a(a+7)(a-6)$.
58. $(m^3+2)(2m-1)$.
59. $a^2(a-b)(a-3)$.
60. $(7+x)(2-x)$.
61. $(17-z)(1-z)$.
62. $(2m^2+3)(m^2-7)$.
63. $(5x-3y)(x+2y)$.
64. $(3m^3-5)(2m^3+9)$.
65. $(3m-4)(3m-4)$.
66. $(5+9a)(5-9a)$.
67. $(a^2b^2+3)(a^2b^2-3)$.
68. $(3+l)(9-3l+l^2)$.
69. $(1-4m)(1+4m+16m^2)$.
70. $(k^2+5l)(k^2-5l)$.
71. $(pq-1)(p^2q^2+pq+1)$.
72. $(2z+1)(4z^2-2z+1)$.
73. $(1+8x)(1-8x)$.
74. $2(5p+1)(25p^2-5p+1)$.
75. $4(5ab^2+1)(5ab^2-1)$.
76. $(9+cd)(81-9cd+c^2d^2)$.
77. $(a+x+1)(a+x-1)$.
78. $(4+b-c)\,(4-b+c)$.
79. $x(3x+2y)(3x-2y)$.
80. $(p-5q)(p+4q)$.
81. $l(l-7)(l+6)$.
82. $(abc+9d)(abc-9d)$.
83. $(4x^2-3y)(16x^4+12x^2y+9y^2)$.
84. $(x-17)(x+19)$.
85. $(x^2+17)(x^2-17)$.
86. $(l+17)(l-16)$.
87. $(10z-3)(100z^2+30z+9)$.
88. $(a+23)(a-13)$.
89. $(a+b+c)(a-b-c)$.

90. $(1 + x - 3y)(1 - x + 3y)$. **91.** $(x^2 + y^2 + 3xy)(x^2 + y^2 - 3xy)$.

92. $(a^2 + a + 2)(a^2 - a + 2)$. **93.** $(b - 29)(b + 27)$.

94. $(x + 2)(x^2 - 2x + 4)(x - 2)(x^2 + 2x + 4)$.

95. $(3y + 2x)(9y^2 - 6xy + 4x^2)(3y - 2x)(9y^2 + 6xy + 4x^2)$.

96. $(x^4 + 1)(x^2 + 1)(x + 1)(x - 1)$.

97. $ab(3a + b)(9a^2 - 3ab + b^2)(3a - b)(9a^2 + 3ab + b^2)$.

98. $a^2(ax + 2y)(a^2x^2 - 2axy + 4y^2)(ax - 2y)(a^2x^2 + 2axy + 4y^2)$.

99. $(a^2 + b^2)(a^4 - a^2b^2 + b^4)(a + b)(a^2 - ab + b^2)(a - b)(a^2 + ab + b^2)$.

100. $(x^2 + 2y^2z^2)(x^2 + 2y^2z^2)$.

101. $(ab + 8)(a^2b^2 - 8ab + 64)$.

102. $(2x + 7)(x + 5)$.

103. $20y(5x + y)(5x - y)$.

104. $\{(a+b)^2 + 1)\}(a + b + 1)(a + b - 1)$.

105. $(c + d - 1)\{(c + d)^2 + c + d + 1\}$.

106. $(1 - x + y)\{1 + x - y + (x - y)^2\}$.

107. $(x - 19)(x + 13)$.

108. $(a + 9)(a - 31)$.

109. $2\{5(a - b) + 1\}\{25(a - b)^2 - 5(a - b) + 1\}$.

110. $2c(c^2 + 3d^2)$. **111.** $9y(4x^2 + 2xy + y^2)$.

112. $(x - 2y)(x + 2y + 1)$. **113.** $(a - b)(a + b + 1)$.

114. $(a + b)(a + b + 1)$. **115.** $(a + b)(a^2 - ab + b^2 + 1)$.

116. $(a + 3b)(a - 3b + 1)$. **117.** $(x - y)\{2(x - y) + 1\}\{2(x - y) - 1\}$.

118. $xy(x + y)(x - y)(x - y)$.

Miscellaneous Examples III-Page 143

1. $x^3 - 2x$. **2.** $42a - 40b + 30c$. **3.** $a^6 - c^6$.

4. (1) 12; (2) $x = 5$, $y = 6$. **5.** $x^3 + 4x - 1$.

6. 72. **7.** $\frac{109}{210}$. **8.** $x^2 + \frac{3}{4}x + \frac{5}{4}$.

9. $2x^2 - x$. **10.** (1) $(ax - 5)(ax + 3)$; (2) $(2m^2 + 9pq)(2m^2 - 9pq)$.

11. (1) $x = -2$, $y = 4$; (2) $x = 5$, $y = -2$. **12.** $\frac{am}{pb}$ miles.

13. $84x^4 + 25x^3 + 101x - 30$. **14.** (1) 7; (2) $-1\frac{1}{2}$.

15. $x^4 + 14x^3 + 27x^2 - 154x + 121$.

16. (1) $(x + 2a)(x - b)$; (2) $(x^2 + 14y)(x^2 - 4y)$.

17. H.C.F. = 7; L.C.M. = $3528a^3b^2c^8$.

18. Rs. 14.

19. $3p$.

21. (1) $m - n = a + c$; (2) $3a^2b^2 + c^3 = p(m + n)$.

22. 8.

23. $6x^2 - xy - y^2$.

24. Apples Rs. 9 a dozen; eggs Rs. 4 a score.

25. $(x - 5)(2x - 3)(x + 1)$.

26. 33.

27. $2x^2 + 9xy - 7y^2$.

28. $x = 2, y = 3, z = 0$.

29. (1) $xy(x + 2y)(x - 2y)$; (2) $(m + n)(m - n)(2m^2 + 3n^2)$.

30. $\frac{bc}{am}$ days, $2\frac{5}{8}$.

XVIII-a. Page 146

1. $a + b$.	**2.** $y + x$.	**3.** $x(x - y)$.	**4.** $2x - 3y$.
5. $x + y$.	**6.** $ab(a - b)$.	**7.** $a(a - x)$.	**8.** $a + 2x$.
9. $b(a + b)$.	**10.** $x - 3y$.	**11.** $a - x$.	**12.** $2x + y$.
13. $2(5x - 1)$.	**14.** $3x + 2y$.	**15.** $x + 1$.	**16.** $y(x - 1)$.
17. $(x - y)^2$.	**18.** $x^2 + a^2$.	**19.** $x + 2y$.	**20.** $x - 3a$.
21. $x + 2$.	**22.** $x - 5$.	**23.** $x - 3$.	**24.** $x - 3$.
25. $3x + 1$.	**26.** $x - 1$.	**27.** $cx + d$.	**28.** $x^2 + y$.
29. $x(a - 3b)$.	**30.** $2x + 1$.	**31.** $x^2(3x + 2)$.	

XVIII-b. Page 150

1. $x^2 - 3x + 2$.	**2.** $x^2 - 13x + 5$.	**3.** $x^2 - 8$.	**4.** $x^2 - 5$.
5. $x^2 + 2x + 1$.	**6.** $x + 3$.	**7.** $a^2 - 2ax + x^2$.	**8.** $x + 1$.
9. $x^2 - 3x + 7$.	**10.** $2x^2 - 7$.	**11.** $3x^2 + 1$.	**12.** $2x^2 - 3$.
13. $3x^2 + 2a^2$.	**14.** $x^3 - ax + a^2$.	**15.** $x^2 + 2ax - a^2$.	
16. $3a^2 - ax - 2x^2$.	**17.** $xy(2x^2 + xy - 3y^2)$.	**18.** $2x^2a^2(2x - 3a)$.	
19. $2x^2(2x + 7)$.	**20.** $6(3x - 5a)$.	**21.** $3x^2 - 2xy + y^2$.	
22. $x^4 + x^3 - 1$.	**23.** $1 + x^3 - x^4$.	**24.** $1 + a$.	**25.** $x(3 + 4x)$.
26. $x^2 - 2x + 1$.	**27.** $2x^2 - 7$.		

XIX-a. Page 154

1. $\frac{3}{2b}$.	**2.** $\frac{b}{c}$.	**3.** $\frac{1}{ax - 1}$.	**4.** $\frac{3b^2c}{20(a - b)}$.
5. $\frac{2x - 3y}{2x}$.	**6.** $4(x - y)$.	**7.** $\frac{1}{2a + 3x}$.	**8.** $\frac{x}{x^2 - 2y^2}$.

9. $\dfrac{x-3y}{x^2+3xy+9y^2}$. 10. $\dfrac{x}{x+1}$. 11. $\dfrac{3x}{x+2}$. 12. $\dfrac{5a}{3b}$.

13. $\dfrac{xy}{x-2}$. 14. $\dfrac{3(a+b)}{a-b}$. 15. $\dfrac{x^2-17}{x^2-5}$.

16. $\dfrac{x+2y}{x^2+xy+y^2}$. 17. $\dfrac{2x+3}{3x+5}$. 18. $\dfrac{a(x-4)}{x+5}$. 19. $\dfrac{x+7}{x+13}$.

20. $\dfrac{3+a}{2}$.

XIX-b. Page 156

The expression in [ ] is in each case the H.C.F. of the numerator and the denominator.

1. $\dfrac{a-2b}{a+2b}[a^2+ab+b^2]$.
2. $\dfrac{x-3}{x+2}[(x-1)^2]$.
3. $\dfrac{a+5}{a+4}[(a-1)(a-2)]$.
4. $\dfrac{x^2+4xy+9y^2}{2x^2+3xy+7y^2}[2x-3y]$.
5. $\dfrac{2a+5b}{3a+5b}[(2a+3b)(a-b)]$.
6. $\dfrac{1-x+2x^2}{1-x+3x^2}[1-x+x^2]$.
7. $\dfrac{x-1}{3x^2+3x+10}[x-1]$.
8. $\dfrac{3a^2+b^2}{4a-b}[a-b]$.
9. $\dfrac{4x^3-ax+a^2}{x^3+a^3}[x+a]$.
10. $\dfrac{2(2x^2-3x-1)}{3x^3+x^2+x-2}[x-1]$.
11. $(2x-3a)^2$.
12. $\dfrac{3x^2-x-2}{3x^2+x-2}[2x+1]$.
13. $\dfrac{5x+2}{7x-4}[x^2-3]$.
14. $\dfrac{2x^2+3x+5}{2x^2+3x-5}[2x^2-3x+5]$.
15. $\dfrac{3(x-3a)(x-4a)}{2(x+3a)(x+4a)}[x-2a]$.
16. $\dfrac{a(x+8a)}{x(x+7a)}[x^2-13ax+5a^2]$.

XIX-c. Page 159

1. $\dfrac{7}{12}$. 2. $\dfrac{ab}{2a-1}$. 3. 2. 4. $\dfrac{a-11}{a-2}$. 5. $\dfrac{4x+3a}{x+2}$.

6. $\dfrac{5a-b}{x(3a-2)}$. 7. $\dfrac{x+2}{x-1}$. 8. $\dfrac{x+1}{x+5}$. 9. $\dfrac{x}{x-2}$. 10. $\dfrac{2x-1}{2x-3}$.

11. $\dfrac{x+1}{x+5}$. 12. $\dfrac{x-1}{4x-7}$. 13. b^2+3b+9. 14. $\dfrac{1}{x+7}$.

15. $8pq-z^2$. 16. x. 17. $\dfrac{x+1}{x-1}$. 18. $\dfrac{x-5}{x-1}$.

19. $\dfrac{x}{y}$. 20. x. 21. $\dfrac{2x-1}{2x-5}$. 22. 1.

23. $\frac{1}{b}$. **24.** $\frac{a+b-c}{b-c-a}$. **25.** $\frac{1}{x-8}$. **26.** $\frac{a-x}{a+x}$.

27. $\frac{m}{n}$. **28.** $x(2+x)$. **29.** $\frac{x+4}{x(x-4)}$. **30.** 1.

31. $a+x$. **32.** $\frac{a^2}{16a^2+4ab+b^2}$.

XX-a. Page 161

1. $x(x+1)$. **2.** $x^2(x-3)$. **3.** $12x^2(x+2)$.

4. $21x^3(x+1)$. **5.** $x(x+1)(x-1)$. **6.** $ab(a+b)$.

7. $xy(2x+1)(2x-1)$. **8.** $6x(3x-1)$. **9.** $x(x+1)(x+2)$.

10. $(x+1)(x-1)(x-2)$. **11.** $(x+2)^2(x+3)$.

12. $(x-1)(x-2)(x-4)$. **13.** $(x-3)(x-1)(x+2)$.

14. $(x+5)(x-4)(x-6)$. **15.** $(x+7)(x-6)(x-5)$.

16. $(x+1)(x+2)(2x+1)$. **17.** $(x+2)(x+3)(3x+2)$.

18. $(x+2)(x+3)(5x+1)$. **19.** $(x+2)(x+8)(2x-1)$.

20. $(x+2)(x-2)(3x-7)$. **21.** $12x(x+2)(2x+1)(4x-7)$.

22. $6x^2(x+7)(3x+5)(3x-2)$. **23.** $20x^2y(3x+1)(5x+1)(4x-1)$.

24. $(x+y)(2x-7y)(4x-5y)$. **25.** $(x-y)^3(3x-2y)(4x-5y)$.

26. $3a^2x(3x-a)(2x+3a)(x+5a)$.

27. $2axy^3(x+3)(4x-1)(3x-2)$.

28. $x^2(3-5x)^2(2+x)^2$.

29. $42a^4b^2(a-b)^3(a+b)(a^2+ab+b^2)$.

30. $m^3n(m^6-n^6)(m-n)^2$.

31. $8c^2(2c-3d)^2(8c^3-27d^3)$.

XX-b. Page 163

1. H.C.F. $x-2$, L.C.M. $(x+1)^2(x+2)(x-2)(x-3)$.

2. $(ax+b)(ax-b)(bx+a)$. **3.** $xy(x-a)(y-b)(y-2b)$.

4. H.C.F. $x(x+3)$, L.C.M. $x(x-1)(x+3)(2x-1)$.

5. $(1+x)^3(1-x)^2$. **6.** $(x-2)(x-4)(x-6)$.

7. H.C.F. $2x+1$, L.C.M. $(2x+1)(x+1)(x-1)(3x+2)(3x-2)$.

8. $ab^2c^2(c+a)^2(c-a)^2$.

9. L.C.M. $y^2(x-y)^2(x^2+xy+y^2)$, H.C.F. $x-y$.

10. H.C.F. $2x-3$. L.C.M. $(2x-3)(3x-2)(x+4)(3x+4)$.

11. $(x+a)^2(x^2+ax+a^2)(x^2-ax+a^2)$.

12. H.C.F. $3x-y$, L.C.M. $(3x-y)(x+y)^2(x-y)^2$.

13. $x-1$.

14. $(a+b)(a-b)(a-2b)(a^2+ab+b^2)$.

15. H.C.F. a^2+xy, L.C.M. $(a^2+xy)(2x+3y)(2x-3y)$.

16. H.C.F. $(x-3)(x-4)$, L.C.M. $(x-2)(x-3)(x-4)(x-5)$.

17. $x-8a$.

18. $105x^2y^2(x+y)^2(x-y)^2$.

XXI-a. Page 167

1. $\frac{4(x+1)}{5}$. **2.** $\frac{13(x-2)}{12}$. **3.** $\frac{25x-16}{56}$.

4. $\frac{17x}{36}$. **5.** $\frac{19x-201}{225}$.

6. $\frac{12x^2+28x-27}{8x^2}$. **7.** 0. **8.** $\frac{3(a+3b)}{8a}$.

9. $\frac{6b^2c+6bc^2+3ac^2+3a^2c-4a^2b+4ab^2}{12abc}$. **10.** $\frac{a^2+3x^2}{2ax}$.

11. $\frac{5x+31}{102x}$. **12.** $\frac{a^4b^2-b^4c^2+a^2c^4}{a^2b^2c^2}$.

13. $\frac{11x^3-18x^2-27x-16}{30x^3}$. **14.** $\frac{x^3+y^3}{x^2y^3}$.

15. $\frac{3y+2z}{yz}$. **16.** $\frac{a^3+b^3+c^3-3abc}{abc}$.

XXI-b. Page 168

1. $\frac{2x+5}{(x+2)(x+3)}$. **2.** $\frac{x+5}{(x+3)(x+4)}$. **3.** $\frac{1}{(x-4)(x-5)}$.

4. $\frac{2(x+6)}{(x-6)(x+2)}$. **5.** $\frac{(a-b)x}{(x+a)(x+b)}$. **6.** $\frac{(a+b)x-2ab}{(x-a)(x-b)}$.

7. $\frac{2}{(x+2)(x+4)}$. **8.** $\frac{4ax}{a^2-x^2}$. **9.** $\frac{8x}{x^2-4}$.

10. $\frac{6}{(x-2)(x-5)}$. **11.** $\frac{ax}{x^2-a^2}$. **12.** $\frac{5x+9}{x^2-9}$.

13. $\frac{x+2y}{4x^2-9y^2}$. **14.** $\frac{3ax}{x^2-4a^2}$. **15.** $\frac{4ab}{4a^2-b^2}$.

16. $\frac{2xy}{x^2-y^2}$. **17.** $\frac{2x^3}{1-x^4}$. **18.** $\frac{x^2+y^2}{xy(x^2-y^2)}$.

19. $\frac{5x^2}{25x^2-y^2}$. **20.** $\frac{x^4+y^4}{xy(x^4-y^4)}$. **21.** $\frac{4a^2}{x(x+2a)}$.

22. $\dfrac{2x^3}{x^2 - y^2}$. **23.** $\dfrac{-2ax}{a^3 - 8x^3}$. **24.** $2b$.

25. $\dfrac{4(x-1)}{(x-2)^2(x+2)}$. **26.** $\dfrac{x^2 + a^2}{ax(x-a)(x+a)^2}$.

XXI-c. Page 170

1. $\dfrac{2}{x+y}$. **2.** $\dfrac{x}{4x^2 - y^2}$. **3.** $\dfrac{1 - 6x^3}{1 - 4x^2}$.

4. $\dfrac{4a^2 + b^2}{4a^2 - 9b^2}$. **5.** $\dfrac{1+a}{9-a^2}$. **6.** $\dfrac{4x-5}{6(x^2-1)}$.

7. 0. **8.** $\dfrac{12a^2 - 4a + 7}{3(4a^2 - 9)}$. **9.** $\dfrac{2(13x+7)}{3(x^2-4)}$.

10. $\dfrac{x^2 + y^2}{x^4 + x^2y^2 + y^4}$. **11.** $\dfrac{2}{(x-4)(x-6)}$.

12. $\dfrac{2}{(x-2)(x-3)(x-4)}$. **13.** $\dfrac{2}{(x-1)(2x+1)(2x+3)}$.

14. $\dfrac{1}{(x-1)(2x+1)(3x-2)}$. **15.** $\dfrac{17a}{(1-2a)(4+a)(3+5a)}$.

16. $\dfrac{23x}{(1+2x)(2+x)(5-9x)}$. **17.** $\dfrac{x+2}{(x+1)(x+3)}$.

18. $\dfrac{1}{x+1}$. **19.** $\dfrac{1}{a+b}$.

20. $\dfrac{3x+2}{(x-2)(x-1)(x+1)}$. **21.** $\dfrac{1}{x+2}$.

22. $\dfrac{8x^2 + 4x - 3}{(x-1)(x+1)(2x+1)}$. **23.** $\dfrac{1}{2x+1}$.

24. $\dfrac{x^2 + 11}{(x-1)(x+2)(x+3)}$. **25.** $\dfrac{2x+13}{(x+3)(x+4)(x-4)}$.

26. $\dfrac{32a^2}{(1-2a)^2(1+2a)}$. **27.** $\dfrac{96x^2}{(3-2x)^2(3+2x)}$.

28. $\dfrac{4x^3}{81 - x^4}$. **29.** $\dfrac{72a}{16a^4 - 81}$. **30.** $\dfrac{1}{1 - x^4}$.

31. $\dfrac{a(a^2 + 2ax + 3x^2)}{4(a^4 - x^4)}$. **32.** $\dfrac{16x}{16 - x^4}$.

33. $\dfrac{x(37 + 172x^3)}{6(1 - 16x^4)}$. **34.** $\dfrac{2a(a^2 + 32x^2)}{3(a^4 - 255x^4)}$.

35. $\dfrac{7a^2 + 45}{6(a^4 - 81)}$. **36.** $\dfrac{x^5}{1 - x^8}$.

37. $\frac{36a^4}{a^8 - 6561}$. **38.** $\frac{2}{x^2(x^2-4)}$.

39. $\frac{1}{(3x-y)(x-3y)}$. **40.** $\frac{2}{(x-1)(x+1)^2}$.

41. 1. **42.** 0. **43.** $\frac{4x}{x^2-1}$.

XXI-d. Page 173

1. $\frac{x-11}{20(x^2-1)}$. **2.** $\frac{1}{1-a^2}$. **3.** $\frac{x+3a}{x+a}$.

4. $\frac{2x-a}{x+a}$. **5.** 0. **6.** $\frac{7x}{1-x^2}$.

7. $\frac{1}{x-3}$. **8.** $\frac{12(2x+1)}{4x^2-9}$. **9.** $\frac{61-21b}{12(1-b^2)}$.

10. $\frac{2}{3(1-a^2)}$. **11.** $\frac{y^5}{x^6-y^6}$. **12.** $\frac{x}{y}$.

13. $\frac{2x}{x+y}$. **14.** $\frac{2x^3}{x^2-4}$. **15.** $\frac{a}{4a^2-25b^2}$.

16. $\frac{b(a+b)}{x^2-b^2}$. **17.** $\frac{2bx}{4x^2-1}$. **18.** $\frac{x+c}{(x-a)(x-b)}$.

19. $\frac{x-c}{(x-a)(x-b)}$. **20.** $\frac{2a}{(x-a)(x-b)}$. **21.** 0.

22. $\frac{4a^3}{x^4-a^4}$. **23.** $\frac{48a^3}{(x^2-a^2)(x^2-9a^2)}$. **24.** $\frac{x^4}{a^8-x^8}$.

25. 0. **26.** $\frac{a^6}{a^8-b^8}$. **27.** $\frac{a-x}{a+x}$.

28. $\frac{a^3}{(a-b)(a^3+b^3)}$. **29.** $\frac{2+x+3x^2}{2(1-x^4)}$. **30.** $\frac{2(x^3+1)}{x(x^3-1)}$.

31. 0. **32.** $\frac{4ab}{a^2-b^2}$.

XXI-e Page 176

1. 0. **2.** $\frac{bc+ca+ab-a^2-b^2-c^2}{(a-b)(b-c)(c-a)}$.

3. $\frac{x^2+y^2+z^2-yz-zx-xy}{(x-y)(y-z)(z-x)}$. **4.** 0.

5. $\frac{2(bc+ca+ab-a^2-b^2-c^2)}{(a-b)(b-c)(c-a)}$. **6.** 0. **7.** 0. **8.** 0.

9. $\frac{2(qr + rp + pq - p^2 - q^2 - r^2)}{(p-q)(q-r)(r-p)}$. 10. 0.

11. 0. 12. $\frac{p(y-z) + q(z-x) + r(x-y)}{(y-z)(z-x)(x-y)}$.

XXII-a. Page 180

1. $\frac{m^2 - nl}{na - mb}$. 2. $\frac{x+y}{y-x}$. 3. $\frac{ad+b}{dx-y}$.

4. $\frac{x+c}{b-x}$. 5. $\frac{3}{4b}$. 6. $\frac{a}{c}$.

7. $\frac{x^2 - y^2}{x^2 + y^2}$. 8. $\frac{c}{ac+b}$. 9. $\frac{ad}{6d+c}$.

10. $\frac{nx}{nx-m}$. 11. $\frac{pn(ad+bc)}{bd(pm+kn)}$. 12. $x - 1$.

13. $\frac{x(x+3)}{x+4}$. 14. $-\frac{x+1}{x^2(x+3)}$. 15. $-\frac{x^2(2x+3)}{x+2}$.

16. $\frac{1}{x}$. 17. $\frac{a^2 - b^2}{2}$. 18. 2.

19. $\frac{y^4}{x^2 + y^2}$. 20. $\frac{1}{2x^2 - 1}$. 21. $\frac{2(a+b)}{a-b}$.

22. $a + x$. 23. $\frac{4}{x^2}$. 24. $\frac{1+x}{1+x^2}$.

25. $\frac{a^2 - a + 1}{2a - 1}$. 26. $\frac{6 + x + 2y}{8x(y+6)}$. 27. $\frac{a(yz+n)}{xyz + nx + mz}$.

28. $1 - x$. 29. $\frac{x^2 - 3x + 1}{x^2 - 4x + 1}$. 30. $\frac{2}{x^2}$.

31. $\frac{a-c}{1+ac}$. 32. $\frac{b}{a}$. 33. $\frac{1}{a+x}$.

34. 4. 35. $8x^2 - 1$. 36. $2x^2$.

XXII-b. Page 183

1. $\frac{x}{3} + \frac{y}{9} - \frac{y^2}{9x}$. 2. $\frac{a^2}{4} - \frac{ax}{3} + \frac{x^2}{2}$.

3. $\frac{a^2}{2b} - \frac{3a}{2} + \frac{3b}{2} + \frac{b^2}{2a}$. 4. $\frac{1}{bc} + \frac{1}{ca} + \frac{1}{ab}$.

5. $\frac{1}{a} + \frac{1}{b} + \frac{1}{c}$. 6. $\frac{a^2}{6} - \frac{b^2}{2} + \frac{1}{3}$.

7. $x - x^2 + x^3 - x^4$; Rem. x^5. 8. $1 + \frac{b}{a} + \frac{b^2}{a^2} + \frac{b^3}{a^3}$; Rem. $\frac{b^4}{a^3}$:

9. $1 + 2x + 2x^2 + 2x^3$; Rem. $2x^4$.

10. $1 + x - x^3 - x^4$; Rem. x^6. **11.** $x - 3 + \frac{9}{x} - \frac{27}{x^2}$; Rem. $\frac{81}{x^2}$.

12. $1 + 2x + 3x^2 + 4x^3$Rem. $5x^4 - 4x^5$.

17. $\frac{x-3}{x-4}$. **18.** $3(a-2x)^2$.

19. $\frac{b^2 - 3b - 2}{b - 6}$. **20.** $\frac{a^2 - 4b^2}{a + 3b}$.

21. $\frac{(2x-3)(2x+7)}{6}$.

XXII-c. Page 184

1. $\frac{4(c-x)}{3(a+x)}$. **2.** $\frac{x(x+a)}{2}$. **3.** $\frac{1}{a^2 + ab - 2b^2}$.

4. $\frac{8xy(x^2+y^2)}{(x^2-y^2)^2}$. **5.** $\frac{4x(2-x)}{(x-1)(x^3+1)}$. **6.** $\frac{x^4}{1-x^8}$.

7. $\frac{1}{x(x+1)^2(1+x+x^2)}$. **8.** $\frac{1-x+x^2}{1+x+x^2}$.

9. $\frac{2x+3}{3(x+6)}$. **10.** $\frac{bx+a}{ax+b}$. **11.** $\frac{ax^3(x^2+a^2)}{x^3+a^3}$.

12. $\frac{a^6}{(a-x)(a+x)^2}$. **13.** $\frac{(x+1)^2}{3x^3+6x^2-x-8}$. **14.** $\frac{a+y}{a^2-y}$.

15. $\frac{2(a^2+a+1)}{a(a+1)(a+2)}$. **16.** $\frac{1}{2(3-2x)}$. **17.** $\frac{4}{1-x^4}$.

18. 1. **19.** $\frac{(2x-1)(x+1)}{(x+2)(x-1)}$. **20.** $\frac{x-2}{4x^2-5x-5}$.

21. $\frac{x}{(x-2a)^2}$. **22.** $\frac{a(a^2+x^2)}{(x-a)(a+x)^2}$. **23.** 1.

24. 1. **25.** $9x - \frac{1}{x}$. **26.** $\frac{a}{2x^2}$.

27. $\frac{1}{2x(2x-1)}$. **28.** $\frac{b^4}{b^2+a^2}$. **29.** $\frac{ab}{a+b}$.

30. x. **31.** x. **32.** bx.

33. $\frac{a^2-b^2}{2}$. **34.** 1. **35.** $\left(x - \frac{1}{x}\right)^2$.

36. 1. **37.** 1. **38.** $\frac{x(x+1)}{x^2+4x+1}$.

39. $\frac{12}{(a^4-4)(a^4-1)}$. **40.** $\frac{3n^2}{(3m+2n)(9m^2-n^2)}$.

41. $\dfrac{1+x+x^2}{(1+x)(1+x^2)(1-x)^2}$. 42. $\dfrac{2x}{(x-2)(x+1)^2}$. 43. $\dfrac{1}{x+y}$.

44. 1. 45. 1. 46. 1.

47. 0.

48. $\dfrac{a^2+b^2+c^2-bc-ca-ab}{(b-c)(c-a)(a-b)}$. 49. 1. 50. 1.

51. 0. 52. $2y+a+b$.

53. $\dfrac{(2a^2+x^2)(a-x)}{a^2x}$. 54. $\dfrac{28(x+4)}{9(x+3)}$. 55. $\dfrac{7(x-4)}{4(x-1)}$.

56. $x+3$. 57. $1+a-a^3$. 58. $-\dfrac{c}{e}$.

Miscellaneous Examples IV. Page 188

1. $-\dfrac{1}{22}$. 2. 6. 3. $abc(b-c)$; -6.

4. 7. 5. $\dfrac{5}{3}$. 6. (1) 232; (2) -29.

7. (1) -19; (2) 0. 8. 1. 9. $-\dfrac{3}{10}$.

10. (1) -12; (2) 1. 11. 1. 12. $8\dfrac{1}{2}$.

13. $98x-2y$; $19\dfrac{1}{3}$. 14. (1) 1; (2) 21.

15. $(x+9)(x+12)$. 16. $(a-7)(a+13)$.

17. $(x-8y)(y-12y)$. 18. $(ab-17)(ab+3)$.

19. $c(c+13)(c-12)$. 20. $n(m-3n)(m-3n)$.

21. $(p^2+7q^2)(p^2-8q^2)$. 22. $(d^2+5c^2)(d+3c)(d-3c)$.

23. $xy(x+6y)(x-7y)$. 24. $(m+13)(m+15)$.

25. $(14-a)(15+a)$. 26. $(19-pq)(3+pq)$.

27. $(x^2+16)(x^2+11)$. 28. $(a^2+14)(a^2-7)$.

29. $(c+27)(c+27)$. 30. $(9-xy)(8+xy)$.

31. $(a^2+2x^2)(a^2+7x^2)$. 32. $(p-12q)(p+9q)$.

33. $2(a^3+12)(a^3-11)$. 34. $x^2(x-9)(x+7)$.

35. $(bc+12)(bc-7)$. 36. $(z+17)(z+17)$.

37. $(a-3c)(a-19c)$. 38. $yz(y-7)(y+13)$.

39. $(2+3x^3)(1-x)(1+x+x^2)$. 40. $(2ab-5)(ab+3)$.

41. $(3p-4)(3p-4)$. 42. $(5+mn)(7+mn)$.

43. $(17+c)(7-c)$. 44. $x^3(2-x)(3-x)$.

45. $(2m+3)(3m-1)$. 46. $(2a-5b)(2a+b)$.

47. $(6p-q)(p-2q)$.
48. $(5x+4z)(4x-5z)$.
49. $(2x^2+3)(4x^3-5)$.
50. $6(2y-1)(y-2)$.
51. $(3ab+4)(4ab-3)$.
52. $(2a^2b-5)(a^2b-2)$.
53. $(7x+8y)(3x-2y)$.
54. $(9m-5n)(2m+3n)$.
55. $(c+a-b)(c-a+b)$.
56. $(a+b-c)(a-b+c)$.
57. $(5x+3y)(25x^2-15xy+9y^2)$.
58. $(ab+7)(a^2b^2-7ab+49)$.
59. $(8b-a^2)(64b^2+8ba^2+a^4)$.
60. $(a+2x-2y)(a-2x+2y)$.
61. $(m+n+1)(m+n-1)$.
62. $2c^2(3c+d)(c-d)$.
63. $(a^2b^2-1+x-y)(a^2b^2-1-x+y)$.
64. $(1+2m)(1-2m)(1-2m+4m^2)(1+2m+4m^2)$.
65. $p^3(1+10q)(1-10q+100q^2)$.
66. $(81+a^2)(9+a)(9-a)$.
67. $(x^2-1+y-z)(x^2-1-y+z)$.
68. $(a+4b-4c)(a-4b+4c)$.
69. $(c-d)(1+2c-2d)(1-2c+2d)$.
70. $(p-4q)(p+4q+1)$.
71. $2[1+4a+4b][1-4(a+b)+16(a+b)^2]$.
72. $(x+3y)(1+x^2-3xy+9y^2)$.
73. $(x+y)(x^2+y^2)$.
74. $(cx-d)(ax+b)$.
75. $(7+a)(2-a)$.
76. $(14x^2+y^2)(7x^2-y^2)$.
77. $(17+a)(3-a)$.
78. $(1+m+p)(1-m-p)$.
79. $(bx-a)(ax-b)$.
80. $(3b-c+4)(3b-c-4)$.
81. $(c+1)(c^2-c+1)(x+1)(x-1)$.
82. $(3x-b)(x+2a)$.
83. $(m-n)(m+n+x)(m+n-x)$.
84. $(a+b)(c+a-b)(c-a+b)$.
85. $(x+2)(x^2-2x+4)(x^2+1)(x+1)(x-1)$.
86. $(x+1)(x+7)(2x-3)$.
87. $(2x+5y)(x-3y)(2x-5y)$.
88. $325a^3b^3(x^2-a^2)^2(x+2a)$.
89. $2x^2-9x+9$.
90. $2x^3(x^2-4)(x^2-16)$.
91. H.C.F. $=a+b+c$, L.C.M. $=(a+b+c)(a-b)(b-c)(c-a)$.
92. $a+b-c$.
93. $(a-b)^2(a+b)$.
95. $(a^4-b^4)(a+b-2c)$.
97. H.C.F. $=(x-7)(x-3)$.
L.C.M. $=(x-1)(x-2)(x-3)(x-4)(x-5)(x-7)$.
98. $\dfrac{1}{(1-x)^2}$.
99. $\dfrac{x-9}{(x^2-9)(x-3)}$.
100. $\dfrac{6x+1}{(2x+1)^2(2x-1)}$.
101. $\dfrac{2}{x}$.

102. $\frac{4}{(1-x^2)^2}$. **103.** 1. **104.** 0. **105.** $\frac{x}{9}$.

106. $\frac{2x-y}{x^2-y^2}$. **107.** $y-x$. **108.** ab.

109. $2(ac+bd)(ad+bc)$. **110.** 1. **111.** 1.

112. $\frac{(x^2+2)(x^4+1)}{x}$. **113.** $\frac{1}{f-q}$. **114.** $\frac{1}{x+1}$.

115. $x(1+x+x^2)$ **116.** $\frac{3abc}{a+b}$. **117.** $a+b$. **118.** 1.

XXIII-a. Page 196

1. 6. **2.** $1\frac{3}{10}$. **3.** $\frac{1}{5}$. **4.** 1.

5. 20. **6.** 2. **7.** $\frac{7}{17}$. **8.** 0.

9. 2. **10.** $-6\frac{5}{6}$. **11.** 5. **12.** 6.

13. $-\frac{8}{11}$. **14.** $-\frac{7}{18}$. **15.** 1. **16.** -10.

17. -4. **18.** $3\frac{3}{8}$. **19.** 3. **20.** 4.

21. 6. **22.** 13. **23.** -7. **24.** 2.

25. $2\frac{1}{2}$. **26.** 4. **27.** $1\frac{1}{2}$. **28.** 14.

29. $\frac{1}{4}$. **30.** $2\frac{1}{4}$. **31.** $\frac{1}{6}$. **32.** 3. **33.** 20.

XXIII-b. Page 198

1. $\frac{2b-3a}{a-5b}$. **2.** $a+b$. **3.** $\frac{b^2-a^2}{2b}$.

4. $\frac{a^2-ab+b^2}{a-b}$. **5.** 3. **6.** $m-n$.

7. $-\frac{ab}{a+b+c}$. **8.** $\frac{a^2-2ab+bc}{c-b}$. **9.** a.

10. $\frac{7bc}{9b+4c}$. **11.** $\frac{2ab}{a+b}$. **12.** $17a$.

13. $\frac{1}{c}$. **14.** $3a+2b$. **15.** $\frac{a+b}{2}$.

16. $\frac{a^2-2b^3}{3a-4b}$. **17.** $\frac{x}{17}$. **18.** $\frac{a^2}{b}$.

19. $\frac{bc^2}{a^2}$. **20.** a. **21.** $a+b$.

22. $\frac{2a}{21}$. **23.** $\frac{a+2b}{2}$. **24.** $\frac{a}{3}$.

25. $\frac{b(2a-b)}{a}$.

XXIII- C. Page 201

1. $x=\frac{al-bm}{a^2-b^2}, y=\frac{am-bl}{a^2-b^2}$. **2.** $x=\frac{nq-mr}{lq-mp}, y=\frac{lr-np}{lq-mp}$.

3. $x=\frac{bc}{a^2+b^2}, y=\frac{ac}{a^2+b^2}$. **4.** $x=\frac{a^2+ab+b^2}{a+b}, y=-\frac{ab}{a+b}$.

5. $x=\frac{a'^2-a}{a'-a^2}, y=\frac{1-aa'}{a'-a^2}$. **6.** $x=\frac{q^2-pr}{qr-p^2}, y=\frac{pq-r^2}{qr-p^2}$.

7. $x=\frac{a+a'}{a'b+ab'}, y=\frac{b'-b}{a'b+ab'}$. **8.** $x=2a, y=2b$.

9. $x=\frac{2}{3}a, y=\frac{1}{2}b$. **10.** $x=\frac{pa}{q}, y=\frac{rb}{p}$.

11. $x=\frac{mm(m+m')}{m^2+m'^2}, y=\frac{mm'(m-m')}{m^2+m'^2}$.

12. $x=\frac{qn}{ql-pm}, y=\frac{pn}{mp-lq}$. **13.** $x=\frac{c(a+b)}{2a}, y=\frac{c(a-b)}{2a}$.

14. $x=a+b, y=a-b$. **15.** $x=3a, y=-2b$.

16. $x=\frac{2aa'b}{ab'+a'b}, y=\frac{2abb'}{ab'+a'b}$.

17. $x=a, y=0$. **18.** $x=m+l, y=m+l$.

19. $x=\frac{a}{b}, y=\frac{b}{c}$. **20.** $x=a+b, y=a-b$.

21. $x=a^3-b^3, y=a^3+b^3$.

XXIII-d. Page 202

1. $\frac{x+1}{x-1}\cdot b, \frac{x-1}{x+1}\cdot a$. **2.** $-\frac{ac}{a+c}$.

3. $2b-a, \frac{b^2}{a}, \frac{ab}{2a-b}$. **4.** $\sqrt{\frac{A}{\pi}}, \frac{C}{2\pi}$.

5. $\sqrt{\frac{3V}{4\pi}}, \sqrt{\frac{A}{4\pi}}$. **6.** $\frac{V}{\pi r^2}, \frac{A-2\pi r^2}{2\pi r}$.

7. $\frac{A}{2r(r+h)}$. **8.** $\sqrt{\frac{3V}{\pi h}}, \frac{A-\pi r^2}{\pi r}$.

9. $r\left(\frac{A}{2}-\pi r^2\right)$.

10. $\frac{2A}{a+b}, \frac{2A}{h}-b$.

12. $\frac{360}{180-N}, 10$.

13. $\frac{MHt^2}{4\pi^2}, \frac{4-H}{t^2H}, \frac{4-H}{t^2M}$.

14. $V=\frac{10.6mT}{76-12T}$.

15. $\frac{Ha^3}{2t^2}$.

16. $\left(\frac{v}{k\sqrt{h}}\right)\left\{\frac{v}{k\left(1-\frac{a}{b}\right)}\right\}^2$.

17. $\frac{A}{\left(1+\frac{r}{100}\right)^n}, 100\left\{\sqrt[n]{\frac{A}{P}}-1\right\}$.

18. $\frac{5bz}{3y}\cdot\frac{1+x}{1-x}\cdot\frac{3ay}{5z}\cdot\frac{1-x}{1+x}$.

19. $\frac{4k-5}{\sqrt{18k^2-4}}$.

20. $\frac{C^2}{4\pi}, 2\sqrt{\pi A}$.

21. $\frac{1}{6}\sqrt{\frac{A^3}{\pi}}, \sqrt[3]{36\pi V^2}$.

22. $\frac{u^2}{u-f}, \frac{v^2}{v-f}$.

23. $(b+1)(b+8)$.

24. $\frac{2}{b-1}$.

25. $\frac{1+q^2}{q-4}, \frac{1+p^2}{p-4}$.

27. $\sqrt{\frac{ab-A}{1-\frac{\pi}{4}}}, \frac{1}{a}\left\{A+\left(1-\frac{\pi}{4}\right)r^2\right\}$.

28. $\frac{ma+nb}{m+n}, \frac{1}{m}\{mc+nc-nb\}$.

29. $C=\frac{100S}{100+P}, S=\frac{C}{100}(100+P), P=\frac{100}{C}(S-C)$.

30. $s=\frac{2ab}{a+b}, b=\frac{as}{2a-s}, a=\frac{bs}{2b-s}, 6$

31. $\frac{2(S-an)}{n(n-1)}, 2a$.

32. Rs $(S+Ik)$, $\frac{2}{I}(T-S)$ years.

33. $C=11\left(\frac{x}{12}+10\right)$, 12 paise.

34. $\pi=(m+r)x, 2$.

35. $h=\frac{x}{y}(m+r), 5$.

36. $C=s(2ac+2bc+ab)$, 10 cm.

37. $\frac{r}{5}\left(p+q-\frac{r}{5}\right)$.

38. $\frac{5\sqrt{5}}{2}$ cm.

39. $n=\frac{T-N}{2}$; 500.

41. $36.9^{\circ 5}C$.

42. $\frac{100}{C}(S-C)$, Rs 152.

43. (ii) 800.

44. $\frac{100R}{n}+5$.

46. (*a*) Rs 1100, (*b*) 4%.

47. Second set.

48. When $u = v = r$.

49. $\frac{pv}{R} - 273$.

50. $233\frac{1}{3}$ c.c.

51. $100 - m_2$.

52. $3, 2\frac{1}{2}, 11\frac{1}{2}$.

53. $\frac{2a(a-kL)}{2a-kL}, \frac{2a(a-s)}{k(2a-s)}, \frac{2a(a-s)}{L(2a-s)}$, $53\frac{1}{3}$kg.

54. $\frac{Wb' - W'b}{bb'(b-b')}$.

55. $c - \frac{t(u-v)}{60}, \frac{t(u-v)}{60} - c, \frac{60(c-D)}{u-v}, \frac{60(c+D)}{u-v}$.

56. $\frac{100P - pd}{p-q}$.

57. $\frac{lt(t-y)}{y}$ km.

58. Rs $\frac{zx(x-y)}{y}$.

59. $\frac{Nx^2}{10000 - Nx}$ dm.

60. $\frac{100}{C(100+r)}[100(S-C) - Cr]$; $\frac{100}{C(100+s)}[100(S-C) - Cs]$.

61. $\frac{P - n(F+b)}{a-b}$.

62. Numerator $\frac{d - cx - e}{x - 2y}$, denominator $\frac{2yd - 2cxy - ex}{x - 2y}$.

63. $\frac{tx^2 + x(y-z)}{tx + y}$.

64. $\frac{R(c-b) + abc}{2c(c-b)}$.

XXIV-Page 210

1. 40. **2.** 60. **3.** 55.

4. Rs 80. **5.** Silk Rs 5, Calico 50 paise per metre.

6. 54. **7.** 42. **8.** 48, 23.

9. $21\frac{9'}{11}$ past one.

10. $17\frac{5'}{11}$ past three.

11. $32\frac{8'}{11}$ past six.

12. $5\frac{10'}{11}$ past two.

13. 378, 216.

14. 15 persons; 5 rupees.

15. 8 metres at Rs 4.50; 16 metres at Rs 4.

16. 17, 15.

17. 3 km per hour.

18. 54

19. $2\frac{1}{2}$ km per hour.

20. $21\frac{9'}{11}$ and $54\frac{6}{12}$ past seven. At $5\frac{5'}{11}$ past

21. $\frac{8}{12}$.

22. 10 p. m. : halfway.

23. $1\frac{1}{3}$ hours. **24.** 200. **25.** 30 km.

26. Rs 36000. **27.** Rs 200. **28.** 4 and 3 litres.

29. $\frac{3}{5}$ and $\frac{2}{5}$ of a litre. **30.** $\frac{pa}{p+q}$ km.

31. 192 and 172 km. **32.** Coffee to chicory as 7 to 2.

33. $c-b$ and $a-c$ kg. **34.** $\frac{c}{2a}, \frac{2c}{b}$ metres. **35.** 60 km.

XXV-a. Page 216

1. ± 5. **2.** ± 4. **3.** $3, -25$. **4.** $1, -25$.

5. $3, 7$. **6.** ± 8. **7.** $3, -6$. **8.** $2, -7$.

9. $9, -4$. **10.** $9, -8$. **11.** $31, -11$. **12.** $20, -11$.

13. $4, -17$. **14.** $13, -12$. **15.** $11, -17$. **16.** $8, 15$.

17. $7, 6$. **18.** $23, -1$. **19.** $6, -\frac{16}{3}$. **20.** $\frac{1}{3}, -\frac{3}{5}$.

21. $\frac{3}{2}, -\frac{1}{3}$. **22.** $\frac{1}{5}, -4$. **23.** ± 9.

XXV-b. Page 219

1. $\frac{11}{5}, -5$. **2.** $11, \frac{11}{3}$. **3.** $3, \frac{7}{6}$. **4.** $\frac{15}{8}, -2$.

5. $\frac{7}{3}, 5$. **6.** $2, -\frac{11}{6}$. **7.** $\frac{3}{4}, -5$. **8.** $\frac{7}{2}, -3$.

9. $\frac{13}{3}, -\frac{11}{3}$. **10.** $\frac{7}{4}, \frac{2}{3}$. **11.** $\frac{3}{4}, -\frac{4}{5}$. **12.** $\frac{5}{8}, -3$.

13. $\frac{5}{7}, -\frac{1}{3}$. **14.** $\frac{9}{10}, -\frac{3}{5}$. **15.** $\frac{13}{6}, -\frac{2}{3}$. **16.** $3, -\frac{7}{5}$.

17. $\frac{a}{3}, -\frac{a}{5}$. **18.** $\frac{3a}{7}, -\frac{a}{3}$. **19.** $\frac{7k}{3}, -\frac{k}{2}$. **20.** $-\frac{5k}{4}, -\frac{2k}{3}$.

21. $\frac{4c}{3}, -\frac{5e}{4}$. **22.** $3, -\frac{4}{3}$. **23.** $5, -\frac{5}{2}$. **24.** $4, \frac{7}{5}$.

25. $3, -1$. **26.** $2, \frac{1}{3}$. **27.** $4, \frac{11}{2}$. **28.** $7, 2$.

29. $11, 2$. **30.** $4, \frac{4}{3}$. **31.** $13, \frac{2}{3}$. **32.** $6, \frac{40}{13}$.

33. $2, \frac{39}{8}$. **34.** $3, -\frac{1}{2}$. **35.** $12, -2$. **36.** $5, \frac{23}{7}$.

37. $3a, \frac{3a}{2}$. **38.** $2c, \frac{11c}{14}$. **39.** $a, \frac{ab}{a-2b}$.

XXV-c. Page 223

1. $\frac{5}{3}, -3.$ **2.** $\frac{3}{2}, -5.$ **3.** $1, \frac{7}{2}.$ **4.** $\frac{3 \pm \sqrt{29}}{2}.$

5. $-4, -\frac{1}{5}.$ **6.** $\frac{7 \pm \sqrt{5}}{2}.$ **7.** $1, -\frac{7}{8}.$ **8.** $\frac{17 \pm \sqrt{89}}{10}.$

9. $7, -\frac{5}{2}.$ **10.** $\frac{1 \pm \sqrt{13}}{6}.$ **11.** $\frac{1}{3}, -2.$ **12.** $3, -\frac{11}{2}.$

13. $\frac{7}{6}, -1.$ **14.** $\frac{7}{4}, \frac{3}{2}.$ **15.** $\frac{7}{11}, -3.$ **16.** $-\frac{6}{5}, -4.$

17. $\frac{9}{10}, -\frac{5}{6}.$ **18.** $\frac{8}{3}, -\frac{3}{4}.$ **19.** $\frac{2}{7}, -14.$ **20.** $\frac{5}{12}, -\frac{3}{8}.$

21. $\frac{3}{5}, -\frac{2}{5}.$ **22.** $\frac{5}{2}, -\frac{7}{2}.$ **23.** $\frac{9a}{4}, -\frac{4a}{3}.$ **24.** $\frac{9a}{4}, \frac{4a}{3}.$

25. $\frac{5b}{3}, -\frac{7b}{3}.$ **26.** $\frac{7b}{6}, -\frac{5b}{6}.$ **27.** $2a, 2b.$ **28.** $2a, -8.$

29. $0, \frac{2a+b}{3}.$ **30.** $0, \frac{b-2}{a}.$ **31.** $\pm 2, \pm 1.$ **32.** $\pm 2, \pm 3.$

33. $1, -2.$ **34.** $3, -2.$ **35.** $\pm 4, \pm\frac{1}{4}.$ **36.** $\pm a, \pm b.$

37. $2, -3.$ **38.** $\pm 3, \pm 4.$ **39.** $3, -2, 4, -3.$ **40.** $4a, -2a, a.$

XXV-d. Page 225

1. 1, −1, −1. **2.** 1, −1, 2. **3.** 1, 2, −2.

4. 1, −3, −5. **5.** 2. −1, −1. **6.** 0, 1, 1, −2.

7. 3, 2, −5. **8.** 5, 2, −7. **9.** 7, −3, −4.

10. $-2a, -2a, 4a.$ **11.** $0, 6a, 6a, -12a.$ **12.** 1.05, −3.05.

13. 3.90, −90. **14.** .66, −1.66. **15.** 18.55, 17.45.

16. 5.99, 1.01. **17.** 3.18, 2.32. **18.** .55, −.22.

19. 1.4, .6. **20.** $\frac{a}{2}(\sqrt{5}-1), -\frac{a}{2}(\sqrt{5}+1)$, 7.416, −19.416.

21. $\frac{1}{2}(a \pm \sqrt{a^2 - 4c^2})$, 13.292, 2.708.

XXVI-a. Page 226

1. $x = 17, 11; y = 11, 17.$ **2.** $x = 37, 14; y = 14, 37.$

3. $x = 53, 21; y = 21, 53.$ **4.** $x = 14, -9; y = 9, -14.$

5. $x = 27, -19; y = 19, -27.$ **6.** $x = 43, -25; y = 25, -43.$

7. $x = 71, 13; y = 13, 71.$ **8.** $x = 33, -41; y = 41, -33.$

9. $x = 52, -74; y = 74, -52.$ **10.** $x = 43, -51; y = -51, 43.$

11. $x = 29, -47; y = 47, -29.$ **12.** $x = 22, -87; y = -87, 22.$

13. $x = \pm 8, \pm 5; y = \pm 5, \pm 8.$ **14.** $x = \pm 13, \pm 1; y = \pm 1, \pm 13.$

15. $x = \pm 4, \pm 7; y = \pm 7, \pm 4.$
16. $x = 13, 3; y = 3, 13.$
17. $x = 10, 5; y = 5, 10.$
18. $x = 9, -5; y = 5, -9.$
19. $x = 12, -6; y = 6, -12.$
20. $x = 11, -8; y = 8, -11.$
21. $x = 9, 4; y = 4, 9.$
22. $x = 5, 4; y = 4, 5.$
23. $x = 7, -4; y = 4, -7.$
24. $x = 10, 4; y = 4, 10.$
25. $x = 12, -2; y = 2, -12.$
26. $x = 1; y = 1.$
27. $x = 4, 3; y = 3, 4.$
28. $x = \frac{1}{a}; y = \frac{1}{b}.$
29. $x = \pm 1; y = \pm 1.$

XXVI-b. Page 229

1. $x = 7, 4; y = 4, 7.$
2. $x = 8, 5; y = 5, 8.$
3. $x = 14, 9; y = 9, 14.$
4. $x = 7, -5; y = 5, -7.$
5. $x = 11, -7; y = 7, -11.$
6. $x = 13, 0; y = 0, -13.$
7. $x = \pm 6, \pm 4; y = \pm 4, \pm 6.$
8. $x = \pm 7, \pm 3; y = \pm 3, \pm 7.$
9. $x = \pm 9, \pm 5; y = \pm 5, \pm 9.$
10. $x = \pm 9, \pm 3; y = \pm 3, \pm 9.$
11. $x = \frac{6}{5}, \frac{8}{3}; y = \frac{8}{3}, \frac{6}{5}.$
12. $x = \pm 6, \pm 5; y = \pm 5, \pm 6.$
13. $x = 4, 2; y = 2, 4.$
14. $x = 7, -3; y = 3, -7.$
15. $x = 5, 3; y = 3, 5.$
16. $x = 4, -2; y = 2, -4.$
17. $x = 8, -2; y = 2, -8.$
18. $x = 5, 1; y = 1, 5.$
19. $x = 5, 1; y = 1, 5.$
20. $x = \frac{1}{6}, -\frac{1}{5}; y = \frac{1}{5}, -\frac{1}{6}.$

XXVI-c. Page 232

1. $x = 4, -\frac{3}{5}; y = 3, -20.$
2. $x = \pm 3; y = \pm 2.$
3. $x = 12, 8; y = 2, -2.$
4. $x = 2, \frac{10}{3}, y = 5, 3.$
5. $x = 4, 7; y = 1, 10.$
6. $x = 4, -3; y = 1, -\frac{4}{3}.$
7. $x = 1, -\frac{71}{17}; y = 4, \frac{112}{17}.$
8. $x = \pm 2, \pm \frac{4}{\sqrt{5}}; y = \pm 1, \pm \frac{3}{\sqrt{5}}.$
9. $x = 2, \frac{5}{8}; y = -7, -\frac{1}{8}.$
10. $x = \pm 4, \pm 6; y = \pm 2, \pm 4.$
11. $x = \pm 3, \pm 4; y = \pm 2, \pm 5.$
12. $x = \pm \frac{3}{2}, \pm \frac{1}{2}; y = \pm \frac{1}{2}, \pm \frac{3}{2}.$
13. $x = \pm 2, \pm 1; y = \pm 1, \pm 2.$
14. $x = \pm 2, \pm 5; y = \pm 3, \pm 6.$
15. $x = \pm 7, \pm \sqrt{3}; y = \pm 2, \pm 3\sqrt{3}.$
16. $x = \pm 3, \pm 36; y = \pm 5, \pm \frac{23}{2}.$
17. $x = 5, 3; y = 3, 5.$
18. $x = 7, -6; y = 6, -7.$

19. $x = 6, -2$; $y = 2, -6$.

20. $x = 7, 1, 4 \pm \sqrt{28}$; $y = 1, 7, 4 \pm \sqrt{28}$.

21. $x = 4, 3, 6, 2$; $y = \frac{3}{2}, 2, 1, 3$. **22.** $x = 2, \frac{2}{3}, 4, \frac{1}{3}$; $y = 2, 6, 1, 12$.

XXVII-Page 236

1. 13. **2.** 45, 9. **3.** 7, 8. **4.** 3.
5. 15, 12. **6.** 9. **7.** 7 hours. **8.** 7, 5.
9. 90 metres, 160 metres. **10.** 55 dm, 30 dm.
11. $36', 60'$. **12.** 6. **13.** 4 rupees. **14.** 20.
15. 60 paise. **16.** 3 dm. **17.** 20 cm.
18. 121 square dm. **19.** Forty paise. **20.** 40, 12; 30, 16 metres.
21. 56. **22.** 50. **23.** 25.
24. 12 km per hour. **25.** 75. **26.** 20, 30 km an hour.
27. 40 and 45 km an hour. **28.** 10 litres.
29. A, 16; B, 14. **30.** Distance, 12 km; rate 8 km an hour.
31. $\frac{a}{2}(-1 \pm \sqrt{5})$. **32.** 3.7 cm, 2.3 cm.
33. $AP = 20.9$ cm, $BP = 12.9$ cm.
35. 8.4 cm. **36.** 2.6 cm, 1.6 cm. **37.** 9 cm, 4 cm.
39. (i) 3, 4; (ii) 5, 6; (iii) 5.2, 0.8; (iv) 5.7, 2.3.

XXVIII-a. Page 240

1. $(x^2 + 4x + 16)(x^2 - 4x + 16)$. **2.** $(9a^2 + 3ab + b^2)(9a^2 - 3ab + b^2)$.

3. $(x^2 + 3xy + y^2)(x^2 - 3xy + y^2)$.

4. $(m^2 + 4mn - n^2)(m^2 - 4mn - n^2)$.

5. $(x^2 + 2xy - y^2)(x^2 - 2xy - y^2)$.

6. $(2x^2 + 9xy - 3y^2)(2x^2 - 9xy - 3y^2)$.

7. $(2m^2 + 6mn + 3n^2)(2m^2 - 6mn + 3n^2)$.

8. $(3x^2 + xy + 2y^2)(3x^2 - xy + 2y^2)$.

9. $(x^2 + 3xy - 5y^2)(x^2 - 3xy - 5y^2)$.

10. $(4a^2 - 6ab + b^2)(4a^2 + 6ab + b^2)$.

11. $\left(\frac{3}{ab} - 1\right)\left(\frac{9}{a^2b^2} + \frac{3}{ab} + 1\right)$. **12.** $\left(6a - \frac{b}{2}\right)\left(36a^2 + 3ab + \frac{b^2}{4}\right)$.

13. $\left(\frac{x}{5} + y\right)\left(\frac{x^2}{25} - \frac{xy}{5} + y^2\right)$. **14.** $\left(\frac{mn}{9} - 1\right)\left(\frac{m^2n^2}{81} + \frac{mn}{9} + 1\right)$.

15. $\left(\frac{ab}{5} + 10\right)\left(\frac{a^2b^2}{25} - 2ab + 100\right)$.

16. $\left(\frac{x}{8}-\frac{4}{x}\right)\left(\frac{x^2}{64}+\frac{1}{2}+\frac{16}{x^2}\right)$. **17.** $(y-3x)(x+y)(x-y)$.

18. $(m-5n)(2n+3m)(2n-3m)$. **19.** $(ax+b)(bx+a)$.

20. $(x^2z^2+y^2)(xy+z)(xy-z)$. **21.** $(a^2+bx)(a+x)$.

22. $(mn-p)(pm-n)$. **23.** $(3ab-2x)(2ax-3b)$.

24. $(2x+3y)(a^2+xy)$. **25.** $(2x-3y)(a^2+xy)$.

26. $\{ax+(a+1)\}\{(a-1)x+a\}$. **27.** $(x-a)(3x-a-2b)$.

28. $\{ax+2(b-c)y\}\{2ax-(3b-4c)y\}$.

29. $\{(a-1)x+a\}\{(a-2)x+(a-1)\}$.

30. $\{(a+1)x-(b-1)y\}(ax+by)$.

31. $(b+c-1)(b^2+c^2+1-bc+c+b)$.

32. $(a+2c+1)(a^2+4c^2+1-2ac-a-2c)$.

33. $(a+b+2c)(a^2+b^2+4c^2-ab-2bc-2ca)$.

34. $(a-3b+c)(a^2+9b^2+c^2+3ab+3bc-ca)$.

35. $(a-b-c)(a^2+b^2+c^2+ab-bc+ca)$.

36. $(2a+3b+c)(4a^2+9b^2+c^2-6ab-3bc-2ca)$.

37. $(x^4-9x^2+81)(x^2+3x+9)(x^2-3x+9)$.

38. $(a^4-4a^2b^2-b^4)(a^2+b^2)(a+b)(a-b)$.

39. $(a+b+c-d)(a+b-c+d)(c+d+a-b)(c+d-a+b)$.

40. $\left(x^4+\frac{1}{16}\right)\left(x^2+\frac{1}{4}\right)\left(x+\frac{1}{2}\right)\left(x-\frac{1}{2}\right)$

41. $(x^8+y^8)(x^4+y^4)(x^2+y^2)(x+y)(x-y)$

42. $(x^3+x^3y^3+y^6)(x^6-x^3y^3+y^6)(x^2+xy+y^2)(x^2-xy+y^2)$
$(x+y)(x-y)$.

43. $\left(\frac{1}{x}+1\right)\left(\frac{1}{x}-1\right)(a-2x)(a^2+2ax+4x^2)$.

44. $(x^2+y^2)(x^4-x^2y^2+y^4)(x-2y)(x^2+2xy+4y^2)$.

45. $(x^2+4)(x^4-4x^2+16)(x+1)(x^2-x+1)$.

46. $\left(\frac{2}{a}+\frac{3}{b}\right)\left(\frac{2}{a}-\frac{3}{b}\right)(a+b)(a^2-ab+b^2)$.

47. $\left(\frac{1}{3x}+\frac{y}{2}\right)\left(\frac{1}{3x}-\frac{y}{2}\right)\left(\frac{xy}{2}-1\right)\left(\frac{x^2y^2}{4}+\frac{xy}{2}+1\right)$.

48. $(x^2+5)(x^2-5)\left(x+\frac{1}{2}\right)\left(x-\frac{1}{2}\right)$.

49. $(x+1)(x^2-x+1)(x^2+4)(x+2)(x-2)$.

50. $(x-1)(x^2+x+1)(4x^2+9)(2x+3)(2x-3)$.

XXVIII-b. Page 244

1. $4x^2 - 49y^2 + 42yz - 9z^2$. **2.** $9x^4 + 26x^2y^2 + 49y^4$.

3. $25x^4 - 115x^2y^2 + 81y^4$. **4.** $49x^4 - 64x^2y^2 + 48xy^3 - 9y^4$.

5. $x^6 - y^6$. **6.** $(x + y)^4 + 4(x + y)^2 + 16$.

7. $16x^2(1 - 4x^2)$. **8.** $48a^2(a^4 - 1)$.

9. $x^6 - 64$. **10.** $x^6 - 729a^6$.

11. $\frac{a^4}{x^2} - 3a^2 - x^2 - \frac{x^4}{a^2}$. **12.** $64x^4(9x^2 - 1)$.

13. $x^8 + a^4x^4 + a^8$. **14.** $1 + x^8 + x^{16}$.

15. $a^{12} - 3a^8x^4 + 3a^4x^8 - x^{12}$. **16.** $1 - 2x^8 + x^{16}$.

17. $x^6 - 14x^4 + 49x^2 - 36$. **18.** $x^6 - 14x^4 + 49x^2 - 36$.

19. $x^6 - 64$. **20.** $a^4 - 18a^2b^2 + 81b^4$.

21. $a^3 + b^3 + c^3 - 3abc$. **22.** $7x + y + z$.

23. $(x^4 - 4a^2x^2 + 16a^4)(x^2 - 2ax + 4a^2)$.

24. $5x + 7y - 6z$. **25.** $x + 5$.

26. $2x(x + 1)$. **27.** $5(x - 13)$.

28. $(x + 3)(x^2 + 2x + 4)$. **29.** $(7x - 3)(x - 1)$.

30. $a - b$. **31.** $x^3 - 3x^2y - 3xy^2 + y^3$.

32. $x^4 - 4x^2yz + 7y^2z^2$. **33.** $1 + 9x^2 + 4y^2 + 6xy + 2y - 3x$.

34. $(x + 1)(x - 3)$. **35.** $(2a - 5)(2a - 7)$.

36. $(x - a)(x - b)$.

37. $a^2 + 9x^2 + 4y^2 - 6xy + 2ay + 3ax$.

38. $9 + 4x^2 + 16y^2 - 8xy + 12y + 6x$.

45. $\frac{m(m^2 + 3n^2)}{4}$. **47.** $(3a^2 + b^2)(a^2 - 3b^2)$.

49. $\frac{1}{16}(9p^2 - 5q^2)(9q^2 - 5p^2)$. **50.** $16ab^3$.

XXIX-a. Page 247

1. $x + c$. **2.** $x^2 - ax + b$.

3. $x^2 + 2bx - ax - 2ab$. **4.** $x^2 - (p + q)x + 2q(p - q)$.

5. $x^2 - (m + n)x + m(m - n)$. **6.** $ax + a + 1$.

7. $x^2 + bx + a^2$. **8.** $2lx - (3m - 4n)$.

9. $(a + 2)x + (a + 1)y$. **10.** $x + b$.

11. $(x + 1)^6 + 3(x + 1)^4 + 3(x + 1)^2 + 1$.

12. $(m + 1)b^2x^2 + (n + 1)(m + 1)abx + (n + 1)a^2$.

13. $(m - 1)x + m$. **14.** $mx - n$.

15. $ap - bq$. **16.** $ax + b$.
17. $2ax - 3$. **18.** $x + 2ab$.
19. $(x^2 - 1)(x^2 - px + y)(x^2 - qx + p)$.
20. $\{px - (p - 1)\}\{(p + 1)x + p\}\{(p + 2)x + p + 1\}$.
21. $\{(a-3)x + a + 1\}\{(a-2)x - a\}\{ax - (a + 4)\}$

XXIX-b. Page 252

1. $x - 7$. **2.** $2 - \frac{1}{m}$. **3.** $a + 2x$.
4. $1 + x - x^2$. **5.** $1 + 2x - x^2$. **6.** $1 + x$.
7. $x - 2a$. **8.** $a - 3x$. **9.** $x - y$.
10. $x^2 + (p-1)\,x - 1$. **11.** $1 + \frac{x}{2} - \frac{x^2}{8} + \frac{x^3}{16}$. **12.** $1 - x - \frac{x^2}{2} - \frac{x^3}{2}$.
13. $2 + \frac{x}{2} - \frac{x^2}{16} + \frac{x^3}{64}$. **14.** $1 - \frac{x}{2} - \frac{5x^2}{8} - \frac{5x^3}{16}$.
15. $a - \frac{x}{2a} - \frac{x^2}{8a^3} - \frac{x^3}{16a^5}$. **16.** $x + \frac{a^2}{2x} - \frac{a^4}{8x^3} + \frac{a^6}{16x^5}$
17. $a^2 - \frac{3x^2}{2a^2} - \frac{9x^4}{8a^6} - \frac{27x^6}{16a^{10}}$.
18. $3a + 2x - \frac{2x^2}{3a} + \frac{4x^3}{9a^2}$. **19.** $x - \frac{a^3}{3x^2} - \frac{a^6}{9x^5}$.
20. $2 + \frac{x}{12} - \frac{x^2}{288}$. **21.** $\frac{1}{a} + 3a^2x - 9a^5x^2$.
22. $1 - 2x + 3x^2$. **23.** $3x^2 - x - 1$. **24.** $4 - x - \frac{x^2}{16}$.

XXIX-c. Page 254

19. 0. **20.** 0. **26.** 0.

XXIX-d. Page 257

1. 0. **2.** 1. **3.** 1. **4.** $a + b + c$.
5. 1. **6.** $\frac{1}{abc}$. **7.** $\frac{1}{abc}$. **8.** 1.
9. d. **10.** $\frac{1}{(x - a)(x - b)(x - c)}$.
11. $\frac{x^2}{(x + a)(x + b)(x + c)}$. **12.** $(a + b + c)^2$. **13.** $-\frac{a + b + c}{3}$.
14. $\frac{1}{3}$. **15.** $a + b + c$. **16.** $bc + ca + ab$. **17.** abc.
18. $(b + c)(c + a)(a + b)$.

XXIX-e. Page 262

1. 5. **2.** 10. **3.** $\frac{b}{a}$. **4.** $\frac{p}{16q}$.

5. $\frac{5c}{b}$. **6.** $\frac{d - a^4}{2a^3 - c}$. **7.** $a + c, b = \frac{a^2}{4} + 2$.

8. 6. **9.** $\pm 3a$. **10.** $\pm\sqrt{\frac{2n}{m}}$. **11.** $b^3 = 27c^2$.

12. $c = a(b - a^2)^2, d = (b - a^2)^3$, whence $c^3 = a^3d^2$.

13. 32. **15.** $(x - 1)(x - 2)(x - 3)$.

16. $(x + 2)(x - 3)(x - 4)$. **17.** $(x + 2)(x + 3)(x + 4)$.

18. $(x - 3)(x - 5)(x + 7)$. **19.** $(x - 2)(x - 5)(x + 7)$.

20. $(x + 1)(x + 2)(x - 11)$. **21.** $(x + 1)(3x + 2)(2x - 1)$.

22. $(x + 2)(3x - 1)(2x - 3)$.

23. $x^6 - x^5y + x^4y^2 - x^3y^3 + x^2y^4 - xy^5 + y^6$.

24. $x^7 - x^6y + x^5y^2 - x^4y^3 + x^3y^4 - x^2y^5 + xy^6 - y^7$.

25. $x^5 + x^4y + x^3y^2 + x^2y^3 + xy^4 + y^5$.

26. $x^8 + x^7y - x^6y^2 + x^5y^3 + x^4y^4 + x^3y^5 + x^2y^6 + xy^7 + y^8$.

27. $x^2 + (a - 2)x + a$. **28.** $(a + 1)x^2 + ax + a - 3$.

29. 6 or $\frac{2}{3}$. **30.** 13. **34.** 3005. **35.** $-37a^3$.

XXX-a. Page 268

1. $\frac{2}{x^{1/4}}$. **2.** $\frac{3}{a^{2/3}}$. **3.** $\frac{4a^3}{x^2}$. **4.** $3a^2$.

5. $\frac{a^2}{4}$. **6.** $\frac{x^{1/2}}{5}$. **7.** $\frac{3c^4x^2}{5a^3y^2}$. **8.** $\frac{x^ab^a}{y^b}$.

9. $\frac{6}{x^{1/2}}$. **10.** $\frac{a^{1/2}}{2}$. **11.** y^2. **12.** $\frac{1}{3a^2x^2}$.

13. $\frac{1}{x^{3/2}}$. **14.** $\frac{x^{3/5}}{4}$. **15.** $2y^{3/2}$. **16.** $x^{5/4}$.

17. $\frac{a}{x^{1/2}}$. **18.** $\frac{1}{a^{2/3}}$. **19.** $\frac{1}{a^2}$. **20.** $\sqrt[5]{x^3}$.

21. $\frac{1}{\sqrt{a}}$. **22.** $\frac{5}{\sqrt{x}}$. **23.** $\frac{2}{\sqrt[x]{a}}$. **24.** $\frac{1}{2\sqrt[3]{a}}$.

25. $2\sqrt[4]{b}$. **26.** $\frac{1}{2\sqrt[3]{c}}$. **27.** $\sqrt[x]{x}$. **28.** $\frac{2}{\sqrt[6]{a^5}}$.

29. $\frac{\sqrt{a}}{2\sqrt[3]{x^2}}$. **30.** $\frac{21}{\sqrt{a^3}}$. **31.** $\frac{2}{\sqrt{a}}$. **32.** $\frac{1}{3\sqrt{a^3}}$.

33. $\frac{4}{\sqrt[3]{x^2}}$. **34.** $\frac{1}{\sqrt[3]{x^{a+2}}}$. **35.** $\sqrt[6]{a^{19}}$. **36.** $\sqrt[5]{a^x}$.

37. $\sqrt[2a]{x^5}$. **38.** $\frac{1}{\sqrt[2a]{x}}$. **39.** $\frac{1}{\sqrt[x]{a}}$. **40.** $\sqrt[6]{a^n}$.

41. 8. **42.** $\frac{1}{32}$. **43.** 25. **44.** $\frac{1}{4}$.

45. $\frac{1}{216}$. **46.** 625. **47.** 9. **48.** $\frac{3}{2}$.

49. $\frac{27}{8}$. **50.** $\frac{2187}{128}$.

XXX-b. Page 271

1. a^6b^9. **2.** $\frac{x^{4/3}}{y}$. **3.** $\frac{1}{y^{2a+3b}}$.

4. $\frac{1}{2x^{1/2}y^{1/2}}$. **5.** $\frac{4}{9a^2x^2}$. **6.** $16ac^4$.

7. $\frac{x^{1/3}}{y^{1/4}}$. **8.** $x^{1/6}$. **9.** $\frac{3ax}{2}$.

10. x^{n-1}. **11.** $\frac{1}{x^{n+1}}$. **12.** $x^{1/a}$.

13. $\frac{1}{a^{2/3}b^{1/2}}$. **14.** $a^{1/2}$. **15.** x^{b+1}.

16. $\frac{1}{x^{1/2}}$. **17.** $\frac{1}{x^2}$. **18.** ab^2.

19. $a+b$. **20.** $\frac{1}{(x^2-y^2)^{3n}}$. **21.** $\frac{1}{a^5}$.

22. $b^{3/2}$. **23.** $x^{1/9}$. **24.** $\frac{a+b}{(a-b)^{1/2}}$.

25. $c^{7/2}$. **26.** $\frac{x^2}{a^3}$. **27.** $\frac{1}{a^{5/3}}$.

28. $ab(b^6-a^6)^{1/3}$. **29.** $a^{n(n-1)}+a$.

30. $x^{n(n-1)}+x^{n-1}$. **31.** $a^{4n(p-q)}$. **32.** x^b.

33. $\frac{x^7}{y^7}$. **34.** $x^{1/7}y^{35/6}$. **35.** 2^{n^3}.

36. $\frac{1}{4}$. **37.** 4. **38.** 1.

XXX-c. Page 273

1. $12x^{2/3}-20x^{1/3}+41-15x^{-1/3}+24x^{-2/3}$.

2. $9a^{4/5}-9a^{2/5}-25+23a^{-2/5}+6a^{-4/5}$.

3. $2c^{2x}-9c^x-34+31c^{-x}-6c^{-2x}$.

4. $8x^{3a} + 14x^{a} - 3x^{-a} - 9x^{-3a}$.

5. $7x^{2/3} - 2x^{1/3} + 1$.

6. $3a^{1/3} - 3a^{1/3} + 2a^{-1}$.

7. $8a^{-2} + 7a^{-1} + 6$.

8. $5b^{1/2} + 4b^{1/6} + 3b^{-1/6} + 2b^{-1/2}$.

9. $7a^{2x} + 3a^{x} - 4$.

10. $c^{2n} - 1 + c^{-2n}$.

11. $3x^{1/2} - 2 + x^{-1/2}$.

12. $5a^{2/3} - 3a^{1/3} + 4$.

13. $2x^{n/2} - 4 + 3x^{-n/2}$.

14. $a^{2x} - 3a^{x} - 2$.

15. $a^{2} + 2a - 16q^{-2} - 30a^{-3}$.

16. $1 - x^{1/6} - 0x^{1/3} + 0x^{2/3}$.

17. $4a^{8/3} - 8a^{4/3} - 5 + 10a^{-4/3} + 3a^{-8/3}$.

18. $x^{1/2} - 2x^{1/6} + 4x^{-1/6} - 8x^{-1/2}$.

19. $1 - 2a - 2a^{3/2}$.

20. $2x^{1/4} - 3x^{-1/12} - x^{-5/12}$.

21. $3x^{-2} - 3x^{-1}y^{1/2} + y$.

22. $2x^{3/4} - 3y^{1/4} + 4x^{-3/4}y^{1/2}$.

23. $9x^{2/3}y^{-1} + 0x^{1/3}y^{-1/2} - 9$.

24. $\frac{1}{4}x^{-1} + 1 - 3y^{1/3}$.

XXX-d. Page 275

1. $x - 4x^{1/2} - 21$.

2. $16x^{2} - 8 - 15x^{-2}$.

3. $49x^{2} - 81y^{-3}$.

4. $x^{m}y^{-n} - x^{-m}y^{n}$.

5. $a^{2x} - 4 + 4a^{-2x}$.

6. $a^{2x} + 2a^{x+1/x} + a^{2/x}$.

7. $x^{a} - x^{-a/2} + \frac{1}{4}x^{-2a}$.

8. $20x^{2a}y^{2b} + 13 - 15x^{-2a}y^{-2b}$.

9. $\frac{1}{9}a^{2/3} - \frac{1}{3} + a^{-2/3}$.

10. $9x^{2a} + 15y^{2b} - 15y^{-2b} - 25x^{-2a}$.

11. $a^{2x} - a^{x} - \frac{7}{4} + a^{-x} + a^{-2x}$.

12. $x^{2/a} + x^{-2/a} + x^{2} - 2 + 2x^{1+1/a} - 2x^{1-1/a}$.

13. $2a + 2(a^{2} - b^{2})^{1/2}$.

14. $a + b + (a-b)^{-1} - 2(a+b)^{1/2}(a-b)^{-1/2}$.

15. $x^{1/2} - 3a^{1/2}$.

16. $x + 3x^{1/2} + 9$.

17. $a^{x} + 4$.

18. $x^{2a} - 2x^{a} + 4$.

19. $c^{x} + c^{-x/2}$.

20. $1 + 2a^{-1} + 4a^{-2}$.

21. $a^{2x} - x^{3}$.

22. $x^{-3} - x^{-2} + x^{-1} - 1$.

23. $x^{4/3} + x + x^{2/3} + x^{1/3} + 1$.

24. $x^{4n} - 0x^{3n} + 4x^{2n} - 8x^{n} + 16$.

25. $x^{2} + 0x^{3/2} + x - 16$.

26. $4x^{2/3} + 36x^{1/3} + 16 - 9x^{-2/3}$.

27. $4 - x^{2/3} + 4x + x^{2}$.

28. $a^{2x} - 49 - 42a^{-x} - 9a^{-2x}$.

29. $a^{1/3}(a^{1/3} - 2b^{1/3})$.

30. 1.

31. $\frac{x^{2/3} - 2}{x^{1/3} + 2}$.

32. $\frac{a^{1/2}}{b}$.

XXXI-a. Page 279

1. $\sqrt[12]{x^4}$. **2.** $\frac{1}{\sqrt[12]{a^6}}$. **3.** $\sqrt[12]{\frac{x}{a}}$. **4.** $\sqrt[12]{a^9}$.

5. $\sqrt[12]{a^{21}}$. **6.** $\sqrt[12]{a^4}$. **7.** $\sqrt[n]{x^{2n/3}}$. **8.** $\sqrt[n]{xa^{2n}}$.

9. $\sqrt[n]{a^{n/2}}$. **10.** $\frac{1}{\sqrt[n]{a^{1/2}}}$. **11.** $\sqrt[n]{x^{n2/3}y^{1/3}}$. **12.** $\sqrt[n]{a^n}$.

13. $\frac{1}{\sqrt[n]{x^{n/2}y^{2n}}}$. **14.** $\sqrt[n]{a^{n/2}x^{n2}}$. **15.** $\sqrt[18]{a^9}, \sqrt[18]{a^{10}}$. **16.** $\sqrt[10]{a^6}, \sqrt[10]{a^6}$.

17. $\sqrt[24]{x^9}, \sqrt[24]{x^{16}}, \sqrt[24]{x^6}$. **18.** $\sqrt[13]{x^3}, \sqrt[12]{x^{10}}$. **19.** $\sqrt[12]{a^3b^4}, \sqrt[12]{a^3b^2}$.

20. $\sqrt[26]{a^{13}x^{26}}, \sqrt[26]{a^6x^4}$. **21.** $\sqrt[6]{125}. \sqrt[6]{121}, \sqrt[6]{13}$.

22. $\sqrt[8]{64}, \sqrt[8]{81}, \sqrt[8]{6}$. **23.** $\sqrt[3]{2}, \sqrt[3]{2}, \sqrt[3]{2}$.

XXXI-b. Page 281

1. $12\sqrt{2}$. **2.** $7\sqrt{3}$ **3.** $4\sqrt[3]{4}$. **4.** $6\sqrt[3]{2}$.

5. $15\sqrt{6}$. **6.** $24\sqrt{5}$. **7.** $35\sqrt{5}$. **8.** $7\sqrt[3]{3}$.

9. $5\sqrt[4]{5}$. **10.** $-9\sqrt[3]{3}$. **11.** $6a\sqrt{a}$. **12.** $3ab^2\sqrt{3ab}$.

13. $-3xy^3\sqrt{4x}$. **14.** $x^3y^{2n}\sqrt[n]{y^5}$. **15.** $xy\sqrt[2p]{x^a}$.

16. $(a+b)\sqrt{a}$. **17.** $2(x-y)^3\sqrt{xy}$. **18.** $\sqrt{242}$.

19. $\sqrt{980}$. **20.** $\sqrt[3]{864}$. **21.** $\sqrt[3]{750}$. **22.** $\sqrt{\frac{14}{10}}$.

23. $\sqrt{5b}$. **24.** $\sqrt{9a^2y}$. **25.** $\sqrt{\frac{3a}{x}}$. **26.** $\sqrt[3]{8ax}$.

27. $\sqrt[4]{2a}$. **28.** $\sqrt[n]{a^2b^2}$. **29.** $\sqrt[p]{ab}$. **30.** $\sqrt{\frac{x}{y}}$.

31. $\sqrt{x^2-y^2}$. **32.** $\sqrt{\frac{a+x}{a-x}}$. **33.** $14\sqrt{5}$.

34. $\sqrt{7}$. **35.** $-12\sqrt{11}$. **36.** $-15\sqrt{3}$. **37.** $7\sqrt[3]{7}$.

38. $11\sqrt[3]{3}$. **39.** 0. **40.** $17\sqrt[3]{2}$. **41.** $20\sqrt{3}-13\sqrt{2}$.

42. $3\sqrt{6}$. **43.** $6\sqrt{7}-15\sqrt{6}$. **44.** $\frac{181\sqrt{3}}{9}$.

XXXI-c. Page 283

1. $14\sqrt{6}$. **2.** $12\sqrt{3}$. **3.** $10\sqrt{3a}$. **4.** $30\sqrt{3}$.

5. $288\sqrt{2}$. **6.** $\sqrt[3]{x^2-4}$. **7.** $3\sqrt{3}$. **8.** $\frac{5\sqrt{2}}{4}$.

9. $-\sqrt{13}$. **10.** $14\sqrt[3]{9}$. **11.** $240\sqrt[3]{4}$. **12.** $\sqrt{6}$.

13. $ab^2\sqrt{ab}$. **14.** $\frac{33}{10}$. **15.** $\frac{1}{10}\sqrt{2}$. **16.** $\frac{2\sqrt{2}}{a}$.

17. $\frac{a-b}{x}$. **18.** 9.8995. **19.** 11.1804. **20.** 3.7796.
21. 19.5959. **22.** 26.8328. **23.** 58.7878. **24.** .8165.
25. .2887. **26.** .0447. **27.** .2566. **28.** 1.5749.
29. .4032.

XXXI-d. Page 284

1. $6x - 10\sqrt{x}$. **2.** $2x - 2\sqrt{ax}$. **3.** $a\sqrt{b} + b\sqrt{a}$.
4. $x + y - \sqrt{x + y}$. **5.** $30 + 12\sqrt{6}$. **6.** $6\sqrt{21} - 46$.
7. $6 + \sqrt{10}$. **8.** $6a - 6x + 5\sqrt{ax}$. **9.** $x - 1 + \sqrt{x^2 - x}$.
10. $x + a - \sqrt{x^2 - a^2}$. **11.** $5a + x - 4\sqrt{a^2 + ax}$.
12. $1 + 8a - 4\sqrt{a + 4a^2}$. **13.** $2a - 2\sqrt{a^2 - x^2}$.
14. $a + x + 2 - 3\sqrt{a + x}$. **15.** $2\sqrt{6}$. **16.** $16 + 6\sqrt{10}$.
17. $4x - 2\sqrt{4x^2 - a^2}$. **18.** $2x^2 + 2\sqrt{x^4 - 4y^4}$.
19. $2m + 2\sqrt{m^2 - n^2}$. **20.** $13a^2 + 5b^2 - 12\sqrt{a^4 - b^4}$.
21. $63 - 18x\sqrt{14 - 4x^2}$. **22.** $8x^2 - 2\sqrt{16x^4 - 1}$.

XXXI-e. Page 286

1. 113. **2.** –166. **3.** 172. **4.** –6.
5. $a - 4b$. **6.** $9c^2 - 4x$. **7.** x. **8.** $2p - q$.
9. $2x$. **10.** $25(x^2 - 3y^2) - 49a^2$.
11. $\frac{11 - 3\sqrt{7}}{2}$. **12.** $\frac{3\sqrt{7} - 2\sqrt{3}}{3}$. **13.** $\frac{19 - 6\sqrt{2}}{17}$.
14. $2 + \sqrt{6}$. **15.** $\frac{\sqrt{xy}}{y}$. **16.** $\frac{\sqrt{5}}{5}$. **17.** $\frac{\sqrt{ax}}{a - x}$.
18. $4 + \sqrt{15}$. **19.** $5 + \sqrt{6}$. **20.** $8 - \sqrt{42}$.
21. $\frac{\sqrt{7} - \sqrt{2}}{5}$. **22.** $3\sqrt{2} - 2\sqrt{3}$. **23.** $x - \sqrt{x^2 - y^2}$.
24. $\sqrt{x^2 + a^2} - a$. **25.** $\frac{1 - \sqrt{1 - x^4}}{x^2}$. **26.** $\frac{7a + b + 8\sqrt{a^2 - b^2}}{3a + 5b}$.
27. $\frac{18 + x^2 - 6\sqrt{9 + x^2}}{x^2}$. **28.** $\sqrt{3}$.
29. $2 - \sqrt{3} = .26795$. **30.** $11 + 5\sqrt{5} = 22.18035$.
31. $\sqrt{5} - \sqrt{3} - .50402$. **32.** $\sqrt{5 + 2} = 4.23607$.
33. $\frac{\sqrt{5}}{2} = 1.11803$. **34.** $\frac{3\sqrt{3} - 5}{2} = .09807$.

XXXI-f. Page 291

1. $\sqrt{5}-\sqrt{2}$. **2.** $\sqrt{10}+\sqrt{3}$. **3.** $\sqrt{7}-1$.
4. $\sqrt{3}+\sqrt{2}$. **5.** $3\sqrt{7}+2\sqrt{3}$. **6.** $\sqrt{10}-2\sqrt{2}$.
7. $4\sqrt{2}-3$. **8.** $2\sqrt{5}+3\sqrt{7}$. **9.** $2\sqrt{11}-\sqrt{3}$.
10. $\frac{1}{2}\sqrt{5}+1$. **11.** $2-\frac{1}{3}\sqrt{3}$. **12.** $5\sqrt{\frac{1}{2}}+\sqrt{\frac{7}{2}}$.
13. $\sqrt[4]{3}(\sqrt{2}+1)$. **14.** $\sqrt[4]{2}(\sqrt{3}-1)$. **15.** $\sqrt[4]{5}(\sqrt{2}+1)$.
16. $\sqrt{2}+1$. **17.** $\sqrt{5}+1$. **18.** $\frac{1}{2}(\sqrt{5}+1)$.
19. $\frac{1}{\sqrt[4]{2}}(\sqrt{3}+1)$. **20.** $\sqrt{3}-\sqrt{2}$. **21.** $\sqrt[4]{2}(\sqrt{5}+\sqrt{3})$.
22. $\sqrt{2}-1$. **23.** $\sqrt{3}+1$. **24.** $\sqrt{5}-1$.
25. $4+\sqrt{3}$. **26.** $\sqrt{5}+\sqrt{3}$. **27.** $\sqrt{7}-\sqrt{2}$.
28. $2\sqrt{2}+\sqrt{3}$. **29.** $2\sqrt{2}-\sqrt{7}$. **30.** $\sqrt{11}+3\sqrt{2}$.

XXXI-g. Page 293

1. 14. **2.** 33. **3.** 20. **4.** 44. **5.** 13.
6. $\frac{6}{5}$. **7.** $\frac{17}{6}$. **8.** 9. **9.** 7. **10.** $\frac{56}{5}$.
11. 144. **12.** 2. **13.** $\frac{121}{25}$. **14.** $\frac{25}{16}$. **15.** 5.
16. 12. **17.** 1. **18.** 9. **19.** 8. **20.** 12.
21. $\frac{1}{51}$. **22.** 1. **23.** 2. **24.** $(b-a)^2$. 25. $\frac{(a-b)^2}{2a-b}$.
26. 0, $a-b$. **27.** 10. **28.** $\frac{5}{2}$. **29.** 2. **30.** ± 1.

XXXI-h. Page 294

1. 49. **2.** 4. **3.** 49. **4.** $\frac{121}{9}$.
5. 16. **6.** 64. **7.** $\frac{64}{9}$. **8.** $\frac{1}{3}$.
9. $\frac{4}{3}$. **10.** 9. **11.** 4. **12.** 1.
13. 4. **14.** 50. **15.** 11. **16.** 3.
17. 6. **18.** 25. **19.** $\frac{1}{4}$. **20.** $\frac{8}{5}$.
21. 6. **22.** 361.

XXXII-a. Page 299

1. 1. **2.** 1 : 2. **3.** 1 : 5. **4.** 9 : 32.

5. $2x : 3y$. **6.** $3b : 4a$. **7.** 6 : 1. **8.** $\frac{1}{5}$.

9. 4 : 1. **10.** 17 : 7. **11.** 3 : 4. **12.** 5 : 4.

16. 21, 28. **17.** 11. **18.** 27.

XXXII-b. Page 304

1. bc. **2.** $\frac{6b^3}{a}$. **3.** $5y^2$. **4.** b.

5. $4x$. **6.** $12xy^2$. **7.** x^2. **8.** ab.

9. $4x^2$. **10.** $6a^2x$. **11.** $9ab^2$. **19.** 8 or $\frac{2}{3}$.

20. $x = 17$, $y = 11$. **21.** 2 or 0. **22.** 5 or 0.

XXXII-c Page 309

1. 54. **2.** 27. **3.** 35. **4.** 21.

5. 10. **6.** $\frac{1}{5}$. **7.** 16. **8.** 18.

12. $3a = 5b$. **13.** $5x = 7y$. **14.** $25x^3 = 27y^2$. **15.** $a^3 = b^2$.

16. 16. **17.** 20. **19.** $y = 6x - 3x^2 + x^3$. **20.** $9\frac{1}{2}$.

21. $\frac{3}{10}$, $y(3x + 20) = 2400$. **22.** 75%, 3.6, 1.2.

25. 1.2, 2.7, 7.5, 10.8. **26.** 60, 12, 6, 4. **27.** $y = \frac{1}{5}x$.

28. $y = \frac{12}{x}$. **29.** $y = 2x - 1$. **31.** $346\frac{1}{2}$ cm.

33. 28.8 km per hour. **34.** 9 : 4. **35.** $1\frac{5}{9}$ cm.

36. 3 metres. **37.** Rs 19600. **38.** $\frac{c^2 - b^2}{b^2 - a^2}d$. **41.** $\frac{3}{8}v + \frac{1200}{v}$.

42. 5 seconds. **43.** 9.6 km, 4.5 metres.

XXXIII-a Page 314

1. 161, 245. **2.** 59, −37. **3.** 34, $89\frac{1}{2}$. **4.** 16.9.

5. $574\frac{1}{2}$, $93\frac{1}{2}$. **6.** 98, 243.6. **7.** 43.

8. −49. **9.** $-40\frac{1}{2}$. **10.** 7.2 . **11.** 9.7.

12. $25x$. **13.** $a + 57d$. **14.** $80a - 79b$. **15.** 964, 9780.

16. 3.2, 25.2. **17.** −387, −18900. **18.** $-9\frac{3}{4}, -99\frac{3}{4}$. **19.** $-41\frac{1}{2}$, −361.

20. 544,4864. **21.** 779. **22.** −483. **23.** $980\frac{1}{2}$.

24. $-5569\frac{1}{2}$. **25.** 493. **26.** 140. **27.** p^3.

28. $a^2(4-a)$. **29.** $\frac{a^2(3-a)}{2}$. **30.** $pq(p-4)$. **31.** 30, 3.

32. 25, −3. **33.** 16, −1. **34.** $24, 2\frac{1}{2}$. **35.** 14, −1.

36. 20, 4. **37.** 7, $2a$. **38.** 20, $-2x$.

XXXIII-b. Page 318

1. 4, 11, 18, … **2.** 13, 10, 7, … **3.** 3, 1, −1, …

4. $1, -\frac{1}{2}, -2, \ldots$ **5.** $4, 5\frac{1}{2}, 7, \ldots$ **6.** −11, 4, 19, …

7. 43. **8.** −95. **9.** $-6\frac{1}{2}$.

10. 68, 65, …26. **11.** $91\frac{2}{3}, 90\frac{1}{3}, \ldots 70\frac{1}{3}$.

12. $-6\frac{13}{15}, -6\frac{8}{15}, \ldots -2\frac{8}{15}$. **13.** 6.4, 5.6, …−5.6.

14. $8\frac{1}{2}, 8\frac{1}{6}, \ldots 2\frac{1}{2}$. **15.** 14 or 15. **16.** 8 or 25.

17. 9 or 86. **18.** 13 or 20. **19.** 7 or 10.

20. 11 or 24. **21.** 12, 13, 14. **22.** 1, 4, 7.

23. 7, 11, 15, 19, 23. **24.** 2, 5, 8, 11, 14. **25.** 131.

XXXIV-a. Page 323

1. 48, 384. **2.** $\frac{1}{2}, \frac{1}{128}$. **3.** $1, \frac{1}{16}$.

4. $-\frac{1}{27}, -\frac{1}{2187}$. **5.** 128, 1. **6.** 1, 625.

7. 512. **8.** −4374. **9.** $\frac{243}{16}$.

10. -3^{2n}. **11.** x^{2p-1}. **12.** $\frac{1}{x^{23}}$.

13. 162, 54, 18. **14.** $\frac{1}{2}$, 2, 8, 32. **15.** $-28, 14, \ldots \frac{7}{8}$.

16. $\frac{16}{27}, \frac{8}{9}, \ldots 3$. **17.** 384, 765. **18.** −1458, −1092 .

19. $\frac{1}{8}, 127\frac{7}{8}$. **20.** $\frac{1}{90}, 12\frac{13}{90}$. **21.** $30\frac{3}{8}, 45\frac{5}{9}$.

22. $\frac{1}{1458}$, $6\frac{1093}{1452}$. **23.** $2\frac{20}{81}$. **24.** $1\frac{601}{1458}$.

25. $\frac{1281}{2560}$. **26.** $\frac{1365}{2048}$. **27.** $5\frac{58}{81}$.

28. $\frac{4369}{8192}$. **29.** $\frac{1}{2}(3^p - 1)$. **30.** $\frac{2}{3}(1 - 2^{2p})$.

31. $\frac{40(3+\sqrt{3})}{3}$. **32.** $\frac{\sqrt{a}(a^a - 1)}{a-1}$. **33.** $\frac{585\sqrt{2} - 292}{2}$.

34. $364(\sqrt{6} + \sqrt{2})$.

XXXIV-b. Page 326

1. 27. **2.** 24. **3.** 1. **4.** $\frac{1}{3}$.

5. 1. **6.** $\frac{64}{65}$. **7.** $\frac{27}{29}$. **8.** $\frac{8}{15}$.

9. $\frac{1}{3}$. **10.** $\frac{1}{6}$. **11.** $\frac{8}{33}$. **12.** $\frac{25}{66}$.

13. $\frac{1}{27}$. **14.** $\frac{5}{8}, \frac{5}{4}, \frac{5}{2}, \ldots$ **15.** $\frac{2187}{256}, \frac{729}{128}, \frac{243}{64}$.

16. $\frac{1}{25}, -\frac{1}{5}, 1, \ldots$ **17.** $\frac{9}{64}, -\frac{9}{32}, -\frac{9}{16}, \ldots$

18. 75, 60, 48. **20.** $\frac{3}{4}, \frac{1}{4}, \frac{1}{12}, \ldots$

21. $\frac{y^2(y^{2n} - 1)}{y^2 - 1} + bn(n+1)$ **22.** $\frac{140 + 99\sqrt{2}}{8}$.

23. $\frac{9(3\sqrt{6} + 2\sqrt{2})}{40}$. **24.** $2n^2(2n+1) - \frac{3}{8}\left(1 - \frac{1}{3^{2n}}\right)$.

XXXV-a. Page 330

1. $\frac{2}{3}$. **2.** $\frac{5}{14}$. **3.** -4. **4.** $\frac{3}{n}$.

5. $-\frac{1}{3}, -1, 1, \ldots$ **6.** $4, 2, 1\frac{1}{3}, \ldots$ **7.** $-\frac{1}{27}, -\frac{1}{26}, -\frac{1}{25}, \ldots$

8. $2\frac{2}{3}$. **9.** $1\frac{6}{7}$. **10.** $\frac{1}{7}$.

11. $\frac{2}{a+b}$. **12.** $\frac{1}{x}$. **13.** $\frac{x^2 - y^2}{x}$.

14. $5\frac{1}{7}, 7\frac{1}{5}$. **15.** 3, 4, 6. **16.** $1\frac{1}{5}, 1\frac{1}{2}, 2, 3$.

19. $36\frac{987}{1024}$. **20.** $17\frac{1}{4}$. **21.** $\frac{p}{2}\{(p+3)a - (p-3)x\}$.

22. $1\frac{46}{1215}$. **23.** 18. **31.** $\frac{a^{2n}-b^{2n}}{b^{2n-1}(a^2-b^2)^2}$.

37. $\frac{2}{3}$. **38.** $\frac{n(n+1)}{2}$. $x+\frac{1}{x}\left(1-\frac{1}{2^n}\right)$.

39. $n(3n+2)$.

XXXV.b. Page 332

1. $64\frac{4}{9}$. **4.** 64. **6.** 35392.

7. $3\frac{1}{2}, 5\frac{1}{2}, 7\frac{1}{2}, 9\frac{1}{2}$. **8.** 50200. **9.** 1152.

10. $\frac{1}{2}n(n+1)$. **11.** 13,9. **12.** 136 secs.

13. $n(n+7)$, 8. **14.** $\frac{1}{2}(3^n-1)$.

17. $d=-\frac{3}{2}$ or $-\frac{1}{2}$, $r=\frac{3}{2}$ or $\frac{1}{2}$. **18.** $x=9$ or 4, $y=6$ or -4.

19. $\frac{n+8}{13-n}$. **20.** Rs 2952. **22.** $29\frac{123}{128}$ dm, 30 dm.

Miscellaneous Examples V. Page 334

1. $\frac{c^{1/12}}{a^{1/3}b^{1/4}}$; 1. **7.** $4\sqrt{2}$. **8.** 5.

10. 52, 78, 91 metres. **12.** (1) $x^{2b}+x^{-2b}$. (2) $(a+b)^2$.

13. $-\frac{32}{7a}$. **14.** (1) $\frac{b^4}{a^2}$. (2) $\frac{7}{8}$. **15.** $\frac{a+b}{x^2-y^2}$.

21. 2. **23.** $-5, -2, 1, 4, 7, 10, 13$.

24. 1, 4, 7, ... **25.** 1. **26.** (1) 275; (2) -1705.

28. $-2, 0, 2, 4, 6$. **29.** $18\left[1-\left(\frac{5}{6}\right)^n\right]$. **30.** 1.

31. $a+b$. **32.** $\frac{3n^2}{2}, \frac{63}{2}, \frac{69}{2}, \frac{75}{2}, \frac{81}{2}, \frac{87}{2}$.

34. (1) $9(19a+64x)$. (2) $\frac{2315}{81}$. **37.** 10.

38. (1) $s=\frac{1-3^{2n}}{4}$; $l=-3^{2n-1}$. (2) $s=-2n$; $l=1-4n$.

39. 1 and 9. **40.** $1+\frac{1}{3}+\frac{1}{9}+\dots$. **41.** 8 and 2.

XXXVI. Page 344

1. Rational.
2. Rational.
3. Equal, but opposite in sign.
4. Imaginary.
5. Imaginary.
6. Equal, but opposite in sign.
7. $x^2 - 2x - 15 = 0.$
8. $x^2 + 20x + 99 = 0.$
9. $x^2 - 2ax + a^2 - b^2 = 0.$
10. $12x^2 - 28x + 15 = 0.$
11. $15x^2 + 2ax - 8a^2 = 0.$
12. $8x^2 - 7x = 0.$
13. $-\frac{1}{2}.$
14. (i) 6, (ii) −7 (iii) 2.
15. $-\frac{a-b}{a+b}.$
17. Sum $\frac{4}{3}$, difference $\frac{2\sqrt{7}}{3}$, sum of squares $\frac{22}{9}$.
19. $\frac{25}{8}.$
20. must not lie between 10 and −10.
21. $k < -\frac{49}{12}.$
22. $(4 - x)(3 + x)$; between −3 and 4.
24. $x^2 - 6x + 4 = 0.$
25. $x^2 + 4x + 1 = 0.$
26. $30x^2 + (6a - 5b)x - ab = 0.$
27. $4x^2 - 16x + 9 = 0.$
28. $(a^2 - b^2)x^2 - 2(a^2 + b^2)x + a^2 - b^2 = 0.$
29. $4abx^2 - 2(a^2 + b^2)x + ab = 0.$
30. $\frac{q^2 - 2pr}{p^2}.$
31. $\frac{q^2 - 4pr}{p^2}.$
32. $-\frac{qr}{p^2}.$
33. $\frac{q^4 - 4prq^2 + 2p^2r^2}{p^4}.$
34. $\frac{qr^2(3pr - q^2)}{p^5}.$
35. $\frac{q(3pr - q^2)}{p^2r}.$
36. $\frac{q}{r^3}(3pr - q^2).$
37. $\frac{q}{p^5}(-q^4 + 5pq^2r - 5p^2r^2).$
***38.** $\frac{1}{pr}(r + 2p)^2.$
40. $P = p(p^2 - 3q), Q = q^3.$
41. (i) $(x - 1)^2 - a(x - 1) + b = 0.$ (ii) $(x + 2)^2 - a(x + 2) + b = 0.$
(iii) $\left(\frac{x}{3}\right)^2 - a\left(\frac{x}{3}\right) + b = 0.$
(iv) $(4x^2 - a(4x) + b = 0.$
(v) $(x^2)^2 - ax^2 + b = 0.$
(vi) $(\sqrt{x})^2 - a\sqrt{x} + b = 0.$

(vii) $b^2x^2 - (a^3 - 3ab)x + b = 0.$

(viii) $x^2 - 3ax + 2a^2 + b = 0.$

(ix) $x^2 - (a^2 + a - 2b)x + b^2 + b + a^3 - 3ab = 0.$

(x) $4x^2 + 6ax + 25b - 4a^2 = 0.$

42. $\frac{176}{5}$. **43.** $p = -2(b + c), q = 4bc.$

44. $p = 45$; $x = 1\frac{1}{2}$ or 15. **45.** $x^2 - bx - a^2 = 0.$

47. 150, $-\frac{53}{97}$. **48.** 14′′, 12′′.

49. (i) $p^2 = 4q.$ (ii) $q = 1.$

(iii) $2p^2 = 9q.$ (iv) $p^2 = 4(q + 1).$

(v) $p = -7.$ (vi) $p = -2q.$

50. $p^2 - 2q$, $x^2 - (p - 2q)x + q^2 = 0.$

51. $8x^2 - 20a^3x - a^6 = 0.$ **54.** $2px^2 - (p^2 + 4q)x + 2pq = 0.$

58. $\frac{9}{5}$. **60.** $-\frac{10}{9}$, -10.

XXXVII-a. Page 352

1. 120, 5040, 56, 300. **2.** (1) 2520. (2) 5040.
3. 8. **4.** 35. **5.** 6. **6.** 36.
7. 7 or 8. **8.** 2100. **9.** 455, 816; $(r = 15)$.s
10. 242880. **11.** 1596000. **12.** 504000.

XXXVII-b. Page 356

1. (1) 9979200. (2) 151200. (3) 166320. **2.** 420, 360.
3. 18. **4.** 1023. **5.** m^n. **6.** 168168.
7. 34650. **8.** 120, 144. **9.** 1296. **10.** 180.
11. 11520. **13.** 78. **14.** $(n-2)(n-3)\,\underline{|(n-2)}$.

16. 8! 7! 5! 4! 4! (about 1.4×10^{13}).

4! 8! 7! 5! 4! 12 (about 7×10^{12}).

17. 35, 324. **18.** 10, 10. **19.** 10!, $\frac{10!}{9}$. **20.** 250.

21. $\frac{n!}{p!}$, 36, 28. **22.** 1980, 660.

23. 4080, 680. **24.** 38. **25.** $\frac{(a+b+c)}{a!b!c!}$.

26. $6\,\underline{|6} = 4320$, $6\,\underline{|7} = 30240$. **27.** 216, 90. **28.** 70, 35.

30. 1728. **31.** $\frac{52!}{(13!)^4}, \frac{1}{41}\cdot\frac{52!}{(13!)^4}$. **32.** 9, 9, 5.

XXXVIII-a. Page 363

1. $x^4 + 8x^3 + 24x^2 + 32x + 16.$

2. $x^5 + 15x^4 + 90x^3 + 270x^2 + 405x + 243.$

3. $a^7 + 7a^6x + 21a^5x^2 + 35a^4x^4 + 35a^3x^4 + 21a^2x^5 + 7ax^6 + x^7.$

4. $a^5 - 5a^4x + 10a^3x^2 - 10a^2x^3 + 5ax^4 - x^5.$

5. $1 - 10y + 40y^2 - 80y^2 + 80y^4 - 32y^5.$

6. $16x^4 + 16x^2y + 6x^2y^2 + xy^3 + \frac{y^4}{16}.$

7. $64 - 96x + 60x^2 - 20x^3 + \frac{15x^4}{4} - \frac{3x^5}{8} + \frac{x^6}{64}.$

8. $a^7 - \frac{21a^6}{b} + \frac{189a^5}{b^2} - \frac{945a^4}{b^3} + \frac{2835a^3}{b^4} - \frac{5103a^2}{b^5} + \frac{5103a}{b^6} - \frac{2187}{b^7}.$

9. $a^9x^9 + 9a^7x^8y + 36a^5x^7y^2 + 84a^3x^6y^3 + 126ax^5y^4 + \frac{126x^4y^5}{a} + \frac{84x^3y^6}{a^3} + \frac{36x^2y^7}{a^5} + \frac{9xy^6}{a^7} + \frac{y^9}{a^9}.$

10. $220x^3.$ **11.** $-448y^5.$ **12.** $21875a^3b^4.$

13. $5440x^3.$ **14.** $\frac{210}{x^6}.$ **15.** $\frac{5103x^4a^5}{16}.$

16. -20 **17.** $\frac{2300b^{22}}{x^{16}}.$ **18.** $-24310x^{25}.$

19. $2x^4 + 36x^2 + 18.$ **20.** $32 - 40x^2 + 10x^4.$

21. 11520. **22.** $-\frac{1001}{256}a^9.$ **23.** 7920. **24.** $\frac{1025024}{81}.$

XXXVII-b. Page 368

1. The 8th. **2.** The 9th.

3. The 2nd and 3rd. **4.** The 7th.

5. The 11th. **6.** The 6th and 7th.

7. $r = 7$; excluding the value $r = 4$, which makes the terms the same.

8. $n = 40.$ **9.** $3r = 3n + 2$.

10. $\frac{2\underline{|m}}{\underline{|m}\,\underline{|m}}.$ **11.** $\frac{2\underline{|n}}{\underline{|n}\,\underline{|n}}x^n.$

12. 65536. **13.** 262144.

14. $\frac{n(n-1).....(n-r+2)}{\underline{|r-1}}a^{n-r+1}(2x)^{r+1},$

$\frac{n(n-1)......(n-r+2)}{r-1!}a^{r-1}(2x)^{n-r+1}.$

15. $a^6 + 6a^5 + 15a^4 + 20a^3 + 15a^2 + 6a + 1.$

$x^6 - 12x^5 + 54x^4 - 112x^3 + 108x^2 - 48x + 8.$

16. $1 + \frac{1}{3}x - \frac{1}{9}x^2 + \frac{5}{81}x^3 - \ldots$ **17.** $1 + \frac{3}{4}x - \frac{3}{32}x^2 + \frac{5}{128}x^3 - \ldots$

18. $1 + \frac{2}{5}x - \frac{3}{25}x^2 + \frac{8}{125}x^3 - \ldots$ **19.** $1 - 6x + 27x^2 - 108x^3 + \ldots$

20. $1 + 3x^2 + 6x^4 + 10x^6 + \ldots$ **21.** $1 - 12x + 90x^2 - 540x^3 + \ldots$

22. $\frac{1}{8} - \frac{3}{16}x + \frac{3}{16}x^2 - \frac{5}{32} + x^3 \ldots .$

23. $1 - x + \frac{3}{2}x^2 - \frac{5}{2}x^3 + \ldots .$

24. $\frac{1}{a^{3/2}}\left(1 + \frac{3x}{a} + \frac{15x^2}{2a^2} + \frac{35x^3}{2a^3} + \ldots\right).$

25. $\frac{315}{128}x^4, -\frac{230945}{65536}x^9.$ **26.** $\frac{99}{2}x^2, \frac{77}{256}x^{10}.$

27. $-4x^3, (-1)^r(r + 1)x^r.$ **28.** $-\frac{21}{1024}x^6, -\frac{1.3.5.\ldots(2r - 3)}{2^r \lfloor r}x^r.$

29. $\frac{b^r}{a^{r+1}}x^r, -\frac{(n - 1)(2n - 1)\ldots\ldots\{(r - 1)n - 1)}{\lfloor r}x^r.$

30. 4.95967. **31.** 4.198998. **32.** 1.98734. **33.** .100504.

XXXIX-a. Page 375

1. $\frac{15}{2}, -15, -1, \frac{5}{2}.$ **2.** $\frac{9}{2}, -4, -\frac{3}{4}, \frac{3}{2}.$

3. $5, \frac{1}{9}, 125000, 1, -\frac{1}{4}, 2.89, .01.$ **4.** $\frac{1}{2}\log a.$

5. $-5 \log y.$ **6.** 3, 2, 0, −1, −1, −4, 1.

7. 1.5705780, $\bar{5}$.5705780, 8.5705780.

8. 7.623, .000007623, 76230000.

9. 2.8627278. **10.** 3.9242793.

11. $\bar{1}$.4082400. **12.** .7658178.

13. .8644286. **14.** $\bar{1}$.4841414.

16. $\log 7 + 4\log 3 = 2.7535832$.

17. $6\log 2 + \frac{43}{6}\log 3 - \frac{11}{6} = 3.3922160.$

18. $\frac{1}{3}\log 2 + \frac{1}{2}\log 3 + \frac{1}{6}\log 7 = .4797536.$

19. $\frac{1}{5}(7\log 2 - 3\log 3 - \log 7) = 1.9661496.$

20. Sixty-nine. **22.** 176.

23. .398742. **24.** .500977.

25. $2 - \log 2 - \log 3 - \log 7 = .3767507.$

26. $\frac{1 + 2\log 3 - \log 2}{\log 3} = 3.46.$ 27. $\frac{5 - 7\log 2}{3 - 2\log 2} = 1.206.$

28. $\frac{3}{1 - \log 2} = 4.29.$ 29. $\frac{2\log 2 - 4\log 3}{4\log 2 - \log 3} = -1.8$ very nearly.

XXXIX-b. Page 379

1. 481.9. **2.** 46.22. **3.** .1396. **4.** .008682.
5. 342.9. **6.** .03892. **7.** 8.119. **8.** 44.22.
9. .6797. **10.** 7.446. **11.** 0.3055. **12.** 3.361.
13. .7783. **14.** 1.923. **15.** 1.444. **16.** 19.97.
17. .2008. **18.** .00008855. **19.** 415. **20.** .7142.
21. 2.887. **22.** 1.997. **23.** 1.936. **24.** 1.973.
25. 1.291. **26.** 9.29; 2560. **27.** 9.076. **28.** 178.1.
29. 16. **30.** 4.616. **31.** 9.529. **32.** ₹ 731.
33. ₹ 514. **34.** 20 yrs. **35.** 20. **36.** 4.77.

XL Page 385

1. 30215. **2.** 25566556. **3.** 244332343.
4. 36641 *tt*. **5.** 3245. **6.** 14320241.
7. 123807; 1101122. **8.** 3*e*7580. **9.** 32099.
10. 30523. **11.** 10000011.
12. $2^9 + 2^8 + 2^7 + 2^6 + 2^5 + 2^3 + 1; 6e^4 + 9e^3 + e^2 + 4e + t.$
13. 1736; 1*t*5; 328108. **14.** 667. **15.** 203.71.
16. 31.573. **17.** .100133.
18. .50213; 404052. **19.** $\frac{7}{9}$. **20.** Five.
21. Nine. **22.** Nine. **23.** Seven.
24. 444; 1425; 3333.

XLI Page 389

2. $\frac{1}{2}\left(x - \frac{x^2}{2} + \frac{x^3}{3} - \frac{x^4}{4} + \ldots\right).$ **8.** $b = a + \frac{a^2}{\underline{|2}} + \frac{a^3}{\underline{|3}} + \frac{a^4}{\underline{|4}} + \ldots$

9. 1.6487. **10.** $\frac{(-1)^{r-1}2^r - 1}{r} x^r.$ **13.** $\frac{2^r + 1}{r} x^r.$

XLII-a. Page 392

1. $2, -3, \frac{-1 \pm \sqrt{-27}}{2}.$ **2.** $2, -\frac{1}{2}, \frac{1}{3}(1 \pm \sqrt{10}).$

3. $\frac{-1 \pm \sqrt{-3}}{2}, \frac{5 \pm \sqrt{21}}{2}.$ **4.** $-2, -\frac{1}{2}.$ **5.** $16, -\frac{4}{3}.$

6. 3, 0. **7.** $2, \frac{15}{4}.$ **8.** $9, \frac{1}{9}.$

9. 3, –2, 1, –6. **10.** $1, \frac{1}{81}$. **11.** 20, 11.

12. 2, –1. **13.** –8, –1, 0. **14.** 0.

15. $2, \frac{3}{2}, \frac{7 \pm \sqrt{33}}{4}$. **16.** $1, 1 \pm 2\sqrt{15}$. **17.** $7, -1, 3 \pm 2\sqrt{2}$.

18. $3, -\frac{7}{2}, \frac{-3 \pm \sqrt{1357}}{12}$. **19.** $\frac{3 \pm \sqrt{5}}{2}, \frac{9 \pm \sqrt{-83}}{6}$.

20. $2, -\frac{1}{2}, \frac{3 \pm \sqrt{505}}{4}$. **21.** $\frac{2}{13}, \frac{8}{7}$. **22.** $a^3, \frac{1}{a}$.

23. $1, \frac{c-a}{a-b}$. **24.** $1, \frac{c(a-b)}{a(b-c)}$. **25.** a, b.

26. $c, \frac{a^2 + b^2 - ac - bc}{a + b - 2c}$. **27.** $p + q$.

28. 8, –2. **29.** $\frac{5}{2}, -\frac{13}{2}$. **30.** a, b.

XLII-b. Page 394

1. $x = 5, y = 2$. **2.** $x = 4, 3; y = 3, 4$.

3. $x = 7, -2; y = 2, -7$. **4.** $x = 8, 2; y = 2, 8$.

5. $x = 12, 3; y = 3, 12$. **6.** $x = 3, y = 6$.

7. $x = \frac{1}{7}, y = \frac{1}{3}$.

8. $x = 4, 1, \frac{1}{2}(-5 \pm \sqrt{41}); y = 1, 4, \frac{1}{2}(-5 \pm \sqrt{41})$.

9. $x = \pm 10, 0; y = \pm 1, \pm \frac{\sqrt{34}}{2}$. **10.** $x = 7; -\frac{35}{4}, y = 3, -\frac{15}{4}$.

11. $x = 5, 2, 1 \pm \sqrt{6}; y = -2, -5, -1 \pm \sqrt{6}$.

12. $x = \frac{3}{4}, 1, 0; y = \frac{3}{4}, 0, 1$.

13. $x = -1, 5 \pm \sqrt{6}: y = -1, 1 \pm \sqrt{\frac{2}{3}}$. [It may be shown that $(x+1)^3 = 27(y+1)^3$].

14. (1) 3, 2; 2, 3. (2) $x = 3, -1; y = 1, -3$.

15. $x = 16, 1; y = 1, 16$. **16.** $x = 17, y = \pm 8$.

17. $x = \pm 3, y = \pm 2, z = \pm 4$. **18.** $x = 5, y = 6, z = 1, u = 4$.

19. $x = \pm 6, y = \pm \frac{8}{3}, z = \pm \frac{3}{2}$. **20.** $x = \pm 5, y = \pm 7, z = \pm 11$.

21. $x = -a \pm 2, y = b \pm 1, z = -c \pm 3$.

22. $x = \pm 5, y = \pm 2, z = \pm 4$. **23.** $x = \pm 7, y = \pm 3, z = \pm 2$.

24. $x = \pm 3, y = \pm 4, z = \pm 2$. **25.** $x = 2, -6; y = 3, -5; z = 0, -2$.

26. $x = 7, y = 2, z = 4.$

27. $x = \pm \frac{1}{2}, 0; y = \pm \frac{1}{3}, 0, z = \pm 1, 0.$

28. $x = 8, 2 ; y = 2, 8 ; z = 4.$

29. $x = 2, -6; y = 5; z = 6, -2.$

30. $x = -5; y = 3, 1; z = 1, 3.$

31. $x = 6; y = 9; 4; z = 4, 9.$

32. $x = \frac{30}{11}, y = \frac{26}{11}.$

33. $x = 3, y = 9, z = 6.$

34. $x = \pm \frac{a(b^2 + c^2)}{2bc}, y = \pm \frac{b(c^2 + a^2)}{2ca}, z = \pm \frac{c(a^2 + b^2)}{2ab}$

XLIII Page 398

1. ₹ 128855000.
2. 87 years nearly.
3. ₹ 1287.50.
4. 20-63 per cent, nearly.
5. ₹ 2001.875.
6. 4 per cent.
7. ₹ 33600.
8. ₹ 11708.40.
9. ₹ 1604.
10. 20 years nearly.

XLIV-a. Page 402

7. 36.
8. 32.
9. 25.
11. 1.2 sq. cm.
12. $y = 3x$. Any point whose ordinate is equal to three times its abscissa.
14. The lines are $x = 5, y = 8$. The point (5, 8).
15. A circle of radius 13 whose centre is at the origin.

XLIV-b. Page 405

21. 32 units of area.
22. 100 sq. cm.
23. 72 units of area.
24. 0.64 sq. cm.

XLIV-c. Page 408

1. $x = 1, y = 5.$
2. $x = 2, y = 10.$
3. $x = 3, y = 12.$
4. $x = 3, y = -2.$
5. $x = 4, y = 2.$
6. $x = 6, y = 8.$
7. $x = -2, y = 4.$
8. $x = 0, y = -3.$
9. $x = -3, y = 0.$
10. At the point (0, 21).
11. $3x + 4y = 7.$

XLIV-d. Page 412

1. $y = x.$
2. (0, 0), (– 4, 2).
5. (2, 1).
6. (i) 1.46, –5.46; (ii) 3.24, – 1.24; (iii) 3.32, 0.68.
7. – 5; 7.
8. $-\frac{1}{4}$; 3.79, – 0.79 ; 4.54, – 1.54.
9. $x = 8$, or 6 ; $y = 6$, or 8.
10. The straight line $3x + 4y = 25$ *touches* the circle $x^2 + y^2 = 25$ at the point (3, 4).

XLIV-e. Page 420

3. Each axis is an asymptote to the curve, which approaches the axis of y much less rapidly than it does the axis of x.

7. $x = 2, \frac{10}{3}; y = 5, 3.$

8. $x = 3, -3; y = 2, -2.$

9. $x = 2; y = -1.$

31. $-1, 1, 2.$

32. $-2, 4.41, 1.59.$

XLIV-f. Page 426

1. 0.52, 2.9, 11.6; 2.75, 2.3, 3.1.

3. 2.080, 2.140.

4. 2.4.

5. $-2, 4; -9.$

9. -5 and 1.

10. $-2, 1, 4.$

12. 26.9, 38, 3.58.

13. 0.477, 0.225, 0.350, 1.538.

14. 3 cm from the point of suspension.

15. 12 kg, 10.7 kg, 9.6 kg, 8 kg, 6 kg. The curve is a rectangular hyperbola whose equation is $xy = 48$.

16. 1.5.

17. $x = -\frac{1}{4}.$

18. (i) 1. (ii) 1, 2, -3.

19. (i) $x = 8, y = 1\frac{1}{2}$ or $x = 1\frac{1}{2}, y = 8$. (ii) $x = 6.43, y = 3.07$.
(iii) $x = 6, y = 2$, or $x = -6, y = -2$.

20. $2, 2, -1.$

22. $1, 1.732, -1.732$. Negative for values of $x < -1.732$; positive between -1.732 and 1; negative between 1 and 1.732; positive for values of $x > 1.732$.

XLIV-g. Page 434

2. (i) 54.1 grains; (ii) 0.2.

3. 39.3; 91.6; $y = 0.393\,x$.

4. 3.85 cm; 17.6 cm.

5. 54.5°F, 86.9°F, $F = 32 + \frac{9}{5}C$.

6. $y = 100 + \frac{x}{10}$, ₹ 350; 4250.

7. 45.96; 39.40.

8. ₹ 2.6; ₹ 3.4.

9. 8.1 cm; 24.375 gm.

10. (i) ₹ 320; (ii) ₹ 580.

11. $y = \frac{10}{11}x - 70$. 112; 168; 78.

12. 5 cm per sec; $5\frac{3}{4}$ secs. $v = 5 + 4t$.

13. 2.49 sq. cm.

14. (i) 15.80 metres; (ii) 48.64 metres.

15. Max. height = 19.48 metres; 4 secs.

16. $P = 0.6\,G - 14.4$; 24.

17. 23; ₹ 33.8.

18. 93.5°E.

20. $y = 0.21x + 1.37$.

21. $y = 0.4x + 1.6$; 9.2 ; 3.

22. $a = 45.7, b = 118.$ Error $= 8.43$ in defect.

23. $8.6; P = 0.14W + 0.2; 225$ kg.

24. $a = \frac{1}{4}; b = 3.2; 12.$ **25.** $a = 3, b = 2.7; 4.25.$

26. $n = 3, c = 27 \times 10^5.$ **27.** $n = 1.5, c = 79500.$

XLIV-h. Page 445

1. 6 p.m.; (i) 3.30 p.m.; (ii) 7.30 p.m.
2. (i) 2 p.m; 2.52 p.m.
3. 47 km from *A*'s starting place at 12.42 p.m., 11.12 a.m. and 2.12 p.m.
4. 27 km.
5. 56 km from London at 3.33 p.m., 3.9 p.m; 3.57 p.m.; 57.6 km.
6. (i) 15 km after *C*'s start, 1 km from Bath;
(ii) 45.........$3\frac{1}{2}$ km......
(iii) half a km behind *A* and *B*.
7. 9 km from Y at 12.48 p.m, 12.18 p.m. and 1.18 p.m.
8. 40 metres. *A* 16 metres ahead, *C* 16 metres behind.
9. 5 secs.
10. 5 hours from the start.
11. 7.36 pm; 3 p.m. and 5 p.m.; 19 km from Y.
12. 7 hours 3.7 p.m.
13. 12.12 p.m. (i) 11 a.m.; (ii) 57 km.
14. 5 km.
15. 4.12 p.m.
16. 10.4 a.m.
17. 400 metres.
18. ₹ 4200. 20 for ₹ 4800.
19. After 10 secs. 400 dm per sec.; 600 dm per sec.
20. 30 years. ₹ 4100, ₹ 3200.
21. 75 in Latin; 80 in Greek. 74 and 50.

Miscellaneous Graphs. Page 449

1. $(2, -3)$. **2.** $(1, 2)$. **4.** $x = 1, y = 18.$

5. 26; 1.28 (approx.). **6.** 9; 9.4. **7.** $(-4, 5)$.

8. $(3, 4), (4, 1), (-3, 2)$. **13.** $2 \cdot 65$, 1.91. **14.** $2 \cdot 79, -1.79.$

15. The pt. $(6, 5)$. **16.** Rs. 123.50; Rs. 5.70; Rs. 13.30.

17. 37; 87 paise. **18.** Rs. 33.80; 6 kg.

19. (i) $x = 2$, or -7; $y = 7$, or -2. (ii) $x = 8$, or 6; $y = 6$ or 8.
(iii) $x = 3$, or -5.8; $y = 5$, or -0.6.
(iv) $x = 5.2$, or -1.3; $y = -2.9$, or 5.7.

20. $6.46, -0.46; 12.$ **21.** 23, Rs. 7.20, Rs. 15.60.

22. Rs. 1.41, Rs. 1.97, Rs. 3.66; 5 hrs, nearly.
23. 3.30, – 0.30. **24.** 18, 40, 51. **25.** 90, 72.
27. 2.60, 5.63, 4.16, 5.77.
28. 6 p.m., 48 km from London. At 4 and 8 p.m. (i) *B* 4 km behind *A*; *C* 6 km behind *B*. (ii) 4.21 p.m.
29. 4.30 p.m, 18 km from O. (i) At 3 and 6 p.m. (ii) 20 km.
30. (i) 1 p.m., 28 km from P, (ii) 20 km; (iii) 11.30 a.m.
31. (i) $29\frac{1}{4}$ and 39 millions. **32.** Rs. 80, Rs. 240.
33. 1.5, –1. **34.** Max. ordinates (= 2) at the points (– 1,2), (1, – 2).
35. – 1.73,0, 1.73.
36. (i) $\left.\begin{array}{l} x = 12, \text{ or } 3 \\ y = 3, \text{ or } 12 \end{array}\right\}$; (ii) $\left.\begin{array}{l} x = 6, \text{ or } -3 \\ y = 3, \text{ or } -6 \end{array}\right\}$; (iii) $\left.\begin{array}{l} x = 2, 3, -3, -2 \\ y = 3, 2, -2, -3 \end{array}\right\}$.
37. 30.4 cm. **38.** $P = 1.1Q + 6$; Rs. 1710; Rs. 1440; Rs. 920.
41. Rs. 17; Rs. 26.50 **42.** $4\frac{1}{2}$ km per hr. **43.** 1.30 p.m.; 3 : 1.
44. 24 min.
45. At 100 km from Bombay. 30 km and 155 km. The quickest run is from Borivali to Dahami Rd by the train from Bombay to Surat.

Miscellaneous Examples VI. Page 454

1. 0. **2.** $-6a - 2b - 4d$. **3.** $\frac{1}{2}x^2 + \frac{1}{2}xy - \frac{2}{9}y^2$.
4. 3. **5.** $4 - 12x + 13x^2 - 6x^3 + x^4$.
6. $4\frac{1}{3}$. **7.** $a - 2$. **8.** $\frac{a^2 + b^2}{a^2 - b^2}$.
9. $x = 15, y = 16$. **10.** 1, 3.
11. $\frac{4}{9}$. **12.** $\frac{13}{12}x^2 - \frac{11}{20}y^2 + \frac{5}{3}z^2$.
13. $x^3 + 24x^2y + 192xy^2 + 512y^3$. **14.** $x^2 - y^2$.
15. 11.
16. **H.C.F.** $(x + 2)(x - 1)$. **L.C.M.** $(x - 1)(x + 2)^2(x^2 + 2)$.
17. $2a^2 - 3a + 3$. **18.** $x = \frac{8b + 7a}{9}, y = \frac{8a + 7b}{9}$.
19. $\frac{x}{a - x}$. **20.** $\frac{5}{3}$. **22.** $x - \frac{3}{4}y$.
23. $-35x + 18y + 17z$. **24.** (1) $(10x - 1)(x + 8)$.
(2) $(3x - y)(3x + y)(9x^2 + 3xy + y^2)(9x^2 - 3xy + y^2)$.
25. 13. **26.** 2. **27.** $x^2 - 1$.

28. $\frac{x-3y}{x+3y}$. **29.** $x = \frac{2}{a}, y = 3b$. **30.** $21\frac{9'}{11}$ and $54\frac{6'}{11}$ past 7.

31. 1. **32.** $\frac{1}{8}x^6 - 8y^6$. **33.** $2a^4 + 12a^2 + 2$.

34. 884. **35.** $\frac{1}{x^2 - y^2}$. **36.** $x = 14, y = 17$.

37. $2x^3 - 3x + 7$. **38.** $x = \frac{2}{3}$.

39. $x(x^3 + y^3)(3x - y)$.

40. 21 25-paise coins, 40 50-paise coins.

41. $8ab$. **42.** $2ab^3 + 3b^4$. **43.** 36.

44. $4x - 5$. **45.** $\frac{a^2 + b^2}{ab(a-b)^2}$. **46.** $2x - \frac{y}{6}$.

47. $x = \frac{1}{2}, y = \frac{1}{3}$; or $x = 0, y = 0$.

48. $\frac{2(x-7)(2x-7)}{(x-2)(x-3)(x-4)(x-5)}$.

49. $(2x+3)(4x+5)(3x-5)(x+2)(x-2)$.

50. Rs. 3.75. **51.** $-5605x + 5589$.

52. $4a^2 - 9b^2 + 24bc - 16c^2$.

54. $6(x+1)(x-3)(x-4)$. **55.** $2(a^2 + b^2)(x^2 + y^2)$.

56. $x = 3, y = 2, z = 1$. **57.** 0.

58. $x = -5$. **59.** $\frac{x^4 + 2y^4}{y^2(x-y)^2(x^2 + xy + y^2)}$.

60. 24 days. **61.** $\frac{3}{2}x^3 - 5x^2 + \frac{x}{4} + 9$.

62. 94. **63.** $\frac{1}{x^2 - 1}$.

64. $\frac{ac}{b}x^2 - \frac{b}{c}x$. **65.** $x = 2\frac{1}{2}$.

66. (1) $(x^2 + 1)(x + 5)$ (2) $(x - 19y)(x + 17y)$.

67. $x = 24, y = 9, z = 5$. **68.** $\frac{2x}{x + 5y}$.

69. $(2a - 3b + 2c)^2$. **70.** 3.

71. $x^2 + y^2 + z^2$. **72.** $-2ab$.

73. 6.

74. (1) $3x(x+9)(x-7)$. (2) $(a+b+1)(a+b)$.

75. $x = \frac{qr}{p^2 + q^2}, y = \frac{pr}{x^2 + q^2}$. **76.** $\frac{2x^2}{8x^3 - y^3}$.

77. $x = 8$.

78. $\frac{x^3 + x^2 - 2}{2x^2 + 2x + 1}$.

79. $\frac{2}{(1 - x^2)^2}$.

80. 640.

81. $1 - 4x - \frac{46}{15}x^2 + \frac{10}{3}x^3$.

82. $\frac{1}{2}$.

83. $\frac{3}{4}x^5 - 4x^4 + \frac{77}{8}x^3 - \frac{43}{4}x^2 - \frac{33}{4}x + 27$.

84. $2a^2b^2(a - 2b)^2(2a + b)^2$.

85. $x = 5$.

86. $\frac{5x^2 - 4x - 8}{3x^2 + 4x + 24}$.

87. $2a^2 + 3a + \frac{3}{a}$.

88. $x = 2ab,\ y = 3ab$.

89. $3(2x - y)(5x + 4y)$.

90. 25 shillings, 30 half-crowns.

91. 0.

92. $x^3 - x^2 + \frac{5}{3}x - \frac{23}{9}$. Rem. $-\frac{169}{9}$.

93. $60(p^6 - q^6)$.

94. (1) $(a - 2b^5)(a^2 + 2ab^5 + 4b^{10})$. (2) $(x^2 + x - 1)(x^2 - x + 1)$.

95. $x = a - 2b$.

96. (1) $\frac{7bc}{13a^3}$. (2) $\frac{y(y^2 - y + 2)}{2(y + 5)}$.

97. $x = 1,\ y = -1,\ z = 0$.

98. $\frac{(y + 1)(y - 5)}{(y - 1)(y - 6)}$.

99. $\frac{2a - 3b + c}{2a - 3c}$.

100. Twelve minutes past four.

101. (1) $5\frac{1}{6}$. (2) -1.

102. (1) $\frac{2(a + x)}{a^2 + ax + x^2}$. (2) $1 + x - x^3$.

103. $a^3 - 3a + \frac{3}{a} - \frac{1}{a^3}$; $a - \frac{1}{a}$.

104. $1 - 5x + 15x^2 - 45x^3$.

105. Rs. 200.

106. $(2a - 3b)(a + b)$.

107. (1) 2 or $\frac{7}{5}$. (2) $\frac{5}{2}$ or $\frac{4}{3}$.

109. $7x^2 - \frac{x}{5} + 3$.

110. $\frac{3}{2a^2}$.

111. $\frac{3x^2 + 7x - 12}{(x^2 - 9)(x^2 - 16)}$; $\frac{1}{(x - 3)(x - 4)}$.

112. **H.C.F.** $x - 5b$. **L.C.M.** $6(x + 3a)(x - 3a)(x - 5b)$.

113. (1) $\frac{ab}{2c}$ or 2d. (2) 9 or -3.

114. 177.

115. 18 km.

116. $(3x + 2y)^2 + (3x + 2y)(2x + 3y) + (2x + 3y)^2 = 19x^2 + 37xy + 19y^2$.

118. (1) $(x + y)(x + y)(x + y)$. (2) $mn(m - n)$.

119. (1) $\left.\begin{array}{ll} x=3, & 1 \\ y=-1, & -3 \end{array}\right\}.$ (2) $\left.\begin{array}{ll} x=7, & -5 \\ y=2, & -2 \end{array}\right\}.$

120. a^2+b^2. **121.** (1) 1. (2) $\frac{x-1}{x^2}$. **122.** $a-b$.

123. 435. **124.** (1) $x=a\pm b$. (2) $x=3$, $y=2$.

125. (1) $\frac{x(x+y+z)}{z(x-y+z)}$. (2) $\frac{3x^2+1}{4x(x^2+1)}$.

126. $x^2+(a+2)x+3$.

127. (1) $(x-3y)(x+8y+1)$. (2) $x\left(x+\frac{2}{x}\right)\left(x-\frac{2}{x}\right)$.

128. $p-\frac{3q}{2p}-\frac{9q^2}{8p^3}$.

129. (1) $x=4\frac{1}{2}$. (2) $x=\frac{b}{a^2-ab+b^2}$, $y=\frac{a}{a^2-ab+b^2}$.

130. $x+a$. **131.** (1) x^{a+b+c}. (2) $x^{5/12}y^{13/12}$.

132. 3 rupees. **134.** $x-4+\frac{2}{x}$.

135. **H.C.F.** x^2+a^2. **L.C.M.** $(x^2+a^2)(x^2-4a^2)$.

136. (1) $-2y$. (2) 3. **137.** $(x-2a)(x^2+2ax+4a^2)(2a+3b)(2a-3b)$.

138. (1) 3. (2) $x=105$, $y=210$, $z=420$. **139.** The difference is 3.

140. $x^3-4y^3-9z^3-12y^{3/2}z^{3/2}$. **141.** 3 hrs. 36 min.

142. (1) $\frac{3}{2}$. (2) $\frac{8}{9}$. **143.** $\sqrt{\frac{x}{y}}+\sqrt{\frac{y}{x}}-1$.

144. (1) $\frac{1}{x^3+1}$. (2) $\frac{a^2+y^2}{a-y}$.

145. (1) $4(\sqrt{2}+\sqrt{3})$. (2) $\sqrt{21}+\sqrt{14}$.

146. (1) $x=\frac{a^2+b^2}{a+b}$. (2) $x=2\frac{1}{2}$ or $-1\frac{3}{4}$, $x=-1\frac{1}{6}$ or $1\frac{2}{3}$.

148. $a^{1/2}-2a^{1/4}x^{1/4}+x^{1/2}$. **149.** c^2+1.

150. Rs. 3.60. **152.** 0. **153.** $\frac{x^2}{(7x+4)(4x-3)}$.

155. (1) $x=7$ or $-\frac{77}{2}$. (2) $x=\pm 5$ or $\pm 2\sqrt{3}$, $y=\pm 3$ or $\pm\frac{\sqrt{3}}{3}$.

156. (1) 0. (2) $x^{7/12}y^{5/6}$. **157.** $(p+1)x-(p-1)$.

158. $\frac{3a}{5b(x^2y^2-1)}$. **159.** (1) $1-2^{2n}$. (2) 3^n-2^n.

160. 5 hrs. 57′, $47\frac{1'}{2}$. **161.** 12.

162. (1) $\left(\dfrac{ab}{2a+b}\right)^2$. (2) $\dfrac{3}{5}$. **163.** 1.

164. 1, $5+\sqrt{7}$.

165. $(3y+2x)(3y-2x)(x+2)(x^2-2x+4)(x^2+2x+4)$.

166. (1) 1. (2) $\dfrac{32}{3}$.

167. (1) 1. (2) $\sqrt{11}-\sqrt{3}$.

168. **H.C.F.** $5x^2-1$.

L.C.M. $=(5x^2-1)^2(4x^2+1)(5x^2+x+1)$.

169. (1) $\dfrac{(a-b)^2}{2b}$. (2) $-2\dfrac{5}{8}, -8\dfrac{5}{8}$.

170. Rs 9 and Rs 12 a dozen. **172.** 0.

173. (1) $\dfrac{x^3+y^3+z^3}{3xyz}$. (2) 1. **174.** 11.

175. (1) x. (2) $2-\sqrt{3}$.

176. (1) $x=\dfrac{69}{20}a$; (2) $x=\pm\dfrac{1}{2}, \pm\dfrac{3}{2}$; $y=\pm\dfrac{3}{2}, \pm\dfrac{1}{2}$

177. $\dfrac{ax+b^2x^2}{a^m+x^n}$. **178.** (1) $c^{13/12}$. (2) 27.

179. 6 km an hour. **181.** $\dfrac{ac-b^2}{a+b-2b}$.

182. (1) x^2+y^2+xy-1. (2) $\dfrac{1}{2x-1}$.

183. $3-2x^2$. **184.** (1) $2x$. (2) 10.

185. (1) 5, 1. (2) $x=6, 2, 4$; $y=2, 6, 4$.

186. 0.

187. (1) $20\dfrac{3}{4}$ or $16\dfrac{3}{4}$. (2) $x=3$ or $\dfrac{1}{2}$, $y=-1$ or $\dfrac{2}{3}$.

189. $(2a+1)x-a$. **190.** $2x-\dfrac{1}{2x}$.

191. $(b+c)(c+a)(a+b)$. **192.** (1) $\dfrac{3x-4}{(x+1)(x^3-1)}$. (2) $\dfrac{2a}{\sqrt{x+a}}$.

194. Began at $16\dfrac{4'}{11}$ past 3, and ended $27\dfrac{3'}{11}$ past 5; walked 2 hours $10\dfrac{10}{11}$ minutes.

196. $\left(\dfrac{p}{q}\right)^{p+q}$. **197.** (1) 47. (2) b. **199.** 20.

200. $9x^2+y^2$. **202.** 17 years.

203. $q = 4$. The other root is 1.

204. $1\frac{5}{6}$ hours.

206. $a = \frac{5}{3}, r = \frac{3}{5}$; or $a = \frac{20}{3}, r = -\frac{3}{5}$.

207. $(-1)^m\left(\frac{x+y}{x-y}\right)^{m-n}$.

208. 30240.

209. Rs 11.90; Rs 695.

211. tt_e0121.

212. $\frac{x}{2} = \frac{y}{3} = \frac{z}{4}$ [zero values are excluded].

214. 9979200; 7560.

215. $32a^5 - 240a^4x + 720a^3x^2 - 1080a^2x^3 + 810ax^4 - 243x^5$. The 3rd and 4th terms.

216. 1.

217. −1.

218. (1) 2, 3, $\frac{5 \pm \sqrt{37}}{2}$; (2) $\pm 1, \pm\sqrt{-3 \pm 2\sqrt{2}}$.

220. 13104000.

222. 2400; 4032000.

223. Number of terms = 6; common difference = 2.

224. (1) $32 - 60a + 45a^2 - \frac{135}{8}a^3 + \frac{405}{128}a^4 - \frac{213}{1024}a^5$;

(2) $1 - x + \frac{1}{6}x^2 + \frac{1}{54}x^3 + \frac{1}{216}x^4$.

225. Senary.

226. $4\frac{2}{3}$; 1.412.

227. 5.039684.

228. 315.

229. (1) $\sqrt{5x}$; (2) $x - \frac{1}{x}$.

230. $x^2 - 10x + 19 = 0$.

231. 2.71405; *tet*.

232. 1.75; 1.75; −2; $\bar{5}.2375439$.

233. *B* overtakes *A* at the end of the 8th day; then *A* overtakes *B* at the end of the 15th day.

234. (1) $x = 21, y = 6$; (2) $x = 4, \frac{56}{9}$; $y = 3, -\frac{11}{3}$; $z = 9, \frac{121}{9}$.

235. $a = 2d$.

236. The 4th and 5th terms.

237. 120; 60.

238. $\bar{3}.698970$; 799340; $\bar{1}.785248$; $x = \frac{22}{17}$.

239. $8x = \sqrt{yz} + 2\sqrt[3]{yz}$.

240. log 2.

241. 14.

244. (1) 3; (2) $\bar{1}.36564$; (3) 22.

245. $\frac{5\cdot 2\cdot 1\cdot 4\cdot 7\ldots\ldots(3r-8)}{3^r\underline{|r}}(2a)^{5/3-r}x^{10/3+r}$.

246. 2880.

249. (1) $a, \dfrac{a(a-b)}{b-c}\left[\text{one root is evidently } a\text{, and the product of the roots is } \dfrac{a^2(a-b)}{b-c}\right]$; (2) $q,\ p-q$.

250. The series is the expansion of $\left(1-\dfrac{1}{2}\right)^{-3/2}$.

Additional Miscellaneous Examples VI

***19a.** $\dfrac{5bk}{3(5b-k)}, \dfrac{4ak}{5(4a-k)}, \pm\dfrac{4a}{5b}$. ***29a.** 3, –5. ***39a.** Rs 3675.

***59a.** $\dfrac{1}{50}p(ab+bc+ca), \dfrac{qabc}{1030}$ kg.

***69a.** $\dfrac{2(x+1)^2}{3x+5}$, $z=1$ or $\dfrac{-1}{4}$; $x=1$ or $-\dfrac{3}{2}$.

***79a.** 99 ; $\dfrac{1}{4}$; Rs 299; 660. ***89a.** $\dfrac{1}{2}$, 30, 6.

***99a.** 1. ***109a.** $3\dfrac{1}{2}$ cm.

***122a.** $-\dfrac{5}{4}$; 1, $-\dfrac{2}{3}$. ***131a.** $\dfrac{x+169}{x+1}$.

***140a.** 15. ***149a.** 1.661 *m*.

***196a.** $dn^2 + n(2a-d) - 2S = 0$; 10.